Guide to Rural England

THE SOUTH EAST OF ENGLAND

Kent, East Sussex, West Sussex and Surrey

By Peter Long

Published by:
Travel Publishing Ltd
Airport Business Centre, 10 Thornbury Road,
Estover, Plymouth PL6 7PP

ISBN13 9781904434818

First Published: 2001
Second Edition: 2004
Third Edition: 2007
Fourth Edition: 2009

COUNTRY LIVING GUIDES:

East Anglia
Heart of England
Ireland
The North East of England
The North West of England
Scotland
The South of England
The South East of England
The West Country
Wales

PLEASE NOTE:

All advertisements in this publication have been accepted in good faith by Travel Publishing and they have not necessarily been endorsed by *Country Living* Magazine.

All information is included by the publishers in good faith and is believed to be correct at the time of going to press. No responsibility can be accepted for errors.

Editor:	Peter Long
Printing by:	Latimer Trend, Plymouth
Location Maps:	© Maps in Minutes ™ (2009) © Collins Bartholomews 2009 All rights reserved.
Walks:	Walks have been reproduced with kind permission of the internet walking site: www.walkingworld.com
Walk Maps:	Reproduced from Ordnance Survey mapping on behalf of the Controller of Her Majesty's Stationery Office, © Crown Copyright. Licence Number MC 100035812
Cover Design:	Lines & Words, Aldermaston
Cover Photo:	View across the water to Bosham, West Sussex © www.britainonview.com
Text Photos:	Text photos have been kindly supplied by the Pictures of Britain photo library © www.picturesofbritain.co.uk and © Bob Brooks, Weston-super-Mare

Foreword

From a bracing walk across the hills and tarns of The Lake District to a relaxing weekend spent discovering the unspoilt hamlets of East Anglia, nothing quite matches getting off the beaten track and exploring Britain's areas of outstanding beauty.

Each month, *Country Living Magazine* celebrates the richness and diversity of our countryside with features on rural Britain and the traditions that have their roots there. So it is with great pleasure that I introduce you to the *Country Living Magazine Guide to Rural England* series. Packed with information about unusual and unique aspects of our countryside, the guides will point both fair-weather and intrepid travellers in the right direction.

Each chapter provides a fascinating tour of the South East of England area, with insights into local heritage and history and easy-to-read facts on a wealth of places to visit, stay, eat, drink and shop.

I hope that this guide will help make your visit a rewarding and stimulating experience and that you will return inspired, refreshed and ready to head off on your next countryside adventure.

Susy Smith

Susy Smith
Editor, Country Living magazine

PS To subscribe to *Country Living Magazine* each month, call 01858 438844

Introduction

This is the fourth edition of *The Country Living Guide to Rural England – The South East* and we are sure that it will be as popular as its predecessors. Peter Long, a very experienced travel writer has completely updated the contents of the guide and ensured that it is packed with vivid descriptions, historical stories, amusing anecdotes and interesting facts on hundreds of places in Kent, East Sussex, West Sussex and Surrey. In the introduction to each village or town we have also summarized and categorized the main attractions to be found there, which makes it easy for readers to plan their visit.

The advertising panels within each chapter provide further information on places to see, stay, eat, drink and shop. We have also selected a number of walks from walkingworld.com (full details of this website may be found to the rear of the guide) which we highly recommend if you wish to appreciate fully the beauty and charm of the varied rural landscapes and coastline of the South East of England.

The guide however is not simply an 'armchair tour'. Its prime aim is to encourage the reader to visit the places described and discover much more about the wonderful towns, villages and countryside of the South East in person. In this respect we would like to thank all the Tourist Information Centres who helped us to provide you with up-to-date information. Whether you decide to explore this region by wheeled transport or on foot we are sure you will find it a very uplifting experience!

We are always interested in receiving comments on places covered (or not covered) in our guides so please do not hesitate to use the reader reaction forms provided at the rear of this guide to give us your considered comments. This will help us refine and improve the content of the next edition. We also welcome any general comments which will help improve the overall presentation of the guides themselves.

For more information on the full range of travel guides published by Travel Publishing please refer to the order form at the rear of this guide or log on to our website (see below).

Travel Publishing

Did you know that you can also search our website for details of thousands of places to see, stay, eat or drink throughout Britain and Ireland? Our site has become increasingly popular and now receives monthly over 160,000 visits. Try it!

website: www.travelpublishing.co.uk

Contents

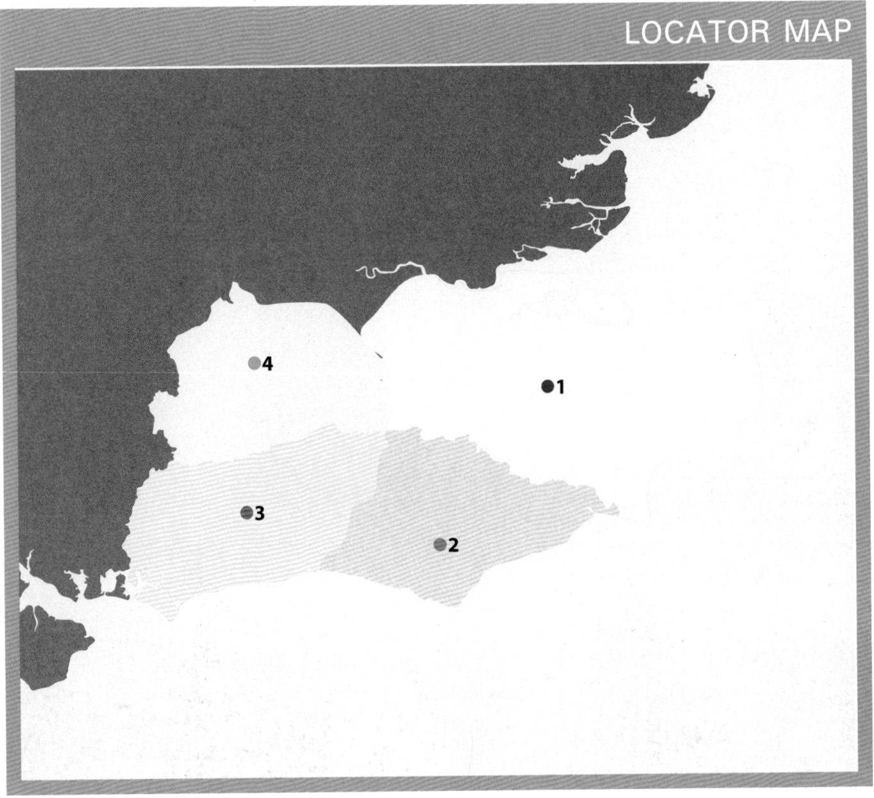

FOREWORD III

INTRODUCTION V

GEOGRAPHICAL AREAS

1 | Kent 3
2 | East Sussex 145
3 | West Sussex 225
4 | Surrey 303

INDEXES AND LISTS

Tourist Information Centres 403
List of Advertisers 406
List of Walks 412
Order Form 413
Reader Comment Forms 415
Index of Towns, Villages and Places of Interest 419

1 Kent

Kent is a land of gardens and orchards, of historic castles and churches, of pretty villages and fine market towns, but above all, it is a land that is inescapably linked to the sea. Its proximity to Europe across the narrow channel means that invaders through the centuries have chosen the Kent coast as a gateway to Britain. The Romans landed here over 2,000 years ago, the Vikings followed almost 1,000 years later and the land was widely settled by the Normans following the defeat of Harold in 1066. All these peoples, and the prehistoric tribes that preceded them, have left their mark on the landscape and the language. Many place names, such as Rochester and Whitstable, are derived from Roman, Saxon or Norman origins. Norman churches and castles in various states of ruin or preservation still stand in the tranquil rural countryside that belies the bloodshed of centuries of successive invasions.

On the south coast, the Cinque Ports were set up in the 11th century as a commercial alliance of significant ports, although silting up of channels over the centuries has left many of them several miles from the sea. Henry VIII established a dockyard at Chatham, which was a major factor in Britain's dominance of the seas in the centuries that followed. The whole length of the Kent coast has been the historic haven of smugglers, and every rocky cove and sheltered bay has seen daring and ruthless smugglers pursued by brave and determined but generally ineffective excise men. In villages across Kent, ancient tales of smuggling are still told and houses, churches and caves are remembered as places where the smugglers' booty was hidden away. However, Kent's maritime tradition did not depend entirely on lawlessness and many villages plied a legitimate trade in fishing. Ancient fishing villages like Deal retain their quaint alleyways and traditional fishermen's cottages around the harbour areas. Whitstable has been famed for centuries for oyster fishing and Whitstable oysters are still regarded as gourmet fare. In the 19th century as the fashion grew for taking holidays by the sea, seaside towns and resorts grew up in former fishing ports like Herne

Hop Farm, Tonbridge

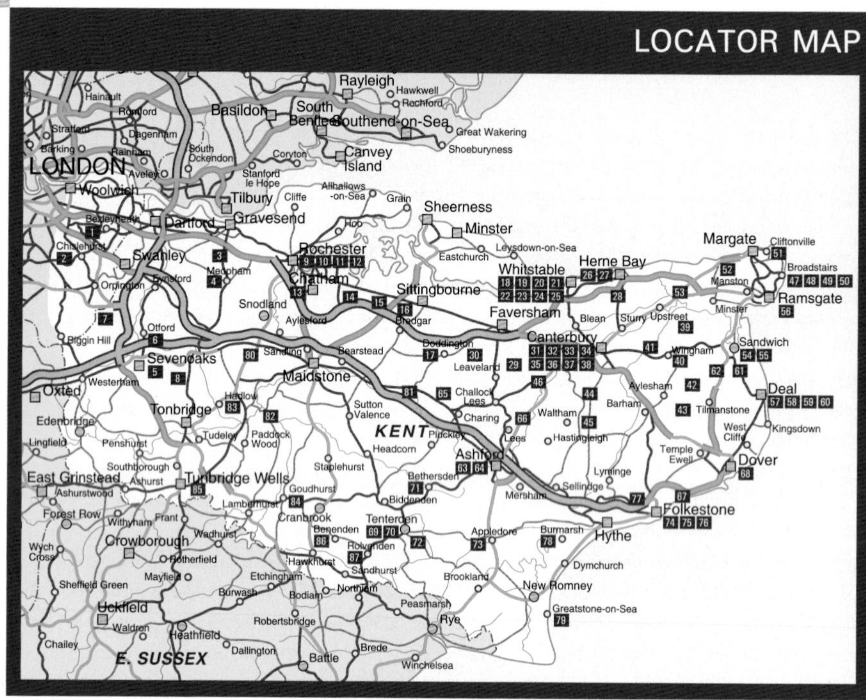

ADVERTISERS AND PLACES OF INTEREST

Accommodation, Food and Drink

7 | Cabbages & Kings, Halstead *pg 20*
15 | B & B At Hartlip Place, Hartlip, nr Sittingbourne *pg 42*
16 | Holly House Bed & Breakfast, Borden, nr Sittingbourne *pg 43*
19 | The Pearsons Arms, Whitstable *pg 47*
21 | Samphire, Whitstable *pg 48*
26 | Bay View Guest House, Herne Bay *pg 51*
27 | The Evening Tide, Herne Bay *pg 52*
28 | West Grange House B & B, Herne Common, nr Herne Bay *pg 53*
29 | The Rose & Crown, Selling, nr Faversham *pg 55*
31 | Castle House Hotel, Canterbury *pg 58*
34 | Yorke Lodge, Canterbury *pg 61*
36 | Sylvan Cottage, Canterbury *pg 62*
37 | Number 7 Longport, Canterbury *pg 63*
38 | Magnolia House, Canterbury *pg 64*
39 | Rose Garden Tea Rooms, Westmarsh, nr Canterbury *pg 66*
41 | The Duke William, Ickham, nr Canterbury *pg 68*
42 | The Griffins Head, Chillenden, nr Canterbury *pg 70*
43 | Yew Tree, Barfreston, nr Canterbury *pg 71*
45 | The Hop Pocket, Bossingham, nr Canterbury *pg 73*
46 | Castle Cottage Chilham B & B, Chilham, nr Canterbury *pg 74*
49 | Merriland, Broadstairs *pg 77*
54 | White Rose Lodge, Sandwich *pg 84*
55 | The George & Dragon, Sandwich *pg 85*
58 | The Bohemian, Deal *pg 88*
61 | Solley Farm House, Worth, nr Deal *pg 94*
62 | The Five Bells, Eastry, nr Sandwick *pg 94*
68 | The Swingate Inn, Swingate, nr Dover *pg 106*
73 | Miss Molletts High Class Tea Room, Appledore *pg 112*
75 | The Whole World Café, Folkestone *pg 115*
77 | Frogholt Bed & Breakfast, Frogholt, nr Folkestone *pg 117*
78 | Haguelands Farm Village, Burmarsh, nr Romney Marsh *pg 120*
83 | Fieldswood Bed & Breakfast, Hadlow, nr Tonbridge *pg 135*

Activities

32 | J.E.M'S Sewing Machine and Needlecraft Centre, Canterbury *pg 59*
50 | Broadstairs Art Courses, Broadstairs *pg 78*
65 | Uplands Riding School, Charing, nr Ashford *pg 98*
74 | Jo Letchford Mosaics, Folkestone *pg 115*
78 | Haguelands Farm Village, Burmarsh, nr Romney Marsh *pg 120*
86 | Hempstead Equestrian Centre, Benenden *pg 143*

Antiques and Restoration

10 | Fieldstaff Antiques, Rochester *pg 31*
52 | Artisan, Birchington *pg 80*
71 | The Antiques Barn, Bethersden, nr Ashford *pg 110*

historic building museum and heritage historic site scenic attraction flora and fauna

Bay. Margate with its glorious sands was one of the first resorts to attract visitors. Even before the railways, pleasure boats brought Londoners to the town in search of sun, sea and sand.

Churchill, Darwin and Charles Dickens all had homes in Kent. Geoffrey Chaucer and Christopher Marlowe, Somerset Maugham and Mary Tourtel, the creator of Rupert Bear, all lived part of their lives in Canterbury. The abbey and cathedral here, along with St Martin's Church, form a fascinating World Heritage Site, the place where St Augustine brought Christianity to England in the 6th century.

Although Kent lies very close to the spreading suburban sprawl of Greater London, much of the county has managed to retain a tranquil rural feel, despite commuter developments. Rolling wooded countryside is dotted with windmills and attractive villages, surrounded by orchards, market gardens, hop fields and countless gardens.

ADVERTISERS AND PLACES OF INTEREST (CONT)

Arts and Crafts

4 | Just Paintings, Meopham *pg 13*
9 | I Dig Dinos, Rochester *pg 30*
11 | Francis Iles, Rochester *pg 32*
12 | Francis Iles, Rochester *pg 32*
14 | Adora Cards & More, Rainham, nr Gillingham *pg 40*
20 | Caxton Contemporary, Whitstable *pg 47*
22 | Frank, Whitstable *pg 48*
32 | J.E.M'S Sewing Machine and Needlecraft Centre, Canterbury *pg 59*
50 | Broadstairs Art Courses, Broadstairs *pg 78*
51 | Lovelys, Cliftonville, nr Margate *pg 79*
56 | Carrera & Bronte, Ramsgate *pg 86*
59 | Swanstitch, Deal *pg 89*
74 | Jo Letchford Mosaics, Folkestone *pg 115*

Fashions

48 | Ritzy Retro, Broadstairs *pg 76*
63 | Ashford Guns & Tackle, Ashford *pg 96*
80 | Baby Bea, Swan Street, nr West Malling *pg 128*

Giftware

6 | Mad Hatters Emporium, Otford, nr Sevenoaks *pg 19*
9 | I Dig Dinos, Rochester *pg 30*
24 | Jane at Graham Greener, Whitstable *pg 50*
25 | Taking The Plunge, Whitstable *pg 50*
35 | Graham Greener, Canterbury *pg 62*
80 | Baby Bea, Swan Street, nr West Malling *pg 128*

Home and Garden

3 | Walnut Hill Nurseries, Longfield Hill, nr Gravesend *pg 12*
6 | Mad Hatters Emporium, Otford, nr Sevenoaks *pg 19*
24 | Jane at Graham Greener, Whitstable *pg 50*
35 | Graham Greener, Canterbury *pg 62*
52 | Artisan, Birchington *pg 80*
56 | Carrera & Bronte, Ramsgate *pg 86*
70 | Wing & a Prayer, Tenterden *pg 109*
72 | Pinecove Nursery, Leigh Green, nr Tenterden *pg 111*
76 | Old English Pine, Folkestone *pg 116*
79 | Greatstone Secret Nursery, Greatstone, nr New Romney *pg 121*

Jewellery

48 | Ritzy Retro, Broadstairs *pg 76*
52 | Artisan, Birchington *pg 80*

Places of Interest

1 | Danson House, Bexleyheath *pg 8*
2 | Chislehurst Caves, Chislehurst *pg 10*
5 | Knole House, Knole, nr Sevenoaks *pg 15*
8 | Ightham Mote, Ivy Hatch, nr Sevenoaks *pg 23*
13 | The Historic Dockyard, Chatham *pg 39*
17 | Doddington Place Gardens, Doddington, nr Sittingbourne *pg 44*
30 | The Belmont Estate and Harris Belmont Charity, Throwley, nr Faversham *pg 56*
53 | Sarre Mill, Sarre, nr Birchington *pg 82*
64 | Godinton House and Gardens, Ashford *pg 97*
67 | The Battle of Britain Memorial, Capel-le-Ferne, nr Folkestone *pg 103*
69 | Kent and East Sussex Railway, Tenterden *pg 108*
82 | Garden Organic Yalding, Yalding, nr Maidstone *pg 134*
85 | Scotney Castle Garden and Estate, Lamberhurst, nr Tunbridge Wells *pg 140*
87 | C.M. Booth Collection of Historic Vehicles, Rolvenden, nr Cranbrook *pg 144*

Specialist Food and Drink Shops

18 | Sugar Boy, Whitstable *pg 46*
23 | The Cheese Box, Whitstable *pg 49*
33 | Sugar Boy, Canterbury *pg 60*
40 | The Little Stour Farm Shop, Wingham *pg 67*
44 | Lower Hardres Farm Shop, Lower Hardres, nr Canterbury *pg 73*
57 | Allotment, Deal *pg 87*
60 | Sugar Boy, Deal *pg 90*
66 | Perry Court Farm Shop, Billing, nr Ashford *pg 99*
78 | Haguelands Farm Village, Burmarsh, nr Romney Marsh *pg 120*
81 | Janson's Deli & Greengrocers, Lenham, nr Maidstone *pg 131*
84 | Taywell Farm Shop, Goudhurst, nr Cranbrook *pg 138*

West Kent

Although the western region of Kent lies so close to the spreading suburban areas of Greater London, it has still managed to maintain an identity that is all its own, illustrated by the offbeat pronunciations of some of its towns and villages. Water dominates much of the history of Kent, reflected in the strong maritime heritage along the banks of the River Thames. The glorious countryside attracts many visitors, yet it still manages to retain a tranquil rural feel. The short crossing to Europe via Dover and the Thames estuary has always made the area one of the first targets for invaders.

Prehistoric remains have been found here along with evidence of Roman occupation at Lullingstone near Eynsford and Croft Roman Villa at Orpington. Danes and Vikings also invaded, and the now picturesque village of Aylesford has, over the centuries, been witness to more than its fair share of bloodshed.

Dartford Church, Dartford

More peaceful times saw the creation of grand manor houses and the conversion of castles into more comfortable homes: this area abounds with interesting and historic places such as Cobham Hall, Knole House, Old Soar Manor, Ightham Mote, Penshurst Place and the magnificent Hever Castle.

Two of these places stand out as being of particular interest. Chartwell, the home of Sir Winston and Lady Churchill from the 1920s until the great statesman's death in 1965, has been left just as it was when the couple were alive and it remains a lasting tribute to this extraordinary man. At Downe, just south of Farnborough, lies Down House, the home of Charles Darwin and the place where he formulated his theories of evolution and wrote his most famous work The Origin of Species by Means of Natural Selection.

Dartford

This urban settlement is best known today as the home of the Dartford Tunnel, which runs for roughly one mile beneath the River Thames, re-emerging on the Essex bank near West Thurrock. Dartford is a place of some historical significance: it stands on the old London to Dover road at the crossing of the River Darent, which is how it got its name Darent Ford.

Local legend has it that Wat Tyler, leader of the Peasant's Revolt, was from Dartford. The revolt was supposedly sparked off by an indecent assault by a tax collector on Tyler's daughter. Deptford, Colchester and Maidstone also lay claim to Wat Tyler. However the historical sources are unreliable and the legend is perpetuated in Dartford, which even has a Wat Tyler Inn.

In the 20th century Dartford changed from Victorian market town to sprawling commuter land with 80,000 residents. Most of the town's older buildings have disappeared down the centuries, victims of war, modern transport systems or the dead hand of urban planning. Holy Trinity church, mainly 18th and 19th century with a Norman tower, a few cottages nearby and a couple of 18th-century buildings on the High Street, including the galleried Royal Victoria and Bull Hotel, are among the few survivors of old Dartford. The church has a memorial to the railway pioneer Richard Trevithick, who died in poverty at the Royal Victoria and Bull (then just the Bull) in 1833. He had been working nearby on new inventions, and his colleagues clubbed together to provide him with a decent funeral.

Around Dartford

CRAYFORD

2 miles NW of Dartford on the A206

World of Silk

This is the point at which the Roman road Watling Street crosses the River Cray. The parish church St Paulinus dates back to the 12th century, but additions have been made over the centuries. A settlement was discovered just to the west of St Paulinus where Iron Age pottery was unearthed.

On the banks of the River Cray, the **World of Silk** provides visitors with an insight into the historic and traditional craft of silk making and the origins of silk are explained. Believed to have been discovered around 1640 by the Empress of China, Hsi-Ling-Shi, silk found its way to Europe along the arduous silk route and, from the humble silk worm through to the beautiful printed fabrics, the whole of the story of this luxury material is explained.

BEXLEYHEATH

3 miles W of Dartford on the A207

Danson Park Hall Place Red House

Lesness Abbey

Despite being located between Dartford and Woolwich, Bexleyheath is somewhat surprising in that, although there was a great deal of development here in the 19th and early 20th centuries, expanses of parkland still remain. As the town's name might suggest, this area was once heathland and, following enclosure in 1814, some of the land managed to escape the hands of the developers. In the heart of Bexleyheath lies one of these areas, **Danson Park** (see panel on page 8), covering more than 180 acres. Originally a private estate, the garden was landscaped by Capability Brown. The Danson Mansion within the park, a Grade I Listed Building, completed in 1762 and designed by Sir Robert Taylor, architect of the Bank of England, is sometimes open to the public. At the centre of the park, a great oak tree, which is over 200 years old, is now designated one of the Great Trees of London.

To the southeast lies **Hall Place**, a charming country house that was built in 1540 for Sir John Champneis, a Lord Mayor of London, and substantially added to around 100 years later. Its later roles include three times a school and, during World War II, an American Army communications centre. Among the parts of the house open to the public are the magnificent Great Hall, Tudor parlour, drawing room and long

Danson House

Danson Park, Bexleyheath, Kent DA6 8HL
Tel: 0208 303 6699
website: www.bexleyheritagetrust.org.uk/dansonhouse

Danson House is primarily the creation of two men: John Boyd, the owner, and his architect Robert Taylor. It reflects a preoccupation with the Golden Age of antiquity and is full of the symbolism of classical mythology. It is a revival of Italian villa design from the area around Vicenza in the second half of the sixteenth century. The leading architect at that time was Andrea Palladio.

In the twentieth century the house fell into an almost ruinous state. In 1995 English Heritage, which had identified the house as 'the most significant building at risk in London' began ten years restoration. The restoration won the Georgian Group National Award in 2004, and the following year the house was formally opened by Her Majesty the Queen, after thirty five years of closure. The grounds were restored as part of the Danson Park project, supported by the Heritage Lottery Fund, in 2006. Shop and refreshments available.

gallery, as well as Bexley Museum and various exhibition galleries. The house is particularly noted for its beautiful award-winning formal gardens on the banks of the River Cray.

One of Bexleyheath's most famous former residents lived at **The Red House** in Red House Lane. Designed by Philip Webb, it was built in 1860 for the newly married William Morris. The interior was decorated by Webb, Morris, Burne-Jones, Madox Brown and Dante Gabriel Rossetti. William Morris described the house as "a joyful nook of heaven in an unheavenly world", while for Rossetti it was "...more a poem than a house - but an admirable place to live in too". The house is in the care of the National Trust.

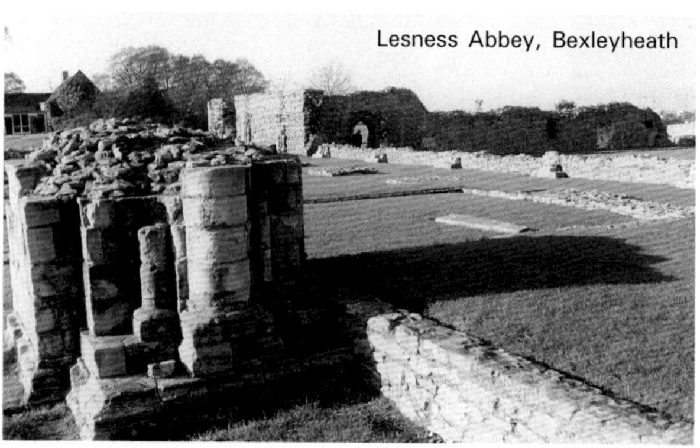

Lesness Abbey, Bexleyheath

The ruins of **Lesness Abbey** are in the area between Belvedere and Abbey Wood. The Augustinians occupied the abbey from 1178 until the 16th century when it was razed to the ground. The foundations excavated in the 20th century give a good idea of the layout of a monastic community.

HEXTABLE

3 miles S of Dartford on the B258

Hextable Gardens & Park

Surrounded by market gardens and orchards, this village is home to **Hextable Gardens**. This heritage centre lies in the former Botany Laboratory of Swanley Horticultural College, believed to be the first horticultural college in the world. The Botany Lab is not listed but is an attractive 1930s white-painted brick building with metal-framed windows, now sensitively restored. **Hextable Park** a charming place specifically designed to attract a wide variety of wildlife and butterflies. Pictorial information plaques aid visitors in identifying the many species found here.

CHISLEHURST

5 miles SW of Dartford on the A208

Chislehurst Caves Chislehurst Common

Petts Wood

Following the arrival of the railways, Chislehurst developed as one of London's more select and fashionable suburbs as businessmen moved here lured by the fresh air and the downland scenery that lies on the doorstep. The town has managed to remain relatively unspoilt by further development thanks, in large part, to **Chislehurst Common**, an oasis of greenery criss-crossed by a number of small roads.

The suburb is also home to **Chislehurst Caves** (see panel on page 10), one of Britain's most interesting networks of underground caverns. There are over 20 miles of caverns and passageways, dug over a period of 8,000 years. The vast labyrinth of caves is a maze of ancient flint and chalk mines dug by hand over the centuries. It comprises three sections that each relate to a specific era and the oldest section, known as the Druids, dates back approximately 4,000 years. The largest section is Roman, while the smallest, and youngest, was excavated some 1,400 years ago by the Saxons. Royalists took refuge here during the Civil War and the pit that was built to trap their Parliamentarian pursuers can still be seen. At the height of the Blitz during World War II, the caves became the world's largest air raid shelter when some 15,000 people hid here from the German bombing raids. Visitors can take a lamp-lit guided tour of the various sections including the air raid shelters, the Druid Altar and the Haunted Pool.

A quiet and pleasant residential area today, Chislehurst has two famous sons: William Willet Junior, the enthusiastic advocate of the Daylight Saving Scheme, who unfortunately died a year before British Summer Time (BST) was introduced in 1916, and Sir Malcolm Campbell, the racing driver and pioneering land and water speed record holder of the 1930s. A memorial to Willet can be found in nearby **Petts Wood** a 150-acre ancient semi-natural woodland with a wide variety of trees. Its neighbour, Hawkwood, is mainly grazed pasture and the whole area forms a 'Green Lung' just 13 miles from the City of London; it is particularly rich in birdlife, fungi and wild flowers.

ORPINGTON

6 miles SW of Dartford on the A224

Bromley Museum Crofton Roman Villa

Once a country village, Orpington changed dramatically in the 1920s and 1930s into the commuter town that it is today. However, thanks to William Cook, a 19th-century local poultry farmer, the town has not lost its rural connections as Cook introduced a breed of poultry - the Black Orpington - that was to

Chislehurst Caves

Old Hill, Chislehurst, Kent BR7 5NB
Tel: 020 8467 3264 Fax: 020 8295 0407
e-mail: enquiries@chislehurstcaves.co.uk
website: www.chislehurstcaves.co.uk

Grab a lantern and get ready for an amazing adventure! Just a short way from central London, close to Bromley in Kent, lie the Chislehurst Caves. Miles of dark mysterious passageways hewn by hand from the chalk, forming a maze covering more than six hectares thirty meters deep, beneath the woodlands and houses of Chislehurst. This is one of the few places left where you actually have your own guide to escort you around, no boring reading posters on the wall here! Things are explained to you, and you can ask questions if you don't understand something. No two tours are exactly the same, as each of the guides has their own unique style. Chislehurst Caves should hold the imagination of even the most easily bored child and if nothing else, there are twenty miles of tunnels to wear them out! There is also a gift shop where you can buy anything from a pencil to a dragon, a licensed café serving home cooked meals, breakfasts, lunches or just tea and cakes and a large free car park.

become famous throughout the farming world in Britain, Europe and beyond.

In the heart of the town, next to the library, stands **Bromley Museum**, which is an ideal starting point for an exploration of this area. Housed in what is a museum piece itself, an interesting medieval building dating from 1290, and surrounded by attractive gardens, Bromley Museum has numerous exhibits and displays that cover the history of the area around Bromley. From prehistoric Stone Age tools, Roman lamps and Saxon jewellery to a re-created 1930s dining room and memorabilia from World War II, there are many interesting items on show. The museum also houses an archaeological collection put together by Sir John Lubbock of nearby Hall Place.

Adjacent to the railway station, and protected from the elements by a modern cover building, is **Crofton Roman Villa**, built around 140 and inhabited for over 250 years. Presumed to have been at the centre of a farming estate, the villa, which was altered several times during its occupation, probably extended to some 20 rooms although the remains of only 10 have been uncovered. Evidence of the underfloor heating arrangements, or hypocaust, can still be seen as, can some of the tiled floors, and there is also a display of the artefacts that were uncovered during the excavations here.

Gravesend

Milton Chantry · Church of St George

The Thames is half a mile wide at Gravesend. This is where ships take on board a river pilot for the journey upstream. It is a busy maritime community, with cutters and tugs helping to maintain a steady flow of river traffic. Gravesend is where the bodies of those who had died on board were unloaded before the ships entered London; but the name Gravesend is not a reference to its being the last resting place of these poor unfortunates, it is derived from 'Grove's End' from the Old

English 'graf' meaning grove and 'ende' meaning end or boundary.

Much of the town was destroyed by fire in 1727. One of the many buildings that did not survive the fire was the parish **Church of St George**, and the building seen today was rebuilt in Georgian style after the disaster. The graveyard is more interesting than the church as this is thought to be the final resting place of the famous Red Indian princess, Pocahontas. Pocahontas was the daughter of a native American chieftain, who reputedly saved the life of the English settler, John Smith, in Virginia. She died on board ship (either from smallpox, fever or tuberculosis) in 1617 while she was on her way back to America with her husband, John Rolfe. A life-size statue marks Pocahontas's supposed burial place in the churchyard.

A building of interest in the town, that did survive the 18th-century fire, is the 14th-century **Milton Chantry**. A chantry is a place set aside for saying prayers for the dead. This small building was the chantry of the Valence and Monechais families. It later became an inn and, in 1780, part of a fort. Milton Chantry is now a heritage centre with fascinating displays detailing the history and varied uses of the building.

Around Gravesend

COBHAM

4 miles SE of Gravesend off the A2

Cobham Hall · Church of St Mary Magdalene · Almshouses · Owletts · Leather Bottle Inn

This picturesque village is home to one of the largest and finest houses in Kent - **Cobham Hall** - an outstanding redbrick mansion that dates from 1584. Set in 150 acres of parkland, and demonstrating architectural styles from Elizabethan, Jacobean, Carolean eras and the 18th century, the house has much to offer those interested in art, history and architecture. The Elizabethan wings date from the late 16th century. The central section of the house is later and here can be found the magnificent Gilt Hall that was decorated by Inigo Jones's famous pupil, John Webb, in 1654. Elsewhere in the house there are several superb marble fireplaces. The beautiful gardens were landscaped by Humphry Repton for the 4th Earl of Darnley. Over the centuries many notable people have stayed here, including English monarchs from Elizabeth I to Edward VIII, and Charles Dickens used to walk through the grounds from his home at Higham to Cobham's village pub. However, perhaps Cobham Hall's most famous claim to fame dates back to 1883 when Ivo Blight, who later became the 8th Earl of Darnley, led the English cricket team to victory against Australia and brought the Ashes home to Cobham. Today, the hall is a private girls' boarding school and is occasionally open to visitors.

Back in the village more evidence can be found of past members of the Cobham family and, in the 13th-century parish **Church of St Mary Magdalene**, a series of superb commemorative floor brasses can be seen that date back to the late Middle Ages. Behind the church are some **Almshouses** that incorporate a 14th-century kitchen and hall that were once part of the Old College that was founded by the 3rd Lord Cobham. He endowed them as living quarters for five priests who were to pray for the repose of his soul. After 1537, when the college was suppressed, the buildings became almhouses for 20 poor men and women from local parishes.

In the heart of the village stands the half-timbered **Leather Bottle Inn**, made famous

WALNUT HILL NURSERIES

Walnut Hill Road, Longfield Hill,
Gravesend, Kent DA13 9HL
Tel: 01474 708106
Fax: 01474 703732
e-mail: nurseries@findwillow.co.uk
website: www.walnuthillnurseries.co.uk

Walnut Hill Nurseries are specialists in specimen trees, shrubs and architectural plants for instant planting. The nursery is owned and run by Adrian Hollingworth and David Bagley, directors of Findwillow Ltd, and is managed by Adrian's daughter Anjuli and horticultural expert Konrad Zelazik. Walnut Hill Nurseries were established in 1981 to provide mature specimens for Findwillow, a main contractor for building and landscaping, and were developed to supply plants to all trade and retail customers. Though primarily a trade nursery selling to landscapers, garden designers and public gardens, Walnut Hill also welcomes the general public, with many special offers for retail customers and a wide range of plants for customers needing a fast and convenient cash & carry service. Three acres of mature and semi-mature container-grown plants include architectural plants and topiary and the site also has three polytunnels. For unusual plant requirements Walnut Hill draws on a network of other growers in the UK and Europe. The nursery has been renovated gradually over the past few years to provide an upgraded irrigation system, better tree and climber tying systems and improved paths, access and standing out areas – all to enhance the quality of the plants and the facilities for visitors.

Walnut Hill Nurseries incorporates a plant hiring service, Willowbean, catering for all shows, events and other occasions large and small. Knowledgeable staff are happy to give advice on planting and plant care at the nursery, which is open from 8am to 4pm Tuesday to Friday and 9am to 1pm Saturday April to October. Delivery can be arranged to all locations in the South East. The location is close to Gravesend, Jeskyns Country Park, Bluewater and Cobham. Customers who can't get to the nursery can order by e-mail through the website, which contains the complete plant and price lists.

by Charles Dickens when he featured his favourite inn in the novel *The Pickwick Papers.* It was at the Leather Bottle Inn that Tracey Tupman was discovered by Mr Pickwick after being jilted by Rachel Wardle.

Close by, just to the north of the village, lies **Owletts**, a lovely redbrick house that was built in the late 17th century by a Cobham farmer. Still retaining a charming sense of rural comfort, the house has an imposing staircase, a notable 17th-century plaster ceiling and a beautiful garden.

MEOPHAM

4 miles S of Gravesend on the A227

Windmill

This pretty village, whose name is pronounced 'Meppam', still acts as a trading centre for the surrounding smaller villages and hamlets. In addition to the well maintained cricket green, the village is home to **Meopham Windmill**, a fully restored black smock mill dating from 1821 that is unusual in that it has six sides. The village was the birthplace of the great 17th-century naturalist and gardener John Tradescant, who introduced many non-native species of flowers and vegetables into England.

SWANSCOMBE

2½ miles W of Gravesend on the A226

This former agricultural village, which has long since been swamped by the growth of industry along the banks of the River Thames, was the site of an important archaeological find in 1935. Excavations in a gravel pit unearthed fragments of a human skull and analysis of the bones revealed that the remains (those of a woman) were around 200,000 years old, making them some of the oldest

JUST PAINTINGS

The Old Bakery, Wrotham Road,
Meopham, Kent DA13 0QB
Tel: 01474 813813 e-mail: justpaintings@btconnect.com
website: www.justpaintings.co.uk

Affordable art in Meopham

Many friends have recommended visiting a gallery in Meopham. What an exciting change to find a gallery that sells paintings rather than prints. Just Paintings are in a lovely old bakery dating from the 1850's, close to Meopham village green on the A227.

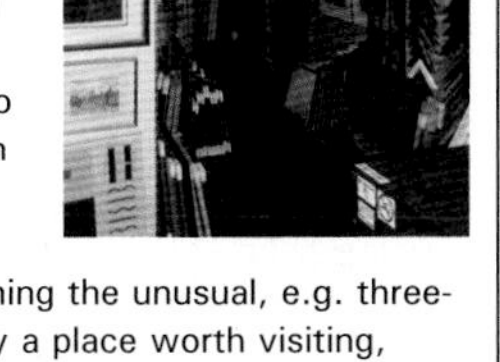

They have been selling a very diverse range of paintings since 1978 - their attitude is they should please most of the people, most of the time. On offer are traditional oil paintings, watercolours and engravings, through timeless Chinese paintings on silk, to contemporary art, and all at very keen prices due to their low overheads. Have a look at their informative web site (www.justpaintings.co.uk.), plus details on how to find them. The business is still run by one of the founders and has been a Fine Art Trade Guild member for over 30 years. Besides selling paintings they have an excellent reputation for custom bespoke picture framing using high quality materials and for their specialist skills in framing the unusual, e.g. three-dimensional items like sugar craft or groups of medals. This is definitely a place worth visiting, with over 300 framed paintings on display and huge stocks in reserve. The gallery is open daily except Saturdays and Bank Holiday weekends, with ample free parking close by.

human remains found in Europe. This riverside settlement also has remnants from more recent historical periods and, while the parish church of Saints Peter and Paul dates mainly from the 12th century, its structure incorporates bricks from Roman times and parts of its tower predate the Norman invasion. Although the church was substantially restored in the Victorian era, making it difficult to detect the original features, it does provide tangible evidence of the many layers of human settlement here along the Thames.

Sevenoaks

Knole House Library Gallery One Tree Hill

With its easy road and rail links to London, and its leafy and relaxed atmosphere, Sevenoaks has come to epitomise the essence of the commuter belt. While this perception is not far from the truth, the town retains a rural feel from the once wooded countryside that surrounded the ancient settlement that stood here some nine centuries ago.

Sevenoaks began as a market town in Saxon times, although an older settlement is believed to have been sited here previously, and it grew up around the meeting point of the roads from London and the Dartford river crossing as they headed south towards the coast.

The first recorded mention of the town came in 1114, when it was called 'Seovenaca', and local tradition has it that the name refers to the clump of seven oaks that once stood here; those trees disappeared long ago but were replaced in 1955 with seven trees from Knole Park. These replacement trees made headline news in the autumn of 1987 when several were blown down in the Great Storm that hit the southeast of England in October.

Rural Sevenoaks changed little over the centuries until the arrival of the railway in 1864, when the town became a popular residential area for those working in London. Despite the development, which was again accelerated when the railway line was electrified in the 1930s, Sevenoaks has managed to maintain its individuality and there are still various traditional Kentish tile-hung cottages to be found here. In the **Sevenoaks Library Gallery** an imaginative programme of contemporary exhibitions of modern art, by both local and international artists, shows that the town does not dwell in the past. The exhibits range from photography and textiles to fine art, and Andy Warhol and John Piper are among the famous names to be featured here over the years.

Not far from the centre of Sevenoaks is another reminder of the town's heritage in the form of the Vine Cricket Ground that lies on a rise to the south. It was given to the town in 1773, but the first recorded match held here - between Kent and Sussex - was in 1782, when the Duke of Dorset (one of the Sackville family of Knole) and his estate workers defeated a team representing All England. This remarkable victory was particularly sweet, as the Duke's team also won a bet of 1,000 guineas! The weatherboard pavilion at the club is 19th century. The Cricket Club pay Sevenoaks Town Council a peppercorn rent, literally two peppercorns per year - one for the ground and one for the pavilion. The council may be required to pay Lord Sackville one cricket ball each year, but only if he asks.

The pride of Sevenoaks is **Knole House** (see panel opposite), one of the largest private homes in England that lies to the southeast of the town and is surrounded by an extensive and majestic deer park. The huge manor house, with its 365 rooms, stands on the site of a much smaller house that was bought by the Archbishop of Canterbury in 1456 and used as an ecclesiastical palace until 1532 when it was taken over by Henry VIII. In 1603, Elizabeth I granted the house to the Sackville family and, although it is now in the ownership of the National Trust, the family still live here. A superb example of late medieval architecture, with Jacobean embellishments that include superb carvings and plasterwork, visitors to Knole can also see the internationally renowned collection of Royal Stuart furnishings, 17th-century textiles, important English silver and works by Van Dyck, Gainsborough, Lely, Kneller and Reynolds. Little altered since the 18th century, it was here that Vita Sackville-West was born in 1892 and, as well as being the setting for Virginia Wolf's novel *Orlando*, it is believed that Hitler intended to use Knole as his English headquarters.

The trees in the 1,000-acre deer park were smashed by the great storm of 1987, and it fell to Lionel Sackville-West and a team of volunteers to plant more than 250,000 trees, mostly beech but with some oak and chestnut. He tended the trees personally until shortly before his death in March 2004, and had the distinction of beating the Queen into third place in a forestry competition for replantings after the storm. Lord Egremont won first prize, but as Lord Sackville commented, "he had professional foresters". In the late 1960s Lord Sackville restored the chapel at Knole, since when it has been used regularly by his family and by Sevenoaks School. Knole has 365 rooms, a handful of which are open to the public.

A very short distance southeast of Sevenoaks stands **One Tree Hill**, a tranquil site with a network of paths that include the Greensand Way, a long-distance footpath linking Haslemere in Surrey with Ham Street, near Dover, in Kent. The name of One Tree Hill originally referred to a single large beech tree that grew near the summit; it was replaced many years ago with a copper beech.

Knole House

Knole, Sevenoaks, Kent TN15 0RP
Tel: 01732 462100
website: www.nationaltrust.org.uk

Knole's fascinating links with Royalty as well as its literary connections with Vita Sackville-West and Virgina Woolf, make this one of the most intriguing houses in England. Thirteen superb staterooms are laid out much the same as they were in the 18th century to impress visitors by the wealth and status of the Sackville family. The house contains Royal Stuart furniture; paintings by Gainsborough and Reynolds as well as many 17th century tapestries. Knole is set at the heart of the only remaining medieval deer park in Kent. Open Apr - Oct. Garden restricted access, please phone for details.

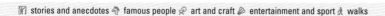

Horsey Common

Distance: *5.7 miles (9.1 kilometres)*
Typical time: *200 mins*
Height gain: *140 metres*
Map: *Explorer 147*
Walk: *www.walkingworld.com ID:552*
Contributor: *Nina Thornhill*

ACCESS INFORMATION:

The walk starts from Hosey Common car park. From the A25 at Westerham follow the signs to Chartwell, which takes you into Hosey Common Road. The car park is on the left, just after the turn for French Street. The walk can also be started from Westerham itself; this may be useful if you arrive by bus, or if you would rather avoid the climb up Hosey Hill on the return to Hosey Common car park. A car park is signposted from the main road (A25).

ADDITIONAL INFORMATION:

The height gain of 140 metres is a bit deceptive, as a total of four hills have to be climbed (making it more like 140 x 4). Westerham has a good choice of pubs, restaurants and tea rooms. There are three historic houses open to the public: the National Trust-owned Chartwell and Quebec House and Squerrys Court. A good place to stop for a picnic is the viewing point at the top of Toys Hill.

DESCRIPTION:

The walk starts just south of Westerham through the wooded Hosey Common, then follows the secluded hamlet of French Street, offering a host of treasures including an oast house and fine views. In 1927, the Westerham Gold was found by workers digging for gravel, this consisted of 14 Iron Age gold staters that were hidden by the Celts. The Greensand Way is followed from here to the National Trust-owned Toys Hill, at just over 800 feet it is Kent's highest point. On a clear day, the Ashdown Forest and South Downs are visible.

From here we start to head west, towards the National Trust-owned Chartwell, home of Sir Winston Churchill for more than forty years. Although the grounds of the estate are not entered, it is still possible to see some interesting outlying buildings and more views.

Another stretch of National Trust countryside is next at Mariners Hill, before climbing up Crockham Hill. This is the woodland section of the walk and continues all the way to Squerrys Park. Here the countryside opens out again to fine views of The High Chart to the west and The Chart to the east. Further on, views of the North Downs and Westerham can be seen. The historic town of Westerham is reached towards the end of the walk.

FEATURES:

Hills or fells, lake/loch, pub, toilets, National Trust/NTS, wildlife, birds, great views.

WALK DIRECTIONS:

1 | From the car park at Hosey Common look for a footpath in the right hand corner, marked by a yellow-arrowed post (there are two paths which go from here but they both join up a little further on). Keep to this path until you reach a fork in about a ¼ mile. At the fork bear left and continue to follow the yellow marker-posts, until another fork is reached close by.

2 | Bear left at this fork. Almost immediately you are faced with a choice of three paths. You need to take the middle one, which is surrounded by little ridges either side. Be careful to stay on this main path as several paths lead off from this one. At a small fork, bear left downhill; in about 20 yards you should arrive at a hollow on the left. Keep left alongside the hollow and after ¼ mile look out for a post and path on the right. Turn right here. When a crossroads is reached, keep ahead. Further on, ignore two paths on the left you should soon arrive at a country lane.

3 | Turn right and walk along the lane, which passes through the hamlet of French Street. At a fork in the road, keep ahead downhill (ignoring the right turn). Some old cottages are passed before reaching another fork. At this fork, keep left to join the Greensand Way, which we follow

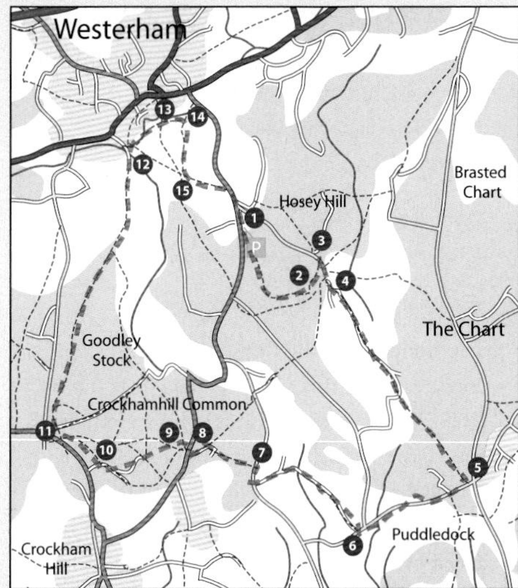

all the way to Toys Hill. Just after climbing uphill, a fork is reached.

4 | Bear right at the fork to take the bridlepath to Toys Hill. Follow the Greensand Way arrows through Toys Hill, ignoring a series of paths going off to the left, until you reach a crossroads. Keep ahead at this crossroads and follow the blue arrows (this is where you part from the Greensand Way). A few paces ahead at a fork, bear right. This path goes downhill to Puddledock Lane.

5 | When Puddledock Lane is reached, turn right and enjoy some breathtaking views. Follow the lane downhill; after passing a small lane on the right at Windswept Cottage, look out for a stile on the right.

6 | Turn right onto this path, which leads to the grounds of Chartwell. When you reach a lane, keep left and head towards an oast house. Keeping the oast house to your right you join a lane. Keep ahead on this lane until you reach a road (Mapleton Road) and turn right into it. Look out for a bridleway on the left, near some houses.

7 | Turn left onto this bridleway to climb Mariners Hill. Stay on the bridleway, ignoring all paths on the right, until the gate of Windmill Bank is reached.

8 | At Windmill Bank take the path ahead through the woods to rejoin the Greensand Way. Keep ahead to reach Hosey Common Road and go straight over to take the path by April Cottage. Soon after you come to a fork.

9 | At this fork, turn left and continue ahead to follow the Greensand Way until you reach a crossroads of paths. At the crossroads, keep ahead to climb up Crockham Hill. Do the same at another crossroads of paths further on. When The Warren house is reached continue to follow yellow arrows. Continue until this track meets a road. You should see a bench on the right.

10 | Turn right here and be sure to follow the yellow Greensand Way markers ahead. Follow this path until a T-junction is reached.

11 | Turn right at this T-junction. The yellow Greensand Way markers are now followed all the way to Westerham (this is no longer the actual Greensand Way, but a route that links Westerham to it). Continue ahead for more than a mile, going over a series of four stiles.

12 | At this, the fifth stile (immediately before the pond), turn left. Another pond is passed on the left. Take the footpath on the right, which goes through a field. Keep to the path along the left-hand side of the field, and in the next field look out for a gate on the left.

13 | Go through this gate. This path leads you along Water Lane to Westerham. When you reach the main road turn right at Mill Street, turn right and re-cross the stream. Keep to the path along the right-hand side and look for a gap in the trees.

14 | Go through the gap and you should see a marker-post just ahead. Turn left here to walk up Hosey Hill. Keep to the left of the field. Go over two stiles and as soon as you pass Glebe House look out for a path on the left.

15 | Turn left and go down this path, which comes out by Hosey Common Road. Turn right at the road and head back to the car park.

Around Sevenoaks

FARNBOROUGH

8 miles N of Sevenoaks on the A21

Just to the south of the village lies High Elms Country Park, a delightful park of woodlands, formal gardens and meadows that was once part of the High Elms Estate.

FRENCH STREET

6 miles W of Sevenoaks off the B2042

Chartwell

A tiny hamlet, tucked away in the folds of narrow, wooded hills, French Street appears to be one of the most hidden away places in Kent, but a particular reason brings visitors here in droves. In 1924, Winston Churchill purchased **Chartwell** as a family home and, with its magnificent views looking out over the Kentish Weald, it is easy to see why the great statesman said of Chartwell, "I love the place - a day away from Chartwell is a day wasted." From the 1920s until his death in 1965, Churchill lived here with his wife, and the rooms have been left exactly as they were when the couple were alive: daily newspapers lie on the table, fresh flowers from the garden decorate the rooms and a box of his famous cigars lie ready. The museum and exhibition rooms contain numerous mementoes from his life and political career, while the garden studio contains many of his paintings along with his easel and paintbox.

The gardens have also been kept just as they were during his lifetime, so visitors can see not only the golden rose walk that the couple's children planted on the occasion of Sir Winston and Lady Churchill's 50th wedding anniversary, but also the brick wall that Churchill built with his own hands. The house is now in the care of the National Trust.

Chartwell, French Street

WESTERHAM

4 miles W of Sevenoaks on the A25

Quebec House Squerryes Court

The building of the M25 has eased the traffic congestion of this pleasant, small town close to the Surrey border and it is now a quieter and calmer place that is more in keeping with its former days as a coaching station. Along the town's main street and around the tiny green are a number of old buildings, including two venerable coaching inns, while, in the town centre, by the green, are two statues of British heroes who had connections with Westerham. The first dates from 1969 and it is a tribute to Sir Winston Churchill, who made his home close by at Chartwell, and the other statue is that of General James Wolfe, who defeated the French at Quebec in 1759. Wolfe was born in Westerham and his childhood home, renamed **Quebec House**, can be found to the east of the town centre. Dating from the 17th century, this gabled redbrick building, now in the care of the National

historic building museum and heritage historic site scenic attraction flora and fauna

Trust, contains portraits, prints and other memorabilia relating to the family, the general and his famous victory over the French.

There has been a house on the site that is now occupied by **Squerryes Court** since 1216 and, in 1658, when the diarist John Evelyn visited the medieval mansion he described it as: "A pretty, finely wooded, well watered seate, the stables good, the house old but convenient." However, this building was not to last much longer, as in 1681 the then owner, Sir Nicholas Crisp, pulled it down and built in its place the glorious redbrick house seen today. Bought by the Warde family in 1731, it remains in their hands today and is perhaps best known for the important collection of 18th-century English and 17th-century Dutch paintings, many of them commissioned by the family. The sumptuously appointed rooms also contain some splendid furniture, porcelain and tapestries, as well as some Wolfe memorabilia. A friend of the family, James Wolfe received his first commission while here, at the tender age of 14. Outside lie superb gardens, restored to their original formal state after the Great Storm of 1987 using a garden plan of 1719.

In Westerham's churchyard is the grave of Sir Peter Nissen, who designed the hut that bears his name and was widely used durring World War II.

OTFORD

3 miles N of Sevenoaks off the A225

Heritage Centre · Becket's Well

Found in a pleasant location beside the River Darent, this village has a history that stretches back to Roman times and beyond - as does much of the Darent Valley. Lying at a crossroads important for many centuries, it was here in 775 that King Offa of Mercia won

CABBAGES & KINGS

The Old Post Office, Church Road, Halstead, Kent TN14 7HE
Tel/Fax: 01959 533054
e-mail: janewhitby@cabbages-and-kings.co.uk
website: www.cabbages-and-kings.co.uk

Built as the village Post Office and general groceries store around 1830, **Cabbages & Kings** is now one of the cosiest B&Bs in the Sevenoaks area. The house is surrounded by the peace and tranquillity of the countryside yet is only a short drive from the M25 (J4), with easy access to many of the county's leading attractions. The transformation of the handsome flint house has been achieved by owner Jane Whitby, who used natural materials – oak, stone, slate – along with sumptuous fabrics and accessories and subtle lighting to create a very comfortable, inviting blend of classic and contemporary. Jane's sure touch and eye for design extends outside to the landscaping and planting of the garden. The bedrooms are decorated and furnished to a very high standard; each has its own individual theme, and all have en suite facilities, flat-screen TV, DVD player and library, clock radio, hairdryer, hot water bottles and tea/coffee tray. Jane's expertise extends into the kitchen, where she produces splendid traditional English breakfast (vegetarian and lighter options available). With a little notice she can provide a picnic and afternoon tea in the garden or by the fire in the sitting room.

the battle that brought Kent into his kingdom; several centuries later, Henry VIII stopped at Otford on his way to the historic encounter with François I of France at the Field of the Cloth of Gold. The King is believed to have stayed the night at one of the many palaces belonging to the Archbishop of Canterbury. The palace at Otford, of which little remains, stood adjacent to the Church of St Bartholomew and opposite the village's duck pond.

The Pond, which lies at the heart of Otford, is itself something of a historic curiosity as it was documented as early as the 11th century and is thought to be the only stretch of water in England to be classified as a listed building. The Otford **Heritage Centre** is just the place to find out more about this interesting village and here can be seen displays on the village's natural history, geology and archaeology, including artefacts from nearby Roman sites and the medieval Archbishop's Palace.

Connections with the Archbishops of Canterbury continue at **Becket's Well**, which once supplied water to the palace and is thought to have miraculous origins. Local folklore suggests that when he was visiting Otford, Archbishop Thomas à Becket was so displeased with the quality of the local water that, to remedy the situation, he struck the ground with his crozier and two springs of clear water bubbled up from the spot.

SHOREHAM

4 miles N of Sevenoaks off the A255

Aircraft Museum

Shoreham is situated beside the River Darent, which features prominently in the village. As well as the footpaths that run along its banks it is also crossed by a handsome hump-backed bridge. Close to this bridge lies the Water House that was the home of Samuel Palmer, the great Romantic painter, for some years. Here Palmer entertained his friend, the poet and visionary William Blake.

On the hillside across the valley can be seen a large cross carved into the chalk which commemorates those who fell in the two World Wars. Shoreham **Aircraft Museum** is dedicated to the Battle of Britain and the air war over southern England. Among the numerous exhibits are aviation relics and home front memorabilia from the 1940s.

EYNSFORD

6½ miles N of Sevenoaks off the A225

Eagle Heights · Lullingstone Castle

Lullingstone Roman Villa · Park & Visitor Centre

The centre of this pretty and picturesque village manages to preserve a sense of history and, crossing the River Darent, there is a small hump-backed bridge and an ancient ford along with a number of old timbered cottages and a church with a tall shingle spire. The ford that gives the village its name has a depth chart that shows that the depth of the ford can reach six feet when the river is swollen with floodwater.

Eynsford Castle, Eynsford

Leslie Hore-Belisha made his home here for a time. It was while Minister of Transport in the 1930s that he gave his name to the Belisha beacon street crossings; he also inaugurated the driving test for motorists.

Tucked away down a lane just a short distance from the village is **Eagle Heights**, Kent's bird of prey centre. Concentrating on explaining the importance of conservation and the birds' environment, the centre hosts free flying shows where visitors can see eagles soaring high above the Darent Valley and watch the condor, the world's largest bird of prey, in flight.

Further down the lane lies **Lullingstone Roman Villa**, although only uncovered in 1949, its existence had been known since the 18th century, when farm labourers uncovered fragments of mosaics that had been pierced as the men drove fence posts into the ground. Perhaps not the largest find in the country, Lullingstone is recognised to be the most exciting of its kind made in the 20th century. The villa, which was first occupied in 80, has splendid mosaic floors and one of the earliest private Christian chapels.

Close by, in a quiet spot beside the River Darent, lies **Lullingstone Castle**, a superb manor house whose 15th-century gatehouse is one of the first ever to be built from bricks. The house remains in the hands of the descendants of John Peche, who built it. John Peche was a city alderman and a keen jouster; he laid out a jousting ground in front of the gatehouse and entertained the young Henry VIII. The house has some fine state rooms, as might be expected of a place with royal connections, as well as family portraits and armour on display. John Peche's jousting helmet is on display in the dining room. The castle is surrounded by beautiful grounds that also house the tiny Norman church of St Botolph. A little further south again lies **Lullingstone Park and Visitor Centre** which incorporates both parkland, with ancient pollard oaks, and chalk grassland. A full programme of guided walks, special events and children's activities take place from the visitor centre, where there is a countryside interpretation exhibition.

FARNINGHAM

8 miles N of Sevenoaks off the A225

Nature Reserve · Darent Valley Path

This attractive village, in the Darent valley, was once on the main London road and much of the Georgian architecture found in the village centre reflects the prosperity that Farningham once enjoyed. A handsome 18th-century brick bridge stands by lawns that slope down to the river's edge, alongside which runs the **Darent Valley Path**, following the course of the river as far as Dartford. Despite its rural appeal, Farningham is close to the M25 and M20 motorway intersection, but **Farningham Woods Nature Reserve** provides a delightful area of natural countryside that supports a wide variety of rare plants and birdlife.

TROTTISCLIFFE

9½ miles NE of Sevenoaks off the A20

Coldrum Long Barrow

As its name, pronounced 'Trossley', implies, this village occupies a hillside position. A pretty, neat village with views over the North Downs, it was the beauty of this quiet place that lured the artist Graham Sutherland to make Trottiscliffe his home (he is buried with his wife in the churchyard).

Just to the north of the village, on high ground that offers commanding views eastwards over the Medway Valley, stands **Coldrum Long Barrow**, some 24 columns of stone that once marked the perimeter of a circular long barrow that was originally 50 feet in diameter. Only four of the huge stones are still standing and, although the large burial mound inside the circle has long since disappeared, this ancient site remains an evocative and mysterious place.

WROTHAM

6 miles NE of Sevenoaks off the A227

This ancient village was once a staging post on one of the important routes southeastwards from London. It was here, in 1536, that Henry VIII received news of the execution of his second wife, Anne Boleyn.

PLATT

6 miles E of Sevenoaks off the A25

Great Comp Garden

This village lies close to **Great Comp Garden**, one of finest gardens in the country and one with a truly unique atmosphere. Around the ruins of the house that once stood here, there are terraces and a sweeping lawn along with a breathtaking collection of trees, shrubs and perennials and tranquil woodland walks. The whole amazing garden was designed and created by Eric Cameron and his wife after they retired in 1957.

IGHTHAM

4½ miles E of Sevenoaks on the A227

Church

This delightful village is a charming place of half-timbered houses and crooked lanes. Inside **Ightham Church** is a mural dedicated to Dame Dorothy Selby, who, according to legend, was instrumental in uncovering the Gunpowder Plot. The story goes that James I showed Dame Dorothy an anonymous letter he had received that hinted at a terrible blow that would soon befall Parliament and, while the king dismissed the letter as the work of a crank, Dame Dorothy, reading between the lines, urged him to take the warning with the utmost seriousness.

IVY HATCH

3½ miles E of Sevenoaks off the A227

Ightham Mote

Just to the south of this small village lies **Ightham Mote** (see panel below), one of England's finest medieval manor houses, owned by the National Trust. Covering some 650 years of history, this beautiful moated house, set in a narrow, wooded valley, dates back to the 14th century. It is constructed around a central courtyard intended as a meeting place which is referred to in its name - 'mote' probably comes from the Old English word meaning 'meeting place'. There is plenty to see here, from the medieval Great Hall and Tudor chapel to the Victorian housekeeper's room and the billiard room. The manor house had a crypt where unlucky prisoners could be simply dispatched by the opening of a sluice gate from the moat. There was also a trap in the floor of a room in the tower from where unsuspecting victims could be dropped into a small dark hole.

An exhibition details the traditional skills that were used during the major conservation programme, that took place here in 1998. The delightful garden and grounds, with their lakes and woodland, provide numerous opportunities for pleasant country walks.

PLAXTOL

4½ miles E of Sevenoaks off the A227

Old Soar Manor   Mereworth Woods

This hilltop village, on a prominent ridge near Ightham Mote, has a charming row of traditional Kentish weatherboard cottages that surround the parish church. Just to the east of the village, and reached via a circuitous succession of narrow lanes, is **Old Soar Manor**, another fine National Trust owned manor house, dating from the late 13th century. The solar end of the old house

Ightham Mote

Mote Road, Ivy Hatch, Sevenoaks, Kent TN15 0NT
Tel: 01732 810378
website: www.nationaltrust.org.uk

Nestling in a sunken valley and dating from 1320, the house has features spanning many centuries. The most extensive visitor route open since Ightham Mote's acquisition by the Trust includes the Great Hall, Old Chapel. Crypt, Tudor chapel with painted ceiling, drawing room with Jacobean fireplace, frieze and 18th-century wallpaper, billiards room and the apartment of Charles Henry Robinson, the American donor. There is an extensive garden and interesting walks in the surrounding woodland. A comprehensive programme of repair begun in 1989 was completed in 2004 and is the subject of a 'Conservation in Action' exhibition in the visitor reception.

survives on a tunnel vaulted undercroft, along with the chapel. An 18th-century redbrick house stands where the original hall was located. While the house itself is charming it is the idyllic setting of Old Soar Manor, with its surrounding orchards and copses, that makes this such a delightful place to visit. The woods grow more dense as they climb the ridge and rise up from the orchards; at the top is one of southern England's largest forests, **Mereworth Woods**. Wild boar once roamed through this forest of oak and beech trees and, though today the wildlife is of a tamer variety, the woods are still enchanting.

MEREWORTH

8 miles E of Sevenoaks on the A228

Found on the southern boundary of Mereworth Woods, the village is something of a curiosity. Early in the 18th century, John Fane, a local landowner, built himself a large Palladian mansion here. He soon found that the village obscured some of his views of the surrounding countryside and so he had the village demolished and moved to a site that could not be seen from his new home. The new village had houses for all the original inhabitants and Fane even built a new church. The architecture of the church owes a lot to the style of Sir Christopher Wren and the result is a faithful copy of St Martin-in-the-Fields in London.

BIGGIN HILL

7½ miles NW of Sevenoaks on the A233

RAF Station

This village is best known for its association with the RAF and, in particular, with the role that the local station played in the Battle of Britain. A Spitfire and a Hurricane flank the entrance to **Biggin Hill RAF Station**. A chapel at the station commemorates the 453 pilots from Biggin Hill who lost their lives during the conflict.

The location of Biggin Hill - high on a plateau on the North Downs - made it an obvious choice for an airfield and the views from here, over the Darent Valley, are outstanding.

The village itself, which sprawls along this plateau, has a particularly interesting church. Saint Mark's was built between 1957 and 1959, using material from the derelict All Saints' Church at Peckham. The windows were engraved by the vicar - Rev V Symons.

DOWNE

7 miles NW of Sevenoaks off the A233

Down House

Found high up on the North Downs and commanding spectacular views, especially northwards towards London, Downe has managed to retain a real country atmosphere. Its central core of traditional flint cottages has not been engulfed by the growing tide of modern suburban housing spreading from the capital. Seemingly at a crossroads between Greater London and the countryside, Downe's natural setting, still evident in the outskirts of the village, also marks something of a boundary as it is poised between the open uplands of the Downs themselves and the more wooded areas of Kent, such as the Weald, further south.

It was in this village, at **Down House**, that one of the world's greatest and best known scientists, Charles Darwin, lived for over 40 years until his death in 1882. Following his five year voyage on *HMS Beagle*, Darwin came back to this house where he worked on formalising his theory of evolution, and it was here that he wrote his famous work *The Origin of Species by*

Means of Natural Selection that was published in 1859. The house is now a museum dedicated to the life and work of this famous scientist and visitors can find out more about his revolutionary theory and gain an understanding of the man himself. The study, where he did much of his writing, still contains many personal belongings, and the family rooms have been painstakingly restored to provide a real insight into Charles Darwin, the scientist, husband and father. 2009 is the bicentenary of the great biologist's birth, and to celebrate the occasion the living laboratory where he developed much of his evolutionary thinking has been re-opened to the public. A newly developed multimedia garden tour, with contributions from Sir David Attenborough, Lord Bragg and the evolutionary biologist Steve Jones, highlights the countryside setting's critical role in the great man's thinking.

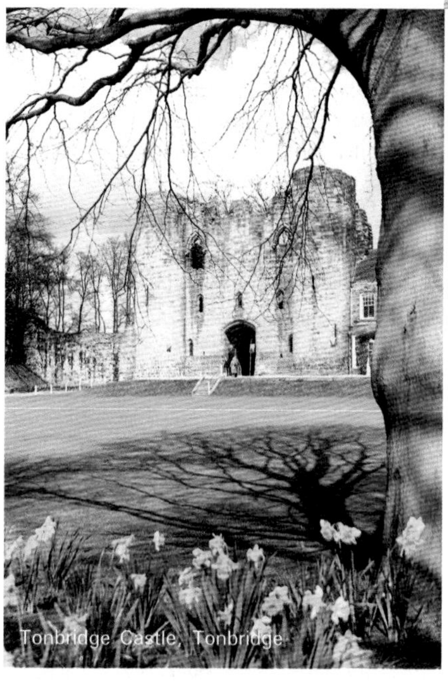
Tonbridge Castle, Tonbridge

Tonbridge

School

This pretty old town stands at the highest navigable point on the River Medway and, as well as having a Victorian cast-iron bridge across the river, the substantial remains of Tonbridge's Norman Castle can be found on a rise in the town centre. The walls of the castle date from the 12th century, while the shell of the keep, along with the massive gatehouse and drum towers, were built in the early 14th century. Within the castle walls is a mound that is believed to have been the site of an earlier Saxon fort that provides further evidence of the importance of the river crossing. The castle was all but destroyed during the Civil War and, today, the ruins are surrounded by attractive landscaped gardens.

While the castle is certainly one of the town's oldest buildings, its most famous institution is **Tonbridge School**, founded in 1553 by Sir Andrew Judd, Master of the Skinners' Company and a former Lord Mayor of London. The school received a charter from Elizabeth I, and on Judd's death the administration was left in trust to the Skinners' Company, the Governors to this day.

Around Tonbridge

TUDELEY

2 miles E of Tonbridge on the B2017

The most striking feature of All Saints Church is a stained-glass window commissioned from Marc Chagall by Sir Henry and Lady d'Avidgor Goldsmith in memory of their daughter Sarah, who drowned in a sailing accident off Rye in 1963. The work was so well received on its installation in 1967 that more were commissioned, the last being installed in 1985, the year of Chagall's death. The glass was made and fitted by Charles Marq of Rheims.

PENSHURST

4½ miles SW of Tonbridge on the B2176

Penshurst Place

With its hilly, wooded setting and Tudor architecture, Penshurst is renowned as being one of Kent's prettiest villages. The houses at its core are all old, dating as far back as the 16th century, and each has its own sense of charm and identity. At the heart of the village, the Church of St John the Baptist appears completely 19th century from the outside, but inside are architectural details from the 13th century onwards. Particularly noteworthy is the carving on a medieval tomb of a supplicant woman. The entrance to the church is by an ancient lychgate. Close by is one of the village's equally ancient houses, a two-storey Tudor dwelling that is particularly quaint with its bulging walls and crooked beams.

Just to the north of the village lies **Penshurst Place**. Set in the peaceful landscape of the Weald of Kent, it is recognised as being one of the best examples of 14th-century architecture in the country. The house was built of local sandstone in 1341 by Sir John de Pulteney, four times Lord Mayor of London. In 1552, Edward VI granted Penshurst Place to his steward and tutor, Sir William Sidney, grandfather of the famous Elizabethan poet, soldier and courtier, Sir Philip Sidney. Additions to the original house over the centuries have seen it become an imposing fortified manor house and it remains in the Sidney family today. Visitors to Penshurst Place have the opportunity to see the magnificent Barons Hall and the impressive staterooms, and a marvellous collection of paintings, furniture, tapestries, porcelain and armour.

The gardens surrounding the house are equally impressive and are a rare example of Elizabethan design. The records here go back to 1346, making this one of the oldest gardens in private ownership, and over a mile of yew hedging separates the walled garden into a series of individually styled 'rooms'. Designed as a garden for all seasons, it provides a riot of colour from early springtime right through to the autumn.

Penshurst Place is also home to a Toy Museum, where the world of the nursery is

Old Village & Church, Penhurst

16th & 17th-century houses, Chiddingstone

brought to life through an interesting collection of dolls, tin soldiers and many other toys that originally belonged to several generations of Sidney children.

Also close by is one of the most modern vineyards in England, Penshurst Vineyards, where adults can enjoy the lovely walks and the wine tastings, and children can see the unusual range of animals, including wallabies and rare breeds of sheep and birds.

CHIDDINGSTONE

6 miles W of Tonbridge off the B2027

Castle

This pretty village, set in pleasant open woodland, is one of the most picturesque in Kent and is owned by the National Trust. Along a footpath behind the main street, which is lined with houses from the 16th and 17th centuries that were built during the village's prosperous period, lies a block of sandstone known as the Chiding Stone. Legend has it that in the past miscreant, vagrants and assorted petty criminals were taken here for public humiliation

Also found in this village is one of Kent's best kept secrets, **Chiddingstone Castle**, a traditional country squire's house that has the appearance of a grand castle. It was in 1805 that Henry Streatfield rebuilt his family home in grand Gothic style. In 1955 the house was bought by Denys Eyre Bower, a self-made man with a passion for collecting. Today, the castle houses Bower's vast and varied collection, covering themes that range from relics from ancient Egypt and artefacts from Japan, to pictures and mementoes from the Royal Stuart dynasty.

BOUGH BEECH

6½ miles W of Tonbridge on the B2027

Reservoir

To the north of this village lies **Bough Beech Reservoir**, whose surrounding nature reserve provides excellent opportunities for bird watching. The reservoir's visitor centre has a series of exhibitions and displays on the local wildlife, the area's hop growing industry and the history of this reservoir.

HEVER

7½ miles W of Tonbridge off the B2027

Castle

This tiny village, set in a delightfully unspoilt countryside of orchards and woodlands, is home to one of Kent's star attractions - **Hever Castle**. The original castle, which consisted of the gatehouse, outer walls and inner moat, was built in the 1270s by Sir Stephen de Penchester,

Hever Castle, Hever

who received permission from Edward I to fortify his home. Some two centuries later, the Bullen (or Boleyn) family purchased the property and added the comfortable Tudor manor house that stands within the castle walls. Hever Castle was the childhood home of Anne Boleyn and the ill-fated mother of Elizabeth I was courted here by Henry VIII. Many of Anne's personal items, including two books of hours (prayer books) signed by Anne, along with other Tudor mementoes, can be seen here.

In 1903, the castle was bought by the American millionaire, William Waldorf Astor, who put his great wealth to use in restoring the original buildings and the grounds - work that included laying out and planting over 30 acres of formal gardens. Visitors are particularly drawn to these award-winning gardens, but the castle also houses fine collections of paintings, furniture, tapestries and objets d'art.

EDENBRIDGE

9 miles W of Tonbridge on the B2026

This small town, found near the upper reaches of the River Eden, a tributary of the Medway, has been a settlement since Roman times and, although the present bridge spanning the river dates from the 1830s, there has been a bridge here since that early occupation. Its High Street is a straight line through the town and across the river. It was originally the Roman road and an important route through the forest of the Kentish Weald. Along its route can still be found some ancient coaching inns some dating from the 1370s - that catered to the needs of travellers. The Crown Inn became notorious in the 17th century as a haunt of the Romney gang of smugglers.

IDE HILL

7½ miles NW of Tonbridge off the B2042

Emmetts Garden

Situated in the upper Darent Valley, this remote little village is the highest spot in Kent at 800 feet above sea level. In the past a beacon on the hill would be used to signal danger to Shooters Hill on the outskirts of London. From its elevated position, Idle Hill commands glorious, panoramic views stretching out over the Weald. During the 16th century its hunting grounds became a secret meeting place for Henry VIII and his future queen, Anne Boleyn of Hever.

Just outside the village, and set on a hillside of mature beech trees, is **Emmetts Garden**, an informal National Trust - maintained garden that boasts the highest tree top in Kent - a 100-foot Wellingtonia planted on Kent's highest point. Noted for its rare trees and shrubs, as well as its rose and rock gardens, Emmetts also offers wonderful views across the Kentish Weald.

North Kent Coast

From Margate, on the northeastern tip of Kent, to Rochester, on the River Medway, the history of the north Kent coastal area has been dominated by the sea. It was invaded over 2,000 years ago by the Romans and, ever since, the land, villages and towns have endured occupation by successive invaders. Many of the place names, such as Rochester and Whitstable, are derived from Roman, Saxon or Norman origins.

The cathedral at Rochester was built on a Saxon site by William the Conqueror's architect Bishop Gundulph, and it was also he who designed the massive fortress of Rochester Castle. While this ancient city, with numerous connections with Charles Dickens, is one of the best known places along the Medway, it is Chatham that really captures the imagination. Henry VIII, looking to increase his sea power, established a dockyard at this originally Saxon settlement. This was the beginning of the Royal Navy that was to be instrumental in the building and maintenance of the British Empire. The Naval Dockyards at Chatham, where Nelson's ship *HMS Victory* was built, and the Napoleonic fortress, Fort Amherst, are two of the best monuments to the great seafaring traditions of England. In conjunction with the naval loyalties of Chatham, Gillingham is the home of the Royal Engineers, and their museum highlights the valuable work that the Corps has done over the centuries in many areas, including civil engineering and surveying.

Further east lie the seaside towns and resorts of Whitstable, Herne Bay and Margate. Certainly the most popular is Margate, the natural destination for many people of southeast London looking for a day beside the sea. While offering all the delights of the seaside, such as amusements, a funfair, candyfloss and fish and chips, Margate is older than it seems. It probably comes as no surprise to learn that the bathing machine was invented in the town. Whitstable, which remains famous for its oysters, presents a calmer and less brash appearance to those looking for a seaside break. With a history that goes back to Roman times, this fishing village, once the haunt of smugglers, has managed to retain an individuality that inspired writers such as Somerset Maugham and Charles Dickens.

Rochester

Castle Cathedral Guildhall Museum

Royal Victoria and Bull Hotel

First impressions of this riverside city are misleading as the pedestrianised main shopping area and steady flow of traffic hide a history that goes back over 2,000 years. Rochester was first settled by the Romans, whose Watling Street crossed the River Medway at this point. To protect this strategic crossing point, they fortified their camp here and, in so doing, created a walled city of some 23 acres. Some five centuries later the Saxons arrived. Still an important strategic town and port, it was at Rochester that King Alfred, determined to thwart Viking sea power, built a fleet of ships and thereby created the first English navy.

Following the Norman invasion in 1066, William the Conqueror, also aware of the importance of the town and its port, decreed

I DIG DINOS

388 High Street, Rochester,
Kent ME1 1DJ
Tel: 01634 406555
mob: 0790 612 4829
e-mail: terence@idigdinos.com
website: www.idigdinos.com

'Fossil Collecting made Easy and Affordable'

I Dig Dinos is the only Dinosaur shop in Kent, and the greatest shop of its kind in the UK. Without a doubt, Terence and Tracy Collingwood own and run one of the most unusual shops you'll ever step inside, a browser's delight and a thoroughly entertaining introduction into the fascinating world of fossils.

The stock, which changes constantly, includes real teeth and bones from such creatures as Tyrannosaurus Rex, African T-Rex, Spinosaurus, Saltasaurus, Oviraptor, Deltadromeus, Sauropods and Triceratops. Genuine dinosaur teeth start at a bargain £2. You'll also find teeth from sharks – Megalodon, Great White, Mako and Otodus. There are ammonites, trilobites, ambers – Baltic, Dominican, Madagascan, Colombian Copal – and fossil plants like Glossopteris, Pecopteris and Neuropteris. All geological ages are represented in this unique place, from Pleistocene to Eocene, Cretaceous, Jurassic, Triassic, Permian right up to the Cambrian.

I Dig Dinos also sells a good range of minerals, including amethyst, agate and fool's gold, and the accessories that every fossil collector needs, such as display boxes and stands. Very much a place for all the family, the shop sells a vast selection of dinosaur-themed toys, games, puzzles and books, along with dig-out kits and hundreds of models.

I Dig Dinos, which is open from 10 to 5.30 Tuesday to Saturday, is located at the Chatham end of Rochester High Street.

Would-be buyers who can't get to the shop can visit the superb website for more fascinating details, online buying and useful links to other sites.

that a castle be maintained here permanently and set his architect, Bishop Gundulph, the task of designing a suitable fortification. Still dominating the city today, **Rochester Castle** is recognised as one of the finest surviving examples of Norman architecture in England. Over 100 feet tall and with walls that are around 12 feet thick, this massive construction comprised four floors from which there were many lookout points. Despite the solidity of the fortress, it has had a very chequered history and over the centuries was subjected to three sieges. In 1215 the rebellious barons were held here by King John for seven weeks. The barons held out despite being bombarded by missiles thrown from huge siege engines, and it was only when the props of a siege tunnel were burnt away and the tunnel collapsed that the barons surrendered. The collapsing of the tunnel also caused the massive tower above to collapse. This was later reconstructed in a round form rather than the original square shape, giving the castle its odd appearance. Rochester Castle was again severely damaged during the Civil War and much of the building seen today is the result of restoration work undertaken in

Rochester Castle, Rochester

FRANCIS ILES

103 High Street, Rochester, Kent ME1 1LX
Tel: 01474 843081
e-mail: nettie@francis-iles.com
website: www.francis-iles.com

Three sisters – Alayne, Nettie and Lucy – own and run **Francis Iles**, a centre of excellence for art, located in a handsome Georgian house in the heart of historic Rochester. The sisters take well-earned pride in offering top-quality work by home-grown and overseas artists that really does provide something for everyone. On the upper two floors they show more than 700 works of art, from traditional oils and watercolours to the more contemporary glass relief and boxed canvases. One of their more esteemed artists was the late Rowland Hilder OBE, who had a lifelong relationship with the Gallery. The Gallery hosts regular and special exhibitions throughout the year and among those planned for 2009 are paintings by Jeremy Sanders, miniatures by Alison Griffin, fantastic stained glass by Leo Amery and collective work by 'Artists of Russia'. Other names associated with Francis Iles include Christopher Jarvis, John Scarland, Ken Turner and Roland Batchelor.

Among the other offerings here are a full restoration service for oils and watercolours, a bespoke framing service run by Fine Art Trade Guild framers and specialist advice on conservation framing. The Gallery is open from 9.30 to 5.30 Monday to Saturday.

FRANCIS ILES

104 High Street, Rochester, Kent ME1 1JT
Tel: 01434 843081
e-mail: advice@artycat.com website: www.artycat.com

The three sisters who run the Gallery at 103 High Street also run this other arm of **Francis Iles**, a mecca for artists and craftspeople, filled with a huge range of art and craft materials. **Artworks** is a store within a store specialising in art materials and equipment for amateur and professional artists. **Craftworks** is a store within a store selling a full range of craft materials for stitchers, knitters, card makers, rubber stampers and other crafters. Both departments include rare and difficult to find items and new products as well as established ranges, and experienced staff are on hand with help and advice on all aspects of arts and crafts. Opening times are 9 to 5.30 Monday to Friday, 9.30 to 5.30 Saturday; customers who can't get to the store can order online or by phone.

The owners offers a comprehensive calendar of workshops, which take place most Saturdays. They also operate an e-mail alert to update clients about forthcoming events. Every other year they stage an Art & Craft Expo held in the Corn Exchange just along the road.

the 19th century. The castle has been brought into the 21st century through an interactive computer programme that takes visitors on a virtual tour of the fortress as it may have looked in medieval times. The tour is located at the Visitor Information Centre in the High Street.

As well as ordering the construction of the massive fortification, William the Conqueror put his architect to the task of building **Rochester Cathedral** on the site of a Saxon church that was founded in 604. Today's building still contains the remains of the 12th-century chapter house and priory, along with other Norman features including the fine west doorway. Like the castle, the cathedral was badly damaged during the Civil War and restoration work was undertaken by the Victorians. The remains of former monastic buildings surround the cathedral and there are three ancient gates: Prior's Gate, Deanery Gate and Chertsey's Gate, all leading on to the High Street.

Rochester Cathedral, Rochester

Not far from Rochester Bridge is the **Guildhall Museum** that covers the history of this city from prehistoric times through to the present day. The Guildhall was built in 1687 and features in Dickens's novel *Great Expectations* as the place where Pip goes to register as an apprentice. The reconstruction of a Medway prison hulk ship, from the turn of the 19th century, covers three floors. It is undoubtedly the most haunting exhibit in the museum depicting the inhuman conditions on board. There are domestic reconstructions of Victorian and Edwardian vintage, and many exhibits relating to Rochester's maritime history. There are scale models of local sailing barges and a diorama of the Dutch raid of the Medway in 1667.

Although the castle, cathedral and river dominate Rochester, the city is perhaps most famous for its connections with the great Victorian novelist, Charles Dickens. The Dickens Discovery Room in the Guildhall Museum in January 2006, is has two very exciting and informative galleries dedicated to the author. There are many related objects on display, text and graphic panels and a multi-lingual touchscreen that highlights other sites of Dickens interest. The audio-visual theatre shows a short film about the author's life and works.

There are many other buildings in the city with a Dickens' connection that are well worth seeking out. The **Royal Victoria and Bull**

Hotel featured as The Bull in *The Pickwick Papers* and again in *Great Expectations* as The Blue Boar. The addition of the 'Royal Victoria' to the hotel's name came in the 1830s following a visit by the as yet uncrowned Queen Victoria in 1836, who was prevented from continuing to London by a violent storm.

The busy port here and the routes to and from London that pass through Rochester have always ensured that the city has a steady stream of visitors. After 11 years in exile, Charles II found himself staying overnight at Rochester while making his triumphal march from Dover to London in 1660. On a less happy note, it was at Abdication House (now a bank on the High Street) that James II, fleeing from William of Orange in 1689, spent his last night in England.

Around Rochester

BORSTAL

1½ miles S of Rochester off the B2097

Found on the eastern side of the elegant Medway Bridge, which carries the M2 over the River Medway, this village gave its name to young offenders institutions when the first prison of this type was opened here in 1908. The original Borstal buildings can still be seen.

STROOD

1 mile W of Rochester off the A228

Temple Manor

Situated on the opposite bank of the River Medway from Rochester, it was here that, during the Roman invasion of Britain masterminded by Claudius from Richborough, the Roman legions were halted by a force of Britons led by Caractacus. After two days, the Romans won the battle but only after Claudius had ordered some of his men to swim the river while others crossed higher up and surprised the Britons from behind.

However, it is as the home of **Temple Manor** that Strood is better known. Built in the 13th century by the Knights Templar, this was originally a hostel where the knights could find shelter, food and fresh horses while going to and from the Crusades. A building of simple design, this is all that survives from an earlier complex that would also have contained stables, kitchens and barns. Sympathetically restored after World War II, the original 13th-century hall, with its vaulted undercroft, and the 17th-century brick extensions have all survived.

A local legend tells that during the bitter feuding between Henry II and Archbishop Thomas à Becket the men of Strood, who were loyal to the king, cut off the tail of Becket's horse while he was riding through the town. Becket suggested that the descendants of those involved

Temple Manor, Strood

in the incident would be born with tails and so, apparently, they were!

As with other Medway towns, Strood has its connections with the sea and, moored at Damhead Creek is *The Medway Queen*, an old paddle steamer that was one of the many thousands of unlikely craft that took part in the evacuation of Dunkirk in 1941.

HIGHAM

3 miles NW of Rochester off the A226

Gad's Hill Place

This scattered village, with its ancient and charming marshland church, is famous for being the home of Charles Dickens - the great novelist lived with his family at **Gad's Hill Place** from 1857, when he bought it for £1,770, until his death in 1870. Dickens made various alterations to the 18th-century house to accommodate his family, in particular, adding a conservatory that has been restored to its former glory. While living at Gad's Hill, Dickens wrote several of his novels. Although the house is now a school, some of the rooms and the grounds that Dickens so loved are open to the public at various times throughout the year. Visitors can see the study where Dickens worked on his novels as well as the restored conservatory, and stroll around the grounds.

COOLING

4½ miles N of Rochester off the A228

This isolated village lies on the Hoo peninsula, an area of bleak marshland lying between the Medway and the Thames. In 1381, John de Cobham of Cooling applied to Richard II to be granted the right to fortify his manor house as, at that time, the sea came right up to his house and he feared a seaborne attack. His fears were well founded, as a couple of years earlier the French had sailed up the river and set fire to several villages in the area. So the king was happy to allow the construction to go ahead. The result of de Cobham's work, which became known as Cooling Castle, can still be seen clearly from the road (although it is not open to the public), but the sea has receded over the years and no longer laps the castle's massive outer walls. In the 15th century, Cooling Castle became the home of Sir John Oldcastle, Lord of Cooling, who was executed in 1417 for the part he played in a plot against Henry V. Shakespeare is said to have modelled his character Falstaff on Sir John.

Close by the substantial castle remains stands St James' Church (redundant but open for visits) where, in the graveyard, can be seen the 13 lozenge-shaped stones that mark the graves of various Comport children who all died of malaria in the 18th century. Not one of the children lived to be older than 17 months and these were, supposedly, the graves of Pip's brothers in Dickens's novel *Great Expectations.*

UPNOR

2 miles NE of Rochester off the A228

Castle

With a river frontage along the Medway and a backdrop of wooded hills, Upnor became something of a resort for the people of the Medway area. However, while this is indeed an ideal place to spend some leisure time, the village has not always been so peaceful. In the 16th century, Elizabeth I ordered the construction of several fortifications along the Medway estuary to protect her dockyard at Chatham from invasion and, in 1559, **Upnor Castle** was constructed. Fronted by a water bastion jutting out into the River Medway, this castle saw action in 1667 when

Lower Upnor

Distance: *3.5 miles (5.6 kilometres)*
Typical time: *90 mins*
Height gain: *37 metres*
Map: *Explorer 163*
Walk: *www.walkingworld.com ID:873*
Contributor: *Ian Elmes*

ACCESS INFORMATION:

From the A228 turn towards Lower Upnor on Upchat Road. Shortly after, turn left onto Upnor Road, at the end of which is a car park.

ADDITIONAL INFORMATION:

There are toilets at the car park in Lower Upnor (starting point).

DESCRIPTION:

A fantastic short walk for those wishing just to get out and about for a little while. The walk takes you along past the Saxon Shore Way by the River Medway at Lower Upnor, returning along field paths back to Lower Upnor. The village of Lower Upnor is ideally suited to relaxed evenings; it boasts two pubs and great views across to the old dockyard at Chatham. It is also a good place to sit and watch the yachts going up and down the river. Just up the road from Lower Upnor is the aptly-named Upper Upnor, which also boasts two pubs and the castle (English Heritage).

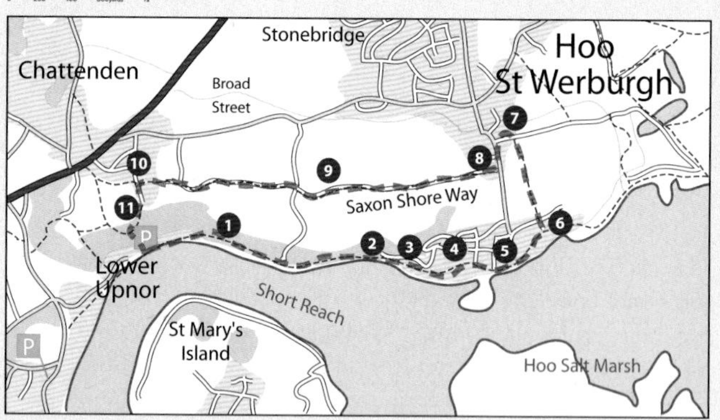

FEATURES:

River, pub, toilets, castle, great views, food shop.

WALK DIRECTIONS:

1 | From the car park at Lower Upnor, turn left along the road towards the Medway Yacht Club. Once at the gate to the yacht club, bear right onto the footpath; be careful here as it can be quite a steep drop into the river if you're not careful. Follow the path past the clubhouse on your left. At the end of the path drop down onto the beach and follow the line of the woods. Continue along the beach past the old Boat House and the old war gun placement towards the Wilsonian Sailing Club, where there is a raised concrete footpath. Continuing on your journey along the beach, you will pass the ruins of an old fortress.

2 | Follow the line of the river; it can be muddy and slippery at this point after high tide. Shortly you will reach a relatively new raised footpath. Continue along this path.

3 | Follow the well-defined footpath past the remains of a wooden ship in the riverbed and past a rather large houseboat named *Anserava* on your right. Continue to the end of the path, past the numerous house barges and through the Hoo Ness Yacht Club.

4 | Once through the gate, follow the track straight ahead, bearing right onto another track just before the white gate. Follow this path past the Saxon Shore Walk marker-post. Continue along the path until it opens out into a car parking area, with mobile homes on the left. Follow the high metal fence and then along the tarmac road past the Riverside Diner.

5 | Continue straight ahead. Should you be hungry or thirsty, there is a supermarket-type shop along the road to the left. Head along the gravel track and through a footpath at the end. Once out in the open, by the

garages on the right, bear right at the house in front of you, following the Saxon Shore marker-post. Follow the path past the yachts and out onto the road. At the end of the path, by the fence, turn right to cross the road and walk along the path between the bus depot and steelworks. Cross the road to take the slightly overgrown footpath to the left of Whitton Marine.

6 | Follow the path and come out at an opening. At the red-windowed factory straight in front of you, turn left along the road. Take the footpath directly in front of you, heading towards three large houses in the distance.

7 | Before the houses, bear left onto another path towards the main road and church. At the main road, turn left and then right onto the farm track by Church Farm Lodge.

8 | Follow this track up the hill, past the vicarage and a few other houses, all the way to the gate at the top.

9 | Go straight ahead at the gate, past the farmhouse on the left and keep straight ahead at the crossroads, taking the track to the right of the chicken-houses. Continue up along the track, ignoring the footpath on the right, past the large house behind the walled railings. Go straight ahead through an enclosed footpath taking you past the gardens of the houses of Elm Avenue.

10 | At the road, turn left and follow the road up the hill.

11 | At the top of the hill (the highest point at 135ft) follow the footpath marker down through the enclosed footpath straight ahead. Instead of following the path to the right, carry straight on to a bench offering fantastic views across the River Medway. Continue along the footpath down towards the river. Bear left at the yellow marker-post. At the bottom, follow the road with the Arethusa Venture Centre on the left and continue along the road, past the toilets and into the car park.

the Dutch sailed up the river with the intention of destroying the English naval fleet. The gun batteries at Upnor were the primary defence against this attack but they proved to be ineffective as the Dutch captured, and made off with, the British flagship the *Royal Charles*.

After this failure, the castle became a magazine and, at one time, more gunpowder was stored here than in the Tower of London. A survey of 1691 counted 5,206 barrels of gunpowder in storage. One of the guns that failed to stop the Dutch has been salvaged from the river and now stands guard outside the entrance to the fort; visitors here can tour the gatehouse and main body of the castle, reliving the Dutch raid through an exciting audio-visual model. The village itself grew up around the castle to provide facilities for the troops stationed there – in 1746 the soldiers were described by one storekeeper as a set of drunken wretches. Needless to say, things are much more peaceful and civilised today.

ALLHALLOWS

8 miles NE of Rochester off the A228

Iron Beacon

This remote village, which takes its name from its small 11th-century church of All Saints, overlooks the River Thames estuary and, beyond, the busy Essex resort of Southend. Nearby is an **Iron Beacon** that was erected in Elizabethan times and it is one of many such beacons that were set up along the coast to warn of imminent invasion. In the 1930s there were plans to develop the coastal strip to the north of the village as a holiday area and, although the resort never quite came to fruition, the Art Deco style railway station still remains and has been put to other uses.

CHATHAM

1 mile E of Rochester on the A2

Fort Amherst Almshouses

Dockyard and Museums

Although there has been a settlement here since Saxon times, it was not until Henry VIII established a dockyard that Chatham began to grow from being a sleepy, riverside backwater into a busy town. The dockyard flourished and was expanded by Elizabeth I during the time of the Armada. Sir Francis Drake, who took part in the defeat of the Spanish fleet in 1588, moved here with his family at the age of six and, while his father was chaplain to the fleet based here, the young Francis learned his sailing skills on the reaches around Chatham and Gillingham. Of the many famous ships that were built at the naval dockyard, perhaps the most famous is Nelson's *HMS Victory*, which was launched in 1765.

The naval connection continued to boost the growth of the town and its present commercial centre originally saw to the needs of navy personnel. Among these was John Dickens, who was employed by the Navy Pay Office. His son, Charles, spent some of his boyhood years at Chatham as the family moved to 2 Ordnance Terrace (now number 11) when Charles was five years old. John Dickens was to provide the inspiration for Charles' character Mr Micawber in *David Copperfield*. Dickens World, at Chatham Maritime, is a themed attraction based on the life, work and times of the author.

Just to the north of the town centre on the banks of the River Medway is **The Historic Dockyard** (see panel opposite), founded by Henry VIII, which became the premier shipbuilding yard for the Royal Navy. Offering over 450 years of history, visitors can appreciate the scale of the 20th-century submarine and battleship dry-docked here as well as the architecture of the most complete Georgian dockyard in the world. Samuel Pepys, the famous diarist, first made reference to the dockyard in his diaries in 1661 and he was here to witness the audacious Dutch raid six years later when Ruyter managed to capture the English flagship, *Royal Charles*. The Ropery at the Historic Dockyard is a building a quarter of a mile long. Rope can be seen being made in the traditional way, using machines dating back to 1811. The 175-year history of the lifeboats is told at the National Collection of the RNLI. The site includes the **Museum of the Royal Dockyard** and three historic warships – the O Class spy submarine *Ocelot*, *HMS Cavalier*, which saw service in World War II, and *HMS Gannet*, a Victorian naval sloop now fully restored and open to the public. The dockyard has been the setting for a number of films over the years, including *The Mummy* and *Tomorrow Never Dies*.

The Chatham dockyards were an obvious target for Hitler's bombers during World War II and, at Fort Amherst Heritage Park and Caverns, which lie close by, the secret underground telephone exchange that coordinated the air raid warnings can be seen. The country's premier Napoleonic fortress, **Fort Amherst** was built in 1756 to defend the naval dockyard from attack by land, and it continued to serve this purpose up until the end of World War II. Today, the fort offers visitors an insight into the daily lives of the soldiers and their families who were stationed here,, through a series of displays and re-enactments in period costumes. The fort's most outstanding feature, and the most interesting, is undoubtedly the underground maze of tunnels and caverns that were used as storage, magazines, barracks and guardrooms,

The Historic Dockyard

Chatham, Kent ME4 4TZ
Tel: 01634 823800 Fax: 01634 823801
e-mail: info@worldnavalbase.org.uk
website: www.worldnavalbase.org.uk

On the banks of the River Medway, lies **The Historic Dockyard** that saw the foundation of the Royal Navy under Henry VIII and, down the centuries, it was the naval power generated here that helped build the British Empire. The Naval Base covers some 400 years of history and visitors touring the site will see the most complete Georgian dockyard in the world along with displays and exhibits that explain the part the dockyard has played in the country's and the world's history. Samuel Pepys, the famous diarist, first made reference to the dockyard in his diaries in 1661 and he was here to witness the audacious Dutch raid six years later when de Ruyter managed to capture the English flag ship, Royal Charles.

Whilst the dockyard exhibitions certainly dwell on past glories, there is plenty more to see here, including the modern spy submarine Ocelot, HMS Cavalier that saw active service during World War II and HMS Gannet the last surviving sloop of the Victorian navy. In a building that is a quarter of a mile long rope can be seen being made in the traditional way whilst the 175 year history of the lifeboats is told at the National Collection of the RNLI. The newly opened Museum of the Dockyard brings together the 400 year history of the World Naval Base and, with so much to see, the steam railway with its audio tour is an excellent way to begin a tour of this impressive site.

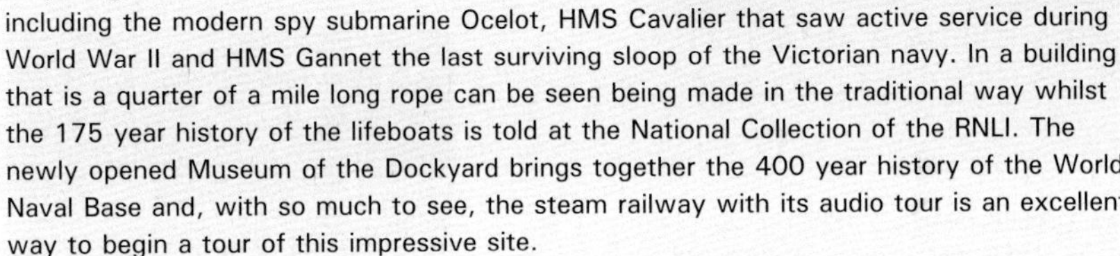

and the guided tour around the underground workings highlights the skills of the military engineers.

The extensive outer fortification, which covers seven acres and includes battlements and earthworks, has been turned into a country park style area where visitors can enjoy a picnic or explore the various nature trails.

Like the dockyard, Fort Amherst has been used as a location by both film and television companies and it was here that Robert de Niro shot the prison cell scenes for *The Mission*, Val Kilmer worked on the remake of the 1960s series *The Saint* and the BBC filmed *The Phoenix and the Carpet.*

In the main part of the town can be found the **Almshouses** that were built by one of the two charities established by the Elizabethan seafarer, Admiral Sir John Hawkins. As well as helping to defeat the Spanish Armada along with Sir Francis Drake, Hawkins was also an inventor and philanthropist and it was he who introduced 'copper bottoms' to help prevent the deterioration of ship's hulls below the waterline. These almshouses were originally designed as a hospital for retired seamen and their widows.

GILLINGHAM

2 miles E of Rochester on the A2

The Royal Engineers Museum

Although there is evidence of both prehistoric and Roman occupation of this area, a village did not really become established here until the 11th century. The oldest part of this, the largest of the Medway towns, is The Green, where the Norman parish church of St Mary stands. It was the establishment of the dockyard at neighbouring Chatham in the 16th century that began Gillingham's expansion as it became a centre for servicing the naval dockyard and depot. As with most towns along the Medway, Gillingham has many links with the sea, and it was the story of the Gillingham sailor, Will Adams, that inspired the novel *Shogun* by James Clavell. In 1600, Adams sailed to Japan and there he befriended Ieyasu, the Shogun, learnt Japanese and was honoured as a Samurai warrior. Beside the A2 is the Will Adams Monument, a fitting tribute to the man who went on to become the Shogun's teacher and adviser.

All things maritime have influenced Gillingham greatly over the centuries, but the town is also the home of one of the most fascinating military attractions - **The Royal Engineers Museum**. This museum reflects the diverse range of skills that the Corps has brought to bear in times of both peace and war. They were the creators of the Ordnance Survey, the designers of the Royal Albert Hall and the founders of the Royal Flying Corps in 1912. The Royal Engineers continue the dangerous work of bomb disposal and throughout the world they build roads and bridges, lay water pipes and assist in relief

work after natural disasters. The courtyard display illustrates the wide variety of activities the Corps has undertaken since the 1940s, while inside are a dignified medal gallery, a reconstruction of a World War I trench and numerous artefacts from around the world acquired by members of the Corps. Both the nearby dockyards and Fort Amherst at Chatham were built by the Royal Engineers. Visitors can see exquisite Chinese embroidery given to General Gordon, Zulu shields from Rorke's Drift and the original battlefield map prepared by the Corps and used by the Duke of Wellington to defeat Napoleon at the Battle of Waterloo in 1815. It was a Royal Engineer, Lieutenant John Chard VC, who played a key role in the defence of Rorkes Drift when the mission, with just 130 men, was attacked by thousands of Zulu warriors. The World War I General, Lord Kitchener, who appeared on the famous recruitment poster campaign, was also a Royal Engineer.

MILTON REGIS

10 miles E of Rochester off the A2

Court Hall Museum · Sailing Barge Museum

Once a royal borough, Milton Regis has been all but incorporated into the outskirts of Sittingbourne. However, in the still well-defined village centre can be found the **Court Hall Museum** housed, as its name might suggest, in a 15th century timbered building that was originally Milton Regis's courthouse, school and town gaol. The museum has displays, photographs and documents that relate to the village and surrounding area.

At Milton Creek lies **Dolphin Yard Sailing Barge Museum**, housed in a traditional sailing barge yard where commercial work is still undertaken. Along with aiming to preserve the barges and other craft that have been used on the local estuaries for hundreds of years, the museum is dedicated in particular to the sailing barge. While the creek provided a means of transport, its waters were also used to power paper mills and paper manufacturing continues in this area today.

SITTINGBOURNE

10½ miles E of Rochester on the A2

Lying close to the Roman road, Watling Street, Sittingbourne was, during the Middle Ages, a stopping place for pilgrims on their way to Canterbury. As a result, the town developed a thriving market that has continued to this day; the town was also a centre for barge making and for paper manufacturing.

It is from here that the Sittingbourne and Kemsley Light Railway runs steam hauled passenger trains along two miles of preserved track. The railway was originally designed to transport paper and other bulk materials but now the journey is taken for pleasure by those fascinated by steam trains and those wishing to view this area of the Kentish countryside at close quarters.

Sittingbourne and Kemsley Light Railway

B&B AT HARTLIP PLACE

Hartlip Place, Hartlip,
nr Sittingbourne,
Kent ME9 7TR
Tel: 01795 842323
e-mail: hartlipplace@btinternet.com
website: www.hartlipplace.co.uk

Outstanding Bed & Breakfast accommodation is just one of the offerings of **Hartlip Place**, a fine south-facing Georgian mansion built by William Bland in 1812. An oasis of calm and comfort, it stands back from the lane in four acres of gardens and woodland that include a 'secret' rose garden and two ornamental ponds. The whole place has a very warm and welcoming feel that is enhanced by many handsome original features, lovely pictures and antiques, and guests can meet not just the family but also the chickens and ducks and peacocks that roam the grounds. The guest accommodation comprises two superbly decorated and furnished rooms: the four-poster room overlooking the front garden has a large en suite bathroom and an open fire in winter, while the large, sunny Indian Room has its own private bathroom just across the corridor. The day starts with an excellent choice for breakfast, and an evening meal can be provided with a little notice.

Since 1989 Hartlip has catered superbly for civil ceremonies and in 2006 it conducted one of the first civil partnership ceremonies. When the weather is suitable the ceremonies (with up to 60 guests) are usually conducted in the loggia next to the large pond with its fountain, with ducks and peacocks among the interested spectators. In the cooler months the formal drawing room is an elegant alternative. Additionally, Hartlip is an ideal venue for receptions for up to 120, usually held in a marquee on the croquet lawn next to the rose garden. The occasion, tailored immaculately to individual requirements, could be anything from a formal sit-down meal to a buffet, a barbecue or a hog roast. The house is located on the outskirts of the village of Hartlip on the edge of the North Downs, a short drive from the M2 (leave at J4) or the M20 (J7, then the A249). First-time visitors should call to get precise directions. There are many places of historic and scenic interest nearby, and Hartlip is also a convenient stopping-off point on the way to or from the Continent, being only 30 minutes from Ashford International Station, 40 minutes from Dover and the Tunnel and 45 minutes from Gatwick Airport.

HOLLY HOUSE B&B

4 ★★★★ (Silver Award)

Wises Lane, Borden, Sittingbourne,
Kent ME9 8LR
Tel: 01795 426953
Mob: 07840067936
e-mail: jane@hollyhousebandb.org.uk
website: www.hollyhousebandb.org.uk

Holly House enjoys a rural location by the village cricket green on the North Downs southwest of Sittingbourne – rural but by no means isolated, as it is a short drive from both the M2 (J5) and the M20 (J7). Built in the late 1960's it has been renovated and redecorated by owner Jane Lee-Frost to provide a lovely Bed & Breakfast base that combines traditional furnishings with a contemporary twist, highlighted by lots of interesting objects collected by the owners in the UK and overseas. The accommodation comprises two double rooms with en suite facilities and a single with private bathroom; all have thermostatically controlled heating, TV, radio-alarm, hospitality tray, hairdryer and quality toiletries. Super breakfasts include fresh baked bread, homemade preserves and produce from local farms and butchers. Jane is a Home Economist and can offer a wide variety of home cooking for evening meals with a little notice. No pets.

DODDINGTON

5 miles SE of Sittingbourne off the A2

Doddington Place

The village is visited by thousands who come to see the magnificent landscaped gardens of **Doddington Place** (see panel on page 44).

The Isle of Sheppey

MINSTER

Abbey Gatehouse Museum

This seaside town on the northern coast of the Isle of Sheppey is an unlikely place to find one of the oldest sites of Christianity in England. However, it was here, on the highest point of the island, that Sexburga, the widow of a Saxon king of Kent, founded a nunnery in the late 7th century. Sacked by the Danes in 855, **Minster Abbey** was rebuilt in 1130 when it was also re-established as a priory for Benedictine nuns. Sometime later, in the 13th century, the parish church of Minster was built, adjoining the monastic church, and so, from the Middle Ages until the Dissolution of the Monasteries, the building served as a 'double church' with the nuns worshipping in the northern half of the building and the parishioners in the other. To the west of this unusual church lies the 15th-century abbey gatehouse, home today to the Minster Abbey **Gatehouse Museum**. Here, the history of Sheppey is told through exhibits of fossils, tools and photographs.

In his Ingoldsby Legends, RH Barham retells the story of the fiery Sir Roger de Shurland, Lord of Sheppey, who in 1300 killed a monk who had disobeyed him. Dodging the county sheriff, Sir Roger swam out on horseback to Edward I's passing ship and received the king's pardon for his wicked act. On returning to shore, Sir Roger met a

DODDINGTON PLACE GARDENS

Church Lane, Doddington, nr Sittingbourne, Kent ME9 0BB
Tel: 01795 886101 Fax: 01795 886363
e-mail: enquiries@doddingtonplacegardens.co.uk
website: www.doddingtonplacegardens.co.uk

Doddington Place Gardens stand in the grounds of an imposing Victorian mansion built for Sir John Croft of the distinguished port and sherry family. The lovely landscaped gardens cover ten acres surrounded by wooded countryside in a designated Area of Outstanding Natural Beauty and are recognised by English Heritage as being of special historic interest.

Among the many highlights for the visitor are a notable woodland garden – spectacular in May and June – that includes many varieties of rhododendron, azalea, camellias and acers; a superbly restored Edwardian rock garden; a formal sunken garden with borders; a spring garden with fruit trees; a fine avenue of Wellingtonia; and a striking two-storey brick and flint folly. Extensive lawns are framed by impressive yew hedges and fine specimen trees, and the avenues provide several themed walks.

The Gardens are open Sunday and Bank Holiday afternoons from Easter Day to the end of September. A tea room serves light snacks, cream teas and hot and cold beverages.

mysterious old hag who foretold that, having saved his life, Sir Roger's horse would also cause his death. On hearing this, the tempestuous knight drew his sword and beheaded his horse. Some time later, while walking on the beach, Sir Roger came across the head of his horse that had been washed ashore. In an angry rage, he kicked the head but one of the horse's teeth penetrated his boot and Sir Roger died later from the infection that developed in the wound. Sir Roger's tomb lies in the abbey church; close to the right foot of his stone effigy can be seen the head of a horse.

EASTCHURCH

2½ miles SE of Minster off the B2231

This village was once the home of the early pioneers of aviation and a young Sir Winston Churchill flew from the old Eastchurch aerodrome. Another early pilot, Lord Brabazon of Tara, was the holder of the first official pilot's licence. The Shorts brothers built the world's first aircraft factory here, later moving to bigger premises at Eastchurch. The Wright brothers came here on a visit, driven from London by Charles Rolls in the first Silver Ghost. Close to the church is a stone memorial to the early pilots, while nearby are the ruins of 16th-century Shurland Hall, where Henry VIII and Anne Boleyn stayed on their honeymoon.

A little way outside the village lies Norwood Manor, a charming old house that dates from the 17th century, although the Northwoode family have lived on this site since Norman times. On display in the house are numerous artefacts that relate to this long established Kentish family.

LEYSDOWN

5 miles SE of Minster on the B2231

Swale National Nature Reserve

A popular seaside place with visitors for many years - Henry VIII loved the Isle of Sheppey so much that he spent one of his honeymoons here - Leysdown is renowned for its sandy beaches, and there are picnic areas and nature trails close by.

A little to the south, on the southeastern tip of the Isle of Sheppey, **The Swale National Nature Reserve** is home to numerous species of wildfowl.

ELMLEY ISLAND

3 miles S of Minster off the A249

Nature Reserve

Situated on the southern coastline of the Isle of Sheppey and overlooking The Swale and the north Kent coast, **Elmley Marshes Nature Reserve** is an area of salt marsh that is home to wetland birds, marsh frogs, numerous insects and many species of aquatic plants.

QUEENBOROUGH

3 miles W of Minster off the A249

Guildhall Museum

A historic town that began as a Saxon settlement, Queenborough became an important wool port and a wealthy borough that was graced by a royal Castle built by Edward III. The town's reliance on the sea for its prosperity also saw its courthouse captured by the Dutch during their invasion of the Medway in 1667. During the 18th century, the town's prosperity continued, based on the increased naval presence after the Dutch invasion. Many fine buildings were built, which still survive. However, the first part of 19th century saw Queenborough decline as enterprising neighbours like Sheerness grew. During World War II, Queenborough became the home of hundreds of mine-sweeping vessels. **The Guildhall Museum**, housed in the building that replaced the earlier courthouse, tells the fascinating story of this town, from Saxon times, through its rise at the hands of Victorian industrialists, to the important role it played during World War II. Queenborough is still a very busy boating centre, with numerous boat builders and chandlers.

SHEERNESS

2½ miles NW of Minster on the A249

Heritage Centre

Overlooking the point where the River Medway meets the River Thames, Sheerness was once the site of a naval dockyard and was the first to be surveyed by Samuel Pepys, who held the position of Secretary of the Admiralty during the reign of Charles II. It was at Sheerness that in 1805 *HMS Victory* docked when it brought Nelson's body back to England after the Battle of Trafalgar. In more recent times, Sheerness has developed into a busy container and car ferry port and most of the Isle of Sheppey's wealth is centred on the town. The naval base was the main reason that a railway line running from Sittingbourne was built; was opened in 1860. The base has gone but the dockyard remains, and large diesel-hauled freight trains regularly use the line.

The **Sheerness Heritage Centre** is housed in a weatherboarded cottage that was built in the early 19th century as a dwelling for a dockyard worker. Despite being constructed of seemingly temporary building materials, the house and its two neighbours have lasted well. Over the years, the cottage has been a baker's shop and a fish & chip shop. The rooms have now been restored to reflect authentic 19th century life and are furnished with genuine pieces from that period. The heritage centre also has an exhibition describing the development of The Royal Dockyard, which closed here in the 1960s.

Whitstable

Museum

Anyone wandering around Whitstable will soon realise that this is not just a seaside resort, but very much a working town centred around the busy commercial harbour that was originally the port for Canterbury. The old-fashioned streets of the town are lined with fisherman's cottages and the winding lanes are linked by narrow alleyways with eccentric names - such as Squeeze Gut Alley - that recall the town's rich maritime past. Sometimes referred to as the 'Pearl of Kent', Whitstable is as famous today for its oysters as it was in Roman times, and it is probable that Caesar himself enjoyed Whitstable oysters. A visit to Whitstable Fish Market will prove that the town's reputation for prime seafood does not stop at oysters. Against a backdrop of fishing boats, nets and lobster pots the market sells a wonderful variety of fresh, sustainable fish and shellfish.

After the Roman occupiers left Britain, the Saxons came to the area and gave the town its name - then Witanstaple, meaning 'an assembly of wise men in the market'. This later became Whitstable. Later, the Normans built the parish church of All Saints, which provided medieval sailors with a key navigation aid. The ownership of the manor of Whitstable in the Middle Ages proved to be something of a poisoned chalice. John de Stragboli was executed for murder, Bartholomew de Badlesmere was hanged for his part in the rebellion against Edward II, and Robert de Vere was convicted for treason. Even in the 16th century, the owner of the manor fared no better when Sir John Gates was executed for his support of Lady Jane Grey over the Catholic Mary Tudor.

Along with oysters and a fishing industry that has lasted over 700 years, the discovery of iron pyrites deposits around Whitstable led to the development of the manufacture of copper to be used for dyeing and making ink and some early medicines. However, it was the

THE PEARSONS ARMS

The Horsebridge, Sea Wall, Whitstable,
Kent CT5 1BT
Tel: 01227 272005
e-mail: bookings@pearsonsarms.com
website: www.pearsonsarms.com

Pearson's Arms is an independently owned and run gastro-pub in a listed 18th century building overlooking the beach. There's plenty of history associated with the spot: the Horsebridge was the original landing place for cargo under sail and the oyster smacks.

The team take great pride in the standard of the food, the variety of beers, wines and cocktails, and provide quality, excellent service and value for money, making it one of the most successful restaurants in the region. The location provides unparalleled views of the famous Whitstable sunsets from the first-floor dining room.

Whitstable is renowned for its seafood, especially oysters and other shellfish, which naturally feature strongly on the menu of modern British dishes, using mainly local producers and suppliers. The cask ales are from the award-winning Ramsgate brewery, and the wine list compiled by Master of Wine, Clive Barlow.

Food is served from noon every day, and Pearson's Arms is available for parties and private hire.

CAXTON CONTEMPORARY

37 High Street, Whitstable, Kent CT9 1AP
Tel: 01227 272444 e-mail: wendyjcroft@btinternet.com
website: www.caxtoncontemporary.co.uk

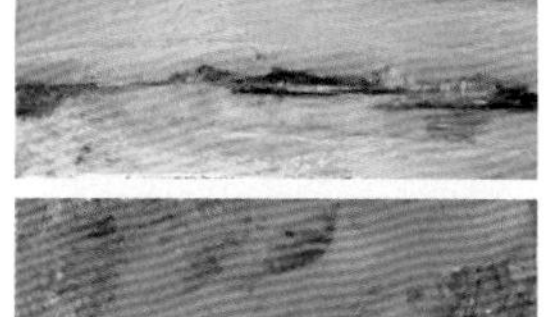

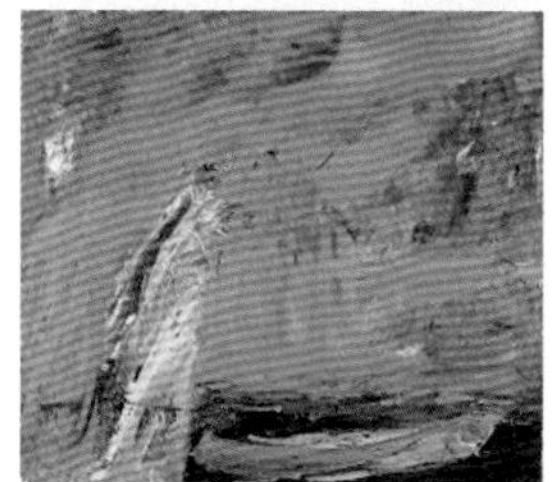

Caxton Contemporary is a modern arts venue situated in the heart of Whitstable, owned and run with energy and enterprise by artist Wendy Croft. Croft saw a gap in the market, realising that Caxton could offer the region more than just another gallery. When the chance arose she took over the shop and printworks that had been in the family for generations and sympathetically renovated it to provide a space, to not only exhibit the best of contemporary fine art, but also to provide a venue where artists can come and work in Whitstables' inspiring environment.

" ... my aim is to encourage dialogue between artists around the country by bringing their work together in Whitstable."

The gallery showcases exceptional works by established and emerging artists, with regular collated exhibitions. Among the artists recently featured are Paul Wadsworth, Suzie Zamit, Virginia Bounds, Simon Tupper, Marie-Claire Hamon, Caroline Underwood, Amanda Thompson, Rowena Harris, Sally Dodd and Elizabeth Armstrong - the comprehensive website gives details and examples of the work of these and others and news of up and coming events. Also on the premises are two exhibition/ workshop spaces and studios that artists can hire to work and exhibit in.

SAMPHIRE

4 High Street, Whitstable, Kent CT5 1BQ
Tel: 01227 770075
e-mail: bookings@samphirewhitstable.com
website: www.samphirewhitstable.com

Samphire is a firm favourite on the Whitstable dining scene. It is an informal, fully-licensed cafe-restaurant sitting among the interesting shops and galleries on Whitstable's busy High Street; a high-quality relaxed place with inviting eclectic décor, painted floorboards and a cheerful mix of old tables and chairs.

The philosophy of providing a high level of quality, friendly efficient service and great value for money that has proved such a success in recent years is evident here.

The food style is modern British, and the produce going into the kitchen is predominantly sourced from local farms, fishermen, gamekeeper and foragers, providing excellent variety and seasonally-changing menus.

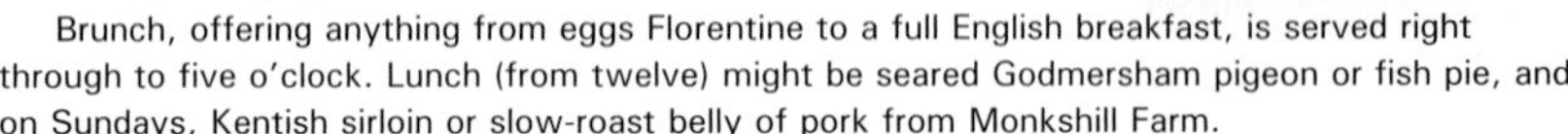

Brunch, offering anything from eggs Florentine to a full English breakfast, is served right through to five o'clock. Lunch (from twelve) might be seared Godmersham pigeon or fish pie, and on Sundays, Kentish sirloin or slow-roast belly of pork from Monkshill Farm.

At five, the supper menu takes over, with dishes such as saddle of venison, pan-roast pollack with bubble & squeak and cockle butter or salsify and pine-nut gratin. There's a well-chosen wine list. Samphire is open from 10am to 10pm, seven days a week.

FRANK

65 Harbour Street, Whitstable, Kent CT5 1AG
Tel: 01227 262500
e-mail: info@frankworks.eu *website: www.frankworks.eu*

Frank can be found in the heart of Whitstable's old town and has rapidly established itself as a destination shop within the bustling independent shopping scene of Harbour Street. The space, a hybrid of gallery and shop, was started by illustrator Mary Claire Smith and her partner Robert Weisz in 2006 with the aim of selling and showcasing the best of British contemporary design, art and craft. Artists and makers include Rob Ryan, Angie Lewin, Cleo Mussi, Julie Arkell and John Dilnot. Frank is dedicated to working with individual makers and independent companies, all from the UK, many Kent-based. The gallery is passionate about promoting young and upcoming artists, designers and makers, as well as those that are more established and collectible. It avoids the mass-produced and concentrates instead on the handmade and the home-made; the original, the quirky and the downright eccentric. From books and badges to jewellery and stationery; from textiles to prints and ceramics to lighting, Frank focuses on sustainable, ethical and environmentally aware retailing.

Although the space itself is small, Frank has garnered much praise in the national press, recently appearing in the Craft section of *Vogue's* 'Secret Address Book', as well as being featured in *The Guardian*, *Elle Decoration* and *Country Living* among many others. "The owners," said *Elle Decoration*, "have a brilliant eye for a cute graphic or whimsical detail." While *Vogue* insisted that "you'll want to take home the lot."

THE CHEESE BOX

60 Harbour Street, Whitstable, Kent CT5 1AG
Tel: 01227 273711
website: www.thecheesebox.co.uk

A modest green frontage in a brick building hides an Aladdin's Cave for cheese-lovers. Dawn Hackett first established her business in her cheese van, plying mainly between Canterbury and Faversham, and when the chance came to set up shop here in Whitstable she jumped at the opportunity.

The **Cheese Box** is a British artisan cheese specialist where Dawn works with UK cheesemakers and developing Kentish cheese producers to offer an unrivalled variety of wonderful British farmhouse cheese. The choice is truly remarkable – cows' cheese, sheep's cheese, goats' cheese, hard, soft, blue, washed rind, rubbed rind – and the owner and staff supply descriptions of milk type, source, contents and background for all the cheeses, which customers can sample and appreciate to the full.

The shop also sells accompaniments to the cheese – bread, crackers, chutneys, sauces, jellies and wines – along with local milk, cream, butter and yoghurt. And the cheese van still operates, on Fridays and Saturdays in Faversham Market.

sea and the associated boat building and repair yards that were to continue to support many of those living in the town. Now many of the yards have gone, but as recently as World War II, ships' lifeboats and other small craft were being built and launched at Whitstable. Going hand-in-hand with the town's maritime connections was the unofficial trade of smuggling, and during the 18th century there were numerous battles between the gangs and the revenue men in and around the town.

While the authorities clamped down hard on this illegal trading, there was one positive spin-off as the smugglers had such an intimate knowledge of the French coastline that Nelson consulted them while planning his naval campaigns.

For a broad picture of the town, past and present, **Whitstable Museum and Gallery** explores the traditions and life of this ancient seafaring community. There are also references and information on the many 'firsts' to which the town lays claim: the first scheduled passenger train ran between Whitstable and Canterbury; the first steamship to sail to Australia from Britain left here in 1837; the diving helmet was invented in the town; and the country's first council houses were built at Whitstable.

Whitstable also has associations with writers and broadcasters. After his parents died, Somerset Maugham came to live with his uncle at Whitstable, and the town features strongly in two of his novels, *Of Human Bondage* and *Cakes and Ale*. Charles Dickens visited here and wrote about the town, and Robert Hitchens, the novelist and journalist, lived at nearby Tankerton. One of the town's

JANE AT GRAHAM GREENER

27 Harbour Street, Whitstable, Kent CT5 1AH
Tel: 01227 277100
website: www.grahamgreener.com

Whitstable has many attractions for the visitor, but for anyone looking for a special gift or a personal treat **Jane at Graham Greener** is the place to head for. The Jane in the name of the shop is Jane Antoniades, who runs the shop with her husband Mario. Jane's flair for decoration and design and her eye for beautiful things are very evident to customers browsing among the lovely items on display. Stunning, sophisticated, modern, traditional, exotic, classic, seasonal....it's all there in the ever-changing stock of desirable things, from beautiful bespoke flowers and garden accessories to homeware, lifestyle products and gift ideas. Flowers and floral design are specialities: customers can choose from the array of cut flowers specially imported from Holland or have a bouquet made up for a special occasion – Mother's Day, Christmas, weddings, birthdays, funerals, corporate – or just for a well-deserved treat. Other stock includes garden tools, accessories and ornaments, olive and bay trees, kids' garden tools and watering cans in bright colours, potted plants, china goods, mirrors, candles, fragrances, soaps, books and cards.

The shop is open 9 to 5 Monday and Tuesday, 9 to 5.30 Wednesday to Saturday and 11 to 4 Sundays and Bank Holidays. The owners have a sister shop, Graham Greener, in Canterbury (qv).

TAKING THE PLUNGE

26 High Street, Whitstable, Kent CT5 1BQ
Tel: 01227 264678
website: www.takingtheplunge.biz

Nicola French-Doyle and Shelly Keeys invite customers to 'Dive into Life' at **Taking the Plunge**, their High Street shop with a cheerful striped canopy and distinctive logo of a diving lady. They opened their shop in September 2008 with the aim of sourcing 'interesting, unusual and gorgeous bits', at affordable prices and often with a retro/vintage theme. The shop has quickly become a great favourite with regular customers and visitors to the town looking for a treat or a special gift. The constantly changing stock includes gifts for all ages (for example, wallets, satchels, cufflinks, footballs, flasks, wash bags, board games, lunch boxes and mugs for boys); jewellery (delicate rings, necklaces and bracelets to commemorate a christening); vintage metal signs; retro telephones; bags, purses, metal wall art, mugs, jugs, plates, chill buckets, place mats, glassware, journals and diaries, flying ducks, vintage button bracelets, clippie kits and old school badges. The owners are great champions of all things British and the iconic Union Jack appears on many items, including bags, mugs, jewellery and Jan Constantine's lovely cushions.

The shop is open from 10 to 5 (to 5.30 on Saturday, to 4 on Sunday). Shoppers who can't get to Whitstable can order on line through the comprehensive website.

more notorious residents was William Joyce, who worked in one of the town's radio shops before travelling to Germany to broadcast Nazi propaganda back to England as Lord Haw Haw during World War II.

Around Whitstable

HERNE BAY

4½ miles NE of Whitstable on the B2205

Museum

Now one of the main resorts on the north Kent coast, Herne Bay was originally a fishing village that became notorious as a haunt for smugglers. Much of the town seen today was laid out in the mid-19th century as it was developed as a resort to attract the Victorian middle classes looking for clean air and safe beaches. It still retains a quiet gentility that is reminiscent of that lost era, and at the **Herne Bay Museum Centre** visitors can discover the history of the town and the story of its famous pier through entertaining displays. The museum also contains relics from prehistoric times such as fossils and stone tools. The Clock Tower, a superb landmark, that stands on the promenade was given to Herne Bay by a wealthy London lady, Mrs Thwaytes, to commemorate Queen Victoria's coronation in 1836.

Just inland, at the ancient Saxon village of Herne, stands Herne Mill, a Kentish smock mill that has recently undergone extensive repair work. Dating from 1789, this particular mill is the latest in a long line that have occupied this site.

THE EVENING TIDE

97 Central Parade, Herne Bay, Kent CT6 5JJ
Tel: 01227 365014
website: www.eveningtide.co.uk

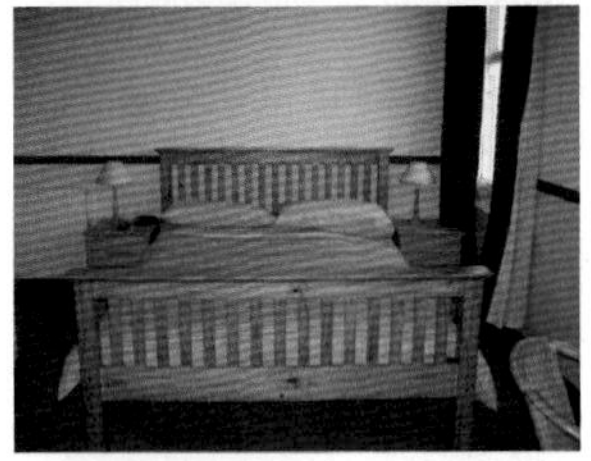

The Evening Tide – a lovely name for a delightful Bed & Breakfast guest house on Herne Bay's Central Parade, just moments from the beach. Resident owners Eric and Colleen have a warm and friendly welcome for all of their guests, and the number of return visits to the house is testimony to its appeal. The accommodation can offer singles, doubles, twins and a family room with bunk beds for the children, all with en suite showers, Freeview TV, DVD and CD players, tea/coffee-making facilities and free wi-fi internet access; some of the rooms enjoy sea views. The day starts with an excellent breakfast – anything from tea and toast to a full English, vegetarian and special diets can be catered for. Herne Bay, which developed from a small fishing village to one of the main resorts on the north Kentish coast, is quieter than some of its neighbours, and an equally good base for a traditional family seaside holiday or for exploring the coast and countryside.

Attractions in and around the town include the heritage museum, the fine old smock mill at Herne, Herne Bay Golf Club (open to non-members), Reculver Country Park and Wildwood Wealden Forest Park. There is also a roller skating rink located on the pier which is home to Herne Bay roller hockey club.

HERNE COMMON

5 miles SW of Whitstable off the A291

Regia Anglorum

Wildwood Wealden Forest Park

Close to the village and found deep in a leafy forest is **Wildwood Wealden Forest Park**, Kent's unique woodland discovery park that is also the home of the only breeding pack of endangered European wolves in Britain. Although wolves have not been living in the wild in this country for many years, tales of the savage packs that once roamed the countryside live on, and at Wildwood stories of the medieval hunters who killed them for bounty and of the fear of travellers alone on dark nights bring back those days. The Saxons called January 'Wulf monat' as this was when the hungry packs were at their most dangerous. However, Wildwood is not entirely devoted to wolves and here in the forest is a reconstruction of a Saxon village, **Regia Anglorum**, where history is brought to life as village members, in authentic costume, go about their daily lives and practise the skills and crafts from centuries ago.

Other wildlife found at Wildwood, includes a badger colony as well as rabbits, polecats, shrews and hedgehogs all living in underground burrows. And in a near natural environment is the park's herd of deer. While this is an interesting, enjoyable and educational place to visit for all the family, much of the work of the park goes on behind the scenes in the area of conservation, and two species in particular,

WESTGRANGE HOUSE B&B

42 Busheyfields Road, Herne Common,
Kent CT6 7LJ
Tel: 01227 740663
website: www.westgrangehouse.co.uk

Just off the A291 and a short drive from the A299 Thanet Way south of Herne Bay, **Westgrange House** is ideally placed for exploring the Kentish coast and countryside, as well as discovering all the history that Canterbury has to offer. Margaret's well-appointed modern redbrick house with its striking steeply raked red-tiled roof has three - five very quiet and comfortable letting bedrooms, three with en-suite. All are tastefully decorated doubles or twins with free-view TV and tea/coffee making facilities that are 4-Star Visit Britain rated. The tariff includes an excellent multi-choice breakfast based as far as possible on local produce.

The coastal resorts of Herne Bay and Whitstable are a short drive away, but even closer is one of the most unusual attractions in the county. Wildwood Wealden Forest Park is home to abundant wildlife, including wolves, badgers, polecats, voles, shrews and hedgehogs, and also houses a reconstruction of a Saxon village.

water voles and hazel dormice, are bred here for re-introduction into the wild.

HERNHILL

5 miles SW of Whitstable off the A299

Mount Ephraim Gardens

A secluded and tranquil village that is surrounded by orchards, Hernhill is home to **Mount Ephraim Gardens**. This family estate also includes a house, woodland and fruit farm. The gardens are essentially Edwardian, offering a good balance between the formal and the informal through such delights as herbaceous borders, topiary, rose terraces, a Japanese garden, a rock garden, a vineyard and orchard trails. There are magnificent views of both the Swale and Thames estuaries from the gardens.

Faversham

Guildhall Chart Gunpowder Mills

Fleur de Lis Heritage Centre

South Swale Nature Reserve

As with many places in this area of Kent, Faversham was first settled by the Romans, who gave the town its name (it comes from 'faber' meaning blacksmith), and it was later inhabited by both the Jutes and the Saxons. Despite this period of turmoil, the town continued to grow, so much so that in 811 King Kenulf granted Faversham a charter and the market still plays an important part in the life of the town today. The Market Place, which is also the junction of three of the town's oldest streets, is dominated by the

Guildhall, which was built in the 16th century. Its open ground floor pillared arcade provided cover for the market. Unusually it has a tower at one end. After the upper floor and tower were damaged by fire in the early 19th century, it was rebuilt in keeping with the original and extended. The clock in the tower was made in 1814 by a clockmaker called Francis Crow, whose workshop was in the Market Place opposite the tower.

Faversham Guildhall, Faversham

Over the centuries, Faversham market has dealt in a wide range of goods, and the town was, for almost 400 years, the centre of the country's explosives industry and **Chart Gunpowder Mills** is a lasting monument to the industry that thrived here between 1560 and 1934. Dating from the 18th century, and now restored, these mills are the oldest of their kind in the world. Chart Mills is an 'incorporating' mill. Incorporating was the process by which the ingredients of gunpowder are incorporated together to become explosive.

Faversham has over 400 listed buildings and one that is well worth seeking out is the 15th-century former inn that is now home to the **Fleur de Lis Heritage Centre**. Here, displays review the past 1,000 years and tell the story of the town's growth and prosperity. Of the numerous artefacts and exhibitions to be seen here one of the more impressive is Abbey Street, a 16th-century thoroughfare that is complete and well-preserved. Also featured are an Edwardian barber shop, a Victorian fireside, a typical village post office, working manual telephone exchange and costume displays.

Close by lies Faversham Creek, a tidal inlet of the River Swale that is inextricably linked with the main town's prosperity as the Creek acted as Faversham's port. A limb of the Cinque Port of Dover, and with a shipbuilding tradition that is so rooted in history that the title of 'The King's Port' is retained as an acknowledgment of the royal gratitude for the provision of navy vessels, Faversham Creek is well worth a visit. Between here and Seasalter, to the east, lies the **South Swale Nature Reserve**, which concentrates on the legacy of natural history of this area. A wide range of wildfowl, including Brent geese, make their home along this stretch of coast. There is a pleasant coastal walk here between Seasalter and Faversham.

Around Faversham

BOUGHTON

3 miles E of Faversham off the A2

Farming World

It is well worth pausing en route to the coast to explore **Farming World** at Nash Court. Almost every aspect of farming is featured here and, with beautiful surrounding countryside and marked trails for walking, there is plenty to keep the whole family amused for hours.

Farming World's extensive breeding programme ensures that there are usually lots of young animals to see, such as lambs, kids, calves and chicks, but it is also home to a variety of rarer breeds such as miniature Shetland ponies, llamas and Britain's smallest breed of cattle.

Along with the animals, the birds of prey and the heavy horses, Farming World has a museum with a fascinating collection of agricultural implements. Throughout the year there are demonstrations on the ancient and traditional skills of farming and other crafts, while specialist talks cover a wide range of subjects, including beekeeping, animal husbandry and falconry.

SHELDWICH

3 miles S of Faversham on the A251

Brogdale National Fruit Collection

Standing at the point where the landscape blends gently from scattered woodlands to open meadows and then farms and orchards, Sheldwich has, at its centre, a Norman parish church with a distinctive squat steeple that is visible from miles around.

Just to the north, at Brogdale, can be found

THE BELMONT ESTATE AND HARRIS BELMONT CHARITY

Belmont House, Belmont Park, Throwley,
nr Faversham, Kent ME13 0HH
Tel: 01795 890202 Fax: 01795 890042
e-mail: administrator@belmont-house.org
website: www.belmont-house.org

At the heart of the **Belmont Estate**, which has been owned by several successive generations of the Harris family, is Belmont House, built in 1769 by Edward Wilks. It was later sold to Colonel John Montresor, who enlarged the park and built the main block of the present house on design by Samuel Wyatt. The house was sold to General George Harris, which is filled with the history of the Harris Family deeds and travels, is open on weekends between Easter and September, with guided tours of the wonderful clock museum on the last Saturday of the month. The gardens and grounds, which can be visited throughout the year, include a large walled kitchen garden and a cricket pitch (available for hire to visiting teams), and the tea room in the courtyard beneath the Clock Tower is open all year at the weekend. The Belmont Estate offers residential and holiday accommodation in Crow Cottage, located in an old cherry orchard, and Pigeon Cottage near the golf course. There are opportunities for workshops and other rural-based commercial enterprises.

the **National Fruit Collection**. Here is the largest collection of fruit trees and plants in the world, with over 2,300 varieties of apples, 550 pears, and numerous plums, cherries and bush fruits, along with smaller collections of nuts and vines that are all grown in the beautiful orchards.

THROWLEY

3 miles S of Faversham off the A251

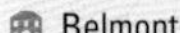

Belmont

Tucked away amid the orchards of Kent and close to the village lies **Belmont** (see panel above), a beautiful Georgian mansion house and estate.

OSPRINGE

1 mile SW of Faversham off the A2

Maison Dieu

This hamlet was a thriving Roman settlement and numerous coins, medallions and household items have been unearthed that suggest that the community was quite sizeable. Various excavated artefacts can be found, along with Saxon pottery, glass and jewellery and relics from medieval Ospringe, at Maison Dieu. The French **Maison Dieu**, meaning God's House, was in common usage in medieval times when a mix of French and English was spoken in England. It meant a house that provided hospitality of various kinds. Such houses would provide a haven for

Maison Dieu, Ospringe

the sick as well as a resting place for travellers on Watling Street.

The exact name of this property was the Hospital of the Blessed Mary of Ospringe. Originally founded by Henry III around 1230, the building served as a combination hospital and hostel for pilgrims on their way to and from Canterbury. As well as having some features still remaining from the 13th century, the house also displays beamed ceilings from the Tudor era. Along with the relics unearthed in the local area, the museum also includes information on the fascinating history of Maison Dieu itself.

TEYNHAM

3 miles W of Faversham off the A2

In 1533, Henry VIII's fruiterer, Richard Harris, planted England's first cherry tree in the village, along with pippins and golden russet apple trees, and thus established Teynham as the birthplace of English orchards. William Lamparde, in his 16th-century Perambulation of Kent, wrote of Teynham as "the cherry garden and apple orchard of Kent". This would appear still to be true, as fruit trees can be seen in every direction.

Canterbury to Sandwich Bay

This ancient land, between the city of Canterbury and the east coast of Kent, has seen invaders come and go, religious houses founded and dissolved under Henry VIII, and the building of great fortresses. Certainly one of the best places to begin any tour of the area is Canterbury itself, the home of the Mother Church of the Anglican Communion, Canterbury Cathedral. The cathedral was founded by St Augustine in the late 6th century, along with an abbey, and both can still be seen today although the cathedral, which still dominates the city's skyline, is actually a Norman structure. The abbey and the cathedral, along with St Martin's Church, the oldest parish church in England still in constant use, form a fascinating World Heritage Site.

However, it is not just ancient buildings that draw visitors to this very special city. There is much else to see here including the places that were known to the city's several famous literary connections: Geoffrey Chaucer, the Elizabethan playwright and spy Christopher Marlowe, Somerset Maugham and Mary Tourtel, the creator of Rupert Bear.

The land between Canterbury and the coast is characterised by pretty villages, while to the south, around Barfreston, was the area of the East Kent coalfield. To the northeast, around Stourmouth, is an area of very fertile land, which is the home of market gardens and orchards. Centuries ago, the Wantsum Channel separated the Isle of Thanet from the rest of Kent. The channel silted up over the centuries becoming marshland. The land seen today is the result of the drainage of the marshland in the 16th and 17th centuries.

This eastern stretch of Kentish coastline supported numerous fishing villages but, with the constant threat of invasion, they became fortified, particularly in 16th century under Henry VIII. Deal Castle remains one of the best surviving examples of Tudor military architecture while its contemporary, Walmer Castle, has been turned into an elegant stately house that is the home of the Lord Warden of the Cinque Ports.

Set up in the 11th century, the Cinque Ports were a commercial alliance of south coast ports but today the title is chiefly ceremonial.

CASTLE HOUSE HOTEL

28 Castle Street, Canterbury,
Kent CT1 2PT
Tel: 01227 761897
e-mail: enquiries@castlehousehotel.co.uk
website: www.castlehousehotel.co.uk

'In the Shadow of the Normans',
'In the Footsteps of the Pilgrims'

Castle House Hotel offers a break to remember in the heart of Canterbury, a holiday that combines Georgian luxury and style, Norman history and modern comfort and convenience.

Built in the 1730s, the house takes its name from the magnificent Norman ruin that stands right opposite, and part of the building is formed from the medieval city wall and the Roman Worthgate. A pretty walled garden to the front originally formed part of the Castle moat – with all this history all around, it's not surprising that the house is part of the official Canterbury City Walk.

Open throughout the year, Castle House has seven very quiet, comfortable and spacious letting bedrooms that provide versatile accommodation – singles, doubles, twins, family rooms, de luxe rooms and a honeymoon suite, all beautifully decorated, with en suite bathrooms and all the expected amenities of TV, clock radio alarm, tea/coffee making facilities, hairdryer and trouser press. Many of the rooms enjoy views of the Castle or the Cathedral. An in-house laundry service is another useful amenity and e-mail and internet facilities are available on request. The tariff includes an excellent cooked-to-order breakfast served in the sunny dining room.

Guests can relax after a day's sightseeing or plan the next day's activities in the peaceful residents' lounge or enjoy a stroll in the beautiful, secluded walled garden. The hotel has secure on-site parking for cars, bicycles and motor bikes, with CCTV an additional security feature.

A converted stable block/coach house to the rear of the main building contains a fully separate, self-contained holiday cottage for up to eight guests.

The lovely Dane John Garden is just round the corner, and the hotel is within easy reach of shops, bars, restaurants and entertainment as well as the numerous historic sights of Canterbury.

Canterbury

St Martin's Church · Cathedral
Roman Museum · Canterbury Festival
Canterbury Tales Visitor Attraction
Museum of Canterbury · St Augustine's Abbey
Kent Masonic Library & Museum

England's most famous cathedral city, and also one of the loveliest, Canterbury lies in one of the most attractive areas of rural Kent. It was here, in 597, that St Augustine founded an abbey, soon after his arrival from Rome, and so lay down the roots of Christianity in England. Lying just outside the city walls, **St Augustine's Abbey** is now in ruins, but there is an excellent museum and information centre here with exhibits on display that have been excavated from the site. Founded in 598, it is one of the oldest monastic sites in Britain. Destroyed at the dissolution of the monasteries in the 16th century, visitors can see the ruins of the original Saxon and Norman churches as well as the remains of Tudor brickwork from a Royal Palace built by Henry VIII. Before Augustine had finished the monastery, he worshipped at St Martin's Church, England's oldest parish church, which was named after the Bishop of Tours, France. The building is believed to date back to Roman times and is still in constant use.

However, both these fine buildings are overshadowed by the Mother Church of the Anglican Communion, **Canterbury Cathedral**, which still dominates the city skyline. Canterbury Cathedral has a tradition of welcoming visitors that goes back to the days of the medieval pilgrimage. St Augustine was sent to England by Pope Gregory the Great and, as the first archbishop, he made

SUGAR BOY

31 Palace Street, Canterbury, Kent Tel: 01227 479545
e-mail: enquiries@sugarboy.co.uk website: www.sugarboy.co.uk

Sugar Boy sells a wonderful variety of everybody's favourite sweets. In this traditional English sweet shop the jolly assistants have a warm welcome for all who pass through the doors. Customers take their pick from over 500 different sweets in shiny jars, weighed on scales, bagged and taken away to be enjoyed by all. The choice runs from blackjacks and shrimps to classy violet creams and much more. Jamie Oliver called Sugar Boy 'the best sweet shop in the world', and in the latest Charlie & the Chocolate Factory film, the sweets were supplied by Sugar Boy.

Canterbury his seat (or 'Cathedra'). The earliest part of the present building is the crypt, dating back to around 1100 and the largest of its kind in the country. On top of this was built the quire that had to be replaced in the 12th century after the original construction was destroyed by fire. Gradually, the building was added to and altered over the centuries. The nave, with its tall columns rising up like trees to meet the delicate vaulted arches, is 14th century, and the 'Bell Harry' tower 15th century.

The windows in the cathedral are magnificent. Fortunately they survived the ravages of Henry VIII's Dissolution of the Monasteries and the wartime bombs that flattened much of the surrounding city. However, the cathedral's library was not so lucky as this was damaged by a German air raid in 1942. The beautiful and historic stained glass at the cathedral had been removed earlier, and only the plain replacement windows were blown out with the force of the blast. Eight of the original 12 12th-century stained glass windows remain intact with amazing jewel-bright colours.

There is a vast amount to see here, from the medieval tombs of kings and archbishops (Lanfranc and St Anselm), to splendid architecture, and the guided tours provide not only information about the building but also of those people who have been associated with it through the centuries. However, it is as the scene of the murder of Archbishop Thomas à Becket that the building is best known. Becket was killed on a December evening in the northwest transept by the knights of Henry II, who supposedly misunderstood the king's request to be rid of this 'troublesome priest'. A penitent Henry, full of remorse for the death of his former friend, later came here on a pilgrimage. Unfortunately,

Canterbury Cathedral, Canterbury

YORKE LODGE

50 London Road, Canterbury, Kent CT2 8LF
Tel: 01227 451243
e-mail: info@yorkelodge.com
website: www.yorkelodge.com

A superb Victorian town house has been beautifully transformed into its current role as a top-quality family-run Bed & Breakfast earning 5 Stars from The AA and English Tourism Council. The building, which dates from 1887 and has recently been fully refurbished, stands on London Road between the A2050 and A290 on the northern side of Canterbury, close to Canterbury West railway station. Its position puts it within a gentle stroll of the city's almost endless attractions and makes it a great base for touring the surrounding area.

The guest bedrooms, each with its own individual décor and furnishing, comprise a single, twin and a number of doubles. Some of the doubles are designated superior, with more space and four-poster beds. One or two extra beds can be added in these larger rooms to provide family accommodation. The rooms retain the style and original features of the late-Victorian era, creating a warm home-from-home atmosphere that combines with all the modern conveniences expected by today's discerning travellers. All the rooms have en suite bathrooms with luxury toiletries. Local produce is to the fore in the traditional English breakfasts, with Continental and lighter options, served in the dining room, which is home to a remarkable and treasured collection of Royal Family, Household, Toy and Tobacco memorabilia. The library, in addition to a wide range of books, has card game and board games for adults and children. The breakfast room opens to a sun terrace where in summer guests can while away an hour or two spotting the wildlife.

Yorke Lodge has its own private off-street parking. Dogs can be accommodated by prior arrangement. The city of Canterbury has more to offer the visitor than almost anywhere in the land, including the Cathedral and other historic buildings, museums, theatres, a county cricket ground, restaurants, shops, walking tours and ghost tours. The coast, at Whitstable and Herne Bay, is a 15 or 20-minute drive away, the seaports and the Channel Tunnels 30 minutes away, and the main road network gives easy access to the castles, gardens and all the other attractions that make Kent such a marvellous place to visit.

GRAHAM GREENER

40 Burgate, Canterbury, Kent CT1 2HW
Tel: 01227 464076

Following on the success of their shop Jane at Graham Greener in Whitstable (qv), Jane and Mario Antoniades opened a sister branch in December 2008 in the heart of Canterbury, opposite one of the entrances to the Cathedral grounds. In three rooms on different levels customers at **Graham Greener** will find a colourful array of beautiful things for the home, for the garden, for a special gift or for a morale-boosting treat. The stars of the show include ready-made bouquets designed and made up by Jane and her team, and delivered daily from their Whitstable shop. They also have a nationwide delivery service, so you can choose what you like in the shop and they will be delivered next day.

In addition to the extensive range of practical homeware, fragrances and gifts of all kinds this shop also sells a selection of jewellery and clothes and several areas dedicated to gifts for men, as well as a children's room filled with toys, games, kids' wear and lots more to delight the little ones.

Shop hours are 10am to 6pm Monday to Friday, 9am to 6pm Saturday and 11am to 5pm Sunday.

SYLVAN COTTAGE

Nackington Road, Canterbury, Kent CT4 7AY
Tel: 01227 765307
e-mail: sylvan5@btinternet.com
website: www.sylvancottage.co.uk

Chris and Jac provide top-quality Bed & Breakfast accommodation at **Sylvan Cottage**, which stands on the B2068 Nackington road south of the historic heart of Canterbury. Their white-painted 17th century cottage has three en suite letting bedrooms. The most recent is a ground-floor room with a walk-in shower and a private patio with access to the garden. The upstairs rooms are ideal for friends or a family group. The day rooms include a recently built lounge area with a log-burning fire and a well-stocked guest kitchen with tea, coffee, juices, a hob, microwave, fridge and laundry facilities. Local produce is used whenever possible in the full English breakfast that starts the day; evening meals are available with a little notice, and evening baby sitting can be arranged.

Sylvan Cottage is an ideal base for exploring the many treasures that Canterbury has to offer or for touring the surrounding countryside on foot, on a bike or by car – the cottage has off-road parking for cars and secure storage for cycles and motorcycles. The Shuttle through the Tunnel is just 20 minutes away.

NUMBER 7 LONGPORT

No 7 Longport, Canterbury, Kent CT1 1PE
Tel: 01227 455367
e-mail: Ursula.wacher@btopenworld.com

Number 7 Longport is a delightful, unexpected hideaway just five minutes from Canterbury Cathedral. The accommodation is quirky and comfortable and the food is locally sourced. The owners always do their best to see that their guests have an enjoyable stay.

The accommodation is contained in a lovely old cottage away from the owners' Georgian house at the bottom of the garden. On the ground floor are a sitting room with a log burning fire, a shower and toilet, while upstairs is a quiet, cosy double bedroom.

Longport is located bang opposite the site of St Augustine's Abbey, off the roundabout at the junction of Lower Chantry Lane and the A257 Sandwich road. Few places not just in the UK but in the World have as rich a history as Canterbury, and there are few places as pleasant as Number 7 Longport for exploring this marvellous city.

Becket's original tomb, said to have been covered in gold and jewels, was destroyed in 1538 by the agents of Henry VIII. However, from the time of his death, in 1170, Canterbury Cathedral has been one of the most famous places of pilgrimage in Europe and it continues to be so today. One of the best examples of ecclesiastical architecture in the country, the whole precincts of the cathedral, along with **St Martin's Church** and St Augustine's Abbey, form a World Heritage Site. The Archbishop of Canterbury is the Primate of All England, attends royal functions and sits in the House of Lords.

By the time that Geoffrey Chaucer was writing his *Canterbury Tales*, some two centuries after the death of Thomas à Becket, Canterbury had become one of the most popular places of pilgrimage after Rome and Jerusalem. Many of the pilgrims set out, on foot or by horse, from London, as did Chaucer himself and, in many cases, the journey seems to have been more of a social event than an act of penance. As well as making the journey at least once himself, as the king's messenger, Chaucer also passed through Canterbury on numerous occasions on his way to the Continent. At the **Canterbury Tales Visitor Attraction** visitors are taken back to the 14th century and invited to embark on the same journey of pilgrimage that was undertaken by the characters in Chaucer's great poem. As they were making the journey, the Knight, the Miller, the Pardoner, the Nun's Priest and the Wife of Bath, along with the other travellers, told tales to keep themselves amused on their journey from the Tabard Inn in London to the shrine of St Thomas à Becket. From the animated farmyard tale of a cock, a hen and a wily old

MAGNOLIA HOUSE

36 St Dunstan's Terrace, Canterbury, Kent CT2 8AX
Tel: 01227 765121
e-mail: info@magnoliahousecanterbury.co.uk
website: www.magnoliahousecanterbury.co.uk

Magnolia House is a late-Georgian property in a quiet residential street on the west side of Canterbury, easily reached from the A2 and A28 and a 10-minute stroll from the centre.

Owner Isobelle Leggett offers first-class Bed & Breakfast accommodation in bedrooms professionally designed to a very high standard. She takes great pride in seeing that her guests have a stay to remember, and the whole place has a particularly warm and friendly atmosphere. The bedrooms, doubles and twins, some with king- or queen-size beds, all have en suite bath or bath and shower, TV, alarm clock-radio, tea tray, milk in the fridge, hairdryer, sewing kit, robes and fluffy towels. Top of the range is the Garden Room on the ground floor, with a four-poster bed and an extra-spacious bathroom with a corner bath.

The house is unlicensed, but a corkscrew, ice and chiller are available for guests who bring a bottle of wine. Full wireless internet facilities are available. Breakfast caters for a variety of tastes and appetites, providing a fine start for a day exploring the city or the Kentish coast and countryside.

fox, to stories of love, chivalry, rivalry and ribaldry, the colourful tales are brought very much to life at this popular attraction. The medieval streets, houses and markets of the pilgrims are faithfully reconstructed, as is Becket's shrine. The Canterbury Tales attraction is located in the former Parish Church of St Margaret. In the High Street stands the Eastbridge Hospital of St Thomas the Martyr, established for pilgrims to Becket's shrine. It survived destruction during the Reformation, finding a new role as an almshouse for 10 poor townspeople.

While Canterbury is certainly dominated by its great cathedral there is much more to the city than first appearances might suggest. The capital of the Iron Age kingdom, Cantii (a name that lives on in the city and in the county name of Kent), the Romans also settled here for a time and, at the **Roman Museum**, there is a fine display of unearthed remains from Durovernum Cantiacorum (the Roman name for Canterbury). This underground museum centres on the remains of a Roman town house and, along with the fine mosaic floors, there are also reconstructions of other Roman buildings, a gallery of household objects that were excavated in and around this ancient site, and some reproduction artefacts that visitors can handle.

Another aspect of life in Kent can be discovered at **The Kent Masonic Library and Museum** where the history of freemasonry over the past 300 years is explored. The vast collections found here cover many aspects of masonic life, and visitors can see numerous pieces of Masonic regalia and a huge library of books covering all aspects of freemasonry. There are also fine

Cathedral Precinct Gate, Canterbury

paintings, glassware and porcelain and the Cornwallis collection of documents and presentation items. The museum has limited opening times.

Housed in the former Poor Priests Hospital, which has some fine medieval interiors, is the **Museum of Canterbury** which presents a full history of the city over the last 2,000 years. From prehistoric times through to Canterbury in World War II, this museum has a great wealth of treasures and award-winning displays. In the same building is a children's museum, featuring celebrities connected with Canterbury such as Rupert Bear, Bagpuss and the Clangers. Canterbury has had many literary connections down the ages, including Mary Tourtel (creator of Rupert Bear), Chaucer, Somerset Maugham (who went to King's School in the city in the 1890s) and the Elizabethan dramatist Christopher Marlowe (at the same school centuries earlier). A contemporary of Shakespeare's and the author of *Dr Faustus* and *Edward II*, Marlowe, the son of a shoemaker, was born in 1564 in George Street, and later went on to Benet (now Corpus Christi) College, Cambridge. As a friend of Sir Francis Walsingham, Elizabeth I's Secretary of State, Marlowe supplemented his literary career by taking an active role as a spy. At only 29 years of age, he was stabbed to death in Deptford following what is officially referred to as a tavern brawl but may well have been a deliberately planned assassination. He is buried at the church of St Nicholas and the church records simply state: "Christopher Marlowe, slain by ffrancis Archer 1 June 1593." Canterbury's main theatrical venue, the Marlowe Theatre, is named after this famous son and, along with the Gulbenkian Theatre at the University of Kent, plays host to the annual **Canterbury Festival** that presents a varied programme of performing arts.

Around Canterbury

FORDWICH

2½ miles NE of Canterbury off the A28

This village was once a busy port for Canterbury on the River Stour, which was tidal to this point. As the river silted up and commercial vessels became larger, Fordwich was robbed of its major economic activity and the once prosperous town became a quiet and peaceful backwater. However, remnants of the bustling trade remain in what is the smallest town in Britain. Its town council meets in one of the smallest Town Halls in the county. Built in Tudor times and sited on the quay, it is timber-framed, with the upper storey overhanging on all sides. On the upper floor was the courtroom and on the ground floor, the jail and the jailer's quarters. There is a fascinating collection of items here including the ancient chest with three locks in which all the town's important documents were kept.

PRESTON

7 miles NE of Canterbury off the A28

Listed in the Domesday Book as Prestetune, which means 'priest's farmstead or manor', the village church of St Mildred had, up until the early 18th century, suffered a period of decline and records show that animals were allowed to graze in the graveyard and that the church services were conducted improperly if they were conducted at all. However, some sort of order was returned to the parish when, in 1711, a house was left to the local church for use as a vicarage on condition that two services were held at the church each Sunday. The church itself is quaint in appearance, 14th century with a 19th-century pyramidal cap on the tower and slightly odd triangular windows. There are also some beautiful 14th-century stained glass windows.

STOURMOUTH

7½ miles NE of Canterbury off the A28

As the village is several miles from the sea, its name seems to make little sense but, centuries ago, this is where the River Stour fed into the Wantsum Channel, the stretch of water that separates the Isle of Thanet from the rest of Kent. In fact, such was the depth of the channel that, in 885, it was the site of a sea battle between King Alfred and Danish raiders, who became trapped in the channel while attempting to attack and capture the City of Rochester.

The Wantsum Channel gradually silted up over the years and, in the 16th and 17th centuries, the resultant marshes were drained by Flemish refugees. Still criss-crossed by a network of drainage ditches today, this land remains very fertile and is now home to market gardens, fruit farms and hop fields.

WINGHAM

6 miles E of Canterbury on the A257

Parish Church · Wingham Wildlife Park

On either side of the long tree-lined High Street that runs through this large village, there are some fine and historic buildings, some of which date back to the reign of Henry VIII. There is an interesting story surrounding the wooden arcade of the **Norman Parish Church**. By the 16th century the building had fallen into a state of acute disrepair and George Ffoggarde, a local brewer, obtained a licence to raise funds for the its repair. However, Ffoggarde embezzled all the £244 that he had collected and so the intended stone arcade, which should have been a feature of the repairs, was replaced with a wooden one that was considerably cheaper. The village became renowned for rebellion as the villagers were not only active in the Peasants' Revolt of 1381 as well as other popular protests, but they also took part in the Swing Riots of 1830, for which several of them were transported to Australia.

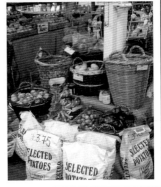

Just to the northeast of the village lies **Wingham Wildlife Park**, which aims to provide safe and secure habitats for many species of bird that are threatened in the wild. Among the many birds here visitors can see waterfowl, parrots, owls and emu while, in the Orchard Aviary, numerous smaller birds live alongside a range of furry mammals. Children will love the Pet Village, where they can mingle with the animals, and the Landscaped

Lake, where they can feed the ducks. A tropical house is home to exotic butterflies and plants.

BEKESBOURNE

3 miles SE of Canterbury off the A2

Howletts Wild Animal Park

Just to the north of the village, and set within 70 acres of beautiful and ancient parkland, lies **Howletts Wild Animal Park**, which was created by John Aspinall and is dedicated to the preservation of rare and endangered species. Here, visitors can see the large family groups of gorillas and breeding herds of Asian and African elephants. Families of rare monkeys can also be seen at the park, along with Indian and Siberian tigers, other large cats and many more endangered animals.

BRIDGE

3 miles SE of Canterbury on the A2

The village stands at a river crossing, where the old Dover Road from London crosses a tributary of the River Stour, which is, obviously, the source of its name. Now by-passed by the main A2 dual carriageway, the village was, for many years, subjected to a constant stream of heavy traffic and the villagers, in the 1970s, caused such a bottleneck while protesting to have the road through the village re-routed that the government relented and the by-pass was opened in 1976.

PATRIXBOURNE

3 miles SE of Canterbury off the A2

This handsome village, with a range of houses

THE DUKE WILLIAM

The Street, Ickham, Kent CT3 1QP
Tel: 01227 721308 Fax: 01227 721244
e-mail: goodfood@dukewilliam.biz
website: www.dukewilliam.biz

Louise White, who runs the **Duke William** with Nicola, has many years' experience in the licensed trade but this is the first pub she has owned. The atmosphere throughout is notably warm and friendly, making it a particularly pleasant place to meet for a drink or a meal, or to enjoy a well-deserved break from the bustle of city life. Real log fires keep things cosy even on the coldest days, and when the sun shines the garden comes into its own – the owners have a welcome for the family, and swings and a slide in the garden will keep the little ones happy. Regular patrons and customers from a widening radius are savouring the delights of a meal in this fine old hostelry.

The kitchen uses local produce as far as possible to produce traditional dishes with a different twist: the choice includes well-priced 2-course lunches, wonderful Sunday roasts, the catch of the day (plaice with lemon and caper butter) and seasonal fresh vegetables to accompany main courses. The inn is open all day from 9.30, making it a popular spot to enjoy a cup of coffee with the morning papers or to pause on a bracing morning walk. The B&B accommodation comprises three en suite rooms with views of the church and countryside.The inn lies on the main street of the village of Ickham, a short drive north of the A257 Canterbury to Sandwich road.

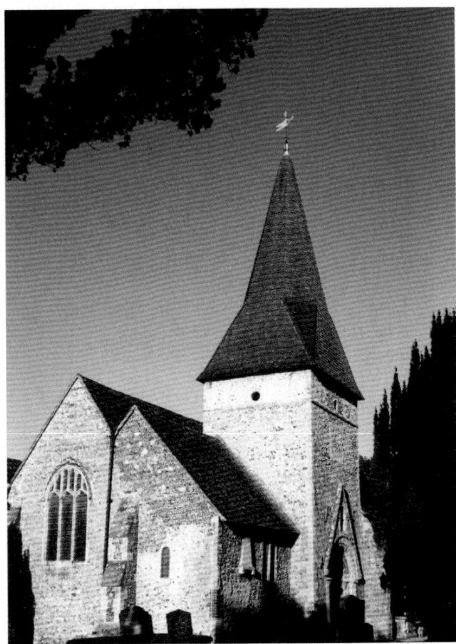

Patrixbourne Church, Patrixbourne

dating largely from the 17th and 18th centuries, also has newer dwellings, built in the 19th century. Carefully constructed in the Tudor style, they blend harmoniously with the existing buildings. The village church dates back to Norman times and has some wonderful carvings including the priest's door with a disfigured saint's head above. Bifrons, now demolished, was the seat of the Marquess of Conyngham, the great favourite of George IV.

AYLESHAM

6½ miles SE of Canterbury off the B2046

Following World War I, the eminent town planner, Professor Abercrombie, set out an ambitious scheme for a new town here that was to provide 2,000 houses. When development began in the 1920s, the plans were scaled down and the village provided 500 dwellings for miners, and their families, who worked in the East Kent coalfield and, in particular, nearby Snowdown Colliery, which closed in 1987.

GOODNESTONE

7 miles SE of Canterbury off the B2046

Goodnestone Park Gardens

Close to the village lies Goodnestone Park, an estate that was originally owned by Brook Bridges, who held an important post in the Treasury during the reign of Charles II. In the 18th century, Jane Austen was a frequent visitor to the house as her brother married Bridges' daughter; during World War II, the house and park were requisitioned by the army and used as a tank repair depot. The estate is now in the ownership of Lord and Lady FitzWalter, and **Goodnestone Park Gardens** are considered some of the best in the southeast of England. The formal gardens around the house contain several old specimen trees and there's a walled garden that still has some of the original 17th-century walls. New planting continues here all the time and beyond the formal garden areas lie mature woodlands and a '1920s' rockery and pond.

NONINGTON

7 miles SE of Canterbury off the B2046

For many years there were several private estates, with grand and imposing houses, situated close to this village and one, Fredville Park, remains to the south of Nonington. Although the superb Georgian house that lay at the centre of this estate was burned to the ground in 1939, the park is still renowned for its collection of fine oak trees and, in particular, the Fredville Oak that is several hundred years old and has a circumference of 36 feet.

THE GRIFFINS HEAD

Chillenden, nr Canterbury, Kent CT3 1PS
Tel: 01304 840325

Jerry and Karen Copestake bought the **Griffins Head** for the excellent reason is that they fell in love with its traditional look and feel. Fifteen years on, the black-and-white slate-roofed building retains all that charm; that's the way they want it, and that's certainly the way their locals want it. It's one of the most delightful places in the whole region to meet old friends or make new friends over a drink, a snack or a meal. The bar is open long hours all day, every day, and freshly prepared traditional pub food is served from 12 to 2 and from 7 to 9, with the succulent Sunday roasts a particularly popular crowd-puller. The pub has a welcome for all the family – there's a separate family room where kids can be kids – and it's also a favourite start point for the local hunt and estate shoots.

The Griffins Head is located at Chillenden, off the B2046 road that links the A257 Canterbury-Sandwich road and the A2 Canterbury-Dover road. Attractions close to the pub include Chillenden Windmill, one of the last surviving open-trestle post mills in the county; Goodnestone Park Gardens; and Nonington Park with its renowned collection of oak trees.

Windmill, Chillenden

CHILLENDEN

8 miles SE of Canterbury off the B2046

Found in a prominent position, just outside this village, is Chillenden Windmill, one of the last open trestle post windmills to be built in England, and one of the last surviving such mills in Kent. It was built in 1868 for Brigadier Speed, who lived at Knowlton Court, although this exposed site has supported windmills for over 500 years. Now restored, and with a complete outward appearance, the mill contains some of the old machinery and is open to the public on occasional days throughout the year.

BARFRESTON

8½ miles SE of Canterbury off the A2

Barfreston's small Saxon church, which dates from the 11th and 12th centuries, is remarkable for its detailed stone carvings, the best examples of which can be seen around the east

YEW TREE

Barfreston, nr Canterbury,
Kent CT15 7JH
Tel: 01304 831000
e-mail: yew.tree@live.co.uk
website: www.yewtree.info

Barfreston was a stopover in the Middle Ages for pilgrims on their way to the shrine of Thomas à Becket at Canterbury. Today, visitors still come to the village to admire the wonderful carvings in the late-Norman Church of St Nicholas and the bell that hangs from a yew tree just outside the church. That famous old tree has given its name to its neighbour, a superb inn that has become a place of pilgrimage for lovers of outstanding food. The west end of the church gives directly on to the garden of **Yew Tree**, a superb place to take a break from a bracing country walk, to enjoy the terrific hospitality and the top-notch food and drink. An inn has stood on the site for centuries, and walking into the present occupant is to take a step back in time, with hop bines, evocative paintings, pine furniture on bare boards in one dining area, carpets and traditional tables and chairs in another, a real fire in the bar. Outside, the terrace tables in the beer garden are a lovely alternative setting for a drink and a meal when the sun shines.

The inn has the services of two Bens, owner Ben Bevan and head chef Ben Williams. Ben Bevan is an ebullient host, a wine expert and a well-known opera singer (his wife is also a singer) with strong links with Scottish Opera – one of his commitments for 2009 is singing the role of Riccardo in Bellini's opera *I Puritani*. Ben Williams, whose CV includes a spell at the Michelin-starred The square in London, sources as many ingredients as possible from local farmers and growers, and his fish comes straight from the nearby Kent ports. His superb British cuisine can be enjoyed seven days a week, every lunchtime (extended hours on Sunday) and Monday to Saturday evenings. Typical bar dishes might include beef & pearl barley broth, plaice goujons with tartare sauce and game sausage rolls with Cumberland sauce. From the lunch menu could come butternut squash risotto, Dover slip sole beurre noisette, ballotine of confit pheasant and warm vanilla rice pudding with a spiced poached pear. The main à la carte menu tempts with the likes of poached duck egg with home-made crumpets, sea salt and black pepper butter; roasted crown of roast pigeon with Savoy cabbage, trio of parsnips and a red wine sauce; and cod with a scallop, mussel & saffron nage.

To accompany the wonderful food are local real ales and a fantastic wine list that includes some exciting new discoveries and purchases from private cellars. The last Sunday of the month brings live jazz to the Yew Tree, featuring house band The Jazz Notes.

door. They represent an array of creatures, scenes from medieval life and religious symbols. An explanatory booklet on these delightful images can be obtained from the nearby public house. There is another curious feature at this church - the church bell is attached to a yew tree in the churchyard.

KNOWLTON

8½ miles SE of Canterbury off the A256

Knowlton Court

The main street through this tiny hamlet leads to **Knowlton Court**, an Elizabethan house remodelled by Sir Reginald Blomfield in 1904. The Lodge was designed by Sir Edwin Lutyens in 1912. Down the years, Knowlton Court has been the home of several military and naval men: the Royalist commander Sir Thomas Peyton lived here at the time of the Civil War while, later, it was the home of Admiral Sir John Narborough. In 1707, Sir John's two sons were drowned off the Isles of Scilly following a naval disaster when navigational error caused the English fleet to be wrecked at night. A tomb in Knowlton Church, designed by Grinling Gibbons, illustrates the scene.

SHEPHERDSWELL

9 miles SE of Canterbury off the A2

East Kent Railway

This old village, which is sometimes referred to as Sibertswold, grew rapidly after 1861 when the London to Dover railway opened and, again, when housing was built here for the miners working at the nearby Tilmanstone Colliery. In 1911, a junction was established for the East Kent Light Railway to serve the colliery and, while the last passenger service ran in 1948, the railway continued its commercial operations until the colliery closed in 1987. Today, the **East Kent Railway** is open once again and carries passengers from the village's charming station to the nearby village of Eythorne. Those visiting the railway will also find a museum of railway memorabilia, a buffet, a gift shop and a miniature railway to add to their enjoyment.

COLDRED

10 miles SE of Canterbury off the A2

The tidy little village of Coldred is one of the highest settlements in East Kent at nearly 400 feet above sea level. Its name may be from Ceoldred, King of Mercia, who supposedly helped the Kentish men against the Saxons, or perhaps from the Old English word for charcoal burning, which was a local industry. Next to the parish church of St Pancras lies a farm that was originally a manor house owned by Bishop Odo of Bayeux, half-brother to William the Conqueror. In fact, both the church and the farm stand on a site that was a fortified Saxon camp of the 8th century - of which a few remains can still be seen. Archaeological excavations in this ancient village have revealed not only finds from Saxon times but also evidence of earlier, Roman, occupation. In later times the village pond was used for witch trials and, in the 1640s, it was recorded that Nell Garlige, an old woman of the parish, was tied up and thrown into the pond where, presumably, she drowned.

CHILHAM

5 miles SW of Canterbury on the A252

North Downs Way

This well-preserved village is one of Kent's showpieces and is often used as a location for filming, particularly the area round the square. The houses here are primarily Tudor and Jacobean and are a delightfully haphazard mix

LOWER HARDRES FARM SHOP

Lower Hardres, nr Canterbury, Kent CT4 5NU
Tel: 01227 700947

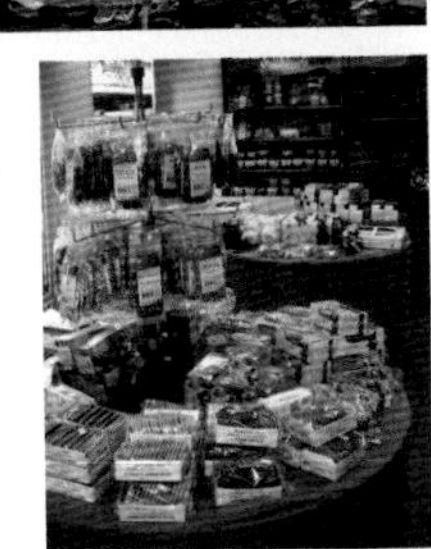

Lower Hardres Farm Shop is a family-run enterprise that takes its name from the little village in which it stands. Simon originally raised calves in his back garden. Simon and Cara moved to the farm in 2002 and added pigs, sheep and hens to the cattle; they opened the farm shop in the summer of 2007. The pigs are saddlebacks – the best for flavour, with fantastic crackling; the cattle are Aberdeen Angus, with natural marbling in their meat and superb flavour – the meat is hung for a minimum of three weeks.

All the meat is prepared on site by a master butcher with more than 40 years' experience in the trade. Visitors can watch him preparing the cuts and joints and making his renowned meat-packed sausages. The hens live in small houses and roam freely outside, so their eggs have lovely deep yellow yolks not seen in eggs produced by larger units. In season the shop also sells game birds, rabbits and venison, and at Christmas supplies turkeys, geese and extra-large chickens.

The farm produces a wide variety of fruit and vegetables with pick-your-own soft fruit, plums and pears available in their seasons. Local producers are very much to the fore in the shop: cheese from Ashmore Cheese in Dargate (the pigs are fed on the whey), cider; jams and chutneys from Wye; bread from Paul Hollywood in Aylesham and ice cream from Bonnington near Ashford. Open from 9am - 6pm (Sun 10am - 4pm).

THE HOP POCKET

Bossingham, nr Canterbury, Kent CT4 6DY
Tel/Fax: 01227 709866

The Hop Pocket is a charming old pub that's the social hub of the little village of Bossingham, off the B2068 a short drive south of Canterbury. Ian, Kim, Nick and Laura, the Pub owners have transformed the Hop Pocket back into a simple country Pub.

Kim and Nick run the kitchen, turning quality ingredients into simple yet satisfying dishes. Their motto is "Good food cooked simply". The main menu offers such delights as Potted Duck, Grilled Scallops in the Shell, Sausage and Mash and Haddock and Chips. The Kitchen makes everything on the premises, even down to the sweet pickle and pickled onions served with the lunchtime ploughmans. The meat and produce are supplied by Lower Hardres farm shop, with the livestock being reared within five miles of the pub and the potatoes used in the hand cut chips coming from the next valley. Now that is really local.

The pub stocks an excellent range of real ales, typically including Shepherd Neame Master Brew and guest ales such as Wadworths 6X, Fullers London Pride and Timothy Taylors to name a but a few.

The Hop Pocket has a new enlarged garden for alfresco sipping and dining with two fires for the winter. Families with children and dogs are always welcome.Open everyday 12am to3pm and 6pm to 11pm.

of gabled, half-timbered houses, shops and ancient inns. A stopping place for pilgrims on their way to the shrine of Thomas à Becket in Canterbury Cathedral, Chilham today plays host to other visitors, many of whom walk the nearby **North Downs Way**.

The village is also the home of Chilham Castle (now privately owned), a Jacobean Mansion built on to a Norman Keep built on Roman foundations. The house was built for Sir Dudley Digges, an official of James I, and the spacious grounds around the castle were first laid out by Charles I's gardener, John Tradescant. They were reworked in the 18th century by Capability Brown. The lodge gates in the village square were added in the 20th century. It was close to Chilham that the Romans fought their last great battle in Britain; the site is known as Julieberrie Downs in honour of Julius Laberius who was killed there in 54BC.

HARBLEDOWN

1 mile NW of Canterbury off the A2

Bigbury Hill Fort

This village was for many pilgrims the last stopping place before Canterbury. The village well, so legend has it, was called Black Prince's Well as the prince believed the waters to have healing properties. Despite drinking a flask of the water each day, the prince died in 1376, probably of syphilis contracted in Spain. The Church of St Nicholas, still known locally as the Leper Church, was built by Archbishop Lanfranc around 1084 as the Chapel for the Leper Hospital, which he founded here. The chapel was extended in the 14th century, and there are four delightful 14th-century stained glass windows in the chancel. The leper hospital was demolished as leprosy disappeared in England; the almshouses next to the church are Victorian.

Near Harbledown is **Bigbury Hill Fort**,

where Caesar fought the local inhabitants in 54BC. The outline of the fort is still clearly visible on the skyline, and the defensive ditches can still be seen. Excavations at the site have unearthed Belgic pottery and iron work, including a slave chain.

BLEAN

2½ miles NW of Canterbury on the A290

Close to the village lies Druidstone Park and Arts Park, where visitors can see a wide variety of animals and birds in a peaceful country setting, as well as a collection of indoor and outdoor sculptures. Along with native species such as otters and owls, the park is also home to more exotic creatures including rhea, mara, wallabies and parrots. Younger children can make friends with the farmyard animals, and there are walks through woodland where the park's herd of deer can be observed. Many of the animals and birds living here have been rescued, and others play an important part in captive breeding programmes. The plant growth in the park provides interest throughout the year, from spring flowers to autumn fungi and winter buds.

Broadstairs

Dickens House Museum

Crampton Tower Museum

Broadstairs was voted second only to St Ives in a recent Guardian readers' and critics' poll of favourite seaside resorts. It grew as an amalgamation of St Peter's inland and Broadstairs and Reading on the coast. It started life as a small fishing village called Bradstow (broad place) and much remains of the historic seafront – the 17th-century timber-boarded Boathouse and Customs House on the jetty, the

RITZY RETRO

York Street, Broadstairs, Kent CT10 1DD
Tel: 01843 600737
e-mail: ritzyretro@btinternet.com
website:
www.stores.ebay.co.uk/ritzy-retro-loves-vintage

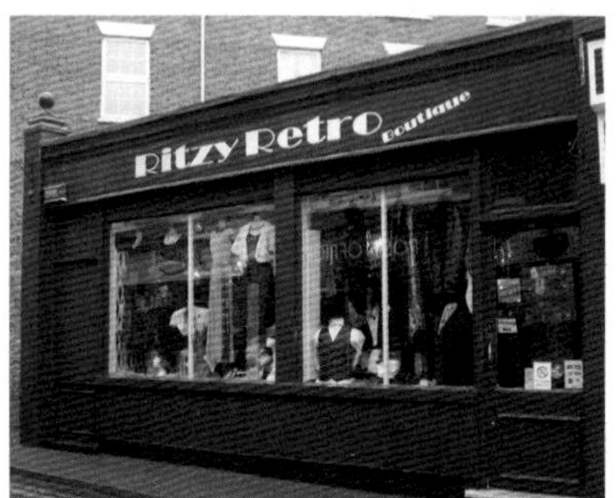

In her youth, Kentish girl Lorraine Tilley loved spending time in a retro shop selling clothes and fabrics from the 1930s to the 1970s. So when the opportunity arose to own and run a shop of her own she naturally jumped at the chance. Located just of the main street of Broadstairs and easy to spot with its dramatic purple frontage, Ritzy Retro is a specialist shop selling clothes, accessories and music from the 1920s to the 1970s.

Everything is authentic, original and one-off, and everyone associated with the boutique is passionate about vintage; since opening in 1999 it has built up a well-earned reputation in the world of vintage fashion and is a member of the prestigious Vintage Fashion Guild. Customers, including celebrities and stylists, come from all parts of the globe to browse and buy in an ambience set by glittering chandeliers and music from the 30s and 40s. Ritzy Retro covers all areas of vintage clothing for men and women, with also some children's clothes. There are vintage day wear, dresses, suits and jackets; glamorous cocktail dresses, evening wear, ball gowns and gorgeous silk opera coats; couture garments, like everything else, in pristine condition; a full range of accessories including shoes, hats, gloves, scarves and costume jewellery, with shelves full of bags, bags and more bags; a sparkling array of evening bags; dinner suits and tail coats for men as well as bespoke city suits, shirts and waistcoats; an amazing collection of ties, cravats and silk hankies, braces, belts and cufflinks.

This marvellous place offers a restoration service as well as customising clients' existing garments to wear to different functions and alterations to garments bought from the shop. Also offered is a personal shopping 'search and find service' for vintage items for men and women.

The online ebay shop (see website above) sells a different range of stock.

Opening hours are Thursday 10 to 4, Friday 10 to 4 and Saturday 10 to 5 all year round, at other times by appointment with a week's notice.

many shops and restaurants located in fishermen's cottages and sheds. The town is well known for its association with Charles Dickens. Those coming in search of Bleak House will find it in Church Road high up on the cliffs at the northern end of the town, overlooking the popular beach at Viking Bay. Charles Dickens spent his summers here for years. He wrote *David Copperfield*, at a desk at the window where from his 'airy nest', he had a splendid view over the English Channel and the Goodwin Sands from his 'airy nest'. The house is no longer open to the public, but the **Dickens House Museum**, the home of Mary Pearson Strong, the inspiration for Betsy Trotwood in *David Copperfield*, is filled with Dickens memorabilia, including letters, costumes, pictures and a collection of prints by Dickens' illustrator Phiz (HK Browne). The town reinforces its links with the great Victorian novelist by holding an annual Dickens Festival – the dates for 2009 are 20th to 26th June. The **Crampton Tower Museum**, housed in the original Broadstairs waterworks, is dedicated to Thomas Russell Crampton, a noted Victorian civil engineer who was the first to lay a working telegraph cable under the English Channel. The Broadstairs Gallery, opened in 2006, focuses on the development of the town in old postcards and photographs. Broadstairs also hosts a Folk Festival in August and a Food Festival in October.

Other notables associated with the town include the politician Sir Edward Heath, who was born here in 1916, and another famous sailor, Sir Alec Rose, who lived in Broadstairs for many years. Writers, too, seem to have found inspiration along this stretch of coast as both Frank Richards, creator of Billy Bunter, and John Buchan, author of the spy thriller, *The Thirty-Nine Steps*, lived here. Buchan wrote the story at a house called St Cuby on Cliff Promenade, and the staircase that gave him the idea for the title stands opposite the house. It comprises 78 steps, but the number was halved by Buchan to provide a catchier title. Viking

BROADSTAIRS ART COURSES

Flint House, 21 Harbour Street, Broadstairs, Kent CT10 1ET
Tel: 01843 861958 Mobile: 07949 884620
email: martin@martincheekmosaics.com
website: www.broadstairsartcourses.co.uk or www.martincheek.co.uk

Martin Cheek has been running Mosaic Courses at Flint House in Broadstairs for many years. Martin is the UK's best known mosaic artist making mosaics to commission and has a wealth of experience and knowledge enabling him to create such exquisite pieces of art. His courses have proved so successful, many participants return frequently. Built in 1720, Flint House has the most enviable position overlooking Viking Bay, the main beach of Broadstairs. With many great restaurants and pubs nearby, as well as fabulous beaches and coastal walks, there is plenty to occupy guests in the evenings. Martin runs his weekend courses and art based holidays in the spacious, light, airy studio with a superb lunch included in the course fee. Numbers are strictly limited in order to give the best level of tuition to participants, so it is advisable to book early in order to avoid disappointment. Other courses held at Flint House include Portrait Painting and Still Life by National Portrait Award Winner Margaret Foreman RBA, Icon Painting by Peter Murphy, and Watercolour Painting by International Watercolourist Cherryl Fountain.

Dates of the various courses are listed on the Broadstairs website, where you will also find a wide choice of nearby, recommended accommodation to suit all budgets.

Bay, is named for the occasion when a Viking ship, now on display at Pegwell Bay, was rowed from Denmark and landed at Broadstairs. There are six other bays – Kingsgate Bay, Botany Bay, Joss Bay, Louisa Bay, Stone Bay and Dumpton Gap, each with its own individual appeal. The North Foreland lighthouse was the last in the country to be permanently manned, being made automatic in 1998.

Around Broadstairs

MARGATE

3 miles NW of Broadstairs on the A28

Museum Salmestone Grange

Shell Grotto

With its long stretch of golden sand, promenades, amusement arcades and candy floss, Margate is very much everyone's idea of a boisterous English seaside resort. This is a well-deserved reputation that has grown up over 200 years. Before the railway brought holidaymakers in droves from London from the 1840s onwards, those looking for a day by the sea came in sailing boats known as Margate hoys. Many Londoners return here time and time again to wander around the old town and take the bracing sea air. With this background as a seaside resort, it is not surprising to find that the bathing machine was reputedly invented here, in 1752, by a Quaker glover and a Margate resident called Benjamin Beale.

However, there is more to Margate than sun, sea, sand and fish & chips. In King Street stands Tudor House, which dates back to the early 16th century and the reign of Henry VIII. It is the oldest house in Margate and holds a collection of seaside memorabilia. Viewing is

LOVELYS GALLERY

248 Northdown Road, Cliftonville, Margate, Kent CT9 2PX
Tel: 01843 292757 Fax: 01843 292758
e-mail: caroline@lovelysgallery.co.uk website: www.lovelysgallery.co.uk

Lovelys has been providing a unique service to artists and art lovers since 1891 and is thriving under Caroline Lovely and her staff who provide expert friendly advice on all aspects of art buying,picture framing and painting. They are rightly proud of being named Art Retailer of the Year 2008 by the Fine Art Trade Guild.

The gallery set over two spacious floors, showcases original paintings,limited edition prints and sculpture from local and internationally acclaimed artists,holds regular art exhibitions and has access to an amazing 50,000 prints worldwide.Beautiful ceramics,pottery,glass and greetings cards are also displayed. Lovelys provide an expert bespoke picture framing service to the highest conservation standards in their own workshop and also offer specialist conservation and restoration of pictures. A wide choice of frames are available. Lovelys are a Winsor and Newton Premier Art Centre and their art and craft department stocks everything an artist,crafter or card making enthusiast might need with an inspirational programme of art and craft demos and workshops throughout the year.

Among the artists showcased on Lovelys excellent website are Doug Hyde,Caroline Shotton, Duncan Macgregor, Rolf Harris, David Shepherd, Fletcher Sibthorp, Sue Howells, Henderson Cisz, Rebecca Lardner, Beryl Cook, John Haskins, John Horsewell, Jean Picton, Jonathan Shaw, Antonio Ianicelli, Brian Jull, Peter Wileman and Jack Vettriano. Open Mon - Sat 9 - 5.30pm.

by appointment only by prior arrangement with **Margate Museum**, located in the Old Town Hall. One of the most unusual and intriguing attractions is the **Shell Grotto**. Discovered in 1835, it is a rectangular chamber whose walls are decorated with strange symbols mosaiced in millions of shells. Margate's Theatre Royal is one of the oldest theatres operating in the country, while the Tom Thumb Theatre on the eastern esplanade at Cliftonville is the smallest old-time music hall theatre in the world.

Just inland lies medieval **Salmestone Grange**, which originally belonged to St Augustine's Abbey at Canterbury. In what is arguably one of the best preserved examples of a monastic grange in England, the chapel, crypt and kitchen can all still be seen.

Another building that has withstood the test of time is Drapers Mill, an old smock corn mill that was constructed in 1845 by John Holman. It continued to be powered by the wind until a gas engine was installed in 1916 and, after being made redundant in the 1930s, the mill was restored to working order in the 1970s.

BIRCHINGTON

6 miles NW of Broadstairs on the A28

All Saints' Church Quex House

This quiet resort, with cliffs and bays, still retains its individuality despite the spread of the Margate conurbation from the east, and it is a particular favourite for families with young children. At **All Saints' Church** there is a monument to one of the most famous British artists of the 19th century, Dante Gabriel Rossetti, the poet and artist who was instrumental in the formation of the

Raphaelite Brotherhood. He lies buried in the doorway and a memorial stone, carved by his mentor, Ford Madox Brown, marks his grave.

About half a mile to the southeast of the village lies **Quex House**, a Regency gentleman's country house that was later expanded into the Victorian mansion seen today. It remains the home of the Powell-Cotton family and visitors looking around the rooms will find that the house still retains the atmosphere of a family home, complete with freshly cut flowers from the garden. A fine collection of period and oriental furniture, family portraits, porcelain and silver can be seen by those wandering through the rooms. One particular member of the family, Major PHG (Percy) Powell-Cotton, was a great explorer, and while he was lured to exotic lands by big game, the major was a true Victorian who also took an interest in the customs and beliefs of the people and tribes that he met on his travels. As a result he put together a vast collection, which the Museum here displays in polished mahogany cases. From dioramas of animals and tribal art, costumes and weapons to European and Chinese porcelains and local archaeological finds, there is a vast range of exhibits from around the world. He once had an uncomfortable brush with a lion, and both the lion and his torn jacket are on display. As well as offering visitors a great deal to see inside the house, Quex is surrounded by some superb gardens, parkland and woodlands that provide the perfect backdrop to this fascinating house. The gardens have wide lawns with mature trees and a walled kitchen garden. John Cotton-Powell's collection of cannons is also displayed in the grounds, where the Waterloo Tower folly, built to house his ring of 12 bells can also be found.

Roman Fort, Reculver

RECULVER

12 miles W of Broadstairs off the A299

Roman Fort · Country Park

Reculver is the site of the Roman Regulbium, one of the forts built in the 3rd century to defend the shores of Kent from Saxon invasion. Sometime later the site was taken over as a place of Christian worship and this early fort provided the building materials for the 7th-century Saxon church that was later extended by the Normans. It was also around this time that the Normans built the two huge towers within the remains of the Roman fort that provided mariners with a landmark to guide them into the Thames estuary. Today, **Reculver Towers and Roman Fort** is under the management of English Heritage, and although there are only a few remains of the fort, the towers still stand overlooking the rocky beach and can be seen from several miles along the coast. **Reculver Country Park** offers visitors a lovely walk to these remains, church and towers, and the park's visitors' centre has some fascinating information on the history and natural history of this stretch of coastline.

As a major historic site, Reculver has seen much archaeological activity over the years and in the 1960s excavation unearthed several tiny skeletons that were buried not far from the towers. It is generally believed that these babies were buried alive as human sacrifices and it is said that on stormy nights the babies can be heard crying out. During World War II, the Barnes Wallace 'bouncing bomb' was tested off the coast of Reculver. Several of these were found on the shore in 1997. Fortunately they did not contain any explosives.

SARRE

12 miles W of Broadstairs on the A28

Mill

This sunken village on the edge of marshland was once an important harbour and ferry point when the Isle of Thanet was indeed an island. Today, it is home to one of the country's few remaining commercially working mills, **Sarre Mill** (see panel on page 82), a typical Kentish smock windmill built in 1820 by the Canterbury millwright John Holman. The addition of first steam and then gas power ensured that Sarre Mill remained in use well into the 20th century but in the 1940s milling ceased here. Fortunately, in the 1980s, the windmill was restored to working order, and today, Sarre Mill is producing high quality stoneground flour and offering tours of the five floors of the mill. It has one set of Derbyshire Peak stones and one set of French Burrs, and most of the original machinery is still in use. There are small farmyard animals that are sure to delight children, and a rare portable steam engine dating from the 1860s that was used to crush apples for cider making. Numerous other items of rural

Sarre Mill

Canterbury Road, Sarre, near Birchington, Kent CT7 0JU
Tel: 01843 847573

Found on high ground just to the northeast of the village is one of the country's few remaining commercially working mills, **Sarre Mill**, a typical Kentish smock windmill. Built in 1820 by the Canterbury millwright John Holman, a steam engine was installed here in 1861 to add further power although it was not until the 1920s that the sails were taken down and the mill wheels were completely powered by the gas engine that was installed in 1907. Milling finally ceased at Sarre in the 1940s and, after being left derelict for decades, the building was purchased in 1985 by the Hobbs family and restoration work was begun.

Today, Sarre Mill is back to working order, producing high quality stoneground flour, and, as well as touring the five floors of the mill, there is plenty more for the whole family to see. There are small farmyard animals, including Victoria, a Tamworth pig, that are sure to delight children and a rare portable steam engine dating from the 1860s that was used to crush apples for cider making. Numerous other items of rural interest, such as old agricultural machinery, farming implements and domestic pieces, are on display here in the exhibition of bygones. A tea rooms provides visitors with the ideal opportunity to enjoy some home-made bread or cake, all made using Sarre Mill flour, whilst, at the mill shop, not only can the flour be purchased but also a wide range of other country goods.

interest, such as old agricultural machinery, farming implements and domestic pieces, are on display in the exhibition of bygones.

MINSTER

8 miles W of Broadstairs off the A299

Abbey · Agricultural & Rural Life Museum

It is likely that there were settlements in the area around this village overlooking Minster Marshes well before the invasion of the Romans, and it is generally accepted that the Isle of Thanet was the first landing place for invading Saxons. Among the many old buildings in the village, some of which date back to the Middle Ages, are the Old House, built in 1350, and the Oak House that is almost as old. One of the country's first nunneries was established at Minster in the 7th century, on land granted to Princess Ermenburga, who is usually better known by her religious name - Domneva. King Egbert, her uncle, gave the land to Ermenburga as compensation when her two brothers were murdered by one of his men, the thane, Thunor. Legend has it that Thunor secured the throne of Kent for Egbert by murdering the two princes, Ethelbert and Ethelred, and he buried their bodies, secretly, in the grounds of the royal palace. The graves were soon found, revealed, so it is said, by mysterious columns of light, and a penitent King Egbert let loose a deer to run free, declaring that all the land that it encircled would be given to Ermenburga. As Thunor watched he became alarmed at the distance that the deer was covering and set out to try halt it but he fell, with his horse into a ditch and was drowned.

In the end, Ermenburga received over 1,000 acres and the story of its acquisition is illustrated in the windows of the parish church of St Mary. Ermenburga founded **Minster Abbey** in 670 and, although the nunnery was later sacked by the Danes, it became part of the estate of St Augustine's Abbey, Canterbury. The monks set about rebuilding the abbey, adding a grange, and much of the Norman work can still be seen in the cloisters and other parts of the ruins. In the grounds of Minster Abbey is Minster's **Agricultural and Rural Life Museum** centred on the Old Tithe Barn, parts of which date back to the 8th century. Agricultural machinery and implements depict farming methods and daily life in a rural community from the early 19th century.

MANSTON

3 miles W of Broadstairs on the B2050

Spitfire and Hurricane Memorial Building

This quiet village, surrounded by rich farmland supports intensive market gardening, was, during World War II, home to one of the country's major airfields. Featuring heavily in the Battle of Britain, RAF Manston was the closest airfield to the enemy coast and, as a consequence, it bore the brunt of the early Luftwaffe air attacks. The **Spitfire and Hurricane Memorial Building**, where the main attractions are the two aircraft themselves, provides visitors with an opportunity to gain an understanding of just what life was like for the pilots and other staff stationed at the airfield in the 1940s. The Spitfire Memorial was officially opened in 1981 to house Supermarine Spitfire TB752, and the Hurricane memorial was officially opened by Dame Vera Lynn in 1988 to house Hawker Hurricane LF751. Photographs and other memorabilia are on sale here, and the cafeteria offers fine views out across the airfield. RAF Manston closed in 1999 and is now a civilian airport called London Manston.

WOODNESBOROUGH

9 miles SW of Broadstairs off the A256

The hill at the centre of the village is Woden-hill derived from the Saxon God Woden, from which the village took its name. In the early 8th century the Battle of Wodnesbeorh took place here between the Saxons and the West Mercians. Legend has it that Woden-hill is actually the burial heap of those who died in the battle. Death certainly seems to have been a feature of Woodnesborough as this is also believed to be the burial place of Vortimer, King of the Saxons, who died in 457. Near the hill is the Parish Church of St Mary, notable for the wooden tower that replaced its spire in 1745.

WORTH

8 miles SW of Broadstairs off the A258

The pond in the centre of this pretty village was once part of a navigable creek that lead out to the sea but, over the centuries, as with much of this coastal strip, the waters have silted up. There are several buildings in Worth with distinctive Dutch architectural features; these were constructed in the 17th century by Flemish and Huguenot refugees who fled from the Continent to escape persecution.

SANDWICH

7½ miles SW of Broadstairs off the A256

Guildhall Museum   Richborough Roman Fort

Sandwich has its origins in Saxon times, when a settlement was established at the mouth of the River Stour. Since those days, the river has silted up and the town now stands a couple of miles from the coast, but its maritime history still lives on. It was one of the original Cinque Ports, hard though it might be to believe

WHITE ROSE LODGE

88 St George's Road, Sandwich,
Kent CT13 9LE
Tel: 01304 620406
e-mail: gillhardy54@hotmail.co.uk
website: www.hydeawaycottage.co.uk
www.whiteroselodge.co.uk
www.littlebeautyparlour.co.uk

When the Hardy family moved to Kent they fell in love with medieval Sandwich but brought their roots of Yorkshire and Cheshire with them in **White Rose Lodge** and **Hyde-a-Way Cottage** where they welcome Bed & Breakfast and Self Catering guests. The guest rooms in White Rose Lodge offer a high standard of décor, furnishings and comfort and have Sky/Freeview TV, DVD player, Wifi, complimentary tea tray, fluffy towels, toiletries and ample wardrobe and drawer space. There are private facilities in high specification shower rooms and bathrooms.

The setting is peaceful and attractive, with a large garden and small orchard and a hot tub in a private part of the grounds. Cereals, fruit and a full English breakfast using local Kent produce is served in the conservatory where guests might get a glimpse of the wildlife that abounds here.

Hyde-a-Way Cottage is a ten minute walk from White Rose Lodge offering a high standard of Self Catering accommodation and can sleep 4/6 people. There is a lovely enclosed garden with patio/BBQ area and it is completely safe for families with children and also pets are welcome.

White Rose Lodge and Hyde-a-Way Cottage are lovely comfortable bases for discovering all that Sandwich and the surrounding area has to offer, including the historic sights and the championship golf courses, but they have another very special asset. Located within White Rose Lodge is a splendid little beauty parlour where guests (and non-residents) can relax and enjoy a massage, reflexology, a Jacuzzi or a variety of treatments. Gillian is a highly qualified beauty and complementary therapist who has been practising for several years in Essex and now here in Kent. Guests can enjoy the most relaxing experience in an atmosphere of calm enhanced by the gentle strains of music and the aroma of essential oils.

today. After the harbour ceased to be navigable, the town turned to cloth manufacturing as its economic mainstay and, with the help of Flemish refugees, once again prospered. This industry has all but ceased and Sandwich has become simply a pleasant and peaceful place, best known for its championship golf course, Royal St George's.

The Sandwich **Guildhall Museum** tells the story of the town from early medieval times onwards, with the help of numerous artefacts dating from as far back as the 13th century. Built in 1576, though much altered in the 20th century, the Guildhall itself can be toured and there are some fascinating historic items including the Moot Horn that was used as far back as the 12th century to summon the people of the town to hear important announcements. The Horn is still used today to announce the death of the monarch and the accession of the successor. Another fascinating item is the Hog Mace, which was used to round up straying animals after the Goose Bell had been rung; all such animals not repossessed by their owners on payment of a fine were passed on to the Brothers and Sisters of St John's Hospital. Sandwich Town Council still meets in the Council Chamber twice a month as it has done for over 400 years. The Mayor's chair dates from 1561.

Elsewhere in Sandwich, visitors can see the Barbican Gate, a turreted 16th century gatehouse that guards the northern entrance into the town, and St Bartholomew's Hospital, which was founded in the 12th century and

THE GEORGE & DRAGON

24 Fisher Street, Sandwich,
Kent CT13 9EJ
Tel: 01304 613106
e-mail: enquiries@georgeanddragon.co.uk
website: www.georgeanddragon-sandwich.co.uk

Brothers Matthew and Mark Philpott came back to Sandwich in the summer of 2008 to re-open the **George & Dragon** as a fine dining restaurant, while retaining its status as a cosy 'local'. Behind its immaculate frontage, with new signage and first-floor window boxes, it's a smart, convivial place to meet friends for a drink or to settle down to a superb meal.

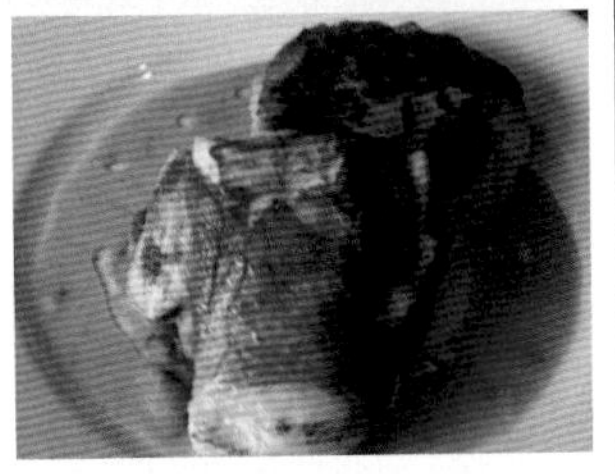

The George & Dragon started life in 1446, since when it has many changes, but in its more than 550 years it has never offered food of such high quality as that provided by chef Mark and his team. The cooking is British with some twists: nothing too complicated, just prime ingredients cooked to perfection. The menu changes constantly and as many as possible of the raw materials that find their way into the kitchen are grown or sourced locally. Typical dishes range from chicken liver & foie gras parfait and rolled meat terrine to cod wrapped in Parma ham with bubble & squeak and parsley sauce, rib eye steak with chips and horseradish béarnaise and braised shoulder of lamb with olive mash. Desserts like rhubarb Eton Mess or apple crumble with cinnamon custard maintain the enjoyment level to the end, and the excellent food is complemented by wines on a well-annotated list. A fine selection of real ales is served in the bar, which is open from 11-3 & 6-11 Mon to Fri and all day Sat and Sun. Food times are 12-2 and 6-9 every day.

consists of a quadrangle of almshouses grouped around an old chapel.

A mile northwest of the town is **Richborough Roman Fort**, believed to date from AD43. These impressive ruins of a fort and supporting township include the massive foundations of a triumphal arch that stood some 80 feet high. The extensive fortifications, which still dominate the surrounding flat land, were designed to repel Saxon invaders and at one time was the most important Roman military base in Britain. The museum here gives a real insight into life during the heyday of this busy Roman town.

RAMSGATE

2 miles S of Broadstairs on the A255

The Grange

For centuries, Ramsgate was a small fishing village until, in 1749, a harbour was built and the town began to grow. After George IV landed here in 1822 (the Obelisk on the East Pier commemorates this historic event), the town adopted the title of 'Royal Harbour'. By the end of the 19th century, its fishing fleet had grown to make it the largest port on the south coast of England. However, at the beginning of World War I, the fishing industry began to decline and, with a seemingly uncertain future,

Ramsgate enjoyed a brief moment of national glory when, in 1940, over 40,000 British troops, evacuated from the Dunkirk beaches by an armada of small boats and vessels, landed here.

The parish church of St George commemorates this important episode in Ramsgate's and England's history with a special stained glass window. The Catholic Church of St Augustine was designed by Augustus Welby Northmore Pugin (1812-1852), best known as the designer of the interior of the Houses of Parliament. He is buried in the church in a tomb chest designed by one of his three sons.

Still dominated by its harbour and shipping, the town is also home to **The Grange**, built by Augustus Pugin in 1843. Now Grade I listed after being restored by the Landmark Trust, it is one of a small group of houses built by great architects for their own use and is unusual in being available to rent.

Just to the south of Ramsgate lies Pegwell Bay, traditionally the landing place of Hengist and Horsa, who led the successful Jutish invasion of Kent in 449. The badge of Kent today has on it a prancing white horse, the image under which these Jutish warriors fought.

Deal

Castle Maritime & Local History Museum

Timeball Tower

This delightful fishing town has changed little in character since the 18th century, thanks in part to its shingle rather than sandy beach, which meant that Deal escaped Victorian development into a full-blown seaside resort. The fishing industry has always played a major role along this stretch of coastline and the roots of that trade are

ALLOTMENT

119 High Street, Deal, Kent CT14 6BB
Tel: 01304 371719
e-mail: allotmentdirect@gmail.com
website: www.allotmentdirect.com

Standing on Deal's busy High Street, **Allotment** is an organic delicatessen selling high-quality fresh organic food and natural products. Esme and Wil's shop prides itself on providing everything a farm shop can offer and more, with the advantage of an easily accessible town centre location. The shelves, boxes and cabinets are filled with a wide range of produce that showcases the finest that the Garden of England has to offer, sourced from carefully selected growers and suppliers. Customers will find an excellent choice of spray-free organic fruit and vegetables, free-range meat, eggs, dairy produce, artisan bread and cakes and organic beers and wines. The selection in the back of the shop includes dry goods and store cupboard items including oils, vinegars and preserves.

Allotment can organise local deliveries of meat, fruit, vegetables and cheese, and also sells boxes of goods and seasonal hampers made to order. Plans for the future include opening a cafe on the premises and a B&B upstairs. Shop hours are 9 to 5.30 Monday to Saturday and 10 to 3 Sunday.

THE BOHEMIAN

47 Beach Street, Deal, Kent CT14 6HY
Tel: 01304 374843
website: www.bohemianbythesea.com

'Specialist Beer Bar & Kitchen'

The Bohemian is a contemporary bar and eating place on a corner site on the coast road opposite Deal's 1950s pier, just seconds from the main A258. Food and drink are naturally the mainstay of the business but they are not the only ingredients that have made this one of the most popular meeting and eating places in the region.

Jonathan Brown, in the hospitality trade for 30 years, is the most sociable of hosts, and he and his partner Coleen guarantee a friendly, lively atmosphere. In 2003 they took over an ailing pub and transformed what had been a run-down boozer called The Antwerp into the super place of today. Jonathan spent many years in London and in Australia, and there's an Oz theme to the beer and wine lists, as well as to the parties and other events that take place here on a regular basis. It's a great place to meet up with friends, but first-timers going in as strangers will soon feel themselves relaxing in good company among the friendly faces and cheerful ambience. In the spacious bar and upstairs dining area with sea views visitors can choose from an impressive range of food and drink, and when the sun shines the tables and chairs set out in the back garden come into their own. Head chef Luke Peters seeks out the best seasonal produce to offer a fine variety of dishes to cater for a variety of tastes and appetites. Super sandwiches (how about merguez on grilled bread with smoked paprika mayonnaise!), sausages, steaks and cod with chips and mushy peas, pork & game terrine and tiger prawns and typical lunchtime fare, while the evening menu tempts with sophisticated choices like seared scallops with truffled pea purée, bordelaise potatoes and alfala shoots; free-range chicken breast with lemon and thyme; mini local fish pie and Ashdown Forest venison.

Wines, mainly from the New World, are available by 200ml and 250ml glass and by the bottle, and there's always a fine selection of real ales, typically including Woodforde Wherry, Deuchars IPA, Sharps Doom Bar and Cornish Coaster and Adnams Broadside. The choice of draught and bottled beers is even more remarkable, with brews from around the world including lots of Oz bottles: Victoria Bitter, Coopers Pale and Sparkling, Little Creatures Pale Ale. Tipplers of the stronger stuff will find a huge rage of premium spirits served in 25 ml or 50ml shots.

Bar hours are 11am to midnight Monday to Friday, 9am to 1pm Saturday, 9am to 11pm Sunday. Food times are 11am to 2.30pm and 6pm to 9pm Monday to Friday, 9am to 2.30pm and 6pm to 9pm Saturday and 9am to 3pm for Sunday brunch.

still very much in evidence. Deal's seafront is one of the most picturesque along the southeast coast and, with its quaint alleyways, traditional fishermen's cottages and old houses, the town is well worth exploring. Deal's pleasure pier was the last to be built in Britain after World War II. It replaced a 1910 structure and was opened by HRH the Duke of Edinburgh in 1957. It offers wonderful views of the seafront and plays host to the World Junior Angling competition. Not surprisingly, given its history, Deal was also the haunt of smugglers whose illegal activities were centred around Middle Street. It was in a house along this street that, in 1801, Nelson's great friend, Captain Edward Parker, died from wounds that he received following a raid on Boulogne. Nelson was a frequent visitor to the town, and he outraged local society by staying at the Royal Hotel with his mistress, Lady Emma Hamilton.

The **Maritime and Local History Museum** is an excellent place to begin as the displays here cover many aspects of the life of the town and its people. Housed in stables that were once used to shelter army mules, the museum has a large collection of real and model boats, figureheads, compasses and other navigational aids, pilots' relics and memorabilia that relate to Deal's seafaring and fishing past. On the site of the old Naval yard stands the distinctive **Timeball Tower** that was built in 1795 and was used to give time signals to ships in the English Channel. The four-storey building had a curious device whereby a black copper ball was dropped down its central shaft at exactly one o'clock to warn ships just off the coast to be ready to set their chronometers. Although this original system has long since been replaced by a modern radio time signal, a

SWANSTITCH

82-84 High Street, Deal, Kent CT14 6EG
Tel/Fax: 01304 366915
e-mail: swanstitch@btinternet.com
website: www.swanstitch.com

Swanstitch is a specialist craft retailer located 150 yards from the beach, at the Old Town end of Deal's High Street. Owned and run by Sylvia Runcie and her daughter Anita Abercrombie, the shop is stocked with all manner of essentials in needlecraft, knitting, haberdashery, cardmaking, scrapbooking, rubber stamping and beading. Two big windows show a little of what's inside, which include a wide variety of wools and yarns and threads, beads and findings, signature samples, papercraft tools, kits for stitching, cross-stitching, needlecraft and tapestry, daylight lamps and frames, patterns and books.....and lots more besides. All the top suppliers are stocked, including Sirdar fashion yarns, Paper Artsy, Illusive Images, Rubber Stamps, DMC, Lanarte and Derwentwater. The owners are on hand with help and advice, and Swanstitch also holds craft workshops for beginners and more advanced crafters. Many of the items in stock can be ordered online, and the website also gives details of the courses. The shop is open from 9 to 4.45 Monday to Wednesday and Friday, 9 to 4.15 Thursday and 9 to 5 Saturday.

SUGAR BOY

10 Broad Street, Deal, Kent Tel: 01304 363626
e-mail: enquiries@sugarboy.co.uk website: www.sugarboy.co.uk

Sugar Boy sells a wonderful variety of everybody's favourite sweets. In this traditional English sweet shop the jolly assistants have a warm welcome for all who pass through the doors. Customers take their pick from over 500 different sweets in shiny jars, weighed on scales, bagged and taken away to be enjoyed by all. The choice runs from blackjacks and shrimps to classy violet creams and much more. Jamie Oliver called Sugar Boy 'the best sweet shop in the world', and in the latest Charlie & the Chocolate Factory film, the sweets were supplied by Sugar Boy.

replica ball still drops down the shaft each day. The tower is also home to a museum devoted to time and telegraphy.

Not far from the Timeball Tower stands the menacing fortress of **Deal Castle**, which was built by Henry VIII in the early 1540s as one of a number of forts designed to protect the south coast from invasion by the French and Spanish, angered over Henry's divorce from his Catholic wife, Catherine of Aragon. The castle was designed to resemble a Tudor rose and the distinctive 'lily-pad' shape can only really be appreciated from the air or by looking at plans of the site. A huge bastion, Deal Castle had 119 guns trained out across the sea and it must have been a very formidable sight to anyone thinking of making an attack. Despite all these precautions, Deal Castle never actually came under attack from foreign invaders and it was not until the Civil War that the fortress saw action. In 1648, it came under fire from the Parliamentarians and, although it was extensively damaged, it stood and was not attacked again until it was hit by a bomb during World War II. At the northern end of the town lies another of Henry VIII's great fortresses, Sandown Castle, but unfortunately time has not been so kind to Sandown and all that remains are some ruined buttresses.

The quiet waters just off the coast of Deal, known as The Downs, create a safe anchorage for ships that might otherwise run aground on the treacherous Goodwin Sands. Down the centuries these sands proved to be a graveyard for unwary vessels, and wrecked ships, with their masts poking above the water, can still be seen at low tide. The sands were mentioned by Shakespeare, in *The Merchant of Venice*, as a place where the merchant lost one of his ships. As many as 50,000 men may have perished on these sands, which have given rise to numerous tales of 'ghost ships'.

Around Deal

WALMER

1½ miles S of Deal on the A258

Castle

This residential seaside town merges almost imperceptibly with its neighbour, Deal, to the north, but Walmer does have its very own, distinct, history. It is firmly believed that it was here, in 55BC, that Julius Caesar and his legions landed in England. However, the town is now best known for its sister castle to Deal. **Walmer Castle**, built as one of Henry VIII's line of coastal defences in the 1540s, has become, over the years, an elegant stately home. Today, it is the official residence of the Lord Warden of the Cinque Ports, a title that has been held by William Pitt the Younger, the Duke of Wellington and Sir Winston Churchill, as well as Queen Elizabeth the Queen Mother. Visitors to this charming place can see the Duke of Wellington's rooms, and even his famous boots, as well as enjoying a stroll around the Gardens. In honour of the Queen Mother's 95th birthday in August 1995, a special garden was planted. One-time owners of the castle, the Beauchamp family, were the inspiration for the Flyte family in Evelyn Waugh's novel *Brideshead Revisited.*

RINGWOULD

3 miles S of Deal on the A258

Centuries ago, this village stood on the edge of a vast forest that extended westwards almost to the city of Canterbury. The oldest building in the village is undoubtedly the 12th century Church of St Nicholas, whose curious onion dome was added to the 17th-century tower to act as a navigation aid for ships in the English Channel. The village's old forge also had maritime connections: iron carriage wheels and chains were made to be used at the naval dockyard in the nearby town of Deal.

ST MARGARET'S AT CLIFFE

5½ miles S of Deal off the A258

Church of St Margaret of Antioch

The Pines Museum

South Foreland Lighthouse

This small town stands on cliffs overlooking St Margaret's Bay. It was, before World War II, a secluded seaside resort with a number of hotels along the beach. It was the home of playwright Noel Coward, and Ian Fleming, the author of the James Bond spy thrillers, later bought Coward's house. As this is the nearest point to the French coast, which lies some 21 miles away, St Margaret's has long been the traditional starting place for cross-channel swimmers and, also because of its position, a gun emplacement was built here during World War II to protect the Channel and ward off any German invasion. St Margaret's possesses an ancient parish church, the 12th-century **Church of St Margaret of Antioch**, which features some interesting rounded arches and an intricately carved doorway.

Just to the south of the town lies **The Pines**, a six-acre park renowned for its trees, plants, shrubs and ornamental lake. The brainchild of a wealthy local builder and philanthropist Fred Cleary, the gardens' imaginative layout includes a Romany caravan, a statue of Sir Winston Churchill and a

Walmer Castle, Walmer

South Foreland

Distance: *5.6 miles (9.0 kilometres)*
Typical time: *180 mins*
Height gain: *107 metres*
Map: *Explorer 138*
Walk: *www.walkingworld.com ID:970*
Contributor: *Ian Elmes*

ACCESS INFORMATION:

Take the A2 towards Dover, turn left heading for Deal, then turn right following the signs to St Margaret's Bay. Plenty of parking space is available.

DESCRIPTION:

A moderate circular walk from St Margaret's Bay, taking in the fantastic views of the English Channel along the clifftops and on past the South Foreland Lighthouse (NT) and up to the viewpoint at Fox Hill Down, overlooking the busy ferry terminal at Dover.

FEATURES:

Sea, toilets, museum, play area, National Trust/ NTS, birds, great views, butterflies, food shop, tea shop

WALK DIRECTIONS:

1 | This walk starts at St Margaret's Bay car park. There is a charge for parking here at the weekends. From the car park, walk back along the road you drove down to the postbox, then take the road straight ahead (looks like an old disused road).

2 | Turn left here along Beach Road, following the sign for the Saxon Shoreway.

3 | Take the left fork at this junction, following the sign to the Saxon Shoreway. Follow the path up the hill - it is very clearly defined. At the top of the hill, bear right to follow the footpath to the top of the cliff. At the top of the hill cross the track to the gate.

4 | Go through the gate and follow the path to the right, going uphill. Beware that the cliffs are dangerous. To the left of you, on a clear day you may well see France. Ahead of you is the South Foreland Lighthouse (National Trust). This was used by Marconi for his first radio transmission. Follow the pathway to the gate at the top, through the gate and turn left, back onto the track you crossed earlier. Continue along the track to the entrance of the lighthouse.

5 | The Lighthouse is National Trust-owned and is open between March and October. Turn left here, following the sign to the Coastal Path and Langdon Cliff. Follow the footpath; there is a diversion as the cliff has eroded as far as the path. Views from here are fantastic, the Port of Dover ahead, together with the cruise terminal.

6 | Follow the track from this point, up and over the undulations of the contours, following the line of the cliff.

7 | Langdon Hole (National Trust). Go over the stile and follow the path straight in front of you. Keep heading toward the three radio masts straight ahead.

8 | Take the steps up the hill towards the coastguard station.

9 | Pass through the kissing-gate and follow the footpath all the way along - great views to the left of the ferry terminal at Dover.

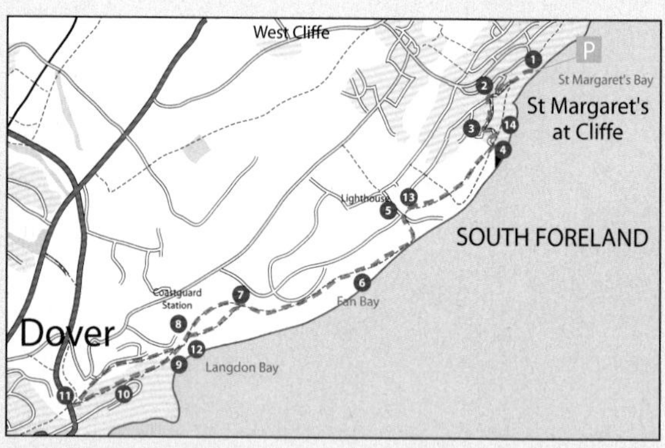

10 | At this point, take the footpath to the left. The pathway opens out and there is a car park to the right. Here you will see many people just sitting watching the ferries - many of them have scanners so they can listen to the conversations between ship and shore.

11 | At the newly formed footpath, turn right to go back up the hill. At the top of the hill, follow the road into the car park of the National Trust. Follow the roadway, through the car park and gate towards the cafe. Follow the path through the triangular bollards and take the left footpath, signposted Saxon Shoreway.

12 | At the kissing gate to Langdon Hole go through and follow the footpath on the right down by the fence. At the end of the fence, follow the footpath straight in front of you, back down the steps and back to the stile at the other end. Just after the stile at the far end, take the right footpath to retrace your steps back to the lighthouse.

13 | At the lighthouse entrance, turn right and keep on the track, past Lighthouse Down, through the gate at the cattle grid and follow it down.

14 | Go through the gate here and follow the track to the left. At the bottom turn right towards the gift shop and garden etc. The tea shop is a nice place to stop for a bite to eat after this wonderful walk. Carry straight on down the road past the postbox and back to the car park at St Margaret's Bay.

waterfall. It is a delightfully tranquil setting in which to enjoy the glorious views over the White Cliffs. Opposite The Pines, and opened in 1989, is **St Margaret's Museum** containing collections of artefacts put together by Fred Cleary relating to local or maritime themes and others of world-wide interest.

A little further south again stands **South Foreland Lighthouse**, the highlight of the White Cliffs and a distinctive landmark overlooking the Straits of Dover. Erected in 1843, the lighthouse was the first to show an electrically powered signal. It was used by the radio pioneer Marconi for his early experiments and it was from here in 1898 that he made the world's first ship-to-shore radio transmission. A guided tour takes visitors around the lighthouse, where its history can be learned and from where there are magnificent long-ranging views.

GREAT MONGEHAM

2 miles SW of Deal off the A258

Hanging from a pole high on the wall of the chancel of the local parish church of St Martin is a helmet said to have been worn at the Battle of Hastings in 1066. More credible is a brass plaque on a pillar that bears a Greek verse written by the poet, Robert Bridges, in memory of his nurse who lies buried in the church.

WEST LANGDON

5 miles SW of Deal off the A256

Langdon Abbey

Close to this small village can be seen the scant remains of **Langdon Abbey**, founded in 1189 by Premonstratensian Canons. After the dissolution, much of the masonry of the abbey was carted to the coast and used in the construction of Henry VIII's coastal defences; a farmhouse was later built on the abbey site.

NORTHBOURNE

3 miles W of Deal off the A256

In the church of this small country village can be found a monument to Sir Edwin Sandys, who was responsible for the drawing up of the constitution of Virginia, in America, and who was born in the village at Northbourne Court. Edwin's son also made a name for himself as he became a prominent and notoriously cruel

SOLLEY FARM HOUSE

The Street, Worth, nr Deal,
Kent CT14 0DG
Tel: 01304 613701
Mob: 07515 852 780
e-mail: solleyfarmhouse@tiscali.co.uk
website: www.solleyfarmhouse.co.uk

An exceptional level of hospitality and quality accommodation is guaranteed at this Five Star, Gold Award Bed & Breakfast with your hosts Sandy and Peter Hobbs providing thoughtful luxury touches at every turn – fresh flowers, toiletries, chocolates, soft towels and robes in the sumptuous ensuite bedrooms. Nestled in the heart of a peaceful conservation area, Solley Farm House overlooks the tranquil village duck pond and an ancient church with Norman origins. This picturesque setting is the perfect base for anyone visiting on business or for a relaxing short break on the East Kent coast. The 18th Century farmhouse is full of character with beamed ceilings and inglenook fireplaces and the property has a large mature garden with gravelled drives to the front and rear, the latter providing secure car parking. Guests are welcome to use the charming walled patio area at the rear of the house to enjoy afternoon tea upon arrival and a delicious breakfast is served in the dining room anytime between 7am and 9am – all fresh organic produce and cooked to order. Two village inns both serving food are within 100 yards and just one mile away is the historic town of Sandwich, boasting a selection of charming coffee shops and restaurants. Perfectly located for discerning golfers, you will find a selection of superb links courses are a few minutes drive away.

***** ***Five Star Gold Award*** ***Michelin Guide 2009***

THE FIVE BELLS

The Cross, Lower Street, Eastry, Sandwich, Kent CT13 0HX
Tel: 01304 611188
e-mail: thefivebellseastry@yahoo.co.uk

Dating back to the 16th Century, **The Five Bells** is situated in the charming village of Eastry near Sandwich surrounded by picturesque countryside. This attractive grade 2 listed building has a brick frontage combined with its Kent peg Tiled roof makes it quite striking to the eye. The friendly owner, Mary Franks, looks forward to meeting new faces and offers a sincere welcome to all customers, adults and children alike. As well as being at the centre of the community, it is well visited by walkers and cyclists who enjoy the excellent food and drink served here. The cosy interior is full of character, exposed beams and an original fireplace create a pleasant atmosphere for guests to drink and dine. Only locally sourced ingredients, from local farmers, are used in the delicious home cooked food served in this friendly hostelry. Reserved eating advisable. Opening hours 11am - 1am Fri - Sat and Sun-Thurs 11am-11.30pm. Pool table and darts are available inside as well as facilities for disabled customers. This establishment also has a seperate function room for celebrations and meetings.

commander in the Civil War on the Parliamentarian side. Although the house that these two gentlemen knew was demolished in the 18th century, the Ornamental Gardens survive and are occasionally open to the public.

EASTRY

4½ miles NW of Deal off the A256

Situated along the Roman road that linked Richborough with Dover, this ancient village has a couple of interesting historic connections. It was here in 1164 that Thomas à Becket hid while waiting to travel to Flanders after his quarrel with Henry II. Lord Nelson also visited the village and one of his officers, Captain John Harvey, lies buried in the local churchyard.

North Downs to Dover

Following the North Downs eastwards to the coast, this area ends, or begins, at Dover, the traditional 'Gateway to England'. As Britain's major cross-Channel port, this is where many start their holiday in England (or leave to go abroad) but the town is well used to 'invaders' and, during the Roman occupation, it was here that they stationed their navy. Dover is still dominated by its castle, set high above the famous White Cliffs; this originally Norman fortress has, over the centuries, been an impressive repellent to foreign foes. While the huge structure of the castle make it a wonderful place to wander around, it is the Secret Wartime Tunnels that attract much of the attention. This is a labyrinthine maze of tunnels cut into the cliffs where, during World War II, the evacuation of Dunkirk was masterminded by Winston Churchill and Admiral Ramsey.

Although defence of the country from sea attack is a key aspect of this stretch of coast, it was overhead that one of the great battles of World War II took place, and close to the coast are both the Battle of Britain Memorial and the Kent Battle of Britain Museum. They each pay tribute, in separate ways, to the courage of the young pilots who fought to win air supremacy over the skies of England and so prevent a German invasion.

It may seem that this area is given over to war, but the idyllic nature of many of the rural villages of the region portray a picture that is both peaceful and tranquil. Inland lie the National Fruit Collection, where literally hundreds of varieties of apples, pears, plums and numerous other fruit trees are grown, and the famous Wye College, the agricultural institution that is now part of the University of London. There are also ancient country houses that open their glorious gardens to the public such as Beech Court Gardens and Belmont.

At the heart of the rural idyll lies Ashford, which, like many places in Kent, has a history that goes back to Roman times. The central location of the town has made it a natural meeting place and, today, with the opening of the Channel Tunnel and its International Station it is beginning to rival Dover for the title 'Gateway to Britain'.

Ashford

Museum Godinton Park

In the heart of the Garden of England, Ashford boasts some fine Georgian houses and is surrounded by countryside, which has inspired such famous writers as HE Bates, Jane Austen and HG Wells. The town itself is dominated by the great central tower of

ASHFORD GUNS & TACKLE (KWG LTD)

Tannery Lane, Ashford, Kent TN23 1PN
Tel: 01233 637717 Fax: 01233 664489
e-mail: guns@k-w-g.co.uk
website: www.k-w-g.co.uk

Ashford Guns & Tackle is superbly geared up to catering for the needs of the local farming community and for followers of country and sporting pursuits. It is part of KWG Ltd, one of the longest established agricultural merchants in the South of England. Ashford Guns was founded in the 1970s and joined KWG in 1998. The Board of Directors are all local farmers, so expertise is in abundant supply in a wide variety of rural matters.

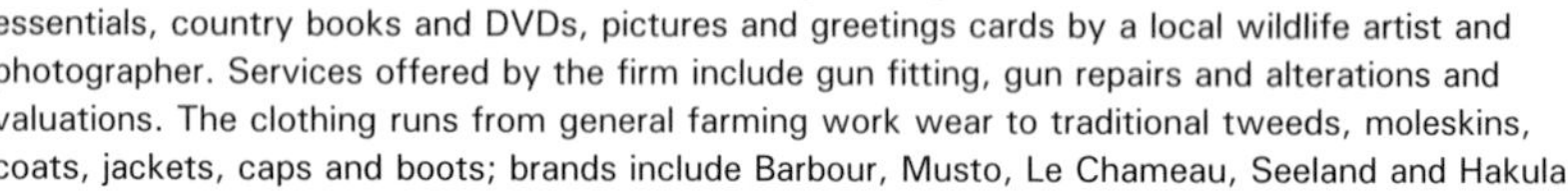

On three floors of a converted Victorian tannery, the stock includes farming supplies, country clothing, guns and other sporting equipment and accessories: air guns, shotguns, rifles, traps, archery equipment, ferreting equipment, dog training essentials, country books and DVDs, pictures and greetings cards by a local wildlife artist and photographer. Services offered by the firm include gun fitting, gun repairs and alterations and valuations. The clothing runs from general farming work wear to traditional tweeds, moleskins, coats, jackets, caps and boots; brands include Barbour, Musto, Le Chameau, Seeland and Hakula.

The oak-beamed gun room features not only guns but interesting displays of taxidermy, curios and works by local artists.

Mary's, its splendid 15th century parish church rising high above the other town buildings, each of its four pinnacles crowned by a golden arrow-shaped weathervane.

Ashford's central location makes it an ideal base from which to visit many of the county's attractions, but it is well worth spending time here and, at the **Ashford Borough Museum**, where visitors can find out more about this interesting and historic place. Housed in Dr Wilks' Hall, which was formerly the Old Grammar School, the museum has a varied collection that ranges from Victorian patchwork to equipment used by the town's fire brigade.

Ashford is the home of the first volunteer Fire Service in the country, formed in 1826 and which purchased its first manual fire engine some 10 years later. In 1925, the first Leyland motor fire engine went into service at Ashford and the funds required to buy the appliance were raised by public subscription.

The town's central location saw a Roman settlement established here in the 1st century and, for several centuries before the Norman Conquest, records show that a town called Esseteford was found here. Growing into a flourishing market town that served the surrounding area, Ashford developed further with the building of turnpike roads and the arrival of the railway. In 1846 the Board of Directors of the South Eastern Railway bought 185 acres of good Kentish countryside on which to lay the foundations of a 'locomotive establishment'. 72 labourers' cottages were built in 1847 and construction of the railway works began. When the old railway companies were grouped in 1923, Ashford became one of the three main works of the Southern Railway dealing with the construction, repair and maintenance of locomotives, carriages and wagons (the others were Eastleigh and Lancing). The railway still influences the town and, with the completion of the Channel Tunnel, a range of Continental European destinations can be reached in just a few hours from Ashford's International Station.

Two miles northwest of Ashford stands **Godinton Park** (see panel below), a Jacobean house built round a 14th-century core. Among the main features are an imposing Great Hall and the Great Chamber with a frieze depicting soldiers doing Dutch pike drill. Here, too, are Chippendale furniture, a Dresden tea service, Worcester and Chelsea china, and a Reynolds portrait of David Garrick.

Around Ashford

CHARING

5 miles NW of Ashford on the A20

There has been a settlement here for centuries and the earliest archaeological evidence is of Iron Age flint workings. Archaeologists suggest that there could well have been a Roman villa close by and the village's name is said to be derived from that of a local Jutish chief. In the late 8th century, Charing was given to Canterbury Cathedral by Egbert II, King of Kent. The manor remained the property of the archbishops until 1545, when Henry VIII confiscated it from Archbishop Cranmer. The little that remains of this

Godinton House and Gardens

Godinton House, Godinton Park, Ashford,
Kent TN23 3BP
Tel: 01233 620773
website: www.godinton-house-gardens.co.uk

Godinton is a superb historic house and garden set in the Kent countryside. A small statue of a horse set in a neat box hedge garden welcomes visitors to an arched porch and panelled oak door. The modest entrance conceals the wealth of history and design at Godinton House. The exterior is Jacobean, the compass gables added in 1620 by the great Captain Nicholas Toke but, within the house, the architectural puzzle is revealed from room to room. The house contains a good country house collection accumulated by its owners; some ancient pieces have been here for many centuries.

There are twelve acres (five hectares) of tranquil gardens at Godinton to be explored and enjoyed, surrounded by parkland studded with stately oaks and chestnuts. Terraced lawns bordered by the famous yew hedge and topiaried box have been softened over the last century by the addition of long, curvy-edged herbaceous borders and ornamental tree and shrub plantings. Wandering through the gardens along broad gravel paths or across the neatly cut lawns (there are no 'Keep off the Grass' signs here) the visitor will discover many surprises. For the more energetic visitor there is a circular walk through the 18th century park and along the Stour river, with wonderful views back to the house and garden. Here an extensive tree planting programme is ensuring the future of the parkland.

UPLANDS RIDING SCHOOL

Waterditch Road, Warren Street, Charing,
Ashford, Kent TN27 0HJ
Tel/Fax: 01233 712259

Uplands Riding School is located in attractive countryside northwest of Charing, a short drive from the A20 and M20. In this delightful setting Samantha Scotcher runs her riding school, welcoming all levels of riders, from nervous and beginners to the more experienced. Facilities on the premises include a sand school, and the fields and lanes of the North Downs are perfect for hacking – a favourite outing can comprise a delightful hack with a visit to one of the pleasant country pubs in the area.

archbishop's palace today dates from the early 14th century, and many of the buildings have been incorporated into a private farm. However, when visiting the parish church of St Peter and St Paul in the village, the archbishop still robes in this ancient palace.

In the Middle Ages, the village lay one day's journey from Canterbury, so Charing became one of the many stopping places, where pilgrims would seek rest, shelter and food on their pilgrimage. Just outside the gates of the manor house was a flourishing market which, due to its antiquity, never required a charter. At the top of the street there are some fine red brick houses dating mainly to the 17th and 18th centuries although Pierce House is 16th century with an even older building beside it, believed to be 13th-century.

Charing Church

PLUCKLEY

5½ miles NW of Ashford off the A20

This charming little village clusters around a tidy little square and the surrounding cottages all have a curious feature - 'Dering' windows. Sir Edward Cholmeley Dering, a 19th century landowner, added these distinctive arched windows to all the houses of his estate because he thought them lucky. One of his ancestors had supposedly escaped from the Roundheads through such a window during the Civil War. He also put them into his own mansion but this appears to be where his luck ended as the great house burnt down. Pluckley featured in the successful TV series *The Darling Buds of May* and according to *The Guinness Book of Records* is the most haunted village in England.

PERRY COURT FARM SHOP

Canterbury Road, Billing, nr Ashford,
Kent TN25 4ES
Tel: 07831 326850 Fax: 01233 812408
e-mail: perrycourtfarm@btconnect.com
website: www.perrycourt.com

The farm shop is a huge converted oast house siutated in the Stoor Valley between Ashford & Canterbury on the A28, also well placed for walkers on the North Downs Way. It is part of the 700 acre farm owned by Martin Fermor, so stocks a wide range of fruit and vegetables grown on the farm which include the enviable 120 varieties of apples and pears. The range varies throughout the year with seasonal produce. This is complemented by local meat and game, cut flowers and a newly opened cheese room, stocking over 80 English Cheeses.

Open everyday 8am - 6pm
a must to visit in this area.

BOUGHTON LEES

2½ miles N of Ashford on the A251

North Downs Way

This delightful village, along with its neighbour Boughton Aluph, lies on the southern fringes of the North Downs, where the wooded hills give way to hedgerows, meadows, fields and a network of narrow, twisting lanes. The long distance footpath, the **North Downs Way**, makes the descent from the higher ground at this point and passes right alongside the parish church of Boughton Aluph. A similar network of footpaths and narrow lanes leads southwards to Boughton Lees.

CHALLOCK

4½ miles N of Ashford off the A251

Beech Court Gardens Eastwell Park

This pretty village high up on the Downs, centred around its wide and spacious green, is set in the dense woodlands known as Challock Forest. Like so many villages with its roots in the Middle Ages, Challock was built around its church in a forest clearing. However, when the Black Plague struck, the villagers moved to a new site, a mile or so from the church. Dedicated to Saints Cosmus and Damian, the church took a direct bomb hit during World War II, but now restored, it is worth visiting, not just for its location but also for the fine wall paintings added in the 1950s as part of the restoration.

Set around a medieval farmhouse, **Beech Court Gardens** provide something of interest right through the year. A riot of colour in the spring when the azaleas, vibernums and rhododendrons are in bloom, the garden has brilliant summer borders and roses while, in the autumn, there are the rich tones of the acers. Well-known for its relaxing atmosphere, the garden has more than 90 named trees, woody areas and extensive lawns.

Just to the south of the village lies **Eastwell Park**, which has a public footpath running through its 3,000 acres. On the northern edge of the vast Eastwell Lake is a ruined church that reputedly houses the bones of Richard Plantagenet, son of Richard III.

STELLING MINNIS

8 miles NE of Ashford off the B2068

Minnis means 'common', and on the edge of what remains of the once great Lyminge Forest, this village has an attractive rural atmosphere. On the outskirts of Stelling Minnis stands Davison's Mill, a smock mill built in 1866 that continued to grind corn commercially until 1970. The mill wheels were rotated by either wind or the mill's 1912 Ruston and Hornsby oil engine, and the museum here has displays of some of the original mill maintenance tools along with other milling implements. It is unlikely that it will ever be able to run wind-powered again, but it is still in working order.

WYE

3 miles NE of Ashford off the A28

College

This attractive old market town on the North Downs has some fine Georgian houses as well as some half-timbered buildings in the area surrounding its 15th-century collegiate church. However, it is not these buildings that have made the town famous but its agricultural college - **Wye College**, now affiliated to the University of London. Occupying the buildings of a priests' college built in 1447 by John Kempe, Archbishop of Canterbury, the college combines teaching with internationally respected research into all areas of agriculture including plants and pests, soils, animals and agricultural economics.

BROOK

3 miles E of Ashford off the A28

Agricultural Museum

A scattered village - once by the sea - in the wooded farmland that lies beneath the North Downs, Brook is home to an **Agricultural Museum** that occupies old farm buildings that stand on a site that dates back to Saxon times. Beginning as a small collection of farm implements and tools that were in the hands of nearby Wye College, the collection has grown and now includes such items as ploughs, man traps, shepherd's crooks and domestic artefacts like butter pats and flat irons. However, it is not just the collection that is of interest here as two of the buildings in which the displays can be seen are worthy of special note. The barn was constructed in the 1370s and its oak framework is particularly interesting, revealing the skills of the craftsmen involved in its construction. It is about 120 feet long and about 30 feet wide, with a Kent peg tile roof. The oast house, dating from 1815, is an early example of one with a round kiln - thought to give the hops more even drying - and it is possibly unique in having four fireplaces rather that just one.

Brook's Church of St Mary has a Norman tower with a winding staircase leading to a first-floor chapel with an altar and wall paintings.

WILLESBOROUGH

1½ miles SE of Ashford off the A20

Now almost swallowed up by the expansion of Ashford, this once rural village is home to Willesborough Windmill, a smock mill that dates back to 1869 and which was restored in 1991. Visitors can take a guided tour around the mill and see just what life was like for a miller at the beginning of the 20th century; the mill is also home to a collection of artefacts that relate to Ashford's industrial heritage.

SMEETH

4½ miles SE of Ashford on the A20

A charming and traditional Kentish village, where authentic country games are still played. Smeeth's name means 'a smooth clearing in the woods' and though, today, most of the woods have long since gone, remains of ancient forests, such as Lyminge to the north, can still be found.

Dover

Castle Maison Dieu Museums

Secret Wartime Tunnels

Roman Painted House

This ancient town, which is often referred to as the 'Gateway to England', is Britain's major cross-Channel port. Many pass through but few stay for long, but with its long history going back to Roman times, it is well worth taking time to explore. It was the Romans who first developed Dover, basing their navy here, and right up to the present day, the town has relied on shipping and seafaring for its prosperity. It was a founder member of Edward I's Confederation of Cinque Ports, and as the old harbour silted up a new one was constructed in the 19th century. Much of the older part of Dover was destroyed by enemy bombs during the World Wars but, among the jumble of modern streets, some of the surviving ancient buildings can still be found.

Situated high on a hill above the cliff tops, and dominating the town from almost every angle, stands **Dover Castle**, dating back to 1180. Although the castle was begun by William the Conqueror, it was under Henry II that the great keep was constructed and the fortress was completed by another surrounding wall that was studded with square towers and two barbicans. Throughout its long life the castle has had an interesting history with one event, in particular, occurring towards the end of the reign of King John. By 1216, the barons had become increasingly frustrated with their king and they invited the heir to the French throne, Prince Louis, to invade and take over. He landed with his army at Dover and laid siege to the castle, which was at that time held by Hubert de Burgh, a baron loyal to King John. Powerful though the castle's walls were, the French managed to gain access to the outer barbican and began to undermine the gate to the inner enclosure. At this point, King John died and the barons declared their allegiance to his successor, Henry III, and Prince Louis went home empty -handed.

Dover Castle, Dover

White Cliffs of Dover, Dover

Today, the castle has much to offer the visitor. It is home to the **Princess of Wales' Royal Regiment Museum**, and there are also the tall remains of the Pharos, a Roman lighthouse, and a small Saxon church within the grounds. However, one of the most spectacular sights and, one of World War II's best kept secrets, are the **Secret Wartime Tunnels** that were cut into Dover's famous White Cliffs, immortalised by Vera Lynn in a morale-boosting World War II song. It was from this labyrinth of tunnels that Winston Churchill and Admiral Ramsey masterminded the evacuation of nearly 350,000 troops from the beaches of Dunkirk. Also in this maze of caves were an operating theatre and underground hospital. Now open to the public and reconstructed to provide the most realistic wartime experience possible, the visitor hears as the lights dim and bombs drop overhead, the atmosphere of wartime Britain is brought back to life.

Back in the heart of Dover, in New Street, another of Dover's popular attractions - the **Roman Painted House**, often dubbed Britain's buried Pompeii. An exceptionally well-preserved town house, thought to date from around 200, the building was used as a hotel for official travellers and the excavated remains have revealed extensive wall paintings and an elaborate underfloor heating system. Discovered as recently as 1970, the house, which has a Roman fort wall built through it, is covered by a modern structure that also houses a major display on Roman Dover. Visitors can try their hand at brass-rubbing on several large and small figures from Roman and medieval times.

The Victorian Town Hall incorporates the magnificent **Maison Dieu**, a hostel for Canterbury pilgrims that was founded in the early 13th century, as well as typically grand Victorian Council Chambers and function rooms.

In the Market Square can be found the area's largest and newest museum, **Dover Museum**, which has an amazing range of items that illustrate the history of the town from prehistoric times onwards. There are artefacts from the time that Dover was a Roman port and fortress, along with finds from one of the most important archaeological sites in Britain, the nearby Buckland Saxon cemetery. The story of Dover as a Cinque Port, the town through both World Wars and numerous Victorian objects all add to the interesting picture of the town that the museum portrays. However, one of the newest exhibits is one of the museum's oldest. After seven years conservation, a 3,500-year-old Bronze Age boat, is now on display.

Just away from the town centre lies the Western Heights, a vast area that stands on what was one of the largest and strongest fortresses in the country. There are some five miles of dry ditches and numerous gun batteries and defences. Some parts date from the late 18th and early 19th centuries, a time when England was expecting to have to defend its shores from French invasion. Other parts date only to World War II. The huge complex has been preserved to include, along with many of the defensive structures, much of the wildlife and the plants that have since colonised the site. The first buildings were erected here in the summer of 1779 and, when Napoleon posed a threat from France, further work was undertaken to strengthen and fortify the area further. The Drop Redoubt is a sunken

Ferry Port, Dover

The Battle of Britain Memorial

Capel le Ferne, Folkestone, Kent CT18 7JJ
Tel: 01304 253286

On a spectacular clifftop position can be found the Battle of Britain Memorial that was built to commemorate those who fought and lost their lives in the summer of 1940. Taking the form of an immense three bladed propeller cut into the chalk hillside with, at its centre, the statue of a lone seated airman, this is a fitting tribute to those young men who so bravely and unselfishly served their country. The memorial was unveiled by HM Queen Elizabeth the Queen Mother in 1993 and an annual memorial day is held here on the Sunday that lies closest to 10th July, the start of the air battle.

The siting of the memorial here is particularly poignant as it was in the skies above, in the summer of 1940, that the RAF struggled to gain air supremacy over the Luftwaffe and so prevent the otherwise inevitable German invasion. The battle, that cost so many their lives, lasted until the end of October and, as well as being the last major conflict over British soil, the victory marked the turning point of World War II. Close to the memorial, by the flagpole that originally stood at RAF Biggin Hill, is a memorial wall on which Winston Churchill's immortal words, "Never in the field of human conflict was so much owed by so many to so Few", are carved. At the adjacent visitors' centre visitors can purchase a range of souvenirs and it should be remembered that this memorial and the site on which it stands relies on public donation for its maintenance. Open daily from 1st April to 30th September, 11am - 5pm.

fortress of the early 19th century that could fire guns in all directions, and St Martin's Battery saw service during World War II. The Grand Shaft is a triple spiral staircase built to allow the soldiers to descend quickly from the Heights to the harbour.

One final place of interest, particularly to those who remember World War II, is the **Women's Land Army Museum**, which pays tribute to the women who served their country by working on the land. Among the numerous exhibits on display are personal letters, uniforms and a wealth of factual information.

Around Dover

CAPEL LE FERNE

5 miles SW of Dover off the B2011

Battle of Britain Memorial

This village, close to the cliffs between Folkestone and Dover, is home to the **Battle of Britain Memorial** (see panel on page 103) that commemorates the fierce 1940 air battle that took place in the skies overhead. The memorial itself takes the from of an immense three-bladed propeller, each blade 38 metres long, cut into the clifftop. The stone figure of a lone pilot is seated on a sandstone base on which are carved the badges of the squadrons that took part in the Battle of Britain.

HAWKINGE

6 miles SW of Dover on the A260

Kent Battle of Britain Museum

Close to the village, at Hawkinge Airfield, can be found the **Kent Battle of Britain Museum**, the home of the country's largest collection of 1940, related artefacts on display to the public. Along with the full size replicas of the planes that played a part in the Battle of Britain - a Hurricane, Spitfire and Messerschmitt have been painstakingly rebuilt from as many original parts as possible - the museum houses an important collection of both British and German flying equipment of that era. Many of the items on display have been recovered from aircraft that were shot down, and there are also weapons, vehicles and exhibits relating to the 'home front' during World War II.

ALKHAM

4 miles W of Dover off the A20

Plans to turn this charming village in the steep Alkham Valley into a large residential area for miners working in the expanding East Kent coalfield never came to fruition, and the village remains much as it has done for centuries. A good place from which to begin a walk in the pleasant countryside around this coastal chalk downland, Alkham is also a pleasant place to stroll around as it has retained its Norman church, 18th-century redbrick rectory, ancient houses and, perhaps most importantly, its old coaching inn.

SWINGFIELD

6½ miles W of Dover on the A260

Butterfly & Garden Centre

At **MacFarlanes Butterfly and Garden Centre** visitors can walk around the tropical green houses, which not only contain exotic plants but also many varieties of colourful butterflies from all over the world that are allowed to fly freely. The life cycle of the butterfly, from the courtship displays, through the egg and caterpillar stages, to the chrysalis and finally the butterfly, are explained and can be observed at close quarters. Exotic plants on which the butterflies live - such as bougainvillaea,

St Radigund's Abbey, River

banana and oleander - can also be studied. For opening times, call 01303 844244.

ELHAM

9 miles W of Dover off the A260

This relatively unspoilt village, whose name is pronounced 'Eelham', is the starting point for a number of footpaths that lead through the Elham Valley. During World War II, the now disused railway line through the village carried an 18-inch 'Boche Buster' gun, actually of World War I vintage, that fired shells seven feet long.

RIVER

1 mile NW of Dover on the A2

Almost a suburb of Dover, this village stands on the banks of a river that has, over the centuries, powered several mills as it meanders its way out to sea. Of those fine old mills, only Crabble Corn Mill survives, a beautiful Georgian mill that still works on a regular basis. Visitors can join a guided tour and see the unique set of automatic 19th-century flour mills. Just to the southwest of the village of River lie the ruins of St Radigunds Abbey, founded by French monks in the 12th century.

TEMPLE EWELL

2½ miles NW of Dover off the A2

This ancient village, in the valley of the River Dour, was mentioned in a charter as long ago as 772 and for centuries it came under the control of successive religious orders: first the Knights Templar, and then the Knights of the Order of St John of Jerusalem. As with the village of River, further down the River Dour, there were once two mills in the valley here that were driven by the Dour's waters.

WOOTTON

6½ miles NW of Dover off the A260

This village was the home of Thomas Digges, the inventor of the early telescope who, during the reign of Elizabeth I, was the builder of the original harbour complex at Dover, now incorporated into the Western Docks. Unfortunately, nothing remains of the manor house, demolished in 1952, that was Digges's home.

DENTON

7 miles NW of Dover on the A260

Denton Court Broome Park

Tappington Hall

This charming village has a green surrounded by pretty half-timbered cottages. Next to the small 13th-century church of St Mary Magdalene, nestling among ancient trees, can be found **Denton Court**, where the poet Thomas Gray was a frequent visitor. Close by are two other interesting, historic houses. **Broome Park**, dating from 1635 and designed

THE SWINGATE INN

Deal Road (A258), Dover, Kent
Tel: 01304 204043
e-mail: info@swingate.com website: www.swingate.com

The **Swingate Inn** is a family-run hotel standing in the lovely Kentish countryside on the A258 a little way north of Dover. The comfortable, practical accommodation provides the perfect base for a relaxing break, a tour of the neighbouring coast and country, a business trip or a pause before or after a trip across (or underneath) the English Channel.

The ten bedrooms, which can be configured as singles, twins, doubles or family rooms, all have en suite facilities, TV, alarm clock-radio, tea/coffee tray and hairdryer. Cots can be provided, blackout curtains guarantee a peaceful night's sleep for even the lightest sleeper and wireless broadband internet connection is available in all the rooms. For a really romantic occasion, the bridal room can be booked with the options of champagne, flowers and chocolates. The Swingate is very much geared to families, and the garden, which is protected by tall trees from the hot sun and strong winds, has an outside bar, a gazebo, picnic tables, a summertime bouncy castle and a climbing tower with a slide.

The bar is well stocked with real ales and other draught and bottled beers, wines, spirits and non-alcoholic drinks, which can be enjoyed on their own or to accompany a snack or a meal. The bar food menu offers sandwiches, salads, jacket potatoes and hot and cold light bites, while the hotel's main eating outlet, the Swingate Stoves, is a fully licensed restaurant specialising in traditional home-cooked food using local produce as far as possible, including fresh seasonal vegetables to accompany the main courses. The Sunday carvery is one of the most popular occasions of the week, and regular theme nights showcase cuisines from across the world.

The Swingate is licensed for civil weddings and partnership ceremonies, which the staff can design and package to suit individual requirements. It is also superbly geared up for a wide variety of functions, from wedding receptions to private parties, stand-up buffets, meetings, conferences, discos, dances and other entertainments.

The Swingate Inn is the perfect place for Continental travellers: the Dover ferry port is just three minutes' drive away, and it's only ten minutes to the Euro Tunnel Terminal. Attractions in the area include beaches and seaside resorts, several golf courses, Dover Castle, the famous White Cliffs, Caesar's landing site and a number of National Trust and English Heritage houses and gardens – and the wonderful, historic city of Canterbury is an easy 20-minute drive away.

by Inigo Jones, was at one time the home of Field Marshal Lord Kitchener, the World War I military leader. The other house, **Tappington Hall**, was built by Thomas Marsh in about 1628. Richard Barham wrote many of his Ingoldsby Legends here, featuring the Ingoldsby family of Tappington-Everard. The hall is associated with several ghost stories. One suggests that it is haunted by a Royalist killed during the Civil War by his brother, who was fighting for the Parliamentarian cause.

BARHAM

8½ miles NW of Dover off the A2

The village is set in a delightful river valley near the point where the woodlands of the North Downs give way to the flatter agricultural lands. This area was first mentioned in the Arthurian legends as being the site of a great battle, and the land around the village was used as a military camp in the early 19th century when an invasion by Napoleon was feared.

WHITFIELD

2 miles N of Dover on the A2

Dover Transport Museum

For centuries this village has stood at an important crossroads where the routes to Canterbury, Dover and Sandwich met and it was also the site of several manor houses. One of the ancient lords of the manor had a particularly unusual service in that it was his duty to hold the king's head whenever he made a Channel crossing and support him through any seasickness to which he might succumb. This village, practically a suburb of Dover, is home to the **Dover Transport Museum**, where a whole range of vehicles, from bicycles to buses, can be seen along with model railways and tramways. Offering a history of local transport, the museum also includes exhibits on the East Kent coalfield and the area's maritime heritage.

Woodlands and Marshes

This southernmost area of Kent is characterised by two diverse landscapes, the woodland, or once wooded, area around Tenterden and the marshlands of Romney and Welland. Often dubbed the 'Jewel in the Weald', Tenterden lies on the eastern border of the Weald and this place, like other villages and towns close by, has the suffix '-den' that indicates a former setting in a woodland clearing. Developed on the wealth of the woollen trade in the Middle Ages and then becoming a key market place for the area, Tenterden has a pleasing mix of old buildings and is an excellent place to begin a tour of southern Kent. Around it are numerous charming villages including the delightful Biddenden, where lived and died the Biddenden Maids, 12th-century Siamese twins. Bethersden has become best known for its marble - a fossil encrusted stone - that has been used in the building work of Kent's two cathedrals and numerous parish churches. At the southern edge of the marshland lies Folkestone, which after the arrival of the railways developed from a little, known fishing village into an important ferry port and fashionable seaside resort. To the south are the delightful former ports of Hythe, Dymchurch and New Romney that were linked in the 1920s by the charming Romney, Hythe and Dymchurch light railway. Finally, there are the remote and isolated marshes, once the haunt of smugglers, today an area of rich farmland and home of the hardy Romney sheep.

Tenterden

Church of St Mildred Museums

Kent & East Sussex Railway

Often referred to as the 'Jewel of the Weald', despite being situated right on the border between the dense woodlands of the Weald and the flatter farmland that leads eastwards to Romney Marsh, Tenterden is a charming town of considerable age. Today's well-earned nickname is, however, a far cry from its earliest days when it was known as 'Tenet-ware-den' or 'pig pasture of Thanet'. Although pigs certainly did well here and in the surrounding area, sheep became more profitable. The town developed quickly as the wool trade grew. In 1331, the far-sighted Edward III prohibited the export of unwashed wool and encouraged weavers from Flanders to settle here and bring their dyeing and weaving techniques to England. The town prospered and became one of the most important centres for the manufacture of broadcloth during the Middle Ages. However, in the 16th century, the fortunes of the clothiers were altered by an act of Parliament and the wool trade began to decline. There are still buildings in the town that were built with the profits of the wool trade, along with elegant 18th-century houses constructed during Tenterden's days as an agricultural market place serving the surrounding towns and villages.

The **Church of St Mildred**, in the heart of Tenterden, dates from 1180, and its most interesting feature is its unusual twin doors at the western end. From the top of its 15th-century tower - some 125 feet above the town - there are panoramic views out across the Weald and to the Channel coast. Another place of prayer, a Unitarian chapel, built in 1695, is particularly interesting as this is where, in 1783, Dr Benjamin Franklin, the American statesman, philosopher and scientist, worshipped. As an apprentice typesetter on his brother's newspaper, Franklin came to England to work in a British printing office for 18 months before returning home to set up his own newspaper. Later, and then acting as an agent for several American provinces, he moved back to England and stayed for 18 years when, as a result of his experiments with electricity and his

WING AND A PRAYER

9 The Fairings, Tenterden, Kent TN30 6QR
Tel/Fax: 01580 761140
e-mail: perrynahome@hotmail.co.uk

In a late-Victorian building just off the main street of Tenterden, **Wing and a Prayer** is filled with a wide range of homeware and gift ideas. Penny Nahome, who opened here in October 2007, sources her stock from near and far, always looking for items of interest that include French and Scandinavian interiors. Much of the furniture comes from France, clothing includes leading brands such as Noa Noa, and other items regularly in stock range from lamps and mirrors to dinner services, candles and jewellery.

invention of the lightning conductor, he was elected a Fellow of the Royal Society.

For a real insight into the history of the town and the local area a visit to the **Tenterden and District Museum** is well worth while. The displays here cover over 1,000 years of history relating to hop-picking, farming, the area of the Weald, the Cinque Ports and Victorian domestic life. Lying close to the town's steam railway, the museum is housed in an interesting 19th-century weatherboarded building that was originally a coach house and stables. Comprising six rooms, on two floors, the museum's collections are extensive and diverse, including exhibits ranging from a 1500BC flint axe head to a re-creation of a typical Victorian kitchen.

Tenterden is also the home of the **Kent and East Sussex Railway** (see panel opposite) that runs for 10 miles between the town and Bodiam just over the county border in East Sussex. When the railway opened in 1900 it was the first full size light railway in the world. It closed to passengers in 1959 and to freight in 1961 but a preservation society was quickly formed and the original route was re-opened in 1974. Today's passengers can journey in beautifully restored carriages dating from Victorian times up to the 1960s, pulled by one of the railway's dozen steam locomotives, travelling through glorious, unspoilt countryside, that will be familiar to anyone who saw the television series *The Darling Buds of May*. Adjacent to the station at Tenterden is the **Colonel Stephens' Railway Museum** where the fascinating story of Colonel Holman Fred Stephens, who built and ran this railway along with 16 other light railways, is told. Well-known natives of Tenterden include William Caxton, the father of printing (b.1422) and David (now Sir David) Frost (b.1939).

Around Tenterden

SMARDEN

5½ miles N of Tenterden off the A262

This ancient Wealden market town's name comes from a Saxon word meaning 'butter valley and pasture' and this charming place has managed to keep its original character, along with some beautiful old half-timbered cottages and houses set along the single main street. A centre for the cloth industry in the Middle Ages, the village's 14th-century church has become known as the 'Barn of Kent' because of its huge roof.

THE ANTIQUES BARN

Greenways Garden Centre, A28 Bethersden, Ashford, Kent TN26 3LF
Tel: 01233 822358
website: www.theantiquesbarn.com

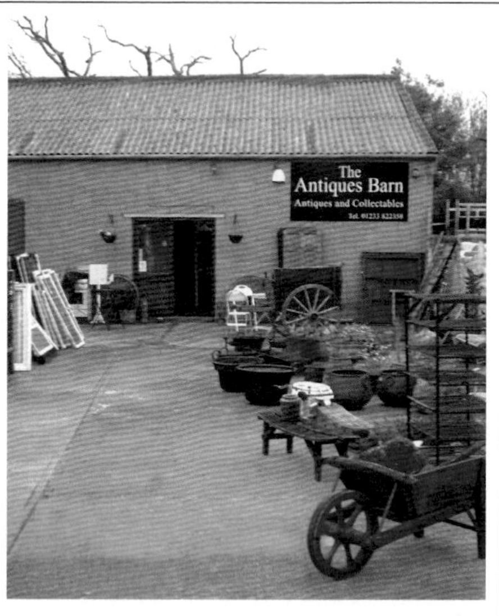

If you're looking for something different and unusual, the **Antiques Barn** is the place for you! There's so much to see and so many browsing opportunities that visitors should allow plenty of time to look around the barn, which is located in the Greenways Garden Centre, well signpostedon the A28 Ashford to Tenterden road.

Owners Tony and Debbie have assembled 21 local stall holders under one roof, selling everything from small ornaments to large pieces of furniture in 3,000 square feet of display space for antiques and collectables. The barn itself is fairly unremarkable, but it's what's inside that makes this place so special. The larger items include furniture for the home and garden in pine, oak and mahogany; there are old garden tools, toys, china and other homeware, baskets and barrows, lighting and mirrors, militaria, jewellery, old books, post cards, cigarette cards....and much more besides.

The stock changes constantly, so every visit is guaranteed to uncover new surprises and delights – perhaps a galvanised bucket, maybe an old horse-drawn cart that would look perfect in a drive or a garden. Whatever the item, Tony and Debbie are always on the lookout for the unusual and the interesting, and they always have a warm welcome for dealers, who come from all over the UK and from overseas. The Antiques Barn's owners and staff don't provide valuations, but they offer various other services, including house and general clearances. The Barn is open from 10 to 5 Monday to Saturday, 10.30 to 4.30 Sunday. There's plenty of off-road parking, and it is not surprising that visitors return time after time to what must rate as one of the fascinating browsing and shopping experiences in the whole region.

PINECOVE NURSERY

Appledore Road, Leigh Green, Tenterden, Kent TN30 7DJ
Tel: 01580 765429

Pinecove Nursery is located in attractive countryside at Leigh Green, a short drive southeast of Tenterden on the B2080 Appledore Road. The nursery is in the excellent care of the Coley family, who took over in 2004 when the previous owners retired. They sell a wide variety of perennials, shrubs and bedding plants, most of them grown at the nursery. Hanging baskets are something of a speciality, and they offer a service for refilling baskets and other containers. During the Christmas period they make beautiful wreaths by hand.

The owners and their staff take justifiable pride in the high standards they maintain at Pinecove Nursery, where they are always ready with friendly, expert advice on all aspects of their trade. The nursery is open Monday to Saturday from 9 to 5, Sunday 10 to 4; closed on Mondays in January, February, August and September.

BETHERSDEN

5 miles NE of Tenterden on the A28

This small village has long been associated with its 'marble' that was quarried in medieval times and used in many of Kent's churches as well as its two cathedrals. Calling the stone 'marble' is a little misleading as it is actually a type of fossil encrusted stone. Although the village is situated on the main Tenterden to Ashford road and had an abundance of local building materials, Bethersden was considered, in the 18th century, to have some of the worst roads in the county.

WOODCHURCH

4 miles E of Tenterden off the B2067

South of England Rare Breeds Centre

In the heart of this large village lies the green around which are grouped several charming typically Kentish houses - including one dating back to Tudor times and others from the Georgian period. It was on this green, in 1826, that a battle took place between a smuggling gang and the Dragoons. The gang members were caught, tried, sentenced and then transported to Australia.

One of the fine buildings to be found here is Woodchurch Windmill, an impressive white smock mill that was constructed in 1820. Fully renovated, and with its original machinery restored to full working order, the mill also houses a display of photographs that tell of its history and illustrate the restoration work. From the mill there are spectacular views over the marshes to the Channel coast. It is open to the public on a limited basis.

Also in Woodchurch is the **South of England Rare Breeds Centre** that, as its name suggests, is home to a large collection of rare British farm breeds, such as the

Lincoln Longwool sheep that date back to Roman times and the Bagot goat that was brought to Britain by the Crusaders. Young visitors can meet many of the centre's animals in the Children's Barn, and there are trailer rides and woodland walks to enjoy, along with a walk-through aviary, a walk-through butterfly tunnel and numerous other attractions for young and old alike.

SMALL HYTHE

2 miles S of Tenterden on the B2082

Smallhythe Place

Hard though it might be to imagine today, this little hamlet was once a flourishing port and shipbuilding centre. In the Middle Ages, the River Rother flowed past Small Hythe and was wide enough and deep enough to accommodate the ships of those days. One of Henry VIII's warships was built here. Today, there is little trace of this village's past life or, indeed, of the river as, even in the wettest weather, it is little more than a tiny stream. One clue, however, to those long ago days lies in the name of the Small Hythe bus stop - The Ferry.

Close to the village lies **Smallhythe Place**, a charming 16th century half-timbered house, best known for being the home of the famous Shakespearean actress Ellen Terry, who lived here between 1899 and 1928. The house, now in the ownership of the National Trust, contains many of her personal items, including some of her stage costumes, and numerous artefacts relating to other great thespians. The house retains many of its original features and, there is a delightful cottage garden and an Elizabethan barn that was adapted into a theatre in the late 1920s.

Small Hythe is also the home of Chapel

MISS MOLLETT'S HIGH CLASS TEAROOM

26 The Street, Appledore, Kent TN26 2BX
Tel: 01233 758555
website: www.missmolletts.co.uk

John and Alexandra Cowell moved to Appledore in 1987 and were joined many years later by Alex's sister Frances and brother-in-law Alan. They had long cherished an ambition to open a tea room to serve as a social centre for the local community and the many visitors to the region, and they realised their ambition in May 2008. **Miss Mollett's High Class Tea Room** serves an excellent variety of snacks and light meals, from toast and crumpets to sandwiches, toasties, soups, quiches, salads and a hot dish of the day, scones, cakes and cream teas. The quality of the enterprise is underlined by bone china and hand-embroidered tablecloths, and the walls are hung with pictures, photographs and mirrors, all for sale. The tea room's name remembers Jessie Blanche Mollett, a distant relative who opened a tea room and guest house elsewhere in the village in the 1930s. Today's tea room was previously an antiques and collectables shop called High Class Junk and before that a High Class Butcher – so they kept the entirely appropriate name! Opening hours are 10 to 5 Tuesday to Saturday; also open on Bank Holiday Mondays.

Down Vineyard, where visitors can walk around the growing vines, tour the herb garden and take in the rural museum.

APPLEDORE

6 miles SE of Tenterden on the B2080

Royal Military Canal

Appledore was originally a port on the estuary of the River Rother. A violent storm in the 13th century changed the course of the river and the resultant silting has left Appledore some eight miles from the sea. However, this did not prevent French raiders, in 1380, arriving here and setting fire to the village's 13th-century church. The **Royal Military Canal**, built in 1806 as a defence against Napoleon, passes through the village. Encircling Romney Marsh, the canal's sweeping bends meant that the whole length of the waterway could be protected by cannon fire and it was designed as a means of quickly flooding the marshland in the event of the expected invasion. However, by the time that the canal had been completed, in 1807, the threat of invasion had ended but, during World War II, when it seemed likely that Hitler would try to land his forces on English soil, pillboxes were built along the length of the canal. Now there is a public footpath running beside the full length of the canal with interpretation panels detailing its history. The canal also provides a wonderful habitat for a variety of wildlife, including dragonflies and marsh frogs.

WITTERSHAM

4 miles S of Tenterden on the B2082

Situated high above the Rother Levels, some 200 feet above sea level, and right in the middle of the Isle of Oxney, Wittersham has been given the affectionate title of the 'Capital of the Isle' despite being not significantly larger, or more important, than many of the area's other villages. The skeleton of a prehistoric iguanadon was uncovered here during World War I and, Wittersham was a mooring site for airships. Nearby lies Stocks Mill, the tallest post mill in Kent, erected on this site in 1781 and restored by the County Council in 1980.

BIDDENDEN

4 miles NW of Tenterden on the A262

All Saints' Church Biddenden Maids

Well recognised as one of the finest villages in the Weald of Kent, Biddenden has an attractive main street, lined with charming half-timbered houses. Ranging from medieval times through to the 17th century, there are many fine examples of period architecture and also some interesting old weaver's houses - situated on the south side of the street to make the most of the available light - that date back to the time when this was a centre of the cloth trade. Now converted into shops, above the door of one of these old houses is a carved wooden head that is said to have come from a Spanish ship, wrecked during the Armada.

At the western end of the main street stands **All Saints' Church**, founded by the Saxons but the oldest parts remaining, such as the nave, chancel and south aisle, date from the 13th century. The tower, which was funded by the thriving cloth trade, was erected in 1400 and it is made from Bethersden marble.

Although this is undoubtedly a delightful place to visit with some fine buildings to see it is the **Biddenden Maids** that arouse most visitors' curiosity. Said to have been born in Biddenden in 1100, Eliza and Mary Chulkhurst were Siamese twins who, despite being joined at both the hip and shoulders, lived to be 34.

Local legend has it that when one of the sisters died the other refused to be separated from her twin, saying, "As we came together we will also go together", and she died some six hours later. The twins bequeathed some land for the poor and needy of Biddenden that is still generating money today. Cakes bearing the womens' images are given to strangers in the village each Easter and a quantity of loaves and cheese, known as Biddenden Dole, are distributed to the poor of the parish.

HEADCORN

7½ miles NW of Tenterden on the A274

Headcorn Manor

Lashenden Air Warfare Museum

This is another of the charming and ancient Wealden villages scattered over this area of the county and, as with many of its neighbours, Headcorn was once a thriving centre of cloth manufacturing. Evidence of this wealth remains in the many fine buildings to be seen here, including Shakespeare House and The Chequers, both excellent examples of Elizabethan timbered buildings. Beyond the large 14th-century church, constructed of local Bethersden marble, lies **Headcorn Manor**, a magnificent Wealden house that has changed little since it was erected some 500 years ago. Despite all this antiquity, Headcorn is also a modern village and it provides shopping facilities for the smaller surrounding communities.

Just to the south of the village, at Lashenden, is the **Lashenden Air Warfare Museum** that commemorates the role played by this area of Kent during World War II and the Battle of Britain in particular. On display are numerous wartime exhibits, from both Britain and Germany, including a V1 flying bomb, ration books and many photographs.

Folkestone

Martello Tower Folkestone Warren

Church of St Mary & St Eanswythe Museum

A port and small fishing village since Saxon times, it was the arrival of the South Eastern railway in 1842 that transformed Folkestone into the elegant resort that it is today. Within a year of the first passenger train service running, passenger ships had started to ferry people across the English Channel to Boulogne; the journey time from London to Paris was just 12 hours. Much of the town dates from the Victorian age, while the wide avenues and formal gardens remain a legacy of the elegant Edwardian era. What is most unusual about this particular seaside resort, however, is that it does not have a recognisable seafront but, instead, it has The Leas, a wide and sweeping promenade with a series of delightful cliff top lawns and flower gardens with a distinctly Mediterranean feel. The name comes from a Kent dialect word meaning an open space. The Leas Cliff Lift, the oldest water-balanced lift in the country, carries people from the cliff tops to the beach below.

Throughout all this development in the late 19th and early 20th century, Folkestone has managed to retain its original ancient fishing village, concentrated in an area known as The Lanterns. One of the oldest buildings in the town is the **Church of St Mary and St Eanswythe** that dates back to the 13th century. St Eanswythe was a Kent princess who founded a nunnery in what is now Folkestone in the 7th century and her bones are buried here. The church also remembers the town's most famous son, William Harvey, in its west window. Born in 1578 in Church Street, a part of the town that was home to traders of cloth and silk, Harvey was a physician to both James I and Charles I but he

JO LETCHFORD MOSAICS

43 The Old High Street, Folkestone, Kent CT20 1RL
Tel: 01303 250717
e-mail: info@joletchfordmosaics.co.uk
website: www.joletchfordmosaics.co.uk

Jo Letchford is a well-known mosaic artist who makes, sells and displays mosaic and runs courses in **Jo Letchford Mosaics**, her premises in Folkestone's Old High Street. A trained artist and teacher, Jo was inspired to take up mosaic work in 1997 after seeing an exhibition by Martin Cheek in Ramsgate Library. She was immediately hooked, and she made her first mosaic from a Martin Cheek kit. Her new career quickly took off and she now produces her own beautiful mosaics, taking her ideas from life, from images, from her love of colour, pattern and texture, from Gustav Klimt and from classical Roman mosaics. The Gallery displays some of her work, which can also be viewed on the excellent website. Jo is very happy to discuss commissions, from pieces to grace the wall or floor of a private house to larger public pieces. The shop, which is open from 10.30 to 4.30 Wednesday to Saturday, sells her kits along with a wide range of Bisazza and porcelain tiles, tools and postcards. The day courses, conducted in the studio in groups of no more than six, are usually held on the second Saturday of the month; phone or look at the website for further details of the courses.

THE WHOLE WORLD CAFÉ

41 The Old High Street, Folkestone, Kent CT20 1RL
Tel: 01303 246999
e-mail: kriordan@ntlworld.com
website: www.thewholeworldcafe.com

'Food & Drink & Art & Music'

Since April 2007 Kath and Nick have been running the **Whole World Café** on the principle that the food they serve should be as fresh and as natural as possible. That commitment generates a menu that changes with the seasons and with the availability of produce. Typical dishes on Nick's vegetarian chalkboard menu might include houmus; goat's cheese and red onion tart; sweet potato, butter bean and tomato lasagne; potato bake; and zingy salads. To accompany the food are organic beers and juices, excellent house wines, smoothies, teas and the best coffee in town. The food is not the only attraction here. The Whole World Café has become a favourite meeting place for lively minds, a popular spot to exchange ideas on issues both local and global, and a gathering place for musicians and artists. The thriving music scene showcases top local talent performing on Saturday evenings – acts regularly taking the stage include a guitar and vocal duo, Latin funk rock and soulful jazz and ballad singers. And the walls of the café are covered with the work of local artists. Opening hours are 9am to 5pm Wed to Thurs, 9am-11pm Fri, 10am-11pm Sat & 10am-3pm Sunday.

OLD ENGLISH PINE

100/102 Sandgate High Street,
Folkestone, Kent CT20 3BY
Tel: 01303 248560

Old English Pine has been trading in Sandgate, on the western edge of Folkestone, for more than 20 years. Owner Andrée Martin, an expert in the furniture business, welcomes visitors, offering them a cup of coffee while they browse at leisure, and she and her staff are always on hand with help and advice on all aspects of caring for pine furniture.

They pride themselves on offering the very finest in pine furniture and associated items, and the stock provides a very wide choice of large and small pieces for every room in the house, as well as outdoor items. A series of well-laid-out rooms open from the entrance, filled with tables, dressers, kitchen shelves and accessories, crockery, curios and antiques. Upstairs are two more floors, with everything from chests of drawers, beds and bookcases to pictures and handsome, ornate mirrors. Some pieces are plain wood, others painted and distressed, for the 'shabby-chic', French château look. The shop provides plenty of furniture catalogues, so if the customer can't find the piece they want in stock, Andrée will do her best to find it. The premises are shared with **Old English Oak**, which stocks an equally impressive selection of high-quality oak furniture. The shop is open from 10 to 6 (11 to 4 Sunday).

is best remembered for his discovery of the circulation of blood in the human body. Unfortunately, it would seem that all of Harvey's medical skills counted for nothing when it came to his own fate for he is reputed to have committed suicide in 1657 after discovering that he was going blind.

The story of the town, from its Saxon roots right through to the present day, is told at the **Folkestone Museum.** The numerous displays and exhibits here range from the early traders, the growth of the medieval port and the town as a smugglers' haven to its development into a fashionable resort. At **Martello Tower No 3**, one of numerous such towers built as a defence against the possible invasion of the country by Napoleon, there is an exhibition that illustrates the measures taken to defend the south coast.

As long ago as the early 19th century, when a French engineer presented Napoleon with plans for a tunnel linking France and England, the idea of such a thoroughfare, then designed for horse-drawn carriages, has captured the imagination. So much so, in fact, that, in 1877 a tunnel was started, from both sides, but work on this ceased, almost before it had begun, because of the public outcry in England. However, in 1986, work on the present Channel Tunnel began. The Channel Tunnel Terminal in England is at Folkestone, where passenger cars, coaches and freight lorries join the trains that take them under the Channel to continental Europe.

A far cry from the bustle associated with the tunnel terminal, **The Folkestone Warren** is a peaceful country park that provides a habitat for numerous birds, insects and small mammals. The clifftop grasslands that were once grazed by sheep and cattle have now been colonised by, in some cases, rare wild flowers, while there are also beautiful plants,

FROGHOLT BED AND BREAKFAST

Wayside Cottage, Frogholt, nr Folkestone, Kent CT18 8AT
Tel: 01303 274181
e-mail: frogholt@googlemail.com website: www.frogholt.biz

The nearest B&B to the Channel Tunnel is located in a tiny rural hamlet, including the oldest thatched cottage in Kent, at the end of a well-kept no-through country lane. Open all year round, **Frogholt B&B** is owned and run by Mary and Stuart Allchurch, who do everything to ensure that their guests have an enjoyable, comfortable stay. Wayside Cottage, their 1950s bungalow, stands in an interesting garden on the site of a gardener's cottage for the nearby manor house. The recently converted accommodation comprises two rooms, a twin and a double, both with en suite facilities, stylishly coordinated soft furnishings, TV, video, radio and beverage tray.

The day starts with a splendid breakfast including eggs from the hens and ducks Mary keeps in the garden. The proximity of the Channel Tunnel and M20 makes Frogholt B&B ideal for travellers to or from the continent. It's also perfect for a quiet break to recharge the batteries. This is good walking and cycling country, and an unusual attraction in the next village, Newington, is the Elham Valley Railway trust, where visitors can see a working model of the Tunnel. The house has plenty of off-road parking and secure cycle storage.

such as Wild Cabbage and Rock Samphire, growing on the chalk cliffs.

Folkestone Racecourse hosts a year-round programme of flat and jump racing.

West of Folkestone

SANDGATE

1 mile SW of Folkestone on the A259

Now more a suburb of Folkestone than a village in its own right, Sandgate is a haven for collectors as its main street is littered with interesting antique shops. This is a peaceful place now but, during the threat of an invasion by Napoleon, no fewer than six Martello Towers were built in the area; these impressive granite structures still overlook the village.

In 1898, the author HG Wells moved to Sandgate, and in 1900, on the proceeds of his successful novels, he moved into Spade House, specially designed for him by CF Voysey. It was here at the foot of Sandgate Hill that he entertained his literary friends and continued to write many of his successful novels, articles and papers advocating social and political change.

HYTHE

4 miles W of Folkestone on the A259

St Leonard's Church · Local History Room

The recorded history of Hythe goes back to 732 when Ethelred, King of the Saxons, first granted it a charter. Its name, which means 'landing place', refers to the time when there was a busy harbour here and Hythe played an important role as one of the Cinque Ports.

However, decline set in as the harbour began to silt up and today this historic town

Beach Lugger & Martello Towers, Hythe

lies half a mile from the sea; no sign of its harbour remains. The skyline is dominated by the Norman tower of **St Leonard's Church**, built in 1080 but much extended in the 13th century. Interesting features include the choir stalls restored by Pearson, and the Victorian pulpit by Street, with mosaics by the Italian Salviati. The crypt houses one of two surviving ossuaries in England (the other is at Rothwell in Northamptonshire). Ossuaries were used to store and honour the bones of the dead when the graveyard became too crowded, and at Hythe over 2,000 skulls and various other assorted human bones, dating back to before the Norman invasion, are on display. For more information on the history of Hythe, the **Hythe Local History Room** is the ideal place to visit. This fascinating museum has numerous artefacts on display and a model of the town dated 1907.

Today, this charming place is best known as one of the terminals for the Romney Hythe and Dymchurch Railway, offering passengers a 14-mile journey by steam train across the edge of Romney Marsh to Dungeness (see under New Romney).

A mile to the north of Hythe lies Saltwood Castle. It is not open to the public but can be seen from a nearby bridleway. It was once the residence of the Archbishop of Canterbury and it was here that Becket's murderers stayed while journeying from France to commit their evil act. More recently, Lord Clark, the famous art historian and presenter of the pioneering TV series *Civilisation*, made this his home when he purchased the estate from Bill Deedes, the veteran journalist. After his death his son, Alan Clark, a Conservative member of Parliament, lived here and undertook considerable restoration work. He died in 1999.

LYMPNE

6½ miles W of Folkestone off the B2067

Castle · Wild Animal Park

Pronounced 'Limm', Lympne was established by the Romans as a port, known as Portus Lemanis, and, in the 3rd century, they built a fort here. Now standing on the site of this ancient fort is **Lympne Castle**, a fortified manor house with Norman towers that has been extensively remodelled since it was first built in the 12th century. In 1905 Sir Robert Lorimer restored the by then almost derelict castle, managing to preserve many original features in the rebuilding. The castle now operates as a hotel for business functions and weddings. From here, there are glorious panoramic views out across Romney Marsh, along the line of the Royal Military Canal and down the coast to Dungeness.

Just beyond the castle lies **Port Lympne Wild Animal Park** that was created by John Aspinall and shares the same aim, of the preserving of rare and endangered species, as its sister park Howletts. The large wild animal wilderness is home to many animals, including Indian elephants, tigers, lions, gorillas and monkeys, and also the largest captive group of black rhino in the world. After taking a safari trailer ride around the park, visitors have the opportunity to discover the delights of the park's historic mansion house, built by Sir Philip Sassoon MP in 1915. A millionaire at 23 and an aide to Lloyd George, he entertained many notables here, including Charlie Chaplin, George Bernard Shaw, TE Lawrence, Edward VIII and Winston Churchill. The house contains the Spencer Roberts Animal Mural Room, where the walls are covered with colourful paintings of exotic animals. Across the hall is the Tent Room decorated in 1934 by Rex Whistler; outside, there are beautiful landscaped gardens.

COURT-AT-STREET

7 miles W of Folkestone on the B2067

The ruined chapel here is connected with the tragic tale of the Holy Maid of Kent, Elizabeth Arton, who in 1525 claimed that she had direct communication with the Mother of God. Her pronouncements made her famous and she was persuaded to enter a convent at Canterbury by clergy seeking to capitalise financially on the increasing public interest in her powers. However, in 1533 Elizabeth made the mistake of suggesting that Henry VIII would die if he divorced his first wife, Queen Catherine, and married Anne Boleyn and she (along with those clerics who had faith in her) was hanged at Tyburn in 1534.

MERSHAM

10 miles NW of Folkestone off the A20

To the southwest of this village lies Swanton Mill, a charming old rural watermill powered by the River East Stour surrounded by a beautiful garden. The restoration work undertaken on the mill has won awards and, today, the mill is still working and produces wholemeal flour.

New Romney

St Nicholas' Church Toy & Model Museum

Romney, Hythe & Dymchurch Railway

Known as the 'Capital of the Marsh', New Romney is an attractive old town with some fine Georgian houses, that was, at one time, the most important of the Cinque Ports. However, in 1287 a great storm choked the River Rother, on which the town stood, with shingle and caused the river's course to be diverted to Rye. The town lost its harbour and its status. Although the Cinque Port documents are still housed at the Guildhall,

New Romney Church, New Romney

HAGUELANDS FARM VILLAGE

Burmarsh, Romney Marsh, Kent TN29 0JR.
Shop: 01303 874727 Bistro: 01303 873535
e-mail: info@aaclifton.ltd.uk
website: www.kentfarmshop.com

Haguelands Farm Village is just one of several excellent reasons for visiting this modern working farm which stands just off the A259 at Dymchurch, a ten minute walk from Dymchurch's splendid sandy beach. The site incorporates a large farm shop, a fishmonger, a conference/training facilities and a bistro which also runs cookery classes. On top of all of this the site now also boasts a PYO vegetable patch and herb garden, a large maize maze with fun yard and picnic area and a selection of interesting animals to interact with, including our herd of Alpaca's which we are currently breeding. To top it all off there is a 5 star, gold accolade bed & breakfast which operates from the familiy farm shop.

The farm shop offers many local delights and there is always something different to take your fancy. Ranging from locally baked bread, local organic and non-organic fruit and vegetables, dairy products, chutneys, pickles, preserves, oils & vinegars, Kentish meat, and much more. Hampers are made to order for Christmas.

A farmers market runs from early spring to late autumn on the 3rd Saturday of every month.

Next to the farm shop is the Romney Marsh fish market. This high-class purveyor of fish to the retail, restaurant and hotel trades started in Battersea in 1996 and sells some 40 varieties of fish and shellfish, ranging from cod, plaice and haddock through to more exotic catches such as squid, red snapper and tilapia. Phone orders can be made on: 01303 874125.

Haguelands kitchen is an open planned bistro, offering tasty dishes, sandwiches, cakes, teas and coffees, all made in our kitchen with fresh local ingredients. There is a warm feel to this oak clad bistro, which also holds numerous cookery classes, promoting healthy eating and encouraging people to get back in the kitchen.

The conference facility on site is available for private functions or business meetings and training days. It comes equipped with overhead projector and Wi-Fi. Teas, coffees sandwiches and lunches can all be made to order from the bistro for your day.

A great attraction for families is the marsh maize maze, which involves hunting for clues in a maze and then finding your way back. Once you're done why not relax in the picnic area whilst the kids let off more steam in the newly fitted fun yard. Also, observe the Alpacas grazing in the adjoining paddock and the rest of the interesting farm animals.

The bed & breakfast side of the farm welcomes holidaymakers and business people for both short and long stays, to relax, to see the local sights, to exercise or to use a stopover en route to the channel ports and the tunnel. The double rooms (non smoking), are equipped with TVs, fridge, drinks tray, trouser press, hairdryer, water, fresh fruit and many other extras. Car parking is off-road with CCTV in operation. The rooms enjoy lovely views over the gardens and countryside. Guests can enjoy a wide range of treatments including massages, reflexology, aromatherapy, facials and waxing.

New Romney now lies a mile from the sea. The sole survivor of the four churches in the town that were recorded in the Domesday Book, **St Nicholas' Church** still dominates the town's skyline with its lofty west tower. Floodmarks that can be seen on the pillars inside the church indicate just how high the floodwaters rose in the late 13th century.

The town is best known as being home to the main station of the **Romney Hythe and Dymchurch Railway**, a charming 15inch gauge railway that was built in the 1920s primarily as an amusement for the dashing racing drivers, Captain Jack Howey and Count Zborowski. It was designed by Henry Greenly, who was on the footplate with the Duke of York (later King George VI) when it opened in 1927. Billed as the 'World's Smallest Public Railway', and running between Hythe and Dungeness, it was not uncommon for train-loads of holidaymakers to find that their carriages were being pulled by a locomotive driven by a famous friend of the Captain. During World War II, the railway was run by the army who used it move both troops and supplies along this stretch of the south coast. Although revived in the post-war boom years, the railway struggled to attract visitors in the 1960s but it was, fortunately, saved by a group of enthusiastic businessmen. Once linked with stations on the Southern Railway but now isolated, the railway is still a delightful way to explore this coastline and makes a fascinating day out for all the family travelling in little carriages pulled by replica steam and diesel locomotives. At the New Romney station can be found the **Romney Toy and Model Museum** housing a wonderful collection of old and not so old toys, dolls, models, posters

GREATSTONE SECRET NURSERY

8 Coast Drive, Greatstone,
New Romney, Kent TN28 8NX
Tel: 01797 364380
e-mail: stevebradshaw@waitrose.com

The mother and son team of Betty and Steve Bradshaw own and run the **Greatstone Secret Nursery**, which is located on the coastal road at Greatstone, close to Dungeness Nature Reserve and the marvellous Romney, Hythe & Dymchurch Railway. Established more than 30 years ago, the Nursery enjoys a tranquil setting behind the owners' house in a third of an acre that includes three polytunnels, a net tunnel and a greenhouse.

The plants on sale, many of them home-grown, include fruit trees and bushes, ornamental trees, conifers, herbaceous perennials, climbing plants, bedding plants for spring, summer and autumn, a large selection of shrubs, fuchsias, acers and ornamental grasses. Also in stock are a selection of soils and growing aids and accessories, terra cotta pots, garden statuary and real oak half-barrels. Parking is easy, and the owners and their helpers are always on hand with help and advice on various aspects of gardening.

and photographs. There are also two magnificent working model railways that are sure to captivate children of all ages.

Around New Romney

ST MARY IN THE MARSH

2 miles N of New Romney off the A259

Set on the lonely and remote flats of Romney Marsh, this village's church steeple is crowned by an interesting ball and weather vane. The ball was obviously used by the villagers for target practice and, during restoration work, honey from the bees who had made their hive in the ball was seen oozing from the bullet holes. In the churchyard lies the simple grave of E Nesbit, the author of many children's books whose most famous work is *The Railway Children.*

BURMARSH

5 miles NE of New Romney off the A259

At the northern end of Romney Marsh, this village is home to one of the area's marshland churches, All Saints' Church, which boasts an impressive Norman doorway that is crowned by a grotesque man's face. Two of the original late 14th-century bells are still rung today, while another, dedicated to Magdalene, has been preserved. At nearby Lathe Barn, children get the opportunity to meet and befriend a whole range of farm animals, including ducks, chicks, barn owls, rabbits, donkeys, calves and sheep.

DYMCHURCH

3½ miles NE of New Romney on the A259

Martello Tower Lords of the Level

This small town's name is derived from 'Deme' the medieval English word meaning judge or arbiter and the town was the home of the governors of Romney Marsh. Known as the Lords of the Level, it was these men who saw that swift justice was carried out on anyone endangering the well-being of marshes and they still meet today. Visitors can find out more about the history of Romney Marsh at the **Lords of the Level**, a small museum housed in the town's old courtroom.

At one time a quiet and secluded village, Dymchurch has become a busy seaside resort with a five-mile stretch of sandy beach and all the usual amusements arcades, gift shops and cafés. However, what does make it rather different from other such resorts is the Dymchurch Wall, which prevents water from flooding both the town and marsh as Dymchurch lies about seven-and-a-half feet below the level of the high tide. A barrier of some kind has existed here since Roman times.

Visitors can go from one formidable defence to another at Dymchurch as the **Martello Tower** here is, arguably, the best example of its kind in the country. Now fully restored and with its original 24-pounder gun, complete with traversing carriage, still on the roof, this is one of the 74 such towers that were built along the coast as protection against invasion by Napoleon. Their name is derived from their 'pepper-pot' shape which is similar in style to a tower that stood at Cape Mortella in Corsica. This was an ironic choice of model as Napoleon himself was born on that Mediterranean island.

From the 1890s onwards the children's author, Edith Nesbit (but always E Nesbit for her novels) came to Dymchurch and other places around Romney Marsh to work on her novels. As well as writing, she would explore the marshland churches, riding first on a bicycle and later in a dog cart.

DUNGENESS

5 miles S of New Romney off the B2075

Nature Reserve Power Station Visitor Centre

This southern-most corner of Kent, with its shingle beach, has been a treacherous headland, feared by sailors for centuries. Originally simple fires were lit on the beach to warn shipping of the dangers around this headland and, in 1615, the first proper lighthouse was erected. As the sea have retreated a succession of lighthouses has been built and today there are two at Dungeness. The Old Lighthouse dates from 1901 and its modern and current successor, Lighthouse number five was opened in 1961. The Old Lighthouse is open to the public and at the top of its 169 steps, there are glorious views out to sea and, inland, over the marshes. As well as the makeshift fishermen's shacks and the lighthouses, the other key building on the headland is **Dungeness Power Station** where, at the Visitor Centre, there is an exhibition on electricity and the generation of nuclear energy. The headland is also home to the **Dungeness Nature Reserve** whose unique shingle flat lands have been described as 'the last natural undisturbed area in the South East and larger than any similar stretch of land in Europe'. This RSPB reserve is noted for the many rare and migrating birds that come here to rest and feed in spring and autumn, and a breeding colony of gulls and terns which nest in summer.

LYDD

3 miles SW of New Romney on the B2076

All Saints' Church Town Museum

Craft Gallery

Like Old Romney, Lydd was once a busy port, linked to the Cinque Port of New Romney, but the changing of the course of the River Rother and the steady build up of land along the marsh put paid to this. Despite the loss of the port trade, and now lying some three miles from the sea, Lydd is an attractive place that has retained many mementoes of its more prosperous past. Along with some fine merchants' houses and the handsome guildhall, the town is home to one of the tallest and longest parish churches in Kent, the 13th-century **All Saints' Church**, often referred to as the 'Cathedral of the Marsh'. While the church was being restored following bomb damage it sustained in 1940, a stone altar that had been thrown out by Reformers was rediscovered; it now stands in the north chancel. Before his meteoric rise to fame, Cardinal Wolsey was the rector of Lydd in 1503.

Housed in the old fire station, **Lydd Town Museum** has a fascinating collection of memorabilia on the history of the town and local area, along with a Merryweather fire engine and an early 20th century horsebus. At Lydd Library, the **Romney Marsh Craft Gallery** has a permanent display of crafts for sale from both Romney Marsh and further afield.

OLD ROMNEY

2 miles W of New Romney on the A259

Romney Marsh Derek Jarman Garden

With its setting in the remote Romney Marsh, this tiny village has a forlorn feel and it is hard to imagine that this place was once a prosperous port. However, the Domesday Book records that Old Romney had three fisheries, a mill and a wharf, thereby indicating that it had a waterfront. As the marsh gained more land from the sea, Romney's position - which had been as a busy island - became landlocked and trading was seriously hampered. So Old Romney lost out to New Romney, which ironically also found itself victim of the gradually accretion of land in the marsh.

Just its name, **Romney Marsh**, is enough to conjure up images of smugglers lugging their contraband across the misty marshland and, for centuries, this whole area profited from the illegal trade that was known locally as 'owling' because of the coded calls the smugglers used in order to avoid the excise men. While Rudyard Kipling has painted a charming and romantic picture of the marsh in his poetry, another writer, Russell Thorndyke, told of a rougher side in his children's novel, *Dr Syn*, published in 1915. As well as being the vicar of Dymchurch, Syn was the leader of a gang of smugglers in the 18th century who killed excise men, fought battles with the militia and stored their contraband in the marshland churches. The film-maker **Derek Jarman** moved to Dungeness in 1987 and created his extraordinary garden. Jarman is buried beneath a yew tree in Old Romney's Church of St Clement.

BROOKLAND

4½ miles W of New Romney on the A259

Church of St Thomas à Becket

Brookland certainly has a name that describes its setting - on the southern fringes of Romney Marsh where the landscape is one of flooded meadows, small ditches and dykes. Despite its location, the village is home to an impressive church, that of St Augustine, said to be built from the timber of local shipwrecks. Inside, the church has some fine features, such as the medieval wall painting of the murder of Thomas à Becket and a cylindrical lead Norman font that is unique in Britain, but the most interesting feature is the church's 13th-century shingled octagonal bell tower. Built in three vertical wooden stages, it stands quite apart from the rest of the church in much the same way as the campanile of an Italian church or cathedral. Architectural historians suspect that the medieval builders feared that the church, built on such damp foundations, would not support the extra weight of a belfry if it was added to the original building.

In the nearby hamlet of Fairfield stands the timber-framed **Church of St Thomas à Becket**. Isolated on the marshes, with the surrounding land frequently flooded, it was at one time accessed mainly by boat. Features include a complete set of box pews and a three-decker pulpit.

BRENZETT

4 miles NW of New Romney off the A259

Aeronautical Museum

This small settlement, lying on the probably Roman Rhee Wall sea embankment, is home to one of the smallest of the marshland churches, St Eanswith's Church. Thought to have been founded in the 7th century, although no traces of the original building surviving, there is an interesting tomb to local

Vampire Aircraft, Brenzett Aeronautical Museum

landowner John Fagge and his son to be seen here. The **Brenzett Aeronautical Museum** houses a unique collection of wartime aircraft memorabilia, including equipment and articles recovered from crash sites.

SNARGATE

5 miles NW of New Romney off the B2080

Church of St Dunstan

In the heart of the Romney Marsh, this village's remote location was the perfect spot for smugglers who plied their illicit trade under the cover of darkness and hid their ill-gotten gains in reed, lined streams or in disused and isolated farm buildings. The 600-year-old parish **Church of St Dunstan**, built in an exposed position, seems, on first sight, to be disproportionately large for the size of this village. However, this extra space was a boon for smugglers as they used it to store their contraband. An excise raid in 1743 uncovered a cask of gin in the vestry and tobacco in the belfry. In the early 19th century, the vicar here was the Rev Richard Barham; during his time at Snargate he wrote his humorous tales, *The Ingoldsby Legends*, some of which relate to the people of the Marsh. As he lived at some distance from the village, Barham was unaware of the nightly activity in and around his church.

STONE-IN-OXNEY

8 miles NW of New Romney off the B2080

Strikingly situated on the eastern flank of the inland island known as the Isle of Oxney, the stone that gives the village its name is Roman and can be found, preserved, in the parish Church of St Mary. Other archaeological remains within the church suggest that this site once served as a temple to Mithras, a Persian deity beloved of Roman soldiers.

The Weald of Kent

The Weald of Kent is a name to be reckoned with and one that conjures up, quite rightly, images of rolling wooded countryside, orchards and hop fields. Cranbrook, often dubbed the 'Capital of the Kentish Weald', is typical of many of the towns and villages of this area. It is a charming place that prospered in the Middle Ages with the growth of the woollen trade and which, when this industry declined, reverted to being a market town serving the surrounding communities.

Further north lies Maidstone, on the River Medway that forms the border between the Kentish Men and the Men of Kent. In bygone days Kent was divided into two parts, East (Men of Kent), administered from Canterbury, and West (Kentish Men), from Maidstone. In 1814 the two came together and Maidstone became the county town. Of the places to visit here, some of the most interesting, such as Allington Castle and the Museum of Kent Life, can be found beside this main waterway just north of the town. Maidstone is also home to a 14th century Archbishop's Palace that was a resting place for the clergy travelling between London and Canterbury and that stands on the site of a building mentioned in the Domesday Book.

Close to the county border with East Sussex lies Royal Tunbridge Wells, a particularly charming town that, unlike many places in the Weald of Kent, was no more than a forest clearing until the early 17th century when health-restoring waters were discovered here. Developed to provide accommodation and entertainment, with the help of Beau Nash, to those coming here to take the waters, the town also received royal patronage that led to the addition of the prefix granted by Edward VII.

In between these key towns, the countryside is dotted with attractive villages and small towns, surrounded by the orchards and hop fields that typify the Weald. This area is also home to two of the most popular attractions in the county, if not England. Situated on two islands and surrounded by glorious gardens, the former royal palace of Leeds Castle, so beloved by Henry VIII, is a wonderful example of Norman defensive architecture that was thankfully restored by Lady Baillie from 1926 onwards. The other is Sissinghurst Castle, the ruin bought by Vita Sackville-West and her husband, Harold Nicholson, in 1930, where they lovingly restored the gardens in the Elizabethan style. There are also other, less famous gardens that are sure to enchant visitors such as Scotney Castle, Groombridge Place and Owl House.

Maidstone

Allington Castle · Carriage Museum

Museum of Kent Life · Museum & Art Gallery

Maidstone grew up on the site of an important meeting place and this is reflected in the town's name that means 'the people's stone'. The River Medway, on which it stands, is the ancient boundary that separated East and West Kent with the Kentish Men living in the west and, to the east of the river, the Men of Kent. This important distinction is still used proudly by many of the county's inhabitants today. Despite being extensively developed in the 20th century, Maidstone has retained many handsome Elizabethan and Georgian buildings. Chillington Manor is a beautiful Elizabethan residence, now home to the **Maidstone Museum and Bentlif Art Gallery**, founded by generous Maidstone Victorian gentlemen and holding one of the finest collections in the south east. The many exhibits here cover a wide range of interests including oriental art, ethnography, archaeology and social history. The museum also has The Lambeth Bible Volume Two, a particularly outstanding example of 12th century illumination, and a real Egyptian mummy. The equally impressive art gallery includes works by both English and continental old masters among its permanent displays. Call 01622 602855 for opening times.

At the **Maidstone Carriage Museum** (under the auspices of Maidstone Museum) visitors can see a marvellous range of horse-drawn carriages that were enthusiastically collected by Sir Garrard Tyrwhitt-Drake, a former mayor of the town, who wanted to preserve this method of transport as it was being replaced by motorcars. The first collection of its kind in Britain, the museum opened in 1946 and it is housed, appropriately enough, in stables that once belonged to the archbishops of Canterbury. Opposite these stables is the Archbishop's Palace which dates

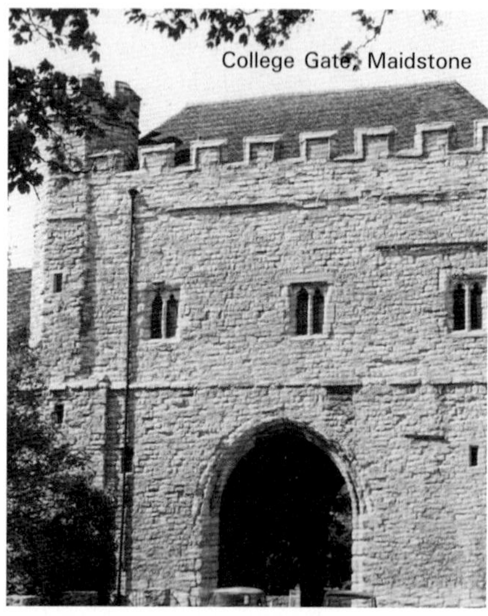
College Gate, Maidstone

from the 14th century and was used by the archbishops as they travelled between London and Canterbury. It is now used for weddings as the Kent Register Office. Close by are the Dungeons, a 14th-century building from which, it is alleged, Wat Tyler, leader of the Peasants' Revolt in 1381, released John Ball, the 'mad priest of Kent'.

Other interesting buildings in the town include the College of Priests, that was founded in 1395, and the early I5th-century Corpus Christi Fraternity Hall, where business was carried out in medieval times and which housed the Grammar School for over 300 years until the Education Act of 1870. Both of these buildings are now in private hands.

Just north of the town centre, at Sandling, on the banks of the River Medway, stands **Allington Castle**, the earliest parts of which are 13th century. However a fire around 1600 destroyed a large part of it and it was not until the early 20th century that it was restored. It was once the home of Sir Thomas Wyatt, one of the 'silver poets' of the 16th century and author of *They flee from me that sometime did me seek*. He shares, with the Earl of Surrey, the credit for introducing into English poetry the sonnet form, popularised by the Italian poet, Petrarch, and later perfected by Shakespeare. It was also at this castle that Henry VIII is said to have first met Anne Boleyn and, now housed in Maidstone Museum, is a chair from the castle that bears the following inscription: "... of this (chay)re iss entytled too one salute from everie ladie thott settes downe in itt - Castell Alynton 1530 - Hen. 8 Rex". The castle is now in private ownership.

Lying on the opposite bank of the Medway from the castle is the **Museum of Kent Life**. Reflecting the unique character of this area of Britain and set in some 50 acres of land at the foot of the North Downs, the open-air museum covers many aspects of the county, including three preserved hoppers' huts remembering the days when families came down from London to spend a working holiday picking hops. Maidstone Millenium Park is a new park running alongside the River Medway, connecting the town centre to the tranquil countryside nearby. Boat trips are available between the Archbishops Palace and the Museum of Kent Life.

Around Maidstone

AYLESFORD

2 miles NW of Maidstone off the A20

Priory Kit's Coty House

This charming village on the banks of the Medway is not only one of Kent's oldest villages, but has also, over the centuries, seen more than its fair share of fighting. Having travelled many miles from Pegwell Bay, the Jutish leaders Hengist and Horsa defeated the ancient Britons here in a great battle in 455. Though Horsa died in the battle, Hengist,

14th Century Bridge, Aylesford

BABY BEA

Mill Yard, Swan Street,
West Malling, Kent ME19 6LP
Tel: 01732 845582 Mob: 07859 074872
e-mail: katherine@babybea.co.uk
website: www.babybea.co.uk

'Baby Bea – Big Ideas for Little People'
'Shopping As Easy As A-Bea-C'
'Small but Perfectly Formed'

When Katherine Vidgen saw a 'baby shop' in Penrith she was very impressed and thought that the South of England needed and deserved something similar. With this in mind, at the end of 2007 she opened **Baby Bea – a Boutique** for 0-5s in the centre of West Malling, in a beautiful courtyard next to the main Post Office. Katherine's philosophy is that buying for a baby should be not a chore but one of the most pleasurable and rewarding shopping experiences. Baby Bea aims to inspire and delight its customers, and the first pleasure of a visit is the building itself: the shop occupies a converted barn with a slate roof, exposed brickwork, wooden cladding and handsome wooden beams. A visit to this stunning boutique is indeed a total delight, whether it's to buy practical baby products or a unique gift for baby to treasure into childhood – and beyond! The customers really love the place: the goods on display are a delight to the eye, there's a squidgy sofa to sink into and you can also purchase a cup of tea or coffee from the tea room above the shop. The inviting atmosphere is enhanced by beautiful lighting, and the shop has excellent feeding and changing facilities.

Katherine and her little daughter Bea have sourced and tried out some of the most imaginative and unusual baby products on the market for their discerning customers, and baby Lucie, born in February 2009, will no doubt soon be playing her part in quality control! The stock really does cover everything for baby, from new-born to five years old, and includes natural and eco nappies, organic baby and mother-to-be skin care products, handmade and unique knitwear, christening outfits, organic clothes and bedding, soft shoes, feeding pillows, sleeping bags and imaginative gifts (including a wide range of Beatrix Potter themed gifts, bespoke paintings and other personalised items such as baby's name worked into a colourful canvas or pine-framed print). The shop also stocks specialist premature baby wear and is the only stockist in Kent of the exclusive Bebe range – an Australian baby clothes company cherished for its gorgeous patterns and prints. Baby Bea is open from 10 to 5 Tuesday to Saturday.

along with his son Aesc, established a kingdom here (Cantware - or 'Men of Kent') and, for the next 300 years, the land was ruled by the descendants of Aesc, the dynasty of the Eskings. Later, in 893, the Danes were seen off by King Alfred while, soon afterwards, in 918, Edmund Ironside defeated Canute and the Vikings at Aylesford.

Aylesford has been an important river crossing for centuries and records recall that there was a bridge spanning the river here as long ago as 1287. However, the beautiful five-arched bridge seen today dates from the 14th century, and from it there is an excellent view of Aylesford's delightful half-timbered, steeply gabled cottages.

In 1242, when the first Carmelites arrived here from the Holy Land, they founded **Aylesford Priory**. After the dissolution of the monasteries in the 16th century, the priory became a private house and was rebuilt in 1675 only to be destroyed by a fire in the 1930s. In 1949, the Carmelites took over the house and, having restored it to its former glory, they re-established the priory - now calling it The Friars to use its traditional name. Today, it is a peaceful and tranquil retreat set in acres of well-tended grounds in which visitors are invited to picnic. The restored 17th-century barn acts as a tea room, as well as a gift and bookshop, while the chapels contain some outstanding modern works of religious art. Still a popular place for pilgrimage, there is also a guesthouse here that offers peace and quiet to individuals, groups and families as well as extensive conference facilities. Just north of the village lies further evidence of the long history of settlement in and around Aylesford in the form of **Kit's Coty House**. Situated on Blue Bell Hill, this is a Neolithic burial chamber (with a capstone lying across three huge upright stones) that is reputed to be the burial site of a British chieftain, Catigern, who was killed by Horsa. The views from the monument, out across the valley to the Medway Gap, make a walk to this site very worthwhile.

Kit's Coty House, Aylesford

DETLING

1 miles E of Maidstone off the A249

Pilgrims Way

Sheltered by the North Downs and by-passed by the main road, this village has remained relatively unspoilt and, today, it is visited by many walking the nearby **Pilgrims Way** footpath. In earlier times, this was an important coaching stop on several major routes that linked Maidstone with Sittingbourne, Faversham and other towns to the north. The High Street, which had been the main thoroughfare for the stagecoaches, is now more tranquil and along here, and elsewhere in the village, there are quaint old cottages to be found. On top of nearby Delting Hill lies the Kent County Agricultural

Show Ground, the venue for the county's major annual agricultural show, and various social events, and where also some World War II buildings still remain from the days when this site was used as an airfield.

BOXLEY

2 miles N of Maidstone off the A249

Very much a hidden village, lying tucked away below the North Downs surrounded by major roads and motorways, Boxley is a small and traditional village of weatherboarded and redbrick cottages. Just outside the village, to the west, lie the remains of Boxley Abbey, now part of a private house and not open to the public, although the abbey's late 13th-century ragstone barn can be seen from the road.

Back in the village stands the 13th-century All Saints' Church, which still retains some features from the original Norman building; inside, visitors can see a monument that recalls the gratitude of one of the village's residents for a cat. In 1483, Sir Henry Wyatt was imprisoned in the Tower of London for denying Richard III's claim to the throne of England. Sir Henry was left to starve to death in one of the tower's cold, damp cells but a cat, by sleeping on his chest at night and bringing him pigeons to eat during the day, saved his life.

OTHAM

3 miles SE of Maidstone off the A274

Despite being only a short distance from Maidstone, this elevated village is a haven of tranquillity with its restored 14th-century church, solid yeomen's houses and surrounding orchards. William Stevens, the eccentric writer who called himself 'Nobody' and founded the society of 'Nobody's Friends' lies buried in the churchyard. Stoneacre, a National Trust property, is a small and charming 15th-century half-timbered yeoman's house, complete with a great hall with a crownpost roof. It was sensitively restored from a state of near dereliction in the early 20th century using windows, fireplaces and wood from other ruined period buildings. The delightful gardens here have been restored to their original cottage style.

HOLLINGBOURNE

4 miles E of Maidstone off the A20

Along with the adjoining hamlet, Eythorne Street, Hollingbourne forms a linear village stretching out below the rising North Downs. Of the two, Eythorne Street is the older and here a number of timber-framed and traditional weatherboarded houses can be found. The 14th-century All Saints Church lies by the village pond. In Upper Hollingbourne is the Grade 1 listed Elizabethan manor house, Hollingbourne Manor, once home to a prominent Kentish family, the Culpepers. This tall Tudor manor house was acquired by Francis Culpeper in 1590.

LEEDS

4½ miles SE of Maidstone on the B2163

Castle

While most people come to the village on their way to see the 'most beautiful castle in the World', it would be a mistake not to spend some time looking around Leeds itself. The village stands on the grounds of a former abbey, that flourished until the dissolution of the monasteries in the 16th century, and many of the older buildings in Leeds, such as its oast houses, Norman Church of St Nicholas, and surrounding farms, were part of the abbey complex.

Leeds Castle, Leeds

Covering almost 1,200 years of history, **Leeds Castle** stands on two islands in the middle of the River Len and, while the peaceful moat is the home of swans and ducks, the castle itself is surrounded by beautifully landscaped gardens. Built on the site of a manor house that was owned by Saxon kings, the present castle was built just after the Norman Conquest and, when Edward I came to the throne, it became a royal palace. Beloved by Henry VIII, Leeds Castle was relinquished by the crown in the mid-16th century and, from then onwards, it has been in private hands. The last owner, an American heiress, Olive, Lady Baillie, bought the estate in 1926 and it is thanks to her vision, determination and hard work that Leeds Castle is so impressive today. It is one of the most popular visitor attractions in the country, with plenty to delight and interest the public both inside and out the gardens. Exhibits include collections of furnishings, tapestries and paintings, as well as an idiosyncratic museum of dog collars. Many of the gardens have been restored including the maze and grotto and the informal and typically English Culpeper Garden. One new garden is particularly interesting - the Lady Baillie Garden, honouring the woman who put so much back into the castle before her death in 1974. Here are planted numerous sub-tropical species like bananas and tree palms that flourish in this south-facing site.

Half-timbered Cottage, Loose

BROOMFIELD

5 miles SE of Maidstone off the A20

This picturesque village in the Len Valley was mentioned in the Domesday Book. In the graveyard of its 12th-century church lie buried several members of both the Wykeham-Martins and Fairfax families of Leeds Castle, along with Frederick Hollands, a 19th-century county cricketer from Broomfield. It is also the home of a spectacular 1,000-year-old yew tree.

LOOSE

2½ miles S of Maidstone off the A229

The older part of this delightful village (pronounced Looze) lies in a narrow little valley and the cottages rise in terraces above the stream. The power of the stream, along with its purity and the availability of Fullers Earth, helped to established a flourishing woollen industry here in the 16th century. As that trade declined, some of the mills were converted to paper making, which change of direction brought about more contact with Maidstone, just to the north. The viaduct that carries the main road from Maidstone across the Loose valley was built by Thomas Telford in 1829 and, along this stretch of road, can be seen large stones that were used, with the help of ropes, to pull heavy wagons up the steep hill.

BOUGHTON MONCHELSEA

3½ miles S of Maidstone on the B2163

Boughton Monchelsea Place

On a ridge overlooking the Weald of Kent, this pleasant village was at the centre of Kentish ragstone quarrying and, not surprisingly, this local building material features heavily here. The quarries, on the edge of the village, have been worked almost continuously for seven centuries, but archaeologists suggest that they were used longer ago than that as both the Romans and the Saxon used the stone in their buildings. Some of these stones were used in the construction of Westminster Abbey, and Henry III ordered a number of cannonballs to be made from Kentish ragstone. Naturally, the village's 13th-century parish Church of St Peter was built with this readily available material. It is also home to one of the oldest lychgates in England - erected in 1470 the gate was built entirely without nails. Local artist Graham Clark designed a modern nativity scene in stained glass for the church's millenium.

To the north of the church lies **Boughton Monchelsea Place**, a beautiful fortified ragstone manor house, originally built in 1567. The house itself is little altered since the late 18th century, retaining 16th-century stained glass windows, Elizabethan wall panellings, a galleried Jacobean staircase and original oak floors and marble fireplaces. To the front, it has breathtaking views of the private deer park and unspoilt countryside. The house is not open to the public.

MARDEN

7 miles S of Maidstone on the B2079

Surrounded by orchards and hop fields, the old part of the village is centred round a main street lined with attractive tile hung and weather-boarded houses. This village was, centuries ago, part of a Royal Hundred and, as it was exempt from the jurisdiction of the County Sheriff, it had its own court. This ancient court house still stands in the old square but the village stocks have been moved and can now be found on display in the porch of Marden's 13th-century church.

STAPLEHURST

8 miles S of Maidstone on the A229

Iden Croft Herbs

There was once a stronghold in the village but, today, all that can be seen is a tree covered mound and little is known of the fortification's history. In 1865, the novelist Charles Dickens was involved in a serious train accident at the point where the track crosses the River Beult, which lies to the east of Staplehurst, and he makes a reference to this in a postscript to his novel *Our Mutual Friend.*

A garden with a difference, **Iden Croft Herbs** has wonderful displays of herbs, aromatic wild flowers and plants that particularly attract butterflies, in both open and walled gardens. It is also home to the national oreganum and mentha collections.

EAST FARLEIGH

2 miles SW of Maidstone on the B2010

Standing on steeply rising ground on the side of the River Medway, East Farleigh is surrounded by orchards and overlooks a graceful 14th-century bridge. It was over this superb five-arched river crossing that Parliamentary soldiers marched in 1648 on their way to capturing Maidstone from the Royalists during the Civil War. One of the most important engagements in the war, the battle left 300 of the King's supporters dead and more than 1,000 taken prisoner. In the churchyard of the village's ancient church, a cross marks the final resting place of 43 hop pickers who died of cholera while working here in 1849. Also in the churchyard can be found the graves of the artist Donald Maxwell and Barbara Spooner, the wife of the reformer William Wilberforce, two of whose sons were vicars here.

Garden Organic Yalding

Benover Road, Yalding, Maidstone, Kent ME18 6EX
Tel: 01622 814650
website:: www.gardenorganic.org.uk

Yalding takes visitors on a journey through the fascinating history and thriving future of gardening, with **18** beautiful themed gardens to explore. For a peaceful place to soak up the atmosphere, you can stroll along the stunning Edwardian herbaceous borders, wander through the woodland or relax at The Henge. Travel from the 13th century Apothecary's Garden to the Tudor Knot Garden, and the Victorian Artisan's Glasshouse to the Dig for Plenty Garden. Free tours, led by knowledgeable volunteers are offered Sunday afternoons from May - September. All of these beautiful gardens are managed using the latest organic gardening methods. Our Garden for Today and LowWater Garden are wonderful examples of what can be achieved by nurturing nature.

YALDING

5 miles SW of Maidstone on the B2010

Organic Gardens

This lovely village's position, at the confluence of the Rivers Medway, Beult and Teise, provides ample irrigation for the fertile soil, so it is not surprising that Yalding lies in one of the largest hop-growing parishes in England. Each of the three rivers here is crossed by its own medieval bridge while the delightful high street is lined with charming weather-boarded houses that date back to the 17th century. At **Yalding Organic Gardens** (see panel above) visitors can see 14 individual gardens, including a Tudor garden, a Victorian garden and a wildlife garden, which illustrate the history of gardening from medieval times through to the present day. Changing ideas and themes down the ages are also highlighted, such as stewardship of resource, the importance of genetic engineering and organic horticulture.

NETTLESTEAD

5 miles SW of Maidstone on the B2015

A quiet village set on a bank above a particularly pleasant stretch of the River Medway, Nettlestead is home to two buildings that are thought to have been founded by Bishop Odo, the half-brother of William the Conqueror. The present parish Church of St Mary was rebuilt in 1420 and it contains some lovely stained glass windows that were greatly damaged in 1763 when a thunderstorm unleashed 10-inch hailstones on the village. Beside the church stands Nettlestead Place. Restored in the early 20th century, this ancient private house still retains its old stone gatehouse and medieval undercroft.

BELTRING

7½ miles SW of Maidstone on the A228

Hop Farm Country Park

This neat little village is home to one of the county's major attractions - the **Hop Farm Country Park**. Situated on a 1,000-acre former hop farm, this agricultural complex was originally a hop-drying centre supplying this major brewery, but it has grown to house a museum, a rural crafts centre and a nature trail. Visitors can learn about the history and purpose of hops in the brewing process (until the 14th century cloves were more commonly used as flavouring) and also about the brewing industry itself. Visitors, particularly children, will also enjoy meeting the famous Whitbread shire horses and the smaller animals at the pets' corner. A collection of agricultural machinery is on display along with an interesting exhibition of rural crafts.

HADLOW

9 miles SW of Maidstone on the A26

Broadview Gardens

Lying in the Medway Valley, this attractive village has a wide main street where a number of its older houses can be found. These, and the rest of the village, are, however, completely overshadowed by the curiosity known as May's Folly. A tower some 170 feet high, this is all that remains of Hadlow Castle, which was built by the eccentric industrialist Walter Barton May over a number of years and was finally finished in the early 19th century. May built the tower so that he would have a view that extended as far as the south coast but, unfortunately, the South Downs made this particular dream of his impossible to realise.

Anyone looking for gardening ideas in the heart of the Garden of England should pay a visit to **Broadview Gardens** where the belief the success of a garden that lies, in its design is firmly held. There are a wide range of gardens to see here - from subtropical, stone and water, oriental and Italian, to mixed borders, cottage, bog and wildlife. Beside the more traditional gardens, there are experimental areas, making this an ideal place to visit for anyone looking for gardening inspiration.

Royal Tunbridge Wells

Church of King Charles the Martyr

Museum Art Gallery

Surrounded by the unspoilt beauty of the Weald, some of the most scenic areas of countryside in England, Royal Tunbridge Wells is a pretty and attractive town that has been a popular place to visit for several hundred years. However, unlike many of the major towns and cities of Kent, Royal Tunbridge Wells has no Roman or ecclesiastical heritage and, during the Middle Ages, when many towns were establishing their trading reputations, it was little more than a forest. The secret of how this charming place gained such prominence lies in the 'Royal' and 'Wells' of its name. In 1606, the courtier, Dudley, Lord North, found natural springs here and rushed back to court to break the news of his discovery of what he declared to be health-giving waters. Soon the fashionable from London were taking the water and spreading the word of their health-restoring qualities but, for three decades, there were still no buildings beside what soon became known as the Chalybeate Spring.

In 1630, Tunbridge Wells received its first royal visitor when Queen Henrietta Maria, the wife of Charles I, came here to recuperate after giving birth to the future Charles II. She and her entourage, like other visitors, camped on the grounds by the springs. The real development of the town into one of the most popular spas of the 18th and 19th centuries was due to the Earl of Abergavenny. In order to increase the popularity of the spa, Beau Nash, the famous dandy who played an important role in the development of another spa town, Bath, came here as Master of Ceremonies in 1735. With Nash at the helm, guiding and even dictating fashion, Tunbridge Wells went from strength to strength and, while royalty had always found the town to their liking, it was not granted its 'Royal' prefix until 1909 when it was bestowed by Edward VII.

The chalybeate spring that was accidentally discovered by Lord North while out riding in what was then Waterdown Forest still flows in front of the Bath House, which was built in 1804 on top of the original Cold Bath. Meanwhile, close to the original springs was a grassy promenade known as The Walks where those coming to take the waters could take some exercise. In 1699 Princess Anne visited Tunbridge Wells with her son, the Duke of Gloucester, who slipped and hurt himself along The Walks. The irate Princess complained and the town authorities tiled over the grass and so created The Pantiles, a lovely shaded walk, lined with elegant shops. The Pantiles were the central focal point for the hectic social life arranged by Beau Nash and there were concerts and balls throughout the season along with gambling houses. Also in this area of the town is the **Church of King Charles the Martyr**, often called the 'Jewel of the Pantiles'. Originally established as a chapel in 1678 for those coming to take the waters, the church has many interesting features, including a charming clock donated to the church in 1760 by Lavinia Fenton, the actress and mistress of the Duke of Bolton. The superb decorative plaster ceiling was designed and begun by John Wetherall and completed by Henry Doogood, the chief plasterer to Sir Christopher Wren.

For a greater insight into the history and development of the town, a visit to the **Tunbridge Wells Museum and Art Gallery**, opened in 1952, is a must. Among the displays and exhibits on natural history and art, there is an exhibition of local history and a collection of Tunbridge ware - the decorative woodwork that is unique to the area. Almost in the centre of the Pantiles is a small square – Fishmarket Square – with a strange little black and white building. The Old Fish Market, dating from 1745, is now the Tourist Information Centre.

Once part of the extensive network of railway lines in Kent and neighbouring East Sussex, Spa Valley Railway is a restored and preserved section of this system that was re-opened in 1996. Now running between Royal Tunbridge Wells, High Rocks and Groombridge, the trains leave Tunbridge Wells West station and take passengers on a pleasant journey through the Wealden countryside.

Around Royal Tunbridge Wells

MATFIELD

5 miles NE of Tunbridge Wells on the B2160

The village name is derived from the Anglo Saxon name 'Matta' and 'feld' meaning large clearing, and appropriately at the centre of this village is one of the largest village greens in Kent. Around it old and new houses blend harmoniously including several fine tile hung, typically Kentish houses and an impressive Georgian dwelling built in 1728.

HORSMONDEN

7½ miles E of Tunbridge Wells on the B2162

It is hard to imagine that this delightful village, tucked among orchards and fields, was once a thriving industrial centre. Although little evidence of this remains today the key to the village's prosperity lies in the pond found just to the west. Known as a furnace pond, it supplied water to the ironworks that flourished throughout the Weald of Kent. Now, nature is reclaiming the pond and it will soon be indistinguishable from other expanses of water in and around the village.

From the village green, known as The Heath, a footpath leads to the village church, some two miles to the west. This is a walk worth making as the countryside is pleasant and, on reaching the church, visitors can see a memorial to John Read, who died in 1847, and is best known for inventing the stomach pump.

GOUDHURST

9 miles E of Tunbridge Wells on the A262

Finchcocks · Bedgebury National Pinetum

Standing on a hill and with sweeping views across the surrounding orchards and hop fields, and especially over the Weald, Goudhurst (pronounced 'Gowdhurst') is a picturesque place that draws many visitors, not

Goudhurst Church, Goudhurst

least because of its main street, lined with traditional tile hung, weatherboarded cottages. The solidity of the village reflects the prosperity it enjoyed when the woollen industry was introduced here in the Middle Ages. The village church, which stands on the hilltop, begun as a chapel in 1119, dates chiefly from the 15th century and, inside, there are many memorials to the leading local family, the Culpepers. The Culpepers were at one time noted ironmasters and made guns for Drake's navy against the Spanish Armada. From the church tower it was said that 51 other churches could be seen on a clear day. This may have been possible when the tower was higher, but whatever the truth of the 51 churches it is certainly possible today to see Canary Wharf Tower in London, which is 40 miles away.

Just to the southwest of the village lies **Finchcocks**, a charming Georgian manor house, with a dramatic frontage, that is named after the family who lived on this land in the 13th century. Built for the barrister Edward Bathurst in 1725, the house has managed to retain many of its original features despite having changed hands several times over the years. In 1970, Finchcocks was bought by Richard Burnett, a leading exponent of the early piano and, today, it is home to his magnificent collection of historic keyboard instruments. The high ceilings and oak panelled rooms are the ideal setting for this collection of beautiful instruments, which includes chamber organs, harpsichords, spinets and early pianos, and whenever the house is open to the public those instruments restored to concert standard, are played. Finchcocks also houses some fine pictures and prints and an exhibition on 18th-century pleasure gardens. Tucked away behind the elegant house are four acres of beautiful gardens, which provide a dramatic setting for outside events. The gardens are mainly of Victorian design, except the walled garden, which was designed in 1992, as an 18th-century Pleasure Garden.

Further south again, and adjoining the county border with East Sussex, lies **Bedgebury National Pinetum**, founded jointly by the Forestry Commission and the Royal Botanic Gardens at Kew in the 1920s. Today, Bedgebury is home to the National Conifer Collection, the largest collection of temperate conifers on one site in the world, where some of the most famous conifers, including large Californian redwoods, are to be found. Bedgebury has a unique habitat that attracts dragonflies, dormice, butterflies and even bats.

LAMBERHURST

6 miles E of Tunbridge Wells on the A21

Scotney Castle   Owl House Gardens

As this village lies on the main road between Royal Tunbridge Wells and Hastings, it once played an important role as a coaching stop but much of the village's prosperity is due to the iron industry of the Weald. The high street here is lined with attractive old houses and other buildings dating from those days. Lamberhurst produced iron railings, which are can be seen along this road and at St Paul's Cathedral. Lamberhurst's 14th century church, set some way from the village centre in the valley of the River Teise, has been remodelled to accommodate a smaller congregation than those it attracted during the years of Lamberhurst's heyday. Today, the village is associated with viticulture and the first vineyard was established here in 1972.

To the northwest of the village lies **Owl House Gardens,** a particularly pretty little cottage whose tenants, according to records dating from 1522, paid the monks at Bayham Abbey an annual rental of one white cockerel. Later the house became associated with night smugglers or 'owlers' (hence its name) who traded English wool for French brandy and avoided the tax inspectors by giving out coded hoot calls. In 1952, the house was bought by Lady Dufferin and, while it is not open to the public, the beautiful gardens that she planted can be visited. There are extensive lawns and walks through woodland of birch, beech and English oak as well as spring bulbs, roses, flowering shrubs and ornamental fruit trees. As this was once the site of the iron works that made some of the fitments for St Paul's Cathedral, there are also hammer ponds which have been creatively converted into informal water gardens surrounded by willows, camellias and rhododendrons.

To the east of the Lamberhurst lies **Scotney Castle** (see panel below), a massive, rust-stained tower that was built by Roger de Ashburnham in 1378 and that now incorporates the ruins of a Tudor house. However, what especially draws people to Scotney are the romantic gardens that are renowned for their autumn colours but are beautiful throughout all the seasons. The water lily-filled moat around the ruins provides the perfect centrepiece to the wealth of plants found in the gardens and there are also delightful countryside walks around the estate.

GROOMBRIDGE

4 miles SW of Tunbridge Wells on the B2110

Groombridge Place

Groombridge Place Gardens

Straddling the county border between Kent and Sussex, it is generally recognised that the Kent side of this village is the prettier and more interesting as this is where the triangular village green lies, overlooked by the tile hung cottages of the Groombridge estate. This charming village centre piece is also overlooked by **Groombridge Place**, a

Scotney Castle Garden and Estate

Lamberhurst, Royal Tunbridge Wells,
Kent TN4 8XX
Tel: 01892 891081
website: www.nationaltrust.org.uk

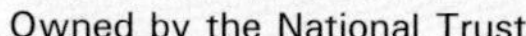

Owned by the National Trust

Scotney is a hidden gem and one of the most romantic gardens in England, this stunning picturesque garden provides a unique backdrop for a fairytale 14th century moated ruined castle. From early in the year snowdrops appear, then swathes of primroses and daffodils cover the lawns sweeping down to the moat, whilst sweet smelling drifts of bluebells line the driveway. Magnificent rhododendrons, azaleas and Scotney's famous Kalmia latifolia follow, and as summer progresses, the breathtaking fragrant white wisteria lazily rambles the walls of the ruined castle. Finally the season comes to a close with the rich autumnal hues of reds and golds from Liquid ambers and Japanese Maples in the garden, coupled with the glorious vibrancy of the new quarry garden and surrounding estate with its ancient parkland and meadow.

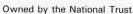

Groombridge Place Gardens Dragon

classical 17th century manor house that stands on the site of a medieval castle. The house is surrounded by superb parkland and **Gardens**, designed by the famous Jacobean diarist John Evelyn in a formal manner. Likened to a series of rooms, the walled gardens are complemented by extensive herbaceous borders while, high above these, there is The Enchanted Forest a magical and imaginative series of mysterious gardens that are a delight to explore.

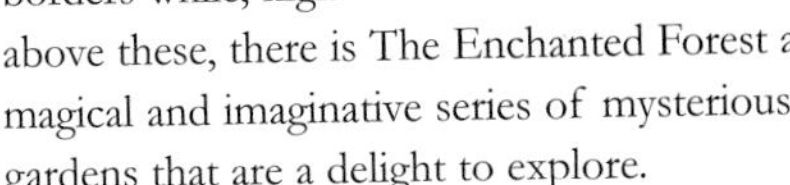

RUSTHALL

1½ miles W of Tunbridge Wells off the A264

Although Rusthall lies on the outskirts of Royal Tunbridge Wells, it has managed to retain some of its original rural character and not become completely engulfed by its much larger neighbour. A lovely common marks the heart of the village and some of the unusual rock structures that can be found in Royal Tunbridge Wells can also be seen here, in particular, there is Toad Rock, a natural rock formation, so called because of its remarkable resemblance to a giant toad balanced atop a rock.

SPELDHURST

2½ miles NW of Tunbridge Wells off the A26

This attractive, chiefly residential, village was mentioned as early as the 8th century and, though close to Royal Tunbridge Wells, still manages to preserve a cohesive sense of village identity and a rural atmosphere. At its heart lies the village church, built on the foundations of a much older Norman church that was struck by lightning in 1791. Great care was taken by the Victorians when the church was rebuilt and it is worth visiting to view the colourful stained glass windows designed by Burne-Jones.

Cranbrook

St Dunstan's Church Museum

Originally a little hamlet lying in the hills close to the source of the River Crane, Cranbrook began to grow in the 11th century, and by the end of the 13th century it was sufficiently well established to be granted a market charter by Edward I. However, it was the introduction of wool weaving from Flanders, in the 14th century that really changed the town's fortunes and, for the next few centuries, Cranbrook prospered. Several old buildings date back to this period of wealth including the church and the Cloth Halls and the winding streets lined with weatherboarded houses and shops. However, the industry began to decline and, by the 17th century, agriculture had taken over and, like other Wealden places, Cranbrook was transformed into a market town serving the needs of the surrounding area.

Often dubbed the 'Capital of the Kentish Weald', one of the best places to start any exploration of the town is at the **Cranbrook Museum** that is housed in a museum piece itself. Dating back to 1480, the museum is a fine example of a timber-framed building that is held together by elaborate joints. Opened in 1974, the displays and exhibitions here cover many aspects of Wealden life, from agriculture and local crafts to Victorian and wartime memorabilia. Naturally the town's reliance on the weaving industry is highlighted and, along with the collection of prints by the 19th-century Cranbrook colony of artists, there is a display of local birds, many of which are now rare.

The parish church, **St Dunstan's**, is believed to have been built on the site of first a Saxon and then a Norman church. Known locally as the 'Cathedral of the Weald', and built between the 14th and 16th centuries, the size of this church reflects the prosperity of the town at the time. Even the stone font is of impressive proportions, designed for total immersion, its base featuring wooden bosses of Green Man. Above the porch, reached by a stone staircase, is a room known as 'Baker's Jail' where, in the reign of Mary Tudor, Sir John Baker, sometimes known as 'Bloody Baker', imprisoned the numerous Protestants he had convicted there, to await their execution. Originally, the room was intended to hold church valuables. Elizabeth Paine, wife of the American philosopher Thomas Paine, is buried in the churchyard.

Although St Dunstan's church tower is tall, the town is dominated by the tallest smock mill in England, Union Mill, which is around 70 feet high. Built in 1814, the windmill was fully restored in the 1960s and in 2003 and, wind permitting, it still grinds corn into the flour that is sold here.

Around Cranbrook

SISSINGHURST

1½ miles NW of Cranbrook on the A262

Castle Gardens

The main street of this village is lined with old weatherboarded houses that have been built over a period of several centuries. Many of the larger houses were erected by prosperous weavers who worked in the thriving industry that was introduced to Sissinghurst during the reign of Edward III.

Sissinghurst is, of course, famous for the lovely gardens that were the creation of the writer Vita Sackville-West and her husband Harold Nicholson. When, in 1930, the couple bought **Sissinghurst Castle**, it was all but a ruin. The castle was originally built in Tudor times by Sir John Baker, who, during the reign of Mary Tudor, sent so many Protestants to their deaths that he became known as 'Bloody' Baker. Such was Sir John's reputation that local legend tells that when two women working at the castle heard him approaching, they hid under the main staircase. From their hiding place they saw that their master was being followed by a servant carrying the body of a murdered woman. As the men climbed the staircase, one of the dead woman's hands became caught in the banisters. Impatient to continue whatever gruesome tasks he was about to perform, Sir John quickly hacked the hand from the body and he and his servant continued up the stairs. Meanwhile, the severed hand fell into the lap of one of the women hiding below.

Later, during the Seven Years War in the 18th century, the castle was used as a prison for 3,000 French troops and, by the time they had left, only a few parts of the original building were left standing. Decades of neglect, and a short time as a workhouse, finally saw the castle descend to the wrecked state of the 1930s.

Restoring what they could of the castle, the couple concentrated on creating the famous **Gardens** that, today, bring so much pleasure to visitors. Laid out in the Elizabethan style, there are a series of formal gardens, or 'rooms', that each have a different theme such as the White Garden where only silver leafed, white flowering plants are grown. Away from this formality there are also woodland and lakeside walks and the estate's oast house is home to an interesting exhibition.

BENENDEN

3 miles SE of Cranbrook on the B2086

This attractive village is strung out along a ridge. It is famous for its girls' public school, also called Benenden, housed in a mock-Elizabethan house dating from 1859 to the west of the village centre. Benenden village itself is well-known for cricket, played on most summer evenings on the large green.

ROLVENDEN

5 miles SE of Cranbrook on the A28

CM Booth Collection of Historic Vehicles

Surrounded by orchards and hop fields, this large village stands on the eastern fringe of the Weald and on the edge of the Isle of

HEMPSTEAD EQUESTRIAN CENTRE

Chittenden Farm, Golford Road, Benenden, Kent TN17 4AJ
Tel: 01580 240086 mob: 07947 256541
e-mail: sally@wealdenpoolsandspas.co.uk
website: www.hempsteadequestrian.co.uk

Sally Reynolds, who owns and runs **Hempstead Equestrian** Centre, has been involved with horses from a very young age, starting in pony clubs and graduating to eventing and show jumping and acquiring a qualification to teach riding at Brockenhurst College.

Standing next to the famous girls' school in 30 acres of grounds, the Centre's main offering is providing exclusive hacking (riding) for all ages in the adjacent, beautiful Hemsted Forest. The Centre's horses and ponies are carefully selected for their ability and temperament, and they clearly enjoy their role as much as the riders. The hacking can be tailored to individual requirements and usually takes place in small groups (no more than four, including the guide in 1¼ hour or 40 minute (lead-rein) sessions.

Private tuition in individual or group lessons is also offered, subject to availability, and visitors should also ask about Own a Pony days and festive fancy dress rides. The Centre is open from 12 to 7 Tuesday to Sunday, otherwise by arrangement.

C.M. Booth Collection of Historic Vehicles

Falstaff Antiques, 63 High Street, Rolvenden, Kent TN17 4LP
Tel: 01580 241234

The main feature here is the unique private collection of Morgan 3 wheel cars. Ten are normally on display, dating from 1913-1935, plus the only known Humber Tri-car of 1904, a1929 Morris van, motorcycles, bicycles and a 1936 Bampton caravan, There are also displays of toy and model cars, signs and other automobilia.

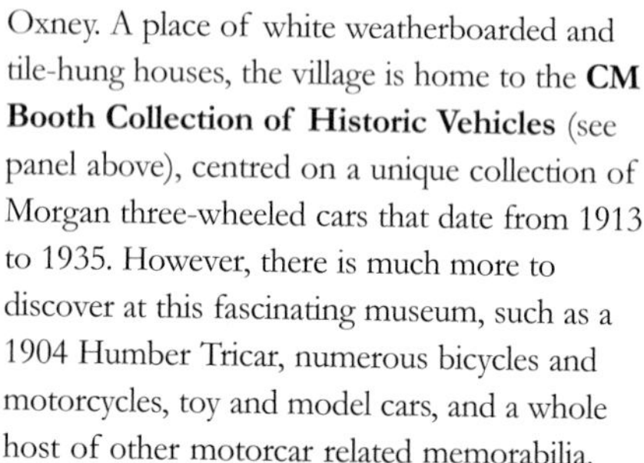

Oxney. A place of white weatherboarded and tile-hung houses, the village is home to the **CM Booth Collection of Historic Vehicles** (see panel above), centred on a unique collection of Morgan three-wheeled cars that date from 1913 to 1935. However, there is much more to discover at this fascinating museum, such as a 1904 Humber Tricar, numerous bicycles and motorcycles, toy and model cars, and a whole host of other motorcar related memorabilia.

Close to the village lies Great Maytham Hall, a charming country house, renovated by Sir Edwin Lutyens, which stands in glorious grounds. At the turn of the 20th century, the novelist Frances Hodgson Burnett, who spent most of her life in America, leased the house. While staying here, she fell in love with the particularly beautiful walled kitchen garden that was to inspire her to write the classic children's book *The Secret Garden*. The garden is open to the public on a limited basis.

SANDHURST

5 miles S of Cranbrook on the A268

Visitors coming here expecting to find the Royal Military Academy will be disappointed as this is located at Sandhurst, Berkshire. However, Sandhurst, Kent, is an attractive place that deserves a visit in its own right. Set in reasonably hilly terrain this feature of the countryside gave rise to the name of a local inn, The Missing Link, which refers to the practice of linking extra horses to the wagons in order to pull heavy loads up the hill.

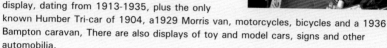

2 East Sussex

Maritime Stade, Hastings

Good Old Sussex by the Sea – in 1912 Rudyard Kipling wrote a poem about it and, five years later, William Ward-Higgs composed an anthemic song. Sussex was all one county then; it's two now, but the appeal that inspired verse and song remains to this day.

East Sussex has been witness to some of the most momentous events in the history of England. The coastal village of Pevensey was the landing place of William, Duke of Normandy, and his army in 1066 and, as every school child knows, William proceeded to defeat Harold near Hastings and claim the crown of England. Hastings and Battle, the town that grew up around the site of the battlefield, have museums and exhibitions on these history-changing events. The victorious Normans soon set about building castles and fortifications from which to defend their new territory, as well as religious buildings, and the area is still rich in Norman architecture.

The south coast was always an obvious target for invasion and, in the days before the Royal Navy, the confederation of Cinque Ports was established to provide a fleet of ships to defend the coast. Many Sussex towns, now some distance from the sea, were part of the confederation. The silting up of the harbours has changed the landscape of the East Sussex coast considerably in the past 1,000 years.

Nowadays, the coast is the preserve of holiday-makers, taking advantage of the generally moderate climate and the bracing sea air. The thriving resorts of Brighton and Eastbourne began life as quiet fishing villages, but developed rapidly at the beginning of the 19th century. Brighton is best known for its exotic Royal Pavilion, designed in magnificent Indian style by John Nash for the Prince Regent. Eastbourne, by contrast, was carefully planned and laid out in genteel style by William Cavendish, the 7th Duke of Devonshire, close to the chalk cliffs of Beachy Head. St Leonards and Bexhill are quieter resorts, but perhaps the most picturesque of all is Rye, with its many medieval buildings.

Away from the coast, on the high ridges of the Weald, is the largest area in southeast England that has never been put to agricultural use. Ashdown Forest was a royal hunting ground and its thriving population of deer made it a favourite sporting place. The

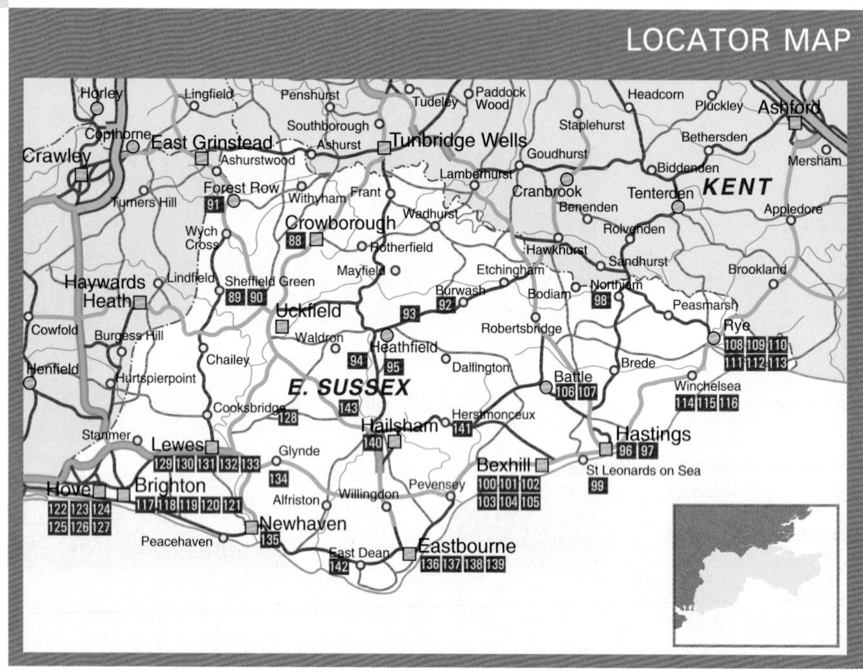

ADVERTISERS AND PLACES OF INTEREST

Accommodation, Food and Drink

88	Yew House Bed & Breakfast, Crowborough	pg 148
89	Trading Boundaries, Sheffield Green, nr Fletching	pg 152
94	Holly Grove Bed & Breakfast, Little Landon, nr Heathfield	pg 160
95	The Brewers Arms, Vines Cross, nr Heathfield	pg 160
96	Minstrel's Rest, Hastings	pg 164
99	Sherwood Guest House, St Leonards-on-Sea	pg 170
100	The Old Manse Bed & Breakfast, Bexhill-on-Sea	pg 171
104	Arden House, Bexhill-on-Sea	pg 173
105	Eve's B & B, Bexhill-on-Sea	pg 174
106	Nobles Restaurant, Battle	pg 175
108	Jeake's House Hotel, Rye	pg 180
110	The Queens Head Hotel, Rye	pg 182
111	Hayden's, Rye	pg 182
116	The Lodge At Winchelsea, Winchelsea	pg 187
117	Terraces Bar & Grill, Brighton	pg 189
123	igigi Café, Hove	pg 194
135	The Garden of Eden, Newhaven	pg 208
136	The Gables Bed & Breakfast, Eastbourne	pg 210
137	Savoy Court Hotel, Eastbourne	pg 210
138	The Cherry Tree Guest House, Eastbourne	pg 211
139	Cromwell House, Eastbourne	pg 212
142	Hikers Rest Coffee & Gift Shop, East Dean	pg 218
143	Pekes Manor House, Golden Cross	pg 224

Arts and Crafts

103	Wa Waa's Wool 'n' Bits, Bexhill-on-Sea	pg 173
107	Battle Wool & Needlecraft Shop, Battle	pg 178
132	Kings Framers, Lewes	pg 202
140	The Pumpkin Patch, Hailsham	pg 213
141	Arts Hut, Herstmonceux	pg 214

Fashions

89	Trading Boundaries, Sheffield Green, nr Fletching	pg 152
101	Vintage Styling by Lily Rose, Bexhill-on-Sea	pg 172
112	The Golden Fleece, Rye	pg 183
121	Pardon my French!, Brighton	pg 192
124	igigi Womens Boutique, Hove	pg 195
125	igigi Menswear, Hove	pg 195

Giftware

89	Trading Boundaries, Sheffield Green, nr Fletching	pg 152
90	Villandry Home, Sheffield Green, nr Fletching	pg 153
91	The Pavilion, Forest Row	pg 155
101	Vintage Styling by Lily Rose, Bexhill-on-Sea	pg 172
118	sixtyseven, Brighton	pg 190
121	Pardon my French!, Brighton	pg 192
126	Second Seed Bespoke Furniture, Unique Interiors and Gifts, Hove	pg 196

historic building · museum and heritage · historic site · scenic attraction · flora and fauna

Eastbourne

network of tracks across the forest goes back to prehistoric times, the Romans built a road straight across it, and the rights of commoners to gather wood for fuel, cut peat and graze cattle, were well established by Norman times. Much of the woodland has been lost, but the remaining forest is protected as an Area of Outstanding Natural Beauty and Site of Special Scientific Interest. The surrounding area is characterised by small towns and villages of weatherboarded cottages, traditional hall houses and unspoilt farmsteads.

Many artists and writers of the 19th and 20th centuries chose to live here. A A Milne set the Winnie the Pooh stories in Ashdown Forest and surrounding area. Virginia Woolf and her husband Leonard lived at Monk's House, Rodmell, while her sister, Vanessa Bell, was at nearby Charleston in Selmeston. The Elms at Rottingdean was the home of Rudyard Kipling until 1902, when he moved to Burwash, and the village of Ditchling was home to several of the leading lights of the Arts and Crafts Movement.

ADVERTISERS AND PLACES OF INTEREST (CONT)

Home and Garden

89 | Trading Boundaries, Sheffield Green, nr Fletching *pg 152*
90 | Villandry Home, Sheffield Green, nr Fletching *pg 153*
91 | The Pavilion, Forest Row *pg 155*
93 | Petals For Plants, Broad Oak, nr Heathfield *pg 159*
101 | Vintage Styling by Lily Rose, Bexhill-on-Sea *pg 172*
102 | Bexhill Linens, Bexhill-on-Sea *pg 172*
109 | Tower Forge Fires, Rye *pg 181*
113 | Forget-Me-Not, Rye *pg 184*
118 | sixtyseven, Brighton *pg 190*
119 | Aramas Interiors, Brighton *pg 190*
121 | Pardon my French!, Brighton *pg 192*
122 | igigi Homewear, Hove *pg 194*
126 | Second Seed Bespoke Furniture, Unique Interiors and Gifts, Hove *pg 196*
127 | Brass Monkeys, Hove *pg 197*
128 | Giganteum, Ringmer *pg 199*

Jewellery

127 | Brass Monkeys, Hove *pg 197*
129 | Punzi, Lewes *pg 200*
130 | The Workshop, Lewes *pg 200*

Places of Interest

92 | Bateman's, Burwash, nr Etchingham *pg 157*
97 | Shipwreck Heriatge Centre, Hastings *pg 165*
98 | Great Dixter House and Gardens, Northiam, nr Rye *pg 167*
120 | Royal Pavilion, Brighton *pg 191*
131 | Historic Days Out in East Sussex, Lewes *pg 201*
133 | Anne of Cleves House Museum, Lewes *pg 203*
134 | Firle Place, Firle, nr Lewes *pg 206*

Specialist Food and Drink Shops

114 | Sutton's Fish Shop, Winchelsea *pg 186*
115 | J Wickens Family Butcher, Winchelsea *pg 186*

Ashdown Forest and the Sussex Weald

This region of East Sussex is centred round the ancient Ashdown Forest, a royal hunting ground that also provided fuel for the area's iron industry. Much of the actual woodland has been lost both as fuel and for shipbuilding. The area is characterised by small towns and villages of weatherboarded cottages, traditional hall houses and unspoilt farms. There is evidence in ancient tracks that the area has been inhabited since prehistoric times, but the exciting discovery of a supposedly 150,000-year-old skull in 1912 at the village of Piltdown was proved some 40 years later to be a clever and complicated hoax.

Over the centuries the area has been notable for many fine houses and castles. The impressive Herstmonceux Castle, home of the Royal Observatory from 1948 until the 1980s, is a magnificent medieval brick fortress, which also provided comfortable living accommodation for its inhabitants; it is set in the most glorious gardens and parkland.

Other houses here have a more personal appeal and one, Bateman's at Burwash, was the home of Rudyard Kipling from 1902 until his death in 1936. A quiet place in a secluded position, the house has been left as it was when Kipling died and is full of his personal possessions. Ashdown Forest and Hartfield are linked with another 20th-century writer, A A Milne. He lived close by and wrote the Winnie the Pooh stories, set in the forest and surrounding area, for the amusement of his son, Christopher Robin.

Crowborough

This Wealden town, on the eastern edge of Ashdown Forest is, at over 750 feet above sea level, one of the highest towns in Sussex.

Before the arrival of the railways in the 1860s, this was a small community of iron smelters and brigands centred around the parish church and vicarage. At the heart of the town is a triangular green where stands the greystone church dating from 1744.

The railways put Crowborough within easy reach of London, so it was gradually transformed into the flourishing residential town it is today. A relatively peaceful place, its convenient location attracted a number of well-known late 19th-century writers, including Sir Arthur Conan Doyle, creator of Sherlock Holmes, perhaps the best-known detective in the world. Conan Doyle's house, high up on Crowborough Beacon, was a country house called Windlesham. Apparently he nicknamed it Swindlesham because of the amount it cost to extend and refurbish it.

Around Crowborough

GROOMBRIDGE

4 miles N of Crowborough on the B2110

Groombridge Place

This unspoilt village straddles the county border with Kent and, while the Sussex part of the village, which grew up around the railway station, has little to offer, the Kent side is particularly charming. The name is said to be derived from the Saxon 'Gromen', meaning man as in bridegroom. Centred round a triangular green, there are attractive 15th and 16th-century estate cottages and a superb manor house **Groombridge Place**, dating from the 17th century. The site on which the foundations were laid is much older and there is some evidence that there was first a Saxon, then a Norman castle here. Built by Charles Packer, the Clerk of the Privy Seal, who accompanied Charles I on his unsuccessful journey to Spain to ask for the Infanta's hand in marriage, Groombridge Place is a splendid redbrick house surrounded by a moat. Set within beautiful terraced gardens, the house has a small museum dedicated to Sir Arthur Conan Doyle, who was a frequent visitor to the house and the surrounding woodland known as the Enchanted Forest. This is indeed a magical place, with a wild wood area, a Celtic Forest, a North American Wood and a Jurassic Valley. The gardens and woodlands are open throughout the summer months. Groombridge Manor was the model for Birlstone Manor in Conan Doyle's *The Valley of Fear.*

HADLOW DOWN

4 miles SE of Crowborough on the A272

Wilderness Wood

This handsome hamlet is surrounded by winding lanes that weave their way through some of the most glorious Wealden countryside. Just outside Hadlow Down, the **Wilderness Wood** is a living museum of woodland management that does much to maintain the crafts and techniques of

Wilderness Wood Visitor Centre

woodland management. Visitors can see the woodland being tended in the traditional chestnut coppices and plantations of pine, beech and fir. The wood is then harvested and the timber fashioned, using traditional techniques, into all manner of implements in the centre's workshops. There are also woodland trails, a bluebell walk and an adventure playground for children.

WALDRON

7 miles S of Crowborough off the B2192

The 13th-century village Church of All Saints has a lovely kingpost roof and, unusually for its age, a very wide aisle and nave, the reason for which has never quite been explained.

BUXTED

5 miles SW of Crowborough on the A272

Buxted Park Hogge House

A village long dominated by the great house of **Buxted Park**, this Grade II listed building was built along classical lines in 1725. Almost destroyed by fire in 1940, it was restored by the architect Basil Ionides. Although altered from its original design, it was sensitively rebuilt using numerous period pieces from other locations. There are doors and chimney pieces by Robert Adam, cabinets and pillars from grand London houses and country mansions, and a particularly fine staircase from a house in Old Burlington Street in London.

In the 19th century, the house was the home of Lord Liverpool who, wishing to give himself more privacy, decided to move the village further away. The villagers were incensed and refused to move, so his lordship retaliated by declining to repair the estate cottages. Eventually the villagers gave way and moved to the village that is now Buxted. However, several buildings have remained in the old location including, at the entrance to the park gates, the half-timbered **Hogge House**. Dating back to the 16th century, the house was once the home of Ralph Hogge, who is said to have been the first man to cast guns in England, in 1543. The much-restored 13th-century parish church also remains in the park's grounds, and the Jacobean pulpit was once used by William Wordsworth's brother, who was vicar here for a time.

MARESFIELD

5½ miles SW of Crowborough off the A22

Before the turnpikes between London and the south coast were laid through the Weald, this was a remote place. However, in the 18th century, its position at a crossroads on the turnpike ensured its development. The tall Georgian Chequers Inn is arguably the village's oldest building and a fine example of its type. Close by is a white-painted iron milestone with the number 41 and four bells and bows in outline. One of a whole chain of such milestones that stood on the old turnpike road, this is a particularly witty one as it refers to the distance, in miles, from Maresfield to Bow Bells in London.

In the neighbouring village of Fletching is one of the loveliest churches in East Sussex. It was here in May 1264 that Simon de Montfort kept vigil the night before he and his troops defeated Henry III at the Battle of Lewes. It is said that some of the knights who fell in the battle are buried in full armour beneath the nave.

PILTDOWN

7½ miles SW of Crowborough off the A272

Though the village itself is not well known, its name certainly is. In 1912, an ancient skull was discovered by a Lewes solicitor and amateur archaeologist, Charles Dawson, in the grounds of Barcombe Manor. At the time, archaeologists the world over were looking for a 'missing link' between man and the ape and the skull seemed to fit the bill. It had a human braincase and an ape-like jaw. The find was believed to be about 150,000 years old, but it was not until the 1950s, with much-improved scientific dating techniques, that the skull was shown to be a fake. It was actually the braincase of a medieval man who had suffered a bone-thickening disease, and the jaw of an orang-utan, both carefully treated to suggest fossilisation. The perpetrator of the hoax was never discovered.

UCKFIELD

7 miles SW of Crowborough on the B2102

Situated in the woodland of the Weald, on the River Uck, this was once a small village at the intersection of the London to Brighton turnpike road with an ancient pilgrims' way between Canterbury and Winchester. When the stagecoaches arrived, a number of coaching inns sprang up. Before this, the village had been a centre of the iron industry thanks to its plentiful supplies of wood and water.

However, despite these advantages, Uckfield remained small until the 19th century, when a period of rapid expansion followed the arrival of the railway.

Several of the old coaching inns survived the move from horse-drawn to steam-powered travel, and among the Victorian buildings there is Bridge Cottage, a very fine example of a 15th-century hall house.

SHEFFIELD GREEN

8 miles SW of Crowborough on the A275

Bluebell Railway   Sheffield Park and Gardens

The village takes its name from the manor house, a Tudor building that was remodelled in the 1770s by James Wyatt for John Baker Holroyd, MP, the 1st Earl of Sheffield. At the same time as creating his mansion, Sheffield Park, the Earl had Capability Brown and Humphry Repton landscape the gardens. While living here, the Earl's great friend Edward Gibbon came to stay during the last months of his life, and it was during this time that he wrote much of his epic *Decline and Fall of the Roman Empire* in the library.

A later inhabitant, the 3rd Earl of Sheffield, was a keen cricketer and was the first to organise the test tours between England and Australia. At the same time he began a tradition that the visiting team come to **Sheffield Park** to play their first match against the Earl of Sheffield's XI. Though the house remains in private hands, the splendid gardens belong to the National Trust and are open to the public. From the mass of daffodils and bluebells in spring, to the blaze of colour from the rare trees and shrubs in

Sheffield Park Gardens

TRADING BOUNDARIES

Sheffield Green, nr Fletching, East Sussex TN22 3RB
Tel: 01825 790200
website: www.tradingboundaries.com

TRADING BOUNDARIES

Trading Boundaries offers an enticing and eclectic mix of furniture and lifestyle products from all over the world.

A passion for sourcing the finest products for its customers – including quality furniture, vibrant textiles, architectural pieces, beautiful jewellery, stunning antiques and artefacts – is the inspiration behind everything it does.

Trading Boundaries is filled with an ever changing collection of wonderful finds; beautiful and often one-off pieces simply unavailable anywhere else – an 'Aladdin's cave' where customers will always find something new and exciting. All products are sourced directly from overseas manufacturers, giving outstanding quality to customers at unmatched prices.

The showroom is complemented by the fully licensed Elephant Café Bar where customers can enjoy a fresh and appealing menu and a year-long programme of live music events.

Providing a tranquil and relaxing shopping environment, the award-winning Courtyard houses a number of high quality shops, offering something for everyone – from children's toys, home wares and furniture to designer women's wear and handbags.

Trading Boundaries is housed in splendid Georgian Grade II* listed buildings in the heart of the Sussex countryside. The former coaching inn is a well known landmark situated in an area of outstanding natural beauty, close to The Bluebell Steam Railway, The Sheffield Park National Trust Gardens and The Ashdown Forest (home of Winnie the Pooh).

Opening times: Mon-Sat 10am – 6pm
Sunday 11am-5pm, Thurs open for breakfast from 8.30am.

On the A275 just north of the Sheffield Park National Trust Garden and the Bluebell Steam Railway.

VILLANDRY HOME

The Courtyard, Trading Boundaries, Sheffield Green, nr Fletching, East Sussex TN22 3RB
Tel: 01825 790890 Mob: 07929 347288
website: www.villandry.co.uk

Villandry is the unique home interiors shop with a wide variety of interesting merchandise to adorn the most discerning of homes. Recently rejuvenated under the ownership of Sarah Cotter, Villandry is located within the grounds of Trading Boundaries, an exclusive array of courtyard shops, surrounding beautiful gardens and featuring the popular Elephant restaurant and cafeteria.

With a veritable variety of goods on display a visit to Villandry is more than just a shopping experience, it offers an opportunity to find exclusive items that will add a certain character to any home, ranging from furniture, linen, crockery, candles, gifts and accessories the list goes on.

Sarah, personally selects her goods from throughout France and other European cities, enjoying exclusive distribution rights to many ranges as well as having established brands such as Linum, Cote Table, Cote Bastide, Le Pere Pelletier and many more.

The constantly changing selection of goods ensures that shoppers return again and again with many regular customers attending VIP evenings to see the newest of products before they go on general sales.

autumn, there is always plenty to look at and enjoy.

Not far from the house, in the village, lies the Sheffield Arms, a coaching inn built by the 1st Earl in the 18th century. Local stories told of a cave behind the inn with an underground passageway to a nearby farmhouse that was used by smugglers and, in order to test out the truth of the tales, three ducks were shut in the cave. After 10 days, one of the ducks reappeared - in the cellars of the farmhouse.

The village is also the terminus of the **Bluebell Railway**, and the cricketing Earl would surely have been pleased with the railway's success today as he was on the board of the Lewes and East Grinstead Railway that originally built the line. For details of the line and timetables call 01825 720825, or visit the website www.bluebell-railway.co.uk.

CHAILEY

9 miles SW of Crowborough on the A275

Chailey Common

This large and scattered parish comprises three villages: North Chailey, Chailey and South Common. Though small, Chailey has some impressive old buildings, including the 13th-century parish church and a moated rectory. To the north, lies **Chailey Common**, a nature reserve covering some 450 acres of wet and dry heathland where Chailey Windmill can be found. Unlike many Sussex windmills, Chailey's splendid smock mill was saved from ruin just in time.

Overlooking the common is Chailey Heritage, which was founded in 1903 as a home for boys with tuberculosis from the East End of London. The home has become a learning centre for children with disabilities and has a worldwide reputation.

NEWICK

9 miles SW of Crowborough on the A272

The village is centred around its large green on which stands an unusual long-handled pump, erected to mark Queen Victoria's Diamond Jubilee in 1897. The actor Dirk Bogarde spent some time in the area and was given his first big acting part in an amateur production here in the 1930s.

Post Mill, Nutley

NUTLEY

5 miles SW of Crowborough on the A22

Nutley Windmill

The village is home to **Nutley Windmill**, Sussex's oldest working windmill. It was restored in 1968 by a group of enthusiasts after it had stood unused and neglected for over sixty years.

ASHDOWN FOREST

3 miles W of Crowborough on the B2026

Ashdown Forest

This ancient tract of sandy heathland and woodland on the high ridges of the Weald is the largest area in southeast England that has never been ploughed or put to agricultural use. The original meaning of 'forest' was as a royal hunting ground and this is exactly what **Ashdown Forest** was. The earliest record dates from 1268, and its thriving population of deer made it a favourite sporting place. However, the area was used long before this, and in prehistoric times there was a network of tracks across the forest. Later, the Romans built a road straight across it and, by the time of the Norman invasion, the rights of the commoners living on its fringes to gather wood for fuel, cut peat and graze cattle were well established.

During medieval times it was a great place for sport and a 'pale', or ditch, was dug around it to keep the deer within its confines. A famous sporting owner was John of Gaunt, Duke of Lancaster, and during his ownership the forest became known as Lancaster Great Park. Henry VIII and James I were frequent visitors in their time. By the end of the 15th century, much of the woodland had been cut down to be used as fuel for the area's iron industry; the forest was neglected during the Civil War and by 1657 no deer remained.

Today, the forest is designated an Area of Outstanding Natural Beauty, a Site of Special Scientific Interest and a Special Protection Area for birds. It is a place of recreation with many picnic areas and scenic viewpoints and open access for walking throughout. The deer have returned and the clumps of Scotch pines that make prominent landmarks on the higher points of the forest were planted in the 19th century.

WYCH CROSS

6 miles W of Crowborough on the A275

Ashdown Forest Llama Park

Marking the western limit of Ashdown Forest, local folklore has it that the village's name is derived from a cross that was erected on the spot where the body of Richard de Wyche, Bishop of Chichester, rested overnight on the journey from Kent to its burial place in Chichester during the 13th century. This is the location of the **Ashdown Forest Llama Park**, one of the top visitor attractions in Sussex. The herd, which arrived here in 1987, now numbers more than 100 llamas and alpacas, and in 2007 they were joined from Sweden by the reindeers Dasher, Dancer and Blitzen. The 30 acres also includes a farm trail, picnic area, adventure play area, coffee shop, knitwear and gift shop, and a museum. The Park is open all year from 10 to 5 (or until dusk if earlier).

FOREST ROW

6 miles NW of Crowborough on the A22

This hillside village in Ashdown Forest is a popular place with walkers and also a good starting point for wonderful forest drives. The village was founded in the late Middle Ages when the forest was still extremely dense in places and provided a thick swathe of vegetation between the Thames Valley and the south coast.

Unusually, many of the village's buildings are older than the parish church, which dates only from 1836. The village is also the proud owner of a stone wall that commemorates a visit made by President John F Kennedy.

HAMMERWOOD

7 miles NW of Crowborough off the A264

Hammerwood Park

Down a potholed lane lies **Hammerwood Park**, a splendid mansion that was built in

1792 by Benjamin Latrobe, the architect of the Capitol and the White House in Washington DC (Latrobe's work was much admired by Thomas Jefferson and he became Surveyor of Public Buildings in 1803). The house has had a chequered history. Divided into flats in the 1960s, it was bought by the rock group Led Zeppelin in the 1970s, and was rescued from ruin in the 1980s.

HARTFIELD

4 miles NW of Crowborough on the B2026

Pooh Corner

An old hunting settlement on the edge of the Ashdown Forest, which takes its name from the adult male red deer, or hart. The village is very closely associated with A A Milne and Winnie the Pooh. Milne lived at Cotchford Farm, just outside Hartfield, and he set his books, which he wrote in the 1920s, in the forest. Designed to entertain his son, Christopher Robin, the books have been delighting children ever since and, with the help of illustrations by E H Shepard, the landscape around Hartfield has been brought to millions around the world.

In the village lies the 300-year-old sweet shop to which Christopher Robin was taken each week by his nanny. Now called **Pooh Corner**, this is a special place to visit for both children and those who remember the stories from their own childhood. Full of Winnie the Pooh memorabilia, the shop caters for all tastes as long as it involves Winnie. All the famous Enchanted Places lie within the parish of Hartfield. Poohsticks Bridge, a timber bridge, crosses the little Posingford Stream in Posingford Wood, which can be reached from a car park off the B2026 Uckfield Road; the bridge was fully restored in 1979. A A Milne wrote only two stories about his son and the bear of very little brain, *Winnie-the-Pooh* (1926) and *The House at Pooh Corner* (1928). But Pooh fans can look forward to an addition to the books, due to be published in October 2009: the challenge for the distinguished author David Benedictus and illustrator Mark Burgess in *Return to the Hundred Acre Wood* is to revive a much-loved series in a way that is sympathetic to the originals without being a pastiche.

WITHYHAM

3½ miles NW of Crowborough on the B2110

This small village, with its church and pub, was the home of the Sackville family from around 1200. The original village church was struck by lightning in 1663. The lightning was said to have come in through the steeple, melted the bells and left through the chancel, tearing apart monuments on its route. Completely rebuilt following the destruction, the church incorporates some original 14th-century features including the west tower. The Sackville Chapel was commissioned in 1677 to house a memorial to Thomas Sackville, who had died aged 13. The marble memorial incorporates life-size figures of the boy and his parents. There is also a memorial to Vita Sackville-West, the poet and owner of Sissinghurst Castle in Kent, who died in 1962.

Burwash

Bateman's

Standing on a hill surrounded by land that is marsh for part of the year, Burwash is an exceptionally pretty village, whose main street is lined with delightful 17th and 18th-century timber-framed and weatherboarded cottages. Among the buildings is Rampyndene, a handsome timber-framed house with a sweeping roof that was built in 1699 by a wealthy local timber merchant. Between the 15th and 17th centuries, Burwash was a major centre of the Wealden iron industry, which brought great prosperity to the village.

However, it is not the village that brings most people to Burwash, though it certainly deserves attention, but a house just outside. In 1902, Rudyard Kipling moved from Rottingdean to **Bateman's** (see panel below) to combat the growing problem of over-enthusiastic sightseers. Located down a steep and narrow lane, the Jacobean house was originally built in 1634 for a prosperous local ironmaster. With its surrounding 33 acres of beautiful grounds, landscaped by Kipling and his wife, it proved the perfect retreat.

Kipling and his wife lived here until their deaths - his in 1936 and hers just three years later - and during his time here the author wrote many of his famous works, including *Puck of Pook's Corner*, the poem *If* and the *Sussex* poems. Now in the care of the National Trust, the rooms of the house have been left as they were when the Kiplings lived here, and among the personal items on display is a watercolour of Rudyard Lake in Staffordshire, the place where his parents met and which they nostalgically remembered at the time of their son's birth in Bombay. Also here is a series of terracotta plaques that were designed by Kipling's father, Lockwood Kipling, and which he used to illustrate his novel *Kim*. Lockwood was an architectural sculptor and went to India as the principal of an art school; he later became the curator of Lahore Museum.

While the family lived at Bateman's their only son, John, was killed on active duty during World War I at Loos, France in 1915. A tablet in the village church remembers the 18-year-old.

Around Burwash

THREE LEG CROSS

4 miles N of Burwash off the B2099

Bewl Bridge Reservoir

In 1975, the Southern Water Authority dammed the River Bewl to create **Bewl Bridge Reservoir**, the largest area of inland water in the southeast of England. A great many buildings were lost under the water but one, the 15th-century Dunsters Mill, was taken down, brick by brick, before the waters rose and re-sited above the high water level. Another couple of timber-framed farm

Bateman's

Burwash, Etchingham, East Sussex TN19 7DS
Tel: 01435 882302
website: www.nationaltrust.org.uk

The interior of this beautiful 17th century Jacobean house, Rudyard Kipling's home from 1902 to 1936, reflects the author's strong associations with the East. There are many oriental rugs and artefacts, and most of the rooms – including his book-lined study – are much as Kipling left them. The delightful grounds run down to the small River Dudwell with its watermill, and contain roses, wild flowers, fruit and herbs. Kipling's Rolls Royce is also on display.

buildings in the valley were also uprooted and sent to the Weald and Downland Museum at Singleton.

The land around Bewl Bridge is a Country Park and has much to offer, including lakeside walks, trout fishing, pleasure boat trips and glorious countryside.

TICEHURST

3½ miles N of Burwash on the B2099

Pashley Manor Gardens

This ancient village is filled with attractive tile-hung and white weather boarded buildings that are so characteristic of the settlements along the Sussex-Kent border. Among the particularly noteworthy buildings here are Furze House, a former workhouse, and Whatman's, an old carpenter's cottage with strangely curving walls. The village is also home to **Pashley Manor Gardens**, which surround a Grade I listed timber-framed house that dates from 1550. With waterfalls, ponds and a moat, these romantic gardens are typically English, with numerous varieties of shrub roses, hydrangeas and peonies adding colour and lushness at every corner. Less formally, there is a woodland area and a chain of ponds that are surrounded by rhododendrons, azaleas and climbing roses. The gardens and house are privately owned, but the gardens are open to the public throughout the summer.

ETCHINGHAM

2 miles NE of Burwash on the A265

This scattered settlement, located in the broad lush valley of the River Rother, was home in the Middle Ages to the fortified manor of the de Echyngham family. Built to protect a crossing point on the River Rother, the house, which stood where the station now stands, has long gone. Just outside the village lies Haremere Hall, an impressive Jacobean manor house now rented for holiday accommodation.

BRIGHTLING

2½ miles S of Burwash off the B2096

Sugar Loaf Mausoleum

The character of this tiny hillside village is completely overshadowed by the character of one of its former residents. It is certainly not unkind to say that the Georgian eccentric, 'Mad' Jack Fuller, was larger than life since he weighed some 22 stones and was affectionately referred to as the 'Hippopotamus'. A local ironmaster, squire and generous philanthropist, 'Mad' Jack, who sat as an MP for East Sussex between 1801 and 1812, was elected only after a campaign that had cost him and his supporters a massive £50,000. Fuller was one of the first people to recognise the talents of a young painter, J M W Turner, and he was also responsible for saving Bodiam Castle from ruin.

However, it is for his series of imaginative follies that this colourful character is best remembered. He commissioned many of the buildings to provide work for his foundry employees during the decline of the iron industry and among those that remain today are Brightling Observatory, now a private house, a Rotunda Temple on his estate, and the Brightling Needle. The 40-foot stone obelisk was built on a rise to the north of the village which is itself 650 feet above sea level.

One of Fuller's more eccentric buildings was the result of a wager. Having struck a bet with a friend on the number of spires that were visible from Brightling Park, Fuller arrived back to find that the steeple of Dallington church, which he had included in the bet, was not visible. In order to win the bet, Fuller quickly ordered his men to erect a 35-foot mock spire in a meadow on a direct line with Dallington, and the monument is affectionately referred to as the **Sugar Loaf**. Perhaps Fuller's greatest structure is his **Mausoleum**, a 25-foot pyramid, which he built in the parish churchyard some 24 years before his death. The story went around that Fuller was buried inside in a sitting position, wearing a top hat and holding a bottle of claret. However, despite the appropriateness of this image of his life, the parish church quashed the idea by stating that he was buried in the normal, horizontal position.

CROSS IN HAND

8 miles W of Burwash on the A267

This intriguingly named settlement lies on a busy road junction that has a post mill standing in the triangle formed by the converging roads. Certainly worth a second glance, the windmill at one time stood five miles away at Uckfield.

CADE STREET

5 miles W of Burwash on the B2096

This hamlet, used as a street market until the early 20th century, is reputed to be the place where the notorious Jack Cade, leader of the Kentish rebellion, was killed in 1450 by the High Sheriff of Kent, Alexander Iden. A stone memorial marks the spot where he fell, and on it is inscribed the moral, 'This is the Success of all Rebels, and this Fortune chanceth ever to Traitors'.

HEATHFIELD

6 miles W of Burwash on the A265

To the east of the town centre lies the large expanse of Heathfield Park, once owned by

HOLLY GROVE B&B

Holly Grove, Little London, Heathfield,
East Sussex TN21 0NU
Tel: 01435 803375
e-mail: jochristie@btinternet.com
website: www.hollygrovebedandbreakfast.co.uk

In the tiny village of Little London, on the A267, **Holly Grove** is the perfect place for a well-earned break. Light and roomy, it stands in south-facing gardens and grounds bordered by a stream in a quiet country lane. The accommodation comprises the Nutcracker Suite, the New Room and the Stable. 2 single beds can be added to the Nutcracker Suite, the New Room is a smaller en suite double and the Stable is a twin room with private bathroom. A heated outdoor swimming pool is a real bonus in the summer months, and guests can sit by the pool, on the terrace or in the garden listening to the birdsong. In the cooler months the open fire in the lounge and the log burner in the Great Space beckon. The Christie family are the most welcoming of hosts and always do their best to ensure that their guests have a pleasant stay – the number of return visits show how well they succeed! They share their home and paddock with cats, dogs and horses; guests can bring their four-legged friends by arrangement, and a spare stable is available if needed. No children under 12. There's excellent walking, riding and cycling hereabouts, and the many varied delights of the Sussex coast and countryside are within easy reach.

THE BREWERS ARMS

Vines Cross, Heathfield,
East Sussex TN21 9EW
Tel: 01435 812288
e-mail: info@brewersarmspub.co.uk
website: www.brewersarmspub.co.uk

Since opening the doors in May 2006 owners/ hosts Tim and Chas Earley have been busy putting the **Brewers Arms** on the gastropub scene. Tim has many years' experience as a chef, with spells at some of the top restaurants at home and overseas, while Chas, also a trained chef, does an excellent job front of house with his passion for real ales and fine wines. The pub brings in the customers with real food at realistic prices, using good seasonal produce mostly shot, reared or grown in Sussex; everything is made on the premises, from the bread to the chutneys and preserves and the luscious hokey pokey ice cream.

This is also very much a friendly local, relaxed and informal, with a warm welcome for all who pass through the door. The bar is open lunchtime and evening and all day Friday, Saturday and Sunday, and food is served every session. The village of Vines Cross is located off the A267 or B2202 a short drive south of Heathfield.

General Sir George Augustus Elliot (later Lord Heathfield), the Governor of Gibraltar and commander of the British garrison that successfully withstood attacks from both France and Spain between 1779 and 1782. Despite the wall surrounding the grounds, Gibraltar Tower, a castellated folly erected on his estate in his honour, can be seen.

Heathfield remained a quiet and undistinguished town until the arrival of the Tunbridge Wells to Eastbourne railway in the 19th century, after which it grew to become an important market town for the local area.

MAYFIELD

6 miles NW of Burwash off the A267

Mayfield Palace

This ancient settlement, one of the most attractive villages in the area, possesses one of the finest main streets in East Sussex, with a number of fine 15th to 17th-century houses. According to local legend, St Dunstan, a skilled blacksmith by trade, stopped here in the 10th century to preach Christianity to the pagan people of this remote Wealden community. While working at his anvil, St Dunstan was confronted by the Devil disguised as a beautiful maiden. When she attempted to seduce the missionary, he spotted that her feet were cloven and grabbed her by the nose with a pair of red-hot tongs. The Devil gave out an almighty scream and beat a hasty retreat. But he soon returned, this time dressed as a traveller in need of new shoes for his horse. Dunstan again saw through the deception and, threatening Satan with his blacksmith's tools, forced him to promise never again to enter a house that had a horseshoe above the door.

St Dunstan became Archbishop of Canterbury in 959 and, some time later, **Mayfield Palace**, one of the great residences of the medieval Archbishops of Canterbury, was built here. Though little remains of the grand palace, a Roman Catholic Convent School incorporates the surviving buildings. St Dunstan also founded here a simple timber church, replaced by a stone structure in the 13th century. It was rebuilt after a fire in the 14th century and again after a lightning strike in the 17th century. The present day Church of St Dunstan is a conglomeration of styles, incorporating a 13th-century tower, a Jacobean pulpit, a font dated 1666, and some 17th and 18th-century monuments to the local Baker family.

WADHURST

5 miles NW of Burwash on the B2099

Church of St Peter & St Paul

This was another great centre of the Wealden iron industry in the 17th and 18th centuries, and it was also one of the last places in Sussex to hold out against the improved coal-fired smelting techniques that had taken root in the north. Though the village **Church of St Peter and St Paul** is not quite built of iron, the floor is almost entirely made up of iron tomb slabs, a unique collection marking the graves of local ironmasters who died here between 1617 and 1772.

Many of Wadhurst's fine buildings date from the iron industry's heyday, including the large Queen Anne vicarage on the main street, built by John Legas, the town's chief ironmaster. In the late 19th century, the village found fame when an important prize fight was held here, with many of the spectators travelling down from London by train to this otherwise rather obscure venue.

The Cinque Ports and the East Sussex Coast

The story of this area of the East Sussex Coast is, of course, that of the events leading up to October 14th, 1066. William, Duke of Normandy, came here to claim the throne of England and, after defeating Harold a few miles from the town of Hastings, this is exactly what he did. Hastings and Battle, the town that grew up around the abbey that was built on the site of the battlefield, have a concentration of museums and exhibitions on the events of the 11th century. The victorious Normans soon set about building castles and fortifications from which to defend their new territory, along with religious buildings. Today this area is still rich in Norman architecture.

The south coast was always susceptible to invasion and, in the days before the Royal Navy, the confederation of Cinque Ports was established to provide a fleet of ships to defend the coast. Many of the towns that were part of the confederation seem unlikely sources of ships today, but the silting up of many of the harbours has changed the landscape of the East Sussex coast considerably in the past 1,000 years.

More recently, the coast has been the preserve of holiday-makers taking advantage of a moderate climate and bracing sea air. St Leonards was created in the 1820s and went on to become a fashionable resort, while the small and more modest Bexhill-on-Sea is home to the impressive De La Warr Pavilion, constructed from steel in the 1930s.

Perhaps the most picturesque of the coastal settlements is the ancient town of Rye. Situated on a hill and once a great haunt for smugglers, the changing fortunes of the town have left it with a great number of handsome old buildings, making it a charming place to visit.

Hastings

1066 Story · The Maritime Stade

Shipwreck Heritage Centre

Fishermen's Museum · Smugglers Adventure

Museum of Local History · Hastings Embroidery

Underwater World

Long before William the Conqueror landed on the beach at nearby Pevensey, Hastings was the principal town of a small Saxon province that straddled the county border between Sussex and Kent. Its name comes from 'Haestingas', a Saxon tribal name, and, during the reign of Edward the Confessor, the town was well known for its sailors and ships. In fact, the town became so important that it even had its own mint. Earlier, during the 9th century, when the Danes were occupying the town, the crowing of a cockerel, awoken by the movements of the townsfolk preparing to surprise their oppressors, alerted the

Hastings Castle

occupying force to the uprising. As a vengeance on all cockerels, the people of Hastings instituted a game called 'cock in the pot', where sticks were thrown at an earthenware pot containing a bird. Whoever threw the stick that broke the pot was given the cockerel as his prize and the game continued to be played each Shrove Tuesday until the 19th century.

The Maritime Stade, Hastings

Following the Battle of Hastings, which actually took place six miles away at Battle, the victorious William returned to Hastings where the Normans began to build their first stone castle in England. Choosing the high ground of West Hill as their site, the massive structure is now in ruins and all that can be seen on the clifftop are the original motte and parts of the curtain wall. Here, too, at Hastings Castle the **1066 Story** is on permanent display. Housed in a medieval siege tent, the exhibition uses audio-visual techniques to tell the story of the Conquest and the Castle. Other attractions include the 'Whispering Dungeons' and the once grand Eastern Gateway.

The West Hill also contains a system of elaborate underground passages, known as St Clement's Cave, where the naturally formed tunnel network has been extended. The caves were leased to Joseph Golding, who spent a great deal of time fashioning the sandstone into sculptures, arcades and galleries, which became one of the town's first commercial sights. Used as air raid shelters during World War II, the caves are now home to the **Smugglers Adventure**, where visitors are told stories of the town's illegal trade by a grizzly old smuggler known as Hairy Jack. After the Conquest, this already important port became a leading Cinque Port, a role it played until the harbour began to silt up in Elizabethan times. Nevertheless, the fishing industry has managed to survive here: **The Stade**, or 'landing place', is home to Europe's largest beach-launched fishing fleet. Boats are pushed across the shingle by tractors to be launched at high tide. On their return, they are pulled back up the beach by winches, and their catches, including herring, mackerel, Dover sole, cod, bass and plaice, are unloaded and sent to the fish market. One of the town's greatest features is the cluster of tall wooden huts used for drying nets and storing fishing tackle. Dating from the 17th century, they are known as net shops or 'deezes'. The Church of St Nicholas, built on the beach to minister to the local fishing community, is now home to the **Fishermen's Museum**, which has as its centrepiece *The Enterprise*, dating from 1912, and one of the last of the town's sailing luggers. Also here, among the displays of fishing tackle, model boats and historic pictures and photographs, is the *Edward and Mary*, the first locally built boat to be fitted

MINSTREL'S REST

21 Greville Road, Ore, Hastings, East Sussex TN35 5AL
Tel: 01424 443500
e-mail: minstrelsrest@hotmail.com
website: www.minstrelsrest.co.uk

Minstrel's Rest is a medieval-themed guest house in the village of Ore, on the northeast edge of Hastings. The location is quiet and peaceful, yet the town centre and the sea front are only five minutes' drive away, making it the perfect base for holidaymakers and business people to relax or explore historic Hastings and 1066 country.

Resident owners Michelle and Phill Wood, who renovated the property from top to toe when they arrived in July 2005, offer comfortable, characterful accommodation in five rooms decorated and furnished in the medieval style that runs through the house. Taliesin the 6th century bard, lends his name to the king-size, four poster en-suite room. Perdigon, Berdic and Blondel, named after a french minstrel and minstrels of William the Conqueror and Richard Lionheart, are en suite doubles, and Taillefer, remembering William's minstrel at the Battle of Hastings, is a twin-bedded room with private bathroom. All have TV, hospitality tray, mini-fridge with fresh milk and juices, and free broadband internet access. An excellent breakfast, including preserves made with home-grown fruit, is served at a Jacobean-style solid oak table using handsome glazed pottery plates and cups.

with an engine. Staying with a maritime theme, the **Shipwreck Heritage Centre** (see panel opposite) is an award-winning museum devoted to the history of wrecked ships. Exhibits on display here include the remains of a Roman ship, a medieval sailing barge sunk on the River Thames in London, the warship *Anne*, beached near Hastings in 1690, and the hull of a Victorian barge. Additional displays cover modern methods that help eliminate the possibility of a shipwreck, including radar and satellite navigation. Next to the Shipwreck Heritage Centre is **Underwater World**, where many of the underwater creatures living off Hastings can be seen. A dramatic glass tunnel under a huge tank allows visitors to walk beneath the ocean – and stay dry.

The old part of Hastings consists of a network of narrow streets and alleyways - or 'twittens' - which lie between West and East Hill. There are two cliff railways, one running up each of the hills. West Hill railway runs underground, taking passengers to Hastings Castle and St Clement's Caves, while the East Hill Railway, the steepest in England, takes passengers to the clifftop and the beginning of Hastings Country Park. This 500-acre park is unlike the clifftops around Eastbourne as the drop here is not sheer, but is split by a series of sloping glens overhung with trees.

The best way to discover the town's many interesting old residential buildings, inns and churches is to take a walk up the High Street and All Saints Street. St Clement's Church, in the High Street, has two cannonballs embedded in its tower, one of which was fired from a French warship, while the Stag Inn, in All Saints Street, has a concealed entrance to a

Shipwreck Heritage Centre

Rock a Nore Road, Hastings, Sussex TN34 3DW
Tel: 01424 437452

This award winning museum is devoted to the history of wrecked ships. Hastings has one of the richest displays of shipwrecks at low tide in Europe. An exciting audio-visual presentation tells the story (the ships featured in the display. These include a medieval sailing barge sunk in the Thames at London; the 70-gun English warship *Anne* beached near Hastings in 1690 during the Battle of Beachy Head; and the Dutch East Indiaman *Amsterdam* that ran aground at Bulverhythe. Additional features include radar, weather satellite, push-button videos and *Primrose*-the last Rye barge. Hearing loop for the deaf. Open all year.

smugglers' secret passage and a pair of macabre 400-year-old mummified cats.

Occupying the old Town Hall, which was built in 1823, the **Museum of Local History** is an excellent place to find information on this historic town. Going right back to the Stone Age, and with a considerable section on the Norman Conquest, the museum also covers the more recent past, including displays on the rise of the Victorian resort, its life as a Napoleonic garrison and its role as a Cinque Port. By contrast, the **Hastings Museum and Art Gallery** on Bohemia Road covers a wider range of exhibits that also take in the county's ancient crafts. Hastings also contains a variety of attractions that are typical of a traditional seaside resort. The 600-foot pier was completed in 1872 and had to be repaired after World War II when, like many piers, it was deliberately holed in two places to prevent it being used as a landing stage for Hitler's forces. According to local legend, the Conqueror's Stone at the head of the pier was used by William the Conqueror as a dining table for his first meal on English soil. The town also has its own version of the Bayeux Tapestry, the **Hastings Embroidery**, made by the Royal School of Needlework and completed in 1966. It was in 1923, in a house in Linton Crescent, that the television pioneer John Logie Baird succeeded in transmitting the image of a man's hand. He later moved to Queens Avenue, later to London and eventually to Bexhill, where he lived in a house near the railway station.

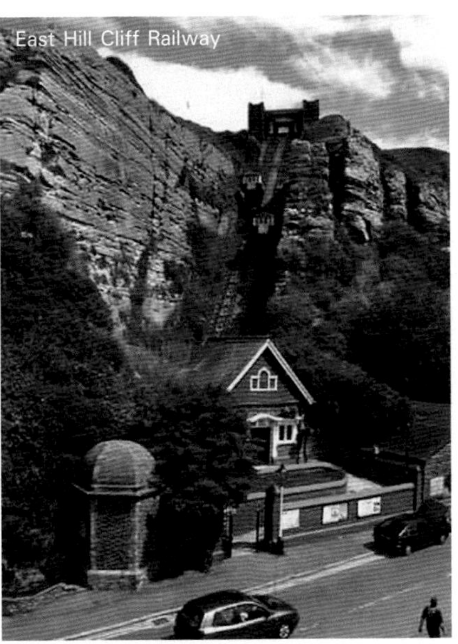
East Hill Cliff Railway

Around Hastings

Brede Place, Brede

WESTFIELD

3½ miles N of Hastings on the A28

This modern redbrick village on the edge of Brede Level has at its old centre weatherboarded cottages and a Saxon church, with a beautiful Norman arch.

Vineyards in this country are still something of a novelty, but the gentle rolling slopes of the South Downs and the high mineral content of the soil are ideal for growing grapes. At Carr Taylor Vineyards, visitors can follow the Vineyard Trail from the vines, to the massive presses that crush two tons of grapes in one load, right through to the bottling plant to see the fascinating process of turning grapes into wine.

BREDE

5 miles N of Hastings on the A28

Situated to the north of the River Brede, this compact village has a long history, shrouded in myth and tales of the supernatural. One particular legend is that of the Brede Giant, based around the 16th-century owner of Brede Place, Sir Goddard Oxenbridge. At over seven feet tall he was certainly a giant and, by all accounts, he was a god-fearing gentleman of the parish. However, some time after his death, stories spread that he was a child-eating monster who was eventually killed by a band of Sussex children who, having got him drunk, sawed him in half - the children of East Sussex holding down one end of him with the children of West Sussex securing the other.

Tombs of the Oxenbridge family can be seen in the small Norman village church, as can a wood carving of the Madonna created by a cousin of Sir Winston Churchill, who died, aged 84, in 1970. This remarkable woman travelled to America, where she learnt to carve in wood while staying for six months on a Native American reservation. In the aftermath of the Russian revolution, she journeyed to Moscow and, staying for two months at the Kremlin, she carved busts of both Lenin and Trotsky.

The more recent Giants of Brede are massive pumping engines hidden behind Baroque and Art Deco buildings in the lovely Brede Valley.

NORTHIAM

9½ miles N of Hastings on the A28

Brickwall House · Great Dixter House

Kent & East Sussex Railway

In this large and picturesque village, characteristic white weatherboarded cottages and a number of fine 17th and 18th-century buildings overlook the triangular green at its heart. Elizabeth I is known to have dined and rested on this green under a great oak tree on her journey through Kent and Sussex in 1573. Her green high-heeled shoes must have been particularly uncomfortable as she took them off here and left them to the villagers, who saved them as a memento of her brief visit. Unfortunately, the vast oak tree, which was said to be over 1,000 years old and was held together by chains and clamps, has died and all that remains of it is its giant stump.

Of the memorable buildings in the village, **Brickwall House** is one of the finest. This imposing 17th-century gentleman's residence was the home of the Frewen family, an old local family who had been living in Northiam since 1573 when the first Frewen came to the village as rector. Well known for its splendid plaster ceilings, it also has a comprehensive series of family portraits from the 17th century. On display in the house are Elizabeth I's famous green shoes, and a sedan chair that belonged to Martha Frewen, who burnt to death in her bedroom in the 1750s. Several members of the family were strict Puritans and one family named their two sons Accepted and Thankful. Despite the handicap of these unusual names, Accepted went on to become first the president of Magdalen College, Oxford, and then the Archbishop of York, while Thankful is remembered for having donated the communion rails to the church in 1683. The church is also home to an impressive 19th-century family mausoleum. Brickwall House, so named because the house and grounds are surrounded by a high stone wall, has some splendid topiary in the gardens, as well as an arboretum and chess garden. Now a private school, the house and grounds are open by appointment only.

Just three miles northwest of Northiam lies **Great Dixter House and Gardens** (see panel below), one of the finest examples of a late medieval hall house, surrounded by a very special garden. Built in the 1450s, the manor house was purchased in 1910 by Nathaniel Lloyd, who then employed Sir Edwin Lutyens to renovate and extend the property. He restored the house to its original medieval

Great Dixter House and Gardens

Great Dixter High Park, Northiam, Sussex TN31 6PH
Tel: 01797 252878
website: www.greatdixter.co.uk

Despite major alterations made about 1595, since removed, the principal medieval features of **Great Dixter House** have remained relatively intact. It is one of the largest surviving timber-framed halls in the country and the fine roof has hammerbeams strengthened with a tiebeam. The fine armourial shields on the hammer beams depict the arms of the Etchinghams, the Dalyngrigges and the Gaynesfords and suggest an approximate building date of between 1440 and 1454.

One of the pleasant features about the gardens is that they lie all around the house. Make a circuit of the gardens and you have made a circuit of the house exterior. Each has good views of the other. Great Dixter nurseries offer a quality service of direct and mail order sales. Most of the plants are raised by the nursery and many can be seen in the fabric of the gardens.

grandeur, as well as adding suitable domestic quarters for an Edwardian household. The Great Hall, constructed of Wealden oak and moved here from nearby Benenden to be incorporated into the building, is one of the largest surviving timber-framed rooms in the country. Many of the original rooms are filled with antique furniture, and there are some very fine examples of 18th-century needlework.

However, it is the gardens that make Great Dixter so special. The imaginative design was laid out by Lutyens and various new features were added, such as the sunken garden, the topiary lawn and the meadow garden. Begun by Nathaniel Lloyd and his wife, Daisy, the gardens were added to by their son Christopher (Christo), who died in January 2006. A regular contributor to gardening magazines, Christopher's lively and inventive approach to horticulture obviously stemmed from working in the gardens. A mixture of formal and wild, there are many rare plant specimens on display here and the gardens are open to the public.

Northiam Station is also on the **Kent & East Sussex Railway**, which was restored in 1990 and has steam trains running through a pleasant rural landscape for 10 miles between Tenterden in Kent and Bodiam during the summer months. At one time too, the River Rother was navigable to this point and barges were brought upstream to be unloaded at the busy quay. This must have been an ancient port as in the 1820s the remains of a Viking long ship were found in the mud by the river where they must have lain hidden since the 9th century.

BODIAM

10½ miles N of Hastings off the B2244

Castle

Situated in the valley of the River Rother, this attractive village, whose name is pronounced 'Bodjem', is home to one of the most romantic castles in the country. In the 1380s, Richard II granted Sir Edward Dalyngrygge a licence to fortify his manor house in order to defend the upper reaches of the then navigable River Rother. Thankfully, Dalyngrygge chose to interpret the licence liberally and thus one of the last great medieval fortresses in England was built. Construction on **Bodiam Castle** was begun in 1385, when the technology of castle building was at its peak and before the use of gunpowder. Completely surrounded by a wide moat, the arrow slits, cannon ports and aptly-named murder holes (through which objects were thrown at attackers below) were never used in anger. However, there was a minor skirmish here in 1484, and during the Civil War the castle surrendered without a shot being fired.

Bodiam Castle

A long period of decay followed in the 17th and 18th centuries until, in 1829, plans to dismantle the castle were thwarted by 'Mad' Jack Fuller of Brightling and a programme of restoration begun. This was started by George Cubitt at the end of the 19th century, and completed by Lord Curzon in 1919. On his death in the 1920s, Lord Curzon left the castle to the National Trust and they continued the restoration programme, including replacing the floors in the towers so that visitors can climb to the top of the battlements and gain a real feel of the security that Bodiam must have offered its inhabitants over the centuries.

GUESTLING THORN

4½ miles NE of Hastings on the A259

With no real village centre and an isolated ancient church found down a small lane, it is hard now to believe that this was probably the meeting place for the important governing body of the Cinque Ports. However, as it lay on neutral territory and was not controlled by any of the ports, it would have been a suitable venue for all the parties concerned.

PETT

4 miles NE of Hastings off the A259

Pett level

Situated on top of a hill, the village overlooks, to the south, **Pett Level**, a vast expanse of drained marshland that now consists of watercourses and meadows. Dotted with small lakes the area provides a suitable sanctuary for wildfowl.

FAIRLIGHT

3 miles NE of Hastings off the A259

Separated from Hastings to the west by its country park, this village is a small settlement of, chiefly, old coastguard cottages. The 19th-century greystone church occupies a magnificent position overlooking the coast and its tower can be seen for miles out to sea. So much so, in fact, that when the weathervane blew down the villagers were inundated with requests from anxious sailors asking for it to be replaced. In the churchyard, among a number of elaborate tombstones, is the rather neglected final resting place of Richard D'Oyly Carte, the founder of the opera company linked with the works of Gilbert and Sullivan.

To the west of the village lies Fairlight Glen, an attractive place where a gentle stream approaches the sea through a steep sided woodland valley. The Lovers' Seat placed here is said to be in memory of a girl who waited on this spot for her lover to return to her from his ship. Unlike many similar tales, this one had a happy ending as, not only did the girl's lover return from overseas unharmed, but her parents also consented to their marriage.

ST LEONARDS

1 mile W of Hastings on the A259

Gardens

St Leonards was created in the 1820s as a fashionable seaside resort by the celebrated London architect, James Burton, who was also responsible for designing much of Bloomsbury. The centrepiece of Burton's plans was the Royal Victoria Hotel, which, although still standing, is now rather overshadowed by the vast Marina Court, built in the 1930s to resemble an ocean liner. Assisted by his son, Decimus, a talented architect in his own right who later designed the Wellington Arch at Hyde Park Corner, London, James Burton went on to create a model seaside town that was designed to attract wealthy and aristocratic visitors.

SHERWOOD GUEST HOUSE

15 Grosvenor Crescent, St Leonards-on-Sea,
East Sussex TN38 0AA
Tel: 01424 43331
e-mail: jimandjeanette@btinternet.com
website: www.sherwoodhastings.co.uk

Enthusiastic owners Jim and Jeanette Morgan extend a warm and friendly welcome to guests at **Sherwood Guest House**, their home opposite West Marina Gardens, the beach and the sea. West St Leonards-on-Sea Station is nearby, and there's easy access to the main road network. The versatile centrally heated accommodation numbers nine rooms – two singles that share a bathroom, a twin, three doubles (two with en suite facilities) and three en suite family rooms. Travel cots and a high chair are available on request; rooms at the front enjoy sea views. The house has a licensed bar, and a multi-choice full English or Continental breakfast is served in the dining room.

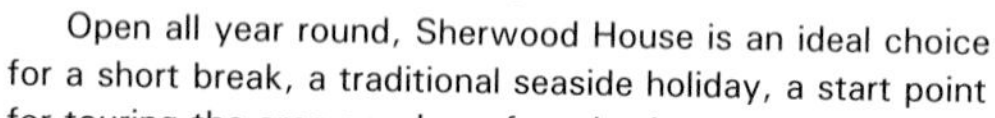

Open all year round, Sherwood House is an ideal choice for a short break, a traditional seaside holiday, a start point for touring the area or a base for a business trip. St Leonards itself is a pleasant spot with some delightful gardens, and its big neighbour Hastings and the area inland are rich in history.

In its heyday, the town's formal social activities took place, behind the Royal Victoria Hotel, in the Assembly Rooms. A classical building, it had a tunnel running between the two so that the hotel could provide suitable refreshments for the wide variety of functions. The Assembly Rooms are now the Masonic Hall. During the Victorian era, this well-organised town even had its own services area. Mercatoria was the tradesmen's quarters and Lavatoria the laundrywomen's.

The delightfully informal **St Leonards Gardens** stand a little way back from the seafront and were originally private gardens maintained by subscriptions from the local residents. Acquired by the local council in 1880, they form a tranquil area of lakes, mature trees and gently sloping lawns that can now be enjoyed by everyone.

In the churchyard of the parish church, which was destroyed by a flying bomb in 1944 and rebuilt in a conservative modern style in the 1960s, lies James Burton's curious tomb - a pyramid vault where he and several other family members are buried.

BULVERHYTHE

3 miles W of Hastings on the A259

A port during the Middle Ages, in the 19th century the noise made by the shingle as it was washed by the tide was called the 'Bulverhythe Bells' and their sound was seen as an indicator of bad weather by local fishermen. Just off the coast, at very low tides, the remains of the wreck of the Dutch East Indiaman *Amsterdam* are clearly visible.

BEXHILL-ON-SEA

5 miles W of Hastings on the A259

De La Warr Pavilion Museum

This small seaside resort became a popular resort in the 1880s thanks in part to the

De La Warr Pavilion, Bexhill-on-Sea

influential De La Warr family, who lived at the original village of Bexhill, just a mile from the coast. The old Bexhill was an ancient place, with its roots well established in Saxon times, when the land around 'Bexlei' was granted to Bishop Oswald of Selsey by Offa, King of Mercia. Fortunately, a good many of the older buildings have survived the late 19th century development including old weatherboarded cottages, a 14th-century manor house and also the part Norman parish church.

Among the many fine buildings, the **De La Warr Pavilion** stands out. Built in the 1930s by Erich Mendelsohn and Serge Chermayeff, it is a fine example of Art Deco, a style that was becoming fashionable at the time. Looking rather like an ocean-going liner, with its welded steel frame, curves, abundance of glass and terraces, the Grade I listed building is one of the most important modernist buildings in Britain. It was commissioned by Earl de la Warr, Mayor of Bexhill from 1932 to 1934, as a 'peoples' palace by the sea'; recently fully refurbished, it offers a year-round cultural

THE OLD MANSE B&B

18 Terminus Avenue, Bexhill-on-Sea,
East Sussex TN39 3LS
Tel: 01424 216151
e-mail: debbie.march@virgin.net
website: www.theoldmansebexhill.co.uk

Debbie and Eric March welcome Bed & Breakfast guests to **The Old Manse**, their handsome home standing in quiet, mature gardens a short walk from the Bexhill seafront. The letting accommodation consists of two beautifully appointed, spacious rooms named after local parks. The Egerton Suite has en suite facilities, an inviting sofa and plasma TV, and the Polgrave Room is a double (a single bed can be added) with a large adjoining private bathroom. Both have splendidly comfortable beds, luxurious furnishings and a well-stocked beverage tray; wireless internet connection is also available. An excellent breakfast, using organic and fair trade produce whenever possible, is served in the smart south-facing dining room, which opens out onto a covered terrace. The choice includes juices, cereals and preserves, a full English main course or several lighter options, including scrambled eggs & smoked salmon. After a days sightseeing guests can relax and enjoy a selection of teas and homemade cakes. All in all, the Old Manse is a very pleasant, civilised base for discovering 1066 Country and all that Bexhill, its neighbours Hastings and Eastbourne and the Sussex countryside have to offer.

VINTAGE STYLING BY LILLY ROSE

50/52 Sea Road, Bexhill-on-Sea, East Sussex TN40 1JP
Tel: 01424 221444
e-mail: lillyrose60@gmail.com
website: www.lilyroseonline.co.uk

Vintage Retro Neo-Retro

In a double-fronted Victorian building a short walk up from the sea, **Vintage Styling by Lilly Rose** is stocked with an eclectic range of clothing, sloes, jewellery, handbags, textiles and quirky vintage items for the home.

Owner Julia Platt has many years' experience in interior design and fashion, combined with a passion for vintage clothing and fabrics, and acquiring the empty premises in April 2008 gave her the chance to bring her creativity and eye for style to Bexhill. Julia has always had strong views on the environment and on Fair Trade and sees value, quality and desirability in items that many would discard. The shelves are a riot of colour and ideas, a browser's delight, with unusual and quirky items, many beautiful, many salvaged and revived, emphasising Julia's stand against the throwaway society. Prominent among the eyecatching items is her own range of 30s and 40s-inspired trousers in linen, silk and cotton and tops and dresses in vintage fabrics. There are satin pyjamas, antique petticoats, silk and lace lingerie, cushions, kitchenalia, art deco lampshades, obscure paperbacks, locally handmade jewellery, beautiful painted healing stones and so much more – and with the stock changing constantly every visit will uncover new surprises and treasures.

BEXHILL LINENS

57 Western Road, Bexhill-on-Sea, East Sussex TN40 1DT
Tel: 01424 212125

'For All Your Household Linens'

Independently owned with old fashioned service.
We can source items the large stores cannot.

That's the motto of **Bexhill Linens**, which has been owned and run since 2005 by Kerry Roe. Kerry has stocked her shop with bed linen in all sizes and style: blankets, sheets and duvet covers in 100% Egyptian cotton and poly/cotton, duvets and pillows in down or microfibre. But there's much more here than just bed linen, including ready made and made-to-measure curtains, café nets, roller and Venetian blinds, tracks and poles, a wide range of throws, cushions and cushion covers, draught excluders, towels and bath sets, tablecloths, napkins, seat pads, covers for chair backs and arm caps, aprons, tea cosies and lots of useful little gifts.

Bexhill Linens are agents for Sibona, Bronte Blankets and Helena Springfield. Shop hours are 9am to 5pm Monday to Saturday, closed at 1pm on Thursday.

programme exploring a range of responses to modernism by artists, architects and designers.

For what would appear today to be a relatively conservative resort, Bexhill was the first seaside town to allow mixed bathing on its beaches - in 1900! A very progressive move then, the gently sloping shingle beaches still offer safe and clean bathing, as well as facilities for a range of watersports. The town has another first: in 1902, it played host to the birth of British motor racing when a race and other speed trials were held here. The huge Edwardian cars - nine-litre engines were not uncommon - flew along the unmade roads around Galley Hill and stopping was a matter of applying the rear wheel brakes, brute force and luck. Among the competitors were some of the best-known names of early motoring,

WA WAA'S WOOL 'N' BITS

22 Parkhurst Road, Bexhill-on-Sea, East Sussex TN40 1DF
Tel: 01424 222488 e-mail: fran@wawaawools.co.uk
website: www.wawaawools.co.uk

The small seaside resort of Bexhill has plenty to interest the visitor, including a mecca for anyone who loves knitting. **Wa Waa's Wool 'n' Bits** is stocked with a wide selection of yarns from top producers like Debbie Bliss, Noro, Adriafil and Bergère de France. Fran wants buying yarn to be a pleasurable experience and has introduced a 'Knit 'n' Natter' concept – customers can exchange knitting and crochet tips over a cup of tea or coffee. She also holds regular evening knitting and crochet classes.

ARDEN HOUSE

28 Manor Road, Bexhill-on-Sea, East Sussex TN40 1SP
Tel: 01424 225068 e-mail: info@ardenhousebexhill.co.uk
website: www.ardenhousebexhill.co.uk

Arden House offers a quiet, civilised break in a central location close to the town centre, the seafront and the railway station. In his elegant 1920s detached house owner Peter Lapham has three well-appointed bedrooms, a double en suite, a twin-bedded/family room and a double with private bathroom. All are handsomely furnished with mainly antique furniture and have bath and shower rooms that have been recently modernised with up-to date facilities. The rooms are also provided with TVs/videos, digital radios, hospitality trays, mineral water and fresh flowers. There is ample parking available to guests. A full and varied breakfast menu, with the emphasis on local produce, is served in the conservatory that overlooks the mature enclosed garden. There's a beautifully relaxing lounge where guests can unwind after a day's sightseeing and plan the next day's activities.

Bexhill has plenty to interest the visitor, including the town museum and the renowned De La Warr Pavilion, a striking 1930s modernist building named after the family who helped to popularise the town as a resort; it offers a year-round programme of exhibitions and events. The surrounding area is rich in both history and breathtaking scenery making it a wonderful place to enjoy a walk. The room rates at Arden House are very reasonable, and discounts are available for stays of three days or longer.

EVE'S BED & BREAKFAST

20 Hastings Road, Bexhill-on-Sea,
East Sussex TN40 2HH
Tel: 01424 733268
e-mail: evesbandb@googlemail.com
website: www.evesbedandbreakfast.com

Eve's Bed & Breakfast is a beautifully restored Victorian house with masses of character and many original features. It has been run since 2003 by Eve and Barry Davis and is a 4-Star Visit Britain rated guest house. The accommodation comprises four roomy comfortable en suite bedrooms – two doubles and two family rooms, each with its own individual decorative theme. The doubles can be booked as singles. Breakfast is served between 7.30 and 9, and an evening meal is available by arrangement. There's free parking in the drive or on the road right outside the house.

Bexhill, a popular seaside resort, is an excellent choice for a traditional family holiday but is a pleasant place to visit at any time of the year. Among the attractions are the fascinating Bexhill Museum and the striking 1930s De La Warr Pavilion, where year-round exhibitions explore a range of responses to modernism by artists, architects and designers. And the area is rich in scenic and historic appeal, with the story of 1066 and the Battle of Hastings very much to the fore.

including H S Rolls, Herbert Austin and Baron Rothschild. The anniversary of this first race was celebrated here each year until quite recently.

To discover more about the history of this seemingly modern but truly ancient settlement a visit to the **Bexhill Museum** is a must. As well as a range of exhibitions on local wildlife, history, geology and archaeology, there are also dinosaur exhibits and even a Great Crab from Japan.

NINFIELD

7 miles NW of Hastings on the A269

Ashburnham Park

To the north of this village, straggled along a ridge, lies Ashburnham Place, a redbrick house that is much less impressive than it once was. The house has been subject to many alterations over the years, including the addition of a new block in the 1960s. However, the landscaped **Ashburnham Park** has survived much as it was conceived by Capability Brown in the 18th century, though a large number of trees were lost in the hurricane of 1987.

Close to the house lies the parish church where there are several monuments to the landowning Ashburnham family. One member of the family, John Ashburnham, was a supporter of the monarchy in the Civil War and he followed Charles I on his last journey to the scaffold in London. Imprisoned in the Tower by Cromwell, the late king's possessions that he was wearing on the day of his death - his shirt, underclothes, watch and the sheet in which his body was wrapped - came into the hands of the Ashburnham family. These relics were kept in the church following the restoration of Charles II to the throne and for many years

NOBLES RESTAURANT

17 High Street, Battle,
East Sussex TN33 0AE
Tel: 01424 774422
e-mail: contact@noblesrestaurant.co.uk
website: www.noblesrestaurant.co.uk

'We created **Nobles Restaurant** to offer our customers a modern dining experience. We regularly change our menus to incorporate the best local and seasonal produce available.'

That's the philosophy of owner/head chef Paul Noble, whose 30 years' experience includes spells at such leading establishments as the Goring and Landmark Hotels in London and the Royal Crescent in Bath. He opened his restaurant in June 2007 in a Grade II listed building in the High Street, a stylish, relaxed setting with cream, green and red walls, a modern red-panelled bar and a pleasant sun terrace. Paul's menus delight with such beautifully prepared and presented dishes such as tempura-battered plaice or lemon sole, blue swimmer crab risotto, a fish mixed grill and an amazing pork dish with chargrilled loin, braised belly and roast fillet served with a faggot of black pudding and chorizo. Desserts like red wine poached pear and steamed syrup sponge pudding keep the enjoyment level high to the end, and the fine food is complemented by a well-chosen, well-annotated wine list and friendly, attentive service led by manager Debbie Grant. Nobles is open for lunch and dinner Monday - Saturday.

were believed to offer a cure for scrofula, a glandular disease called King's Evil.

BATTLE

6 miles NW of Hastings on the A2100

- Battle Abbey
- Prelude to Battle Exhibition
- Museum of Local History
- Yesterday's World
- Battle of Hastings Site

This historic settlement is, of course, renowned as being the site of the momentous battle, on October 14th 1066, between the armies of Harold, Saxon King of England, and William, Duke of Normandy. The Battle of Hastings actually took place on a hill, which the Normans called 'Senlac', meaning 'lake of blood', and even today some believe in the myth that blood seeps from the battlefield after heavy rain. However, any discolouration of the water is, in fact, due to iron oxide present in the subsoil. The battle was a particularly gruesome affair, even for those times, and it was not until late in the afternoon that Harold finally fell on the field. However, what happened to

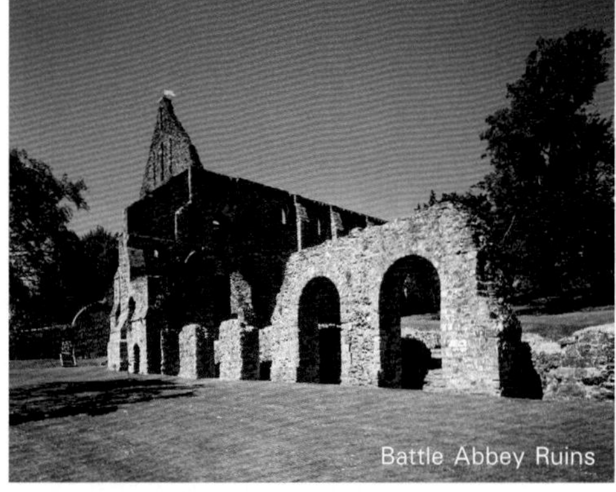
Battle Abbey Ruins

Battle to Bexhill

Distance: *5.3 miles (8.5 kilometres)*
Typical time: *150 mins*
Height gain: *60 metres*
Map: *Explorer 124*
Walk: *www.walkingworld.com ID:206*
Contributor: *Jacky Rix-Brown*

ACCESS INFORMATION:

Battle is on the main railway line from Hastings to London, and Bexhill is on the railway line between Hastings and Eastbourne. Bus service 395 runs between Battle and Bexhill, and other buses connect each town with Hastings. Parking in Battle may be tricky, but the walk finishes at a large car park in Bexhill, so best advice is to park there, walk to Bexhill Town Hall Square and take the bus to Battle.

ADDITIONAL INFORMATION:

In 1066, William, Duke of Normandy, landed at Pevensey. King Harold marched south to defend his land, but was defeated by William in the Battle of Hastings, which was fought at Senlac Hill. William founded a monastery there, and round it grew the town of Battle. The 1066 Country Walk connects Battle with Pevensey, Rye, Hastings and Bexhill. These five historic towns abound with interesting places to visit. In Battle: abbey, museum, ancient church, pubs and eating places, shops and tourist information centre. In Crowhurst: Fore Wood nature reserve, ancient church, 1000-year-old yew tree. In Bexhill: museum, ancient church, bathing beach, shops, pubs, eating places and tourist information centre.

DESCRIPTION:

Appropriately for the scene of the Battle of Hastings in 1066, the town of Battle is the hub of the 1066 walks. The main walk is from Pevensey to Rye via Battle. This spur takes you from Battle almost due south to the seaside town of Bexhill-on-Sea. It begins on Senlac hill where Battle Abbey marks the place where King Harold fell. But before you start, the town is well worth exploring, with many interesting places to visit.

The walk takes you out through rolling hills, passes through a woodland nature reserve and the sleepy village of Crowhurst with its ancient church and centuries old yew tree.

Having crossed small streams in the early part of the walk you come to the low marshy lands formed by the streams that run into the Coombe Haven. The latter part of the walk takes you through the quiet residential streets of Bexhill. It ends at a car park beside a park in which are a museum and the ruins of a manor.

FEATURES:

River, sea, toilets, museum, church, castle, wildlife, birds, flowers, great views.

WALK DIRECTIONS:

1 | From the front of Battle Abbey, walk west past the Pilgrims Rest restaurant (formerly the Abbey hospice). The road ends in a track and the 1066 walk symbol points the way along the track beside a wood.

2 | Where the ways divide be careful as two routes are both 1066 walk! Ignore the right fork to Pevensey and take the left to Bexhill. Initially, this stays alongside the wood. Continue over a hill, across a stream and onwards until you meet a tarmac track near a road.

3 | On reaching the track, cross straight over (as shown by arrow of 1066 symbol) and over a stile onto a path that runs between a fence and hedge, parallel to a road. Be careful! The stile from the path leads straight onto a road that can be quite busy, as well as being on a blind bend with another road leading off and a drive alongside – quite a road safety hazard. Cross the main road and go down the side road directly opposite the end of the path.

4 | Soon leave the side road (Talham Lane), taking the right fork towards Peppering Eye Farm (private road). Continue past the farm and other houses, ignoring paths to right and left, and go up hill towards woods.

5 | At a major junction of paths, near a cottage at the start of woods, go left, then keep right (effectively forking, rather than turning, left) as shown by 1066 symbol. On emerging from wood, turn left downhill with the footpath. (The track ahead here is not a right of way.) Cross the stream and enter another wood. On entering this wood, bend right on the main track, going south. Keep your eyes skinned, this is the Fore Wood Nature Reserve. There was an Elephant Hawk Moth larvae beside the path when we were there. Stay on the main track through the wood.

6 | Here the map doesn't fully match the ground. In the wood just past a pond on the left (not on map) you reach a fork in the path. Keep right and go to

the stile at the edge of the wood, where the familiar 1066 symbol directs you forward. Cross the field and bear left up the hill on the obvious track and continue to the road.

7 | Turn right onto the road through Crowhurst village. Here I suggest deviating from the 1066 walk to go through the village. Go right into the church and pass its ancient yew. Go right round the church and leave the churchyard at the bottom gate and turn right down the hill. Cross the stream and up the other side (on the road) past the millennium memorial garden. Keep left at the fork. Ignore the first footpath on the right. Where the road bends sharp left go right over a style onto the footpath beside a stream. You are now back on the 1066 way. Continue on this path by the stream for about a kilometre.

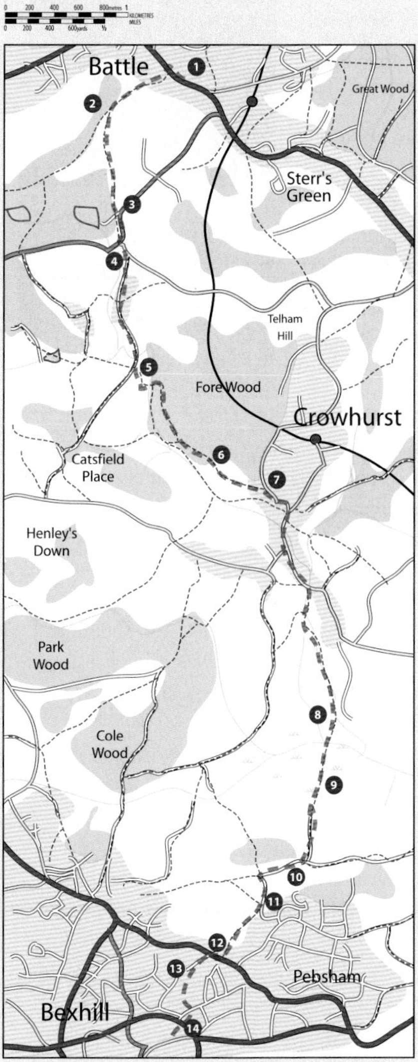

8 | Just past the track to Adam's Farm, the main track curves left beside the stream. Turn right, as shown by 1066 sign, to follow a zig-zag path to the bridge. The ground is marshy so keep to the path even though it takes you right then left. There are actually two bridges across adjacent watercourses. From the bridges continue south across the marshland, noting the embankments where a railway line used to cross on a long viaduct.

9 | Approach the stile, which is hidden in a corner under a tree. Once over it, continue up a dry valley beside the hedge with the railway embankment to your left, then on across an open field, rising to cross the course of the old railway. Follow the track up, past Little Worsham farm, where it is more of a road.

10 | At the T-junction turn right and pass a low building with a red tiled roof. After about 400m, at another junction, turn left toward Upper Worsham Farm. Continue about 150m.

11 | Look out a fork, where the main track continues south and another track forks right to the farm. In the angle of the fork, almost hidden by the hedgerow, and just to the right of a telegraph pole, there is the stile. Climb this and continue on a well-walked path across the field, over a stream and on beside a hedge until you come to a busy road, the A2036.

12 | With care, cross the main road directly, and enter an enclosed footpath between gardens. Follow this for about 300m until it meets a road at right angles.

13 | On emerging onto a residential road, do not take the continuation of the path between gardens, but turn left along the pavement (as signed 1066). Continue to the next road junction and turn right (another 1066 sign). Follow this road to its end.

14 | Take the footpath that leaves the end of the road going left up onto a bridge across a very busy trunk road, A259. On the far side of the bridge, the footpath takes you back to the right to the end of another road. This road leads you straight to the car park where the walk ends.

BATTLE WOOL & NEEDLECRAFT SHOP

2 Mount Street, Battle,
East Sussex TN33 0EG
Tel: 01424 775073
e-mail: battlewools@tiscali.co.uk

Battle Wool & Needlecraft Shop is the creation of Shelagh Duffill, who took over an 18th century weatherboarded shop close to the high street in 1989. Since then it has 'grown like Topsy' and Shelagh has the valued assistance of long-serving staff Jenny, Carol, Gill and Lynn, who are always ready with help and advice.

The stock includes a wide range of craft materials, knitting wool, needles, patterns and accessories; embroidery, needlecraft and tapestry supplies; haberdashery; beading supplies, and an enormous variety of craft books. An Aladdin's Cave!

She also runs two clubs: Knit & Knatter, held from 11am to 1pm on the second and fourth Saturdays of the month, and Bead & Banter, 1pm to 3pm on the first and third Tuesdays of the month. Both these clubs meet at the Kings Head pub opposite the shop. There is a large car park close by, its entrance is just a long Mount Street.

Harold's body remains a mystery. One story tells how it was buried by his mother at Waltham Abbey in Essex, while another suggests that William the Conqueror wrapped it in purple cloth and buried it on the cliff top at Hastings.

After the battle and subsequent victory, William set about fulfilling his vow that, if he were victorious, he would build an abbey. Choosing the very spot where Harold fell, **Battle Abbey** was begun straight away and was consecrated in 1094. Throughout the Middle Ages, the Benedictine abbey grew increasingly more wealthy and powerful as it extended its influence over wider and wider areas of East Sussex. This period of prosperity, however, came to an abrupt end in 1537 when Henry VIII dissolved the monasteries. The abbey buildings were granted to Sir Anthony Browne and, during a banquet to celebrate his good fortune, a monk is said to have appeared before Sir Anthony announcing that his family would be killed off by fire and water. The prophecy was forgotten as the family flourished until, some 200 years later, in 1793, the home of Sir Anthony's descendant, Cowdray Hall near Midhurst, burnt to the ground. A few days later another member of the family was drowned in the River Rhine in Germany.

Although little of the early Norman features remain, Battle Abbey has much to offer the visitor. The most impressive part is the Great Gatehouse, a magnificent medieval abbey entrance built around 1338. The **Prelude to Battle Exhibition** introduces visitors to the site and its history. This is followed by a video on the Battle of Hastings. Other on-site attractions are a children's themed play and picnic area and an educational Discovery Centre. Battle Abbey is the staging ground for an elaborate Reenactment of the Battle of Hastings every October, which draws hundreds of specialist performers from around Europe. The 1066 Country Walk passes through Battle on its route between Pevensey and Rye.

There is more to Battle than the abbey and the battlefield, and any stroll around the streets will reveal some interesting buildings. The **Battle Museum of Local History** is an excellent place to discover more about the lives of those who have lived in East Sussex through the ages. There is also a replica of the Bayeux Tapestry. Opposite the abbey, and housed in a 600-year-old Wealden hall house and new exhibition centre, is **Yesterday's World**, where 100,000 objects are displayed in authentic room settings covering the period from 1850 to 1950. The exhibits include replicas of a Victorian kitchen, a 1930s country railway station, an English country garden, a grocer's, a chemist's, a wireless shop, a bicycle shop and the 1930s-style Nippy's Tea Room.

SEDLESCOMBE

6½ miles NW of Hastings on the B2244

This former flourishing iron founding settlement is a now a pleasant and pretty village, stretched out along a long sloping green, where the parish pump still stands under a stone building dating from 1900. The interior of the village church, on the northern edge of the village, retains its seating plan of the mid 17th century, which lays out the hierarchy of this rural society in no uncertain terms. The front pew was retained for the Sackville family, with the other villagers seated behind; right at the back, the last few pews were kept for 'Youths and Strangers'.

To the southeast of the village, centred around an adapted 19th-century country house, is the internationally renowned Pestalozzi Children's Village. Founded in 1959 to house children from Europe who had been displaced during World War II, the centre follows the theories of the Swiss educational reformer, Johann Heinrich Pestalozzi. This influential gentleman believed that young people of all nationalities should learn together, and took into his care orphans from the Napoleonic Wars. The village now takes children from Third World countries, who live here in houses with others from their country under the care of a housemother of the same nationality. After studying for their first degree, the young adults return to their own countries where their newly learnt skills can be put to excellent use in the development of their homelands.

ROBERTSBRIDGE

10 miles NW of Hastings off the A21

Situated on a hillside overlooking the valley of the River Rother, the village's name is a corruption of Rothersbridge. In the 12th century an annexe to a Cistercian Abbey was founded here by the river, and today some of the buildings, now part of a farm, can still be seen. The unusually high pitched roof protects the remains of the abbot's house and other ruins stand in the garden. Robertsbridge has long been associated with cricket and, in particular, the manufacture of cricket bats. The village establishment of Grey Nicholls has made bats for many of the sport's famous names, including W G Grace, who once stayed at The George Inn in the village.

HURST GREEN

12 miles NW of Hastings of the A21

Merriements Gardens

Set in four acres of gently sloping Weald

farmland, close to the village, **Merriments Gardens**, is a place that never fails to delight its visitors. A naturalistic garden, where the deep borders are richly planted according to the prevailing conditions of the landscape, it nurtures an abundance of rare plants. By contrast, there are also borders that are planted in the traditional manner of an English garden, and colour-themed using a mix of trees, shrubs, perennials and grasses.

Rye

Lamb House · Rye Castle Museum
Mermaid Inn · Rye Harbour Nature Reserve
Heritage Centre · Landgate

This old and very picturesque town was originally granted to the Abbey of Fecamp in Normandy, in 1027, and was only reclaimed by Henry III in 1247. It became a member of the confederacy of the Cinque Ports, joining Hastings, Romney, Hythe, Dover and Sandwich as the ports that were a key part of the south coast's maritime defence, and became a full Head Port in the 14th century. Over the years, this hill top town, which overlooks both the Rother estuary and the Romney Marshes, was subjected to many raids, including one by the French in 1377, which left no non-stone building standing. As a result, the rebuilt town is one of the prettiest in England, with timber-framed houses, some with jettied upper storeys. The harbour suffered the same fate as many others along the south coast as it silted up, and was moved further down the estuary. **Rye Harbour Nature Reserve**, on the mouth of the River Rother, is a large area of sea, saltmarsh, sand and shingle, which supports a wide range of

JEAKE'S HOUSE HOTEL

Mermaid Street, Rye, East Sussex TN31 7ET
Tel: 01797 222828 Fax: 01797 22623
e-mail: stay@jeakeshouse.com
website: www.jeakeshouse.com

Jeake's House Hotel caters admirably for discerning guests who want to capture the sense of history about the town while enjoying high standards of comfort and relaxed hospitality. Guests can look forward the warmest of welcomes from resident owners Jenny Hadfield and Richard Martin, along with their adorable Tonkinese Yum Yum and Monte. Jenny created the B&B from three separate houses on one of the most delightful cobbled streets of Rye. The galleried dining room was once a religious meeting place: its pews now furnish the bar and the old baptismal font still lies under the floorboards. The bedrooms are named after literary and artistic figures associated with the town – Conrad Aitken, Elizabeth Fry, Malcolm Lowry, Radclyffe Hall. Most have en suite bathrooms and they all have telephone, television, drinks tray, fluffy towels and dressing gowns. The day starts with an excellent choice for breakfast, including such very English treats as oak-smoked haddock, kippers and devilled kidneys. Rye is a charming place to visit at any time of the year, and Jeake's House offers discounts for stays of any two nights between November and March (not Christmas or New Year).

both plant, animal and bird life. One of the most unusual plants is the Least Lettuce, which flowers in late-July and only shows itself in the morning.

Rye's prominent hill top position was a factor in making it a strategically important town from early times. A substantial perimeter wall was built to defend the northern approaches, and one of its four gateways, the **Landgate**, still survives today. This imposing structure is all that remains of the fortifications erected by Edward III in the 1340s.

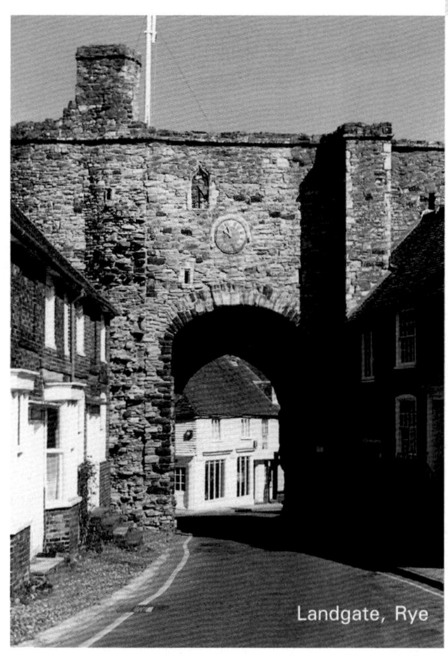
Landgate, Rye

Found in the heart of this ancient town, Durrant House Hotel is a charming, spacious Georgian residence that played a strategic role in the history of Rye. Built for a local gentleman in the 17th century, the house was, like so much of the town, at the centre of the smuggling trade. However, in the 18th century,

THE QUEENS HEAD HOTEL

19 Landgate, Rye, East Sussex TN31 7LH
Tel: 01233 770394

Situated by one of the ancient gateways on Rye's perimeter wall, the **Queens Head Hotel** is a great place for a drink, a meal or a well-earned break. It was first licensed in 1636 and has been part of Rye's hospitality scene ever since. Formerly called the Two Brewers, it acquired its present name because it stood on the site occupied by Queen Elizabeth I and her court when they came to inspect the town's defences.

Since December 2005 it has been in the excellent care of Claire and Stephen Clare. In the three bars of this atmospheric free house a fine selection of real ales and lagers is always on tap; the public bar is a favourite local meeting place with a convivial ambience, a pool table, darts, pinball, juke box and big-screen TV for the major sporting events. A good choice of bar snacks – eggs Balmoral, hot buttered prawns, peppered chicken strips – is served lunchtime and evening, while in the 60-seat restaurant a full à la carte menu proposes such delights as plaice on the bone, sea bass, sizzling curries and juicy steaks.

For guests taking a break to discover the many attractions of Rye and the surrounding area, the Queens Head has five comfortable letting rooms, four with en suite facilities, one with a four-poster. Bar hours are 11 to 11 (Friday and Saturday to midnight, Sunday from 12). Food is served from 12 to 3 and 6 to 9 (all day Sunday with traditional roasts).

HAYDEN'S

108 High Street, Rye, East Sussex TN31 7JE
Tel: 01797 224501
e-mail: haydens_in_rye@mac.com
website: www.haydensinrye.co.uk

Hayden's is a small, family-run, environmentally friendly Bed & Breakfast establishment that also incorporates a coffee shop and restaurant. In the heart of Rye, it offers a comfortable, luxurious setting in which guests can relax and unwind, whether it's for a short break, a coffee or a meal. The four guest suites, the Red Room, the Chocolate Room, Kingfisher Room and the Silver Room, are large and very comfortable, with en suite bathrooms and seating areas. The restaurant is open for evening meals on Friday and Saturday throughout the year. The chef seeks out the finest local, seasonal and (where possible) organic produce for the menus, which are traditional English with a contemporary twist. Local produce is highlighted by Romney Marsh lamb, Rye Bay plaice and organic beef pies made in Udimore.

Hayden's is the ideal base for exploring the many attractions of Rye, including the Museum, the Heritage Centre, the Mermaid Inn, Lamb House and Rye Harbour Nature Reserve.

the property was bought by Sir William Durrant, a friend of the Duke of Wellington, and gained respectability. During the Napoleonic Wars, it was an operations centre for the defence of the Channel port and a relay station for carrier pigeons bringing news of the victory at Waterloo.

The town grew prosperous in the late medieval period due to the activities of its fishermen and the merchant fleets that traded with continental Europe. But the loss of the harbour through silting denied Rye the chief means of earning a living and the town fell into decline. Visitors today very much benefit from this turn of events as Rye still retains a large number of medieval buildings that would undoubtedly have made way for new structures if the town had been more prosperous.

Naturally, being a seafaring town, there is an abundance of old inns, and the **Mermaid Inn**, an early timbered building down a cobbled street, is one of the most famous. Rebuilt in 1420 after the devastating French raid over 40 years before, the inn was the headquarters of the notorious Hawkhurst Gang in the 18th century. The most infamous band of smugglers on the south coast in their day, they reputedly always sat with their pistols close to hand in case of a sudden raid by the excisemen.

Another interesting building is a handsome Georgian residence **Lamb House**, built by a local wine merchant, James Lamb, in 1723 and now in the care of the National Trust. The family was well known in the town and not without a certain influence. Not long after the house was built, the family were involved in an infamous murder when, in 1743, a local butcher named Breads killed James Lamb's brother-in-law by mistake. His intention had been to murder James, then the town's Lord Mayor, against whom he held a grudge. Tried and found guilty, Breads was hanged on a gibbet and his bones were stolen to be used as a cure for rheumatism. Only his skull remains and it can be seen, along with the gibbet, in Rye Town Hall.

More recently, Lamb House was the home of the novelist, Henry James. He saw it in 1896 and fell in love with it; he rented it for a while, then bought it for £2,000 and lived in it until his death in 1916. Many of his personal possessions are on show in the house, including his massive French writing desk and a painting of him by Burne-Jones. Upstairs is the panelled bedroom where George I spent a night in 1726 on his return from the continent to open Parliament. A storm drove his ship onto Camber Sands and James Lamb, the

Ypres Tower, Rye

FORGET-ME-NOT

72 Church Square, Rye, East Sussex TN31 7HF
Tel: 01797 222330
e-mail: sarah@forgetmenotrye.com
website: www.forgetmenotrye.com

Forget-Me-Not is a delightful lifestyle and giftware shop in a fine old corner building opposite St Mary's Church. Sarah Hastings, who acquired the business in April 2008, has lost no time in making her mark, sourcing unusual and interesting items from new places and choosing as far as possible goods made in England. The constantly changing stock includes a wide variety of clothing, including hand-made baby clothes and ladies nightwear, bedding, quilts, cushions and throws and cushion covers, curtains and ties, hangers and hanging organisers, table cloths and table mats, coasters and napkins and napkin rings, food covers, jugs and candle snuffers, lampshades, vintage tins and soft toys. There are gemstones and handmade bracelets and necklaces, oils, soaps and lotions, foam baths and bath salts, hand creams and moisturising creams. For art-lovers, Forget-Me-not keeps a selection of limited edition prints featuring, among others, Emma Ball, Claire Davies, Sheila Gill, Maureen Jordan and Patricia Hall. Customers who can't get to the can shop online by way of the excellent website.

Mayor at the time, offered him shelter. Henry James was also responsible for laying out the gardens and he invited many of his friends to the house, including H G Wells, Rudyard Kipling, G K Chesterton and Joseph Conrad. The literary associations do not end there as, in the 1920s, the property was leased to E F Benson, who is best remembered for his Mapp and Lucia novels, which include descriptions of the town, thinly disguised as 'Tilling'. Benson was also for a time the Mayor of Rye. (The cartoon character Captain Pugwash was also conceived in Rye.) One of the town's oldest surviving buildings is Ypres Tower, which forms part of the **Rye Castle Museum**, the other part being in East Street. The collection concentrates on the town's varied past and includes exhibitions on smuggling, law and order and the iron industry. On the second site, there is an old fire engine, pottery made in the town, nautical equipment and much more that tells the full history of Rye. Combining the traditional craft of model-making with the latest electronic techniques, the **Rye Heritage Centre** presents a model of the town, complete with light and sound, that transports visitors back through the ages.

Around Rye

PLAYDEN

1 mile N of Rye off the A268

Royal Military Canal

This smart hamlet has a rather battered old 12th-century church, with a shingle broach spire. Inside there is an unusual memorial to a 16th-century Flemish brewer, Cornelius Roetmans. A refugee from Spanish persecution in the Low Countries, he settled in the area along with a community of Huguenots and carried on his trade as a brewer. After his death, he was remembered in the church by a memorial slab carved with beer barrels and mash forks - the tools of the brewing trade. In the chancel is a memorial to the men of *HMS Barham*, sunk in 1941. The country lanes to the northeast of Playden lead to the start of the **Royal Military Canal**, an unusual waterway built in 1804 as part of the defences against a possible invasion by Napoleon. A 20-mile towpath between Rye and Hythe offers easy and attractive walking along the fringes of the now drained Walland and Romney Marshes.

CAMBER

3 miles SE of Rye off the A259

Camber is a small village lying on the western edge of Romney Marsh and is famous for its beach of golden sands. It was known as a good place for smugglers - goods were landed on Camber beach as the dunes provided cover for those taking part. The Excise built a Watch House in the early 1800s, which is now adjacent to the Lydd Ranges. The village has seen a lot of development since World War II with the building of bungalows on the sand dunes.

WINCHELSEA

2½ miles SW of Rye on the A259

Camber Castle   Court Hall Museum

Though Winchelsea lies only a short distance from Rye, there could be no greater contrast. While Rye is a place of tourist bustle, Winchelsea is a quiet place that time seems to have forgotten. An ancient Cinque Port and one of the smallest towns in England, Winchelsea lay several miles to the south until the 13th century. This site was engulfed by the

SUTTON'S FISH SHOP

Sea Road, Winchelsea, East Sussex TN36 4LA
Tel: 01797 226261

Since 1970 Hugh Sutton has been running the shop that has borne the family name since 1932. Hugh's father created the business, selling the fish he caught, the game he shot, the vegetables he grew and the preserves and honey (from their own bees) that his mother made.

Fish and shellfish caught in Rye Bay are still the mainstay of the shop, on sparklingly fresh display behind the cheerful red and white striped blind. Dover and lemon sole, cod, plaice, skate, crab and scallops are among the favourites that bring customers from many miles around. Sutton's also stocks a selection of French fish soup and bisques. Seasonal game is another speciality, including wild boar (steaks and sausages), venison, rabbit, hare, wild duck, pheasant, partridge and quail.

Locally grown fruit and vegetables are on show outside at the front of the shop, and there's always a selection of pure fruit juices. Customers can always expect a warm, friendly welcome at Sutton's, which is open all day, every day including bank holidays and Sunday. Closed Tuesday.

J WICKENS FAMILY BUTCHER

Castle Street, Winchelsea, East Sussex TN36 4HU
Tel: 01797 226287

Jamie Wickens was born in Uckfield and served his apprenticeship there before establishing **J Wickens Family Butcher** here in Winchelsea in 1987.

Everything is of the very best quality, and Jamie is known for many miles around for his speciality sausages. They come in about two dozen varieties and among the favourites are pork & leek, pork & sage, pork & apple, venison & apple, beef with tomato & onion and lamb with rosemary & garlic. Traditional cuts of Sussex beef are beautifully dressed and presented in the long display case, along with prime pork and Romney Marsh lamb. One of the major suppliers of the shop is Elms Farm in Winchelsea, where Stephen and Anne Rumsey produce top-quality beef, lamb and pork. The chickens are organically raised, and Jamie is a licensed dealer in game, selling pheasant, partridge, mallard, pigeon, woodcock, venison, wild boar, hare and rabbit in their seasons. Other items not to miss are traditionally cured bacon, superb beef, pork and game pies and a choice of 40+ English and Continental cheeses.

J Wickens Family Butcher is a worthy recipient of many local and national awards from the National Federation of Meat Traders as well as being numbered among Rick Stein's Food heroes. The shop is open every day except Sunday.

Strand Gate, Winchelsea

sea after a series of violent storms. The 'new' Winchelsea stands on a hill and was built to a rigid grid pattern laid out by Edward I. The ambitious rectangular plan of 39 squares - a feature that can still be seen some 700 years later - became the home of about 6,000 inhabitants, nearly 10 times the number of residents here today.

For a short time in the 14th century, Winchelsea prospered as the most important Channel port, but nature took its toll and the town lost its harbour. As a result of the Black Death and constant raids by the French, the town declined into almost complete obscurity. It was not until the mid 19th century that a successful recovery plan was put together to restore the town to something like its former grandeur and historic beauty.

Winchelsea Court Hall Museum illustrates events that led to the town's prosperity, culminating in it being made a Head Port of the confederation of Cinque Ports, and its gradual decline. The museum is

THE LODGE AT WINCHELSEA

housed in one of the oldest surviving buildings, close by the ruins of a 14th-century Franciscan Friary.

Just to the east of the town lies **Camber Castle**, a fine example of the coastal defences built by Henry VIII in the 16th century. The fortress, reached by a walk across the sands, seems rather far inland today, but when it was built, it held a commanding position on a spit of land on one side of the Rother estuary.

BECKLEY

4½ miles NW of Rye on the B2088

When Alfred the Great died in 900, he referred to lands at 'Beccanleah' in his will and there was certainly a Saxon church here. A medieval building with a Norman tower now stands on the site. Inside there are two grotesque stone heads with leaves protruding from the mouths that were known as 'jack in the greens'. On still nights, it is said that Sir Reginald Fitzurse can be heard riding furiously to the church for sanctuary after taking part in the murder of Thomas à Becket.

Brighton and the East Sussex Downs

This coastal area of East Sussex centres around the thriving resorts of Brighton and Eastbourne. Both began life as quiet fishing villages but, following Royal visits, they developed rapidly at the beginning of the 19th century. Brighton, the favoured holiday resort of the Prince Regent, is best known for the lavish Royal Pavilion, a splendid monument to exotic architecture and design. However, its Lanes, the narrow streets and alleyways of the old village, are a real treat for antique lovers.

Eastbourne has none of the grand architecture of its rival. Carefully planned and laid out by William Cavendish, the 7th Duke of Devonshire, this is a genteel resort close to the spectacular chalk cliffs of Beachy Head.

The county town of Lewes dates back to Saxon times and it benefited greatly just after the Norman Conquest, when both a great castle and the important St Pancras Priory were founded here by the Norman William de Warenne. Another coastal village, Pevensey, was the landing place of William, Duke of Normandy, and his army in 1066.

Although many of the inland towns and villages have their roots in Saxon England they are also linked with artists and writers of the 19th and 20th centuries. Virginia Woolf and her husband Leonard lived at Monk's House, Rodmell, until Virginia's death in 1941, while her sister, Vanessa Bell, maintained her eccentric household at nearby Charleston, in Selmeston. The Elms at Rottingdean was the home of Rudyard Kipling until his success as a novelist forced him to move to a more secluded location in 1902, and the village of Ditchling was home to a group of artists and craftsmen at the centre of the Arts and Crafts Movement.

Brighton

Royal Pavilion · The Dome · Preston Manor · Metropole Hotel · Sea Life Centre · Church of St John · Toy & Model Museum · Stanmer Park & Rural Museum · Theatre Royal · Booth Museum of Natural History · Pier

Before Dr Richard Russell of Lewes came here in the 1750s, this was an obscure little south coast fishing village called Brighthelmstone, dating back to medieval times. Dr Russell, a believer in the benefits of sea air and water, published a dissertation on The Use of Sea

TERRACES BAR & GRILL

Unit 8, Madeira Drive, Brighton,
East Sussex BN2 1PS
Tel: 01273 570526
e-mail: sales@the-terraces.co.uk

Showcasing the best of British cooking with some Mediterranean influences, **Terraces Bar & Grill** enjoys an unbeatable setting on the seafront just along from the Pier. There are truly stunning views from the terrace, where customers can enjoy anything from a glass of wine or a cup of perfect Segafredo coffee to a snack or a full meal. Light breakfast are served until noon, and the main menu runs from small plates – super sandwiches, mezze platter, baked camembert, chorizo with a poached egg and salad – to seafood dishes (traditional fish & chips, oysters, fricassee) and meaty main courses typified by gourmet burgers, lamb chops, corn-fed chicken and rib eye steak. Sunday lunch brings a selection of roasts served with all the trimmings. A spacious, self-contained area on a lower level is available for hire for parties, wedding receptions, formal dinners, corporate events, product launches or business meetings – free wireless broadband is on hand. Options run from informal buffets to sit-down meals, and the area can cater for groups of 10 to 240. Terraces Bar & Grill (TBG) is open from 11am - 11pm (Sun 10am - 10.30pm).

Water in Diseases of the Glands. Russell set about publicising the village as a place for taking sea air, bathing and even drinking sea water in order to gain relief from ailments and diseases. He also promoted the medicinal virtues of the mineral waters of St Ann's Well at Hove. By the time of the Prince Regent's first visit to the village, at 21 years of age in 1783, it was already becoming a popular place, but still remained concentrated around the old village of Brighthelmstone. The effect of royal patronage on the village was extraordinary and the growth here was rapid. By the time of the Prince Regent's last visit to Brighton, some 47 years after his first, the place had been completely transformed.

The Prince Regent, later to become George IV, was so taken with the resort that he first took a house here and then built his extraordinary **Royal Pavilion** (see panel on page 191). The small farmhouse on the site was transformed in 1787 by architect Henry Holland into a neoclassical building with a dome and rotunda. (Henry Holland was a partner of Capability Brown and married his daughter.) John Nash was employed to rebuild and enlarge Holland's building in a magnificent Indian style. Based on a maharajah's palace, complete with minarets, onion-shaped domes and pinnacles, the Royal Pavilion has been the best-known Brighton landmark for almost 200 years. The interior of the palace is one of the most lavish examples of Regency chinoiserie in the world. The detail in the decoration is astonishing, with imitation bamboo everywhere. Even the kitchens have flamboyant cast-iron palm trees.

The gardens surrounding this seaside pleasure palace are also the work of John Nash, though one ancient oak tree here is said to be the one in which Charles II hid after the Battle of Worcester. Although this is an unlikely claim,

sixtyseven

67 Dyke Road, Brighton, East Sussex BN1 3JE
Tel: 01273 735314
e-mail: jo@shopatsixtyseven.co.uk
website: www.shopatsixtyseven.co.uk

On the corner of Dyke Road and Clifton Road, in the Seven Dials district of north Brighton, **sixtyseven** is a treasure trove of gorgeous gifts, gift wrap, cards, toys, jewellery, lighting, chocolates and furniture. Owner Joanna Weeks is following in the footsteps of her grandparents, who ran a similar shop in Southsea. She sources the great majority of her stock in the UK, with much of it the work of talented Sussex craftspeople. Among the impressive variety of goods on display – the choice changes all the time – are bags and satchels by Moth and Neoma; jewellery by Ridley & Dowse; organic bath and baby products by local firm Roots & Wings; candles, wooden toys, games and colouring books; flower presses; tea towels and mugs by Pearl & Earl; scarves; cards by local artist Shyama Ruffell: Momiji dolls; Ercol furniture from the 50s and 60s; and delectable chocolates made by Chocoholly of Hove. There's no better place to browse and find a treat or a special gift than sixtyseven, which is generally open from 10.30 to 5.30 Tuesday to Saturday.

ARAMAS INTERIORS

86 Dyke Rd , Brighton , East Sussex BN1 3JD
Tel: 01273 711009
e-mail: gemma851@btinternet.com

Dyke Rd lies at the heart of the Seven Dials area of Brighton,a mile north of the city centre at a point where seven streets meet.The area is filled with fabulous places to eat , but anyone seeking out the best in lifestyle items, home ware and collectibles with a period feel to the place to head for is ARAMAS at number 86. Behind it's newly signed frontage this fascinating place is filled with desirable objects all carefully sourced.Objects both large and small at prices to suit all pockets.The owner of the shop is Gemanica St Clair, whose career started in a family business in Oxford specialising in Antique Furniture and French polishing.Furniture is very much still at the heart of ARAMAS , focusing on antique chairs, along with handmade Vintage Fabric soft furnishings.Cushions , Bolsters , Blankets.ARAMAS also offers a hand embroidered monogram service as well as a traditional upholstery service.All gifts purchased are wrapped beautifully at no extra cost.Stock changes regularly and among the smaller items are perfect pampering treats, quality scented candles , handcrafted soaps and organic essential bath oils.

the tree certainly predates Nash's splendidly laid-out grounds. Beginning life as the Royal Pavilion's stables, and once housing a riding school, **The Dome**, dated 1805, is now a superb concert hall. Another part of the complex has been converted into the **Brighton Museum and Art Gallery**. Opened in 1873, this outstanding museum houses collections of both national and international importance. Among the marvellous displays are Art Nouveau and Art Deco furniture, decorative art, non-western art and culture, archaeology from flint axes to silver coins, paintings by both British and European masters, musical instruments, costume and design.

The creation of the Royal Pavilion and the almost permanent residence of the Prince Regent in the resort certainly sealed Brighton's fate as a sought-after seaside location and the town rapidly expanded - westwards until it met up with Hove, and eastwards to Kemp Town, laid out by Thomas Reid Kemp, a local lord of the manor in the 1820s. Another notable feature of Brighton is Royal Crescent, an early example of town planning. Built in the late 1790s, this discreet row of little houses was built to face the sea rather than have their backs turned towards the coast as was the norm at the time.

For many visitors to Brighton a trip to The Lanes, the warren of narrow streets that represent what is left of the old village, is a must. Today, these tiny, twisting alleys are the preserve of smart boutiques, antique shops and restaurants. The old Parish Church standing outside the old part of Brighton is shown in ancient pictures as an isolated building. It has long since been engulfed. In the churchyard is a curious gravestone to Phoebe Hessel. Born in 1713, she served in the army as a private and, after her retirement, she came to Brighton where she died, aged 108, in 1821.

Another church worth visiting is the Roman Catholic **Church of St John** in Kemp Town. However, it is not for any ancient feature that visitors make their way here but to see the last resting place of Mrs Fitzherbert, who died in 1837. Maria Anne Fitzherbert, twice a widow,

Royal Pavilion

Brighton, Sussex BN1 1EE
Tel: 01273 290900
website: www.royal.pavilion.co.uk

Indian architecture contrasts with interiors inspired by China in this breathtaking Regency palace. Built for King George IV, the Royal Pavilion was also used by William IV and Queen Victoria. Originally a farmhouse, in 1787 architect Henry Holland created a neo-classical villa on the site. It was transformed into Indian style by John Nash between 1815 and 1823.A £10 million restoration scheme has returned the palace to its full Regency splendour with lavish decorative schemes. The centrepiece of the Banqueting Room is a huge chandelier held by a silvered dragon illuminating a table laid with dazzling Regency silver-gilt. The Music Room is equally stunning, with lotus-shaped lanterns hanging from a high domed glided ceiling.

Preston Manor, Brighton

was secretly married to the future George IV in London in 1785. They honeymooned in Brighton, where Mrs Fitzherbert took a house, said to be linked to the pavilion by an underground passage. Their marriage had to remain a secret as it was completely in breach of the Royal Marriages Act. Eventually, the Prince Regent, who could not acknowledge her publicly without renouncing the throne, broke off their affair in 1811. The Church of St Bartholomew has one of the highest naves in the country, and the Church of St Michael contains fine windows by Burne-Jones, Webb, Morris and Kempe.

Just a short distance from the seafront lies **Preston Manor**, a delightful old house, now restored and refurbished in the style of an Edwardian gentleman's residence. Beginning life as a 13th-century manor house, set within beautifully landscaped grounds, the manor was rebuilt in the 1730s and much extended in 1905. Laid out on four floors, there are some 20 rooms to explore, from the attics and nursery on the top floor to the servants' quarters, kitchens and butler's pantry 'below stairs'. The dining room is dominated by a case filled with an amazing collection of Buddhist Chinese lions. Within the pleasant grounds are a walled garden, a pets' cemetery and a croquet lawn.

Another lesser known place of interest in Brighton is **Stanmer Park and Rural Museum**, a 200-acre country park centred around the fine early 18th-century mansion that was once the home of the Earls of Chichester. The park now contains a large municipal nursery as well as glasshouses where flowers are grown. Behind Stanmer House is a unique collection of agricultural implements, including blacksmith's and wheelwright's tools. The late 17th-century well house, which was designed to supply water to the house and was originally powered by oxen, can also be seen here.

For those wishing to take a step back into

their childhood, the **Brighton Toy and Model Museum**, under the arches of Brighton station, is the place to go. A fascinating display of trains, dolls, teddy bears, planes and much more will delight all members of the family - young and old. The world of natural history can also be discovered in Brighton, at the **Booth Museum of Natural History**, the creation of Edward Booth, a Victorian ornithologist. His original collection of some 500 species of bird, assembled between 1865 and 1890, has been extended by displays of butterflies, fossils and animal skeletons. The Sea Life Centre concentrates very much on live creatures and has the longest underwater viewing tunnel in Europe. The tunnel winds through a series of underwater habitats where both fresh and sea water creatures can be viewed. Although this is an up-to-the-minute centre, some of the original 19th-century display cases are still in use in this Victorian building. Few visitors to the city leave without taking a walk along **Brighton Pier**. The Palace Pier, one of the most famous in the land, was opened in 1901. It was designed by R St George Moore and built by James and Arthur Mayoh to replace Samuel Brown's Chain Pier, the world's first pleasure pier, which was the terminus of the cross-channel ferry service to Dieppe; it was destroyed by a storm in 1896 while awaiting demolition. A plaque on the sea wall below Marine Parade marks the site of this pier, and its two entrance kiosks, rescued from the storm, now flank the land end of the present pier. The **Theatre Royal**, opened in 1807, is one of the country's best and loveliest provincial theatres. The arts certainly flourish in Brighton, and the annual Brighton Festival, held each May, is one of the largest in the country. A popular feature on the seafront is the Volks railway, the first electric railway in the country. It was designed by Magnus Volk, Brighton Corporation's Electrical Engineer, and opened on August Bank Holiday 1883. It runs for about a mile from the Aquarium (close to the Pier) to Black Rock and the Marina, the largest in Europe. Volk was also responsible for bringing the telephone service to Brighton.

Naturally, Brighton also has a wealth of places to stay, from small bed and breakfast establishments to splendid five star hotels. Side by side on the front, are two superb hotels that symbolise Victorian holiday luxury, the white-painted Grand Hotel, built in the 1860s, and its neighbour, the **Metropole Hotel**, completed in 1890. In 1896 it marked the finish of the Emancipation Run, celebrating the abolition of the rule that every motorised vehicle had to be preceded by a man carrying a red flag. In commemoration the London to Brighton Veteran Car Run takes place each year, on the first Sunday in November.

Around Brighton

HOVE

W of Brighton on the A259

13 Brunswick Place · Museum & Art Gallery · British Engineerium · Foredown Tower

Nestling at the foot of the downs, and now joined to Brighton, Hove is a genteel resort with Regency squares - such as Brunswick and Palmeira - and broad tree-lined avenues. An interesting project that is still in progress is the restoration of **13 Brunswick Place**, a Regency house dating from 1820. The work is being carried out by a group of enthusiasts called the Regency Town House. A former fishing village, major development of Hove took place in the early 19th century when the seafront was built with its distinctive terraces. As well as the usual attractions of a seaside

IGIGI HOME-WEAR

37A Western Road, Hove, East Sussex BN3 1AF
Tel: 01273 775257
e-mail: igigi@igigigeneralstore.com website: www.igigigeneralstore.com

igigi General Store is a beautiful and inspirational space filled with an eclectic mix of vintage and antique pieces. The furniture ranges from simple dining chairs and tables to Victorian reading and nursing chairs upholstered locally in hand woven linens.

The store also houses ranges such as hand-blown glassware from Belgium by Henry Dean, silver plated classic cutlery from France and ceramics from across the globe including Royal Staffordfshire and Wonkywear from South Africa and much more. Please visit our website for more info and register for up dates (see above).

Monday to Saturday 10am to 6pm & Sunday 11am to 4.30pm

IGIGI CAFE

31A Western Road, Hove, East Sussex BN3 1AF
Tel: 01273 775257
e-mail: igigigeneralstore.com website: www.igigigeneralstore.com

The **igigi cafe** sits above the General Store at the top of the magnificent sweeping staircase. Whether you enjoy a healthy stew or soup of the day the cafe really does cater for all tastes. For breakfast dippy eggs and hot buttered soldiers are a favorite whilst the Welsh rarebit served with fresh green salad and roasted tomatoes speaks for its self. While our organic cream teas and homemade cakes are second to none.

Special 'Two for Tea' vouchers can be purchased for that special occasion. Freshly brewed Monmouth coffee is served all day.

Monday to Saturday 10am to 5pm & Sunday 11am to 4.30pm

IGIGI WOMENS BOUTIQUE

37 Western Road, Hove, East Sussex BN3 1AF
Tel: 01273 734160
e-mail: igigi@igigigeneralstore.com
website: www.igigigeneralstore.com

igigi Women's boutique has been established on the Western Road, Hove for over 10 years. It is well known throughout East Sussex for carrying a fine collection of classic contemporary fashion and stocking a wide range of sizes from 8 to 18.

We specialise in niche designer brands from Scandinavia, France, Italy and the UK. The collections include soft pallets of natural earthy colours which change with the seasons. Every piece has a hidden twist which brings a contemporary feel to our great classics.

Our experienced staff will help you create the perfect wardrobe, for both every day or evening wear. An in-house tailoring service is also available.

Monday to Saturday 10am to 6pm &
Sunday 11am to 4.30pm

IGIGI MENSWEAR

31A Western Road, Hove, East Sussex BN3 1AF
Tel: 01273 775257
e-mail: igigigeneralstore.com
website: www.igigigeneralstore.com

The long awaited menswear collection has finally arrived in the basement at the General Store.

The quirky emporium has a dark and masculine feel to it making it a great setting for the collection. Classic antique chairs and vintage pieces mingle with jackets and suits chosen for their natural fibers in sumptuous cashmeres, linens, cottons and denim.

With well chosen accessories , scarves , bags ,belts and wallets, there is certainly plenty to choose from for either yourself or a gift.

Designers include; Ally Cappelino for leather goods, Doctor Harris for traditional toiletries and clothing labels such as Albam, Hartford & 120% Lino. These bring a much needed and unique collection for men.

Monday to Saturday 10am to 6pm &
Sunday 11am to 4.30pm

town, Hove is home to the Sussex County Cricket Club and hosts teams from all over the world at their ground.

The **Hove Museum and Art Gallery** contains a whole host of exhibits on the history of the town. There is also a superb collection of 20th-century paintings and drawings and 18th-century furniture. (The splendid wooden pavilion, Jaipur Gateway, an elegantly carved structure that was transported to England from Rajashtan in 1886, has recently been moved to the other side of the building.) For history of a different kind, the **British Engineerium**, housed in a restored 19th-century pumping station, has all manner of engines - from steam-powered to electric. Many of the model and life size displays still operate and the museum's working beam engine is powered up on a regular basis. The Giant's Toolbox is a hands-on display of gears and levers, cylinders and pistons that visitors can discover for themselves. Hove Ikon Gallery includes an exhibition about the Turin Shroud and paintings by local artist Norma Weller.

For one of the most spectacular views of the South Downs a visit to **Foredown Tower** is a must. Housed in a beautifully restored Edwardian water tower, there is a viewing gallery with Sussex's only operational camera obscura and a mass of computers and countryside data that tell the story of the local flora and fauna, as well as the geography of the night sky.

Also in Hove, and rather out of place with the grand Regency squares and avenues, is West Blatchington Windmill. Built in the 1820s and still with all its original machinery working on all five floors, the mill has been fully restored.

SECOND SEED BESPOKE FURNITURE, UNIQUE INTERIORS & GIFTS

94 Portland Road, Hove,
East Sussex BN3 5DN
Tel: 01273 323078
e-mail: shop@secondseed.com
website: www.secondseed.com

Bespoke handmade furniture and inspirational interiors and gifts are the stock in trade of **Second Seed**, which has graced one of Hove's main shopping streets since May 2008. Joint-owner Paul Soden creates stunning handmade pieces from a variety of reclaimed and recycled materials, notably including old sea groynes from along the Southeast coastline. The shapes and colours of these sea-weathered timbers inspire a vast array of furniture for the home and garden.

The shop's name is derived from the theory of wood originating from seed. Working with old wood gives it a second life in a different form, a second seed creation. Each tree is individual and each piece of wood unique, so that even if the size and design of two or more pieces are the same each will have its own unique characteristics. Commissions are invited and shoppers are welcome to visit the workshop. In addition to these marvellous designs Second Seed stocks an original selection of fairly priced homeware and inspirational gifts, including log baskets made from old timbers or old tyres, cast-iron or wrought-iron table tops, French porcelain tableware, Polish glassware and Danish candles and tea light holders.

As well as watching the fascinating milling process, visitors can view an exhibition of agricultural equipment, which includes an oat crusher and a threshing machine.

DITCHLING

6 miles N of Brighton on the B2116

Anne of Cleves' House · Ditchling Beacon · Ditchling Common Country Park · Museum

This historic village, known as 'Diccelingas' in Saxon times, has records going back to 765. Once part of a royal estate belonging to Alfred the Great, it was passed on to Edward the Confessor and then to the Norman William de Warenne. The oldest building here, the parish Church of St Margaret of Antioch, dates from the 13th century, though details from before the Norman Conquest can still be seen in the nave.

Close by the village green and opposite the church, stands Wings Place, an unusual Tudor house, also known as **Anne of Cleves' House**. There is no record that the fourth wife of Henry VIII ever stayed here, but she is thought to have acquired the property as part of her divorce settlement.

At the beginning of the 20th century, this pretty village, at the foot of the South Downs, became the home of a lively group of artists and craftsmen including Eric Gill, Sir Frank Brangwyn and Edward Johnston. Today, it remains a thriving artistic community with many studios and galleries.

To the north of the village lies **Ditchling Common Country Park**, a splendid nature reserve and beauty spot, with a lake, stream and nature trails. Meanwhile, south of Ditchling lies the 813-foot summit of **Ditchling Beacon**, the third highest point on the South Downs. Once the site of an Iron Age hill fort, and almost certainly occupied by the Romans, the beacon was used as a vantage point from which fires were lit to warn of the coming of the Spanish Armada. A magnificent place from which to view much of this area - southerly over the coast and northwards over the Weald - the beacon was given to the National Trust in memory of the owner's son, who was killed in 1940 during the Battle of Britain.

Visitors wanting to discover more about the locality's long and interesting history should make a point of calling in at the superb **Ditchling Museum**, which is located in the Victorian former village school. From the Iron Age there has been evidence of settlement in this area, and the museum's Attree Room shows archaeological finds from prehistoric sites nearby and remains of Roman pottery dug up to the east of the village. It also displays the history of the parish church and of 17th-century non-conformist worship in the village. As this remarkable village has an important place in the English Arts and Crafts movement, the museum features an important collection of work by 20th-century artists and craftspeople, including stone carver and typographer Eric Gill, calligrapher Edward Johnston, painter and poet David Jones, weaver Ethel Mairet, silversmith Dunstan Pruden and artist Frank Brangwyn. The village school itself opened in 1838, and the schoolmaster's garden is stocked with fruits, flowers and vegetables as it would have been in the days of the first schoolmaster, George Verrall. The life of the village, at home and on the farm, is shown in the schoolmaster's cottage.

PLUMPTON

6 miles NE of Brighton on the B2116

Plumpton Place Racecourse

The village is divided in two by the railway line: the modern Plumpton Green and the old village of Plumpton. Plumpton Green, to the north, grew up around the railway station and is the home of the popular **National Hunt Racecourse**. Spectators arriving by train should look out for the Victorian signal box, which has been designated a listed building following the valiant efforts of local railway enthusiasts to preserve it.

Old Plumpton is centred around its flint-built church which dates from the 12th century. The elegant moated 16th-century **Plumpton Place** was substantially remodelled by Sir Edwin Lutyens in the 1920s. The then owner, Edward Hudson, was a wealthy magazine proprietor who had already commissioned Lutyens to renovate his other country property, Lindisfarne Castle, off the Northumberland coast. A previous Tudor owner, Leonard Mascall, was a great cultivator of apples, a tradition that is still maintained at the East Sussex Agricultural College here in Plumpton.

The site of an early Bronze Age settlement can be found up a footpath opposite the college and, nearby, is a sandstone block that commemorates the Battle of Lewes, where Simon de Montfort defeated Henry III in 1264.

HAMSEY

8 miles NE of Brighton off the A275

This must have once been an important place for, in 925, King Athelstan held a meeting of his counsellors at Hamsey Manor. Today, though, all that remains of this hamlet is the old church that is reached through the yard of a 400-year-old farm.

BARCOMBE

9 miles NE of Brighton off the A275

Set on the banks of the River Ouse, which is tidal as far as this point, Barcombe is a tranquil place that was a favourite picnic place with the Edwardians. As well as fishing and picnicking, artists would come here to paint the dilapidated mill buildings in this splendid Ouse Valley setting. There is evidence that the Romans were here, and the village was described as having a church and three and a half mills in the Domesday Book. The half mill was one that spanned the river so the other half was accredited to the village of Isfield.

The parish church of St Mary once lay at the heart of the village but, as the Black Death came to the area, the village was devastated and those who survived rebuilt their houses a mile away to the north. There are marvellous views of the South Downs from the churchyard.

RINGMER

9½ miles NE of Brighton on the B2192

This spacious village, familiar to anyone arriving at Glyndebourne by car, is one of the earliest recorded settlements in Sussex. Though nothing remains of the Saxon church that once stood close to the village's enormous green, there has been a place of worship here for over 1,000 years. The present church was built in 1884 by William Martin after fires in the 16th and 19th centuries had burnt down the previous buildings. Inside the church is a poignant memorial to the village's cricket team. During World War I they joined up en masse to fight at the front and, of the 34 club members who went to France, only six returned alive.

During the 17th century, this rural village

PUNZI

27 Station Road, Lewes, East Sussex BN7 7DB
Tel: 01273 475476
e-mail: margherita@margheritahale.co.uk

Artist/craftswoman Margherita Hale has been exhibiting and selling in Lewes for more than 20 years, and since 2004 she has been based at her shop **Punzi** just off the High Street (A277). Here she designs, makes and sells a range of beautiful gemstone jewellery in a wide range of styles and colours at affordable prices. Her creations include earrings, necklaces and pendants, each a unique and desirable work of art, and most items can be tailored to customers' individual requirements. Many feature unusual gems, including amazonite, iolite, kyanite, red garnet and yellow opal. As well as the lovely gemstone jewellery Margherita also sells many interesting rough and polished stones and fossils from all over the world and her own oil paintings. Commissions are welcome and the shop offers a same-day necklace repair service.

THE WORKSHOP

164 High Street, Lewes,
East Sussex BN7 1XU
Tel/Fax: 01273 474207
website: www.theworkshoplewes.com

The Workshop is owned and run by Jonathan Swan, a distinguished jeweller with many years' experience. He was made a Freeman of the Goldsmiths' Company in 1989 and has won several prestigious awards, the most recent being the Goldsmiths Craft & Design Award for Innovation in 2003. The Gallery is recommended as among the countries best by the Crafts Council and is a showcase for his work and for the work of more than 70 contemporary jewellers. The Workshop also accepts commissions, identifying and developing exactly what the customer requires. They also run jewellery classes spread over 4 evenings a week in the workshop behind the gallery.

The Workshop is easily identified with its bold blue frontage on the High Street. The earliest part of the building dates from around the 9th or 10th century, making it some 300 years older than its near neighbour the Castle. The Workshop is open from 9.30 to 5 Monday to Saturday.

played, in a roundabout manner, an important part in the history of America. Two young women of the parish married men who went on to become influential figures in the birth of the United States. Guglielma Springett, the daughter of Sir William, who supported Parliament during the English Civil War, married William Penn, the founder of the State of Pennsylvania, while Ann Sadler married John Harvard, the founder of Harvard University.

Ringmer's most famous inhabitant was Timothy, a tortoise. He belonged to the aunt of the 18th-century naturalist Gilbert White. During his visits to see his aunt, White became fascinated by Timothy's activities. After his aunt's death, White continued to study the tortoise and, in *The Natural History of Selbourne*, he describes the tortoise's lethargic movements. Timothy's carapace can be seen in the Natural History Museum in London.

LEWES

7 miles NE of Brighton on the A27

Castle Martyrs' Memorial

Anne of Cleves' House Barbican House

The county town of East Sussex, Lewes is an historic settlement that occupies a strategically important point where the River Ouse is crossed by an ancient east to west land route. Much of the town's street plan dates from Saxon times. It was one of the Saxon capitals visited by Alfred the Great and it was considered important enough to be allowed to mint currency. The Norman invasion in the 11th century and William the Conqueror's success at Battle, however, really saw Lewes grow in stature.

HISTORIC DAYS OUT IN EAST SUSSEX

Tel: 01273 486260 Fax: 01273 486990
e-mail: admin@sussexpast.co.uk
website: www.sussexpast.co.uk

Thomas Paine House - The house at 92 High Street, Lewes once lived in by the revolutionary writer Tom Paine, is open for guided tours by appointment. (Tel: 01273 486260).

Anne of Cleves House Museum - This beautiful 15th century timber-framed house was given to Henry VIII's wife, Anne of Cleves. The kitchen and bedroom are furnished in Tudor period with costumes for children to enjoy. Exhibitions tell the story of Lewes from the medieval to modern times. Complete your visit with a stroll around the period-style garden. (Tel: 01273 474610). Joint tickets available with Lewes Castle.

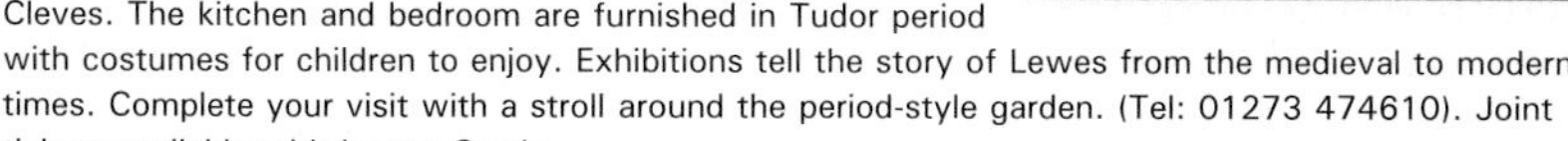

Lewes Castle & Barbican House Museum - Lewes Castle was built soon after the Norman Conquest of 1066. Magical views of Lewes, the Downs and the River Ouse reward everyone who climbs to the top of its high towers. Barbican House Museum, opposite the Castle, tells the story of Sussex from the Stone Age to the end of the medieval period. Displays include a delightful model of Lewes. (Tel: 01273 486290)

Michelham Priory - The house was once part of the original priory and is now surrounded by beautiful gardens and a Moat Walk. Also see the working forge, Rope Museum and restored Medieval watermill. Enjoy a meal in the licensed restaurant or book a tour of the house. (Tel: 01323 844224.)

Michelham Priory, Lewes Castle and Anne of Cleves House are used for weddings and civil ceremonies. See www.sussexpastweddings.co.uk.

Lewes Castle

Because of their closeness to the English Channel, William gave the Sussex estates to his most trusted barons, and the lands around Lewes were granted to his powerful friend, William de Warenne. De Warenne and his wife Gundrada began the construction of **Lewes Castle** and founded the great Priory of St Pancras. Today, a substantial part of the castle remains, including a section of the keep and two towers dating from the 13th century. During the early 19th century, the castle was owned by the Kemp family and they are responsible for the elegant Georgian façade to the Barbican House.

Overshadowed by the Barbican Gate, the house is now home to the **Barbican House Museum** where relics found in the area, from prehistoric times through to the Middle Ages, are on display. Here, too, is the Lewes Town Model, a sound and light show based round a model of 19th-century Lewes. Splendid views over the town are the reward for climbing to the roof of the keep.

Little remains of the Priory of St Pancras. Built on the foundations of a small Saxon church, the priory and a great deal of land were given to the abbey of Cluny in Burgundy. At its height, the priory had a church as large as Chichester Cathedral, with outbuildings on the same scale, but all were destroyed at the time of the Dissolution of the Monasteries in the 16th century.

During the 14th century, a feud developed between the 4th Earl de Warenne and Lord Pevensey. In order to settle their differences, the two met, one May morning, under the walls of Lewes Castle. As they fought, Lord Pevensey cornered de Warenne and, as he was about to drive home his sword, Lady de Warenne began to pray to St Nicholas to save his life and she vowed that, should her husband be spared, her first-born son would not marry until he had placed St Nicholas' belt on the tomb of the Blessed Virgin in Byzantium. At that moment, Lord Pevensey slipped and, as he fell, de Warenne drove home his sword. Years went by before the earl's eldest son, Lord Manfred, became engaged to Lady Edona and, halfway through a banquet to celebrate the 21st anniversary of de Warenne's victory, a vision of the combat appeared to all the guests. Understanding at once that the vow must be fulfilled before their son's wedding, the earl and his wife sent Manfred to Byzantium. For over a year Lady Edona waited for him to return and, finally, his ship was sighted off Worthing. A welcoming party gathered and then, with every one watching, the ship struck a hidden rock and sank with all hands. Lady Edona, watching the ship go down, gave out a sigh and sank to the ground dead. A plinth stands in memory of Lady Edona, who was buried where she fell.

Beside the priory ruins is a bronze memorial by the sculptor Enzo Plazzottia that was commissioned to commemorate the 700th anniversary of the Battle of Lewes. Fought on Offham Hill, the Battle of Lewes took place in May 1264, between the armies of Henry III and Simon de Montfort. The night before the battle, de Montfort and his troops were said to have kept vigil in the church at Fletching, while Henry and his men had a wild, and in some cases drunken, evening at the castle. Whether this was the reason for the king's defeat or whether it was down to bad military tactics is open to debate.

Anne of Cleves House Museum

52 Southover High Street, Lewes, Sussex BN7 1JA
Tel: 01273 474610
e-mail: pro@sussexpast.co.uk
website: www.sussexpast.co.uk

The oldest part of this beautiful timber-framed house was built in the fifteenth century. It was given to Henry VIII's fourth wife, Anne of Cleves, as part of her divorce settlement but she never lived in the house. The kitchen and bedroom are furnished in period style. The Lewes Gallery tells the story of Lewes from the fifteenth century to modern times, the role of local resident Tom Paine, the Lewes Bonfire Night traditions and the story of the Snowdrop Inn. Another gallery illustrates the important Wealden iron industry and there are also displays of everyday domestic objects.

Another monument in the town is the **Martyrs' Memorial** erected in 1901 in memory of the 17 Protestant martyrs who were burnt to death on Lewes High Street during the reign of the Catholic queen Mary Tudor. The mainly Protestant inhabitants of Lewes found an outlet for their resentment at this treatment after the foiling of the Gunpowder Plot and the Bonfire Celebrations, which still take place here, are elaborate affairs.

Like Ditchling, Lewes has an **Anne of Cleves House** (see panel on page 203). In this case, an early 16th-century Wealden hall house that, again, formed part of Henry VIII's divorce settlement with his fourth wife. Also like the house in Ditchling, it is unlikely that the queen ever set foot in the building. Today, it is open to the public and the rooms are furnished to give visitors an idea of life in the 17th and 18th centuries.

In 1988, the Railway Land Wildlife Trust was founded to establish a Local Nature Reserve, a 60-acre wildlife sanctuary within easy walking distance of the town centre.

GLYNDE

9½ miles NE of Brighton off the A27

Glynde Place · Mount Caburn

Situated at the foot of **Mount Caburn**, this small and attractive village is home to a splendid house and an ancient church. Overlooking the South Downs, **Glynde Place** was built in 1579 for William Morley out of flint and Normandy stone that was brought across the Channel in barges. The most notable family member was Colonel Herbert Morley, a Parliamentarian, who was also one of the judges at the trial of Charles I. Fortunately for the family, Morley did not sign the king's death warrant and so, at the Restoration, the family was able to gain a pardon for him from Charles II. The house passed by marriage into the Trevor family and, in 1743, it was inherited by the Bishop of Durham, Richard Trevor. He left the exterior of the house untouched, while turning the interior into a classical 18th-century residence.

At the gates to the house stands the church built by the bishop in 1765 to the designs of Sir Thomas Robinson. Having recently visited Italy, Robinson was very enthusiastic about Renaissance architecture and, as a result, the church has a coved rococo ceiling, box pews and a gallery.

The village is also the home of the black-faced Southdown sheep, first bred here by John Ellman, who lived here between 1753 and 1832. A benevolent farmer, he built a school for his labourers' children and, when they married, he gave the couple a pig and a cow. He even allowed the single labourers to lodge under his own roof. However, Ellman would not allow a licensed house in the village, though he didn't mind if his men brewed their own beer at home.

The distinctive Mount Caburn, to the west of Glynde, can be reached along a footpath from the village. Many thousands of years ago, this steep sided chalk outcrop was separated from the rest of the Downs by the action of the River Glynde. This process created a mound about 500 feet in height whose natural defensive properties have not gone unnoticed over the centuries. The earthwork defences of an Iron Age hillfort can still be made out near the summit and there is evidence of an earlier Stone Age settlement.

GLYNDEBOURNE

9½ miles NE of Brighton off the B9192

Opera House

Glyndebourne, a part Tudor, part Victorian country house, just a mile north of Glynde village, is now the home of the world famous **Glyndebourne Opera House**. In the early 1930s, John Christie, a school master, music lover and inheritor of the house, married the accomplished opera singer Audrey Mildmay and, as regular visitors to European music festivals, they decided to bring opera to England and their friends. In the idyllic setting of their country estate, they built a modest theatre and, in 1934, Glyndebourne first opened with a performance of Mozart's *Marriage of Figaro*. Audrey sang the role of Susanna, lady's maid to the Countess Rosina. Their scheme was not an overnight success: on the second night, when *Cosi fan Tutte* was performed, the audience was very sparse. Fritz Busch was the conductor and Carl Ebert the producer. Joined later by Rudolf Bing, they enlarged the theatre in 1939, doubling the capacity from 300 to 600. The opera house reopened after the War with a performance of Benjamin Britten's *Rape of Lucretia*, and in 1947 the premiere of Britten's Albert Herring was staged, with Britten himself conducting. Since those days, Glyndebourne has gone from strength to strength and, as well as extending the theatre further, the repertoire has also been widened. Today, each summer season, from May to August, sees opera-lovers venturing here dressed in evening wear and laden with picnic hampers, to enjoy a wide range of opera in a unique setting and to eat their picnics in the grounds during the long interval.

WEST FIRLE

10 miles E of Brighton off the A27

Firle Place · Firle Beacon

Though the village is known as West Firle, there is no East Firle - or any other Firle - in the area. A feudal village of old flint cottages at the foot of the South Downs, it is dominated by **Firle Beacon** to the southeast, which rises to a height of 718 feet. As one of the highest points in the area, the importance of this vantage point has long been recognised. It was used by the Admiralty for a fire beacon to warn of the approaching Spanish Armada in the 16th century, and remains of a Stone Age long barrow and a group of Bronze Age round barrows have been found on the summit. There was also a Roman observation point here. Today, the summit can be reached by taking a small detour off the South Downs Way, and the breathtaking views make the climb well worth while.

Back in the village, and set in its own idyllic parkland, is **Firle Place** (see panel on page 206), the home of the Gage family for over 500 years. Built by Sir John Gage in the 15th century, this marvellous Tudor manor house was greatly altered some 300 years later and today it will be familiar to many who have seen it as a backdrop for major feature films or as a location for TV series. Still very much a family home, today owned by the 7th Viscount, its rooms contain a wonderful collection of European and English Old Masters, as well as some rare and notable examples of French and English furniture and Sèvres porcelain. The magnificent deer park, which surrounds the house, was landscaped by Capability Brown in the 18th century and features a castellated tower and an ornamental lake. It is open to the public in the summer.

RODMELL

7 miles E of Brighton off the A26

Monk's House

This little village of thatched cottages is thought to have got its name from 'mill on the road' and, though no mill can be found here

FIRLE PLACE

Firle, nr Lewes, East Sussex BN8 6LP
Tel: 01273 858307 Fax: 01273 858188
e-mail: gage@firleplace.co.uk
website: www.firleplace.co.uk

Set in idyllic parkland, **Firle Place** has been the home of the Gage family for more than 500 years. It was built in the 15th century by Sir John Gage, using Caen stone thought to have been rescued from a monastery dissolved by Henry VIII. The original Tudor building was remodelled in the 18th century and now has the look of French chateau. Still the Gage family home, it contains a wonderful collection of English and European Old Masters, including Gainsborough, Kneller, Reynolds, Guardi, Van Dyck, Moroni, Rubens, Tintoretto, Teniers and Zoffany. Other treasures include fine English and European furniture and an impressive collection of Sèvres porcelain. Firle Place is open to visitors on Wednesday, Thursday and Sunday afternoons between June and September, also Easter, May & August Bank Holiday Sundays and Mondays. The licensed Terrace Restaurant is open for lunch and tea, and private dinners can be booked in the Tudor Great Hall or the terrace area.

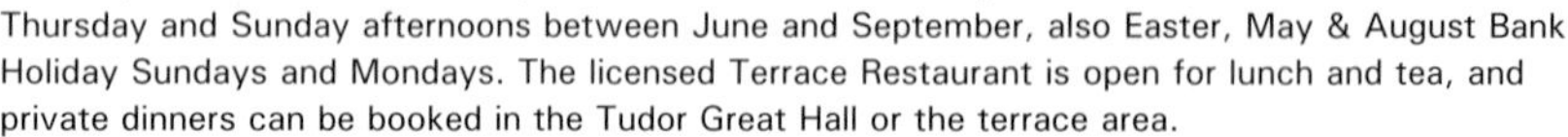

The deer park, which was landscaped by Capability Brown, features a castellated tower and an ornamental lake. The house lies at the foot of the Sussex Downs off the A27 Lewes-Eastbourne road – take the turning marked Firle Village.

today, there is a Mill Road and, in the small 12th century church, there is a reference to the village's old name 'Rodmill'.

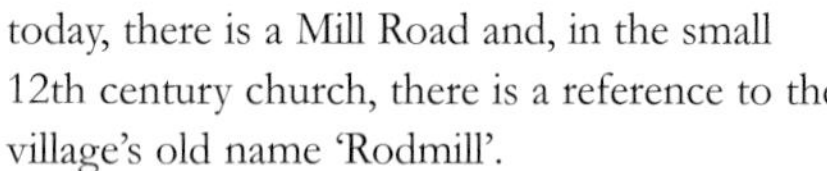

However, the village's main claim to fame is that it was the home of Virginia and Leonard Woolf from 1919 until her death in 1941. The couple, escaping the confining intellectual world of the Bloomsbury set in which they were influential figures, settled at **Monk's House**, a delightful early 18th-century farmhouse that is now in the hands of the National Trust and open briefly in the summer. The garden, which is lush with hollyhocks, dahlias and hydrangeas, gives good views over the downs across the River Ouse.

During her time here, Virginia wrote many of her best remembered works, but throughout her life she suffered great bouts of depression and mental illness. Finally, in 1941, she took her own life by wading into the river with her pockets full of stones. Surprisingly for the disappearance of such a well-renowned figure, her body was not discovered for three weeks, and only then by some children playing on the riverbank. Her ashes, along with those of her husband, who stayed in Rodmell until his death in 1969, are scattered in the garden.

SOUTHEASE

7 miles E of Brighton off the A26

This tiny village, in a dip on the Lewes to Newhaven road, was first mentioned in a Saxon charter of 966, when King Edgar granted the church and manor here to Hyde Abbey in Winchester. Some 100 years later, at the time of the Domesday Survey, this was a flourishing village that was assessed as having 38,500 herrings as well as the usual farm produce. Inside the early 12th-century church is a copy of King Edgar's charter. The original is in the British Museum in London. There is also an unusual organ built by Allen of Soho and installed in 1790. The only other organs of this kind known to be still in existence are in Buckingham Palace and York Minster.

TELSCOMBE

6 miles E of Brighton off the A26

Telscombe was once an important sheep rearing and a racehorse training centre. In fact, the last man in England to be hanged for sheep stealing, in 1819, is believed to have come from the village. In 1902, the racing stables at Stud House trained the winner of the Grand National - Shannon Lass. The horse's owner, Ambrose Gorham, was so delighted with the win that he rebuilt the village church and each Christmas gave every child of the parish a book and a pair of Wellington boots.

PIDDINGHOE

7½ miles E of Brighton off the A26

Set on a wide curve of the River Ouse, this village - pronounced 'Piddnoo' by its older inhabitants - is a picturesque place, with a host of 17th-century cottages and pleasant riverside walks. It was a great place for smugglers in days gone by. Today, however, the ships and boats that tie up at the quayside below the church belong to deep sea anglers and weekend sailors. The golden fish weather vane on top of the church tower was referred to by Kipling as a dolphin, but is actually a sea trout.

NEWHAVEN

9 miles E of Brighton on the A26

Newhaven Fort Museum

Planet Earth Exhibition

Newhaven itself is a relatively new settlement and it replaces the much older village of Meeching. Inhabited since the Iron Age, when a fort was built on Castle Hill, Meeching lay beside the River Ouse. However, in 1579 a great storm altered the course of the river and its outlet to the sea moved from Seaford to near Meeching. Thus Newhaven was established at the new river mouth and it is now one of the county's two main harbours (the other is at Shoreham-by-Sea) with an important cross-Channel passenger service and also a cargo terminal.

Newhaven's rise began in the 19th century and it grew steadily busier once the rail link with London was established in 1847. Two of the earliest visitors to use the passenger steamer service to Dieppe were the fleeing King and Queen of France, Louis Philippe and Marie Amelie, who stayed at the Bridge Inn in 1848 after their sea journey before continuing to London by train where they were met by Queen Victoria's coach and taken to Buckingham Palace. In order to maintain their anonymity, the couple registered themselves at the inn under the

Newhaven Harbour

THE GARDEN OF EDEN

2 Coronation House, High Street, Newhaven, East Sussex BN9 9PR
Tel: 01273 515913
e-mail: edenchadwick@aol.com

Owner Eden Chadwick found a deliciously apt name for her café situated in a parade of shops on the main thoroughfare in Newhaven. Opened in 1999, the **Garden of Eden** is a bright, sociable eating place, smartly refurbished in 2008, with seats for 40 inside, a few more in the hidden rear patio area and a couple of seats outside on the pavement. It's a great place to meet friends or to take a break from shopping or the office, and it's also a favourite spot with tourists and passengers from the ferry.

Food is typical café fare, with almost everything prepared and cooked on the premises, and the all-day breakfast combinations, the hot and cold lunches and the home-made cakes and biscuits are particularly popular. The Garden of Eden also offers a takeaway service.

The café is open from 8am to 4pm Monday to Saturday (closed Wednesday) and from 10 to 2 on Sunday.

rather original names of Mr and Mrs Smith.

Also in the 19th century, during one of the periodic French invasion scares, **Newhaven Fort** was built. Consisting of a ring of casements constructed around a large parade ground, the fort was equipped with modern guns during World War II; it received several direct hits from German bombs. Today, it is a Museum where visitors can explore the underground tunnels and galleries and view the displays of wartime Britain. The **Newhaven Local and Maritime Museum**, in Garden Paradise, contains a wealth of information relating to Newhaven's port, the town's history and its role in wartime. Here also is the **Planet Earth Exhibition**, which explores the world of natural history from millions of years ago to the present day. Displays trace the origins of the Earth through fossils and minerals; one of the most remarkable exhibits is a fossil dinosaur egg found in China, which was laid nearly 100 million years ago and preserved in a flood before it could hatch.

PEACEHAVEN

9 miles E of Brighton on the A259

If nearby Newhaven is a recent town, Peacehaven must be considered just a fledgling village. The brainchild of wealthy businessman, Charles Neville, it was planned and designed during World War I, when the intention was to call the new town Anzac on Sea in honour of the Australian and New Zealand troops who were stationed here before going off to fight in the trenches. However, after the Armistice, it was renamed Peacehaven which very much caught the mood of the time. Laid out in the grid pattern, and with no immediate connection with either the South Downs or the coast, it remains a quiet place off the usual south coast tourist itinerary.

Along the cliff top promenade there is a 20-foot monument to King George V that also marks the line of the Greenwich Meridian.

ROTTINGDEAN

3 miles E of Brighton on the A259

North End House · The Elms · The Grange

Built in a gap in the cliffs between Newhaven and Brighton, Rottingdean was, naturally, a key place for smugglers at one time. However, more recently, it became the home of more artistic citizens. The artist Sir Edward Burne-Jones lived here for the last 20 years of his life in the rambling **North End House** by the green. During his time in Rottingdean, Burne-Jones designed seven windows for the originally Saxon parish church of St Margaret that were made up by William Morris. After his death in 1898 (he was buried in St Margaret's churchyard), his wife maintained her high profile in Rottingdean and in 1900 caused uproar when she hung anti-war banners from her windows following the Relief of Mafeking.

Lady Burne-Jones was also Rudyard Kipling's aunt, and he lived here, at **The Elms**, for five years before moving to Bateman's in 1902. Overlooking the village pond, the gardens of The Elms are open to the public. Surrounded by old stone walls are formal rose gardens, wild and scented gardens and a wealth of rare plants. At the Museum of the Rottingdean Preservation Society, at **The Grange** in Rottingdean, there is a Kipling Room with a reconstruction of his study in The Elms, and other exhibits devoted to his work. It was while living here that Kipling wrote the *Just So Stories*, *Kim* and *Stalky & Co*, and his feelings for his beloved Sussex are summed up in his well-known poem about the county:

God gives all men all earth to love,
But, since man's heart is small,
Ordains for each one spot shall prove
Beloved overall.
Each to his choice, and I rejoice
The lot has fallen to me
In a fair ground - in a fair ground -
Yea, Sussex by the sea!

Stanley Baldwin and Enid Bagnold, author of *National Velvet*, also spent time in Rottingdean, and another famous resident was J Reuter, a German bank clerk, who started a pigeon post to bring back news from abroad that expanded into the internationally respected worldwide news agency. He is buried in the churchyard of St Margaret.

Eastbourne

Martello Tower · Heritage Centre

Museum of Shops · Military Museum

RNLI Museum

Beachy Head and Countryside Centre

This stylish and genteel seaside resort, which has managed to avoid both becoming too brash or disappearing into shy gentility, takes its name from the stream, or bourne, which has its course in the old reservoir in the area of open land that is now known as Motcombe Gardens. When George III sent his children here in the summer of 1780, it was, in fact, two villages, the larger of which lay a mile inland from the coast. Slowly the villages were developed and merged, but it was William Cavendish, later the 7th Duke of Devonshire, who really instigated Eastbourne's rapid growth as a seaside resort from the 1850s onwards.

As much of the land belonged to the

THE GABLES BED AND BREAKFAST

21 Southfields Road, Eastbourne, Sussex BN21 1BU
Tel: 01323 644600
e-mail: chrissymills@hotmail.co.uk info@gablesbandb.co.uk
website: www.gablesbandb.co.uk

Situated only a few minutes away from Eastbourne's town centre, is the delightful **Gables Bed and Breakfast.** Personally run by Chrissy and Andy Mills, all guests are assured of the most warm and friendly welcome. This charming, detached, Edwardian property, with it's pretty garden, is conveniently situated in a residential area with many restaurants and traditional pubs nearby, as well as a theatre, cinema and main line railway station. Close to The South Downs Way, the Cliffs of Beachy Head and many other local attractions, it is an ideal base for visitors exploring this beautiful part of the country. Everything possible is done to ensure guests of a comfortable, enjoyable stay. The three bed-roomed residence, (one king, one twin and one double) has a modern feel to it while retaining a cosy, informal atmosphere. A selection of continental, as well as English breakfasts, are served in the bright, pleasant breakfast room with all food made from the finest ingredients, free range eggs and home-grown fruit when in season. There is a no smoking policy in guest rooms and all public areas and it is a gay friendly B & B.

SAVOY COURT HOTEL

11-15 Cavendish Place, Eastbourne, East Sussex BN21 3EJ
Tel: 01323 723132
Fax: 01323 737902
e-mail: info@savoycourthotel.co.uk
website: www.savoycourthotel.co.uk

The **Savoy Court Hotel** is a 18th Century listed building 50 meters from the Pier and Beach. It is a short stroll from the shopping centre and Train Station. The friendly management and staff and the hotel's amenities make this an excellent base for a weekend or longer break, a traditional family holiday or business trip. The two stars hotel has a lift and the guest accommodation comprises of 29 comfortable appointed bedrooms. All have en-suite facilities, TV, alarm clock-radio and hospitality tray and iron board and hairdryer ad available on request. Wireless Internet connection is available free of charge. Permits can be obtained from the hotel staff for street parking. The classic bar and restaurant are open to both residents and non-residents – traditional English cuisine is the basis of the menu. Other public rooms include reception room and function room and the hotel has a large rear garden. Eastbourne is a lovely place to take time to explore with numerous attractions for all ages and a wide a variety of interests. Notable among these are the Heritage Centre, the Martello Tower and the RNLI Lifeboat Museum, and few visitors will not want to leave the area without a trip to the spectacular cliffs at Beachy Head. Discounts for groups. Check website for special offers.

Cavendish family, the expansion was well thought out and managed agreeably, which created the elegant town of today, well known for its delightful gardens. Among the first buildings that Cavendish had constructed are the handsome Regency style Burlington Hotel, St Saviour's Church, the town hall and the extremely elegant railway station. The classic pier was built in the 1880s and it remains one of the finest seaside piers in the country.

Eastbourne Town

There are, however, several buildings that pre-date the intervention of William Cavendish. The original parish church, inland from the coast, dates from the 12th century though it stands on the site of a previous Saxon place of worship. The development of the old village into a seaside resort is told at the **Eastbourne Heritage Centre**. In the centre of Eastbourne is the **Museum of Shops** with its Victorian streets, room-settings and displays depicting shopping and social history over the past 100 years.

As a coastal town, during the scare of French invasions at the beginning of the 19th century, Eastbourne had its own defences. The

Martello Tower No 73, one of 103 built along the south coast, is also referred to as the Wish Tower. Another Napoleonic defence, the Redoubt Fortress, was built between 1804 and 1810 on the seafront. Now the home of the **Military Museum of Sussex**, the exhibitions here cover some 300 years of conflict on land, sea and in the air. Highlights include, relics from the charge of the Light Brigade at Balaklava and Rommel's staff car from World War II.

Lifeboat Museum, Eastbourne

The sea has always played an important part in the life of the town, from its early days as a fishing village, and now as a resort offering a safe beach environment. Naturally, the lifeboats have played an important role through the years and, close to their lifeboat station, is the **RNLI Lifeboat Museum**. Here the history of the town's lifeboats, from 1853 onwards, are charted through a series of interesting exhibits, including photographs of some of their most dramatic rescues.

While the town is undoubtedly a charming and delightful place to explore and enjoy, most people wish to see **Beachy Head**. One of the most spectacular chalk precipices in England, with a sheer drop of over 500 feet in places, this very famous natural landmark lies just to the southwest of the town. The grand scale of the cliffs is brought home by the sight of the lighthouse, completely dwarfed at the cliff base. On the cliff top is the **Beachy Head Countryside Centre**, which focuses on downland life from the Bronze Age onwards, and includes numerous wildlife displays. This is also the end (or the beginning) of the South Downs Way, the long distance bridleway that was first established in 1972.

Around Eastbourne

POLEGATE

4 miles N of Eastbourne on the A27

Windmill & Museum

The village grew up in the 19th century around a railway junction and, today, it is almost a suburb of Eastbourne. Visitors generally make for the Polegate **Windmill and Museum**, a splendid redbrick tower mill, built in 1817, and one of the few tower mills open to the public (though on a limited basis). Restored as early as 1867, all its internal machinery is in working order and here, too, is a small but fascinating museum of milling.

HAILSHAM

7 miles N of Eastbourne on the A295

This market town, which first received its charter in 1252 from Henry III, is a pleasant town where the modern shopping facilities sit comfortably with the chiefly Georgian High Street. Once a thriving centre of the rope and string industry, Hailsham had the dubious honour of supplying all the rope for public executions. Now, its rope and string are put to less lethal uses. It maintains its rural roots and the three-acre cattle market is one of the largest in East Sussex.

HERSTMONCEUX

9 miles NE of Eastbourne on the A271

Castle & Gardens Science Centre

Herstmonceaux Castle

Herstmonceux Castle was built on the site of an early Norman manor house in 1440 by Sir Roger Fiennes, treasurer to Henry VI. This is a remarkable building on two counts: it was one of the first large scale buildings in the country to be built of brick and it was also one of the first castles to combine the need for security with the comforts of the residents. As the castle was built on a lake there was added protection, and the impressive gatehouse, with its murder holes and arrow slits, presented an aggressive front to any would-be attackers.

Later, the castle passed into the hands of the Hare family, who presided over a long period of decline for Herstmonceux, which culminated in most of the interior being stripped to provide building materials for another house in 1777. The castle lay semi-derelict for 150 years before a major programme of restoration was undertaken in

ARTS HUT

Gardner Street, Herstmonceux, East Sussex BN27 4LE
Tel: 01323 831831
e-mail: anna@artshut.com
website: www.artshut.com

Arts Hut is the studio gallery of artist Anna Wilson-Patterson situated in the picturesque village of Herstmonceux. Anna's current paintings are inspired by country life: walking her dog at dawn and dusk has ensured that she meets fascinating locals, with two feet, four feet or exotic feathers. Invitations to nearby farms, yards, fields and barns have inspired her tiny mono-prints and collages, and also exciting and colourful life-size portraits of poultry and cattle. Visitors will also find seasonal collections of distinctive work by other local artists – for anyone who is inspired by home-grown rural art with a contemporary twist, this is definitely a place to seek out. Built in 1727, the premises, which were previously the Old Sweet Factory, have been restored to include an elegant beamed gallery showing original drawings, paintings, prints and sculpture. Within Anna's studio are displays of smaller items – ceramics, wood, textiles and glass. In the cottage Sculpture Garden are large metal, stone and ceramic pieces. Arts Hut is *the* place to find a personal treat or a gift for a special friend among the wide range of original and unique artefacts: dramatic landscapes; poultry, cattle, sheep and pig prints; flocks of ceramic birds and some very dotty pots and textiles. Arts Hut is open 9 - 5pm Wednesday - Saturday.

the 1930s under the supervision of a Lewes architect, W H Godfrey. His careful and inspired work saw the turrets and battlements restored to their former glory and, today, the castle is as when first built in its delightfully romantic setting (not open to the public). **Herstmonceux Castle Gardens**, the 500 acres of grounds around the splendid moated castle, are open for most of the summer.

Mint House, Pevensey

In 1948, the Royal Observatory at Greenwich was looking for somewhere to move to away from the glow of the street lights of London. It moved here and, after 20 careful years of planning and building, they opened the gigantic Isaac Newton telescope in the grounds. Although the Royal Observatory has moved on, the castle now contains the **Herstmonceux Science Centre**, where, among the domes and telescopes that the astronomers used between the 1950s and the 1980s, visitors can experience the excitement of viewing the heavens. There are also hands-on displays and an Astronomy Exhibition tracing the history and work of the world-famous Royal Observatory.

PEVENSEY

4 miles NE of Eastbourne on the A259

Castle · Mint House · 1066 Country Walk

On the coast, in the shelter of Pevensey Bay, Pevensey was the landing place for invading Roman legions and it was here they built a fortification to protect their anchorage. The fortress of Anderida, built around AD280, was one of the first south coast defences. William the Conqueror landed here with his troops prior to the Battle of Hastings and left his half brother, Robert, behind while he went off to defeat Harold. Robert built a Norman fortress here, which was joined, in the 13th century, by a stone curtain wall. **Pevensey Castle** seemed well able to withstand attack. Following the Battle of Lewes, Simon de Montfort laid siege to the castle without success. However, the structure gradually fell into disrepair although it was brought back into service, briefly, during the advance of the Spanish Armada and again during World War II. Today, the castle is besieged only by visitors who can explore the ruins and follow its history, from the days of the Romans to the mid 20th century.

In the rest of the village there are several fine medieval buildings including the **Mint House**, a 14th-century building that lies outside the castle gates. Coins have been minted on this site since 1076 and, though it is now an antiques showroom, visitors can see the priest's secret room and King Edward VI's bedroom. Any self-respecting old building has a ghost and the Mint House is no exception. In the 1580s an Elizabethan woman, the mistress of the London merchant Thomas Dight, lived at the house. Coming back unexpectedly, Dight found her in bed with her lover. Incensed with jealousy, Dight ordered

East Dean

Distance: *6.0 miles (9.6 kilometres)*
Typical time: *180 mins*
Height gain: *17 metres*
Map: *Explorer 123*
Walk: *www.walkingworld.com ID:590*
Contributor: *Martin Heaps*

ACCESS INFORMATION:

The start and end point are easily accessible from Eastbourne town centre with a bus stop only a few yards away. For the energetic, the start point can be accessed by walking from the town centre along the A259 towards Brighton, but the climb up East Dean Hill can be taxing.

DESCRIPTION:

An easy walk on grassy downland paths and farm tracks. Navigation is straightforward and paths are well marked. The climb up East Dean Hill can be taxing but is certainly rewarding.

FEATURES:

Sea, pub, toilets, National Trust/NTS, great views.

WALK DIRECTIONS:

1 | The start of the walk is well-defined, just a few yards from the bus stop. Walk along the grassy path towards the sea and enjoy the fine views over Eastbourne and further east towards the Pevensey Marshes and Hastings. The Royal Sovereign Light can be seen out to sea.

2 | The triangulation point soon comes into view with the dew-pond nearby. Bear right towards the road and keep to the right to reach Waypoint 3.

3 | Be careful when crossing the road as it does get busy, especially in summer. Pass through the gate and after a short while you are walking amongst the sheep. Please keep your dog on a lead. The path can get muddy, particularly around the gates. Continue to follow the path to the wonderfully-named Crapham Bottom and into East Hale Bottom. There is a newly-built pumping station, which has been built in sympathy with the area. Walk on through the next gate and past a group of farm buildings to join a concrete track at Cornish Farm.

4 | The track leads directly towards Belle Tout, a disused lighthouse and now a residential home. Follow the path to the road, cross to join the path and turn right towards Birling Gap.

5 | Walk through the car park towards the toilet block and turn left onto the stony track.

6 | A gradual climb to Went Hill, but be careful not to miss the path on the right leading downhill towards East Dean. The path bears right to a gate and then past several houses to become a narrow road. The road emerges on to the village green and the Tiger pub is a welcome sight.

7 | The Tiger has a wide range of meals and refreshments and the green can be used for picnics.

8 | Facing The Tiger, walk to the left and onto the main road. At the road turn right and on the left is Downsview Lane. This track runs parallel to the road through the golf course and back to the start of the walk.

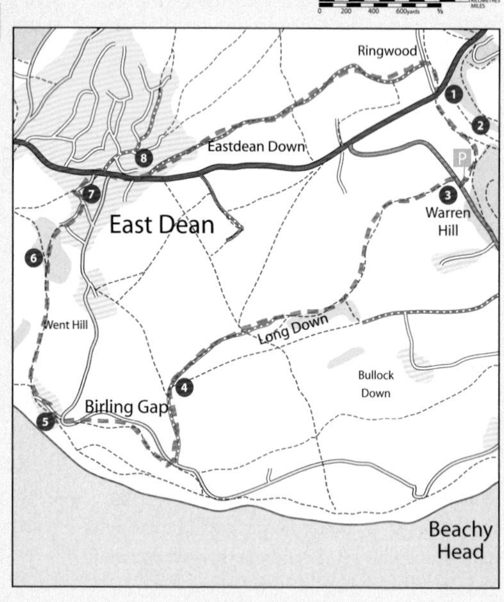

his servants to cut out her tongue and hold her while she was made to watch her lover being roasted to death over a fire. The lover's body was thrown into the harbour and the mistress lead to an upstairs room where she starved to death.

In the days prior to the founding of the Royal Navy, Pevensey served as one of the nation's Cinque Ports - that is to say, it was granted certain privileges by the Crown in return for providing ships and men in defence of the south coast. The **1066 Country Walk** runs for 31 miles through beautiful countryside from Pevensey Castle to Rye by way of Battle. The Walk is an ideal way of learning about the history of the Norman invasion. There are both small wooden posts and signposts throughout the route.

Inland, lies the area of drained marshland known as the Pevensey Levels. At one time this was an area of tidal mudflats that were covered in shallow salt pans. Since then it has been reclaimed for agricultural use and is now covered in fertile arable fields.

WESTHAM

4 miles NE of Eastbourne on the B2191

This pretty village is home to one of the most ruggedly beautiful churches in Sussex, dating from the 14th century and much patched and braced over the years. Inside the church there is a memorial to John Thatcher, who died in 1649 and left his estate to the 'Old Brethren' in the hope that Roman Catholicism would one day be the religion of England once more.

EAST DEAN

3 miles W of Eastbourne off the A259

South Downs AONB Seven Sisters

This charming village at the foot of the South Downs is one of the county's most picturesque, with its village green surrounded by flint cottages, a pub and an ancient church.

During the 18th century, the local parson, Jonathan Darby, is said to have made a cave in the nearby cliffs from which he could display a huge lantern on stormy nights to warn sailors of the hidden rocks. However, some say that the reason for his retreat to the caves was actually to get away from Mrs Darby!

View from Seven Sisters

Just south of the village, right on the coast, is Birling Gap, a huge cleft in the cliffs that offers the only access to the beach between Eastbourne and Cuckmere Haven. Naturally, this was a great place for smugglers who landed their contraband here before making their way

HIKERS REST COFFEE AND GIFT SHOP

Village Green Lane, East Dean, East Sussex, BN20 0DR
Tel: 01323 423733
e-mail: kimshearer@btconnect.com
website: www.beachyhead.org

The Hikers Rest Coffee and Gift Shop is everything it says in its name and more! A perfect position for walkers and visitors to the area, The Hikers Rest is situated on the beautiful village green, a great starting point for your walk over to the cliff tops and the nearby Seven Sisters.

Open since March 2007, this welcoming café and gift shop offers tasty light lunches and sandwiches all of which are freshly prepared in the 'farmhouse' kitchen. For those who have a sweet tooth there is also a selection of delicious cakes and cream teas. With a great selection of coffee's and tea's plus wines and beers for those who want something stronger, there is something for everyone. Inside there is seating for 40,plus comfy sofa area. There is further seating on the patio as well as benches on the nearby village green. Alternatively the friendly staff can prepare a picnic for you to takeaway and enjoy on your walk.

Free parking close by and toilet facilities for the disabled make this a practical spot for all visitors. The Gift Shop offers a wide range of gifts and paintings. Open Tues - Fri 10am - 4.30pm & Sat/Sun 10am - 5.30pm.

up the steep steps to the cliff top. This stretch of the coast, during the 18th century, was controlled by a particularly notorious gang led by Stanton Collins. He had his headquarters in Alfriston, and on one particular night, the gang are said to have moved the lumps of chalk from the cliff path so that pursuing customs officers could not find their way. One unfortunate officer fell over the cliff edge but miraculously held on by his fingertips. The gang came upon him and stamped on his fingertips, causing him to fall to his death. Stretching between Birling Gap and Cuckmere Haven in the **South Downs Area of Outstanding Natural Beauty** are the gleaming white cliffs of the **Seven Sisters**, huge blocks of chalk that guard the coast between Eastbourne and Seaford. The downland is home to a wide variety of birds, including the skylark, and butterflies. There are traces here of ancient settlements, including a Beaker settlement at belle Tout, east of Birling Gap, and Bronze Age barrows at Belle Tout and Crowlink.

FRISTON

3½ miles W of Eastbourne on the A259

This is rather more a hamlet than a village, as only a part Norman church and a Tudor manor house can now be found around the village pond. The churchyard, however, is interesting as it contains the grave of the composer and virtuoso violin and viola player Frank Bridge, one of the pioneers of 20th century English music and also the mentor and teacher of Benjamin Britten. Born in Brighton, Bridge lived in Friston for much of his life though he died in Eastbourne in 1941 - the south door was placed here in his memory. Britten was his pupil from the age of 12 and

Countryside at Friston

dedicated his *Sinfonietta* to his teacher. Later, he wrote *Variations on a Theme of Frank Bridge*, which became a popular classic. The village pond, too, has a claim to fame as it was the first in the country to be designated an ancient monument.

To the north and west of the village lies Friston Forest, 1,600 acres of woodland planted in 1927 by the Forestry Commission. Among the fast-growing pine trees slower-growing broad-leaved trees have also been planted. There is a waymarked circular tour through the forest.

WEST DEAN

5 miles W of Eastbourne off the A259

Charleston Manor

Though the village is only a couple of miles from the south coast and close to Eastbourne, its position, hidden among trees in a downland combe, gives an impression that it is an isolated, timeless place. King Alfred is thought to have had a palace here, and no more idyllic spot could be found for such a place. Alfred is also said to have kept a great fleet here on the River Cuckmere, which in his day formed a much deeper and wider estuary.

The village is now the home of **Charleston Manor**, an ancient house built in 1080 for William the Conqueror's cupbearer. Recorded in the Domesday Book as Cerlestone, the house has been added to over the years and forms the centrepiece of a remarkable garden. Planted in the narrow valley, just north of Westdean's centre, the parterres and terraces give the garden something of a Continental look and feel.

SEAFORD

8 miles W of Eastbourne on the A259

Museum Seaford Head

Once a thriving port on the River Ouse, Seaford was also a member of the confederation of Cinque Ports. Following a great storm in the 16th century, which changed the course of the River Ouse, Seaford lost its harbour and also its livelihood to the newly established Newhaven. Traces of the old medieval seafaring town can still be seen around the old church but, overshadowed by Brighton and Eastbourne on either side, the town never gained the status of its neighbours. The building of the esplanade in the 1870s did bring some development as a modest resort, but the constant pounding of the sea, particularly in winter, has kept the development small.

However, during the threat of a possible French invasion in the early 19th century, Seaford was considered important enough to be the site of the most westerly Martello Tower - this one is number 74. Today it is the home of the **Seaford Museum of Local History**, and among the exhibits in this friendly and lively museum are a World War II kitchen, radio sets and mementos from shipwrecks. The tower's contemporary cannon stands on the roof, from where there are magnificent views over the town and beyond.

To the west of the town lies **Seaford Head**, an excellent place from which to view the Seven Sisters (see under East Dean page 217). The local nature reserve here is home to over 250 species of plants and the reserve supports a wealth of wildfowl on its extensive mudflats, meadowland and downland. A footpath runs to the Seven Sisters Country Park.

JEVINGTON

3½ mile NW of Eastbourne off the A22

This old smugglers' village was established during the time of Alfred the Great by another Saxon called Jeva. Inside the parish church, which can be found along a tree-lined lane, there is a primitive Saxon sculpture. The tower dates from the 10th century. During the 18th century, when smuggling was rife in the area, the local gang brought their illegal goods up here from Birling Gap and stored them in the cellars of the village rectory. The gang used the local inn as their headquarters - conveniently their leader was the innkeeper who was also the ringleader of a group of highwaymen; he was finally caught and hanged in the 1760s.

ALFRISTON

6 miles NW of Eastbourne off the A27

Star Inn · Market Cross

Cathedral of the Downs · Clergy House

Alfriston is one of the oldest and best preserved villages in Sussex. The settlement was founded in Saxon times and it grew to become an important port and market town on the River Cuckmere. The old market cross still stands in the square, one of two left in the county (the other is in Chichester). However, it has not escaped the ravages of time as it was smashed by a lorry and repaired by replacing the shaft.

One of the oldest buildings remaining in the town is the **Star Inn**, built in the early 15th century as a resting place for pilgrims on their way to and from the shrine of St Richard at Chichester. Inside can still be seen the original medieval carvings of animals on the ceiling beams. Another ancient inn, the **Market Cross**, had no fewer than six staircases, and during the 19th century was the headquarters of the notorious gang of smugglers led by Stanton Collins (see also under East Dean). Though he was never arrested for smuggling, Collins was eventually caught for sheep stealing and, as punishment, was transported to Australia. It was tales of Stanton Collins and other local gangs that inspired Rudyard Kipling, living at nearby Rottingdean, to write his atmospheric poem, *A Smuggler's Song*.

The former prosperity of the town is reflected in its splendid 14th-century parish church that is often referred to as the **Cathedral of the Downs**. As recently as the 1930s, local shepherds would be buried here with a scrap of raw wool in their hand - a custom that served to inform the keeper of the gates of heaven that the deceased's poor church attendance was due to his obligation to his flock.

Beside the church is the thatched and timbered **Clergy House**, the first building to be acquired - for £10 - by the National Trust, in 1896. A marvellous example of a 14th-century Wealden hall house, its splendid condition today is due to the skilful renovation of Alfred Powell, who managed to save both its crown pot roof and the original timbers. Visitors to the house can see an interesting exhibition on medieval construction techniques. The house is surrounded by a magnificent and traditional cottage garden that includes rare flowers grown since Roman times and almost lost to cultivation.

By contrast, to the north of the village lies Drusillas Park, a child-friendly zoo that is certain to delight the whole family. As well as housing over 90 species in imaginative and naturalistic enclosures, it also has a creative play area, a train ride and attractive gardens.

WILMINGTON

5 miles NW of Eastbourne off the A27

Priory   Long Man

This delightful village, with its mix of building styles, is home to the historic remains of **Wilmington Priory**. Founded in the 11th century by William the Conqueror's half brother, Robert de Mortain, as an outpost of the Benedictine Abbey of Grestain in Normandy, the priory was already in steady decline by the time of the Dissolution. Many of the buildings were incorporated into a farmhouse, but other parts remain on their own including the prior's chapel, which is now the parish church of St Mary and St Peter.

Cut into the chalk of Windover Hill is Wilmington's famous **Long Man**, which took its present form in 1874. There is much debate about the age of the Long Man and archaeologists and historians have been baffled for centuries. The earliest record of this giant is dated 1710, but this is inconclusive as it could be prehistoric or the work of an artistic monk from the local priory. However, what is known is that, at over 235 feet high, it is the largest such representation of a man in Europe. The giant, standing with a 250-foot shaft in each hand, is remarkable, as the design takes account of the slope of the hill and appears perfectly proportioned even when viewed from below. Covered up during World War II, as the white chalk was thought to be a navigation aid to German bombers, the Long Man was outlined in concrete blocks in 1969.

ALCISTON

7½ miles NW of Eastbourne off the A27

Dovecote

This quiet hamlet, which once belonged to Battle Abbey, became known as the 'forgotten village' after its inhabitants left following the ravages of the Black Death and settled close by. The villagers left, among other buildings, a 13th-century church, which had been built on a hill on the foundations of a Saxon structure to avoid flooding, and 14th-century Alciston Court, that was once used by the monks. During the Middle Ages, the tenant farmers paid a rent to the abbot of Battle in the form of one tenth of their annual farm output and, at harvest time each year, this was brought to the abbey's vast medieval tithe barn that still looms in front of the church. After the village was abandoned, Alciston Court became a farmhouse. The remains of a large **Medieval Dovecote** can also be seen close by. During the winter, large numbers of pigeons would be kept here to help supplement the villagers' dreary winter diet.

SELMESTON

8 miles NW of Eastbourne off the A27

Charleston

This ancient hamlet, which is sometimes pronounced 'Simson', was the site where, during the 1930s, archaeologists discovered tools, weapons and pottery fragments in the churchyard, thought to date from the New Stone Age. However, though the finds are interesting in themselves, Selmeston is better remembered as being the home of Vanessa Bell, the artist. Vanessa moved here to **Charleston** in 1916, with her art critic husband, Clive, and her lover, fellow artist Duncan Grant.

Charleston, Selmeston

Over the next 50 years, the intellectual and artist group that became known as the Bloomsbury Group frequented the house. David Barnett, John Maynard Keynes, E M Forster, Lytton Strachey, Roger Fry and Virginia and Leonard Woolf, who lived not far away at Rodmell, were all frequent visitors. During the 1930s, the interior of the house was completely transformed as the group used their artistic skills to cover almost every wall, floor, ceiling, and even the furniture, with their own murals, fabrics, carpets and wallpapers. They hung their own paintings on the walls, including a self-portrait of Vanessa Bell and one of Grace Higgens, the valued housekeeper, along with works by Picasso, Renoir, Sickert, Derain, Henry Lamb and others. The garden of the house, too, was not forgotten and a delightful walled cottage garden was created at the same time with carefully laid out mosaic pathways, tiled pools, sculptures and a scented rose garden. Following Duncan Grant's death in 1978, a trust was formed to save the house and garden, restoring them to their former glory. This unique task has been described as "one of the most difficult and imaginative feats of restoration" to be carried out in Britain. A Day in the Life of Charleston is an award-winning tour exploring the details of a working day at Charleston and includes an opportunity to see the kitchen and Vanessa Bell's studio.

UPPER DICKER

8 miles NW of Eastbourne off the A22

Michelham Priory   Priory Gardens

This hamlet, which overlooks the River Cuckmere, is centred around a minor crossroads in an area that was once known as 'Dyker Waste'. In 1229, Augustinian canons chose this as the site for the beautiful **Michelham Priory**. Founded by Gilbert de Aquila, the Norman Lord of Pevensey, the six-acre site is surrounded on three sides by the River Cuckmere and on the other by a slow flowing moat - England's longest water-filled medieval moat. The slow moving water is still used to power an old mill where traditionally ground flour is produced in small batches. A splendid gatehouse to the priory was added in the 14th century and the priory continued to flourish until the Dissolution of the Monasteries.

After the Dissolution, the priory came into the hands of first the Pelham family and then the Sackville family who, in the 300 years of their ownership, incorporated some of the priory's buildings into a Tudor farmhouse that went on to become the focal point of a large agricultural estate. Today, the grand Tudor farmhouse rooms are furnished with a collection of Dutch paintings, Flemish tapestries and old English furniture, and the gatehouse, topped by the Pevensey coat of arms, is home to a working forge.

Michelham Priory Gardens are equally interesting and cover a range of styles. To the south of the house is a physic herb garden containing plants that were, and still are, grown for their medicinal and culinary benefits. There is also a re-created cloister garden, which illustrates the ability of the original monks to combine a pleasing garden with one that requires little maintenance. An Elizabethan Great Barn can also be found in the grounds of the priory, as can the medieval watermill, and the river and moat attract a variety of waterfowl throughout the year.

LAUGHTON

11 miles NW of Eastbourne on the B2124

This scattered village, isolated on the Glynde Levels, was once home to flourishing marble mines, potteries and a brickworks. Laughton Place, built in 1534, was one of the first brick buildings constructed in Sussex. The interior of the village church, which lies some way from the village centre, is dominated by a stone war memorial that features a soldier and sailor, both carved in minute detail.

HALLAND

13 miles NW of Eastbourne on the A22

Bentley House & Motor Museum

Just to the south of Halland lies the fascinating **Bentley House and Motor Museum**. Covering some 100 acres of beautiful Sussex countryside, the estate cleverly combines a wildfowl reserve, a stately home and a museum in order to provide a fun day out for all the family. Originally a modest 17th-century farmhouse, Bentley was transformed into a splendid Palladian mansion by the architect Raymond Erith, who also oversaw the restoration of 10, 11 and 12 Downing Street in the 1960s. Exquisitely furnished throughout, the house is particularly renowned for its Chinese Room and the Philip Rickman gallery, which contains a collection of over 150 wildfowl watercolours by the celebrated Sussex artist.

The formal gardens surrounding the house are laid out in a series of rooms, separated by yew hedges, and they often follow a colour theme. Beyond the house are the grounds and a woodland walk through the cool tranquillity of Glyndebourne Wood. The Motor Museum comprises a superb collection of privately owned vintage cars and motorcycles, which follow the history of motoring from its infancy in the Edwardian era to an elegant modern Lamborghini.

The waterfowl collection, which includes swans, geese, ducks and flamingos, was begun in the 1960s by Gerald Askew. The emphasis at the wildfowl centre is on conservation and breeding, particularly of the world's endangered birds.

EAST HOATHLY

12 miles NW of Eastbourne off the A22

Situated some 20 miles from West Hoathly, this compact village was immortalised by Thomas Turner in his *Diary of East Hoathly*. Although the village church was almost completely rebuilt in the mid 19th century, the 15th-century squat tower remains from the original building. Known as a Pelham Tower, because it was built by the local Pelham family,

PEKES MANOR HOUSE

Nash Street, Golden Cross,
East Sussex BN27 4AD
Tel: 020 7352 8088
e-mail: pekes.afa@virgin.net
website: www.pekesmanor.com

Pekes Manor House and the surrounding properties on the 28-acre estate offer exceptional self-catering accommodation in lovely countryside. It was a Monsieur de Peke, an aide to William the Conqueror, who built the first house on the site, a large one-room Norman hall. Only his name survives, but what now stands on the site is an eight-bedroom residence dating in the main from 1550. The superb interior retains many original features, including beams, panelling and beautiful period furnishings.

The eight bedrooms are serviced by four bathrooms and there are three reception rooms. The oldest part is the kitchen, which retains oak beams, the original brick floor, a large hearth and lattice windows. Down the years, the house passed through the hands of several farming families before being bought in 1908 by the grandfather of the current owner Eva Morris. He restored the property and the neighbouring properties and created a beautiful garden, including a walled vegetable garden and a croquet lawn. The Edwardian Wing, originally a cowshed, was converted in 1911 to make a drawing room and library for the manor house and now provides quiet and comfort in two bedrooms.

Elsewhere on the estate are several equally distinctive self-catering properties, with accommodation varying from 4/5 to 11 guests. The largest is the Oast House, a 'fairy tale' property with two circular towers and its own jacuzzi. Tudor Cottage, built in 1937; Mounts View Cottage – with a state-of-the-art barrel sauna on the terrace; and Gate Cottage with its own garden.

the structure has a belt buckle carved on it on either side of the door. This distinctive emblem was awarded to Sir John Pelham for his part in capturing King John of France at Poitiers in 1356. One of the door emblems has a deep slit in it that was supposedly caused by a bullet fired at Sir Nicholas Pelham in the 17th century. The failed murderer is said to have been a Cavalier, Thomas Lunsford, who joined the French army after being exiled for the attempted murder. He returned to Britain to fight with the king during the Civil War, then emigrated to America and died in Virginia in the 1650s.

CHIDDINGLY

10½ miles NW of Eastbourne off the A22

This small village is dominated by the 15th-century spire of its church, which, at 130 feet, is a useful local landmark. Inside the church is a impressive monument to Sir John Jefferay, Baron of the Exchequer under Queen Elizabeth, who lived at nearby Chiddingly Place - a once splendid Tudor mansion that is now in ruins.

However, his memorial is overshadowed by that of his daughter and son-in-law, who both appear to be standing on drums. Tradition has it that the Jefferay family once laid a line of cheeses from their manor house to the church door so that they would not get their feet wet. So the large discs of Sussex marble could, in fact, be a reference to those cheeses!

Curiously, the monuments have lost hands and fingers over the years as enraged locals knocked them off, thinking that the family were related to Judge Jeffreys, who presided at the Bloody Assizes.

3 West Sussex

For the most part (the major development round Gatwick Airport is one of the few exceptions), West Sussex remains an essentially rural landscape dominated by the South Downs, a magnificent range of chalk hills. The South Downs Way, a 100-mile bridleway along the crest of the hills from Winchester to Beachy Head, offers panoramic views across the Weald to the north and the sea to the south. It traces the long history of this area along ancient trails, passing Bronze Age barrows and Iron Age hill forts. On the coast, Chichester, the county town, once a busy haunt of smugglers, is now a thriving sailing centre, while the small fishing villages of the past are quiet holiday resorts like Littlehampton, Bognor Regis and Worthing. The ancient woodland of the West Sussex Weald is now a landscape of pastures and hedgerows and small country villages. The trees were felled for fuel to drive the furnaces of the iron industry, which flourished here for centuries. The legacy of this prosperous industry can be seen in the wealth of elaborate buildings, particularly churches, built from the profits.

Chichester Cathedral

Evidence of early human habitation and culture abound in this area. The Romans settled in Chichester in the 1st century, and it later became a great medieval religious centre with a fine Norman cathedral. At Fishbourne, the Roman remains of a splendid palace built for the Celtic King Cogidubnus were discovered in 1960. At Arundel, the original Norman motte and double bailey design of its magnificent castle is still visible, as well as the alterations and additions of subsequent generations. Norman churches are everywhere, often little altered over the centuries. In the tiny village of Sompting, there is a Saxon church with a pyramid capped tower, unique in England. Near Ardingly, Wakehurst Place is the striking Elizabethan mansion of the Culpeper family, with a magnificent collection of trees and shrubs. Wakehurst Place is also home to the Millennium Seed Bank, a project that aims to ensure the continued survival of over 24,000 plant species worldwide. Petworth House is an elegant late 17th century building, reminiscent of a French château with a garden landscaped by Capability Brown. Close to East Grinstead, the remarkable Victorian country house, Standen, has been sensitively restored to its

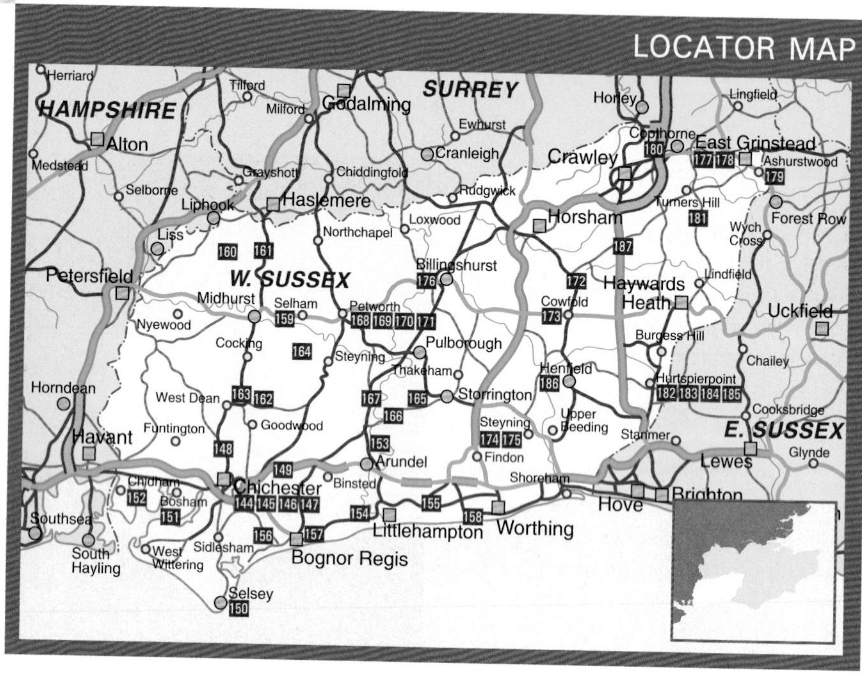

ADVERTISERS AND PLACES OF INTEREST

Accommodation, Food and Drink

148 | West Faldie Bed and Breakfast, Lavant, nr Chichester *pg 233*
151 | Millstream Hotel and Restaurant, Bosham, nr Chichester *pg 240*
154 | Field Place Country House Bed & Breakfast, Climping, nr Arundel *pg 247*
157 | White Horses Bed & Breakfast, Felpham, nr Bognor Regis *pg 251*
160 | Woodmansgreen Farm, Linch, nr Liphook *pg 260*
161 | The Kings Arms, Fernhurst *pg 260*
162 | Woodstock House Hotel, Charlton, nr Chichester *pg 262*
164 | Country House Accommodation, Withy, nr Graffham *pg 263*
167 | The Barn at Penfolds Bed and Breakfast, Bury, nr Arundel *pg 274*
168 | Coco Café & Sugar Lounge, Petworth *pg 276*
171 | The Horse Guards Inn, Petworth *pg 278*
173 | Camelia Botnar Homes & Gardens, Cowfold *pg 282*
174 | Uppingham Bed and Breakfast, Steyning *pg 285*
175 | Michael's Country Kitchen, Steyning *pg 286*
176 | Burdfield's Country Market & Tea Room, Billingshurst *pg 287*
181 | The White Hart Restaurant & Bar, West Hoathly *pg 296*
184 | Clayton Wickham Farmhouse, Hurstpierpoint *pg 298*
186 | No 1 The Laurels Bed and Breakfast, Henfield *pg 300*

Activities

152 | Chichester Canal Trading Ltd, Chidham, nr Chichester *pg 241*
155 | Wood Design Workshops & Mettle Studios, Angmering, nr Arundel *pg 248*
178 | Charlotte Rose, East Grinstead *pg 291*

Antiques and Restoration

180 | Antique Chandeliers, Copthorne *pg 295*

Arts and Crafts

145 | Eternal Maker, Chichester *pg 228*
150 | Amanda's, Selsey *pg 237*
155 | Wood Design Workshops & Mettle Studios, Angmering, nr Arundel *pg 248*
156 | Rose Green Centre of Art & Craft, Aldwick, nr Bognor Regis *pg 250*
158 | Verité Gallery, Goring-by-Sea *pg 257*
169 | Stringers Gallery, Petworth *pg 276*

Fashions

183 | Emmie Boutique, Hurstpierpoint *pg 297*

Giftware

156 | Rose Green Centre of Art & Craft, Aldwick, nr Bognor Regis *pg 250*
170 | Artful Teasing, Petworth *pg 277*
173 | Camelia Botnar Homes & Gardens, Cowfold *pg 282*
178 | Charlotte Rose, East Grinstead *pg 291*

original Arts and Crafts Movement style.

Many great artists and literary figures have found this region inspirational. Turner loved to paint its landscapes and harbours. H G Wells, Anthony Trollope and Tennyson all lived here. The composer Edward Elgar wrote his famous cello concerto at Fittleworth in 1917. And at Hurstpierpoint, at the Elizabethan mansion, Danny, Lloyd George and his war cabinet drew up the terms of the armistice that ended World War I.

Petworth House

Within easy reach of London by rail or road, but not so near as to suffer too much from commuter belt blight, served by an international airport and close to channel ports for travel to the continent, it is no surprise that many notable people continue to make their homes here. Few places so elegantly combine 21st century convenience with the unspoiled charm of a rich historic heritage.

ADVERTISERS AND PLACES OF INTEREST (CONT)

Home and Garden

173 | Camelia Botnar Homes & Gardens, Cowfold *pg 282*
179 | The Forge & General Blacksmith, Ashurst Wood, nr East Grinstead *pg 294*
180 | Antique Chandeliers, Copthorne *pg 295*
182 | Hurstpierpoint Cookshop, Hurstpierpoint *pg 297*
185 | Polka Dot Interiors, Hurstpierpoint *pg 298*

Jewellery

155 | Wood Design Workshops & Mettle Studios, Angmering, nr Arundel *pg 248*
177 | The Jewellery Workshop Sussex Ltd, East Grinstead *pg 290*
178 | Charlotte Rose, East Grinstead *pg 291*
183 | Emmie Boutique, Hurstpierpoint *pg 297*

Places of Interest

144 | Historic Days Out in West Sussex, Chichester *pg 228*
146 | Chichester Cathedral, Chichester *pg 229*
149 | Tangmere Military Aviation Museum, Tangmere, nr Chichester *pg 235*
152 | Chichester Canal Trading Ltd, Chidham, nr Chichester *pg 241*
153 | Arundel Wildfowl and Wetlands Centre, Offham, nr Arundel *pg 246*
163 | Weald and Downland Open Air Museum, Singleton, nr Chichester *pg 262*
165 | Parham House and Gardens, Parham, nr Pulborough *pg 269*
166 | Amberley Museum and Heritage Centre, Amberley, nr Arundel *pg 271*
172 | Leonardslee Gardens, Lower Beeding, nr Horsham *pg 281*
187 | Nymans House and Gardens, Handcross, nr Haywards Heath *pg 301*

Specialist Food and Drink Shops

159 | Farm Fresh Express, Selham *pg 259*
168 | Coco Café & Sugar Lounge, Petworth *pg 276*
176 | Burdfield's Country Market & Tea Room, Billingshurst *pg 287*

HISTORIC DAYS OUT IN WEST SUSSEX

Tel: 01273 486260 Fax: 01273 486990
e-mail: admin@sussexpast.co.uk
website: www.sussexpast.co.uk

Fishbourne Roman Palace - See the remains of a 1st century Roman palace near Chichester with the largest collection of *in-situ* Roman floor mosaics and a variety of Roman archaeological finds. Take a Behind the Scenes Tour of the Collections Discovery Centre where you can handle some of the collections' artefacts. Plenty of free parking, café and special events all year.

The Priest House - A 15th century timber-framed house in the picturesque Wealden village of West Hoathly, containing domestic objects displayed in furnished rooms. It stands in a traditional cottage garden with over 170 herbs.

Marlipins Museum - A delightful local museum in Shoreham-by-Sea with displays on silent film, early transport and maritime history.

ETERNAL MAKER

89 Oving Road, Chichester, West Sussex PO19 7EW
Tel: 01243 788174 Fax: 01243 531032
e-mail: sales@eternalmaker.com
website: www.eternalmaker.com

Anna Hodgson is the hands-on owner of **Eternal Maker**, an aptly named shop that attracts craftspeople from all over the region. The extensive and ever-changing stock includes thousands of samples, 1,500 bolts of fabrics, felting, sewing and needlework kits, cross-stitch, bag making and card making supplies, locally made buttons, bead and button jewellery, rubber stamping, patchwork quilting, threads and yarns, inks and papers, patterns, magazines and books and much, much more.

Anna and her team are major suppliers to other craft shops and go to craft events and knitting and stitching shows all over the UK and Ireland. They also run, at the shop, regular crafts classes covering such topics as papercraft, scrapbooking, bag making, felting and quilting. Eternal Maker is located on the B2144, 500 yards from the A27 Chichester Bypass. Shop hours are 10 to 5 Tuesday to Saturday.

Chichester

Cathedral · Pallant House

St Mary's Hospital · Guildhall

Pallant House Gallery · Canal

Festival Theatre · District Mueum

Royal Military Police Museum

Set on the low-lying plain between the south coast and the South Downs, Chichester, the county town of West Sussex, was founded by the Romans in the 1st century AD. The invading Roman legions used the town as a base camp, christening it Noviomagus, the new city of the plain, and both the city walls and the four major thoroughfares - North, South, East and West Streets - follow the original Roman town plan. They cross at the point where a fine 16th century octagonal Market Cross now stands, an ornate structure built in 1501 by Bishop Edward Story to provide shelter for the many traders who came to sell their wares at the busy market.

The city walls, originally consisting of raised earthwork embankments built in an irregular 11-sided shape, were constructed around AD200. Over the subsequent centuries alterations and improvements were made and, today, the remaining walls largely date from medieval times, and large sections still form the boundary between the old and new city. After the Romans left, the Saxons arrived in about AD500, and the modern name of Chichester is derived from Cissa's ceaster after the Saxon King Cissa.

Chichester also has a long and colourful ecclesiastical history and, although St Wilfrid chose nearby Selsey as the site of the area's first cathedral, the conquering Normans, who moved all country bishoprics to towns, built a new cathedral on the present site in the late 11th century. Resting on Roman foundations, the construction work began in 1091 and the finished building was finally consecrated in 1184. A fire just three years later all but destroyed the cathedral and a rebuilding programme was started by Richard of Chichester in the 13th century. A venerated bishop who was canonised in 1262, Richard was subsequently adopted as the city's patron saint.

Lying in the heart of the city, **Chichester Cathedral** (see panel below), a centre for Christian worship for over 900 years, is unique

Chichester Cathedral

West Street, Chichester, Sussex PO19 1PX
website: www.chichestercathedral.org.uk

Chichester Cathedral is a magnificent building which has stood at the centre of Chichester for nearly 1000 years. A wonderful combination of the ancient and the modern, it holds a number of treasures including the 12th century Lazarus Reliefs and works by Sutherland, Chagall and Piper. The magnificent building is also a tourist attraction and, throughout the year, visitors are welcomed from all over the world. Built to the glory of God, the building is the mother church of the Diocese of Chichester which covers East and West Sussex. Services take place daily.

THE DINING ROOM AT PURCHASE'S

31 North Street, Chichester,
West Sussex PO19 1LY
Tel: 01243 537352
Fax: 01243 780773
e-mail: info@thediningroom.biz
website: www.thediningroom.biz

The citizens of Chichester are not the only ones to enjoy the superb food at **The Dining Room at Purchase's**, as the talents of chef-proprietor Neil Rusbridger and his team bring diners from many miles around. This gourmet haven is located in a beautiful Georgian building in the heart of Chichester that is also home to the UK's oldest family run wine merchants, Arthur Purchase & Son, established in 1760. Comprising restaurant and wine bar, The Dining Room is open Monday to Saturday for lunch (12 to 3), for pre-theatre supper from 5.30 and for dinner from 7.30 (last orders 8.45). The interior combines an elegant period feel with some eyecatching contemporary touches, including a stylish modern bar counter and a huge Ordnance Survey map of the city on one wall.

There are two non-smoking dining areas, one of them a charming conservatory looking out over the leafy walled garden. The menu caters for all tastes and appetites, and the food is complemented by a fine selection of wines (including a connoisseur's list) and courteous, attentive service. Local and organic ingredients are used as much as possible, and the team of chefs under Neil provide a wide variety of dishes, from Danish open sandwiches and hot and cold tapas to fresh fish and shellfish, the finest British meat, game and poultry, zingy fresh salads and much more.

The only problem facing diners is a pleasant one – what to order from a main menu that's filled with mouthwatering possibilities. Some typical delights: Selsey crab 'au gratin', with ginger and leeks, topped with gruyère cheese; diver-caught scallops with grilled bacon (starter or main course); terrine of foie gras with an apple and cider brandy jelly; duck confit with jasmine, cherry brandy and sultana sauce; a classic omelette Arnold Bennett; Scotch beef fillet served on a smoked field mushroom with Roquefort butter or a red wine & shallot sauce; sun-dried tomato & lemon couscous with grilled summer vegetables and saffron. The Dining Room is also the perfect place for a wedding or private party.

on two counts. Firstly, it is the only medieval English cathedral that can be seen from the sea rather than being secluded by its own close and, secondly, it has a detached belfry. The existing tower was thought not to have been sturdy enough to take the cathedral bells and another separate building was needed. In 1861, the cathedral spire blew down in a storm and demolished a large section of the nave. The present 277-foot spire was designed by Sir Gilbert Scott, in keeping with the building's original style, and can also be seen for miles around from all directions.

Among the treasures within the cathedral is the Shrine of St Richard of Chichester along with some fine Norman arches, a set of 14th-century choir stalls and some excellent modern works of art. There is an altar tapestry by John Piper, a stained glass window by Marc Chagall and a painting by Graham Sutherland of *Christ Appearing to Mary Magdalene*. However, the most important treasures to be seen are the Norman sculptures: *The Raising of Lazarus* and *Christ Arriving in Bethany*, which can be found on the south wall. The ashes of the composer Gustav Holst were buried in the north transept of the Cathedral. The Prebendal School, the cathedral choir school, is the oldest school in Sussex and stands alongside the main building.

From the Middle Ages until the 18th century, Chichester was a major trading and exporting centre for the Sussex woollen trade, and some handsome merchants' houses were built on the profits from this trade. The city's oldest building, **St Mary's Hospital**, dating from the 13th century, was established to house the deserving elderly of Chichester.

The almshouses that were built into the hospital walls are still inhabited and the chapel has some unique misericords. The city's **Guildhall**, built in the 1270s as the church of the Franciscans, is also well worth seeing. Later becoming Chichester's town hall and law courts it was here, in 1804, that William Blake, poet, painter and inveterate hater of authority and the establishment, was tried with high treason for having "uttered seditious and treasonable expressions". He was acquitted. Today, it is home to a display telling the story of the building and the surrounding Priory Park in which it stands.

There are also some fine Georgian buildings to be found here and, in the area known as The Pallants, lies **Pallant House**. A fine example of a redbrick town house, it was built in 1713 by the local wine merchant Henry 'Lisbon' Peckham, and the building is guarded by a wonderful pair of carved stone birds, which have given rise to its local nickname -

Market Cross, Chichester

the Dodo House. Another curious feature is the observation tower on the house from which Peckham would look out for his merchant ships returning laden with goods from the Iberian Peninsula. Today, the house is the **Pallant House Gallery**, one of the finest galleries outside London, with each room reflecting a different period. Among them is one of the best collections of Modern British Art in the world, with works by Royal Academicians past and present including Peter Blake, Patrick Caulfield, R B Kitaj and Joe Tilson.

One of the city's most distinctive modern buildings can be found at Oaklands Park, close by the city walls. The **Chichester Festival Theatre** was opened in 1962 and the splendid hexagonal building has since gained a reputation for staging the finest classical and contemporary drama, opera and ballet. The theatre and the cathedral are the focal points of the annual Chichester Festival. The **Royal Military Police Museum** is housed in the Keep at Roussillon Barracks, Broyle Road, and is a must for anyone interested in military history. The various exhibitions trace the entire history of the Redcaps from Tudor times to recent conflicts. Display cases contain life-size models of military policemen dressed in the varieties of uniforms they have used at different times and in different parts of the world. Also included are maps, weapons and communications equipment used in various theatres of operations.

Once a busy port, the city is now a haven for boat lovers and yachtsmen, with 12,000 resident boats in one of Europe's largest marinas. From the bustling harbour visitors can take a boat trip around this stretch of sheltered water with its sand dunes, mudflats, shingle and woodlands providing habitats for varied sea birds. A particularly pleasant waterside walk takes in the city's impressive canal basin, along the **Chichester Canal** (see panel on page 241) to Chichester Harbour. The canal opened in 1822, taking vessels up to 150 tons from Arundel to Portsmouth. The last commercial cargo travelled the route in 1928 but now, after restoration work, this shorter stretch provides a delightful walk with a cruise boat at the other end on which to make the return journey.

Housed in an 18th-century corn store, **Chichester District Museum** explores local history through displays and hands-on activities. Visitors can find out about local geology and prehistory, including Boxgrove Man, believed to have lived around 500,000 years ago. Part of a human shinbone and two human feet, the earliest remains of human-like species found in Britain, can be seen. They were discovered during excavations in the 1990s along with bones of butchered animals and tools. Life in Roman, Saxon and medieval Chichester is also revealed. There are displays on Chichester during the Civil War and visitors can see how the city changed during Georgian and Victorian times. The story is brought right up to date with displays on Chichester since 1900.

Around Chichester

MID LAVANT

2 miles N of Chichester on the A286

This attractive village, along with its neighbour East Lavant, is named after the small river that flows from Singleton into Chichester Harbour. There are spectacular views from here northwards over the South Downs and it is said that these were the inspiration for the

WEST FALDIE B&B

Lavant, Chichester, West Sussex PO18 0BW
Tel: 01243 527450 website: www.west-faldie.com

West Faldie is a handsome traditional Sussex flint house where resident owner Hilary Mitten has two attractive en suite bedrooms for Bed & Breakfast guests. The rooms are very quiet and comfortable, and the setting is delightful, with a beautiful garden giving way to open farmland. The house stands just off the A286, a couple of miles north of Chichester, is an ideal base for a well-earned break or discovering the many nearby places of interest, including Goodwood (horseracing and motor sports), the Chichester Festival Theatre and the Weald & Downland Open Air Museum. Children over 12 and pets are welcome. Closed Dec - Jan.

Woods at West Stoke, nr Mid Lavant

words "England's green and pleasant land" that appear in William Blake's poem *Jerusalem*.

GOODWOOD

3 miles NE of Chichester off the A285

Goodwood House · Good wood Racecourse

This is not a village, but the spectacular country home of the Dukes of Richmond, **Goodwood House**. It was first acquired by the 1st Duke of Richmond (the natural son of Charles II and his beautiful French mistress, Louise de Keroualle) in 1697, so that he could ride with the local hunt. The original, modest hunting lodge still remains in the grounds, but has been superseded by the present mansion, built on a grand scale in the late 18th century for the 3rd Duke by the architect James Wyatt. At the same time the splendid stables were added. Refurbished by the Earl and Countess of March, several rooms in this impressive house, including the state apartments, are open to visitors. The state apartments are magnificent examples of the luxury of the period with an Egyptian state dining room, grand yellow drawing room and an elegant ballroom. Among the items on display are two *Views of the Thames from Old Richmond House* by Canaletto, the *Lion and Lioness* by Stubbs, fine Sèvres porcelain collected by the 3rd Duke while he was Ambassador to Paris, gruesome relics from the Napoleonic Wars and French and English furniture.

Viewers of the BBC television drama *Aristocrats* will recognise the house as it was used as the location for the series. Not only was the drama filmed here, but the story was that of the independent-minded and glamorous daughters of the 2nd Duke of Richmond. The girls grew up both at Goodwood House and at the Duke's London residence, Richmond House, and the whole

Cass Sculpture Park, Goodwood

family were enthusiastic leaders of early Georgian society. Goodwood House was the setting for Sarah's banishment from society and it was also here that Kildare wooed Emily. On display in the house is a painting by George Stubbs, which features Caroline's husband, Lord Holland, and the Meissen snuff box the couple gave to the duchess four years after their elopement.

The house is the focal point of the Goodwood Estate, some 12,000 acres of downland, which also incorporate the world-famous **Goodwood Racecourse**. A favourite venue with the rich, racing has taken place here for nearly 200 years and, in particular, the Glorious Goodwood meeting. First introduced by the 4th Duke of Richmond in 1814, just 12 years after racing began here, this prestigious five-day meeting is one of the major events in the calendar and has long been a much anticipated part of the summer season. Further, the estate contains a golf course, motor racing circuit, children's adventure play area, sculpture park and a new Rolls-Royce factory. Highlights of the year for motoring and motor racing enthusiasts are the Festival of Speed held in June and the Revival Meeting in September.

HALNAKER

3½ miles NE of Chichester on the A285

Halnacker House

Pronounced Hannacker, this village was the seat of the influential and powerful De La Warr family. The present **Halnaker House**, designed by Edwin Lutyens in 1938, is a splendid modern country house. Just to the north lies the original Halnaker House, which was allowed to fall into decay around 1800. Built in medieval times, the old house was originally the home of the De Haye family who were also the founders of Boxgrove Priory.

Above the village, on Halnaker Hill, stands an early 18th-century tower windmill, Halnaker Windmill, which was painted by Turner. It remained in use until 1905 when it, too, was allowed to fall into ruin. In 1912, Hilaire Belloc mentioned the windmill in a poem where he compares the decay of agriculture in Britain with the neglected mill. The exterior was restored in 1934 and the windmill was used as an observation tower during World War II. It was restored once again in 1955 by the county council.

BOXGROVE

2 miles NE of Chichester off the A27

Priory

This attractive village is home to the remains of **Boxgrove Priory**, a cell of the Benedictine

Lessay Abbey in France, which was founded around 1115. Initially a community of just three monks, over the centuries the priory expanded and grew into one of the most influential in Sussex. However, all that remains today are the Guest House, Chapter House and the Church, which is now the parish Church of St Mary and St Blaise. Its sumptuous interior reflects the priory's former importance and, before the Dissolution of the Monasteries, the De La Warr Chantry Chapel was built like a 'church within a church' to be the final resting place of the family. Unfortunately, Henry VIII forced De La Warr to dispose of the priory and the family was eventually buried at Broadwater near Worthing. Though it is still empty, the extravagant marble chapel has survived.

In 1993, a fascinating discovery was made by local archaeologists who unearthed prehistoric remains in a local sand and gravel pit. Among the finds was an early hominid thigh bone and, although there is still some debate over the precise age of the bone, the find has been named Boxgrove Man (see Chichester Museum page 232).

TANGMERE

2 miles E of Chichester off the A27

Military Aviation Museum

The village is still very much associated with the nearby former Battle of Britain base, RAF Tangmere and, although the runways have now been turned back into farmland or housing estates, the efforts of the pilots are remembered at the local pub, The Bader Arms (named after pilot Douglas Bader) and the **Tangmere Military Aviation Museum** (see panel below). The museum, based at the airfield, tells the story, through replica aircraft, photographs, pictures, models and memorabilia, of military flying from the earliest days during World War I to the present time. The Battle of Britain Hall tells its own story with aircraft remains, personal effects and true accounts from both British and German pilots of those desperate days in 1940. On display are two

Tangmere Military Aviation Museum

Tangmere, nr Chichester, West Sussex PO20 2ES
Tel: 01243 790090
website: www.tangmere-museum.org.uk

Tangmere Military Aviation Museum was established in 1982 on the old RAF Tangmere airfield. From its beginnings in 1916, through its illustrious service as one of Britain's front line fighter bases during WW2 and on to its key role as home to the world speed record breaking aircraft of the High Speed Flight in the post war years it has occupied a unique place in aviation history.

The museum contains countless fascinating exhibits. Here you can see priceless historic aircraft such as Neville Duke's world record breaking Hawker Hunter, actual equipment used by the brave SOE agents who were carried into occupied France on 'black Lysander' flights from Tangmere, flight simulators where you can try your hand at flying, a full sized replica of the very first Spitfire prototype and more. Much more. There is something for all the family to see and do.

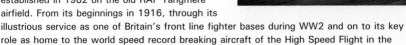

St Wilfrid's Chapel, Norton

historic aircraft, each of which beat the World Air Speed record in their day – one is the Hawker Hunter of Neville Duke. Finally, it was while at RAF Tangmere during World War II that H E Bates completed his novel *Fair Stood the Wind for France* about a bomber crew shot down over occupied France.

NORTON

6 miles S of Chichester on the B2145

One of the original communities that made up Selsey, Norton's first church was probably built on, or close to, the site of the cathedral that St Wilfrid erected when he became Bishop of the South Saxons in AD681. Following the Norman Conquest, the country bishoprics were moved into the towns and Selsey's bishop transferred to Chichester. In the 1860s, the decision to move the medieval parish Church of St Peter from its isolated site to Selsey was taken. But, according to ecclesiastical law, a church chancel cannot be moved, so it remains here as St Wilfrid's Chapel.

SIDLESHAM

4 miles S of Chichester on the B2145

Pagham Harbour Nature Reserve

A pleasant village, which is home to the information and interpretation centre for **Pagham Harbour Nature Reserve**. The harbour was formed when the sea breached reclaimed land in 1910 and it is now a well-known breeding ground for many rare birds. The tidal mud flats attract an abundance of wildfowl and also many species of animals and marine life. Sidlesham Ferry is the starting point for guided walks around this important conservation area.

SELSEY

7 miles S of Chichester on the B2145

Windmill Lifeboat Museum Selsey Bill

Once an important Saxon town, fishing has been the main stay of life here for many centuries. However, according to accounts by the Venerable Bede, St Wilfrid, while Bishop of the South Saxons, discovered that the Selsey fishermen were unsuccessful and such was their shortage of food that they were prepared to throw themselves off nearby cliffs. St Wilfrid taught them to fish and the town has thrived ever since; at one time, only Selsey crabs were served on the liner QE2.

Now a more modest town, yet still a popular resort, the main street looks much as it did in the 18th century. The Sessions House, where the Lord of Selsey Manor held court, was probably built in the early 17th century though it contains the exposed beams and wooden panelling of an earlier age. There are also several thatched cottages to be seen, including the 18th-century cottage and the 16th-century farmhouse known as The Homestead. Perhaps, though, the most impressive building here is **Selsey Windmill**.

AMANDA'S

153 High Street, Selsey, West Sussex PO20 0QB
Tel: 01243 607968

Next to Boots on Selsey's High Street, **Amanda's Hobbie Hideout** is filled with ideas to satisfy creative appetites. Among many hundreds of craft products in Amanda Bridge's delightful shop you'll find paints and papers, pens, crayons, inks, rubber stamps, wools, tapestry, clay, wax and kits for making cards, jewellery and cross stitch. Also in stock are toys and games, jigsaw puzzles, beach balls, buckets and spades, fishing nets and Christmas decorations. Saturday morning brings classes on a variety of craft subjects.

Today's mill was built in 1820 as the previous late 17th-century timber construction had suffered greatly from weather damage. A tower mill built from local red bricks, though it ceased milling flour in 1910, the mill continued to grind pepper into the 1920s. Now rescued and restored, it is a pleasant local landmark.

With so many of the townsfolk depending on the sea for their living, the Lifeboat Station was established here in 1860. The present building was erected 100 years later and there is also an interesting little **Lifeboat Museum**.

For many years, the town's East Beach was a well-known site for smuggling, which was a full-time occupation for many local inhabitants in the 18th century. In fact, while the French were in the throes of their revolution, the villagers of Selsey were busy smuggling ashore over 12,000 gallons of spirits. Much later, during World War II, East Beach was used as a gathering point for sections of the famous Mulberry Harbour that was transported across the Channel as part of the D-Day landings. Just inland from the beach, now on a roundabout, is a small building called the Listening Post. During World War I it was used as a naval observation post, with personnel listening out for the sound of invading German airships, and as such it acted as an early warning system long before radar was established.

A gruesome reminder of Selsey's smuggling past is Gibbet Field. The bodies of two smugglers, John Cobby and John Hammond, who had been executed for their crimes in 1749, were hung in chains from the gibbet that once stood in this field, as a grim warning to others who might follow in their footsteps.

Geographically, **Selsey Bill**, the extreme southwest of Sussex, is an island, with the English Channel on two sides. Pagham Harbour to the northeast and a brook running from the harbour to Bracklesham Bay cuts the land off from the remainder of the Manhood Peninsular. However, Ferry Banks, built in 1809, links the Bill with the mainland. Over the centuries this part of the coastline has been gradually eroded and many of the area's historic remains have now been lost beneath the encroaching tides.

EARNLEY

6 miles SW of Chichester off the B2198

Rejectamenta · Earnly Gardens

This charming small village is home to **Earnley Gardens**, a delightful five acres of themed gardens, exotic birds and butterflies. It also has a fascinating small museum of ephemera. **Rejectamenta**, the museum of 20th-century memorabilia, displays thousands of everyday items reflecting the changes in lifestyle over the past 100 years. There is everything here from old washing powder packets and winklepickers, to stylophones and space hoppers.

WEST WITTERING

7 miles SW of Chichester on the B2179

Cakeham Manor House   East Head

West Wittering and its larger neighbour, East Wittering, both lie close to the beautiful inlet that is Chichester's natural harbour. A charming seaside village, West Wittering overlooks the narrow entrance to the harbour and this former fishing village has developed into a much sought-after residential area and select holiday resort. Here, too, lies **Cakeham Manor House**, with its distinctive early 16th-century brick tower that was once the summer palace of the bishops of Chichester. A splendid part-medieval, part-Tudor and part-Georgian house, it was in the manor's studio that Sir Henry Royce, of Rolls-Royce, designed many of his inventions.

Both villages have easy access to excellent sandy beaches and the headland that forms the eastern approach to Chichester Harbour, **East Head**, which is now a nature reserve, a sand and shingle spit that supports a variety of bird, plant and marine life; marram grass has been introduced to the sand dunes to help reduce the ravages of the sea and wind. It is one of the last pieces of natural coastline in the county and is an ideal place to walk, play and sunbathe, or simply to admire the yachts that anchor off the northern end. It is also a very important place for wildlife.

ITCHENOR

5 miles SW of Chichester off the B2179

Originally a Saxon settlement called Icenore, in the 13th century the villagers of Itchenor built a church that they chose to dedicate to St Nicholas, the guardian of seafarers. As the village overlooks the sheltered waters of Chichester Harbour, shipbuilding was an obvious industry to become established here and, as early as the 1600s, there was a shipyard at Itchenor. The last ships built here were minesweepers during World War II, and the village today is a busy sailing and yachting centre as well as being the customs clearance port for Chichester Harbour.

BIRDHAM

4 miles SW of Chichester on the A286

Sussex Falconry Centre

The setting for Turner's famous painting of Chichester Harbour (which can be seen at Petworth House), this delightful place is as charming today as it was when the views captured the great artist's imagination. Here, too, can be found the **Sussex Falconry Centre**, which was originally set up as a breeding and rescue centre for indigenous birds of prey. In 1991, the centre started to exhibit the birds to the public and, as well as viewing and watching the birds fly, visitors can also take advantage of the centre's falconry and hawking courses.

West Wittering Beach

FISHBOURNE

2 miles W of Chichester on A286

Roman Palace

This unremarkable village would not appear on anyone's list of places to visit in West Sussex if it was not for the splendid Roman remains discovered in 1960 when a new water main was cut. **Fishbourne Roman Palace** was built around AD75 for the Celtic King Cogidubnus, who collaborated with the Roman conquerors. As well as taking on the role of Viceroy, Cogidubnus was rewarded with this magnificent palace with underfloor heating, hot baths, a colonnade, an ornamental courtyard garden and lavish decorations. This was the largest residential building north of the Alps, and among the superb remains are a garden and numerous mosaic floors, including the famous Cupid on a Dolphin mosaic.

As well as walking through the excavated remains of the north wing, visitors can see the formal garden, which has been replanted to the original Roman plan. When the palace was first constructed, the sea came right up to its outer walls and the building remained in use until around AD320 when a fire largely destroyed the site. The history of the palace, along with many of the artefacts rescued during the excavations, can be discovered in the site museum, where there is also an exhibition area on Roman gardening.

Mosaic, Fishbourne Roman Palace

BOSHAM

3½ miles W of Chichester off the A286

Bosham Walk Craft Centre

Pronounced Bozzum, this pleasant village is well known for both its history and its charm. Though it was the Irish monk Dicul who built a small religious house here, Bishop Wilfrid is credited with bringing Christianity to the area in AD681 and Bosham is probably the first place in Sussex where he preached. Later, in the 10th century, Danish raiders landed here and, among the items that they stole, was the church's tenor bell. As the Danes left and took to their boats, the remaining bells were rung to sound the all-clear and to indicate to the villagers that they could leave the nearby woods and return to their homes. As the last peal of bells rang out, the tenor bell, in one of the Danish boats, is said to have joined in and, in doing so, capsized the boat. Both the bell and the sailors sank to the bottom of the creek and the place is now known as Bell Hole. Whether the story is true or not, Bosham certainly has its fair share of local legends as the village has strong associations with King Canute. It was here, on the shore, that the king, in the early 11th century, is said to have ordered back the waves in an attempt to demonstrate his kingly powers. King Canute's daughter is also buried in the once important Saxon parish church.

King Harold sailed from Bosham in 1064 on his ill-fated trip to Normandy to appease his rival for the English throne, William of Normandy. However, Harold's plans

MILLSTREAM HOTEL & RESTAURANT

Bosham Lane, Bosham, nr Chichester, West Sussex PO18 8HL
Tel: 01243 573234
Fax: 01243 573459
e-mail: info@millstream-hotel.co.uk
website: www.millstream-hotel.co.uk

In the heart of historic Bosham on the shores of Chichester Harbour, the **Millstream Hotel** combines the style and elegance of an English country house with the charm and character of an 18th century malthouse cottage. It offers the highest levels of comfort, service and hospitality and is a holder of the coveted Visit Britain Gold Award. Each of the 35 enchanting guest bedrooms has its own individual appeal, and all are decorated and furnished to an impressively high standard. Two particularly charming rooms are suites with private gardens, located in the thatched Waterside Cottage.

The cosy bar is the perfect place to unwind – perhaps to meet other guests, to have a game of cards or to enjoy a quiet read by the fire. In fine weather, afternoon tea or an aperitif on the lawn is guaranteed to put the daily grind of city life far into the background. The hotel is open to residents and non-residents for morning coffee, light and full lunches, afternoon cream teas and candlelit dinners. In the fine restaurant, overlooking the garden and millstream, a wide-ranging menu of English and European dishes is served, with the emphasis on top-quality fresh local produce. The chefs pay great attention to both preparation and presentation in dishes that range from starters such as a game terrine of venison, pigeon and duck or pan-seared scallops with crispy bacon, to main courses such as grilled whole sea bream served with herb butter and breast of Gressingham duck served with prune and brandy sauce. There's always a good choice for vegetarians, and desserts like praline crème brulée and iced pineapple and ginger parfait set the seal on a meal to remember.

Bosham is a lovely place to spend time discovering (see photograph on the front cover of this guide). Now a popular base with yachtsmen, its maritime connections go back famously to the day when King Canute found that the waves had little regard for his majesty's authority. Canute's daughter is buried in the Saxon church. The town also has plenty of interesting old buildings, shops and a craft centre, and the Millstream Hotel is the ideal base for getting to know this delightful place.

CHICHESTER CANAL CRUISES

Chidham, Chichester, West Sussex PO18 8TL
Tel: 01243 576701
e-mail: bookings@chichestercanal.com
website: www.chichestercanal.com

The **Chichester Canal** was completed in 1822, taking vessels of up to 150 tons on their journey from Arundel to Portsmouth. The last commercial cargo was carried in 1906, but the canal has been restored as a major leisure facility. It runs for nearly four miles from Chichester city walls to the harbour, and there are plans to extend it to the sea lock.

The headquarters of **Chichester Canal Cruises**, with office, shop and café, is located 2 minutes from Chichester rail and bus station, signposted off the main A27 Chichester bypass. The narrow boat *Egremont* runs round trips along the canal four times a day, and the wide-beamed *Richmond* can be hired for parties, with lunch, cream teas or evening trips with seats for up to 42. In 2009 the owners plan to market monthly sundowner and music cruises (Tel: 01243 377405).

Apart from the cruises the canal is a great place for walking or cycling on the towpath, hiring a rowing boat or canoe, fishing, painting or taking part in the regular wildlife tours and talks.

went awry when he was taken captive and made to swear to William to aid his claim to the crown - a promise which, famously, Harold did not keep. It was the breaking of the promise that caused William to set forth with his army a couple of years later. As a result, Harold's lands in Sussex were some of the first to be taken by the conquering Norman army and Bosham church's spire can be seen alongside Harold's ship in the Bayeux Tapestry.

An important port in the Middle Ages and, particularly, between the 1800s and the 20th century when it was alive with oyster smacks, today's Bosham is a place for keen yachtsmen as well as a charming place to explore. The narrow streets that lead down to the harbour are filled with elegant 17th and 18th-century flint and brick buildings among which is the **Bosham Walk Craft Centre**. This fascinating collection of little shops selling all manner of arts, crafts, fashions and antiques within an old courtyard setting, also holds craft demonstrations and exhibitions throughout the season.

Low Tide at Bosham

Stoughton

Distance: *4.3 miles (6.9 kilometres)*
Typical time: *105 mins*
Height gain: *146 metres*
Map: *Explorer 120/Landranger 197*
Walk: *www.walkingworld.com ID:2092*
Contributor: *Sylvia Saunders*

ACCESS INFORMATION:

From Emsworth A27(T) take the B2148, B2147 then the B2146 turning off right to Walderton and Stoughton. You will see the sign for St. Mary's Church at the green. Park at the end of the green in the marked out triangle on the road. Have no fear of blocking the bus stop as, sadly, the buses stopped running a few years ago.

DESCRIPTION:

When most people arrive at the quiet village of Stoughton they cannot resist walking in the outstandingly beautiful Kingley Vale Nature Reserve. However, this walk takes you up and over the hill on the opposite side of the road where the views and the woodland are just as spectacular, but much quieter. You will be unlucky if you don't spot some deer on this walk.

FEATURES:

Hills or fells, pub, church, wildlife, birds, flowers, great views, butterflies, woodland.

WALK DIRECTIONS:

1 | Take the lane to the right of the tree and village notice board. After a short distance you will see two tracks on your right hand side. The first one leads up to the church. Ignore this. Turn right up the second track, signposted 'bridleway' with the telephone box on the left hand side of it. Near to the top of the hill there is a track off to your right, ignore this and follow the bridleway as indicated by the post. As you begin to drop, ignore the footpath off on your left and all other trackways, following the well signed route to the lane.

2 | Cross straight over the lane and follow the bridleway uphill. After a short distance you will arrive at a set of fingerposts. Ignore the bridleway off to the left and carry straight on up the hill ignoring all other tracks. The route is clearly marked along the way with wooden posts. At the top of the hill you arrive at a T-junction with another track.

3 | Cross straight over here taking the footpath through Lyecommon. Pass the idyllic Keeper's cottage where you can usually find a kindly placed drink of water for thirsty dogs. After passing a couple of other cottages you will arrive at a wooden gate and stile. At the time of walking the stile was overgrown but the gate was wide open. Pass straight through and you will soon arrive at a choice of routes.

4 | Take the lower track to the left as indicated by the footpath sign. Walk downhill until you come to a track bearing right. Turn right as indicated. After a short distance you will arrive at another track. Turn right here. After a short distance you will arrive at a fingerpost sign by a big beech tree. Turn left here and the track soon opens out into a field. Walk through this field with the trees on your right hand side. The main trackway bends off to the right out of this

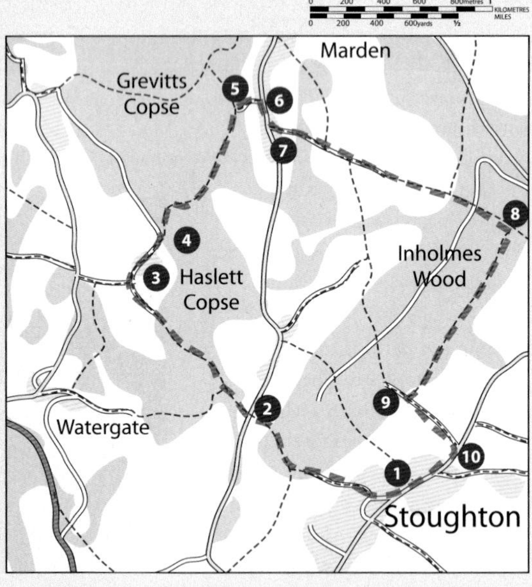

field. Carry on straight ahead still walking on the right hand side of the field edge. As you climb this gentle rise, look at the trees on the other side of the field. They look like they have all had their foliage carefully trimmed to the same length at the bottom. Study the bottoms of them carefully and you may see some deer looking back at you! Look at the green open area beyond the field ahead. There is often a herd of them to be seen here as well. You may well see one of the local celebrities... an albino deer. The track leaves the field and you will shortly arrive at a fingerpost sign.

5 | Turn right here. When the track bends to the left, follow it, ignoring the track on your right, which leads into a field entrance. You will soon arrive at metal gates with a stile.

6 | Go over the stile and turn right down the lane. After about 200 metres there is a track on the left hand side with a sign to Tumblecroft and Black Barn cottages. The bridleway fingerpost is opposite, but was hardly visable when I last walked here as it was overgrown at the time.

7 | Turn left here. Walk along this track, pass the cottage and ignore both footpaths. The track then opens up into fields. Carry on walking straight ahead keeping the trees on your left hand side. Here you must be quiet! Have a good look around - there may well be deer to be seen in these fields. Walk along to the end of the field where you will find a wooden marker post. Turn right here walking through the woods. The track descends and crosses over a wide track. Soon you will get a first glimpse of the view over to Kingley Vale. Now look out for the footpath marked with a wooden post off to your right. Be careful that you don't miss it as the wooden post is tucked around the corner a little.

8 | Turn right here. This path was beautiful before the devastation of the 1987 storm. For years afterwards it was decimated, but now I believe it is even more lovely than it ever was! The views are better and the more open woodland has allowed a wealth of wild flowers to flourish. Carry on until the path divides, with one path bending uphill to the right and another more minor path carrying straight on. Carry straight on here and in a few metres the path will bring you out into a field with more outstanding views. Walk along the top edge of this field with the trees on your right. When you reach the other side of the field you will see a fingerpost directing you into a shady track.

9 | Turn left onto this track and walk downhill to the road.

10 | Turn right and walk along this quiet road back through the village of Stoughton. Shortly after you pass the Hare and Hounds you will find yourself back at your starting point.

WALDERTON

6 miles NW of Chichester off the B2146

Stanstead House   Garden Centre

Just to the west of the village lies **Stansted House**, a splendid example of late 17th-century architecture, built on the site of Henry II's 11th-century hunting lodge. Stansted has played host to a variety of distinguished guests, including royalty, over the centuries. The house was built on its present site in 1668 for Richard Lumley - probably by the architect William Talman. Heavily altered in the following two centuries, it was burnt to the ground in 1900 but, in 1903, the house was rebuilt to the exact plans of Richard Lumley's grand mansion.

Now open to visitors, on a limited basis, the house is home to the late Lord Bessborough's collection of paintings and furnishings, including some fine 18th-century tapestries. The Below Stairs Experience transports visitors to the old kitchen, pantry, servants' hall, living quarters and wine cellars. The surrounding grounds are renowned for their peace and tranquillity and the **Stansted Park Garden Centre** in the original walled garden has restored Victorian glasshouses, including a palm house, camellia house, fernery and vine house.

EAST ASHLING

3 miles NW of Chichester on B2178

Nature Reserve

A couple of miles to the north of East Ashling lies **Kingley Vale National Nature Reserve**, which contains the largest forest of yews in Britain. The trees were protected until the mid 16th century as they were used for making long bows, England's successful weapon against crossbows. Yews are a long-lived species - 100 years is nothing in the life of a yew tree. Here at Kingley Vale, there are several 500-year-old trees, although most of the forest is made up of yews approaching their first century. Towards the summit of Bow Hill, the trees give way to heather and open heathland and it is here a group of four Bronze Age burial mounds, known as the King's Graves or Devil's Humps, can be found.

Arundel

Castle Cathedral Wildlife & Wetland Centre Museum & Heritage Centre

A settlement since before the Romans invaded, this quiet and peaceful town, which lies beneath the battlements of one of the most impressive castles in the country, is a strategically important site where the major east-west route through Sussex crosses the River Arun. It was one of William the Conqueror's most favoured knights, Roger de Montgomery, who first built a castle here, on the high ground overlooking the river, in the late 11th century. With a similar plan to that of Windsor castle, **Arundel Castle** consisted of a motte with a double bailey, a design which, despite several alterations and much rebuilding, remains clearly visible today. The second largest castle in England, it has been the seat of the Dukes of Norfolk and the Earls of Arun for over 700 years.

It was damaged in 1643 when, during the Civil War, Parliamentarian forces bombarded it with canons fired from the church tower. A programme of restoration took place during the late 18th century to make it habitable once more. A second programme of rebuilding was undertaken 100 years later by the 15th Duke of Norfolk, using profits from the family's ownership of the newly prosperous steel town of Sheffield. Unfortunately, all that remains today of the original construction are the 12th-century shell keep and parts of the 13th-century barbican and curtain wall.

However, the castle is still an atmospheric place to visit. The state apartments and main rooms contain some fine furniture dating from the 16th century and there are some excellent tapestries and paintings by Reynolds, Van Dyck, Gainsborough, Holbein and Constable on show. Also on display are some possessions of Mary, Queen of Scots, and a selection of heraldic artefacts from the Duke of Norfolk's collection. The title Duke of Norfolk was first conferred on Sir John Howard in 1483, by his friend Richard III. Carrying the hereditary office of Earl Marshal of England, the Duke of Norfolk is the premier duke of England.

Perhaps the most gruesome item to be seen at the castle can be found, not surprisingly, in the armoury. The Morglay Sword, which measures five feet nine inches long, is believed to have belonged to Bevis, a castle warden who was so tall that it was said he could walk from Southampton to Cowes without getting his head wet. In order to determine his final resting place, Bevis, so the story goes, threw his sword off the castle's battlements and, half a mile away, where the sword landed, is a mound that is still known as Bevis's Grave.

The period of stability that the castle brought to the town in the late medieval times turned Arundel into an important port and market town. In fact, the port of Arundel was mentioned in the Domesday Book and it continued to operate until the 20th century when it finally closed in 1927 - the last Harbour Master was moved to Shoreham and the port transferred to Littlehampton.

Arundel Castle

It was also during this peaceful period that the 14th-century parish Church of St Nicholas was built, a unique church in that it is divided into separate Catholic and Anglican areas by a Sussex iron screen. Despite religious persecution, particularly during the 16th century, the Fitzalan family and the successive Dukes of Norfolk remained staunch Catholics. So much so, that the 15th Duke, who was responsible for the 19th-century rebuilding of the castle, also commissioned the substantial Catholic Church of St Philip Heri, which was designed by J A Hansom and Son, the inventors of the Hansom cab, in 1870. In 1965, this impressive building became the seat of the Catholic bishopric of Brighton and Arundel and was renamed the **Cathedral of Our Lady and St Philip Howard**. (Sir Philip was the 13th Earl of Arundel who died in prison after being sentenced to death by Elizabeth I for his beliefs.) Each June, the cathedral hosts the two-day Corpus Christi Festival during which a carpet of flowers is laid out on the entire length of the aisle.

Other historic sites in the town include the Maison Dieu, a medieval hospital outside one of the castle's lodges, founded by Richard Fitzalan in 1345. Dissolved by Henry VIII 200 years later, this semi-monastic institution combined the roles of clinic, hotel and almshouse. For a greater insight into the history of the town and its various inhabitants down the ages, the **Arundel Museum and Heritage Centre** is well worth a visit. With imaginative use of models, old photographs and historic artefacts, the story of Arundel, from Roman times to the present day, is told.

Just to the north of the town, is the **Wildlife and Wetland Centre** (see panel on page 246), a wonderful place that plays host to a wide variety of ducks, geese, swans and other migratory birds from all over the world. Visitors can experience the wetlands from the water and keep an eye out for water voles and other wetland species while gliding along the waterways on one of the guided Wetlands Discovery Boat Safaris. The Eye of the Wind wildlife art gallery shows a continuous programme of local and national wildlife artists, and visitors can enjoy excellent food in the Waters Edge restaurant. The Centre is part of the Wildfowl & Wetlands Trust founded in

Arundel Wildfowl and Wetlands Centre

Mill Road, Offham, Arundel, West Sussex, BN18 9PB
Tel: 01903 883355 Fax: 01903 884834
e-mail: info.arundel@wwt.org.uk website: www.wwt.org.uk

Have a fantastic day out seeing, feeding, and learning about wetland birds and wildlife, and at the same time help the **Wildfowl & Wetlands Trust** to conserve wetland habitats and their biodiversity. WWT was founded in 1946 by the artist and naturalist Sir Peter Scott and is the largest international wetland conservation charity in the UK. WWT Arundel is one of 9 centres and it consists of more than 60 beautiful acres of ponds, lakes and reed beds. It is home to over 1,000 of the world's most spectacular ducks, geese and swans, many of which are rare or endangered, including the world's rarest goose, the Nene, which was saved from extinction by WWT. Also see the New Zealand Blue Ducks - this is also the only site in the world outside of New Zealand where Blue Ducks have successfully bred.

You can enjoy an atmospheric stroll through the reed beds on the boardwalk, or watch wild birds from one of the many hides. Kids can follow the themed Discovery trail through the grounds. WWT Arundel also features the award winning recreation of the volcanic Lake Myvatin, complete with lava formations, waterfalls, and it's native duck the common Scoter which is part of a specialist breeding programme. Inside the centre is the new Eye of the Wind wildlife art gallery which shows a continuous programme of local and national wildlife artists, many of whom host art workshops at the centre. You can enjoy superb homemade food in the Waters Edge Restaurant situated in the main viewing gallery overlooking swan lake, or browse through the gift shop or *In Focus* (telescope and binocular specialists) shop.

1946 by the artist and naturalist Sir Peter Scott; the trust is the largest international wetland conservation charity in the UK.

Around Arundel

BURPHAM

2 miles NE of Arundel off the A27

This charming and attractive downland village of flint and brick-built thatched cottages overlooks the River Arun and provides excellent views of Arundel Castle. The peace and quiet found here seems far removed from the days when the Saxons built defensive earthworks in an attempt to keep the invading Danes at bay. Later, during the Middle Ages, one of the farms on nearby Wepham Down was a leper colony and the track leading down into the village is still known as Lepers' Way.

LYMINSTER

1½ miles S of Arundel on the A284

Knuckler Hole

Lyminster is an ancient settlement of flint cottages and protective walls, which appears as Lullyngminster in Alfred the Great's will of AD901. From the village there is a marvellous view of Arundel Castle across the water meadows of the lower River Arun. Local legend has it that the deep pool, known as the **Knuckler Hole**, which lies northwest of Lyminster church, was once inhabited by a savage sea dragon, whose only food was fair maidens. This monster was said to have terrorised the local population to such an extent that the King of Wessex offered half his kingdom and his daughter's hand in marriage to the man who killed the beast. The dragon was finally slain after a terrible fight though there is some confusion regarding the identity of the brave dragon slayer. This was either a gallant young farm boy known as Jim Pulk, or a handsome knight. The early Norman coffin slab in the north transept of the church is where the conquering hero was finally laid to rest and it is still known as the Slayer's Stone.

LITTLEHAMPTON

3 miles S of Arundel on the A284

Museum

This is a charming maritime town at the mouth of the River Arun. Signs of Roman occupation have been discovered here and the local manor is mentioned in the Domesday Book. Following the Norman invasion, Littlehampton became an important Channel port (declining considerably in the 1500s), exporting timber from the Sussex Weald and importing stone from Caen,

WOOD DESIGN WORKSHOPS AND METTLE STUDIOS

Roundstone Bypass, Angmering, nr Arundel, West Sussex BN16 4BD
Tel: 01903 776010

A long wooden building by the A259 Littlehampton to Worthing road is home to adjoining enterprises **Wood Design Workshops** and **Mettle Studios**. Furniture designer/maker Brendan Devitt-Spooner blends traditional skills and contemporary design in furniture that catches the eye and gives many years of pleasure. He specialises in solid wood pieces using the finest hardwoods available, and much of the timber is seasoned naturally outside the workshop. He concentrates on commissions, so it is fitting that his work is very varied in style, size and timbers used. He makes dining tables, chairs, bookcase and cabinets alongside more unusual bespoke pieces for corporate clients. In the showroom prospective clients can see exhibition pieces on display, and they can also see current commissions being made in the workshop.

e-mail: devittspooner@ntlworld.com website: www.brendandevitt-spooner.co.uk

Lorraine is a jeweller working in printed aluminium combined with precious and non-precious materials. She uses traditional printmaking techniques adapted for use on the metal, to express her passion for colour and decorative design, and her metal-smithing skills to transform the materials into three dimensional forms, creating unusual, bold but lightweight jewellery, influenced by her interest in gardens and our natural surroundings, and also a love of textiles. Works range from tiny iridescent spiral rings, to glorious neckpieces and tiaras, and everything in between. Lorraine is a qualified and experienced teacher and runs one and two-day workshops for both beginners and those with some experience. She is a member of the Sussex Guild.

e-mail: l.gibby@btinternet.com

Designer / Pewtersmith Fleur Grenier designs and makes her work from the Mettle Studios workshop where she works predominantly in lead-free pewter. She produces a wide range of items varying from tableware, cheeseknives, salt and pepper; Giftware, Clocks, mini spirit levels and also one-off sculptural pieces. Fleurs range of work is on display at the workshop and can be bought direct or commissions can be taken for a bespoke item.

Fleur also runs one-day workshops, where you can learn how to work with pewter. The course is suitable for beginners or experienced metalworkers, runs from 10am – 4pm with a maximum of 2 people, so you are guaranteed individual attention. For further details about the course and date please check the website. *website: www.fleurgrenier.co.uk*

France. It was here, too, that Queen Matilda arrived from France, in 1139, to stake her unsuccessful claim to the English throne occupied by Stephen.

Now a quiet and pleasant coastal town and a popular holiday resort, though not as fashionable as many of its larger neighbours, Littlehampton has all the ingredients for a traditional seaside break. There is a large amusement complex, a boating marina, a promenade and a harbour. Littlehampton Fort was built in 1854 to protect the entrance to the River Arun. Although the site is fenced off and heavily overgrown, it is visible from the path and there is a plaque with historical details. However, the town's most charming feature is, undoubtedly, the large green, which lies between the seafront and the first row of houses.

In the old manor house in Church Street, **Littlehampton Museum** tells the history of the town, including its maritime past, through a series of informative displays. The Body Shop Headquarters lie just outside the town, which is the birthplace of both the company and its founder Anita Roddick. Another attraction, The Look and Sea Visitor Centre, is great fun for all the family with interactive displays, games and superb panoramic views. It takes you on a voyage of discovery showing how Littlehampton has developed over thousands of years.

FORD

2½ miles S of Arundel off the A259

Situated on an ancient ford crossing of the River Arun, this village is dwarfed by the prison on the site of an old RAF station. This does little to spoil the splendid and isolated setting of the Saxon church that stands alone by the river.

YAPTON

3½ miles SW of Arundel on the B2233

Set amid the wheatfields of the coastal plain, this village has a charming 12th-century church, the tower of which leans at an alarming angle.

BOGNOR REGIS

6 miles SW of Arundel on the A259

Museum Birdman Rally

Towards the end of the 18th century, Sir Richard Hotham, a wealthy London milliner, sought to transform Bognor from a quiet fishing village into a fashionable resort to rival Brighton. He set about constructing some imposing residences, including The Dome in Upper Bognor Road, and even planned to have the town renamed Hothampton. Unfortunately, the fashionable set of the day stayed away and Hotham's dream was never realised - at least not in his lifetime. However, in 1929, George V came to the resort to convalesce following a serious illness and, on the strength of his stay, the town was granted the title Regis (meaning 'of the King'). "Bugger Bognor" was allegedly a retort made by King George in his last illness when a courtier tried to cheer him up by saying that he would soon be well enough to travel to Bognor to recuperate. Candidates for his actual last words include, "How is the Empire?" and "God damn you!" (when a shot of morphine was painfully administered). Today, the town is a pleasant coastal resort with some elegant Georgian features, traditional public gardens, a promenade and safe, sandy beaches. The Pier, one of the oldest in Britain, was originally 1,000 feet in length but is now shorter: the pavilion end sank in 1965, and a 20-metre mid-section was swept away in a storm in 1999. Opposite the

Pier, The Steyne has many handsome Regency buildings and a drinking fountain commemorating Queen Victoria's Diamond Jubilee. The large central Hotham Park is another feature of this charming town where visitors can enjoy concerts given at the bandstand, clock golf and tennis. The naturally planted gardens are perfect to stroll in, picnic or just watch the squirrels. An ice house was the 18th-century 'fridge' of the Hotham Park Estate. **Bognor Regis Museum**, housed in Hotham Park lodge, plays tribute to Sir Richard Hotham as well as telling the story of the famous bathing machine lady, Mary Wheatland. Mary Wheatland was a well-known Bognor Regis character. Born in 1835 in the nearby village of Aldinbourne, she hired out bathing machines as well as teaching children to swim. She also saved many souls from drowning, for which she received medals and recognition from the Royal Humane Society. The sea air and exercise must have done the eccentric lady a great deal of good as she lived to be 89 years old. The Museum incorporates a Wireless Museum where visitors can try their hand at Morse code.

Perhaps, more than anything else, the resort is known for its 'Birdmen' and the annual international **Birdman Rally**. The competitors, in a variety of classes, take it in turns to hurl themselves off the pier in an attempt to make the longest unpowered flight and so win the coveted competition.

FELPHAM

5 miles SW of Arundel off the A259

This is the village to which the poet and artist, William Blake, moved, along with his wife and sister, in 1800 to undertake some engraving work for William Hayley, a gentleman of the

WHITE HORSES B&B

Clyde Road, Felpham,
West Sussex PO22 7AH
Tel: 01243 824320
e-mail: bellamy@btinternet.com
website: www.whitehorsesfelpham.co.uk

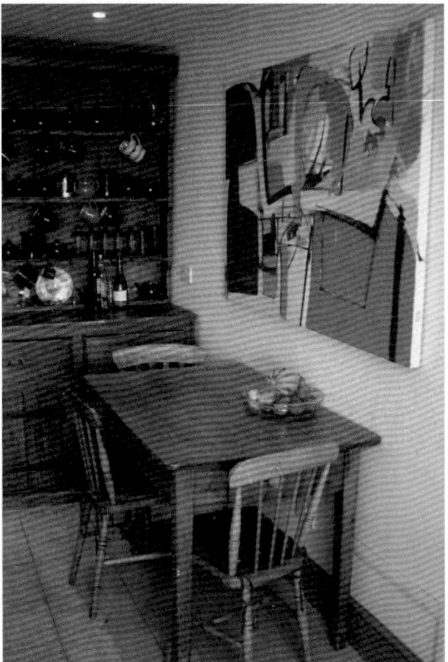

White Horses offers bright, roomy, contemporary Bed & Breakfast accommodation a few steps from the seafront with its promenade, cafés, pubs, restaurants, putting green, tennis court and children's play area. The resident owners of this lovely 100-year-old brick and flint house are Mark and Jacky Bellamy. They have lived in the area for many years and since 2001 they have been running this super B&B. Mark and Jacky have created a comfortable mix of the traditional and the contemporary, a relaxed ambience that brings back guests year after year. Many original features remain, including the sash windows and a dresser that was actually built into the house. On the lovely wooden floor in the dining room stain marks can be seen around the nails, a legacy of the time when the sea came in! The house has four letting rooms, two doubles and a twin/double with spacious showers and a family room with its own big bathroom. Each room has its own colour scheme and two of them, Yellow and Grey, enjoy sea views – the proximity of the beach is emphasised by touches such as natural pine furniture and beach pebbles on the blind cords. A cot can be provided for any room. All rooms have teletext TV, and wi-fi and internet/e-mail access is available. Days at White Horses begin with a freshly prepared breakfast that includes a fresh fruit salad, freshly baked bread and eggs, bacon, sausages and mushrooms supplied by local shops and farm shops. Vegetarian and gluten-free diets can be catered for with a little notice. The poet and artist William Blake lived for some time in Felpham.

Art is still strong here, and nowhere is that more in evidence than at White Horses, where all the rooms – day rooms, bedrooms, even the bathrooms – feature striking pieces of artwork. Much of it is Jacky's own original work, contemporary paintings and drawings produced in her studio in the garden, but other local artists are also displayed, including Felpham sculptor Dick Martin. Felpham lies on the A259 a mile east of Bognor Regis.

period. The cottage where the Blakes lived can still be seen down Blake's Road, and it was here that he wrote "Away to sweet Felpham for Heaven is there", which recalls the view of the sea from his window, and *Jerusalem*, later set to music by Sir Hubert Parry who lived along the coast at Rustington. Blake left the village a few years later after being acquitted of a charge of treason.

WALBERTON

3 miles W of Arundel off the B2132

Down a narrow country lane, this pleasant village has obviously been settled for centuries as the local parish church is built on Saxon foundations and it still contains an ancient Saxon tub-shaped font.

FONTWELL

3½ miles W of Arundel off the A27

Racecourse Denman's Garden

The village is well known to followers of horse racing as it is home to the pleasantly situated **Fontwell Park National Hunt Racecourse**. First opened in 1921, the unusual 'figure of eight' track holds around 15 meetings between August and May and remains a firm favourite with jumping enthusiasts. Fontwell is also home to **Denman's Garden**, a beautifully sheltered, semi-wild, 20th-century garden where the emphasis in planting has been on colour, shape and texture and which can be visited all year round.

EARTHAM

5 miles NW of Arundel off the A285

The village was the home of the 19th-century Member of Parliament, William Huskisson, who was famously knocked down and killed by Stevenson's Rocket during its inaugural run in 1830. He thereby acquired the dubious honour of being the world's first recorded victim of a railway accident.

SLINDON

3 miles NW of Arundel off the A29

Slindon Estate

With a dramatic setting on the side of a slope of the South Downs, the name Slindon is derived from the Saxon word for sloping hill. This picturesque village has splendid views over the coastal plain to the English Channel and numerous lovely old cottages. As an excellent observation point, it has been occupied from Neolithic times and many fine examples of early flint tools have been found in the area.

The village was the estate village for Slindon House. Today, the **Slindon Estate** is owned by the National Trust and most of the village, the woodlands and Slindon House (now let to Slindon College) come under its care. The largest Trust-owned estate in Sussex, there is plenty to see here as well as excellent opportunities for walking and birdwatching. Slindon House was originally founded as a residence for the Archbishops of Canterbury. (Archbishop Stephen Langton, a negotiator and signatory of the Magna Carta, spent the last weeks of his life here in 1228.) Rebuilt in the 1560s and extensively re-modelled during the 1920s, the house is now a private boys' school. The estate's wonderful post office is an amalgamation of two 400-year-old cottages and is the village's only remaining thatched building. The focal point of the village is the crossroads where a tree stands in a small open area close to the village church. Dating from the 12th century, this charming flint-built church contains an unusual reclining effigy of a Tudor knight, Sir Anthony St Leger, the only wooden carving of its kind in Sussex. Finally, just to the north lies the cricket field where Sir Richard Newland is said to have refined the modern game over 200 years ago.

From the village there is a splendid walk around the estate that takes in the ancient deer park of Slindon House as well as other remains such as the summerhouse. The magnificent beech trees in the woodland were once highly prized and their seeds were sold worldwide. Unfortunately, the severe storm of October 1987 flattened many of these splendid trees, some of which had stood for 250 years. Though most of the fallen trees were cleared, some were left, and the dead wood has provided new habitats for a whole range of insects and fungi. Birds and other wildlife also abound in the Slindon woodlands and, in May, the woodland floor is a carpet of bluebells.

Also at the Slindon Estate is Gumber Bothy Camping Barn, a stone tent now fully restored by the National Trust, which provides simple overnight accommodation just off the South Downs Way. Originally an outbuilding of Gumber Farm, a secluded working farm in the folds of the South Downs, the bothy is available to anyone over the age of five who enjoys the outdoor life.

Worthing

Museum and Art Gallery

Worthing has been inhabited since the Stone Age and, until the mid 18th century it was a small and isolated fishing community. The popularity of sea bathing in the late 18th century made Worthing an ideal location, not far from London or Brighton, but far enough away to be relaxing and unspoilt. The royal stamp of approval came in 1798 when George III sent his teenage daughter, Princess Amelia, to Worthing to rest her lame knee. Her visit initiated a period of rapid development. Few examples of Georgian Worthing survive but it is worth wandering along Warwick Street and Montague Place.

The town grew steadily throughout the 19th century until 1893, when its worst typhoid outbreak kept holiday-makers away and it became a ghost town. During the 20th century, an extensive development programme was begun and the town became more residential with its boundaries expanding.

Throughout much of the 19th century, Worthing remained a popular resort with both royalty and the famous. It was here, in the summer of 1894, that Oscar Wilde wrote *The Importance of Being Earnest* and immortalised its name in the central character, Jack Worthing. A plaque on the seafront marks the site of the house where he wrote the play in just 21 days. Worthing's Pier, one of the country's oldest, was built in the early 1860s. An elegant construction with a 1930s pavilion at the end, it has, during its lifetime, been blown down, burnt down and blown up; it was named Pier of the Year 2006 by the National Piers Society. Of the more recent buildings to be found here, the English Martyrs Catholic Church, just west of the town centre, is notable in having a reproduction of the Sistine Chapel ceiling; it was painted in 1933 by local artist Gary Bevans and is two-thirds the size of the original.

Beach House Park contains some really beautiful flower beds and an unusual memorial to wartime carrier pigeons. The Park is the home of the English Bowling Association, and five international class greens are used for National Championships and Open Tournaments in the summer.

For an insight into Worthing's past a visit to the **Worthing Museum and Art Gallery** is essential. The Local History and Downland

Gallery tells the story of the town's development over the years. The museum is also home to nationally important costume and toy collections. No visit would be complete without a wander around the museum's stunning Sculpture Garden.

As Worthing expanded it also swallowed up a number of ancient nearby settlements including Broadwater with its fine cottages and Norman church, and West Tarring where the remains of a 13th-century palace belonging to the Archbishops of Canterbury now double as the village hall and primary school annexe.

Around Worthing

HIGH SALVINGTON

1½ miles N of Worthing on the A24

This village, now almost entirely engulfed by Worthing, is home to the last survivor of several windmills that once stood in the area. High Salvington Windmill, a black post mill, was built between 1700 and 1720 and its design is one that had been used since the Middle Ages - a heavy cross-shaped base with a strong central upright (or post) around which the sails and timber superstructure could pivot. The mill stopped working in 1897 but, following extensive restoration in the 1970s, it has now been restored to full working order. It is open on a limited basis with afternoon tea available.

FINDON

3 miles N of Worthing off the A24

Cissbury Ring

An attractive village, Findon's main square is surrounded by some elegant 18th-century houses. Situated within the South Downs Area of Outstanding Natural Beauty, Findon is famous for being the venue of one of the two great Sussex sheep fairs - the other is at Lewes. Markets have been held on Nepcote Green since the 13th century, and the Findon Sheep Fair has been an annual event each September since the 18th century. The village has a festival atmosphere and thousands of sheep change hands here during the fair. Despite a gap year in 2001 due to foot and mouth disease, the fair has returned to business as usual.

From Findon there is also easy access to **Cissbury Ring**, the largest Iron Age hillfort on the South Downs. Overshadowed only by Dorset's Maiden Castle, this impressive hilltop site covers an area of 65 acres and is surrounded by a double rampart almost a mile in circumference. Archaeologists have estimated that over 50,000 tons of chalk, soil and boulders would have had to be moved in the fort's construction, which would indicate that this was once a sizeable community in the 3rd century BC. However, the site is much older than this as Neolithic flint mines, dating back 6,000 years, have also been discovered here, which makes Cissbury one of the oldest industrial sites in the country. Cissbury Ring is set on a chalk promontory that offers expansive views of countryside and coastline from Beachy Head to the Isle of Wight.

COOMBES

4 miles NE of Worthing off the A27

This tiny settlement of just a few houses and a farm is worthy of a visit if just to see the village church, which stands in the farmyard. An unassuming Norman church, it contains some exceptional 12th-century murals in many shades of red and yellow that were only uncovered in 1949 and are believed to have been painted by monks from St Pancras Priory,

Lewes. Just to the north of the hamlet lies Annington Hill from where there are glorious views over the Adur valley and also access to a section of the South Downs Way footpath.

SHOREHAM-BY-SEA

4½ miles E of Worthing on the A259

Shoreham Fort Marlipins Museum

There has been a harbour here, on the River Adur estuary, since Roman times and, though evidence of both Roman and Saxon occupations have been found, it was not until the Norman period that the town developed into an important port. At that time, the River Adur was navigable as far as Bramber and the main port was situated a mile or so upstream where the Norman Church of St Nicholas, with some notable Norman figure carvings, still stands today.

However, towards the end of the 11th century, the river estuary began to silt up and the old port and toll bridge were abandoned in favour of New Shoreham, which was built at the river mouth. Again, the Normans built a church, the Church of St Mary, close to the harbour and both churches remain key features of the town. The old town lapsed into the life of a quiet village while, during the 12th and 13th centuries, New Shoreham was one of the most important Channel ports. It was here in 1199 that King John landed with an army to succeed to the throne of England following the death of Richard the Lionheart, and, in 1346, Shoreham was asked to raise 26 ships, more than both Dover and Bristol, to fight the French. Perhaps, though, the town's most historic moment came in 1651, when Charles II fled to France from here, following defeat at the Battle of Worcester, on board the ship of Captain Nicholas Tettersell.

The new port flourished until the 16th century when, once again, silting, in the form of a shingle spit, which diverted the river's course, had disastrous economic consequences. The next 200 years or so saw a period of decline in Shoreham, which was only relieved by the rise in popularity of nearby Brighton and the excavation of a new river course in 1818. To reflect its new importance, **Shoreham Fort** was constructed at the eastern end of the beach as part of Palmerston's coastal defence system. A half-moon shape, the fort was capable of accommodating six guns, which could each fire 80 pounds of shot. The fort has been restored and is now open to visitors who will also have a superb view of the still busy harbour.

The history of Shoreham-by-Sea, and in particular its maritime past, are explored at **Marlipins Museum**. The museum is interesting in itself, as it is housed in one of the oldest surviving non-religious buildings in

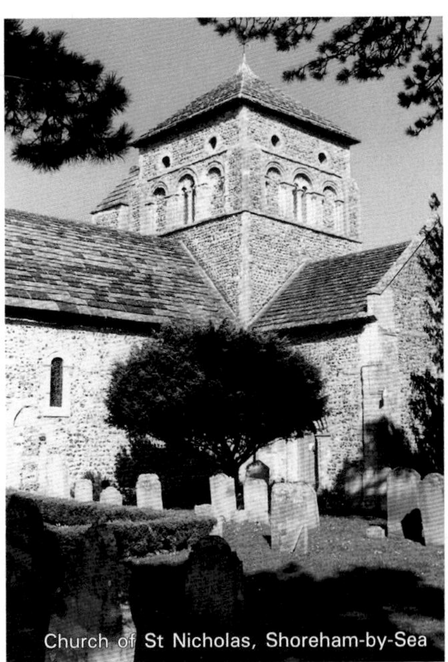

Church of St Nicholas, Shoreham-by-Sea

the country. A Norman customs warehouse, an unusual knapped flint and Caen stone patterned façade was added in the 14th century, and it has a single 42-foot beam supporting the first floor.

Though the town's past is, undoubtedly, built upon its port, Shoreham Airport was opened in 1934 and is the country's oldest commercial airport. It remains a major base for recreational flying and the delightful Art Deco terminal acts as a departure lounge and arrivals hall for many business passengers who are travelling to and from the Channel Islands and Western Europe.

NORTH LANCING

3 miles E of Worthing off the A27

This attractive downland village, with its curved streets, has one of the most ancient Saxon names in Sussex. It is derived from Wlencing, one of the sons of Aella, who led the first Saxon invasion to the area in AD477. Apart from the old flint cottages on the High Street, the 13th-century church adds to the timeless atmosphere of the village. However, North Lancing is dominated by a more recent addition to its skyline - Lancing College. Set high up on a beautiful site overlooking the River Adur, the college was founded in 1848 by Nathaniel Woodward, whose aim was to establish a group of classless schools. By the time of his death in 1891, there were 15 such schools in the Woodward Federation. Of the buildings at Lancing College, the splendid 19th-century Gothic-style chapel is the most striking and is considered to be one of the finest examples of its kind.

SOMPTING

2 miles E of Worthing off the A27

This village, the name of which means marshy ground, has, as its pride and joy, a church that is unique in Britain. Built on foundations, which can be traced back to AD960, the Church of St Mary has a distinctive spire that consists of four diamond-shaped faces that taper to a point. Known as a Rhenish helm, the design was popular in the German Rhineland, but is not found elsewhere in this country. In 1154, the church was given to the Knights Templar who completely rebuilt it except for the spire, which they left untouched. Just over 150 years later, the building came into the hands of their rivals, the Knights Hospitallers, who were responsible for the present design of the church as they returned it to its original Saxon style.

GORING-BY-SEA

1½ miles W of Worthing on the A259

Highdown Gardens

Until the arrival of the railway in the mid 19th century, this was a small fishing village. However, the Victorians love of a day by the

Lancing College, North Lancing

seaside saw the rapid growth of Goring and today it is a genteel place with a pleasant suburban air.

To the northwest stands the cone-shaped Highdown Hill, which, although only 266 feet high, stands out above the surrounding coastal plain. Its prominent nature has made a much sought-after vantage point over the centuries. It has been an Iron Age hillfort, a Roman bath house and a Saxon graveyard.

Close by, **Highdown Gardens** are the creation of Sir Frederick and Lady Stern, who spent over 50 years turning what was originally a chalk pit into this splendid garden. One of the least known gardens in the area, Highdown has a unique collection of rare plants and trees, which the couple brought back from their expeditions to the Himalayas and China in the mid 20th century. The garden was left to the local borough council on the death of Sir Frederick in 1967, and it has been declared a national collection.

On the south side of the main A27 is Castle Goring, built for the grandfather of the poet Percy Bysshe Shelley. It is not exactly a castle, although the castellated frontage and the arched windows with their elaborate tracery are believed to be based on Arundel Castle. The south frontage is quite different with pillars and pediments resembling a Roman villa. The building is currently a private English language school.

The West Sussex Downs

The southern boundary to this part of West Sussex is the South Downs, a magnificent range of chalk hills extending for over 100 miles. The South Downs Way, a long distance bridleway follows the crest of the hills from Winchester to Beachy Head at Eastbourne and, whether taken as a whole or enjoyed in sections, it provides splendid views of this Area of Outstanding Natural Beauty, as well as a wealth of delightful rural hamlets and villages to discover.

To the north of the Downs lies Midhurst, the home of the area's most famous ruin - Cowdray House. Though the once splendid Tudor mansion has been reduced to a shell following a fire in the late 18th century, the ruins provide a haunting backdrop to the parkland's famous polo matches. In better condition are Uppark, where H G Wells spent many hours in the great library as a boy, and Petworth House, an elegant late 17th-century building that is very reminiscent of a French château.

Other great names from the world of the arts have also found this region inspirational. The novelist Anthony Trollope spent his last years at South Harting, the poet Tennyson lived under the wooded slopes of Black Down, and the composer Edward Elgar visited Fittleworth several times and wrote his famous cello concerto while staying there in 1917.

Midhurst

Cowdray Cowdray Park

Midhurst Grammar School

Though this quiet and prosperous market town has its origins in the early Middle Ages, its name is Saxon and suggests that once it was surrounded by forest. It was the Norman lord, Savaric Fitzcane, who first built a fortified house here, on the summit of St Ann's Hill, and, though only a few stones remain today, the views from this natural vantage point over the River Rother are worth the walk.

The town of Midhurst grew up at the castle gates. By 1300, when the de Bohuns (the then lords of the manor) moved from their hilltop position the town was well established. Choosing a new site by the river in a coudrier, or hazel grove, gave the family the name for their new estate - **Cowdray**. In the 1490s, the estate passed, by marriage, to Sir David Owen, who built the splendid Tudor courtyard mansion. However, due to rising debts, he was forced to sell the house to Sir William Fitzwilliam, Lord Keeper of the Privy Seal at the court of Henry VIII. He and his family added the finishing touches and, when complete, the magnificent house was a rival to Hampton Court. Indeed, the house played host to many notable visitors including both Henry VIII and Elizabeth I who were frequently entertained here. Even though the house is in ruins following a devastating fire in 1793, it is still a splendid monument to courtly Tudor architecture. Thousands of visitors come to **Cowdray Park** to watch the polo matches that take place every weekend and sometimes during the week from May until September.

Back in the town, on the opposite side of the River Rother from Cowdray Park, there are some impressive buildings. The 16th-century timber-framed Market Hall stands in front of the even older Spread Eagle Inn, an old coaching inn dating from the 1400s, where Elizabeth I is reputed to have stayed. Nearby is the famous **Midhurst Grammar School**, founded in 1672 by Gilbert Hanniman and now a successful comprehensive school. Though the centre of the town has migrated away from its old heart around the market

Cowdray Manor, Midhurst

square and the church, the custom of ringing the curfew each night at eight o'clock from the heavily restored church continues and is said to be in memory of a legendary commercial traveller. While endeavouring to reach Midhurst, the traveller got lost in the local woods at dusk and, on hearing the sound of the church bells, was able to find his way safely to the town.

For most people visiting Midhurst, it is through the books of H G Wells that they feel that they already know the town. Herbert George's maternal grandmother came from Midhurst, and his mother worked at nearby Uppark where, as a young boy, Wells spent many hours in the library. At the age of 15, H G was apprenticed to a chemist in the town and also enrolled at the Grammar School for evening classes. Though he left Midhurst for some years, Wells later returned to the school as a teacher. As well as providing the inspiration for his most famous book *The Invisible Man*, Midhurst has been the setting for many of his short stories including *The Man Who Could Work Miracles*. The great novelist and science fiction writer obviously had fond

WOODMANSGREEN FARM

Woodmansgreen Farm, Linch, Liphook,
Hampshire GU30 7NF
Tel: 01428 741250
e-mail: peterandmary@woodmansgreen.fsnet.co.uk

The Woodmansgreen Farm offers bed and breakfast accommodation located in a beautiful old Sussex farmhouse. With 4 bedrooms and 2 ensuite bathrooms, visitors are able to experience the beauty surrounding them. This is wonderful walking countryside. The owners Peter and Mary Spreckley have their own chickens, which provide the most beautiful eggs for breakfast. They have a heated, outdoor swimming pool (May-August). There is nearby entertainment such as Polo at Midhurst and Goodwood for both horses and cars. The accommodation at the farm varies from two twin rooms, sharing a bathroom and a double room with ensuite, located in the farmhouse. There is also a granary room, which is separate from the main house and features a double bedroom,private shower room and toilet. There is a guest sitting room with TV and open fireplace for comfort, as well as bicycles available to explore the local area.

THE KINGS ARMS

Midhurst Road, Fernhurst,
West Sussex GU27 3HA
Tel: 07810 771 461
e-mail: david.butler@powdertain.co.uk

The Kings Arms is a popular dining pub with accommodation located on the A286 on the Midhurst side of Fernhurst. The kitchen produces a fine variety of freshly cooked food to cater for appetites large and small. Sandwiches and jacket potatoes come with interesting fillings like smoked salmon with cream and chives or bacon, brie and cranberry. Typical main dishes run from wild mushroom risotto to trout with almonds and a prawn butter sauce and ribeye steak matured for 28 days. To accompany the food or to enjoy on their own there's a good choice of local beers, and a good wine list that includes several organic wines. The pub has a large restaurant but diners can enjoy their meals anywhere inside or out in the garden under parasols.

The 17th century pub has two bars and a function room that's an ideal venue for wedding receptions and other celebrations – a marquee can be set up in the garden. For guests taking a break in this pleasant part of the world the Kings Arms has six en suite double rooms adjacent to the main building.

recollections of his time in the town for he wrote in his autobiography: "Midhurst has always been a happy place for me. I suppose it rained there at times, but all my memories of Midhurst are in sunshine."

Around Midhurst

EASEBOURNE

1 mile N of Midhurst on the A272

This delightful estate village, which has some superb half-timbered houses, was the home of an Augustinian convent of the Blessed Virgin Mary. Founded in the 13th century, the convent prospered until 1478, when the prioress and some of her nuns were accused of gross immorality and squandering the convent's funds on hunting and extravagant entertaining. All that remains today of the priory is the church, now the parish church. Another interesting building here is Budgenor Lodge; built in 1793, it was a model workhouse and has now been converted into apartments.

FERNHURST

4½ miles N of Midhurst on the A286

Black Down

Just to the east of this pretty village, with its assorted tile hung cottages surrounding the green, lies **Black Down**, rising abruptly from the Sussex Weald. A sandstone hill covered in heather, gorse and silver birch that is an ideal environment for a variety of upland birdlife, the summit is the highest point in Sussex and from here there are views over the Weald and South Downs to the English Channel.

A particularly fine viewpoint lies on the southern crest, and one of the footpaths up the hill has been named locally as Tennyson's Lane, after the famous poet who lived in the area for 20 years. At one time a Royal navy signal tower stood on Tally Knob, a prominent outcrop to the southeast of the Temple of the Winds. A development of the tried and tested system of fire beacons, in 1796 the Admiralty introduced the Shutter Telegraph here as a more sophisticated means of passing messages between Portsmouth and London. Though ingenious, the system was found to be impractical and was soon abandoned.

To the west of Fernhurst, an Augustinian priory, on a smaller scale than the magnificent Michelham Priory near Upper Dicker, was founded in the late 12th century. At the time of the Dissolution of the Monasteries the priory became a farmhouse. One of the first floor rooms, which was originally the prior's chamber, is decorated with Tudor murals and, although it is a private house, Shulbrede Priory is occasionally open to the public.

LURGASHALL

4½ miles NE of Midhurst off the A283

This delightful rural village has, as a backdrop, the wooded slopes of Black Down, where Tennyson lived at Aldworth House. The village's largely Saxon church has an unusual loggia, or porch, outside where those who had travelled from afar could eat and rest before or after the service.

LODSWORTH

2½ miles E of Midhurst off the A272

Situated on the River Lod, a small tributary of the River Rother, this old community has some fine buildings including a 13th-century manor house and an early 18th-century Dower House. The whitewashed village Church of St Peter lies on the outskirts of Lodsworth, and

WOODSTOCK HOUSE

Charlton, nr Chichester, West Sussex PO18 0HU
Tel/Fax: 01243 811666
e-mail: info@woodstockhousehotel.co.uk
website: www.woodstockhousehotel.co.uk

Woodstock House is a fine converted farmhouse set in the heart of the South Downs. Owners Sandra and Nick Ansley, here since 2006, welcome guests with tea and cake on arrival before taking them to their bedrooms. Thirteen well-appointed en suite rooms, set around a garden courtyard, comprise doubles, twins and a family room. Two rooms are on the ground floor, one with a view of the garden, the other overlooking Levin Down, part of which is a nature reserve. WIFI is available in all the public rooms and most of the bedrooms. The courtyard garden is the perfect spot to indulge in a glass of wine after a day's walking or sightseeing. For during the winter months there is a comfortable lounge for relaxing by an open fire. There's a very good choice for breakfast, and evening meals are served on Friday and Saturday. Rural but certainly not isolated, Woodstock House offers an ideal base for walking, golf or riding holiday or visits to the many attractions of the region: horseracing and motor sports at Goodwood, the theatre and dockyard at Chichester, polo at Cowdray Park , the Weald & Downs Open Air Museum, the National Trust's Petworth House and Uppark. With its location and facilities, Woodstock is a favourite venue for functions and reunions of all kinds. Charlton lies 6 miles north of Chichester, a mile east of Singleton off the A286 Chichester-Midhurst road.

Weald and Downland Open Air Museum

Singleton, Chichester, Sussex PO18 0EU
Tel: 01243 811348
website: www.wealddown.co.uk

Set in 50 acres of beautiful Sussex countryside is a very special place to wander amongst a fascinating collection of nearly 50 historic buildings dating from the 13th to the 19th century, many with period gardens, together with farm animals, woodland walks and a picturesque lake. Rescued from destruction, the buildings have been carefully dismantled, conserved and rebuilt to their original form and bring to life the homes, farmsteads and rural industries of the last 500 years. Many of the interiors have been furnished, recreating the way the buildings were used by their owners centuries ago: seven historic gardens show the herbs, vegetables and flowers grown to meet the needs of rural households from medieval to Victorian times.

Demonstrators regularly show their skills and everyone you meet will be happy to talk about how people lived and worked. Discover the skills of the early carpenters, find out about traditional building techniques and learn how we help to conserve rural crafts. Children will enjoy the freedom to roam in safety and gain hands-on experience of the Museums buildings, gardens and animals.

just to the north is St Peter's Well, the water of which is said to have healing qualities.

DUNCTON

5 miles SE of Midhurst on the A285

Sheltered beneath Duncton Hill, beside Burton Park (previously St Michael's Girls' School), stands a small church on the wall of which can be seen the Royal Arms of King Charles I dated 1636.

SINGLETON

5½ miles S of Midhurst on the A286

Weald & Downland Open Air Museum

Lying in the folds of the South Downs, in the valley of the River Lavant, Singleton, owned by Earl Godwin of Wessex, father of King Harold, was one of the largest and wealthiest manors in England. Little remains here from Saxon times, except an ancient barn on the village green, though the 13th-century church was built on the foundations of its Saxon predecessor. Inside the church, in the south aisle, is a memorial to Thomas Johnson, a huntsman of the nearby Charlton Hunt who died in 1744. There are also two interesting monuments to two successive Earls of Arundel who died within two years of each other in the mid 16th century.

Singleton is also the home of the famous **Weald and Downland Open Air Museum** (see panel opposite), which has over 40 historic rural buildings assembled from all over southeast England. All the buildings in the museum, which was founded by J R Armstrong in 1971, were at one time under threat of demolition before being transported here and reconstructed.

The buildings vividly demonstrate the homes and workplaces of the past and include Titchfield's former Tudor market hall, farmhouses and agricultural buildings from the 15th and 16th centuries, hall houses, a Victorian toll house from Bramber, a schoolroom from West Wittering, labourers' cottages, a working blacksmith's forge and the watermill from Lurgashall, which produces flour every day for sale in the shop and use in the lakeside café. Several interiors have been furnished as they may have been during the building's heyday. Visitors can take a look at the Tudor farmstead, with its fireplace in the middle of the hall, traditional farmyard animals and gardens, and the Victorian schoolroom, complete with blackboard, benches and school bell. To complement the buildings, five historic gardens have been carefully researched and planted, using traditional methods, to demonstrate the changes and continuities in ordinary gardens from 1430 to 1900.

This enchanting and unusual collection is situated in a delightful 50-acre park on the southern edge of the village. The museum also arranges demonstrations of rural skills and children's activities' days where traditional games, trades and crafts of the past, such as basket making and bricklaying, can be enjoyed.

WEST DEAN

6 miles S of Midhurst on the A286

The Trundle · West Dean Gardens

Just to the south of this pretty community of flint cottages, the land rises towards the ancient hilltop site known as **The Trundle**. One of four main Neolithic settlements in Sussex, the large site was fortified during the Iron Age, when massive circular earth ramparts and a dry ditch were constructed. Named after the Old English for wheel, the site now enjoys fine views over Chichester, Singleton and Goodwood Racecourse.

The Trundle, West Dean

Amidst the rolling South Downs, **West Dean Gardens** reproduces a classic 19th-century designed landscape with its highly acclaimed restoration of the walled kitchen garden, the 16 original glasshouses and frames dating from the 1890s, the 35 acres of ornamental grounds, the 40-acre St Roche's arboretum, and the extensive landscaped park. All the areas of this inspiring and diverse garden are linked by a scenic parkland walk. A particular feature of the grounds is the lavishly planted 300-foot Edwardian pergola, designed by Harold Peto, which acts as a host for a variety of climbers including roses, clematis and honeysuckle. The beautifully restored Victorian glasshouses nurture vines, figs and soft fruits, as well as an outstanding collection of chilli peppers, aubergines, tomatoes and extensive floral displays.

CHILGROVE

6 miles SW of Midhurst on the B2141

To the north of this village, which is situated in a wooded valley, lies Treyford Hill, where a line of five bell-shaped barrows known as the Devil's Jump can be found. Dating back to the Bronze Age, these burial mounds - where the cremated remains of tribal leaders were interred in pottery urns - received their descriptive name as a result of the local superstitious habit of attributing unusual, natural features of the landscape to the work of the Devil.

WEST MARDEN

9 miles SW of Midhurst off the B2146

This picturesque place, much loved by artists, is the largest of the four Marden hamlets, which are all linked by quiet country lanes. North Marden, itself only a tiny place, is home to the Norman Church of St Mary, which is one of the smallest in the county, while Up Marden's minute 13th-century church, which stands on the ancient Pilgrims' Way between Winchester and Chichester, is only a little bigger. It is quite plain and simple apart from its Victorian Gothic pulpit. Of the four Mardens, East Marden is the most village-like and, on the village green, there is a thatched well house with a notice reading, "Rest and be Thankful but do not Wreck me". As the well is still very much in existence, the advice has been heeded down the centuries.

COMPTON

8 miles SW of Midhurst on the B2146

A tranquil settlement of brick and flint buildings, Compton lies under the steep slope of Telegraph Hill. Close to the hill is a grassy mound, which is, in fact, a Neolithic long barrow, known locally as Bevis's Thumb. This mysterious burial site was named after a local giant, Bevis (the same Bevis who threw his sword from the battlements of Arundel Castle), who had a weekly diet of an ox washed down with two hogsheads of beer.

SOUTH HARTING

6 miles W of Midhurst on the B2146

Uppark · Durford Abbey · Harting Down

One of the most attractive villages of the South Downs, South Harting has ancient thatched cottages and elegant redbrick Georgian houses. The spire of the local church is, famously, covered in copper shingles, the bright verdigris hue of which can be seen from several miles away, acting as a signpost to this handsome place. Outside the church stand the ancient village stocks, along with a whipping post, and inside, there are several monuments, including a set of tombs of the Cowpre family and one commemorating the life of Sir Harry Fetherstonhaugh of Uppark. In the

South Harting Church

churchyard is a memorial by Eric Gill to the dead of World War I.

South Harting can boast of being the home of the novelist Anthony Trollope for the last two years of his life. Though here only a short time before his death in 1882, Trollope wrote four novels while in South Harting and his pen and paper knife can be seen in the church.

The village stands at the foot of **Harting Down**, beneath the steep scarp slope of the South Downs ridge, which is traversed by the South Downs Way. This spectacular long distance footpath and bridleway stretches for nearly 100 miles, from Winchester to Beachy Head and, here, the path skirts around Beacon Hill. At 793 feet above sea level, the hill is one of the highest points on the Downs. Harting Down is one of the largest areas of ancient chalk downland owned by the National Trust. This sheep-grazed local nature reserve and Site of Special Scientific Interest is home to a wide range of species, and the dew pond at the bottom of the valley is a haven for interesting wildlife including frogs and dragonflies.

Just south of the village lies the magnificent house, **Uppark**, a National Trust property that is superbly situated on the crest of a hill. However, the climb up to the house was so steep that, when the house was offered to the Duke of Wellington after his victories in the Napoleonic Wars, he declined as he considered the drive to the mansion would require replacing his exhausted horses too many times. The house was built in the late 1680s for Lord Grey of Werke, one of the chief instigators of the Duke of Monmouth's rebellion of 1685. Lord Grey was let off with a fine and he retired from his none too illustrious military career and concentrated on building his house to the latest Dutch designs. As well as being a splendid house architecturally, the building of the house on this site was only made possible with the help of a water pump invented by Lord Grey's grandfather that brought water up to the hilltop from a low-lying spring.

It was a mid 18th century owner, Sir Matthew Fetherstonhaugh, who created the lavish interiors by decorating and furnishing the rooms with rare carpets, elegant furniture and intriguing objets d'art. At his death in 1774, Sir Matthew left his estate to his 20-year-old son, Sir Harry, who, with his great friend the Prince Regent, brought an altogether different atmosphere to the house. He installed his London mistress, Emma Hart (who later married Sir William Hamilton and became Lord Nelson's mistress), and carried on a life of gambling, racing and partying. However, in 1810, Sir Harry gave up his social life and, at the age of 70, married his dairymaid, Mary Ann, to the amazement and outrage of West Sussex society. He died, at the age of 92, in 1846, and both Mary Ann and then her sister, Frances, kept the house just as it had been during Sir Harry's life for a further 50 years.

This latter era of life at Uppark would have been remembered by the young H G Wells who spent a great deal of time here as his mother worked at the house. As well as exploring the grounds and gardens laid out by the early 19th-century designer Humphry Repton, Wells had a self-taught education from Uppark's vast stock of books.

After the upper floors of the house were destroyed by fire in 1989, the National Trust undertook an extensive restoration programme and reopened the house to the public in 1995. Luckily, most of the house's 18th-century treasures were rescued from the fire and the fine pictures, furniture and ceramics are on view again in their original splendid settings.

Also close to South Harting lies the site of the now demolished **Durford Abbey** - an isolated monastery founded in the 12th century by a community of Premonstratensian monks, a strict vegetarian order founded in 1120 by St Norbert at Premontre, France. Unlike other orders of their time, which grew wealthy on the income from their monastic estates, life at Durford seems to have been very much a struggle for survival. In fact, so harsh was the monks' existence here that, on the monasteries' dissolution in the 16th century, is was described by a commissioner as "The poorest abbey I have seen, far in debt and in decay". Although little of the abbey remains today, the monks of Durford succeeded in leaving an important legacy in the form of two 15th-century bridges over the River Rother and its tributaries. (During the medieval period it was a duty of religious houses to provide and maintain such bridges.) Both Maidenmarsh Bridge, near the abbey site, and Habin Bridge, to the south of Rogate, are worth a visit, and the latter, which consists of four semicircular arches, still carries the road to South Harting.

TROTTON

3 miles W of Midhurst on the A272

This pleasant village lies in the broad valley of the River Rother, once a densely wooded area known for its timber and charcoal. The impressive medieval bridge in the village dates back to the 14th century and is still carrying modern day traffic. The money for the bridge was given by Lord Camoys, who accompanied Henry V to Agincourt. Inside the parish church is a memorial to Lord Camoys, who died in 1419, and his second wife, Elizabeth Mortimer, who was the widow of Sir Henry 'Harry Hotspur' Percy. Here, too, can be found the oldest known memorial to a woman, a floor brass of Margaret de Camoys, who died here in around 1310.

Pulborough

Nature Reserve

This ancient settlement has grown up close to the confluence of the Rivers Arun and Rother and it lies on the old Roman thoroughfare, Stane Street. Although it was a staging post along the old route between London and Chichester, and was strategically located near the rivers, it was never developed like its rivals over the centuries. It remains today a pleasant and sizeable village, popular for its freshwater fishing. The centre of Pulborough, on the old Roman route, is now a conservation area with several fine Georgian cottages clustered around the parish church, which occupies a commanding hilltop position.

Just southeast of the village lies the **RSPB Pulborough Brooks Nature Reserve** where there is a nature trail through tree-lined lanes, leading to views overlooking the restored wet meadows of the Arun Valley.

Around Pulborough

KIRDFORD

5½ miles N of Pulborough off the A272

This village, with its square green surrounded by stone cottages and tree-lined main street, has more the feel of a small town. Like its neighbour, Wisborough Green, Kirdford was a centre for glassmaking between 1300 and

1600 and the village sign incorporates diamonds of locally made glass. Iron smelting also prospered here for 100 years from the mid 16th century, which this accounts for the rather lavish extensions to the village's original Norman church.

Wisborough Green Village Pond

LOXWOOD

8 miles N of Pulborough on the B2133

Wey and Arun Junction Canal

This pleasant village, which lies off the beaten track and close to the county border with Surrey, is on the **Wey and Arun Junction Canal**, which opened in 1816 and linked London with the south coast. The coming of the railways saw an end to the commercial usefulness of this inland waterway and, in 1871, it was closed. However, certain stretches have been restored and it is now possible to cruise along one of the country's most attractive canals, or stroll along the peaceful towpath.

The village is also associated with the Christian Dependants, a religious sect founded by preacher John Sirgood in the 1850s. The group were nicknamed the 'Cokelers' because of their preference for cocoa over alcohol, and their chapel and burial ground can still be seen in Spy Lane.

WISBOROUGH GREEN

5½ miles N of Pulborough on the A272

Church of St Peter ad Vincula

Fishers Farm Park

This pretty Sussex village has a large rectangular green, surrounded by horse chestnut trees, around which stands half-timbered and tile-hung cottages and houses. Nearby, the village **Church of St Peter ad Vincula** is particularly interesting as the original Norman building, to which the 13th-century chancel was added, has walls almost five feet thick and a doorway 13 feet high. The suggestion is that this was an Anglo-Saxon keep that was later enlarged into a church as the doorway is tall enough to admit a man on horseback. During the Middle Ages, this curious church was a centre of pilgrimage as it contained several relics, including the hair shirt, comb and bones of St James and a crucifix with a drop of the Virgin's milk set in crystal.

The village is set in the undulating country of the Weald and, to the west of Wisborough Green, there are two areas of preserved woodland that give an indication to today's visitors of how most of the land north of the Downs would have looked many thousands of years ago. Looking at the countryside now it is hard to imagine that, in the 16th and 17th centuries, this area was an important industrial centre. Thanks to the seemingly limitless supply of trees for fuel, iron foundries and forges prospered here right up until the time of the Industrial Revolution. A plentiful supply of high quality sand from the coast supported a number of early glassworks. During the 16th century, Huguenot settlers from France and the Low Countries introduced new and improved methods of glass manufacture and the industry flourished until the early 17th century when lobbying by shipbuilders and iron smelters led to legislation banning the glassmakers from using timber to fire their furnaces.

Fishers Farm Park brings together the delights of the rural farmyard with the excitement of an adventure playground. As well as the combine harvester and pony rides, there is a whole assortment of animals, ranging from giant shire horses to goats, lambs and rabbits. For those who seek more mechanical diversions there is a merry-go-round from the 1950s and up-to-the-minute go-karts.

WEST CHILTINGTON

3 miles E of Pulborough off the A283

Church of St Mary

Built around a crossroads in the twisting lanes of the Wealden countryside, this neat and compact village centres on the village green, which is dominated by the delightful and relatively unrestored **Church of St Mary**. Famous for its medieval wall paintings discovered in 1882, this charming Norman church has an oak shingled spire and a roof of Horsham stone. Beside the churchyard gate are the old village stocks and whipping post.

COOTHAM

3 miles SE of Pulborough on the A283

Parham

The village is synonymous with **Parham** (see panel below), the most western and the grandest of the Elizabethan mansions that were built below the northern slopes of the Downs. Just west of the village and surrounded by a great deer park, the estate belonged in medieval times to the Abbey of Westminster and, at the Dissolution of the Monasteries, it passed into the hands of the Palmer family. As was customary, the foundation stone of the great mansion was laid by a child, in this case the two-year-old son of Thomas Palmer.

In 1601, Thomas Bysshop, a London lawyer, bought the estate and for the next 300 years it remained with that family. In 1922, the house and park were purchased by a son of Viscount Cowdray, Clive Pearson and, in 1948 Mr and

Parham House & Gardens

Storrington, near Pulborough, West Sussex RH20 4HS
Tel: 01903 742021
e-mail: enquiries@parhaminsussex.co.uk
website: www.parhaminsussex.co.uk

Idyllically situated in the heart of a medieval deer park, on the slopes of the South Downs, is Parham - an Elizabethan manor house with a four-acre walled garden and seven acres of 18th century Pleasure Grounds. There is an important collection of paintings, furniture and needlework contained within the light, panelled rooms which include a Great Hall and Long Gallery. Each room is graced with beautiful fresh flower arrangements, the flowers home-grown and cut from the walled garden.

Open on Wednesday, Thursday, Sunday and Bank Holiday afternoons from April- September, and Sunday afternoons in October. Licensed lunches and cream teas, picnic area, shop and plant sales area.

Mrs Pearson opened the property to the public. The splendid Elizabethan interiors have been restored to their former glory, including the magnificent 160-foot Long Gallery (its ceiling painted by Sir Oliver Messel), the Saloon, the Great Hall and the Great Parlour, and exceptional collections of period furniture, oriental carpets, rare needlework and fine paintings are on show. The Great Room is largely dedicated to Sir Joseph Banks, the noted botanist and patron of science, who accompanied Captain Cook on his journey to the Pacific in 1768. Banks was also a President of the Royal Society and was one of the founders of the Royal Botanical Gardens at Kew. The paintings here include masterpieces by Stubbs and Reynolds.

The grounds at Parham have also been restored and contain lawns, a lake, specimen trees, fine statuary and a magnificent four-acre walled garden with an orchard, a 1920s Wendy House, and greenhouses where plants and flowers are grown for the house. The house and gardens are open to the public on certain days of the week between April and October. Parham hosts many events during the year, including the Garden Weekend held in July and the Autumn Flowers at Parham event in September, which celebrates the tradition of flower-arranging started by the Hon Mrs Clive Pearson in the 1920s. The Garden Shop sells an impressive variety of plants, many of them unusual and all home-grown.

STORRINGTON

3½ miles SE of Pulborough on the A283

Church of St Mary   South Downs Way

This old market town has a jumble of architectural styles from its small heavily restored Saxon church through to 20th-century concrete buildings. However, from Storrington there is good access to the **South Downs Way** long distance footpath via Kithurst Hill. It was this beautiful surrounding countryside that inspired Francis Thompson to write his poem *Daisy* while he was staying in a local monastery; the composer, Arnold Bax, also lived in the area between 1940 and 1951.

The much-restored **Church of St Mary** has, inside, a Saxon stone coffin on which is the marble effigy of a knight, thought to have been a crusader. When the author A J Cronin moved to the old rectory in the 1930s, he used this legend as the basis for his novel *The Crusaders*.

SULLINGTON

4½ miles SE of Pulborough off the A283

Long Barn   Sullington Warren

This hamlet is home to a 115-foot **Long Barn**, which rivals many tithe barns that were such a feature of the medieval monastic estate. An exceptional building with a braced tie beam roof, the barn, which is privately owned, can be viewed by appointment. Just outside Sullington is **Sullington Warren** - owned by the National Trust, this expanse of open heathland was once used for farming rabbits and it now offers superb views across the South Downs. The Warren has nine prehistoric round barrows, all listed as Ancient Monuments.

AMBERLEY

4 miles S of Pulborough on the B2139

Castle   Museum   Amberely Wild Brooks

An attractive village of thatched cottages situated above the River Arun, Amberley is an ancient place whose name means 'fields yellow with buttercups'. Lands in this area were granted to St Wilfrid by King Cedwalla around AD680 and the village church of today is thought to stand on the foundations of a

Amberley Castle

Saxon building constructed by St Wilfrid, the missionary who converted the South Saxons to Christianity. Later, in the 12th century, Bishop Luffa of Chichester rebuilt the church and it still has a strong Norman appearance.

At around the same time as the church was being rebuilt, a fortified summer palace for the Bishops of Chichester was also constructed. During the late 14th century, when there was a large threat of a French sea invasion, Bishop Rede of Chichester enlarged the summer palace and added a great curtain wall. Still more a manor house than a true castle, **Amberley Castle** is said to have offered protection to Charles II during his flight to France in 1651.

During the 18th and 19th centuries, chalk

Houghton

Distance: *4.3 miles (6.9 kilometres)*
Typical time: *150 mins*
Height gain: *25 metres*
Map: *Explorer 121*
Walk: *www.walkingworld.com ID:76*
Contributor: *Nicholas Rudd-Jones*

ACCESS INFORMATION:

North Stoke, South of Amberley Station and B2139 from Storrington. Can start walk at marker 8 from Amberley station if no car (on Pulborough line from London), otherwise in North Stoke, park near phone box.

ADDITIONAL INFORMATION:

Note the River Arun is tidal and very prone to flooding - check before you start.

DESCRIPTION:

A circular walk based around the River Arun, taking in delightful villages of North and South Stoke. A good walk for kids.

FEATURES:

River, pub, church, wildlife, great views.

WALK DIRECTIONS:

1 | Take footpath to right off the small road next to phone box and post box. Climb two stiles, cross track and continue on grassy path downhill. At bottom of field, the path becomes gravelled.

2 | Cross footbridge; path swings right. Climb stile and turn left at river.

3 | Climb stile and cross bridge; follow track past houses and St Leonard's Church in South Stoke. Join road; swing left past barn on right.

4 | Turn right off road and take bridleway behind barn. At next bridleway signpost turn left. Follow stony track (glimpses of river below to right). Pass through gate and turn right at field; follow path around field edge.

5 | Pass gate back into woods. Continue past a metal gate on the left: this is the entrance to Arundel Park, an interesting diversion if you have time. Follow path along the river, passing under white cliffs.

6 | At end of path, pass through metal gate and join road uphill into Houghton village. There is a path marked along the river's edge straight to Houghton bridge, but when we walked it was completely flooded and impassable — could be worth exploring as a short cut in drier weather. At the crossroads, the George and Dragon pub is a short walk along the road to the left: lovely garden. Cross B2139 and take minor road signed to Bury (marked Houghton Lane on map) across fields.

7 | Turn right when South Downs Way crosses road. On reaching the river, follow round to the right, until you reach Amberley bridge on west bank. Turn left over the bridge. Take footpath halfway across the bridge on the right, heading south.

8 | Cross a subsidiary bridge, then turn right back alongside the river.

9 | Climb a stile and shortly afterwards take the path to left.

10 | On reaching the North Stoke Road, turn right, and you are back at the starting point.

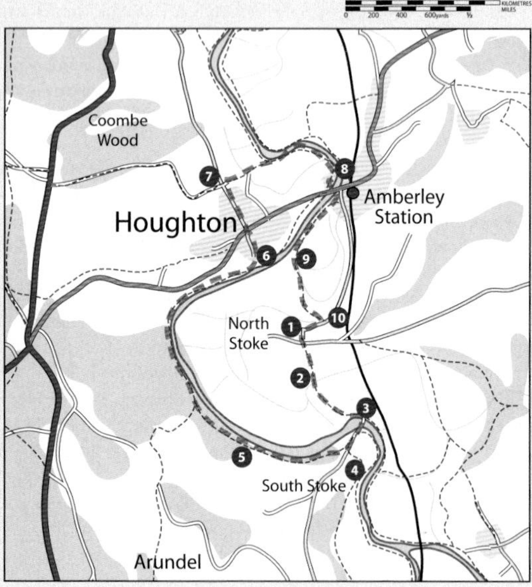

was quarried from Amberley and taken to the many lime kilns in the area. Later, large quantities of chalk were needed to supply a new industrial process, which involved the high temperature firing of chalk with small amounts of clay to produce Portland cement. Situated just to the south of Amberley, and on the site of an old chalk pit and limeworks, is **Amberley Working Museum** (see panel on page 271), which concentrates on the industry of this area. This is very much a working museum, on a site of 36 acres of former chalk pits, and visitors can ride the length of the museum on a workmen's train and see the comprehensive collection of narrow-gauge engines, from steam to electric. The history of roads and road-making is also explored, and in the Electricity Hall is an amazing assortment of electrical items from domestic appliances to generating and supply equipment. In the workshop section, there are various tradesmen's shops including a blacksmith's, pottery, boatbuilder's and a printing works.

To the north of Amberley there is a series of water meadows known as the **Amberley Wild Brooks**. Often flooded and inaccessible by car, this 30-acre conservation area and nature reserve is a haven for bird, animal and plant life. The trains on the Arun Valley line cross the meadows on specially constructed embankments, which were considered wonders of modern engineering when the line was first opened in 1863.

HARDHAM

1 mile SW of Pulborough on the A29

Church of St Botolph

This tiny hamlet, on the banks of the River Arun, is home to the Saxon **Church of St Botolph**, which is famous for its medieval wall paintings. Considered some of the finest in England, the oldest of the paintings dates from around 1100, and among the scenes on view are images of St George slaying the dragon and the Serpent tempting Adam and Eve. The murals are thought to have been worked by artists based at St Pancras Priory in Lewes, who were also responsible for the paintings at Coombes and Clayton.

At one time Hardham had a small Augustinian monastic house and the site of Hardham Priory can be found just south of the hamlet. Now a farmhouse, the priory's cloisters have been incorporated into a flower garden. From here a footpath leads to the disused Hardham Tunnel, a channel, which was built to provide a short cut for river barges wishing to avoid an eastern loop of the River Arun.

Hardham Priory

BIGNOR

5 miles SW of Pulborough off the A29

Roman Villa

The main thoroughfares of this pretty village are arranged in an uneven square and, as well as a photogenic 15th-century shop, there are some charming ancient domestic buildings to be seen. In 1811, a ploughman working on the east side of the village

THE BARN AT PENFOLDS BED & BREAKFAST

The Street, Bury, nr Arundel,
West Sussex RH20 1PA
Tel: 01798 831496 Fax: 01798 831251
e-mail: info@thebarnatpenfolds.co.uk
website: www.thebarnatpenfolds.co.uk

Howard and Susie Macnamara, who have lived here since the 1980s, have recently created high-quality Bed & Breakfast accommodation that combines period appeal with modern comforts. The ancient thatched barn, which stand down a quiet lane next to the owners' 17th century cottage, was once part of the Norfolk Estate; for many years it was occupied by Sidney Penfold, blacksmith and farrier. On the ground floor is a single room with its own bathroom and shower, while above are two double rooms with good-sized bath/shower rooms and a single with a shower room. All have quality furnishings, digital TV and tea/coffee making facilities. Guests have the use of a bright day room with French windows opening on to the garden. The hosts provide a good choice for breakfast, which can be enjoyed in the dining room or at the large farmhouse kitchen table. Children over 12 are welcome; no pets. The little village of Bury, signposted off the A29 a few miles north of Arundel, close to the River Arun at the foot of the South Downs.

unearthed a Roman Mosaic Floor, which proved to be part of a **Roman Villa** built at the end of the 2nd century AD. This is one of the largest sites in Britain with some 70 Roman buildings surrounding a central courtyard. It is thought that the find was the administration centre of a large agricultural estate. The villa, being the home of a wealthy agricultural master, was extended throughout the time of the Roman occupation and the mosaic decoration of the house is some of the finest to be seen in this country.

Unlike the Roman excavations at Fishbourne, this remains relatively undiscovered by tourists and, charmingly, the exposed remains are covered, not by modern day structures, but by the thatched huts that were first built to protect them in 1814. The 80-foot mosaic along the north corridor is the longest on display in Britain, and among the characters depicted are Venus, Medusa and an array of gladiators. The Bignor Roman Villa Museum houses a collection of artefacts revealed during the excavation work as well as a display on the history of the Roman settlement and its underfloor heating system or hypocaust.

FITTLEWORTH

2½ miles W of Pulborough on the A283

Brinkwells

An acknowledged Sussex beauty spot, this village has retained much of its charm despite its position on the main Pulborough to Petworth road. Its narrow roads wind through woods, passing an old mill and bridge, lovely old cottages and lanes leading to the surrounding woods and heath. This rural idyll has been popular with artists over the years, particularly around the turn of the century. In the Swan Inn, the local hostelry, there is a number of paintings of local views, supposedly left by artists in return for their lodgings.

Well known among anglers, the village has excellent fishing on the River Rother and further downstream, where it joins the River Arun.

In the middle of woodlands is **Brinkwells**, a thatched cottage, once home to the village's most famous visitor, the composer Edward Elgar. He first came here in 1917, when he wrote his much-loved cello concerto, and returned for the last time in 1921. Appropriately, the Jubilee clock in the village church has a very musical chime.

STOPHAM

1 mile NW of Pulborough off the A283

Stopham House · Stopham Bridge

This charming place, where a handful of cottages cluster around the early Norman church, lies on the banks of the River Rother. The family home of a distinguished local family who can trace their ancestry back to the Norman invasion, **Stopham House** is still here, as is the splendid early 15th-century bridge, which the family were instrumental in constructing. The impressive **Stopham Bridge** is widely regarded as the finest of its kind in Sussex and, though the tall central arch was rebuilt in 1822 to allow masted vessels to pass upstream towards the Wey and Arun Canal, the medieval structure is coping well with today's traffic without a great deal of modern intervention.

Stopham Bridge

Petworth

Petworth House · Cottage Museum

This historic town, though now a major road junction, still has many elements of an ancient feudal settlement - the old centre, a great house and a wall dividing the two. Mentioned in the *Domesday Book*, where it appeared as Peteorde, this was a market town; the square is thought to have originated in the 13th century, and its street fair dates back to 1189. Between the 14th and the 16th centuries this was an important cloth weaving centre and a number of fine merchants' and landowners' houses still stand today. Daintrey House, which has a Georgian front façade and Elizabethan features to the rear, has magnificent iron railings around the front garden. Another house, Leconfield Hall, built in 1794 on the site of a former covered market, was the courthouse and council meeting place before becoming a public hall. On the north wall can be seen a replica bust of William III, attributed to the Dutch sculptor Honore Pelle, one of only four such pieces in the country. The original can be seen in Petworth House. The garden of Lancaster House, close by, is said to have been used as a hiding place for the church silver during the time of Cromwell.

As well as taking time to wander the streets here and see the many

COCO CAFÉ & SUGAR LOUNGE

Saddlers Row, Petworth,
West Sussex GU28 0AN
Tel: 01798 344006
website: www.cococafeandsugarlounge.com

Behind the brown-and-white frontage of a corner building in Saddlers Row is a veritable paradise for chocolate lovers. Proprietor Nichole Peet, who hails from Oregon, has long had a desire to open a chocolate shop, with further inspiration provided by seeing the film *Chocolat*. Her **Coco Café & Sugar Lounge** is filled with myriad delights, headed by chocolates – individual or in bars – from the UK, Belgium, France and the USA. There are sweets in old-fashioned jars, fudge and cakes and biscuits, croissants and lunchtime quiche.

Drinks include numerous wonderful chocolate concoctions – white, dark and milk, with flavours such as cinnamon, honey, rum, bourbon and vanilla. The walls of this magical place are hung with paintings and photographs by local artists, all for sale, Shop hours are 9 to 6 Monday to Saturday and 10 to 5 Sunday.

STRINGERS GALLERY

Stringers Hall, 94 East Street, Petworth, West Sussex GU28 0AB
Tel: 01798 343179
e-mail: lesliemartin@talktalk.net
website: www.stringers-gallery.co.uk

Part of a handsome 17th century house on the main route through Petworth, **Stringers Gallery** supplies artwork and artists' materials to the local community, to West Sussex and to art lovers everywhere. Owner Leslie Martin, who took over and expanded what was primarily a picture framing business, stocks a wide range of fine art supplies, from paints and oils and brushes to sketch pads and cartridges, tapes and adhesives, greetings cards, reference art books, picture and photo frames, and canvases made in the workshop on the premises. The Gallery also sells rare and antique prints as well as paintings by contemporary artists in oils, acrylic and watercolours. Featured artists include Louise Mizen (horses a favourite subject), Toby Meader (sheep), Peter Ward (animals, birds, fish, butterflies), Andrew Dandridge (Sussex scenes) and Doro Huelin (flora and fauna in oils). Services offered by the Gallery include creating portraits of pets and people from photos, photocopying and web searches, and art courses on various topics can be arranged. Situated in a lovely part of the country that provides abundant inspiration for artists, Stringers Gallery is open from 10 to 5.30 Tuesday to Saturday.

interesting houses, cottages and other buildings, visitors should not miss the **Petworth Cottage Museum**. Housed in a 17th-century cottage of the Leconfield estate it has been restored to the days of 1910 when it was the home of Maria Cummings, seamstress at nearby Petworth House and a widow with four grown-up children. The cottage re-creates her domestic setting, including her bedroom, sewing room, a copper boiler in the scullery and a 'Petworth' range for cooking and heating. However, what brings most visitors to Petworth is the grand estate of **Petworth House**, now owned by the National Trust. Built between 1688 and 1696 by Charles Seymour, the 6th Duke of Somerset, on the site of a medieval manor house belonging to the Percy family, Petworth House is a simple and elegant building that has more the look of a French château than an English country house. Both French and English architects have been suggested. The construction of the house was completed by the Duke's descendant, the 2nd Earl of Egremont, who

Deer in Petworth Park

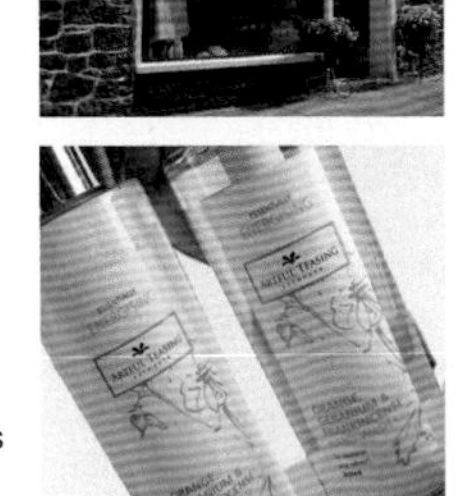

had the grounds and deer park landscaped by Capability Brown in 1752. The Grand Entrance Gates display the twin figures of Gog and Magog, symbols that have been used on the Town Seal since 1894.

Today, the house is home to one of the finest art collections outside London and the layout of the house, with one room leading directly into another, lends itself perfectly to life as an art gallery. Among the works on view are paintings by Rembrandt, Van Dyck, Hobbema, Cuyp, Holbein, Reynolds, Gainsborough and Turner, who was a frequent visitor to Petworth House. On a less grand scale, in decoration terms, the servants' block is also open to the public and provides an interesting insight into life below stairs.

Just south of the estate is the Coultershaw Water Wheel and Beam Pump, one of the earliest pumped water systems, installed in 1790 to pipe water two miles to Petworth House. Restored to full working order by the Sussex Industrial Archaeology Society, it is now open to the public on a limited basis.

TILLINGTON

1 mile W of Petworth on the A272

Dating back to the days before the Norman Conquest, the village appeared in the Domesday Book as Tolinstone. Tillington lies beside the western walls of Petworth House. The local landmark here, however, is All Hallows' Church and, in particular, its tower. Built in 1810, the tower is topped by stone pinnacles and a crown that is very reminiscent of the lower stage of the Eiffel Tower. Known as a Scots Crown, the church and its tower have featured in paintings by both Turner and Constable.

The West Sussex Weald

This area, to the north of the South Downs, is called a weald, a word that is derived from the German word wald, meaning forest. This would suggest an area covered in woodland and, though some areas of the great forest remain, the landscape now is one of pastures enclosed by hedgerows. From the Middle Ages onwards, until the time of the Industrial Revolution, the area was very much associated with iron working and, less so, glassmaking. The trees were felled for fuel to drive the furnaces and streams were dammed to create hammer ponds. The legacy of this once prosperous industry can be seen in the wealth of elaborate buildings and, particularly, the splendid churches built on the profits of the industry.

Those interested in visiting grand houses will find that this region of West Sussex has several to offer. Close to East Grinstead, Standen, a remarkable Victorian country house now restored to its original glory, is a wonderful example of the Arts and Crafts Movement. The low half-timbered 15th-century house, the Priest House, at West Hoathly, was built as an estate office for the monks from St Pancras Priory, Lewes. Now restored, it is open to the public as a museum filled with 18th and 19th-century furniture. The magnificent Elizabeth mansion, Danny, at Hurstpierpoint, has a very special place in history as this is where Lloyd George and his war cabinet drew up the terms of the armistice to end World War I. In private hands today, the house is occasionally open to the public.

Near Ardingly lies Wakehurst Place, a striking Elizabethan mansion built by the Culpeper family in 1590. Now leased to the Royal Botanical Gardens at Kew, the magnificent collection of trees and shrubs in the grounds are well worth seeing. Other great gardens can also be found in this region of West Sussex, including Leonardslee at Lower Beeding, which was laid out in the late 19th century by Sir Edmund Loder and Hymans, and created with the help of the 19th-century gardening revivalists William Robinson and Gertrude Jekyll.

Horsham

Museum Christ's Hospital School

This ancient town, which takes its name from a Saxon term meaning 'horse pasture', was founded in the mid 10th century. Some 300 years later, Horsham had grown into a prosperous borough and market town, which was considered important enough to send two members to the new Parliament established in 1295. Between 1306 and 1830, Horsham, along with Lewes and Chichester, took it in turns to hold the county assizes. During the weeks the court was held in Horsham, large numbers of visitors descended on the town giving it a carnival atmosphere. Public executions were also held here, either on the common or on the Carfax, including one, in 1735, of a man who refused to speak at his trial. He was sentenced to death by compression, and three hundredweight of stones were placed on his chest for three days. When the man still refused to speak, the gaoler added his own weight to the man's chest and killed him outright. The Carfax today is a thriving pedestrianised shopping centre and nothing is left of the horrors of its past.

Horsham's architectural gem is The Causeway, a quiet tree-lined street of old buildings that runs from the Georgian fronted town hall to the 12th-century Church of St Mary, where can be found a simple tablet commemorating the life of Percy Bysshe Shelley, a celebrated local inhabitant. Here, too, can be found the gabled 16th-century Causeway House - a rambling building that is now home to the **Horsham Museum**, a purpose for which its layout is ideal. This excellent museum offers a treasure trove of local history displayed in some 24 galleries, including re-creations of a Sussex farmhouse kitchen, a wheelwright's and a saddler's shop and a blacksmith's forge. Concentrating on local history in particular, the vast and varied collection includes toys, costumes, photography, arts and crafts, a crime and punishment gallery, and many aspects of town life. There are surprises at every turn, from dinosaur bones to a Cambodian bronze Buddha, and a Canadian salmon caught by the artist Millais. With its galleries and exhibition spaces with constantly changing displays, as well as two walled gardens, it's no surprise that the Museum has been called 'a small V & A'.

Just two miles southwest of Horsham lies the famous **Christ's Hospital School**, a Bluecoat school that was founded for poor children, in Newgate Street, London, in 1552 by Edward VI. In the 18th century the girls moved to Hertford and in 1902 the boys moved here to Horsham. The girls joined them here in 1985. The present buildings incorporate some of the original London edifices. Bluecoat refers to the traditional long dark blue cloak that is still worn by the pupils.

Around Horsham

RUSPER

3 miles N of Horsham off the A264

This secluded village of tile hung and timbered cottages grew up around a 13th century priory. Rusper Priory is long gone and the only reminders of it are the medieval tower of the church and the graves in the churchyard of a prioress and four sisters. The church was rebuilt in the mid 19th century by the Broadwater family, whose wealth came from their piano manufacturing business. Lucy Broadwater, who died in 1929 and to whom there is a memorial tablet in the church, was a leading figure in the revival of English folk music.

GATWICK AIRPORT

7½ miles NE of Horsham off the A23

The airport opened to commercial air traffic in 1936 when the first passengers took off for Paris. The return fare was the equivalent of £4.25, which included the return first-class rail fare from Victoria Station, London, to the airport. A month later the airport was officially opened by the Secretary of State for Air. He also opened the world's first circular air terminal here which was immediately christened The Beehive. During World War II, Gatwick, like all other British airports, was put under military control and was one of the bases for the D-Day operations.

After the war, the terminal buildings were extended and, in 1958, the new airport was reopened. Among Gatwick Airport's notable firsts was the pier leading from the terminal to the aircraft stands giving passengers direct access to the planes, and Gatwick was the first airport in the world to combine air, rail and road travel under one roof.

Gatwick Airport Skyview gives visitors the chance to see behind the scenes of this busy airport through its multimedia theatre.

CRAWLEY

6½ miles NE of Horsham on the A23

A modern town, one of the original new towns created after the New Towns Act of 1946, Crawley is really an amalgamation of the villages of Three Bridges and Ifield with the small market town of Crawley. Though much has been lost under the new developments, Crawley probably dates back to Saxon times, though it remained a quiet and unassuming place until the late 18th century. A convenient distance from both London and Brighton, it was used by the Prince Regent and his friends as a stopping-over point when they commuted between the south coast resort of Brighton and the metropolis. However, the coming of the railways took away the need of a resting place and so Crawley returned to its quiet life. In the churchyard of the Franciscan friary is the grave of Lord Alfred Douglas, the intimate friend of Oscar Wilde. He lies beside his mother, who supported him when his father cut off his allowance during his friendship with Wilde.

MANNINGS HEATH

2 miles SE of Horsham on the A281

Just north of the village lies St Leonard's Forest, one of the few wooded heathland areas to survive the long term ravages of the timber fuelled iron industry of the Weald.

CAMELIA BOTNAR HOMES & GARDENS

Littleworth Lane, (Off the A272), Cowfold,
West Sussex RH13 8NA
Tel 01403 864773
e-mail: sales@cameliabotnar.com
website: www.cameliabotnar.com

Tucked away, just outside of Cowfold in the heart of West Sussex is Camelia Botnar Homes & Gardens. Exhibiting superb showroom displays of award-winning Ironwork, traditional handcrafted furniture in oak, maple, beech and pine, hand-thrown terracotta & studio ceramics together with an extensive range of high quality plants all in a 5 acre nursery, so you can be sure your visit will be worthwhile. All our products are finished to a high standard and we are happy to quote on bespoke orders to give your home or garden that unique experience. Our gift shop has an exceptional range of high quality, unusual and good value gifts & greetings cards.

Explore our nursery with our huge selection of trees, shrubs, bedding and baskets to bring colour into your garden.

Our Camelia Botnar Bistro is open daily for breakfasts, lunches, snacks, teas and mouth-watering Sunday roasts. We are now a popular destination where you can expect attentive service and freshly prepared home-made food with a seasonal menu created by our chefs. We are licensed to sell alchohol so you can enjoy a glass of wine or beer with your meal. For reservations ring 01403-864588. Our website shows our menus and special offers **www.cameliabotnar.com**

We do offer **'Tour, Talk and Tea'** afternoons for coach parties and large groups given by our specialists in horticulture, please ring 01403 864773 for further information. We are open 7 days a week Mon-Fri 9am-5pm, Sun 10am-4pm.

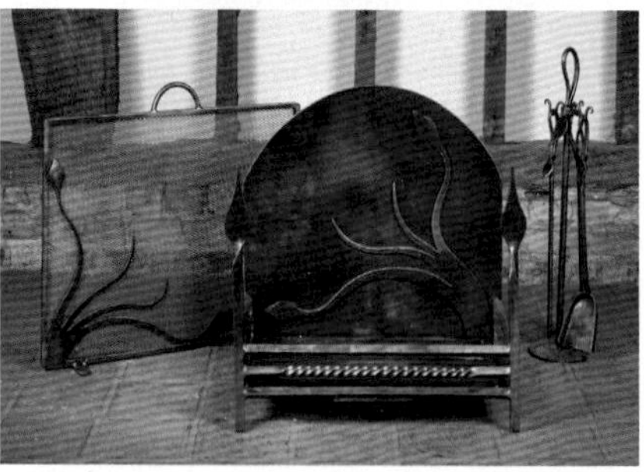

Rising in places to around 500 feet, the forest lies on the undulating sandstone ridge that is bounded by Horsham, Crawley and Handcross. According to local folklore, St Leonard's Forest is the home of the legendary nine-foot-long dragon that roamed the heath and terrorised the surrounding villagers. Coincidentally, some dinosaur bones were discovered nearby in 1822 by Mary Mantell.

LOWER BEEDING

3 miles SE of Horsham on the B2110

Leonardslee Gradens

The name of the village, along with that of its near namesake Upper Beeding, to the south, is somewhat confusing. Lower Beeding is actually situated on the summit of a hill, while Upper Beeding lies in one of the lowest parts of West Sussex. However, this can be explained by looking at the derivation of the shared name. Beeding is derived from the Old English 'Beadingas', which means 'Beada's people' and the Upper and Lower refer to the importance of, rather than the geographical positions of, the two settlements.

Just to the south of the village lies the beautiful **Leonardslee Gardens** (see panel on page 281), in a natural valley created by a tributary of the River Adur. Laid out by Sir Edmund Loder who began his task in 1889, the gardens are still maintained by the family and are world-famous for the spring displays of azaleas, magnolias and rhododendrons around the seven landscaped lakes. Deer and wallabies live in the semi-wild habitat around the small lakes. There are several miles of walks around this large area as well as small gardens, including a bonsai garden, to enjoy. The Loder family collection of motor vehicles, dating from 1889 to 1900, is an interesting and informative display of the various different designs adopted by the earliest car constructors.

COWFOLD

4 miles SE of Horsham on the A272

Church of St Peter St Hugh's Charterhouse

This picturesque village of cottages clusters around the parish **Church of St Peter**, which holds one of the most famous brasses in Sussex. Dating back to the 15th century, the life-size brass is of Thomas Nelond, Prior of Lewes in the 1420s, and the brass, along with its elaborate canopy, is over 10 feet long.

Looking at Cowfold today it is hard to believe that is was once an important centre of the iron industry. The abundance of timber for fuel and reliable streams to drive the bellows and heavy hammers made this an active iron smelting area from medieval times through to the end of the 18th century. In order to secure a steady supply of water to these early foundries, small rivers were dammed to form mill or hammer ponds and a number of disused examples can still be found in the surrounding area.

Just to the south of Cowfold and rising above the trees is the spire of **St Hugh's Charterhouse**, the only Carthusian monastery in Britain. Founded in the 1870s, after the order had been driven out of France, the 30 or so monks of this contemplative order live cut off from the rest of the world behind the high stone walls. Each monk has his own cell, or hermitage, complete with its own garden and workshop, and the monks only emerge from their solitude for services and dinner on Sunday.

UPPER BEEDING

13 miles S of Horsham off the A2037

A sprawling village of cottages along the banks of the River Adur, during the Middle Ages, Upper Beeding was the home of Sele Priory, a Benedictine religious house founded in the late 11th century by William de Braose.

Though a quiet place today, in the early 19th century an important turnpike road passed through Upper Beeding and the old village toll house, one of the last in the county to remain in service, is now an exhibit at the Weald and Downland Museum, Singleton.

BRAMBER

13 miles S of Horsham on the A283

St Mary's House | Castle

Visitors seeing Bramber for the first time will find it hard to imagine that, during Norman times, this small, compact village was a busy port on the River Adur estuary but its demise came as the river silted up. The name Bramber is derived from the Saxon 'Brymmburh' meaning fortified hill, and when William de Braose built his castle on the steep hill above the village it was probably on the foundations of a previous Saxon stronghold. Completed in 1090, the castle comprised a gatehouse and a number of domestic buildings surrounded by a curtain wall. An important stronghold while the port was active, the castle was visited by both King John and Edward I. However, the castle did not survive the Civil War. It was all but demolished by the Parliamentarians.

St Mary's House, Bramber

Today, the stark remains of **Bramber Castle** can be seen on the hilltop and the site is owned by English Heritage.

During the 15th century, the lands of the de Braose family were transferred to William Waynflete, the then Bishop of Winchester and founder of Magdalen College, Oxford. It was Waynflete who was responsible for constructing **St Mary's House**, in 1470, a striking medieval residence that was first built as a home for four monks who were bridge wardens of the important crossing here over the River Adur. Now a Grade I listed building, this is a classic half-timbered dwelling with fine wood panelled rooms, Elizabethan trompe l'œil paintings and medieval shuttered windows. However what remains today is only half of the original construction, which also acted as a resting place for pilgrims travelling to Chichester or Canterbury.

Following the Dissolution of the Monasteries, the house came into private ownership and was refurbished as a comfortable residence for a well-to-do family. The Painted Room was decorated for a visit by Queen Elizabeth I in 1585 and the room in which Charles II rested before fleeing to Shoreham and then France is known as the King's Room. For a time at the end of the 19th century St Mary's House became part of the social scene when owned by Algernon Bourke, the owner of White's Club in London. His wife was called Gwendolen and their names were 'borrowed' by Oscar Wilde for two characters in his play *The Importance of Being Earnest*. Lovingly restored, and with charming topiary gardens, the house was the setting for the Sherlock Holmes story *The Musgrave*

Ritual and it has also featured in the *Dr Who* TV series.

Before the Reform Act of 1832 swept away the rotten boroughs, this tiny constituency returned two members to Parliament. This was despite the fact that, at one time, Bramber only had 32 eligible voters! One Member of Parliament who benefited from the unreformed system was William Wilberforce, who was more or less awarded one of the Bramber seats in recognition of his campaigning work against slavery.

Steyning Church

STEYNING

13 miles S of Horsham off the A283

Museum

This ancient and historic market town, whose main street follows closely the line of the South Downs, was founded in the 8th century by St Cuthman. An early Celtic Christian, Cuthman travelled from Wessex eastwards pushing his invalid mother in a handcart. On reaching Saxon Steyning, the wheel on the handcart broke as they passed Penfolds Field and the nearby haymakers laughed and jeered as the old lady was thrown to the ground. St Cuthman cursed the field and the unhelpful haymakers, and the heavens are said to have opened and torrential rain poured down and spoilt their labours. To this day, it is said to rain whenever Penfolds Field is being mown. St Cuthman took his calamity as a sign that he should settle here and he built a timber church.

By the late Saxon period Steyning had grown to become an important port on the then navigable River Adur and, as well as being a royal manor owned by Alfred the Great, it also had a Royal Mint. By 1100, the silting of the river had caused the harbour to

MICHAEL'S COUNTRY KITCHEN

The Old Bakery, Cobblestone Walk, Steyning,
West Sussex BN44 3RD
Tel: 01903 810000
e-mail: michaelscountrykitchen@btconnect.com

Rosaline Barr and her son Michael took over a lovely old bakery and created a beautiful, traditional tea room in a charming, atmospheric cobbled walk. Local produce is the basis of the excellent sweet and savoury delights served throughout the day, seven days a week. The choice includes sausages from her brother's Brighton Sausage Company, meat from Roberts Family Butchers in Steyning, free-range eggs, sandwiches, hot dishes and scrumptious cakes and pastries. The owners also have a greengrocers shop and a wholefood shop.

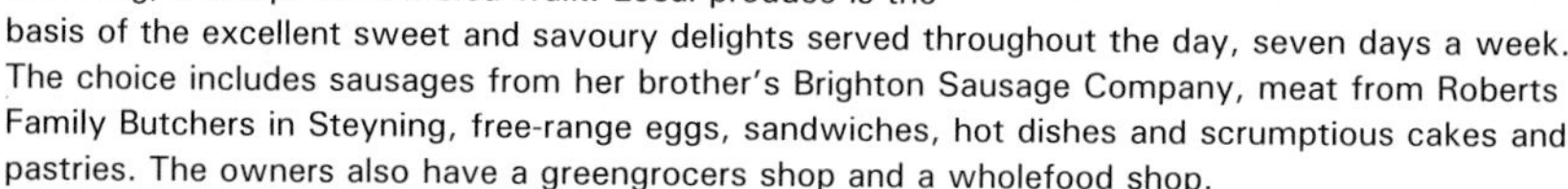

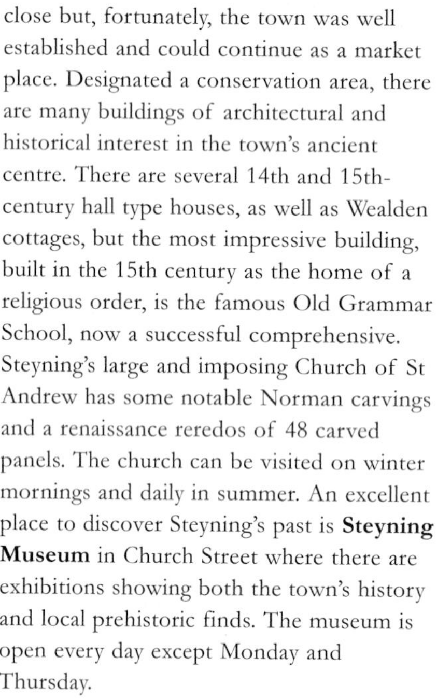

close but, fortunately, the town was well established and could continue as a market place. Designated a conservation area, there are many buildings of architectural and historical interest in the town's ancient centre. There are several 14th and 15th-century hall type houses, as well as Wealden cottages, but the most impressive building, built in the 15th century as the home of a religious order, is the famous Old Grammar School, now a successful comprehensive. Steyning's large and imposing Church of St Andrew has some notable Norman carvings and a renaissance reredos of 48 carved panels. The church can be visited on winter mornings and daily in summer. An excellent place to discover Steyning's past is **Steyning Museum** in Church Street where there are exhibitions showing both the town's history and local prehistoric finds. The museum is open every day except Monday and Thursday.

Steyning's close proximity to the 100-mile South Downs Way and the Downs Link (a long-distance bridleway that follows the course of the old railway line to Christ's Hospital near Horsham and on in to Surrey), makes this a lovely base for both walking and riding holidays.

SHIPLEY

6 miles S of Horsham off the A272

King's Land

As well as its pretty 12th-century village church, this pleasant village also features a small disused toll house and a distinctive hammer pond that, in the 16th century, would have supplied water to drive the bellows and mechanical hammers in the adjacent iron foundry. However, Shipley is perhaps best known for being the former home of the celebrated Sussex writer Hilaire Belloc. He lived at **King's Land**, a low rambling house on the outskirts of the village, from 1906 until his death in 1953 and, appropriately enough, as a lover of windmills, he had one at the bottom of his garden. Built in 1879, Shipley Mill is the only remaining working smock mill in Sussex and, while being the county's last, it is also the biggest. Open to the public on a limited basis, the mill was completely restored and returned to working order after the writer's death.

Belloc is not the only connection that Shipley has with the arts, for the composer John Ireland is buried in the churchyard of the village's interesting church, built by the Knights Templar in 1125.

WASHINGTON

12 miles S of Horsham off the A24

Chanctonbury Ring

Standing at the northern end of the Findon Gap, an ancient pass through the South Downs, this village's name is derived from the Saxon for 'settlement of the family of Wassa'. A pretty place, with a varied assortment of buildings, Washington stands between the chalk downland and the sandstone Weald. The village gets an honourable mention in Hilaire Belloc's West Country Drinking Song:

They sell good beer at Haslemere
And under Guildford Hill.
At Little Cowfold as I've been told
A beggar may drink his fill:
There is a good brew in Amberley too,
And by the bridge also;
But the swipes they take in at Washington Inn
Is the very best beer I know.

Just southeast of the village, and not far from the South Downs Way, lies one of the county's most striking landmarks - **Chanctonbury Ring**. An Iron Age hillfort, the site is marked by a clump of beech trees, planted in 1760 by Charles Goring who inherited the hill along with Wiston Park. Many of the trees suffered during the October hurricane of 1987, though sufficient remain to make this an eye-catching sight on the horizon. Meanwhile, the part 16th and part 19th-century mansion of Wiston House is now leased by the Foreign Office and, though it is not open to the public, views of the house and the park can be seen from the road leading to village church.

The countryside around Chanctonbury Ring inspired the composer John Ireland who, towards the end of his life in the 1950s, bought Rock Mill, which lies below the hill. A converted tower mill, a plaque on the wall records that Ireland lived the happiest years of his life here before his death in 1962.

BILLINGSHURST

6½ miles SW of Horsham on the A272

This attractive small town, strung out along Roman Stane Street, was, in the days before the railways, an important coaching town and several good former coaching inns, including the 16th-century Olde Six Bells, can still be found in the old part of the town. The Norman parish Church of St Mary has a 13th-century tower, but most of the rest of the building dates from the 15th to 16th centuries apart from some unfortunate Victorian restoration to the east end.

ITCHINGFIELD

3 miles SW of Horsham off A264

The parish church in this tiny village has an amazing 600-year-old belfry tower, the beams of which are entirely held together with oak pegs. During a restoration programme in the 1860s, workmen found a skull, said to have been that of Sir Hector Maclean, on one of the belfry beams. A friend of the vicar of the time, Sir Hector was executed for his part in the Jacobite Rising of 1715 and, presumably, his old friend thought to keep his gruesome souvenir in a safe place. In the churchyard of this early 12th-century building is a little priest's house, built in the 15th century as a resting place for the priest who rode from Sele Priory at Upper Beeding to pick up the parish collection.

RUDGWICK

5½ miles NW of Horsham on the B2128

A typical Wealden village of charming tile-fronted cottages, the 13th-century village church has a fine Sussex marble font in which the shells of sea creatures have been fossilised in the stone.

WARNHAM

2 miles NW of Horsham off the A24

Field Place

This small, well-kept village is best known as the birthplace of the poet Percy Bysshe Shelley. He was born in 1792 at **Field Place**, a large country house just outside the village, where he spent a happy childhood exploring the local countryside and playing with paper boats on the lake at the house. Famously, the young poet was cast out of the family home by his father who did not approve of his profession, and while there are many Shelley memorials in the parish church, Percy does not have one. Shelley was drowned when sailing his boat in a storm in the Gulf of Spezia off the west coast of Italy. His body was washed up on the beach some days later and he was cremated on the beach in the presence of Byron, whom he had recently visited at Livorno. His ashes are buried in Rome, though his heart lies in his son's tomb in Bournemouth.

Haywards Heath

On first appearances, Haywards Heath appears to be a modern town, situated on high heathland. However, the conservation area around Muster Green indicates where the old settlement was originally based. A pleasant open space surrounded by trees, which is believed to takes its name from the obligatory annual 17th-century custom of mustering the militia, the green was the site of a battle during the Civil War. Here, too, can be found Haywards Heath's oldest building, the 16th-century Sergison Arms, which takes its name from the landed family who once owned nearby Cuckfield Park.

The modern town has grown up around the station to which Haywards Heath owes its prosperity, as the two nearby villages of Lindfield and Cuckfield both refused to allow the railway to run through them when the line from London to the south coast was laid in the 19th century.

Around Haywards Heath

LINDFIELD

1 mile NE of Haywards Heath on the B2028

Old Place

This famous beauty spot is everyone's idea of

the perfect English village: the wide common was once used for fairs and markets, the High Street leads up hill to the church and there are some splendid domestic buildings from tile-hung cottages to elegant Georgian houses. The village is also home to **Old Place**, a small timber-framed Elizabethan manor house that is said to have been Queen Elizabeth's country cottage, and the cottage next door is said to have been Henry VII's hunting lodge. Sited on a hill top, the 13th-century village church with its large spire was a useful landmark in the days when the surrounding area was wooded. Beside the churchyard is Church House, which was originally The Tiger Inn. During the celebrations after the defeat of the Spanish Armada in 1588, the inn supplied so much strong ale to the villagers that the bell ringers broke their ropes and cracked one of the church bells. The inn was one of the village's busy coaching inns in the 18th and 19th centuries when Lindfield was an important staging post between London and Brighton.

Wakehurst Place, Ardingly

ARDINGLY

3½ miles N of Haywards Heath on the B2028

Wakehurst Place Reservoir

Ardingly is chiefly famous for being the home of the showground for the South of England Agricultural Society. Although there is some modern building, the old part of the village has remained fairly unspoilt. Ardingly College, a public school, founded by the pioneering churchman Nathaniel Woodard in 1858, is a large redbrick building with its own squat towered chapel. The village church, around which the old part of Ardingly is clustered, dates from medieval times though there is much Victorian restoration work. Inside can be found various brasses to the Tudor Culpeper family while, outside, the churchyard wall was used, in 1643, as a defensive position by the men of Ardingly against Cromwell's troops who came to take the Royalist rector.

To the west of the village, a tributary of the River Ouse has been dammed to form **Ardingly Reservoir**, a 200-acre lake that offers some excellent fishing as well as waterside walks and a nature trail.

Just north of Ardingly, at the top end of the reservoir, lies **Wakehurst Place**, the Tudor home of the Culpeper family, who arrived here in the 15th century. The present house, a striking Elizabethan mansion, was built in 1590 by Edward Culpeper, and the house and estate were eventually left to the National Trust in 1963 by Sir Henry Price. Over the years, but particularly during the 20th century, the owners of Wakehurst Place have built up a splendid collection of trees and shrubs in the natural dramatic landscapes of woodlands, valleys and lakes. Now leased to the Royal Botanic Gardens at Kew, the 500-acre gardens are open to the public throughout the year. As well as the varied and magnificent display of plants, trees and shrubs, visitors can take in the exhibitions in the house on local geology, habitats and woodlands of the area. Wakehurst Place is also home to the Millennium Seed Bank, a project that aims to ensure the continued survival of over 24,000 plant species worldwide.

To the southeast of Ardingly lies the village of Horsted Keynes, the final resting place of Harold Macmillan, Prime Minister from 1957 to 1963. He is buried in the family plot at St Giles' Church.

WORTH

8 miles N of Haywards Heath off the B2036

Worth Abbey · Church of St Nicholas

For those with a particular interest in historic churches, the ancient settlement of Worth, which is now all but a suburb of Crawley, is well worth a visit. Considered by many to be one of England's best churches, the Saxon **Church of St Nicholas** was built between 950 and 1050. The massive interior is dominated by three giant Saxon arches. Salvin built the tower in 1871 and also restored the chancel.

The Benedictine monastery and Roman Catholic boys' public school, **Worth Abbey**, to the east of Worth, was originally built as the country house of a wealthy tycoon. Paddockhurst, as it was known, was built by Robert Whitehead, a 19th-century marine engineer, who invented the torpedo. It was greatly added to by the 1st Lord Cowdray who purchased the property from Whitehead in 1894. Using Paddockhurst as his weekend retreat, Lord Cowdray, who had amassed a fortune through civil engineering works, spentthousands of pounds on improving the house, including adding painted ceilings and stained glass. After his death, in 1932, the house was purchased by the monks as a dependent priory of Downside Abbey, Somerset; it became an independent house in 1957.

EAST GRINSTEAD

10 miles N of Haywards Heath on the A22

Church of St Swithin · Standen

Saint Hill Manor · Town Museum

Situated 400 feet above sea level on a sandstone hill, this rather suburban sounding town has a rich history that dates back to the early 13th century. East Grinstead was granted its market charter in 1221. Throughout the Middle Ages, it was an important market town

CHARLOTTE ROSE

54 High Street, East Grinstead, West Sussex RH19 3AS
Tel: 01342 318877

Charlotte Rose is a centre of healing and complementary therapies located on East Grinstead's High Street. Open Monday to Saturday from 9.30, it offers a new concept of a healing and therapy centre run on the basis of love and light, peace and intuition. In comfortably furnished therapy rooms the offerings include Indian Head Massage, Reflexology, Reiki, Crystal Healing and Feng Shui, all given by multi-talented, experienced therapists whose aim is to help and heal on all levels – emotional, spiritual and physical. Charlotte Rose also sells a selection of jewellery, crystals and gifts.

as well as being a centre of the Wealden iron industry. The name, Grinstead, means 'green steading' or 'clearing in woodland' and, though Ashdown Forest is a few miles away today, it was once a much more extensive woodland that provided much of the fuel that contributed to the town's prosperity.

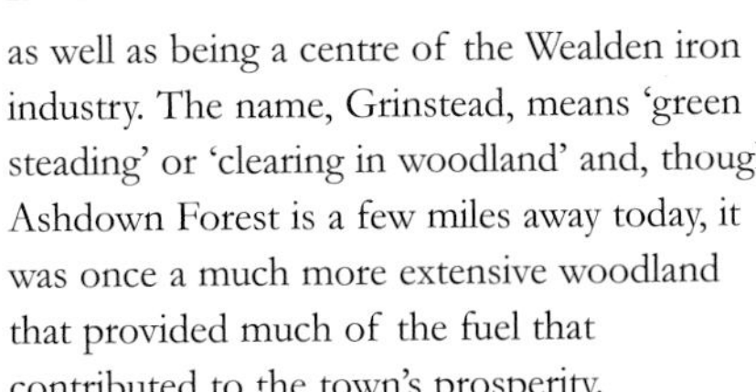

Although there is much modern building here, the High Street consists largely of 16th-century half-timbered buildings - and this is where the splendid Sackville College can be seen, set back from the road. This is not an educational establishment as the name might suggest, but a set of almshouses, founded in 1609 by the Earl of Dorset. A Grade I listed building, the dwellings, built for the retired workers of the Sackville estates, are constructed around an attractive quadrangle and it still provides accommodation for elderly people. Guided tours of the building are available. The parish **Church of St Swithin** stands on an ancient site but it only dates from the late 18th century as the previous church was declared unsafe after the tower collapsed in 1785.

Beside the porch are three grave slabs in memory of Anne Tree, John Forman and Thomas Dunngate, Protestant martyrs who were burnt at the stake in East Grinstead in 1665.

Before the Reform Act of 1832, only the occupants of East Grinstead's 48 original burgage plots (long, narrow housing allotments) were eligible to vote, making this one of the county's most rotten boroughs. As was common practice elsewhere, the local landed family, the Sackvilles, would ensure that they acquired enough votes to guarantee a comfortable majority.

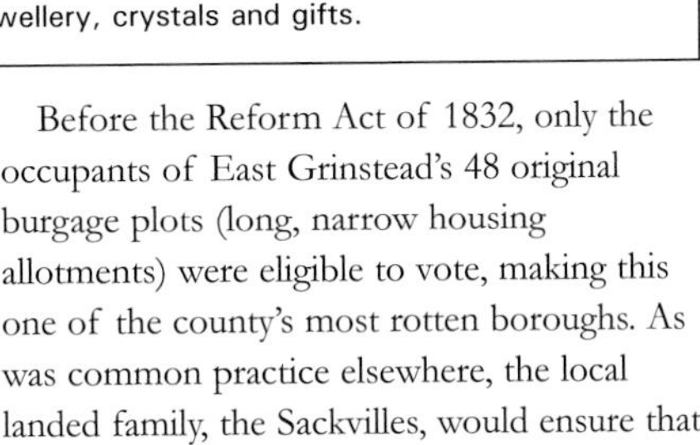

The arrival of the railways in 1855 ended a period of relative decline in the town and, today, East Grinstead is a flourishing place. Perhaps, however, the town will always be remembered for the pioneering work carried out at the Queen Victoria Hospital during World War II. Inspired by the surgeon, Sir Archibald McIndoe, great advances in plastic and reconstructive surgery were made here to help airmen who had suffered severe burns or facial injuries. Following McIndoe's death in 1960, the McIndoe Burns Centre was built to further the research, and the hospital remains the centre of the Guinea Pig Club, set up for and by the early patients of the pioneering surgeon.

The **Town Museum**, housed in East Court, is a fine building that was originally constructed as a private residence in 1769. An interesting place, which tells the story of the town and surrounding area, as well as the life

Horsted Keynes

Distance: *5.9 miles (9.4 kilometres)*
Typical time: *220 mins*
Height gain: *40 metres*
Map: *Explorer 135*
Walk: *www.walkingworld.com ID:1076*
Contributor: *Matthew Mayer*

ACCESS INFORMATION:

By car, there is free parking at Horsted Keynes and Sheffield Park. You can reach Kingscote Station, the northern terminus of the Bluebell Railway, by bus from East Grinstead Station. Buses also run to Horsted Keynes on Saturdays and Sundays.

ADDITIONAL INFORMATION:

Make sure you check the timetable if you are planning to travel using the Bluebell Railway. Phone 01825 722370 (24 hours) or visit www.bluebell-railway.co.uk.

DESCRIPTION:

Starting from the Bluebell Railway station at Horsted Keynes, the route heads first through pretty Horsted Keynes Village. It then heads south through woodland and farmland, crossing the railway at one point. Following the West Sussex Border Path for some of its route, the walk then heads east towards Sheffield Park station, the southern terminus of the Bluebell Railway. The railway uses original steam locomotives to give today's visitors a taste of the 'Age of Steam'. From Sheffield Park, it is possible to return to Horsted Keynes by the railway.

FEATURES:

Lake/loch, pub, toilets, birds, food shop, public transport, tea shop, woodland.

WALK DIRECTIONS:

1 | Starting from outside Horsted Keynes Station, turn left following the sign 'Car Park and Picnic Area'. Continue along the road at the rear of the car park.

2 | Take the first right turn towards the wooden gates. Pass through the metal kissing-gates on the right of the wooden gates, down a wooded path. Ignore a gate on the right and instead continue over a stile, following the public footpath signs, past a field and over another stile. You reach a minor road. Turn left and cross over into the drive of the first house on the other side (Leamlands Barn).

3 | Walk up the drive and take the path through the metal gate (quite heavy, lift it up to swing it). At the rear of the properties, turn right along the grassy path. At the field boundary, cross over into the next field and follow the path round to the left and over a stile. A public footpath sign confirms the route. At the crossroads, go straight on, following the public footpath sign. You cross over a small bridge and then, at the end of the path, three more bridges lead onto a track.

4 | Turn right along the track, passing a small lake on your left. At the crossroads take the minor path ahead, following the red arrow (High Weald Circular Walk). You cross over a farm track but stay on the waymarked path. You cross over one stile, then pass into a wide path between two fields.

5 | At the end of the path, turn right into this road. At the junction go straight across past the 'No Vehicles' signs. At the top of the hill cross over the main road into Horsted Keynes. There are two pubs (the Green Man and the Crown) along the road on the left. Continuing with the walk, take the left fork down Chapel Lane, passing some tennis courts. At the junction go straight on along Wyatts Lane. The road curves to the right, following signs for 'West Sussex Border Path' (WSBP).

6 | At the turnings to Wyatts and Milford Place, take the track straight ahead. You emerge onto another track to turn right and keep on the WSBP. There are several right turns, which you should ignore, as you walk through a small wood. When you emerge from the wood, the path climbs a small hill. At the top of the hill, turn left along the WSBP.

7 | Turn right up the road. Stick to the road until you reach a T-junction, where you should take the left fork to reach the main road.

8 | Head right along the road for around 100m. Take the next left towards Kidborough Farm. Take the right fork off the path at the 'No Horses' sign and skirt along the side of the field and into a small

wood. When you emerge from the wood you pass through two fields before reaching the road.

9 | Turn right along the road.

10 | Just past 'Town Place', turn left into the field and skirt round it on the left-hand side. You soon pick up the footpath signs, which lead you across the field. Take the stile and bridge at the corner of the field and turn right on the path onto which you emerge.

11 | Just before you reach the railway line, you reach this junction. Don't take the path ahead, which ends up running parallel to the railway line. Instead, look for the footpath sign in the bushes on your right. This path takes you across the railway on a bridge. Then follow the signs across the next field. Cross over this stile at the far end of the field. Two more stiles take you to the road.

12 | Turn left down the road, past the Sloop pub. Turn left down this driveway to Bacon Wish and Field Cottage, regaining the WSBP. Pass over a stile into the wood on a wide track.

13 | About 120m into the wood, bear right down this smaller path, staying on the WSBP. The wide track straight on through the forest is not a public right of way. Follow the small path through the wood, over a small stile.You exit the wood over a stile at this signpost. The signpost points you diagonally left across the open space towards another wooden signpost, which you should head straight for.

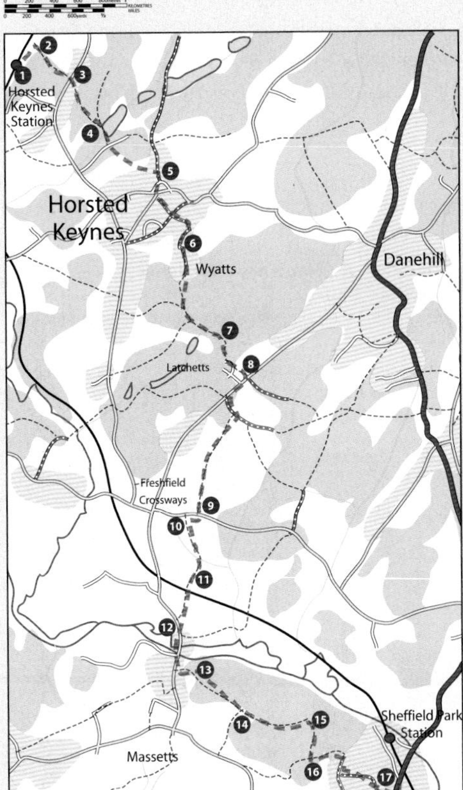

14 | At the three-way signpost, leave the WSBP and follow the public footpath sign left across the open space towards the wood, where there is another stile. Go over the stile and follow the path, well marked with yellow arrows, through the wood. About 500m into the wood, follow the arrows right down this path. Shortly afterwards, turn right onto a wider track.

15 | Shortly afterwards, bear left down this path, following the yellow arrows. The path continues through the wood, descending a slight slope; watch your footing! At the end of the path cross over the stile, bringing you to the edge of a large field.

16 | Turn left and make your way along the edge of the field by the trees. When you reach two small benches at the corner of the wooded area, carry on straight ahead on the track to the wooded area on the far side of the field. Carry on skirting along the wood to the corner of the field. Cross over the stile and turn right across the grass through the wooden gate. Follow the road left at the fork, past a caravan park and farm buildings. Continue until you reach the main road.

17 | Turn left along the road. You pass the entrance to Express Dairies. About 100m further on on the left is the entrance to Sheffield Park station. From here, it is possible to catch a train back to Horsted Keynes station where the walk began.

of its inhabitants, the Greenwich Meridian passes through the town at this point.

To the south of East Grinstead lies **Standen**, a remarkable late Victorian country mansion that is a showpiece of the Arts and Crafts Movement. Completed in 1894 by Philip Webb, an associate of William Morris, for a prosperous London solicitor, the house was constructed using a variety of traditional local building materials. Morris designed the internal furnishings such as the carpets, wallpapers and textiles. Now fully restored, the house, owned by the National Trust, can be seen in all its 1920s splendour, including details such as original electric light fittings. Open to the public, the house is set in a beautiful hillside garden with views over Ashdown Forest and the valley of the Upper Medway. The Bluebell Railway runs from near Standen, offering a pleasant journey by steam train through the Sussex Weald to Sheffield Park, the railway's headquarters, via the 1930s station at Horsted Keynes (see walk on page 292).

Nearby **Saint Hill Manor**, one of the finest sandstone buildings in the county, was built in 1792 by Gibbs Crawfurd, the grandfather of the man who brought the railway to East Grinstead in the mid 19th century. Other owners of the house include the Maharajah of Jaipur and Mrs Neville Laskey, a generous lady who accommodated the RAF patients of Sir Archibald McIndoe. L Ron Hubbard, the author and founder of the Church of Scientology, was the house's last owner and it was he who oversaw the work to restore the manor to its former glory,

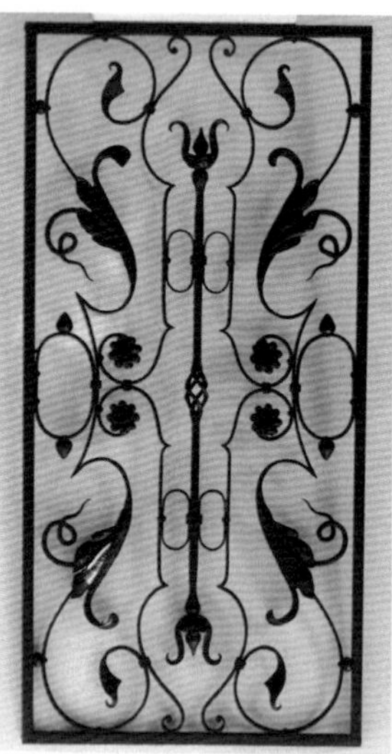

ANTIQUE CHANDELIERS

Copthorne Business Park, Copthorne, West Sussex RH10 3HX
Tel: 01342 717836
e-mail: info@antiquechandeliers.co.uk
website: www.antiquechandeliers.co.uk

Antique Chandeliers is an undisputed leader in its field, an Aladdin's Cave of top-quality antique chandeliers and other lighting located in a small business park ten minutes' drive from the M23 by way of the A26. Upwards of 50 chandeliers in all shapes and sizes are usually in stock, fully restored by experts and dating mainly from the period 1840s to 1950s.

Owners Susan and Douglas Frost, who have been running this unique enterprise since 1993, have also assembled a fine collection of other lighting, equally carefully sourced, including wall lights, ceiling lights and lanterns, like the chandeliers, these too are in a variety of materials, from crystal and glass to bronze, brass, silver plate and iron.

including the Monkey Mural that was painted in 1945 by Sir Winston Churchill's nephew, John Spencer Churchill. The house and gardens are open to the public.

WEST HOATHLY

5½ miles N of Haywards Heath off the B2028

Priest House

Situated high on a ridge overlooking the Weir Wood Reservoir to the northeast, this historic old settlement grew up around an ancient crossing point of two routes across the Weald. The squat towered village church was begun before the Norman Conquest and, inside, there are a number of iron grave slabs of the Infield family from nearby Gravetye Manor. In the churchyard, on the south wall, is a small brass in memory of Anne Tree, one of the 16th-century East Grinstead martyrs. Lying in woodland just north of the village is Gravetye Manor, a splendid Elizabethan stone house built in 1598 for the Infield family, who were wealthy, local iron masters. In 1884, William Robinson, the influential garden designer and gardening correspondent of *The Times*, bought the house and over the next 50 years created the splendid gardens, following the natural contours of this narrow valley. Today, the manor is a first-class country house hotel.

The village's most impressive building is undoubtedly the **Priest House**, a low half-timbered 15th-century house probably built as the estate office for the monks of Lewes Priory who owned the manor here. This would originally have been one vast room but, in Elizabethan times, it was altered to a substantial yeoman's house. It is now a museum belonging to the Sussex Archaeological Society, filled with 18th and

THE WHITE HART RESTAURANT & BAR

Ardingly Road, West Hoathly, West Sussex RH19 4RA
Tel: 01342 715217
website: www.thewhitehartinn.info

Landlady Dottie Esdaile and her head chef Freddie Bodeau put a premium on quality and value for money at the **White Hart Restaurant & Bar**, which stands on the B2028 six miles from the M23 south of Gatwick. The striking property comprises an atmospheric 14th century main building and a fine16th century barn with a lofty timbered roof; log fires in inglenook fireplaces keep things cosy in the cooler months, and when the sun shines the delightful wooded garden comes into its own. Bar and restaurant menus provide plenty of choice for all appetites and tastes, featuring top-quality meat from butchers in East Grinstead and Crawley Down and fruit and vegetables from the best local sources or Covent Garden. The bar menu offers sandwiches, ploughman's platters, jacket potatoes, salads and traditional favourites like liver & bacon, beer-battered cod, fish pie, scampi, ham & eggs, lasagne, burgers and steaks. Typical dishes on Freddie's restaurant menu might be seared scallops with a cider sauce, duck breast with blueberry sauce, smoked haddock & rocket risotto and braised lamb shank with a parmesan crust and chorizo mash. The fine food is accompanied by well-kept ales and an excellent wine list with many available by glass (two sizes) or bottle. The White Hart is open every lunchtime and Tuesday to Saturday evenings. Families and dogs welcome.

19th-century furniture and a fascinating collection of kitchen equipment, needlework and household paraphernalia. The museum is set in a classic English country garden with a formal herb garden containing over 150 culinary, medicinal and folklore herbs.

BURGESS HILL

3 miles SW of Haywards Heath on the B2113

This small town, which has recently undergone much central redevelopment, owes its existence to the arrival of the railway in the mid 19th century. Compared to many of the settlements in the surrounding area, Burgess Hill is a relatively new addition to the landscape. It does, however, have a particularly spacious cricket pitch and some older buildings remaining from what was once a small settlement.

KEYMER

5½ miles SW of Haywards Heath on the B2116

Situated between two tributaries of the River Adur, this old village was once a centre of smuggling. In 1777 over £5,000 worth of goods were seized by customs. Keymer is, however, better known for its famous works that are still producing handmade bricks and tiles. Surprisingly, though, the double spire of Keymer's Church of St Cosmas and St Damian (patron saints of physicians and surgeons) is covered not with tiles, but with wooden shingles.

HURSTPIERPOINT

5½ miles SW of Haywards Heath on the B2116

College

Surrounded by unspoilt countryside, this

pretty village, which takes its name from the Saxon for wood - hurst - and Pierpoint after the local landowning family, was mentioned in the Domesday Book. The narrow High Street here is particularly attractive with some fine Georgian buildings and a tall Victorian church, designed by Sir Charles Barry, the architect of the Houses of Parliament. Another imposing building, dominating the countryside to the north of the village, is **Hurstpierpoint College** chapel. Like nearby Lancing and Ardingly, the school was founded in the 19th century by Nathaniel Woodard.

To the south of the village lies the ancestral home of the Norman Pierpoint family. They settled here in the 11th century close to their powerful relative William de Warenne and Danny was, in those days, a modest hunting lodge situated below the grassy mound of Woolstonbury Hill. In the mid 15th century,

HURSTPIERPOINT COOKSHOP

55-57 High Street, Hurstpierpoint, West Sussex BN6 9TT
Tel: 01273 832909
e-mail: sales@ukcookshop.co.uk
website: www.ukcookshop.co.uk

Amateur and professional cooks will find everything they need for their kitchens in the **Husrtpierpoint Cookshop**, which occupies a prominent corner site by a mini-roundabout on the town's main street. Pots and pans, casseroles and tagines, cake tins and baking trays, graters and slicers and mincers, cutters and peelers, corkscrews and colanders, cutlery, storage tins and jars, measuring spoons, aprons, Aga accessories, cook books.......All the top brands are stocked, and customers who can't get to the shop can do their shopping online.

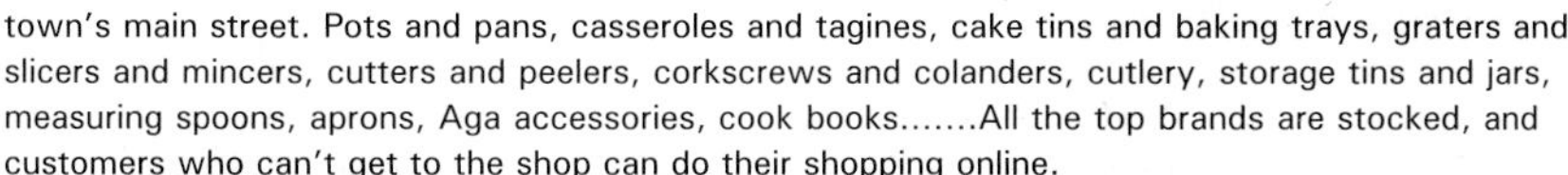

EMMIE BOUTIQUE

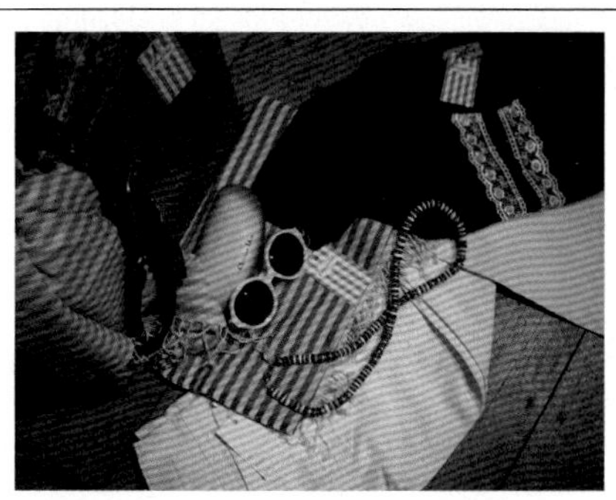

123 High Street, Hurstpierpoint,
West Sussex BN6 9PU
Tel: 01273 835147
e-mail: emily@emilyboutique.co.uk
website: www.emmieboutique.co.uk

Emily Webster, a Fashion designer in london, opened **Emmie Boutique** in a prominent position in Hurstpierpoint's attractive High Street and has been an amazing success. Already the local ladies are appreciating the choice and value's emmie offers. Emily's philosophy: 'Shopping should not be stressful; it should be fun and enjoyable, allowing you the time and freedom to try out new styles with no pressure.' The boutique stocks a wide range of knitwear, dresses, separates and co-ordinates in super fabrics with a wide range of styles to suit all ages, along with an equally impressive choice of shoes, bags, scarves, suitcases and other accessories. Brands usually on the shelves include Traffic People, Almost Famous, Anonymous by Ross & Bute and Hush Pyjamas. Luxury Italian and American jeans by James Jeans and J Brand fly off the shelves, and other exceptional lines include stunning leather shoes by Mellow Yellow, bags and shoes by Jackson Twins, bath and beauty products by Branche d'Olive, True Grace candles and jewellery from Kate Beesley and Alex Monroe.

the family had to flee after the then owner, Simon de Pierpoint, deliberately murdered some of his serfs, and the house was burnt to the ground in retaliation. The site stood empty until, in the late 16th century, Elizabeth I granted the estate to George Goring who built the impressive classic Elizabethan E-shaped mansion seen today.

However, the history of Danny remains a somewhat turbulent story as Goring, a staunch Royalist, was forced to give up his splendid mansion at the end of the Civil War. It was the Campion family, coming here in the early 18th century, who added the Queen Anne south-facing façade as well as remodelling the interior by lowering the ceiling in the Great

CLAYTON WICKHAM FARMHOUSE

Belmont Lane, Hurstpierpoint, West Sussex BN6 9EP
Tel: 01273 845698
e-mail: Susie@cwfbandb.co.uk website: www.cwfbandb.co.uk

Susie and Mike Skinner have been offering top-quality Bed & Breakfast accommodation at the tranquil **Clayton Wickham Farmhouse**. Their restored 14th century home stands down a private lane half a mile from the centre of Hurstpierpoint, within three acres of gardens and grounds including a croquet lawn and tennis court. There are three beautiful en suite rooms (one four-poster) in the main house and two in an adjacent building. A lovely Aga-cooked breakfast is something to look forward to and private dinner parties can be arranged.

POLKA DOT INTERIORS

59 High Street, Hurstpierpoint, West Sussex BN6 9RE
Tel: 01273 831421 e-mail: polkadotinteriors@live.co.uk
website: www.polkadotinteriorsllp.com

December 2008 saw the opening of an important addition to the shops on Husrtpierpoint's High Street. Opposite the church on the mini-roundabout, **Polka Dot Interiors** is stocked with a fabulous, eclectic mix of contemporary and classic furniture, home accessories, unusual gifts, fabrics, bespoke Sussex oak tables and chairs, blinds, curtain poles and lampshades made to order.

Behind the black-and-beige frontage on the High Street and Cuckfield Road, Christine Bugden and her son Charles have assembled a splendid variety of items large and small that help to add the finishing touches to a home. They offer a 10-day service for curtains (500+ fabrics to choose from); curtain poles in an almost endless choice of shapes, sizes and colours; furniture ranging from bespoke media units in wood or chrome to superb Union Jack leather chesterfields and extending oak dining tables with Gothic chairs; spot lamps and table lamps, tripod lamps with black, chrome or matt brass finish; and lampshades made to measure – any size, shape or colour, plain or pleated. Homes in West Sussex and beyond can look forward to a total transformation and a new lease of life after their owners visit this outstanding new enterprise, which is open from 9.30 to 5.30 Monday to Saturday.

Hall and adding a grand, sweeping staircase.

Danny's finest hour came, in 1918, when the Prime Minister, Lloyd George rented the house, and it was here that the terms of the armistice with Germany were drawn up to end World War I. A plaque in the Great Hall commemorates the meetings held here by Lloyd George's war cabinet, during which time, Lloyd George was known to have walked up Woolstonbury Hill to seek peace and solitude. The house also saw service during World War II when it was occupied by British and Commonwealth troops.

CLAYTON

6 miles SW of Haywards Heath on the A273

This small hamlet, which lay on a Roman road between Droydon and Portslade, is home to a rather ordinary Saxon church with some early medieval wall paintings, undoubtedly the work of the renowned group of artists from St Pancras Priory, Lewes.

The settlement lies at one end of a mile-long railway tunnel, which was constructed in the 1840s to take the still busy London to Brighton track. An engineering wonder of its day, the northern end of Clayton Tunnel is dominated by a large Victorian folly, Tunnel House, built in a grand Tudor style to house the tunnel keeper.

On a hill overlooking Clayton stand two windmills, known rather unimaginatively as Jack and Jill. The larger of the pair, Jack, is a tower mill dating from 1896. It fell into disuse in the 1920s and, now without its sails, has been converted into an unusual private residence. Jill, a post mill that originally stood in Brighton, was brought here by oxen in 1852, has been fully restored and is still capable of grinding corn.

PYECOMBE

7 miles SW of Haywards Heath on the A23

This ancient village stands on a prehistoric track that runs along the South Downs from Stonehenge to Canterbury. Home to one of the smallest downland churches, this simple, Norman building has a 12th-century lead font that survived the Civil War by being disguised by the crafty parishioners in a layer of whitewash.

Pyecombe is renowned among farmers, and particularly shepherds, as being the home of the best possible shepherd's crook, the Pyecombe Hook. It was the crook's curled end, known as the guide, that made the Pyecombe Hook so special as it was a very efficient mechanism for catching sheep – though it was hard to fashion. Throughout the 19th and early 20th centuries, the village forge turned out these world-famous crooks and, though they are no longer made today, several rare examples can be seen in Worthing Museum.

POYNINGS

8 miles SW of Haywards Heath off the A281

Devil's Dyke

Once an iron working village, Poynings lies in a hollow below the steep slopes of Dyke Hill on top of which is situated an Iron Age hillfort. Just south of Poynings, and close to the hill, is one of the South Downs greatest natural features - the **Devil's Dyke**. Local legend has it that this great steep-sided ravine was dug by the Devil to drown the religious people of Sussex. Working in darkness, intent on digging all the way to the coast, he was half way to the sea when an old woman climbed to the top of a hill with a candle and a sieve. The light of the candle woke a nearby cockerel, whose crowing alerted the Devil. Looking up, the devil saw the candle light through the sieve and fled thinking that the sun was rising.

Interesting archaeological features range from Bronze Age burial mounds to 19th-century lime kilns. During Victorian times, the Devil's Dyke became a popular place from which to view the surrounding downlands. A railway was built to connect the village with Brighton and a cable car was installed over the ravine. The cable car has now gone but the site is still a popular place with motorists, walkers and hang-gliding enthusiasts.

SMALL DOLE

10 miles SW of Haywards Heath on the A2037

Woods Mill

Just to the north of this small downland village, is **Woods Mill**, the headquarters of the Sussex Trust for Nature Conservation. As well as a nature reserve and the nature trail around the woodland, marshes and streams, the site is also home to an 18th-century watermill, which houses a countryside exhibition.

EDBURTON

10 miles SW of Haywards Heath off the A2037

Church

This tiny hamlet is named after Edburga, the granddaughter of King Alfred, who is said to have built a church here in the 10th century. However, the present **Church of St Andrew** dates from the 13th century and, inside, can be seen one of only three lead fonts remaining in the county. Though battered and dented from the days of the Civil War, when it was used as a horse trough, the font escaped being melted down for ammunition. On top of the steep downland escarpment, which rises to its highest point here, stands Castle Ring, a mound and ditch that are the remains of an 11th-century fort.

CUCKFIELD

1 mile W of Haywards Heath on the A272

Borde Hill Gardens

Borde Hill Gardens, Cuckfield

Pronounced 'Cookfield', this small country town dates back to Saxon times and though it would be particularly charming if the name were to have been derived from the Saxon Cucufleda meaning 'a clearing full of cuckoos', it is more likely that it means 'land surrounded by a quickset hedge'. Situated on the side of a hill, during the 11th century, Cuckfield belonged to the Norman, William de Warenne, who had a hunting lodge and chapel here.

To the north lies **Borde Hill Gardens**, a splendid, typically English garden of special botanical interest set in some 200 acres of spectacular Sussex parkland and woods. Colonel Stephenson Clarke, by funding plant

Nymans House and Gardens

Handcross, nr Haywards Heath, West Sussex RH17 6EB
Telephone: 01444 405250
website: www.nationaltrust.org.uk

One of the great gardens of the Sussex Weald, with rare and beautiful plants, shrubs and trees from all over the world. Wall garden, hidden sunken garden, pinetum, laurel walk and romantic ruins. Lady Rosse's library, drawing room and forecourt garden also open. Woodland walks and Wild Garden.

Garden is open Mar-Oct, closed Monday & Tuesday except Bank Holidays. Licensed tearoom/restaurant and shop.

hunting expeditions to China, Burma, Tasmania and the Andes, established the collection of plants and trees, which is still maintained by the Colonel's descendants. With displays carefully planted to offer a blaze of colour for most of the year, this garden is well worth exploring.

HANDCROSS

7 miles NW of Haywards Heath on the B2114

Nymans · High Beeches Gardens

Close to this little village, which stood on the old London to Brighton road, are two glorious gardens. To the southeast lie the superb National Trust-owned gardens of **Nymans** (see panel on page 301). Though much of the house that stood on this estate was destroyed by fire in 1947, the empty shell provides a dramatic backdrop to one of the county's greatest gardens. At the heart of Nymans is the round walled garden, created with the help of the late 19th-century gardening revivalists William Robinson and Gertrude Jekyll. Elsewhere, the gardens are laid out in a series of 'rooms', where visitors can walk from ont to the other taking in the old roses, the topiary, the laurel walk and the sunken garden.

Just northeast of Handcross is another smaller, though no less glorious garden, **High Beeches Gardens**. Here, in the enchanting woodlands and water gardens, is a collection of rare and exotic plants, as well as native wild flowers in a natural meadow setting.

4 | Surrey

Surrey's proximity to the capital and its transport links have defined much of its history. The Thames winds through Surrey, and many of the present-day villages and towns developed as riverside trading centres in the medieval period or earlier. As the Thames led to the development of earlier villages, the arrival of the railway in the mid 19th century saw new ones spring up, while others expanded out of all recognition. Rail lines and major roads fan put through the whole area from London, with the latest contribution to the road system being the M25.

However, Surrey is full of historical traces. Great houses, as well as royal and episcopal palaces, were built here from medieval times, and many villages have evidence of Saxon, Celtic, Roman and even late Stone Age settlements. The site of one of England's defining moments, the signing of the Magna Carta in 1215, is at the riverside meadow of Runnymede. The most impressive of all buildings along the Thames is Hampton Court, where Henry VIII expanded Cardinal Wolsey's already magnificent palace.

Farnham, with its lovely Georgian architecture and 12th-century castle, is the largest town in southwestern Surrey, while Guildford, the ancient county town of Surrey, is an obvious base for travellers interested in exploring Surrey. Guildford has been the capital of the region since pre-Norman times, and the remains of Henry II's castle and keep provide commanding views over the surrounding area. The old Georgian cobbled High Street incorporates the Tudor Guildhall, with its distinctive gilded clock. Woking, like many Surrey towns, was transformed by the arrival of the railway in the 19th century. The Victorian influence is evident in many of the larger houses built by Norman Shaw and other proponents of the Arts and Crafts style. The more ornate style of Victorian architecture, designed to reflect the prosperity of a confident imperial power, is also represented in the two massive buildings funded by Thomas Holloway - Royal Holloway College and the Holloway Sanatorium, which are near Egham in the

Albury Village

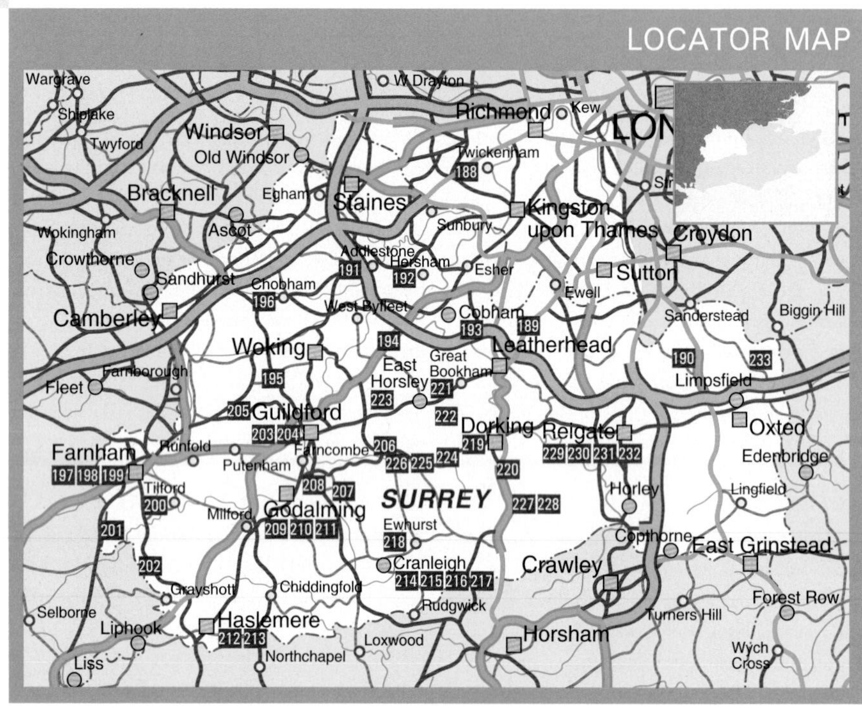

ADVERTISERS AND PLACES OF INTEREST

Accommodation, Food and Drink

192 | The Dining Room, Hersham *pg 327*
197 | Henny's, Farnham *pg 346*
201 | The Blue Bell Inn, Dockenfield, nr Farnham *pg 354*
205 | Littlefield Manor, Littlefield Common, nr Guildford *pg 359*
206 | The Compasses Inn, Gomshall, nr Guildford *pg 361*
214 | Cromwell Coffee House, Cranleigh *pg 373*
215 | One Forty, Cranleigh *pg 374*
220 | The Royal Oak, Stonebridge, nr Dorking *pg 377*
221 | Taste Deli & Café, Great Bookham, nr Leatherhead *pg 380*
225 | The Stephan Langton, Abinger Common *pg 385*
227 | The Six Bells, Newdigate, nr Dorking *pg 389*

Activities

196 | Chobham Rider & The Saddle Room, Chobham *pg 343*
224 | Bury Hill Fisheries, Westcott, nr Dorking *pg 384*

Antiques and Restoration

208 | Memories Antiques, Bramley, nr Guildford *pg 364*

Arts and Crafts

202 | Art & Sold, Miscellanea, The Sculpture Park, Brokenbog and Art & Investment, Churt, nr Farnham *pg 355*

Fashions

196 | Chobham Rider & The Saddle Room, Chobham *pg 343*
203 | The Mad Hatter, Guildford *pg 358*
204 | The Dress Boutique, Guildford *pg 358*
213 | Meeka, Haslemere *pg 371*
215 | One Forty, Cranleigh *pg 374*
230 | Gorgeous, Reigate *pg 392*
231 | Noa Noa, Reigate *pg 393*

Giftware

189 | Bumbles, Ashtead *pg 315*
207 | Jeni Wren Cookware & Kitchen Gifts, Shamley Green *pg 363*
215 | One Forty, Cranleigh *pg 374*
218 | Dragonfly, Ewhurst, nr Cranleigh *pg 376*
230 | Gorgeous, Reigate *pg 392*
232 | Camel & Yak, Reigate *pg 394*

Home and Garden

195 | Horti. Halcyon, Fox Corner, nr Worplesdon *pg 339*
198 | The Lighting Agency, Farnham *pg 347*
207 | Jeni Wren Cookware & Kitchen Gifts, Shamley Green *pg 363*
208 | Memories Antiques, Bramley, nr Guildford *pg 364*
209 | Katherine Letts Interiors, Godalming *pg 364*
211 | The Greenhouse, Godalming *pg 367*
212 | Objets d'Art, Haslemere *pg 371*
216 | Fenestra Interiors, Cranleigh *pg 375*
217 | Youngs of Cranleigh, Cranleigh *pg 375*
218 | Dragonfly, Ewhurst, nr Cranleigh *pg 376*

historic building · museum and heritage · historic site · scenic attraction · flora and fauna

north. The best of Edwardian architecture is well represented throughout Surrey by the work of Sir Edwin Lutyens, often working in partnership with the eminent gardener Gertrude Jekyll.

Hampton Court

This varied architectural heritage belies the notion that Surrey is nothing more than a collection of anonymous suburbs of London. Much of Surrey is indeed the capital's commuter belt and conurbations like Kingston and Croydon spread out into a vast hinterland of suburbia. However, around Guildford and Dorking, and near the Sussex border, there are small towns and wayside villages amid rough Down and Weald uplands or thickly wooded hillsides. The countryside is varied, from the well-maintained plantation of Kew Gardens, possibly the most famous gardens in the world, to numerous parks, greens, heaths, commons and open land. Rich farming areas give way to expanses of heath and woodlands with networks of paths for walkers and cyclists. The famous Hog's Back section of the A31 is one of the most scenic drives in the southeast, with excellent views north and south as it follows the ridge between Farnham and Guildford through some of Surrey's most unspoilt countryside.

ADVERTISERS AND PLACES OF INTEREST (CONT)

219 | The Rug Centre, Dorking *pg 376*
229 | Alans Plants, Reigate *pg 392*
230 | Gorgeous, Reigate *pg 392*
232 | Camel & Yak, Reigate *pg 394*

Jewellery

189 | Bumbles, Ashtead *pg 315*
210 | Jewelled Ltd, Godalming *pg 365*
212 | Objets d'Art, Haslemere *pg 371*
213 | Meeka, Haslemere *pg 371*
230 | Gorgeous, Reigate *pg 392*
231 | Noa Noa, Reigate *pg 393*

Places of Interest

188 | The Museum of Rugby, Twickenham *pg 307*
190 | East Surrey Museum, Caterham *pg 319*
193 | Painshill Park, Cobham *pg 330*
194 | RHS Garden Wisley, Wisley, nr Woking *pg 337*
199 | Farnham Maltings, Farnham *pg 348*
200 | Rural Life Centre, Tilford, nr Farnham *pg 350*
202 | Art & Sold, Miscellanea, The Sculpture Park, Brokenbog and Art & Investment, Churt, nr Farnham *pg 355*
222 | Polesden Lacey, Great Bookham, nr Leatherhead *pg 381*
224 | Bury Hill Fisheries, Westcott, nr Dorking *pg 384*
233 | Titsey Place, Titsey, nr Oxted *pg 401*

Specialist Food and Drink Shops

191 | Crockford Bridge Farm Shop, Addlestone, nr Weybridge *pg 321*
221 | Taste Deli & Café, Great Bookham, nr Leatherhead *pg 380*
223 | F Conisbee & Son, East Horsley *pg 382*
226 | Kingfisher Farm Shop, Abinger Hammer, nr Dorking *pg 386*
228 | Tanhouse Farm Shop, Newdigate, nr Dorking *pg 390*

Northeast Surrey

Kingston-upon-Thames Bridge

Surrey's proximity to London often leads people to assume that it is nothing more than a collection of anonymous suburbs extending south and west from the capital. Indeed much of what had originally been (and which steadfastly continues to consider itself) Surrey was absorbed by London in the boundary changes of 1965. Growing conurbations such as Kingston and Croydon house and employ thousands. Rail lines and major roads fan out through the area from London.

However, this northeast corner of Surrey is also full of historical traces, some well known and others truly hidden gems. Great houses, as well as royal and episcopal palaces, were built here from medieval times, and many villages have evidence of Saxon, Celtic, Roman and even late Stone Age settlements. The countryside is varied, from the well-maintained plantation of Kew Gardens to the rough Down and Weald uplands to the south, and numerous parks, greens, heaths, commons and open land in between. The sound of birdsong ringing through the woods and the click of a cricket bat on a village green are as much a part of this stretch of Surrey as the whirring suburban lawnmower.

Kingston-upon-Thames

Chapel of St Mary Magdalene Museum

The first impression most people have of Kingston is of high-rise office blocks and its famous by-pass, giving it the sense of being totally urbanised and something of a modern creation. However, Kingston has been a thriving market town since the Middle Ages, the first of only four Royal Boroughs in England and Wales. In AD838 it was referred to as 'that famous place called Cyningestun in the region of Surrey'. The Guildhall, built in 1935, is solid and functional but, nearby, beside the 12th-century Clattern Bridge over the River Hogsmill, stands the Coronation Stone, said to have been used in the crowning of up to seven Saxon kings. Records show that Kingston was a prosperous town in Anglo-Saxon times. In the Domesday survey of 1086 it is recorded as having a church, five mills and three salmon fisheries.

Kingston has been a river crossing place since medieval times, the present stone bridge replacing the old wooden bridges in 1828. Regular street markets have been held on a site by the bridge since the 17th century, and around the market a well-preserved medieval street plan can be explored. Kingston parish church was completely rebuilt in neo-Gothic style in the 19th century, but its interior still contains many medieval monuments. On the London Road, however, is a real medieval relic

- the **Chapel of St Mary Magdalene**, dating from the 14th century.

Guided walks of Kingston's historical heritage start from the Market Place every Sunday in summer. The **Kingston Museum**, in a Grade II listed building in Wheatfield Way, tells the story of Kingston from earliest times to the present in the 'Ancient Origins' and 'Town of Kings' galleries. The new Eadweard Muybridge Gallery examines the life and work of the man whose work on animal locomotion was instrumental in the development of cinematography, and the Art Gallery showcases the work of professional artists and amateur groups. The Museum is open daily, except Wednesday and Sunday.

The district of Coombe, to the east of Kingston, was rebuilt by prosperous Victorians. Large houses, built in a variety of architectural styles, came to symbolise the solid financial standing of their owners. Unfortunately, few of these houses survive apart from their impressive gate lodges, but there are a few exceptions such as Coombe Pines in Warren Cutting.

John Galsworthy began the development of Coombe Hill, and two of his own houses survive - Coombe Leigh, which is now a convent, and Coombe Ridge, today a school. Galsworthy's son was the famous novelist and set Soames Forsyte's house in Coombe.

Around Kingston

TWICKENHAM

4 miles N of Kingston on the A310

The Twickenham Museum · Museum of Rugby

Ham House · Orleans House and Gallery

Marble Hill House

Lying on the west side of the Thames just a few miles north of Hampton Court Palace, Twickenham is a thriving community that makes the most of its riverside setting. Perhaps more than anything else Twickenham

The Museum of Rugby

Twickenham Stadium, Rugby Road,
Twickenham, Surrey TW1 1DZ
Tel: 020 8892 8877 Fax: 020 8892 2817
website: www.rfu.com

Few would dispute that sport has an appeal that crosses gender, age and racial barriers. But few people would connect the thrills and spills of top level competition with the standard museum environment.

How can a museum compete with drama, excitement and appeal of live sport? The answer is simple: today's sports museums with their hands on exhibits and interactive screens and sounds are more than just testaments to facts and figures, but living breathing ways of connecting with the unrivalled excitement that only sport can provide.

You can find out all about rugby, its history and its star players by visiting **The Museum of Rugby**, Twickenham. The word's finest collection of rugby memorabilia is housed at the Museum of Rugby, which takes visitors through the history of the sport from 1823 to the present day. The Museum also offers fans a tour of Britain's most famous Rugby Stadium.

is renowned as the headquarters of Rugby Union Football in Britain, a role it has played since 1907. The recently rebuilt stadium hosts England home internationals as well as the annual Varsity match between Oxford and Cambridge. The **Museum of Rugby** allows visitors to savour the history and atmosphere of the sport. Running through the players tunnel is enough to get many people's blood rushing, and the museum provides a full account of Twickenham right up to its latest renovations. Located in an 18th-century waterman's cottage on the Embankment, **The Twickenham Museum** celebrates the rich local history of Twickenham, Whitton, the Hamptons and Teddington.

Marble Hill House, Twickenham

Montpelier Row and Sion Row, wonderfully preserved 18th-century terraces, are some of the fine old houses in the heart of Twickenham. At Strawberry Hill, just to the south of Twickenham, is the villa bought by the author Horace Walpole in 1749 and remodelled into a 'gothic fantasy', which has been described as 'part church, castle, monastery or mansion'. It is internationally recognised as the first substantial building of the Gothic Revival. Strawberry Hill is now St Mary's University College, a teachers' training college, but it is open for pre-booked tours, any day except Saturday, in summer. Those eager to pursue other historical associations from that era can find the tomb of the poet Alexander Pope in the Twickenham churchyard.

Orleans House and Gallery, which houses one of the finest art collections outside London's national collections, enjoys an enviable location in a woodland garden on the riverside between Twickenham and Richmond. The charming 18th-century garden pavilion is named after its most famous resident, Louis Philippe, Duc d'Orléans. The original house was demolished in 1926 and the outbuildings converted in 1972 to house the Borough art collection established by Mrs Nellie Ionides. Next door is **Marble Hill House**, a Palladian villa designed by Roger Morris and completed in 1729 for George II's mistress, Henrietta Howard. Visitors can walk in the 66 acres of riverside grounds, take a look at the furniture and paintings displayed in the house, and enjoy a cream tea in the café.

On the opposite riverbank, accessible by passenger ferry for most of the year, is **Ham House**, built in 1610 and enlarged in the 1670s. Now in the hands of the National Trust, Ham's lavish Restoration interiors and magnificent collection of Baroque furniture provide a suitable setting for the popular summer ghost walks. It has extensive grounds, including lovely 17th-century formal gardens.

RICHMOND

5 miles N of Kingston on the A307

Museum Richmond Hill

Richmond is an attractive shopping centre with the usual chain stores and a number of small specialist and antique shops. However, the lovely riverside setting along a sweeping curve of the Thames, and the extensive spread of Richmond Park, help to retain a strong sense of its rich and varied history.

A good place to get acquainted with old Richmond is Richmond Green, a genuine village green, flanked on the southwest and southeast edges by handsome 17th and 18th-century houses. The southwest side has an older, and more royal, history. It was the site of a palace that passed into royal possession in 1125, when it was known as Shene Palace. The palace was destroyed by Richard II in 1394 but subsequent kings had it rebuilt in stages. The site, right by the green, made it an ideal spot for organising jousting tournaments. The rebuilding and extensions reached their peak under Henry VII, who renamed the palace after his favourite Earldom, Richmond in Yorkshire. Elizabeth I died in the palace in 1603. Sadly, the only surviving element of the palace is the brick gatehouse beside the village green.

Just off the northeast flank of the green is Richmond Theatre, an imposing Victorian building with an elaborate frontage facing the street. Richmond Riverside, a redevelopment scheme dating from the late 1980s, stretches along the Thames. It comprises pastiche Georgian buildings complete with columns, cupolas and facades and includes houses, offices and commercial premises. Among the modern buildings, however, there remain a few of the original Georgian and Victorian houses, including the narrow, three-storey Heron House, where Lady Hamilton and her daughter Horatia came to live soon after the Battle of Trafalgar. The riverside walk ends at Richmond Bridge, a handsome five-arched structure built of Portland stone in 1777 and widened in the 1930s. It is the oldest extant bridge spanning the Thames in London.

Richmond's Old Town Hall, set somewhat back from the new developments at Richmond Bridge, is the home of the **Museum of Richmond**, a fascinating privately-run museum that provides a unique perspective on Richmond's history and has special significance in English life. The museum's permanent displays chronicle the story of Richmond, Ham, Petersham and Kew - communities that grew and prospered along the Thames downstream from Hampton Court. The collections of the Museum of Richmond concentrate on different aspects of this history, detailing the

Richmond Bridge

rich heritage from prehistoric times through to the present.

Special features and detailed models focus on some of the most noteworthy buildings, such as the Charterhouse of Shene, which was the largest Carthusian Monastery in England. The information about Richmond Palace is a bit of English history in microcosm. A number of displays concentrate on the luminaries who have made Richmond their home over the years. Among the roll call of the great and the good are Sir Robert Walpole, Sir Joshua Reynolds, Lady Emma Hamilton, George Eliot, Virginia Woolf, Gustav Holst and Bertrand Russell.

The steep climb of **Richmond Hill** leads southwards and upwards from the centre of Richmond. The view from Richmond Terrace has been protected by an Act of Parliament since 1902. The Thames lies below, sweeping in majestic curves to the west through wooded countryside. Turner and Reynolds are among the many artists who have tried to capture the essence of this scene, which takes in six counties. A little further up the hill is the entrance to Richmond Park. These 2,500 acres of open land, with red and fallow deer roaming free, were first enclosed by Charles I in 1637 as a hunting ground. Set amidst this coppiced woodland is the Isabella Plantation, noted for its azaleas and rhododendrons. The Park was designated a National Nature Reserve in 2000.

KEW AND KEW GARDENS

7 miles N of Kingston off the A310

National Archives · Royal Botanic Gardens

Kew, lying just a couple of miles north of Richmond, on a pleasant stretch of the Thames, is a charming 18th-century village, favoured by the early Hanoverian kings. They built a new palace here and the handsome 18th-century houses, which still surround Kew Green, were built to accommodate the great and the good of the royal circle. The **National Archives** in Kew holds 900 years of historical records, including the *Domesday Book*.

However, Kew is best known for the **Royal Botanic Gardens**, arguably the most famous gardens in the world. Princess Augusta, mother of George III, laid out an eight-acre botanical garden on the grounds of Kew Palace in 1759. Tranquil and spacious, this garden, now extending over 300 acres, has become an important botanical research centre. Over a million visitors a year are attracted to view the 40,000 species of plants and 9,000 trees that grow here in plantations and glasshouses. The most famous and oldest glasshouse, built in 1848, is the Palm House, which includes most of the known palm species.

Kew Palace

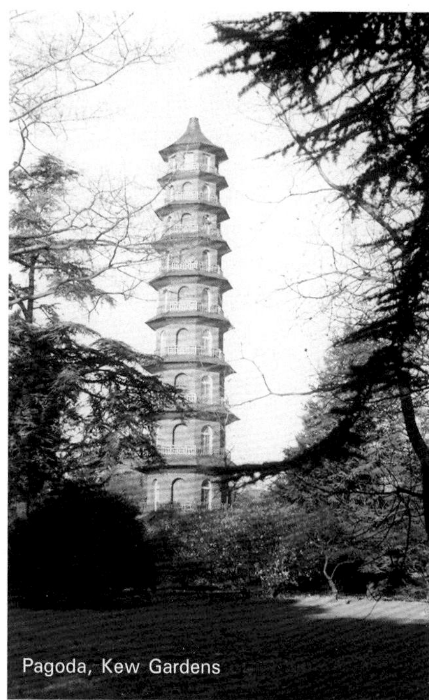

Pagoda, Kew Gardens

Nearby is the Water Lily House, full of tropical vines and creepers overhanging its lily pond. The Princess of Wales Conservatory, which opened in 1987, houses plants from 10 different climatic zones, from arid desert to tropical rainforest.

Here at Kew is Britain's smallest royal residence. The three-storey Kew Palace built in 1631, sometimes nicknamed the Dutch House because of its Flemish-bond brickwork, measures only 50 feet by 70 feet. Queen Caroline acquired it for her daughters in 1730. The only king to have lived in this tiny royal residence was George III, confined here in 1802 during his infamous madness. Behind the palace is a restored 17th-century garden, with labels identifying the herbs and their uses.

Another Kew landmark is the octagonal, 10-storey Chinese Pagoda standing 163 feet high. Originally, the building was flanked by the Turkish Mosque and the Alhambra, all designed by Sir William Chambers, Princess Augusta's official architect. The ground floor is 50 feet across, with each storey reducing in size until the 10th storey is 20 feet by 10 feet. Built as an exotic folly in the fashion of the times, it now serves a more practical purpose as a landmark for visitors. The co-founder and director of the gardens, Sir William Jackson Hooker and his son Sir Joseph Dalton Hooker, are both buried in the churchyard of St Anne, Kew Green. Here, too, lie the artist Thomas Gainsborough and the portrait painter John Zoffany.

MORTLAKE

7 miles N of Kingston on the A205

Mortlake is best known as the finishing point of the Oxford and Cambridge Boat Race. Although it was once an attractive riverside village, it is now dominated by a large brewery building. However, a series of handsome 18th-century houses stand along Thames Bank, towards Chiswick Bridge, and the famous Victorian explorer Richard Burton is buried in an unusual tent-shaped tomb in the cemetery.

WIMBLEDON

3 miles E of Kingston on the A219

All England Lawn Tennis, Croquet Club & Museum

Wimbledon Common

To most people Wimbledon is synonymous with the All-England Lawn Tennis Championships held each year at the end of June and in early July. However, the grounds of the **All England Lawn Tennis and Croquet Club** are open throughout the year and the **Wimbledon Lawn Tennis Museum** has a range of exhibits from the languid era of long flannel trousers, to nail-biting tie-breaks and disputed line calls. But there is more to Wimbledon than tennis. In fact, the Championship fortnight is a time to avoid Wimbledon, since tennis fans throng the streets and every route in and out is clogged with traffic.

The centre of Wimbledon is a thriving commercial area, with stores lining the High Street. Here, cheek by jowl with anonymous 1960s buildings, are a few gems. Eagle House, just west of the National Westminster Bank building, was built in 1613. Its Jacobean appearance, with three large bay windows by its central entrance, still conveys a harmonious grandeur, which in its day would have dominated its neighbours. From Wimbledon itself, Wimbledon High Street climbs steeply to the west towards Wimbledon Village, which has more of a boutique and bistro feel to it. Handsome residential streets lead off the High Street on its climb, and there are expansive views looking east across South London.

Further above Wimbledon Village is **Wimbledon Common**, covering more than 1,000 acres, criss-crossed by walking and riding trails, home of the Wombles and one of the capital's largest areas of public access. At the southwest corner is an Iron Age mound called Caesar's Camp, although it is not Roman, but dates from around 250BC. Archaeological evidence indicates that people have occupied this area since the Paleolithic era, some 3,000 years ago. However, it did not become common land with legal public right of access until the Wimbledon and Putney Commons Act of 1871, after local residents opposed Earl Spencer's intention to enclose it.

NEW MALDEN

2 miles S of Kingston on the A2043

Just a few miles east of Hampton Court, and just south of both Richmond Park and Wimbledon Common, lies New Malden. Excellent road and rail connections link this neat suburb with Central London as well as points south. New Malden makes a good base for exploring the nearby sights, particularly easy by public transport, avoiding traffic and parking problems.

There are a few surprises lurking in this corner of suburbia. Just by the church on Church Road is the redbrick Manor House, dating from the late 17th century. Further along, to the northeast, is a duck pond, flanked by the Plough Inn. This pub seems modern, but its core was built more than 500 years ago.

SURBITON

1 mile S of Kingston on the A307

Surbiton is a well-heeled suburb adjoining Kingston, which escapes much of the traffic and commercial build-up that bedevils its northern neighbour. Handsome properties and good transport connections to London and the south coast make Surbiton one of the most desirable locations in the London commuter belt. Surbiton was called Kingston New Town and Kingston-on-Railway as it developed in the early 19th century. Most of the public buildings date from this period and the architecture of churches such as St Andrew and St Matthew are good examples of the Gothic Revival that was so dominant at the time.

The A307 follows the course of the Thames through Surbiton, with lovely views of Hampton Court Park on the opposite bank of the river. Hampton Court Palace is just over a mile away.

Kingston to Croydon

CHEAM

5 miles E of Kingston on the A217

Lumley Chapel

Roughly equidistant between Kingston and Croydon, Cheam is one of the prettier suburbs of this area, retaining a green and leafy feel, largely due to the number of substantial houses with large gardens. Several houses in Cheam open their gardens as part of the National Gardens Scheme Charitable Trust.

As with so many other parts of Surrey where London has encroached, Cheam has lost much of its overtly medieval elements, but careful detective work can lead to some pleasant surprises. St Dunstan Church, built in the 1860s, is a large and uninspiring Victorian building, but its courtyard contains the surviving portion of the medieval parish church - the **Lumley Chapel**, which was the chancel of the old church. The roof inside was remodelled in 1582 by Lord Lumley, who also commissioned the three finely carved marble and alabaster tombs. A series of delightful and well-preserved brasses commemorate Cheam notables from the 15th and 16th centuries.

Whitehall is a timber-framed building built around 1500. The history of the house and of those who lived in it over its 500 years is displayed inside.

CARSHALTON

6 miles E of Kingston on the A232

Honeywood Heritage Centre

The heart of old Carshalton is clustered around two ornamental ponds, which were created in the 18th century from the old mill pond and an adjoining area of wetland. The Portland Stone bridge was probably designed by the Italian architect Giacomo Leoni for Thomas Scawen, who owned nearby Stone Court. Part of his estate remains as Grove Park, bought by the council in the 1920s "to preserve it as an open space … and to obtain control of the beautiful ornamental waters which form such an attractive centre to the area". Around this area are several fine old houses with grounds that are open to the public.

One of them, Carshalton House, now Saint Philomena's School, was finished in 1713 for Sir John Fellowes, a governor of the South Sea Company. The house is imposing, especially when first seen on the road from Sutton. It is a solid affair of red and yellow brick standing two storeys high, with an attic storey above the cornice. The harmonious, yet restrained look of the house is exactly the effect that so appealed to architects at the time of Queen Anne. The porch, built about 50 years later, with its Corinthian columns reflects a renewed love of classical embellishment. Outside is an impressive early 18th-century water tower, which blends in with the architecture of the main house. It housed a water-powered pump that lifted water from the river into a cistern, which fed the house.

The **Honeywood Heritage Centre** stands beside the upper pond. The original building is 17th century, but was considerably extended at the turn of the last century. Inside it is furnished in Edwardian style, including the paint colours, and has displays on local history including stucco and pottery from Nonsuch Palace.

Two miles south of Carshalton, on the Downs, is a public park with some majestic trees. These formed part of the grounds of a stately home, The Mansion, which was destroyed in an air raid in 1944. It was the home of the 12th Earl of Derby, founder of the famous horse race that bears his name.

BEDDINGTON

7 miles E of Kingston off the A235

Carew Chapel

Croydon Airport, which was located east of Beddington village, closed down in 1959, leaving room for the development of several housing estates, which tend to dominate the village. However, traces of Beddington's past are visible in its Church of St Mary, a large building, which was probably begun in the 11th century. The local landowner, Sir Nicholas Carew, left money for rebuilding the church in the late 14th century, and the **Carew Chapel** bears his name. He, along with many of his descendants, is commemorated in brasses in this chapel and in the chancel of the church. One of the most attractive later additions is the organ gallery, built in 1869. The player's space is screened like a minstrel's gallery.

CROYDON

9 miles E of Kingston on the A23

The Palace St John the Baptist Church

Waddon Caves Fairfield Halls

Looking at the high-rise flats and offices, one-way systems and traffic lights and trams, it is hard to imagine that Croydon was not much more than a large village less than two centuries ago. That historic past seems to have been obliterated in a headlong rush to development.

Yet, as with so many other large British towns, first impressions can be deceptive. Nestling beneath some of the most modern high-rises are some much older buildings, including some brick almshouses built in 1599 and now overshadowed by their modern neighbours. More intriguingly, and certainly worth seeking out, are the remains of the palace that was the summer residence of the Archbishops of Canterbury. **The Palace** was built in the 11th century by Archbishop Lanfranc. It was considerably altered and expanded in subsequent centuries but remained an official residence until 1757. The Palace is now part of the Old Palace School for girls, but the public can see some of the oldest surviving elements, including the Norman undercroft and the 15th-century banqueting hall.

St John the Baptist Church is the largest parish church in Surrey, with a two-storey porch and fine tower. Its enormous size puts it in a league with St Mary Redcliffe in Bristol and St Martin in Salisbury. The 15th-century church burnt down in 1867, but was rebuilt by 1870 on the old foundations in a style that largely matches the earlier church. Some original elements of the medieval church remain in the restored tower and the south porch.

Croydon also has a handsome arts complex, the **Fairfield Halls**, which flank one edge of a modern flower-filled square in the heart of Croydon. It comprises a main concert hall, the Peggy Ashcroft Theatre, the Arnhem Art gallery and a general-purpose lounge that doubles as a banqueting hall. **Waddon Caves**, along Alton Road, was the site of late Stone Age and Iron Age settlements, which were inhabited until the 3rd or 4th century AD.

Epsom

Epsom Downs

The old market and spa town of Epsom is a prosperous residential centre that lies on the edge of London's southwestern suburbs. In the early 17th century, it was observed that cattle were refusing to drink from a spring on the common above the town and subsequent

BUMBLES

90 The Street, Ashtead, Surrey KT21 1AW
Tel: 01372 276219
website: www.bumblesofashtead.co.uk

Gifts, greeting cards and gems, presents of all kinds, homeware and lifestyle ideas – all this and more await shoppers at **Bumbles**, which stands on the main street of the busy market town of Ashtead, near Epsom on the A24. Barbara Kay founded the shop in 1991, since when she has built up a great reputation for seeking out items that are a bit out of the ordinary, and with the stock changing all the time every visit will unearth new delights and surprises. Typical of the unique appeal of the place are silver and well-sourced fashion jewellery, while other items range from unusual gift ideas for men & women, handmade baby shoes, Welsh love spoons, heat-resistant glass trays, plus photo frames, toys and teddies to Bronnley products, bags, and jewellery boxes as well as a variety of stationary, writing products and clocks.

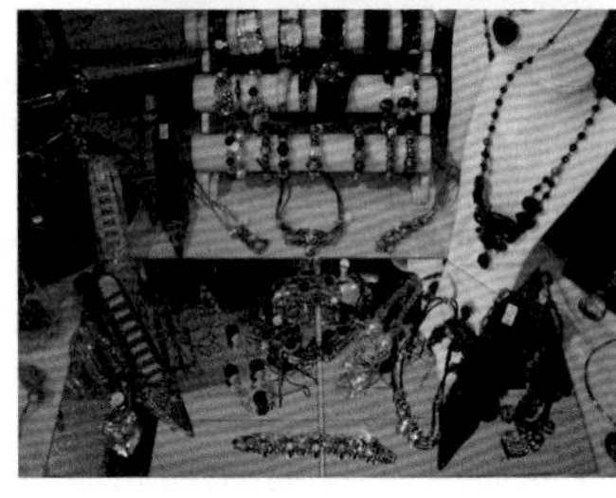

tests revealed the water to be high in magnesium sulphate, a mineral believed to have highly beneficial medicinal properties. As the fashion for 'taking the waters' grew towards the end of the century, wealthy people from London came in increasing numbers to sample the benefits of Epsom salts and the settlement grew from a small village to a town with its own street market, a charter for which was granted in 1685.

By the end of the 18th century, the popularity of Epsom's spa was on the decline, but by this time, the town's pleasant rural location within easy reach of the City of London was already starting to attract well-to-do business people; a number of substantial residential homes were built in and around the town during this period, several of which survive to this day. A lively street market continues to be held every Saturday in Epsom High Street, a wide and impressive thoroughfare, which contains some noteworthy old buildings, including a Victorian clock tower.

Epsom's other main claim to fame is as a horse racing centre. Each year in early June, the Downs to the southeast of the town take on a carnival atmosphere as tens of thousands of racing enthusiasts come to experience the annual Classic race meeting and the colourful fun fair that accompanies it. Informal horse racing took place on **Epsom Downs** as long ago as 1683 when Charles II is said to have been in attendance. Racing was formalised in 1779 when a party of aristocratic sportsmen led by Lord Derby established a race for three-year-old fillies, which was named after the Derbys' family home at Banstead, the Oaks; this was followed a year later by a race for all three-year-olds, the Derby, which was named after the founder himself, although only after he won a toss of a coin with the race's co-founder, Sir Charles Bunbury. (Had Lord Derby lost, the race would have become known as the Bunbury.)

Bourne Hall Museum, Ewell

The Oaks and the Derby were a great success and soon achieved classic status along with the St Leger at Doncaster, the earliest to be established in 1776, and the 1,000 Guineas and 2,000 Guineas at Newmarket, established in 1814 and 1809 respectively. The Derby family has maintained its connection with the Derby and the Classics down the years, and in 2004 the 19th Lord Derby won the Oaks with Ouija Board, who was to become one of the best and best-loved mares ever to race.

Around Epsom

EWELL

2 miles N of Epsom on the A240

Bourne Hall Museum

It comes as something of a surprise to find shades of Xanadu in this leafy town lying just north of Epsom. Nonsuch Park is a reminder of a grand plan that Henry VIII had to build the finest palace in Christendom. The magnificent Nonsuch Palace was almost finished at Henry's death. Unfortunately, it was demolished in 1682 and all that remains is the fine park, which surrounded it, noble in stature and perspective, but singularly lacking its intended focal point.

A few other historical attractions make Ewell worth visiting. There is an ancient spring, which was discovered in the 17th century. The 18th-century Watch House, on Church Street, was once the village lock-up. It is shaped like a small cube, with two narrow doorways under an arch. Its mean and spartan appearance alone must have deterred would-be felons.

Ewell Castle, now a school, is not a medieval fortification. It was completed in 1814 in what was known as the Gothic style. Crenellated and stuccoed, it gives the appearance of a real castle, but the effect is somewhat lessened by its location so close to the road. In addition, **Bourne Hall Museum** is well worth a visit. Overshadowed by the trees of a Victorian park, the museum is housed in a striking circular building that was considered revolutionary when it was built in the 1960s. The open-plan galleries have displays drawing on a collection of more than 5,000 items acquired over the years through the generosity of local people.

BANSTEAD

3 miles E of Epsom on the A217

All Saints Church

Banstead is one of the many small towns of Surrey that alert travellers from London that they are entering the real countryside. With the expansion of the southeast, particularly since World War II, new suburbs have emerged, and even towns that were themselves once suburbs have now created their own ring of smaller satellites.

Banstead is one of the exceptions to this creeping urbanisation, and the Green Belt Act of 1938 has helped it retain much of its original country feel. It stands at the edge of the rolling green Downs that provide ideal riding country. The high street has its fair share of nationally known outlets, but there is still a sense of local flavour and pride in its locally-run firms.

All Saints Church is a small flint and stone parish church, which was built in the late 12th century and early 13th century. It has a squat appearance, with a low, broad tower and a shingled spire. Like many Surrey churches it was renovated in the 19th century. In this case, the Victorian intervention was restrained, and the church now looks much as it must have done in the late Middle Ages. Just north of the church is a circular well. With its large roof, it formed something of a focal point in medieval times.

The Downs near Banstead are ideal for rambling. Traces of late Stone Age huts were found here, and the Galley Hills are formed by four bowl barrows from the same period.

CHIPSTEAD

7 miles E of Epsom on the A23

A mixture of architectural styles give Chipstead an unusual appearance, as it constitutes a mixture of Victorian model village combined with a few older houses and a good measure of suburban development. Some handsome cottages border a crossroads and there is a pretty ornamental pond in the centre. For a taste of real Victoriana though, it is worth making a short detour about half a mile south to view Shabden, a mansion built in the French Renaissance style but with a large timber porch added. The overall effect is a jarring mixture of styles that contrives to make an unattractive house out of potentially attractive ideas.

Chipstead Church

COULSDON

7 miles E of Epsom on the A23

St John the Evangelist Church

Farthing Down

Downlands Circular Walk

Coulsdon is a pretty village that has managed to keep recent housing developments - notably Coulsdon Woods - discreetly removed from the traditional centre. There are pretty cottages in the heart of the village and some of the

Chaldon Church

more substantial farmhouses nearby can be traced to the 15th century. **St John the Evangelist Church**, on the corner of the village green, was built in the late 13th century. The tower and spire were built more than 200 years later, but the interior has some well-preserved elements from the original church. Most notable of these is the sedilla, with its circular piers and pointed arches. A sedilla was a seat for (usually three) priests and always located on the south side of the chancel.

The countryside around Coulsdon has more than its share of history. Traces of a 2nd century AD Romano-British settlement have been found on the ridge along **Farthing Down**, and 14 barrows on the ridge are the evidence of a 6th-century Saxon burial ground. A number of iron knives, swords and other weapons have been dug up from the site. Coulsdon Common, on the way to Caterham, is a tranquil and largely undeveloped spot. Since Saxon times it has been common land given over to grazing, its soil deemed too poor for cultivation.

The **Downlands Circular Walk** conveniently begins and ends at The Fox, an attractive pub facing Coulsdon Common.

CHALDON

8 miles E of Epsom off the A23

It is well worth making the detour to Chaldon, two-and-a-half miles to the west of Caterham, to have a look at the 11th-century church of St Peter and St Paul, which stands within striking distance of the old Pilgrim's Way. An unassuming flint-built structure with little to commend it (other than, perhaps, its south tower and shingled spire), the interior contains one of the most outstanding medieval wall paintings still in existence in Britain. Executed in creamy white on a deep red-ochre background, the mural covers the entire west wall of the church. It is believed to have been painted around 1200, but was covered over during the Reformation and remained undiscovered until 1870. The Chaldon Doom, as it has become known, depicts gory scenes from the Last Judgement; a 'Ladder of Salvation' can be seen reaching up to the Kingdom of Heaven from purgatory, a place where horrific punishments are meted out by fork-wielding devils to those guilty of having committed the Seven Deadly Sins. Realistic looking cauldrons, manned by infernal kitchen staff, await the wicked.

CATERHAM

8 miles E of Epsom on the B2031

East Surrey Museum · Tupwood Viewpoint

The route into Caterham town centre from the south passes close to Foster Down, a section of the North Downs Way, which incorporates the impressive **Tupwood**

East Surrey Museum

1 Stafford Road, Caterham, Tandridge, Surrey CR3 6JG
Tel: 01883 340 275
e-mail: es@emuseum.freeserve.co.uk
website: www.eastsurreymuseum.org

The East Surrey Museum is a museum at the heart of the Tandridge community with an exciting display of archaeology, social history and geology as well as an ongoing programme of fun events and temporary
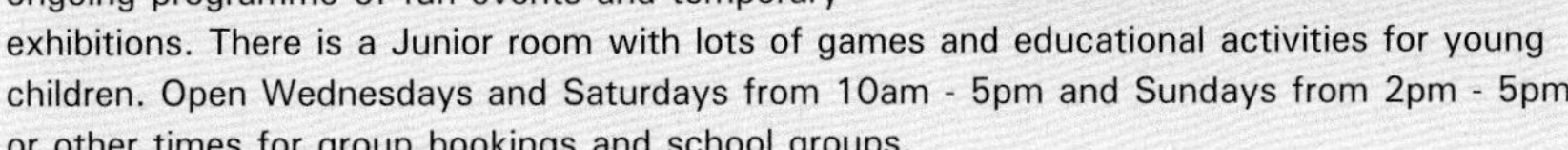
exhibitions. There is a Junior room with lots of games and educational activities for young children. Open Wednesdays and Saturdays from 10am - 5pm and Sundays from 2pm - 5pm or other times for group bookings and school groups.

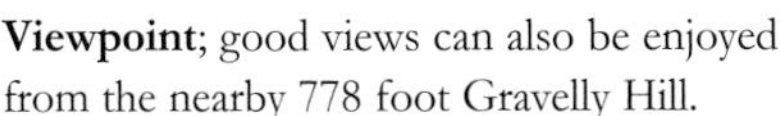
Viewpoint; good views can also be enjoyed from the nearby 778 foot Gravelly Hill.

Caterham itself is a modern and prosperous residential town, which at first glance seems to have little to offer the casual visitor. On the other hand, the town is something of a time capsule. Until 1856 Caterham was a remote Downs village. The arrival of the railway in that year changed everything and the town developed around it and the barracks, which were built in the 1870s. The railway was never extended, so Caterham is a terminus rather than a through station. As such, the 19th-century town plan remains unchanged. Near Caterham Railway Station is the **East Surrey Museum** (see panel above) in Stafford Road, which offers an interesting insight into the natural history and archaeology of the surrounding area, as well as a collection of objects that recall the area's rural past.

WARLINGHAM

8 miles E of Epsom on the B269

Successful enforcement of Green Belt policy since World War II has helped Warlingham retain much of its green and leafy look, and it is hard to imagine that it lies just a few miles south of bustling Croydon and its built-up suburbs. Warlingham's real fame stems from its church, All Saints, or more specifically two historic events that took place in it. The new English prayer book, authorised by Edward VI, was first used in the parish church. Its compiler, Archbishop Cranmer, attended the service. Four centuries later Warlingham parish church was chosen to host Britain's first televised church service. The church itself was restored and enlarged in Victorian times, but dates from the 13th century. It still contains many old elements, including a 15th-century wall painting of Saint Christopher and a 15th-century octagonal font.

Modern housing has replaced most of the traditional cottages in the heart of Warlingham but there are a few survivors from past centuries. The Atwood Almshouses, a two-storey cottage flanked by single-storey cottages, were built in 1663. The vicarage nearby was built in the same year.

TATSFIELD

10 miles E of Epsom off the B269

Tatsfield, high up on the Downs, is something of a curiosity as well as testament to the enduring power of hyperbole in advertising. In the 1920s a group of small, unassuming cottages sprang up in the wooded landscape just north of the old village green. The verdant setting, combined with the hilly location, led to a promotional campaign urging prospective house buyers to "Come to London Alps".

South of the green is St Mary's, the parish church, which dates from about 1300. It stands on its own, commanding panoramic views south over the Weald.

WALTON ON THE HILL

5 miles S of Epsom off the A217

The Hill referred to in the name of this village is one of the many rolling hills that comprise the North Downs. Travellers heading south from London have a real sense of space by the time they reach Walton, and the upland farms strengthen this impression. Buildings - both residential and commercial - have the harmonious redbrick look so typical of this part of Surrey. They were built mainly in the Victorian era, but some of the earlier buildings were constructed from flint, hanging tiles and weather-boarding.

Walton Manor, built in the 1980's, is a good example of the tile-hung style and it was built in the 1890s. Its appearance shows the influence of the decorative Arts and Crafts movement, typified by architects such as Norman Shaw. Embedded in one end, however, are the walls of a stone-built manor house of the 14th-century; a two storey hall and chapel protrude from the east of the house.

The view south from the centre takes in the extent of the Downs, with the North Downs Way - the traditional Pilgrim's Way to Canterbury - running along the ridge on the other side of the broad valley. In the foreground are the rolling grounds of the championship golf course.

North Surrey

The Thames winds through Surrey to the north of Weybridge and many of the present-day villages and towns developed as riverside trading centres in the medieval period or earlier. Romans marched through this part of Surrey during their conquest of Britain, possibly following the trail of the Celts who were already ensconced there. Saxons left their mark later, bequeathing a number of place names, which duly entered the Domesday Book in the 11th century. The most impressive of all buildings along this - and perhaps any - stretch of the Thames is Hampton Court. Here, Henry VIII, England's larger than life monarch acquired and substantially expanded Cardinal Wolsey's palace until it was fit to match his own personality.

The human mark is much in evidence on this landscape, and for every area of suburban sprawl there seems to be a corresponding architectural gem. It might be a sensitively preserved church, as in Thorpe, or even an unlikely high street survivor such as the Salvation Army Youth Centre in Sunbury-on-Thames, the newest incarnation of an impressive mansion.

Just as the Thames led to the development of medieval and earlier villages, so too did the arrival of the railway in the mid 19th century. New villages sprang up, while others expanded out of all recognition. The 20th-century's contribution to the regional transport theme is the M25, which provides the western and southern border for the area covered in this section.

Relatively compact, yet full of interesting detail and constant surprises, this north-central section of the county is a microcosm of Surrey itself.

Weybridge

Elmbridge Museum · Brooklands Museum

Although in many people's minds the epitome of a comfortable and modern commuter belt settlement, Weybridge is a surprisingly long-established settlement. The town takes its name from the bridge over the River Wey on the highway to Chertsey, and there is evidence of such a bridge existing as early as 1235. Tradition also links Weybridge with Julius Caesar, and many historians believe he crossed the Thames near here in 55BC.

The town once possessed a palace, Oatlands Park, in which Henry VIII married his fifth wife, Catherine Howard, in 1540; 110 years later, the building was demolished and the stone used in the construction of the Wey Navigation. Weybridge stands at the northern end of this historic inland waterway, which was one of the first examples of its kind when it was completed in 1670. It extends for almost 20 miles southwards to Godalming and incorporates large sections of the main river.

The middle of the 17th century, during the interregnum, also saw a remarkable development in Weybridge. The Diggers, a radical left-wing group, attempted to build a commune on St George's Hill, although they were thwarted by angry commoners.

Elmbridge Museum, situated in the library in Church Street, is an excellent source of information about the history - and

prehistory - of Weybridge. A wide range of exhibits takes in archaeological artefacts, old maps, photographs and paintings of the district. The costume collection is particularly interesting, as it consists of clothes worn by local residents from the late 18th century to the present day.

In 1907, the worlds first purpose-built motor racing track was constructed on the Brooklands estate near Weybridge, and in the years that followed, this legendary banked circuit hosted competitions between some of the most formidable racing cars ever made. A frequent visitor in the 1920s was Count Zborowski, racing a series of cars he designed; they were all called Chitty Chitty Bang Bang. The first British Grand Prix took place here in 1926, when the fastest lap was achieved by Sir Henry Seagrave in a Talbot. The Campbell Circuit was designed by record-breaking driver Malcolm Campbell in the 1930s. With the outbreak of World War II, the site was given over to the production of aircraft, including Hurricane fighters and Wellington bombers; racing came to an end, the track fell into disrepair and Brooklands never again regained its once pre-eminent position in British motor racing.

In recent years, the circuit has undergone something of a revival with the opening of the **Brooklands Museum**, a fascinating establishment centred on the old Edwardian clubhouse, now restored to its pre-war elegance. There is a collection of the famous cars that raced here, and archive film and memorabilia of the circuit's heyday. Bicycles also raced on this circuit and a display of Raleigh bicycles and accessories charts the company's story from its inception in 1886 to the present day. The Wellington Hangar, built across the finishing straight of the track, houses a collection of Brooklands-built aircraft including a World War II Vickers Wellington, salvaged from Loch Ness and carefully restored.

Around Weybridge

WALTON-ON-THAMES

2 miles NE of Weybridge on the A244

Church of St Mary

Standing almost directly opposite Shepperton on the other side of the Thames is Walton-on-Thames. This unassuming London suburb has a surprisingly long and varied pedigree. As with many of the riverside communities along this stretch of the river, Walton has a claim to be the site where Julius Caesar forded the Thames during his second invasion of Britain. Hard archaeological evidence for this claim is scant, but there is ample proof that there was a settlement here during the Saxon period. Walton appears as Waletona in the Domesday Book when the town was recorded as having a church, a fishery and two mills.

In 1516 Henry VIII granted the residents two fairs a year, and they continued until 1878. Walton's relations with Henry were ambivalent. However, in 1538, Walton along with surrounding communities, became incorporated with Henry VIII's Chase of Hampton Court, into what amounted to a private royal hunting preserve. Walton was outside the perimeter fence, but it was forced to comply with forest law, which had a detrimental effect on cultivation. Luckily for the residents of Walton, this arrangement was discontinued when Henry died.

Until 1750 the Thames could only be crossed by ferry or ford, but in that year the first bridge was built. This original structure, a wooden toll bridge built by Samuel Dicker, was replaced by several other bridges until the present iron one was built in 1864.

The part Norman **Church of St Mary** stands on the highest point of the town. It contains a remarkable memorial to Richard Boyle, the Viscount Shannon, which was sculpted by Louis Roubiliac in the mid 18th century.

In Manor Road is the handsome and imposing Manor House of Walton Leigh, a timber-framed brick building that dates from the medieval period. Old records indicate that John Bradshaw, President of the Court that sentenced Charles I to death, lodged here.

EAST & WEST MOLESEY

3 miles NE of Weybridge on the B369

Molesey Hurst

Molesey can trace its history to the 7th century, when grants of land were made to Chertsey Abbey. Among the abbey's estates was 'Muleseg', which meant Mul's field or meadow. The identity of Mul is lost in the mists of time, but his name is commemorated in two riverside communities.

The prefixes east and west, relating to Molesey, were not used until the beginning of the 13th century. In the *Domesday Book* Molesey was recorded as comprising three manors tenanted by knights who had arrived with William the Conqueror. East Molesey was originally part of the parish of Kingston-upon-Thames, but its growing independence led to its separation from Kingston under a Special Act in 1769.

East Molesey's location just opposite Hampton Court Palace provided a valuable source of income for residents, and ferries did good business until the first bridge spanned the Thames here in 1753. The Bell Inn, one of the loveliest inns in Surrey, dates from the 16th century, right at the beginning of Molesey's links with Hampton Court. Matham Manor, about four centuries old, is another link with the past. The Old Manor House, although handsome and impressive, is something of a misnomer. It originally served as the parish workhouse and was never a manor.

West Molesey is a continuation of East Molesey. It is much larger than its parent, but it occupies an even prettier stretch of the Thames. The parish church stands on a site where there has been a church since the 12th century. The present church is largely a legacy of the Victorian era, although the 15th-century tower remains. Inside are some other artefacts from the medieval era, including the piscina. This is a small basin in a wall niche by the altar and was used for cleaning sacramental vessels.

Molesey Hurst, a low, open stretch of land, lies along the Thames in the north of the parish. The land was once used for sporting activities such as archery, cricket, golf and even illicit duelling. It can also claim a cricketing first. It was here, in 1795, that a player was first given out leg-before-wicket.

HAMPTON COURT

4 miles NE of Weybridge on the A309

Palace

Hampton Court Palace occupies a stretch of the Thames some 13 miles southwest of London. In 1514, Thomas Wolsey, the Archbishop of York, took a 99-year-lease on the buildings at Hampton Court. Wolsey created a magnificent residence with new kitchens, courtyards, lodgings, galleries and gardens. Until 1528 he maintained Hampton Court as his home as well as for affairs of

Bushy Park, nr Hampton Court

Charles I, was imprisoned here after the Civil War. Charles II built accommodation for his mistress at the southeast corner of the palace.

Approached through Trophy Gate, Hampton Court gives an immediate impression of grandeur and scale. The courtyards and buildings to the left still contain a number of grace-and-favour apartments. Two side turrets contain terracotta roundels with the images of Roman emperors, which date from Wolsey's time. Anne Boleyn's gateway, opposite Base Court, is carved with the initials H and A, for Henry and Anne. The many courtyards and cloisters cover six acres in a mixture of Tudor and Baroque styles, with fascinating curiosities such as Henry VIII's Astronomical Clock.

state. However, by then, Wolsey had fallen from favour with Henry VIII and found himself forced to appease the monarch by giving him his house. Henry comprehensively rebuilt and extended the palace over the following 10 years to accommodate his wives, children and court attendants. Although much of Henry VIII's building work has been demolished over time, the Great Hall and the Chapel Royal survive, the latter still in use as a place of worship. The Great Hall, which Henry had completed in 1534, having forced the builders to work night and day, has mounted stag heads and fine tapestries lining the walls beneath the intricate hammerbeam roof. It was the scene of theatrical productions during the reigns of Elizabeth I and James I, and among the performing troupes was that of William Shakespeare. Also intact are the enormous Tudor Kitchens, with the huge fireplaces and assortment of ancient cooking utensils that would have been used in the 16th century to prepare a feast fit for a king. During the 17th century, the Stuart kings lived here both as monarchs and prisoners. James I enjoyed the hunting in the park, while

William III and Mary II made the first major alterations to the palace since Tudor times. They commissioned Sir Christopher Wren to rebuild the king's and queen's apartments on the south and east sides of the palace, although the queen's apartments were left unfinished at the queen's death. King William's apartments remain one of the most magnificent examples of Baroque state apartments in the world. Almost destroyed in a terrible fire in 1986, there followed an ambitious restoration project to return them to the way they were when completed for William in 1700. They can now be seen in their original glory, still furnished with the fine furniture and tapestries of the day. An exhibition under the colonnade in Clock Court near the entrance to the King's

Apartments details the history of the state rooms including the restoration.

The grand Queen's Staircase leads to the Queen's Guard Chamber. The Queen's state rooms run along the east wing of Fountain Court and include the Queen's Drawing Room and the Queen's Bedroom. The Queen's Gallery contains ornate marble fireplaces with mantelpieces decorated with images of doves and Venus. Gobelins tapestries, on the theme of Alexander the Great, hang from the walls. Life-sized marble guardsmen flank the main chimneypiece. Hampton Court Palace contains a large part of the Royal Collection of art works, including many 16th, 17th and early 18th-century pieces.

There are over 60 acres of gardens to explore at the palace including the Great Vine and the newly restored Privy Garden. Shrubberies that were allowed to grow in the Privy Garden in the 19th century have been removed to reveal the ancient formal beds and pathways. An exhibition on the East Front tells the story of the gardens and explains the restoration of the Privy Garden, opened in 1995. From the Privy Garden you can visit William III's magnificent Banqueting House and the Lower Orangery where Andrea Mantegna's Triumphs of Caesar are displayed. The Broad Walk runs from the Thames for half a mile past the east front and is lined with herbaceous borders. Just off the walk to the left and inside is the Tudor Tennis Court, a Real Tennis court built for Henry VIII, who was a keen player. To the north of the Palace is the famous Maze, planted in 1714 within William III's 'Wilderness' of evergreen trees. The Maze is extremely popular and can be surprisingly difficult to negotiate. Further along the Thames Path stands Garrick's Temple. Commissioned by the actor David Garrick to house a statue of Shakespeare, it now contains a replica of the statue and an exhibition celebrating Garrick's career and life in Hampton.

Hampton Court

THAMES DITTON

4 miles E of Weybridge on the A309

St Nicholas' Church

Thames Ditton is one of the two Dittons that lie along the Thames south of Hampton Court. The name probably derives from the 'dictun', or farm by the dyke, and there were already a Saxon church and five manors in the area at the time of the Domesday Book. The heart of Thames Ditton dates mainly from the 19th century, but the harmonious blend of redbrick and occasional black-timbered buildings along the High Street helps put visitors in mind of the town's earlier history.

A flower-decked path leads to **St Nicholas' Church**, which was first mentioned in the 12th century - roughly the time when Ditton was divided into two parishes. The building is of flint and stone and the interior contains a font decorated with mysterious motifs that still puzzle historians.

Thames Ditton benefited from its proximity to Hampton Court Palace and the church contains the grave of Cuthnert Blakeden, "Serjeant of the confectionary to King Henry the Eighth".

LONG DITTON

5 miles E of Weybridge on the A309

There is a peculiar lack of logic in the naming of the two Dittons; Thames Ditton is actually longer than Long Ditton, but this more easterly village has a longer history than its neighbour. St Mary's Church, in the heart of Long Ditton, is a relative newcomer, having been built in 1880, but it stands close to the site of a Saxon church built long before the Dittons separated into two parishes.

Long Ditton is a scattered parish, with only a few vestiges left of its extensive history. Much of that history, however, can be gleaned from a close look inside St Mary's. The interior of the church features monuments to the Evelyn family, who put Long Ditton on the map in the 16th and 17th centuries. George Evelyn, grandfather of the famous diarist John Evelyn, acquired the local manor in the late 16th century and set about establishing gunpowder mills in the area. Business for gunpowder was booming, so to speak, in this turbulent period and the Evelyns amassed a huge fortune, eventually spreading their business further afield within Surrey.

OATLANDS

1 mile E of Weybridge on the B374

'The land where oats were grown' gave its name to the Tudor palace in Oatlands Park. This was already an established residence when Henry VIII forced its owner to cede him the title in 1538. Henry was in a rush to build a palace for his new queen, Anne of Cleves, although Ann never lived at Oatlands. However, the palace did become the home of subsequent monarchs, including Elizabeth I, James I and Charles I. In fact, it was Charles who is said to have planted the proud cedar tree that stands beside the drive of what is now the Oatlands Park Hotel; he was celebrating the birth of his son, Prince Henry of Oatlands.

HERSHAM

2 miles E of Weybridge on the A307

Anglo-Saxons were the likeliest first settlers of Hersham, although prehistoric flint tools have been found on what is now Southwood Farm. In the 12th century, the village was spelt Haverichesham and probably pronounced 'Haverick's Ham'. Two major events have shaped Hersham's history. The first occurred in 1529 after Henry VIII acquired Hampton Court from Cardinal Wolsey. Henry decided that his new estate lacked one of its necessities

THE DINING ROOM

10 Queens Road, The Village Green,
Hersham, Surrey KT12 5LS
Tel: 01932 231686
website: www.thediningroom.co.uk

Anyone who thinks that great British cooking is a thing of the past has clearly never experienced the delights of a visit to **The Dining Room**. This wonderful restaurant is a conversion of two Victorian village shops, and the five interconnecting parlour-like rooms are decorated in warm, highly individual style, with Indian silk colours, candles, chandeliers, fireplaces, shelves filled with old books, cabinets filled with country artefacts and bistro-style cutlery and crockery on scrubbed wooden tables. There are seats for 50 in the delightful patio garden. In this buzzy, relaxed atmosphere the menu is a tribute to the very best of British cuisine, with old favourites such as cheese pot, steak & kidney pudding, lamb & mint pie, smoked haddock with a mustardy cheese rarebit, spotted dick & custard, marmalade pudding and gooey toffee crumble. Other dishes have a more contemporary ring, including cod in a bag with pea pesto, goat's cheese tartlet with red onion marmalade and caper & polenta scone topped with Scottish smoked salmon. The superb food is complemented by an excellent wine list. The Dining Room is located by the village green at Hersham, a short drive from the A3. It is open for lunch and dinner Monday to Friday, dinner Saturday and lunch Sunday.

- a deer park - so he set about buying adjacent land and encircling the area with a perimeter fence. Other villages, including Weybridge and Esher, were on the edge of the park and escaped being enclosed, but Hersham was not so lucky. Not surprisingly, Hersham had a well-developed anti-royalist streak by the time of the Civil War, and one of Cromwell's prominent aides, Captain John Inwood, lived there.

Politics and warfare apart, Hersham continued largely untouched by the outside world until the 19th century. Until 1804, when it was enclosed by Act of Parliament, much of the land around Hersham Green was open heathland. The arrival of the railway in 1838 - the second major event to shape Hersham - led to a huge rise in its population. Development accompanied this boom and much of Hersham's original appearance was altered completely. Local residents, however, would not let the process rip the heart out of their village and Hersham Green was actually enlarged in 1878. Despite extensive redevelopment of the centre in 1985, the charm of the village has been maintained in many of the older buildings around the village green. The village green is still used for a variety of local functions, including a popular Summer Fayre with traditional entertainment.

CLAYGATE

4 miles E of Weybridge off the A3

Standing on a rich geological seam where dense London clay meets Bagshot sand, Claygate is well named. For many years this rich earth provided a living for many local men, who would have to bear the brunt of jibes from neighbouring villagers about working in the Claygate 'treacle mines'. Taunts notwithstanding, Claygate did supply the raw material for countless bricks and fireplaces.

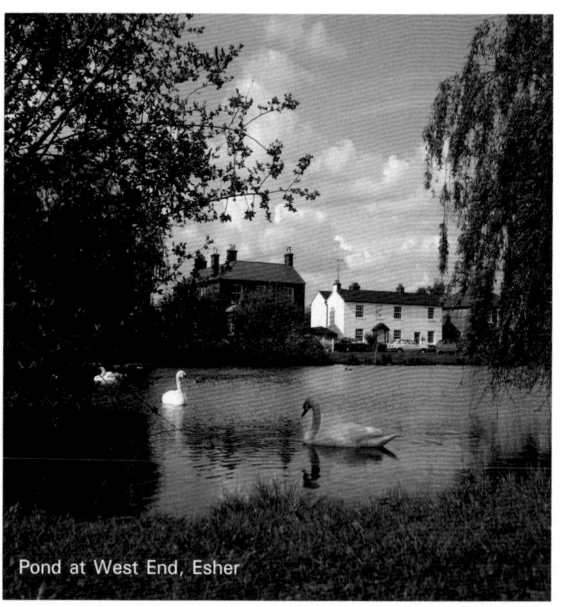
Pond at West End, Esher

Claygate can trace its origins to the Saxon times when it was a manor within the parish of Thames Ditton. In the early Medieval period the estate passed into the ownership of Westminster Abbey, which retained possession until Henry VIII dissolved the monasteries. Henry simply added it to his estates in Hampton Court.

Constrained for centuries by monastic, then royal control, Claygate remained largely unchanged as a tiny community until the 19th century. In 1838, however, Claygate Common was enclosed, enabling residents to enlarge the village considerably. One of the first orders of business was to erect their own church, Holy Trinity, to save the two-mile walk to Thames Ditton.

Ruxley Towers is an interesting building that dates from around the same period. It has a Gothic tower, built in 1830, which is decorated with a frightening display of gargoyles.

ESHER

4 miles E of Weybridge off the A3

Claremont House Sandown Park

Claremont Landscape Garden

Esher's recorded history goes back to Anglo-Saxon times. During the reign of Henry VIII, Hampton Court dominated all the surrounding manors including Esher. The railway arrived in Esher during the 19th century, after which it quickly became a popular residential area for wealthy city businessmen.

Esher is the home of **Sandown Park**, where high-class horse racing is staged all year round. Created in 1875 by Sir Wilfred Brett, it soon attracted all the great and good of the racing world including the royal family. This part of Surrey nearest to London is well supplied with racecourses, with, in addition to Sandown, Kempton Park near Sunbury and Epsom.

Near here, and well worth a visit, is the beautiful National Trust-owned **Claremont Landscape Garden**, which lies on the southern side of the A307 Portsmouth road within a mile of the town centre. Begun in 1715, it is believed to be one of the earliest surviving examples of an English landscape garden. Later in the century, it was remodelled by William Kent, whose work was continued by Capability Brown. Over the years, some of the greatest names in garden history, including Sir John Vanbrugh and

Charles Bridgeman, were involved in its creation. The grounds were designed to include a number of striking vistas and contain a grassed amphitheatre, grotto, lake and an island with a pavilion. Nearby **Claremont House** was designed in the 1700s by Vanbrugh and substantially remodelled in 1772 for Clive of India. Capability Brown, Henry Holland and John Soane all had a hand in this work, which Clive had little opportunity to enjoy, as he died by his own hand in 1774. In 1816 the house was acquired for the Prince Regent's daughter and her husband, the future King of the Belgians. Queen Victoria was a regular visitor, and worshipped at St George's Church on the estate. The part 16th-century church has an unusual three-tier pulpit, a very grand pew designed by Vanbrugh for the Duke of Newcastle, and a marble monument to Princess Charlotte of Wales. The Princess was George IV's heir and would have succeeded him had she not died in childbirth at the house in 1817.

COBHAM

4 miles SE of Weybridge off the A3

Painshill Park Bus Museum

Cobham, now a busy residential town, with densely settled residential streets, is found in the *Domesday Book* as 'Coveham'. However, it does possess some fine period buildings, which dominate a bend of the River Mole on the southeastern side of the town. An impressive 19th-century water mill stands on the site of earlier mills dating back to the Middle Ages. The redbrick building has now been restored to full working order. Cobham is also home to the **Cobham Bus Museum**, which houses the largest collection of London buses in the world. Cedar House, built in the mid 18th century, is a solid and well-proportioned brick building, which actually changes height halfway along its front. To the rear is a medieval section, which includes a large tracery window. About a mile north of Cobham is Foxwarren Park, a bizarre house with eerie gables and multi-coloured bricks. It was built in 1860, and contemporary Victorian architects were known to introduce a bit of macabre humour into some of their designs. In this case it is hard to decide whether the intended effect was self-mocking or whether the gloomy appearance conformed to the owner's tastes.

One mile west of Cobham is **Painshill Park** (see panel on page 330), a white 18th-century house in a fine setting on a hill. The house is impressive, but Painshill is more noted for its grounds, which were laid out by the Hon Charles Hamilton, son of the Earl of Abercorn, in the 1740s. These grounds were a talking point in the mid 18th century and were praised by luminaries such as Horace Walpole. Hamilton had let his imagination conjure up a series of landscapes and ornaments that created a profoundly Romantic atmosphere. An ornamental lake lay in front of a Gothic brick abbey, while on an island in the lake were various tufa sculptures and perpendicular cliffs leading down to the water. Hamilton even built a hermitage, and then went one stage further by installing a hermit in it. The mounting catalogue of expenses took its toll on Hamilton, however, and he eventually went bankrupt. Although many of the features in the grounds are gone, it remains an amazing spectacle. The walk around the lake, takes in a Gothic temple, Chinese bridge, a ruined abbey, a Turkish tent, and a waterwheel. The planting at Painshill makes it a gardener's

Painshill Park

Portsmouth Road, Cobham, Surrey KT11 1JE
Tel: 01932 868113
e-mail: info@painshill.co.uk website: www.painshill.co.uk

This once barren heathland was transformed by the celebrated plantsman and designer, the Hon Charles Hamilton, into one of Europe's finest 18th-century landscape gardens. Hamilton conjured up a mysterious and magical place in which to wander- the equivalent of a 20th-century theme park where fashionable society could wander through a landscape theatre. Staged around a huge serpentine lake there are surprises at every turn - a Gothic Temple, Chinese Bridge, Ruined Abbey, a Grotto, Turkish Tent, Gothic Tower and a magnificent waterwheel.

When Hamilton eventually ran out of money, he discharged his debts by selling the estate in 1773. It then had a succession of owners and was eventually sold off in lots in 1948. By 1981 the gardens were derelict and overgrown, but Elmbridge Borough Council, conscious of the importance of Painshill, purchased 158 acres with a view to restoring them and opening them to the public. The subsequent ongoing restoration has been a great success and most of the principal features of the garden are open for viewing. The restoration has been a slow process requiring lots of detailed and painstaking research, inlcuding archaeological excavation, documentary research and the identification and dating of trees, tree stumps and historic paths. From this, detailed plans are created to show what the estate would have looked like in the 18th century and all the later stages to the present day.

Now the historic circuit is a signposted two-mile long route that an 18th-century visitor would have followed to view all the attractions of the garden. A shorter path round the lake passes delights such as the ruined abbey, boat house and crosses the Chinese bridge. The new visitor centre restaurant is named Hamilton's after the man who made it all possible. The shop is a cornucopia for present and souvenir buyers containing everything from trugs and dibbers to umbrellas, food, china, books, honey and beeswax candles and Painshill wine.

delight as it changes with the seasons. The landscape is enhanced by cedars and original 18th-century plantings, including tiers of shrubs, flowerbeds and a vineyard.

OXSHOTT

4 miles SE of Weybridge off the A3

Oxshott Woods

Taking its name from the Old English for Occa's Wood, Oxshott's history as a settlement stretches back thousands of years. A flint found on Oxshott Heath is believed to date back to 8000BC, making it the oldest tool ever discovered in the area. Another fascinating find in **Oxshott Woods**, now displayed in the British Museum, is an intricately carved Anglo-Saxon bronze brooch of the early 10th century. Oxshott remained a small hamlet set in woods and heather until the 1880s, when the completion of the Surbiton to Guildford Railway ushered in an era of growth and development. Some stretches of woodland have withstood the tide of new roads and houses, notably Oxshott Heath and Princes Coverts, which is a woodland owned by the Crown Estate. In the middle of Princes Coverts is a square redbrick building that was erected in the 18th century over a medicinal spring known as Jessop's Well. The mineral content of the spring water was said to compare with that of Cheltenham, but despite the Royal connection and the salubrious waters, Oxshott somehow never achieved true spa status.

Perhaps Oxshott was considered a bit too dissipated, because for many years it was mildly notorious for having two public houses but no church. This imbalance between sacred and profane was partly offset in 1912, when St Andrew's Church was erected.

STOKE D'ABERNON

5 miles SE of Weybridge off the A3

St Mary's Church Slyfield Manor

Like Cobham, the northern part of Stoke d'Abernon is undistinguished; however, the older southern part, which reaches down to the River Mole, contains a fine mid 18th-century part-Palladian, part-baroque manor house, and an exceptional parish church that is believed to be among the oldest in the country.

The south wall of **St Mary's Church** is believed to date back to the days of St Augustine in the 7th century, and indeed it has been found to contain brickwork and cornices belonging to a Roman structure, which once stood on the site. There are also traces of an early Saxon lord's gallery and one of the oldest monumental brasses in Britain, that of Sir John d'Abernon who was buried in 1277. The church, with its wonderful mixture of styles is part-medieval with the magnificent walnut pulpit dating back to the early 17th century.

About half a mile south of Stoke d'Abernon is **Slyfield Manor**, which was built in the 17th century but incorporated a late medieval timber-frame building. Garden walls, with original archways, blend with the painstaking brickwork of the house to create an effect that reminds many visitors of the work of Inigo Jones, particularly in Covent Garden.

WHITELEY VILLAGE

2 miles SE of Weybridge on the B365

A mile-and-a-half to the southwest of Weybridge, and close to the St George's Hill residential area much-favoured by famous media personalities, lies the remarkable Whiteley Village. This unique 230-acre model village was founded on the instructions of the proprietor of a famous Bayswater department store, William Whiteley, who was shot in 1907. He left one million pounds in his will to house the elderly poor. The charitable community was designed to be entirely self-contained with its own churches, hospital and shops, and was laid out in an octagonal pattern around a green containing a memorial to the project's benefactor. The buildings are Grade II listed and of great architectural interest. The site has been planted with a great many trees and flowering shrubs, and is at its best in late-spring and summer. It is a private estate and not open to the public.

CHERTSEY

3 miles NW of Weybridge on the A320

Museum

Chertsey is an ancient riverside town, which has altered almost beyond recognition over the centuries. The town once boasted a formidable abbey, whose influence stretched over a wide area of southern England. When it was demolished following the Dissolution of the Monasteries, its stone was used to build Hampton Court Palace and later, the River Wey Canal.

One of the abbey bells now hangs in the parish church, St Peter; at one time it was used to sound the evening curfew and is associated with a local romantic legend concerning Blanche Heriot, a young Chertsey woman who, on hearing that her lover was to be executed at the sound of the curfew bell, climbed into the tower and clung onto the tongue until his pardon arrived. This heroic action was commemorated in the ballad *The Curfew Must Not Ring Tonight* by the American poet Rose Hartwick Thorpe.

Chertsey Museum, housed in a fine Regency building near the Thames, has a large collection of items of both local and national interest including a 10th-century Viking sword and a fascinating costume display exploring 300 years of high fashion. The museum closed for a time recently for a programme of renovation and extension but has now re-opened.

Despite the upheavals that Chertsey has undergone, it still manages to preserve some lovely woodland scenery, with a number of green fields and commons including Chertsey Mead. A well-proportioned, seven-arched bridge spans the River Thames in the centre of the town.

THORPE

6 miles NW of Weybridge off the M25

Many of the streets in Thorpe are walled, screening residential buildings and small parks, and planning authorities succeeded in preserving this feature - unique in Surrey - despite a postwar building boom. There are some ancient elements in St Mary Church, including a plain 12th-century chancel arch. An 18th-century monument to Elizabeth Townsend features a praying cherub designed by Sir Robert Taylor. Old brick cottages line Church Approach. Some of the larger buildings in Thorpe betray its farming background. Spelthorne St Mary, on Coldharbour Lane, is a solid 18th-century residence with a half-timbered barn dating from a century earlier. The Village Hall, to the east of Church Approach, was converted from a 17th-century brick barn.

SHEPPERTON

3 miles N of Weybridge on the B376

Over the centuries Shepperton has capitalised on its strategic riverside location, and today's thriving market town is testimony to the entrepreneurial spirit of previous generations. It grew from its origins as a straggling collection of homesteads to become a bustling way station for west-bound traffic from London. This status was firmly established by the 15th century, and many of the lovely houses around the Church Square Conservation Area date from that period, or shortly afterwards.

Staines Riverside

This century brought a new wave of development, as the famous Shepperton Film Studios were built in the 1930s. Handy for London's Airport, first at Croydon then at Heathrow, Shepperton presented itself as an ideal site for a film venture. International stars were collected from their transatlantic flights or from their Mayfair flats. Moreover, Shepperton's position at the edge of the Green Belt meant that "rural" location shots could be managed just a few miles from the studios themselves. Recent films made here include *Shakespeare in Love* and *Hilary and Jackie*.

STAINES

6 miles N of Weybridge on the A30

Museum · Great Thorpe Park

The ancient town of Staines stands at the point where the old Roman road from London to the southwest crossed the Rivers Thames and Colne, and in the 17th and 18th centuries, it became an important staging point on the old coaching routes to the West Country. When walking beside the Thames, look out for the London Stone that was erected in 1285 to mark the boundary of the city's authority over the river. The old part of Staines contains some noteworthy buildings, including the part 17th-century church of St Mary and the town hall built in Flemish-style on the Market Place.

The **Spelthorne Museum**, located in the old fire station of Staines, tells the story of Staines and its extensive history. Archaeological excavations in the 1970s confirmed that Staines stood on the site of the Roman settlement of Pontes.

The museum contains Iron Age and Roman artefacts and archaeological evidence, as well as re-creations of life in Roman times, and provides a useful chronology for the successive riverside settlements on this site. There is a re-creation of a Victorian kitchen, a collection of brewing and bottling equipment and the Staines Linoleum display devoted to the company that first made linoleum.

The M25 to the south of Staines passes close to **Great Thorpe Park**, a 500-acre leisure park that has been built on an area of reclaimed gravel pits. The park incorporates a shire horse centre, a series of historic reconstructions of life in ancient Britain, and a permanent theme park containing some of the latest roller coaster rides and fairground attractions.

LALEHAM

5 miles N of Weybridge on the B376

Riverside Park

Located only a few miles from bustling Staines, and only minutes north of the M3, Laleham sits on the banks of the Thames, with one of London's larger reservoirs backing onto it. A triangular green lies near the river, reached by Ferry Lane. It is a pretty village with many 18th and 19th-century houses. Facing the green is a pair of early 18th-century houses, Muncaster House and The Coverts.

Parts of All Saints Church at Laleham are 16th century, but it is said to stand on the site of a Roman temple. Laleham's best-known son is Matthew Arnold, who is buried in the churchyard. **Laleham Riverside Park** was formerly the grounds of Laleham Abbey, which belonged to the Lucan family. Water understandably plays a large part in activities here, with boat hire available just a few hundred yards west of the trim Victorian centre.

LITTLETON

5 miles N of Weybridge on the B376

Littleton has undergone a number of dramatic changes in the past four decades and today it is hard to find much of the original village lying south of the huge reservoir serving the capital. New houses, car parks and a school have replaced what had been a harmonious medieval ensemble of church, rectory, manor farm and manor house.

Luckily, of this group, the church remains intact. St Mary Magdalene is built of brick and dates back to the 13th century. The brick is a 16th-century addition, the original nave and chancel had been made of ragstone and flint rubble. This modification constituted a decided visual improvement. The west tower was built at a later date; like the earlier modifications it is of brick, giving the church a cohesive appearance. Inside there are a number of curiosities, including a late medieval locker and a complete restored set of pews from that same period. The ornate choir stalls are said to have come from Winchester.

SUNBURY-ON-THAMES

3 miles N of Weybridge off the M3

With its high-rise office blocks and modern shopping precincts, today's Sunbury-on-Thames seems a far cry from its origins as a 10th-century 'burgh' built by the Saxon Lord Sunna. It developed as a medieval market town for a riverside district stretching from Chertsey all the way to Kingston, and these bastions of commerce have simply kept pace with the passing of time. The local inhabitants seem happy enough to have retained the town's trading essence, even if it does mean that many of Sunbury's period buildings have long since been replaced.

However, few of the town's period buildings remain, including the Salvation Army Youth Centre, which had been Sunbury Court, an 18th-century mansion with Ionic decoration. A yew tree in the churchyard of the 18th-century St Mary Church featured in *Oliver Twist* by Charles Dickens. Between Sunbury Court and the church are some handsome Georgian residences.

Northwest Surrey

The northwest corner of Surrey, lying to the west of the M25 and stretching westwards to the Berkshire and Hampshire borders and given a southern limit by the A3, shows the county's countryside coming into its own. Rich farming areas give way to expanses of heath and dotted woodlands, once the haunt of highwaymen but now safe for ramblers - as long as they steer clear of the well-marked military areas.

Woking is the principal town in this area, like many Surrey towns an established centre that was transformed by the arrival of the railway in the 19th century. The Victorian influence is strong throughout this part of Surrey, evident in many of the larger houses built by or under the auspices of Norman Shaw and other proponents of the Arts and Crafts style, which blossomed as a reaction against poor-quality, mass-produced building materials.

The more ornate style of Victorian architecture, which seemed to be the embodiment of a prosperous nation flexing its imperial muscle, is also represented in the two massive buildings funded by Thomas Holloway, Royal Holloway College and the Holloway Sanatorium, which are near Egham in the north. That same northern extremity contains the site of one of England's defining moments, the signing of the Magna Carta in 1215 at the riverside meadow of Runnymede.

Woking

Woking is a commuter town on the main railway line to Waterloo. In fact it was the railway that defined the present appearance - and location - of Woking. The original village was what is now called Old Woking, and when the railway arrived in 1838, the station was built two miles away in what was then open heathland. Most of the heart of Woking dates from the middle of the 19th century, but among these Victorian-era buildings is an unexpected 'first'. The first purpose-built mosque to be founded in Britain - Shah Jehan Mosque - can be found in Woking's Oriental Street. The construction of this unusual onion-domed structure was largely financed by the ruler of the Indian state of Bhopal who visited the town in 1889. Woking was involved in another first, the beginnings of science fiction. H G Wells' Martians, in his 1898 novel *War of the Worlds*, landed on Horsell Common in Woking. The impressive Martian sculpture in the town centre was raised to commemorate the centenary of the book. Standing seven metres tall, the alien sculpture dominates its location. Even the paving around it is patterned to represent shock waves from the impact of the alien pod landing.

Old Woking is a former market town, which is now incorporated into the southeastern suburbs of its more modern neighbour. This is an old settlement, dating from the Saxon period and mentioned in the Domesday Book. Old Woking had the good fortune to be listed as a personal possession of the king and therefore it did not need to pay taxes. Its streets contain some noteworthy old buildings, including the 17th-century old Manor House, and the part Norman parish church of St Peter, which has a late-medieval west tower. On the western edge of Woking is the largest cemetery in the country. Brookwood Cemetery was opened in 1854 by the London Necropolis and National Mausoleum Company to relieve the overcrowded cemeteries of London. It was served by special funeral trains that ran from Waterloo Necropolis Station, next to the main Waterloo Station. The service soon built up to a train a day, each carrying up to 48 bodies (as well as

Newark Priory, Pyrford

grieving friends and relatives) on what the railway workers called the 'stiffs express'. This station was bombed in 1941 and was never rebuilt. Brookwood is a good place for spotting famous graves: among its many thousands of occupants are St Edward the Martyr; Margaret, Duchess of Argyle, the society beauty who was the subject of Cole Porter's song *You're the Top*; the bandleader Carroll Gibbons; the painter John Singer Sargent; the writers Rebecca West and Dennis Wheatley; Alfred Bestall, for 30 years the illustrator of the Rupert Bear stories; and the murderess Edith Thompson. (The body of Dodi Fayed was buried here briefly before being moved to the Fayed family estate.)

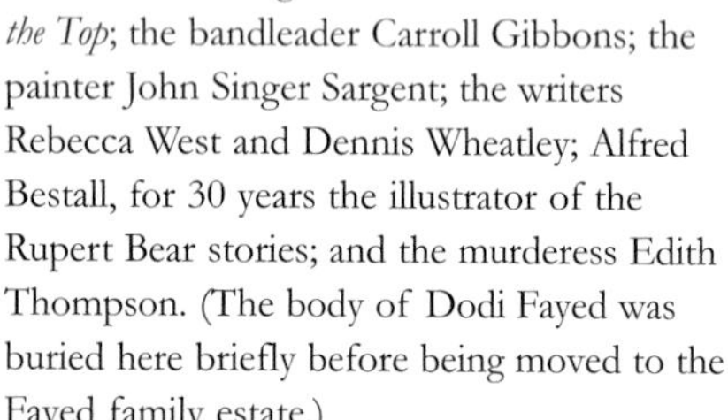

Around Woking

PYRFORD

1 mile E of Woking on the B382

Church of St Nicholas · Newark Priory

Located roughly midway between Woking and Byfleet is Pyrford, which manages to retain many aspects of its village character despite being no more than a couple of miles from its larger neighbours. It is set in meadows along the River Wey, with most of its original redbrick cottages still forming a core near the church. This parish church, the largely Norman **Church of St Nicholas**, has been preserved over the centuries without being the victim of intrusive restoration work. The south wall of the nave contains some unusual wall paintings of the Flagellation and Christ's Passion, which were painted around 1200. Research work carried out in the 1960s uncovered some even earlier murals beneath these paintings. The murals depict horsemen, as well as a mysterious procession of men carrying staves.

About half a mile along the B367, to the south of Pyrford, is **Newark Priory**, an evocative ruin set in fields along the banks of the Wey. The priory was a house of Austin Canons who founded it in the 12th century. Like other monastic settlements, it was a victim of the dissolution under Henry VIII. Unlike others, however, it was never converted into a private residence. Instead its walls were broken down for use in local buildings, although some of its features - including the east window - are said to have been taken to Ockham. Today, only the walls of the south transept and those of the presbytery still stand, and visitors must use their imagination to work out where in the surrounding corn fields there might once have been the remainder of the monastic buildings.

WISLEY

3 miles E of Woking off the A3

RHS Garden

The Royal Horticultural Society's internationally renowned **Wisley Garden** (see panel below) lies on the north side of the A3, one mile to the northwest of Ockham. As well as containing a wide variety of trees, flowering shrubs and ornamental plants, this magnificent 250-acre garden incorporates the Society's experimental beds where scientific trials are conducted into new and existing plant varieties. Wisley also acts as a centre for training horticultural students, and offers a wide range of plants, books, gifts and gardening advice at its first-class plant centre and shop.

RIPLEY

2 miles E of Woking off the A3

Just a mile or so to the southwest of Wisley is the attractive village of Ripley, a former staging post on the old coaching route between London and Portsmouth. The main street contains a number of exceptional brick and half-timbered buildings, including the charming Vintage Cottage with its unusual crown post roof.

RHS Garden Wisley

Woking, Surrey, GU23 6QB
Tel: 0845 260 9000
website: www.rhs.org.uk

The Royal Horticultural Society's garden at Wisley has 240 acres of beautiful and practical garden ideas. A gardener's paradise, the richly planted borders, luscious rose gardens and exotic glasshouses are a joy to wander through. But the garden also provides a test bed for countless cultivation methods and in a series of model gardens various growing conditions are applied. When the RHS was given Wisley in 1903, only a small part of the estate was cultivated as a garden, the remainder being woods and farmland. George Ferguson Wilson designed the original garden in 1878 as the 'Oakwood experimental garden' to try to grow difficult plants. Over the years as the garden expanded it has still remained true to the original concept.

Recent developments include the Walled Garden (West) planted with tender perennials, shrubs and climbers. The rich selection of plants from around the world has been chosen for their foliage. Cascades of water, streams and pools, terracotta pots and wrought iron work set against mellow York paving add to the architectural planting. Wooden seating designed by Julian Chicester allows visitors to enjoy the sights and scents of this unusual garden. The Temperate Glass House has been recently re-organised with a section of dry bright conditions, a central section for temporary displays and the remaining part designed around a waterfall and pools with damp, shady conditions. A new feature for Wisley is a bonsai collection in a minimalist Japanese style garden. It is on the site of the former Garden for the Disabled and is easily accessible for wheelchairs.

Most of the attractive houses lie on the gracefully curving High Street. Unusually, the long and wedge-shaped village green lies beside the street on the west side. The village seems to have grown away from the green rather than around it as in most English villages.

SUTTON PLACE

2 miles SE of Woking off the A3

Sutton Place

Sutton Place was the creation of Sir Richard Weston, a protégé of Henry VIII who was a Knight of the Bath, a Gentleman of the Privy Chamber and eventually Under-Treasurer of England. He had accompanied Henry to France for the famous meeting at the Field of the Cloth of Gold in 1520, so in every respect he had the right to expect to live in sumptuous surroundings that reflected his high standing.

The house he had built, after receiving the grant of the Sutton estate in 1521, is seen by many critics as one of the most important English houses to be constructed in the years after Hampton Court was completed. It was built to describe almost a perfect square, with sides measuring about 130 to 140 feet surrounding a central courtyard. The north side was demolished in the 18th century, so today's house appears to comprise a two-storey, redbrick central building with two long projections. Symmetry is important in **Sutton Place**, as English architects were busy putting to use the elements of the Italian Renaissance in their buildings. Doorways and windows are balanced in each wing.

The Italian influence is particularly evident in the terracotta ornamentation of the windows, and even more dramatically in a series of terracotta panels depicting cherubs over the entrance. Terracotta had been first used as an architectural feature, mainly as faience, in Hampton Court in 1521. Sutton Court was built probably no more than a decade later - records show that Henry VIII was a guest in 1533 - so it was obviously at the forefront of this style of ornamentation. It is the exterior, with its strict adherence to Renaissance tenets, that makes Sutton Place so fascinating. Inside, there have been alterations and additions that make the effect less wholly linked to one period.

Sir Geoffrey Jellicoe, the most renowned British landscape gardener of the century, partially completed a visionary garden for Sutton Place's then owner, the oil tycoon Stanley Seeger. Inspired by the philosophy of Carl Jung, Jellicoe created a series of symbolic gardens around the grand Elizabethan house. The most notable survival is the yew-enclosed garden, which contains a vastly enlarged marble abstract 'wall' sculpture based on a small maquette by Ben Nicholson. The yew walk is one of the garden's finest features.

WORPLESDON

3 miles SW of Woking on the A322

Worplesdon retains a sense of its rural past in its setting on the edge of heaths, despite the threat posed by the expansion of Guildford, which is just a couple of miles to the south. A number of brick houses dating from the early 18th century surround the triangular green, which is up on a hill. One of these houses displays a brick front, of around 1700, tacked on to a timber frame, creating an unusual effect.

St Mary's Church, standing above the village, was mentioned in the *Domesday Book*. Although clumsily restored in the Victorian era, the oldest part is 11th century and it retains a number of interesting features from

HORTI. HALCYON

Heath Mill House, Heath Mill Lane, Fox Corner, Worplesdon, Surrey GU3 3PR
Tel/Fax: 01483 232095
e-mail: hortihalcyon@btconnect.com
website: www.hortihalcyon-organic.co.uk

Horti. Halcyon sells over 60 varieties of vegetables, herbs and fruit grown on site or locally throughout the year. Horti is short for Horticultural and Halcyon is the first name of the senior partner Halcyon Broadwood, who runs the enterprise with her daughter Miranda. The land on which they grow has been in the same family since 1935 so is guaranteed never to have been intensively farmed. As a company Horti Halcyon has been growing and selling since 1996, starting with a small market stall in Worplesdon. Currently they deliver more than 100 organic boxes per week, regularly attend Farmers' Markets to sell their vegetables and baked goods, and also offer a catering service for buffets, parties and weddings using organic ingredients (see website for further details).

They try to put themselves in the position of the customer, knowing that no customer wants to pay for a box that contains items they don't like. All new customers are invited to give notice of any produce that they dislike which will be kept on record so that it is not included in their boxes. They are also concerned about miles and emissions, so they ensure that bought-in produce is sourced as locally as possible. They offer essentially two box options:

The Standard Box, an ongoing weekly or fortnightly box containing at least seven types of seasonal vegetables chosen from a wide selection.

The Special Orders Box is where the customer supplies us with their shopping list and we will deliver what has been ordered –subject to availability. This can be set up as a standing order or we will await your order and only deliver when an order is received.

Customers can pay by credit/debit card over the phone or by cash or cheque on delivery. The website gives up-to-date information on prices, recipes, maps and information on organic farming.

Outside the delivery area, customers can come in person and buy from the farm, where the shop is open from 9 to 4 Monday to Friday. The easiest way into the farm is from the B3032 Fox Corner-Pirbright road.

the medieval period. Chief among these is the late 15th-century tower, which is compact and well proportioned. At its base is a tower arch over an intricately carved door.

PIRBRIGHT

3 miles W of Woking on the A324

Pirbright is a village that is first recorded in 1166 as Perifrith, a compound of the two words 'pyrige' (pear tree) and 'fryth' (wooded country). It remained a hamlet of scattered homesteads until the 19th century, when the railway's arrival in 1840 led to a boom in the population and a corresponding burgeoning of new construction.

Despite the rapid increase in the village population, and thanks also to the enlightened Green Belt policies of this century, Pirbright has managed to keep most of its rural aspect. The huge village green that forms its core is in fact a wedge of the surrounding heathland. Pirbright contains many listed buildings, including several medieval farmsteads. Information about these, as well as a selection of excellent walks, is contained in a lovingly produced booklet available from the vicarage.

FARNBOROUGH

7 miles W of Woking off A331

Air Science Museum

Farnborough lies just over the border in Hampshire and although it is largely a commercial and shopping - rather than historical - centre, it is worth visiting for its links with the Royal Aircraft Establishment. These ties are explained fully at the **Farnborough Air Science Museum**, with its interactive displays and historical material. Other attractions include the bi-annual Air Show, a working monastery, and the tombs of Napoleon III, his wife and his son.

FRIMLEY

7 miles W of Woking off the M3

Basingstoke Canal Visitors Centre

Frimley is an extremely old village on the Hampshire border and a site of several important prehistoric and Roman finds, which are displayed at the Surrey Heath Museum in Camberley. Much of the more recent history, unfortunately, has been less well-preserved and the old sense of the village's coaching significance has been erased with a series of housing developments over the past four decades. The area around Frimley Green, however, gives some indication of what Frimley looked like in the late medieval period. Cross Farmhouse is one of the oldest surviving houses, its timber and brick structure containing elements dating from the 15th century. The parish church of St Peter dates only from 1825, but its churchyard contains the graves of many famous people. Among them is Francis Bret Harte, the American novelist whose wanderings around the world led him to settle eventually in England.

Just south of Frimley, and also hugging the Hampshire border, is the village of Mytchett, which has also suffered from some unthinking urban planning.

The **Basingstoke Canal Visitors Centre**, which lies just east of Farnborough and only five minutes from the M3, offers a tranquil and relaxing way in which to discover the charming countryside. Visitors can take a leisurely trip on a narrowboat, gaining a fascinating insight into the points of interest from the informative guide. The Canal Exhibition provides an in-depth account of how barge skippers lived a century ago and how the Basingstoke Canal, and its wildlife habitats, have been conserved more recently.

CAMBERLEY

7 miles W of Woking off the M3

Sandhurst Surrey Heath Museum

Prior to 1807, when the famous Sandhurst Royal Military Academy was relocated nearby, the substantial town of Camberley did not exist, and indeed its oldest part, the grid-patterned York Town, was constructed to house the academy's first instructors. (Lying just across the Berkshire border, **Sandhurst Academy** is set around a group of buildings designed in neoclassical style by James Wyatt.)

Although now resembling many other large towns with its High Street chains and modernised pubs, Camberley still displays much of the care and attention that marked its development in the mid-Victorian era. Unlike other towns, which sprang up willy-nilly, usually with the advent of the railway, Camberley had a measured growth and the town expanded along the lines of the grid shape of York Town. Shops and workers' houses predominated north of the railway line, while to the south were the larger houses of prosperous merchants set among stands of mature trees. These latter houses, many of which are good examples of the Arts and Crafts style of architect Norman Shaw and his followers, still stand, although recent housing developments have encroached on much of the wooded areas.

The story of the development of Camberley and the surrounding area is well told at the **Surrey Heath Museum** on Knoll Road. Most of the exhibits have been designed to tell this story from a child's point of view, but adults will also enjoy seeing some of the curiosities and original documents from the 19th century. There are also displays on heathland crafts, the archaeology of the area and the notorious highwaymen who preyed on unwary travellers.

BISLEY

3 miles W of Woking on the A322

Surrounded by farmland and heaths, Bisley remains resolutely small-scale and unassuming. It is within easy reach of Camberley to the west and Woking to the east, but luckily much of the traffic comes in the form of ramblers who are equipped with the well-marked books of pub walks in the vicinity. Bisley's contribution to the pub supply is the Fox Inn, which stands opposite Snowdrop Farm, where a well-marked trail crosses the A322. Having crossed the A322, the trail cuts southwestwards across Bisley Common, where annual marksmanship competitions are held on the rifle ranges, past the pretty little Stafford Lake and into Sheet's Heath. Even making this short walk, which in fact is part of one of the longer pub trails, gives a good indication of the native landscape. Here the land is more or less in its natural state, with scrubby low bushes and bracken indicating why it was the more fertile soil east of the A322 that was so sought after for cultivation.

The attractive church of St John the Baptist likewise stands to the west of most houses in Bisley, giving it an almost lonely appearance. It is built of local sandstone with a short tiled spire topping its wooden tower.

LIGHTWATER

7 miles W of Woking off the M3

Country Park

For many Londoners, Lightwater represents the first taste of countryside outside the metropolis. It has the advantage - from the visitor's point of view - of lying within easy reach of the M3. By turning south off the motorway, instead of north to Bagshot, drivers soon enter a countryside defined by heaths and scattered woodlands. Bagshot Heath, once a rough area peopled by highwaymen and duellists, begins at the western edge of Lightwater, and the village of Donkey Town lies just to the south, its name providing some confirmation of the area's rural nature.

Lightwater Country Park is over 57 hectares of countryside, with two colour-coded trails guiding walkers across open areas of natural heath, and through pine and birch woodlands. There is also a Trim Trail fitness circuit set among pine woods. The steep climb to the summit of High Curley is rewarded by panoramic views of the surrounding countryside. Heathland Visitor Centre has a fascinating collection of exhibits about the history and natural history of this stretch of West Surrey countryside.

BAGSHOT

7 miles W of Woking on the A30

On the western edge of Surrey, on the Berkshire border, lies the ancient village of Bagshot, which Daniel Defoe described as "not only good for little but good for nothing". Bagshot today largely bears out Defoe's description, but the village centre and the Church Road area are now Conservation Areas. The village was on the main coaching route from London to the west and was a bustling post stop, catering for thousands of travellers every year. In 1997, two wall paintings, dating from the turn of the 17th century, were discovered in a 14th-century building. The paintings, which had been concealed behind wall panels, cover two walls and are now protected behind glass.

WINDLESHAM

7 miles NW of Woking on the A30

Windlesham, lying in a setting of heath and meadow, is far prettier than its larger southern neighbour Bagshot. Victorian brick buildings - including some larger examples of the 'prosperous merchant' variety - line the heath, and one of the most attractive houses in Windlesham is Pound Cottage on Pound Lane. This timber-framed, 17th-century cottage has a lovely thatched roof, which comes down in hips to the ground floor ceiling. Like much of Surrey Heath, Windlesham was once part of Windsor Great Forest and developed as a traditional farming community centred around several manors and the church. Like Bagshot, Windlesham contains two conservation areas.

CHOBHAM

3 miles NW of Woking on the A3046

Enjoying a peaceful location just five minutes drive from Woking town centre is the attractive community of Chobham. The village is a Conservation Area and the High Street has developed over the centuries into an attractive and generally harmonious stretch of buildings, the oldest dating back to the 16th century. The street itself curves up a hill, with the parish church of St Lawrence punctuating the row about halfway along. The original church was built in the 11th century, but a restructuring in 1170 was the first of many alterations, including the tower, added around 1400, and the Victorian extension of the side aisle, that have left the church of St Lawrence more of an assembly of disparate elements than a harmonious whole.

VIRGINIA WATER

7 miles N of Woking on the A30

Windsor Great Park · Valley Gardens

Savill Garden

From Camberley, the A30 runs along the northeastern border of the county to Virginia Water, a surprising diversion, which lies in the heart of the Surrey stockbroker belt. The 'water' referred to is a mile-and-a-half long artificial lake, which is set within mature woodland at the southern end of **Windsor Great Park**; it was created by Paul and Thomas Sandby, two accomplished Georgian landscapers who were also known for their painting. The picturesque ruins standing at the lakeside are genuine remains of a Roman temple that once stood at Leptis Magna in Libya. The **Valley Gardens** also contain an unusual 100-foot totem pole, which was erected here in 1958 to mark the centenary of British Columbia. A little further to the north, the **Savill Garden** is renowned as one of the finest woodland gardens in the country covering around 18 hectares. Begun by Eric Savill in 1932, it has continued to develop with various additions over the years, including herbaceous borders, a bog garden and a temperate glasshouse.

Holloway Sanatorium, now renamed Crossland House, was designed by the Victorian architect W H Crossland for the eminent businessman and philanthropist Thomas Holloway. It was built to house middle-class people afflicted with mental disease. Holloway Sanatorium looked to the continent for inspiration, to the architecture of Bruges and Ypres. The result was a brick and stone Gothic structure that stood as the epitome of high Victorian fashion, ironically constructed after the popularity of that overblown style had begun to ebb. This Grade I listed building had fallen into dereliction, when in 1998, it was sensitively restored as part of a prize-winning housing development at Virginia Park.

ENGLEFIELD GREEN

8 miles N of Woking on the A30

The green that gives Englefield Green its name is large and attractive, flanked by a number of interesting houses, including some several centuries old. The aptly-named Old House dates from 1689, and most of it is a tribute to the redbrick symmetry so beloved of that period. Next to it is Englefield House, built in the late 18th century. This is more of a curiosity, since it seems that the architect was unclear whether his brief called for something classical, neo-Gothic or Venetian. Castle Hill is the largest building around Englefield Green. Extended in the 19th century, the original building was a 'Gothic' structure, built for Sir John Elwell. When the common lands were enclosed in 1814, the green survived as open land on account of the wealth and influence of its surrounding residents.

EGHAM

8 miles N of Woking on the A30

Royal Holloway College

Skirted by the River Thames and the historic fields of Runnymede, Egham is near a number of points of real interest. The centre of Egham is not particularly noteworthy, although the area by the Swan Hotel at the Staines Bridge is attractive, with a pretty row of old riverside cottages.

The Swan Sanctuary at Egham took over an area of disused land at Pooley Green in 1989 and consists of nursing ponds, rehabilitation lakes, and various facilities for cleaning and caring for injured swans. All birds are returned to the wild as soon as they are fit.

Between Egham and Englefield Green is one of Surrey's more memorable buildings, **Royal Holloway College**. It is a huge Victorian building, modelled on the Chateau du Chambord in the Loire Valley in France. Opened by Queen Victoria in 1886, it was one of the first colleges for women in the country. Like the Holloway Sanatorium at Virginia Water, it was designed by W H Crossland for Thomas Holloway. Holloway made his fortune from Holloway's Patent Pills in the 1870s. He was an entrepreneur and philanthropist, his wife a passionate believer in women's education. Holloway's generous ideas on lodging - each student was allocated two rooms - dictated the enormous size of the building. In the form of a double quadrangle, it measures 550 feet in length and 376 feet across. Inside, the formal rooms include a remarkable library, and a picture gallery housing a collection of Victorian paintings by artists such as Millais, Landseer and Frith. It is now part of the University of London.

RUNNYMEDE

10 miles N of Woking on the A30

Magna Carta Site Air Forces Mamorial

A meadow beside the River Thames to the north of Egham is where King John was forced to sign the **Magna Carta** in 1215. The historic Runnymede Site and nearby Cooper's Hill are contained within a 300-acre tract of land that is now under the ownership of the National Trust. Runnymede was an open space between the King's castle at Windsor and the camp of the rebel barons at Staines. The king was forced to agree to protect the barons from certain injustices, but the important principle was established that the king, as well as his subjects, could be governed by the law.

The area contains three separate memorials: a domed neoclassical temple that was erected by the American Bar Association to commemorate the sealing of the world's first bill of democratic rights, a memorial to John F Kennedy, and the **Air Forces Memorial**. Many come to see this memorial commemorating the men and women of the Commonwealth Air Forces killed in World War II who have no known grave. From its position on Coopers Hill, above the river, it commands splendid views over the Thames Valley and Windsor Great Park. The river below is populated by slow-moving motor cruisers and pleasure craft, and river trips to Windsor, Staines and Hampton Court can be taken from Runnymede, daily between May and October, and at weekends during winter. The nearby Runnymede Pleasure Ground offers a range of children's leisure activities in a pleasant riverside setting.

Runnymede Site

Farnham and the West

Farnham, with its lovely Georgian architecture and battle-worn castle, is the largest town in southwestern Surrey, where the heel of the county extends westwards into Hampshire. Apart from Farnham, however, there are no large towns in this corner of the county, and its charms lie more in the array of attractive villages, scattered farmhouses, woodlands and open heaths in some of the hilliest parts of the southeast.

History plays an important role in this area, with Civil War battle cries still almost audible from the walls of Farnham Castle, and the hint of plainsong hanging in the still air around the ruins of Waverley Abbey. "Stand and deliver" would seem to be a more appropriate sound to hear in the wilder sections of the southern extremity, and the Gibbet Memorial on Hindhead Common is a tangible reminder of the fate that awaited those highwaymen who had the misfortune to meet the long arm of the law.

The famous Hog's Back section of the A31 forms the northern edge of the area covered in this section. This lovely stretch of road is one of the most scenic drives in the southeast, affording excellent views north and south as it traverses the ridge between Farnham and Guildford. Indeed, looking south from the Hog's Back provides an aerial perspective of many of the sites covered in the following pages, or at least the countryside surrounding them. The panorama is best viewed from the grassy verge by the side of the A31 at one of the many lay-bys.

Farnham

Castle · Museum · Maltings

The most westerly town in Surrey is Farnham, a market town of particular architectural charm with its 12th-century castle overlooking Georgian houses in the river valley below. This fine old settlement stands at the point where the old Pilgrims' Way from Winchester to Canterbury crosses the River Wey, and it has long been an important staging post on the busy trading route between Southampton and London. Remains of Roman, Saxon and Stone Age dwellings have been found within its boundaries. The town first became a residence of the Bishops of Winchester during Saxon times and, following the Norman conquest, the new Norman bishop built himself a castle on a pleasant tree-covered rise above the centre of the town. The castle is a blend of the fortified and residential. It underwent a number of alterations, most notably in the 15th century when the decorated brick-built tower was added, and it remained in the hands of the Bishops of Winchester from the 12th century until 1927.

Farnham Castle has been visited on a number of occasions by the reigning English monarch and was besieged during the English Civil War. Today, it is approached along Castle Street, a delightful wide thoroughfare of Georgian and neo-Georgian buildings laid out to accommodate a traditional street market. The old Norman keep, now owned by English Heritage, is open to the public at weekends during the summer, and guided tours of the Bishops Palace take place on Fridays. The residential part of the castle is now occupied by Farnham Castle International Briefing and Conference Centre.

HENNY'S

5 Downing Street, Farnham, Surrey GU9 7PB
Tel: 01252 728254 Fax: 01252 715910
e-mail: info@hennyscafe.co.uk
website: www.hennyscafe.co.uk

Farnham is a charming market town, with a 12th century castle, a fascinating museum and a thriving arts and community centre. **Henny's** is one of the favourite places in the town to take a break or meet friends for a coffee, a snack or a light meal. The warm inviting atmosphere and calming surroundings at Hennys makes it the most talked about place in Farnham. Owner Henny (Henrietta) Corker takes great pride in serving freshly prepared food, locally sourced as far as possible, and she has the assistance of very friendly, welcoming staff. The menu has 30 covers, with some relaxed window seats for sipping a cup of coffee while looking out on Farnham life. The menu offers sandwiches, baguettes and paninis filled to order with a variety of freshly prepared homemade fillings along with fresh, appetising salads, homemade soups and hot jacket potatoes. For the sweet tooth Henny's can offer a good selection of delicious cakes baked fresh daily, including flapjacks, chocolate brownies and Hennys famous millionaire slices, all accompanied by a variety of teas, coffees and other hot and cold drinks. Henny's is open from 9 to 4.30 Monday to Saturday.

THE LIGHTING AGENCY

Lion & Lamb Yard, Farnham, Surrey GU9 7LL
Tel/Fax: 01252 719192
e-mail: info@thelightingagency.co.uk
website: www.lightingagency.co.uk

The Lighting Agency is located in a charming, atmospheric building in a classic English cobbled yard. The display area is filled to the brim with an amazing selection of all kinds of lighting, from new and vintage chandeliers to table lamps, wall lamps, bathroom fittings, ceiling fittings and outdoor lanterns and lamps in bronze, nickel, crystal, glass and other materials. One of the most sought-after lines is the Olive range – a simple, contemporary collection for today's cosmopolitan lifestyle. Many of the new items on display are unique to the Lighting Agency, most of which can be modified to individual customer's requirements. There's always an interesting collection of revamped and electrified chandeliers, lamps and lanterns, with up to 100 on display at any one time.

Some of the table lamps have a classic look that's perfectly in place here in the Surrey/Sussex borders, while others have a smart, edgy contemporary appeal, offering a sophisticated 'London' look at provincial prices. A wide range of lampshades complements on the spot purchases or can be personalised and sent to the buyer. The Lighting Agency was founded by Alistair Henderson in 2001, since when he has maintained its individuality and its reputation for quality, service and its unique range of decorative lighting, whether new, vintage or reconditioned.

Alistair also owns sister establishment **The Curtain Agency**, specialising in made-to-measure curtains and blinds, quality secondhand curtains, fabrics, wallpapers and accessories. One branch is just round the corner at 103 West Street (Tel: 01252 714711), another at 231 London Road, Camberley (Tel: 01276 671672).

Farnham Castle

Farnham contains a number of other interesting historic buildings, including a row of 17th-century gabled almshouses. The informative **Farnham Museum** is housed in Willmer House in West Street, an attractive Grade I listed townhouse dating from 1718. The house has many original features including a pleasant walled garden at the rear. As well as some fine wood panelling, carvings and period furniture, the museum contains some interesting archaeological exhibits and a unique collection of 19th-century glass paperweights.

Farnham Maltings (see panel below) in Bridge Square is a thriving arts and community centre, which is housed in a listed early 18th-century building, thought to have been a tanyard. The writer and agriculturalist William Cobbett (*Rural Rides*) was the son of a Farnham labourer. He was born in a hostelry - now named after him - on Bridge Square and is buried beside his father in the churchyard of St Andrew.

Farnham Maltings

Bridge Square, Farnham, Surrey GU9 7QR
Tel: 01252 726234 Fax: 01252 718177
e-mail: info@farnhammaltings.com
website: www.farnhammaltings.com

Over 300,000 people visit **The Maltings** every year. They come to performing and visual arts events, courses and workshops; visit the monthly markets, trade fairs; or belong to one of the 40 or so societies which meet regularly there. But, whilst the Maltings has built up its reputation as an arts and community centre only since 1975, its history stretches back to the 18th century.

The earliest surviving document relating to the Maltings is dated 1729, but there is evidence of two previous owners. In those days it was a tanyard. In 1830 Robert Sampson set up as a maltster in the then separate East Wing. He was succeeded in business by his son, Sampson Sampson, whose sign can still be seen on the end of his cottage at 18 Bridge Square. Meanwhile, the tanyard was sold to John Barrett, who converted it into a brewery.

The building stood empty for 12 years before it was turned ino an arts and community centre. The conversion so far comprises the Great Hall, the Barley Room, Malt Room, Tannery, Main Bar, Forum, Maltings Gallery & Studio, Long Kiln Room, Dance Studio, South West Kiln, the East Wing Studios, Dressing Rooms, and Playgroup Studio. In1991 fully retractable theatre style raked seating in the Great Hall was installed.

Around Farnham

WAVERLEY ABBEY

2 miles E of Farnham on the B3001

Abbey

Lying within easy striking distance of Farnham are the atmospheric ruins of **Waverley Abbey**. Dating from the 12th century, this was the first Cistercian abbey to be built in England. The first church was completed in 1160 and destroyed during the Dissolution of the Monasteries. Its monumental floor plan was only revealed after excavations this century. There is little in the way of architectural detail remaining at the site apart from some frater arches. However, architectural historians have suggested that this early church might well have inspired the famous Gothic churches of Tintern, Fountains and Rievaulx abbeys.

The Abbey remains are open during daylight hours and are said to have provided the inspiration for Sir Walter Scott's romantic novel, *Waverley*, published in 1814 during his stay at the nearby Waverley Abbey House, whose imposing structure was built with stone taken from the abbey in 1723.

Waverley Abbey

TILFORD

3 miles E of Farnham off the B3001

Rural Life Centre

A lovely two mile riverside walk from Waverley Abbey leads to Tilford, an attractive village that stands at the confluence of the two branches of the River Wey. The monks of Waverley are believed to have been responsible for rebuilding Tilford's two medieval bridges following the devastating floods of 1233, during which the abbey itself had to be evacuated. At the heart of Tilford stands a triangular village green, which features a 900-year-old oak tree with a 25 foot girth that is known as the King's or Novel's Oak; a pleasant early 18th-century inn can be found nearby. Tilford's parish church of All Saints hosts a regular spring festival of early church music. In Reeds Road to the southwest of Tilford is the **Rural Life Centre** (see panel on page 350). The centre, a great place for all the family to visit, is a museum of past village life from 1750 to 1960, set in 10 acres of gardens and woodland and housed in purpose-built and reconstructed buildings, including a chapel, village hall and cricket pavilion. Among the crafts featured is wheelwrighting, of which the centre's collection is probably the finest in the country.

RUNFOLD

2 miles E of Farnham on the A31

Runfold marks the beginning of the large tracts of woodland that dominate much of the landscape between Farnham and Guildford. A well-marked turning off the A31 indicates the small road

Rural Life Centre

Old Kiln Museum, Reeds Road, Tilford,
Farnham, Surrey GU10 2DL
Tel: 01252 795571 Fax: 01252 795571
e-mail: info@rural-life.org.uk
website: www.rural-life.org.uk

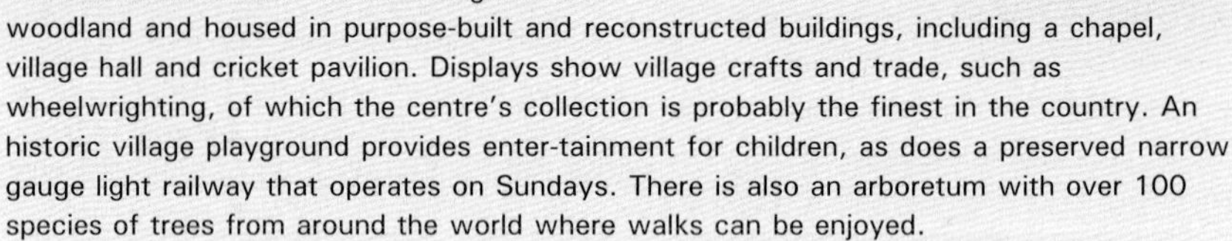

The Rural Life Centre is a museum of past village life covering the years from 1750 to 1960. It is set in over 10 acres of garden and woodland and housed in purpose-built and reconstructed buildings, including a chapel, village hall and cricket pavilion. Displays show village crafts and trade, such as wheelwrighting, of which the centre's collection is probably the finest in the country. An historic village playground provides enter-tainment for children, as does a preserved narrow gauge light railway that operates on Sundays. There is also an arboretum with over 100 species of trees from around the world where walks can be enjoyed.

The centre is open 11am-5pm, Wednesday to Sunday and Bank Holidays from March until October and during winter months it is open 11am-4pm, Wednesday and Sunday only. Picnic areas can be found around the site and there is also a cafe and a gift shop.

that winds south into the village. Runfold, like its immediate - and even smaller - neighbour Seale, was essentially a mixed farming community in the medieval period, and this way of life is displayed in Manor Farm, which lies between the two villages.

TONGHAM

2 miles E of Farnham on the A31

Tongham lies at an important junction where Surrey meets Hampshire. Aldershot lies just west across the border, which is marked by the A331. With the busy A31 linking Farnham and Guildford lying just to the south, Tongham is hard pressed to retain any sense of the country. That it manages to do so is to the credit of the planners, who have ensured that many of its timber-framed cottages are still seen to good effect. Look out for the distinctive curved braces (the timbers linking walls and roof) on some of these cottages. Tongham boasts its own brewery, called the Hogs Back Brewery, which can be seen after the hill to the east of the town and the stretch of the A30 that continues to Guildford. It is famous for its TEA (or Traditional English Ale) and is based in an 18th-century barn where they brew the beer in the traditional way.

HOG'S BACK

4 miles E of Farnham on the A31

The Hog's Back is the name given to the ridge that dominates the landscape between the level ground surrounding Guildford (looking north) and the wooded, more undulating terrain looking south towards Hindhead. Motorists refer to this stretch of the A31 as the Hog's Back, and the four-mile stretch between Tongham and Compton is well served with picnic stops and the occasional lay-by from where you can admire the views.

The hamlet of Wanborough on the northern side of the A31 contains one of the smallest churches in Surrey. Built by the monks of Waverley Abbey, it stands in the shadow of a massive monastic tithe barn.

The old manor house was constructed between the 15th and 17th centuries on the site of a pre-Norman manor and was used during World War II to train secret agents.

PUTTENHAM

5 miles E of Farnham off the A31

The Hog's Back village of Puttenham lies stretched out along the route of the old Pilgrims' Way. An attractive mixture of building styles, the village contains a restored part Norman church, several fine 15th and 16th-century cottages, an 18th-century farm with a number of period outbuildings and oast houses, and an impressive Palladian mansion, Puttenham Priory, which was completed in 1762.

The mixture of building styles arose because of Puttenham's location, where chalk gives way to sandstone. Cottages use one or other, or both these materials, and the effect is enlivened with brickwork, usually dating from the 18th century.

ELSTEAD

5 miles E of Farnham on the B3001

The attractive village of Elstead lies surrounded by farmland and crossed by the River Wey. In fact it is this crossing that makes Elstead noteworthy. Its rough stonework bridge dates from the medieval period, crossing the river in a series of five graceful arches. It has a brick parapet, making the overall effect one of solidity and strength. Unfortunately, the medieval effect is lessened somewhat by the modern bridge that runs parallel to it on the north side. Nevertheless, the bridge marks a delightful entrance to the village itself.

On the lane leading from the old bridge to the village green is the Old Farm House, a large timber-framed building that was completed in the 16th century. The green itself is compact and triangular and a small cul-de-sac leads from it to the 14th century Church of St James, which was overly restored in the 19th century.

Just west of the centre is Elstead Mill, an 18th century water mill. It stands four storeys high, its brick structure topped with a Palladian cupola. Six classical columns support a small lead dome at the very top. It is now a restaurant, and much of the machinery, including a working water wheel, is displayed within.

PEPER HAROW

6 miles E of Farnham off the A3

Church of St Nicholas Peper Harrow House

Peper Harrow Farm

Peper Harow is a small village lying just west of the A3 in completely rural surroundings. It has a number of interesting cottages reinforcing its rustic charm, as well as one of the best collections of Surrey farm buildings at **Peper Harow Farm** just outside the centre of the village. Of particular interest is the large granary, built around 1600. It stands - resting on its 25 wooden pillars - at the centre of a quadrangle at the heart of the farm.

The **Church of St Nicholas**, in the centre of the village, was built in Norman times but was massively restored in the 19th century. The restoration, however, was conducted by A W N Pugin, and there is great care evident throughout. St Nicholas represents something of a find for students of architecture since it appears to be one of the few churches where Pugin sought to create a Neo-Norman effect, rather than the higher-flown Gothic style. The ancient yew tree in the churchyard is probably more than 600 years old.

Frensham Common

Distance: *5.8 miles (9.3 kilometres)*
Typical time: *180 mins*
Height gain: *45 metres*
Map: *Explorer 145*
Walk: *www.walkingworld.com ID:1059*
Contributor: *Tony Brotherton*

ACCESS INFORMATION:

Car parking is at Frensham Great Pond car park. Access is from lane to west of pond: signs from A287 for Frensham Great Pond are unobtrusive, but signs for Frensham Pond Hotel are rather less so. Car park is extensive in its woodland setting and it may be possible to park facing the pond.

ADDITIONAL INFORMATION:

Frensham Great and Little Ponds were created some 800 years ago as fish ponds. The surrounding lowland heath supports rare creatures such as the Dartford warbler, sand lizard and silver-studded blue butterfly. The entire area of Frensham Common is an SSSI.

DESCRIPTION:

This is a truly satisfying walk of great variety, embracing water features, rolling green hills and National Trust heathland, with glorious views.

FEATURES:

Hills or fells, river, lake/loch, pub, toilets, National Trust/NTS, wildlife, birds, flowers, great views, butterflies, food shop.

WALK DIRECTIONS:

1 | From car park walk, downhill to bottom right-hand corner to locate sandy waterside path. Follow path, with Frensham Great Pond on left, to reach lane. Lane bends left. At stream and sign 'Bacon Lane', cross to bridleway.

2 | Follow bridleway through woods, with first lake, then River Wey to left. At fork, either take lower, or keep to higher path - they merge further on. Proceed as far as arched bridge.

3 | Cross river and continue along path to stile at minor road. Turn right along road as far as pair of cottages, then take bridleway on left and follow path winding gently uphill. Path eventually joins lane at Orchard End, then continues as bridleway, still rising, to reach The Blue Bell pub.

4 | Continue walk to road at Batts Corner. Turn right, then right again along gravel drive at 'Highlands' sign, as far as footpath signed to right over stile.

5 | Cross couple of paddocks before entering woods via stile in corner. Proceed along woodland path with fields to right, emerging onto open ridge with fine views on either side of wooded Surrey Hills.

6 | Follow line of trees to re-enter woods, now on descending path. At stile, enter field and go left to near corner and further stile at entrance to woods.

7 | Enter woods once more, to exit by stile into field. Keep to right-hand side round field until, just past house, crossing stile and passing through wooden latch-gate onto drive and lane, to reach crossroads.

8 | Cross here and go ahead. Road becomes track, then footpath leading to bridge over stream. Now climb bank and bear half-right into field to reach three-way signpost. Go ahead on path into next field, with barbed-wire fence on left; t ninth and last stile, descend through wooded strip to main A287 road at The Mariners pub.

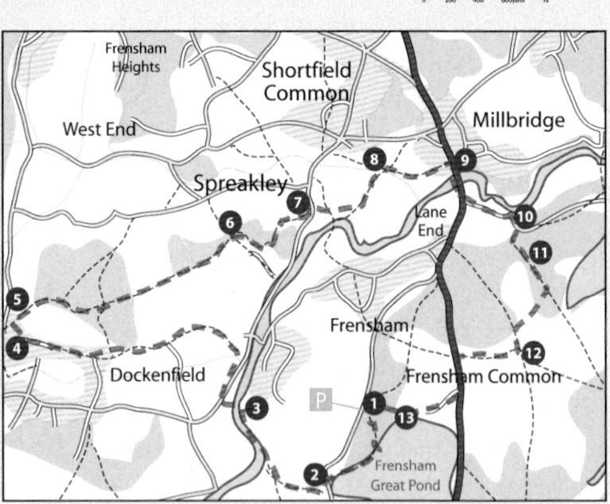

9 | Resume walk by crossing road and going downhill to bridge over river. Continue along to Priory Lane. Walk down lane until it bends sharp left; here turn right into sandy car park leading onto Frensham Common.

10 | At top of small rise, turn right to follow orange arrows denoting Two Ponds Way Trail.

11 | For climactic finish of this walk, follow path across common with Frensham Little Pond coming into view on left. With Great Pond now visible to right, continue along main or parallel subsidiary path through heather and gorse until, at highest point of common, you reach sign for 'Path 43' on right.

12 | Descend on 'Path 43', then go left along 'Path 1', which runs alongside main road. Cross with care to reach path across common leading to refreshments and information room by Frensham Great Pond.

13 | Car park is now close by.

The other big attraction in the village is **Peper Harow House**, a Grade I listed building dating from 1768 and now converted into flats. It is a cube-shaped manor house, the bottom two storeys soberly classical. An extra floor was added in 1913 along with some Baroque ornamentation that clashes with the style of the original building. The outbuildings are almost as impressive as the house itself, in particular the three-sided stables. The park surrounding the house was designed by Capability Brown in 1763.

FRENSHAM

3 miles S of Farnham off the A28

St Mary's Church was moved in the 13th century from its previous site on low ground beside the River Wey. The chancel walls were part of the original building. The tower is 14th-century, with massive diagonal buttresses, but the whole church was subject to a major restoration in 1868.

The village of Millbridge lies just to the north of Frensham, and like Frensham it is set in heaths with occasional farmland dotted around it. The A287 to the south of the village runs between Frensham's Great and Little Ponds, two sizeable National Trust-owned lakes which provide good bird-watching and recreational facilities. These are now contained within a 1,000-acre country park that incorporates four prehistoric bowl barrows and the Devil's Jumps, three irregularly shaped hills whose origin, like many other unusual natural features, is attributed to Satan.

Little Pond, Frensham

THURSLEY

6 miles SE of Farnham off the A3

St Michael's Church

Thursley is an exceptional village, which takes its name from the Viking god Thor and the Saxon word for field, or lea. The settlement was once an important centre of the Wealden iron industry and a number of disused hammer ponds can still be seen to the east. These artificial lakes

THE BLUE BELL INN

Batts Corner, Boundary Road, Dockenfield,
nr Farnham, Surrey GU10 4EX
Tel: 01252 792801
e-mail: alexneil@hotmail.co.uk
website: www.bluebellpub.com

The Blue Bell is a family-run country pub located off the A325 at Batts Corner, Dockenfield, a few miles south of Farnham. It stands in two attractive acres that include a large beer garden and a terrific children's play area made of wood. The Neil family aim to produce the best home-made food in the area with service to match and a lovely relaxed atmosphere. The pub is not tied to any brewery or company, so it can offer a unique menu and dining experience that breweries and chains cannot match.

Alex Neil has more than 35 years experience in the trade, having been head chef in some of London's top hotels. He was apprenticed in France and Switzerland and started his main career in London's Park Lane Hilton Hotel. Quality and value for money are paramount, and their aim is more than fulfilled with an exceptional choice of food to cater for all tastes and appetites.

Everything is made on the premises, with no short cuts: sauces come from their own stock, reduced the proper way, with no flour and definitely not a packet or cube to be seen. Sandwiches made with a variety of breads provide tasty, satisfying quick meals, with interesting fillings like smoked bacon and field mushrooms or sirloin steak on ciabatta with chunky chips and a salad garnish. The all-day blackboard menu proposes pub favourites such as steak & mushroom pie, sausages with fried onions and mash, the Blue bell burger and battered cod with chips, mushy peas and tartare sauce, along with Cajun chicken Caesar salad or seared salmon with a saffron cream sauce. Friday brings an additional fish menu with the likes of tuna niçoise salad or sea bass with sun-dried tomato risotto and a lemon cream sauce. The children's menu, with small portions of 'grown-ups' dishes, rightly treats children as budding gourmets, and everyone should leave room for a scrumptious dessert – perhaps rich chocolate sponge or lemon tart. Meals can be enjoyed in the main restaurant, the bar, the snug or, when the sun shines, at picnic benches out in the garden.

The fine food is complemented by an excellent selection of fine wines, and local real ales include Tongham Tea and their own Blue Bell Bitter. Alex's son, also called Alex, does a great job front of house, with a warm welcome for all who come to this exceptional pub.

ART & SOLD, MISCELLANEA, THE SCULPTURE PARK, BROKENBOG AND ART & INVESTMENT

Crossways, Churt, nr Farnham, Surrey GU10 2JA
Tel: 01428 714014 Mob: 07831 500506
Fax: 01428 712946
e-mail: eddiepowell@miscellanea.co.uk
website: www.artandsold.co.uk

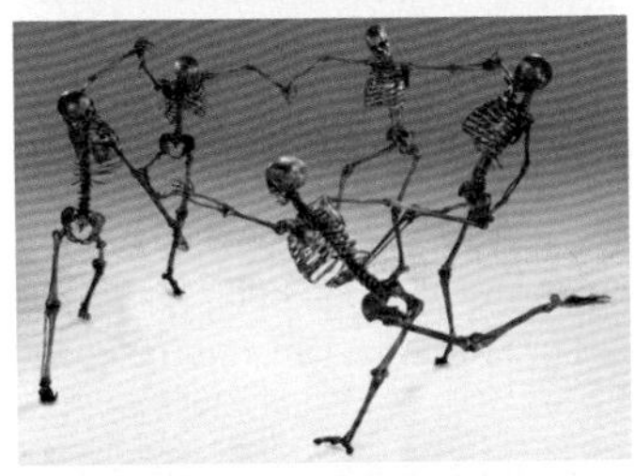

Art & Sold is the umbrella name for a variety of enterprises founded by Eddie Powell. Miscellanea on the A287 north of Hindhead offers a unique one-stop shopping experience for all interior and exterior design and decoration requirements. The well-laid out space is filled with items large and small for the house and home or for a very special gift. Art & Sold incorporates **Miscellanea**, specialising in the design of bespoke bathrooms, bedrooms and kitchens. The choice of bathrooms is perhaps the largest in the world, with every conceivable option from 14th century medieval style to 21st century high tech and everything in between; the choice includes rare and discontinued colours that are unavailable elsewhere.

Apart from the furniture, there's a bewildering choice on display, including glassware, mirrors, paintings, prints and photographs, sculpture, metalwork, lighting, textiles, fabrics, ceramics, rugs, tiles, murals and quirky items such as twirly glass vases, pictures on glass or cloth, strange headdresses and Spitting Image puppets. The thousands of items available for delivery or collection from the warehouse share Eddie's traditional values of quality, reliability and service for today's lifestyle.

The businesses are open from 8.30 to 5 Monday to Friday, 9.30 to 4 Saturday. **Art for Investment** proposes a variety of ways to invest through discretionary purchases of paintings, prints, photographs and sculptures. **Brokenbog** is a vast warehouse where they endeavor to supply any colour and style ever made in bathware.

THE SCULPTURE PARK

Tel: 01428 605453 Fax: 01428 609871
e-mail: eddiepowell@thesculpturepark.co.uk
websites: www.thesculpturepark.com; www.miscellanea.co.uk; www.brokenbog.com; www.artandinvestment.com

Close to the warehouse, in Jumps Road, Eddie has one of the chief visitor attractions in the area. The **Sculpture Park** is considered the most atmospheric sculpture park in Britain, with 150 renowned sculptors, living or dead, responsible for over 200 sculptures for sale within ten acres of arboretum and wildlife-inhabited water gardens. From classical to conceptual, they cater for all budgets, from private or commercial ornamental to serious investment. The Park is open from 10 to 5 Monday to Sunday and on Bank Holiday Mondays.

provided power to drive the mechanical hammers and bellows in the once-bustling iron forges. Today, the village is a tranquil place arranged around a green containing an acacia tree that was planted as a memorial to William Cobbett, the Georgian traveller and writer who is best remembered for his book describing riding tours of England, *Rural Rides*, which was published in 1830. Thursley is also the birthplace of the celebrated architect Sir Edwin Lutyens who, at the age of only 19, converted a row of local cottages into a single dwelling, now known locally as the Corner.

Thursley's two principal thoroughfares, the Lane and the Street, contain a wide variety of noteworthy domestic buildings. The latter leads to **St Michael's Church**, a part Saxon structure that was heavily restored by the Victorians. The spire and belfry are 15th-century and are supported by massive timber posts with tie-beams and arched braces, a good example of late-medieval engineering.

The churchyard contains the grave of a sailor who was murdered on Hindhead Heath in 1786 by three men he had gone to help. Although the villagers never discovered the victim's name, they gave him a full burial and erected an inscribed stone over his grave.

Two interesting old buildings stand near the church, the half-timbered and tile-hung Old Parsonage and the part timber-framed Hill Farm, both of which date from the 16th century.

THE DEVIL'S PUNCHBOWL

7 miles S of Farnham off the A3

The Devil's Punchbowl, probably Surrey's best-known natural feature, is a steep-sided natural sandstone amphitheatre through which the busy A3 Guildford to Petersfield road passes four miles to the southeast of Frensham Great Pond. It was formed by springs cutting down into the soft rock. As usual, Lucifer's name is invoked in the place name, but the origins might have more to do with real events than with superstition. The deep valley provided excellent cover for thieves and highwaymen, and even in coaching days passengers would look on the natural wonder with a mixture of awe and apprehension. On one of the paths is a memorial to the brothers of W A Robertson, both killed in the World War I. The Robertson family gave the Devil's Punchbowl to the National Trust to commemorate the men's sacrifice.

HINDHEAD

7 miles S of Farnham on the A28

Hindhead stands near the top of a ridge and, at 850 feet above sea level, is the highest village in Surrey. Perhaps surprisingly, it has only been in existence since the late 19th century. Before that it was known primarily as a site for highwaymen planning their next heist while taking cover in the steep wooded countryside.

The town grew up along the Portsmouth Road (now the A3) and the buildings date mainly from a concentrated period in the 1890s. Shops were built along the Portsmouth Road, and a number of comfortable residences were dotted through the surrounding woodlands. Most of these houses still enjoy leafy settings, even if today the appearance is somewhat tamer. The late-1890s construction date means that these residences reflect the influence of the Arts and Crafts movement. Most of them derive from the designs of Norman Shaw, the movement's great proponent. One of the best examples of this style is Thirlestane on the Farnham Road. Making the most of the south-facing situation, as well as the height, this V-shaped house faces southwest so that most of it acts as a suntrap. A deliberately rough exterior, combined with the hanging tiles, typify the attention to quality materials, while the deliberately asymmetrical nature of the two wings suggests the freedom of spirit associated with that period.

HINDHEAD COMMON

7 miles SE of Farnham off the A3

Hindhead Common

Lying just to the east of Hindhead itself is **Hindhead Common**, comprising a largely untamed collection of wild heathlands, pinewoods and steep valleys. The National Trust owns 1,400 acres of Hindhead Common and maintains a series of trails and paths that takes visitors through evocatively named sites such as Polecat Copse, Golden Valley, Hurt Hill and Stoatley Green. On the summit of Gibbet Hill is a granite monument marking the spot where the gibbet stood. The glorious views across both the North and South Downs were the last earthly memories of the thieves and murderers who were executed here.

Guildford and the South

Guildford, with its prominent setting on a hill visible from the A3, is an obvious base for travellers interested in exploring the southwestern section of Surrey that extends down to, and then traces, the West Sussex border. Like the area around Farnham, this area contains some of Surrey's most unspoilt countryside. Rough, hilly, thickly wooded in places, the landscape comes as close as anywhere in the county to fitting the descriptive term 'wild'.

The interaction between landscape and human society provides the background for some of the most interesting sights covered in the following pages. From time-worn remnants of prehistoric hill forts to medieval bridges along the Wey Valley, and even including some of the modern architecture to be found among Guildford's hilly streets, the imprint of necessity-driven design is everywhere. Is it any wonder that Sir Edwin Lutyens cut his teeth, architecturally speaking, with his designs for houses occupying hilly sites or tucked in narrow valleys?

The settlements become decidedly smaller and more scattered as the Sussex border is neared. It is in these villages, many no more than hamlets, that visitors can appreciate just how even the earliest settlers scraped a living, and how later inhabitants developed crafts that exploited the rich natural surroundings.

Guildford

Cathedral Castle Museum

River Wey Navigations

The route into Guildford from the northwest passes close to **Guildford Cathedral**, one of only two new Anglican cathedrals to have been built in this country since the Reformation (the other is Liverpool). This impressive redbrick building stands on top of Stag Hill, a prominent local landmark that enjoys panoramic views over the surrounding landscape. The building was designed by Sir Edward Maufe with a superb high-arched interior and begun in 1936. However, work was halted during World War II, and members of the local diocese had to wait until 1961 for the new cathedral to be finally consecrated. Guided tours and restaurant facilities are available all year round. In 1968, the University of Surrey relocated from London to a site on

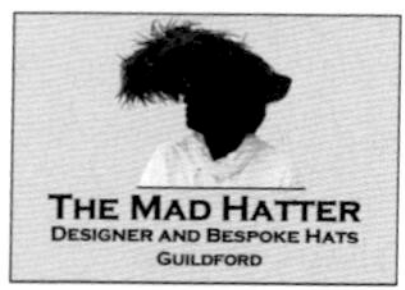

THE MAD HATTER

12 Castle Street, Guildford,
Surrey GU1 3UW
Tel: 01483 566845
e-mail: jonescarolien@hotmail.com
website: www.themadhattermillinery.com

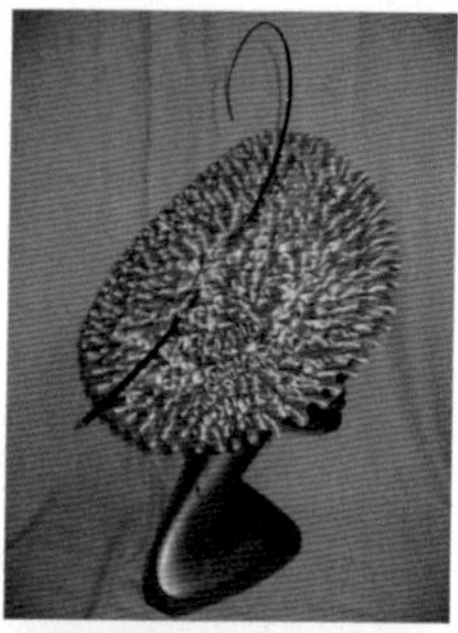

The Mad Hatter is a rare and wonderful treasure haven offering a dizzying collection of hats, cocktail pieces and fascinators for every imaginable occasion. Featuring a wide range of international designers, the hats come in an amazing array of colours. Alternatively, milliner Carolien Jones can design and create a truly unique hat especially for you or re-trim hats to perfectly compliment your outfit. Whatever the event, be it a wedding, a day's racing at Ascot or Henley Royal Regatta, you are sure to find the perfect hat here.

Other luxurious accessories and finishing touches are also available at the Mad Hatter. A range of pashminas and stunning Italian double skin umbrellas anticipate the unpredictable elements of a British summer, whilst the beautiful straw and linen sun hats will keep you cool should the sun decide to make an appearance. The winter months are also taken care of with a range of fashionable winter and rain hats. Even gentlemen will be pleased to find a selection of trilby and panama hats. The Mad Hatter also stocks a range of non-irritant and super soft sun-block hats to protect delicate skin through hair loss in a variety of fashionable styles.

THE DRESS BOUTIQUE

10 Castle Street, Guildford,
Surrey GU1 3UW
Tel: 01483 306103
e-mail: info@thedressboutique.co.uk
website: www.thedressboutique.co.uk

Dress, a delightful independently owned boutique, first opened its doors on Castle Street in November last year. The shop aims to provide an alternative to the host of chain stores that now dominate Guildford by offering individual yet highly wearable collections from a carefully chosen range of designers. To do this they have brought together a stunning variety of talent from the world of women's fashion. Affordable yet unusual day wear from the likes of Legatte, Splendid and Nanette Lepore combines comfort with fashion and style.

Exciting and innovative statement pieces have been selected from labels such as Marithe Francois Girbaud, Heymann and Ischiko. Timeless and sophisticated, their designs are perfect for the ageless woman who wants clothing that will make a statement for more than one season.

And a shop called Dress wouldn't be complete without an outstanding evening wear range. Dresses by Dina Bar-el are often seen gracing the red carpet and are the epitome of chic femininity. Service is friendly and helpful styling advice is always available from experienced staff. The shop is open six days a week and you are assured of a warm welcome.

a hillside to the northwest of the cathedral. Pleasant and leafy, the campus contains a number of striking buildings including the university library and art gallery.

From the university, it is only a mile to the heart of Guildford, the ancient county town of Surrey. Guildford has been the capital of the region since pre-Norman times, and in the 10th century it even had its own mint. Henry II built a **Castle** here on high ground in the 12th century, which later became the county jail. Today, the castle remains and the ruined keep provide a fascinating place from which to view the surrounding area. Those visiting the town for the first time should make straight for the old High Street, a wonderful cobbled thoroughfare of Georgian and older buildings that rises steeply from the River Wey. Perhaps the most noteworthy of these is the Guildhall, a Tudor structure with an elaborately decorated 17th-century frontage, which incorporates a belltower, balcony and distinctive gilded clock.

Abbot's Hospital, a little further along, is an imposing turreted almshouse, which was built in 1619 by the Guildford-born Archbishop of Canterbury, George Abbot; at the top of the High Street, the Royal Grammar School dates from the early 1500s and was subsequently endowed by Edward VI.

A number of interesting streets and alleyways run off Guildford High Street, including Quarry Street with its medieval St Mary's Church and old Castle Arch. The latter houses the **Guildford Museum**, an informative centre for local history and archaeology, which also contains an exhibition devoted to Lewis Carroll, the creator of *Alice In Wonderland* who died in the town in 1898. He is buried in Mount Cemetery. A charming

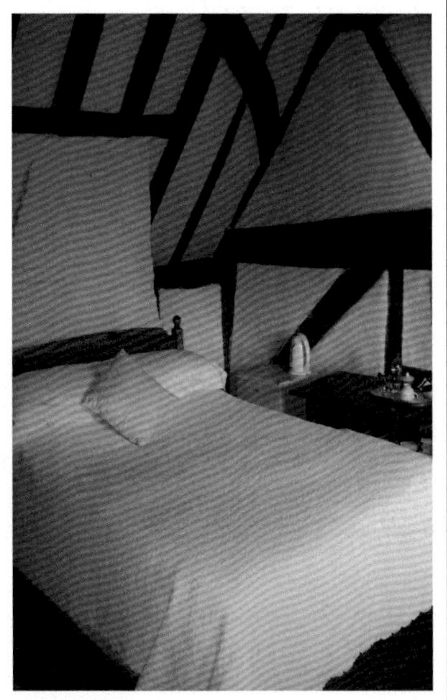

bronze memorial to Lewis Carroll (real name Charles Lutwidge Dodgson), which is composed of a life-sized Alice chasing the White Rabbit into his hole, can be found on the far bank of the River Wey, midway between the two footbridges. The well-known Yvonne Arnaud Theatre stands in a delightful riverside setting at the foot of the castle mound on the town side of the river. As well as offering top-quality productions, the theatre has an excellent bar, coffee lounge and restaurant, which remains open throughout the day. On Wharf Road, the Visitor Centre at Dapdune Wharf is the centrepiece of one of the National Trust's most unusual properties, the **River Wey Navigations**. Exhibits and displays tell the story of Surrey's secret waterway, one of the first British rivers to be made navigable. It was opened for navigation in 1653, connecting London to Guildford, and was extended to Godalming in 1764. The 20-mile stretch of navigations and towpaths between Godalming and the Thames at Weybridge is popular with walkers, cyclists and boaters. Visitors can see where the great Wey barges were built, and climb aboard one of the last survivors, *Reliance*. See also under Shalford.

Around Guildford

CLANDON PARK

5 miles E of Guildford on the A247

Clandon Park

Set in the farming countryside east of Guildford and south of Woking is the National Trust-owned **Clandon Park**. This magnificent country mansion was designed in the 1730s by Giacomo Leoni, a Venetian architect, who combined Palladian, Baroque and European styles to create one of the grandest 18th-century houses in England. The interior is renowned for its magnificent two-storey marble hall, sumptuous decoration and fine Italian plasterwork depicting scenes from mythology. The Gubbay collection of furniture and porcelain is also housed here, along with the Ivo Forde collection of humorous Meissen figures. The surrounding parkland was landscaped by Capability Brown in characteristic style, and includes a parterre, grotto and brightly painted New Zealand Maori house.

Clandon Park House

GOMSHALL

5 miles E of Guildford on the A25

This once industrialised community has a Victorian heart and was an important centre of the tanning and leather-working industries. The old packhorse bridge over the River

THE COMPASSES INN

Station Road, Gomshall, nr Guildford,
Surrey GU5 9LA
Tel: 01483 202506
website: www.thecompasses.co.uk

'Purveyors of Fine Food, Ale and .... Music'

For the locals and a growing band of regulars from farther afield, all roads point to **The Compasses Inn**, a lovely pub nestling under the North Downs in fine walking country. Landlady Fiona Morley has a warm, genuine welcome for all who pass through the door, whether it's for a drink, a snack or a leisurely evening meal. Food is served all day from 12 to 9 (12 to 6 on Sundays and Bank Holidays) in the bar or in the restaurant, which can be reached through the bar or direct from the pub's roadside entrance. The all-day choice includes sandwiches, jacket potatoes, ploughman's platters and 'meals for little people' – cod goujons, honey roast ham and super steak and chicken pies served in smaller portions for smaller appetites. Bigger portions of those super pies, along with burgers. Steaks and fish specials, make up the locally sourced homecooked traditional pub menu. To accompany the food or to enjoy on their own are fine wines and real ales, including three brews from the Surrey Hills Brewery in Shere, near Guildford. Friday night is music night, with live performances from top local groups.

Tillingbourne dates from the 1500s, and the manor house at the southern end of the village from the early 1700s.

SHERE

6 miles E of Guildford off the A25

Church of St James · Museum

Shere is one of the loveliest, and consequently most visited, villages in Surrey. Thankfully now bypassed by the A25, it lies at the foot of the North Downs in the river valley that is particularly known for the growing of watercress, a plant that requires a constantly flowing supply of fresh water. The village **Church of St James** dates from the 12th century and was tastefully restored in the 1950s. Among its many noteworthy features are the 13th-century Purbeck marble font, the St Nicholas Chapel, and an unusual hermit's cell built in the 14th century for a local woman who asked to be confined there for life.

The churchyard is entered through an impressive lych gate designed by Lutyens, and close by stands the White Horse Inn, one of the many fine 16th and 17th-century buildings to be found in the village. The **Shere Museum** in the Malt House contains an interesting collection of local artefacts, and the Old Farm behind the church is an open farm, which, at weekends, offers hands-on demonstrations of traditional farming techniques.

ALBURY

4 miles E of Guildford on the A28

Albury Park

Albury dates largely from the last century and was constructed in fanciful neo-Gothic style as an estate village for nearby **Albury**

Park. This large country mansion was built on the site of a Tudor manor house in the early 18th century and was much altered by Pugin in the 1840s. (Pugin also designed the south transept chapel in the Church of St Peter and St Paul, which stands on the estate. It was a mortuary chapel for Henry Drummond, the estate's owner.) The most eccentric feature of the house is its collection of chimneys, 63 of them built for only 60 rooms in an amazing variety of shapes and sizes. Although the mansion has now been converted into flats, the estate gardens are open to visitors and are well worth a look. They were laid out by the diarist John Evelyn at the turn of the 18th century, and feature a series of terraced orchards that rise above the house to the north. A number of smaller communities nestle around Albury.

CHILWORTH

3 miles E of Guildford on the A28

Chilworth Manor

Chilworth is a former munitions and paper-making centre whose church, St Martha on the Hill, had to be rebuilt in 1850 following an explosion in the nearby gunpowder works. The result is a genuine success and shows great flair and sensitivity. There was no attempt made to copy the original exactly, but the resulting reconstruction remains true to the Norman spirit of the destroyed church. On the hill to the south of the church are five circular banks, each about 100 feet in diameter, which have been identified as early Bronze Age henge monuments.

Chilworth Manor was built in the 1600s on the site of a pre-Norman monastic house. The exterior is a medley of styles, but its 17th-century gardens are complete, running up the side of the hill in terraces.

SHALFORD

3 miles S of Guildford on the A281

Water Mill Great Tangley

Wey & Arun Junction Canal

The residential community of Shalford contains a fascinating **Water Mill** that operated from the early 1700s right up to World War I. Once powered by the waters of the Tillingbourne stream, this exceptional tile-hung, four-floored structure retains most of its original machinery. During the 1930s, it was bought and restored by Ferguson's Gang, a secretive group of conservationists who hid their identities behind eccentric *noms de plume* and who eventually donated the water mill to the National Trust.

Shalford stands near the northern entrance to the **Wey and Arun Junction Canal**, an ambitious inland waterway constructed in 1816 to connect the Thames with the English Channel. Conceived during the Napoleonic wars as a way of avoiding attacks on coastal shipping, unfortunately it opened too late to fulfil its function and was soon superseded by the railways. A towpath providing some delightful walks runs along almost two-thirds of the canal's 36-mile length, a significant proportion of which has now been fully restored by enthusiastic teams of volunteers.

About a mile south of Shalford is **Great Tangley**, one of the finest 16th-century half-timbered houses in Surrey. The exterior is made up of roughly square panels each with four curved diagonal braces. This combination creates a star shape for each panel, which is repeated across the sides of the house.

BLACKHEATH

4 miles SE of Guildford off the A248

Set in the hills above Albury, this tidy Victorian hamlet gives the visitor a sense of remoteness despite being within easy striking distance of Guildford. Blackheath has some fine late-Victorian buildings. One of the most interesting is Greyfriars, a Franciscan monastery built in neo-Gothic style in 1895. The church and dormitories of this stone-built structure are contained under one roof. Another Victorian curiosity is the somewhat austere timbered residence, the Hallams.

WONERSH

4 miles SE of Guildford off the A248

Chinthurst Hill

Wonersh is a former weaving centre with a fine 16th-century half-timbered inn, the Grantley Arms, located along the high street, which presents a cheerful and harmonious appearance with its medley of brick, stone, tile-hanging and half-timbered buildings. An imposing Lutyens house, **Chinthurst Hill**, is just a few minutes' walk northwest of the heart of the village. Lutyens used the local Bargate stone to create a Tudor effect, the work being completed in 1895, before he had developed his own distinctive style. The house occupies a lovely hillside site and the terraced garden was planted by Gertrude Jekyll.

BRAMLEY

3 miles SE of Guildford off the A248

Millmead

Despite being largely Victorian, Bramley has some attractive Georgian and Regency residential buildings. These appear somewhat haphazardly through the long winding street that forms the nearest thing to a core of the village. There are two Lutyens houses in Bramley. The small, L-shaped **Millmead**, a National Trust property, is located south of Gosden Green. It was built for the gardener

MEMORIES ANTIQUES

High Street, Bramley, nr Guildford, Surrey GU5 0HB
Tel: 01483 892205 Mob: 07790 121037
website. www.memoriesantiques-andcurtains.co.uk

Wendy Camfield has been operating in Memories Antiques since 1985 and has built up a large and loyal clientele. Her commitment is to provide ideas and inspiration for people to add the finishing touches that make a house a home.

Memories specialises in period brown and painted shabby chic furniture for any room setting plus silver, jewellery and lighting. But there's much more besides with an ever-changing stock of designer secondhand curtains (Colefax and Fowler, Nina Campbell etc) and seasonal garden furniture and accessories. Wendy also offers a free search and find service so if customers have seen something they like - perhaps in a magazine - she will do her best to trace it. The National Trust have two attractions nearby, Winkworth Arboretum and Shalford Mill, which are both one and a half miles from Bramley and many people combine these with a trip to Memories Antiques for a special gift or personal treat. The shop is open from 10 - 5 Tuesday to Saturday and also by appointment on Sunday or Monday. Bramley is located on the A281, three miles south of Guildford.

KATHERINE LETTS INTERIORS

103 High Street, Godalming, Surrey GU7 1AQ
Tel: 01483 860106
Fax: 01483 428484

Since the mid-1980s, **Katherine Letts Interiors** has established itself as one of the leading outlets for interiors and homeware. Owner Kate Christopherson who has many years' experience in the design industry runs the shop with the valued assistance of her mother Sue and sister Diana. Their presence allows Kate to visit clients in their homes with advice on all aspects of soft furnishings, helping them to add the finishing touches that make a house a home.

The shop is stocked with a wide variety of wallpaper, curtain and upholstery fabric books (Colefax and Fowler, Jane Churchill, Osborne & Little, Zoffany, Romo) offering a bespoke curtain, blind, upholstery and soft furnishings service. Also in stock at this excellent shop are accessories for the home, including china and decorative gifts (Emma Bridgewater, East of India, Bombay Duck).

Gertrude Jekyll between 1904 and 1907 and traces of her original garden still survive. About half a mile north is Little Tangley, a late 19th-century house to which Lutyens added a porch and staircase hall in 1899. The Stables, which is now a private house called Edgton, was one of the architect's first works.

Godalming

Munstead Wood Charterhouse
Museum Winkworth Arboretum

The old market town of Godalming was once an important staging post between London and Portsmouth and a number of elegant 17th and 18th-century shops and coaching inns can still be found in the High Street. A market was established here in 1300 and the town later became a centre for the local wool and textile industries. Perhaps the most interesting building in the old centre is the former town hall, affectionately known as The Pepperpot, which was built at the western end of the High Street in 1814. This unusual arcaded building once contained an interesting museum of local history, but the **Museum** is now opposite the Pepperpot at the fascinating Wealden House, parts of which date from the 15th and 16th centuries, but which also has Victorian and Georgian additions. The museum has displays on geology and archaeology as well as local history, including a display detailing Godalming's claim to fame as the first town to have a public electricity supply. Two of Godalming's most renowned former residents – Gertrude Jekyll, the gardener, and Sir Edwin Lutyens, the architect – are celebrated in a gallery exhibition and there is a Jekyll-style garden. The timber-

Guildford to Godalming

Distance: *5.0 miles (8.0 kilometres)*
Typical time: *180 mins*
Height gain: *50 metres*
Map: *Explorer 145*
Walk: *www.walkingworld.com ID:31*
Contributor: *Daisy Hayden*

ACCESS INFORMATION:

Train from Waterloo to Guildford 40 mins. Return from Godalming to Waterloo 50 mins. 2 or 3 trains per hour.

DESCRIPTION:

This is a beautiful, relaxing and easy walk along the River Wey, including the Godalming navigations. The open valley is National Trust Land, and the scenery is varied and unspoilt. There are plenty of pubs and tea shops for refreshments in Guildford and Godalming, and toilets two thirds of the way along the walk at Farncombe Boatyard. (There is also a tea shop here, unfortunately it is usually closed.) Wear boots or wellies as the path is muddy.

FEATURES:

Toilets, National Trust/NTS, birds.

WALK DIRECTIONS:

1 | Turn right out of Guildford Railway station (you only need to cross over the line if arriving at Guildford on the train towards London). Walk 200 yards down Park Street, crossing Farnham Road to arrive at the church seen in the distance.

2 | Turn left into High Street and pass in front of the Church, to reach a pub, The White Horse, on your right. Turn right down steps in front of the pub (the steps are just before this bridge). Go through the beer garden, and take the riverbank path to the right (behind pub sign and evergreen tree). Continue along the riverbank for 100 yards until you reach a white bridge. Cross this bridge towards Millmead Lock

3 | Do not cross Millmead Lock. Stay on the path, following the sign to the right (sign says Godalming 4½m) Pass the Jolly Farmer pub on the opposite bank. Cross this bridge, past the boathouses, and follow the path. Here the river loops to the left, then curves right (along line of trees on horizon). Follow the path on the right to join the river by a bridge, or take the longer way round, following the bend of the river to end up at the same bridge. Turn right to cross this bridge to follow the path along the riverbank.

4 | Continue along the path on the right. This part of the walk is particularly peaceful and charming, and only 15 minutes from Guildford town centre. Path gets muddy here.

5 | Continue over this bridge and along the path, looking back towards Guildford at St Catherines Lock. Cross the bridge to visit the nature reserve, otherwise continue on the riverside path

6 | The Gomshall line crosses the river here on this impressive bridge. Continue on the path under the bridge.

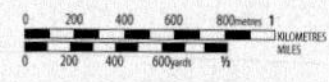

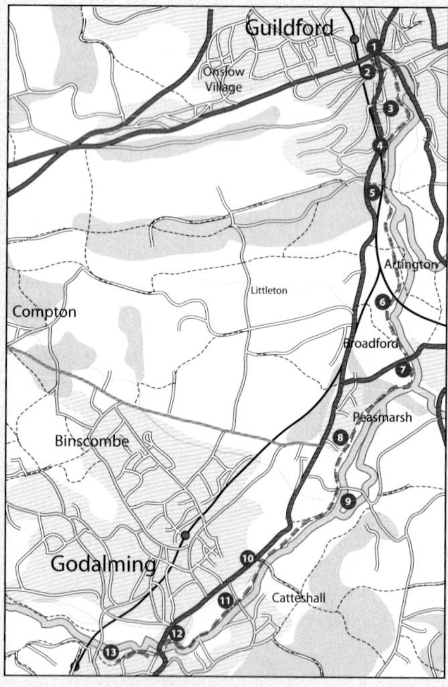

7 | Not a very pretty view, but a landmark anyway. Cross over the A248 at Broadford bridge and keep following the path ahead. Beware: fast traffic!

8 | Opening Unstead lock. Children may want to watch or help boatpeople operate the lock gates.

9 | Cross the road over a bridge to follow this footpath sign. Caution; fast traffic!

10 | Continue past this old brick footbridge.

11 | Looking back towards Guildford at Farncombe boathouse (boat hire here). Carry straight on over the bridge towards Godalming.

12 | Follow the path to the car park, then turn left over the bridge. Just after the bridge, go straight ahead and up this street. Turn right at the top for the main high street and shops and refreshments. Follow signs to station, which is right at the far end of the high street.

13 | Alternatively, just after the bridge, turn right along Bury Road for 200 yards. Take the path right off the road, on the left of St Peter and Paul Church, for the train station.

framed house once belonging to Gertrude Jekyll can be found in dense woodland on the opposite side of town. **Munstead Wood** was designed for her by Lutyens in characteristic rural vernacular style and partially constructed of Bargate stone, a locally quarried hard brown sandstone that was much loved by the Victorians. Lutyens also designed the tomb in which Gertrude Jekyll is buried in the churchyard at Busbridge, just south of Godalming.

Godalming's part Norman parish church of St Peter and St Paul is also built of Bargate stone, as is **Charterhouse**, the famous public school, which moved from London to a hillside site on the northern side of Godalming in 1872. Among its most striking features are the 150-foot Founder's Tower and the chapel designed by Giles Gilbert Scott as a memorial to those killed in World War I.

Three miles along the B2130, to the southeast of Godalming, lies the renowned **Winkworth Arboretum**, a 95-acre area of wooded hillside, which was presented to the National Trust in 1952. The grounds contain two lakes and a magnificent collection of rare trees and shrubs, many of them native to other continents. Hascombe, one mile further on, is another characteristic Surrey village with great charm.

Winkworth Arboretum

Around Godalming

LOSELEY PARK

3 miles N of Godalming off the B3000

Loseley House

Loseley Park, a handsome Elizabethan country estate, was built in 1562 of Bargate stone, some of which was taken from the ruins of Waverley Abbey. **Loseley House** is the former home of the Elizabethan statesman, Sir William More. Both Elizabeth I and James I are known to have stayed here, and the interior is decorated with a series of outstanding period features, including hand-painted panelling, woodcarving, delicate plasterwork ceilings, and a unique chimney-piece carved from a massive piece of chalk. The walled garden is a beautiful place to take a stroll, the surrounding gardens contain a terrace and a moat walk, and the nearby fields are home to Loseley's famous herd of pedigree Jersey cattle. Visitors can take a trailer ride to the traditional working dairy farm, where they can see the Jersey herd being milked every afternoon and discover the history of the estate.

Loseley House and Rose Gardens

COMPTON

4 miles N of Godalming off the B3000

The historic community of Compton was once an important stopping place on the old Pilgrims' Way. The village possesses an exceptional part Saxon church, St Nicholas, with some remarkable internal features, including a series of 12th-century murals, which were only rediscovered in 1966, an ancient hermit's, or anchorite's, cell, and a unique two-storey Romanesque sanctuary, which is thought to have once contained an early Christian relic.

Compton is also renowned for being the home of the 19th-century artist G F Watts, a largely self-taught painter and sculptor whose most famous work, *Physical Energy*, stands in London's Kensington Gardens. At the age of 47, Watts married the actress Ellen Terry, but the couple separated a year later. Then, at the age of 69, he remarried, this time to Mary Fraser-Tytler, a painter and potter 33 years his junior who went on to design Watts' Memorial Gallery, which today contains over 200 pieces of the artist's work, along with the Watts Mortuary Chapel, an extraordinary building that was completed in 1904 and is decorated in exuberant Art Nouveau style. The Watts Gallery is a fascinating place to visit, housing a unique collection of his paintings, drawings and sculptures. The nearby memorial chapel is also worth visiting.

EASHING

1 mile W of Godalming off the A3100

The Meads

The tiny hamlet of Eashing is noted for the lovely medieval Eashing Bridge, which has segmented arches and uses cutwaters, pointed upstream and rounded downstream, to stem the flow of the river. It is one of several surviving Wey Valley bridges of that period, the others being at Elstead and Tilford. Just to the east of the bridge is **The Meads**, an ancient house of two distinct parts. Half of it is 16th century, with timber framing and an original Tudor doorcase. The other is 18th century and brick and stone, with small dark chips of stone set in the mortar.

WITLEY

4 miles S of Godalming on the A283

Old Manor Tigburne Court

Witley Common Information Centre

The historic village of Witley comprises an attractive collection of fine tile-hung and half-timbered buildings loosely arranged around the part Saxon church of All Saints, a much-altered structure that contains some rare 12th-century frescoes and a delicately carved 13th-century font, and incorporates a 17th-century tower. The present village inn, the White Hart, was constructed in Elizabethan times to replace an even earlier hostelry. It is believed to be one of the oldest inns in the country, and at one time stood adjacent to a market place, which hosted a busy Friday market.

Witley's **Old Manor** was visited by a number of English monarchs, including Edward I and Richard II, and the village centre contains some delightful 15th and 16th-century timber-framed houses, many of which are hung with characteristic fishtail tiles. These include the Old Cottage, Red Rose Cottage (so-called because the lease granted on Christmas Day 1580 called for an annual rent of one red rose), and Step Cottage, a former rectory that was once the home of the Reverend Lawrence Stoughton; this worthy gentleman died aged 88 after serving the parish for 53 years and outliving five wives.

At one time, Witley was a summer haven for artists and writers, the best known of whom is perhaps George Eliot, who wrote her last novel, *Daniel Deronda*, here between 1874 and 1876. Her home, the Heights, was designed by Sir Henry Cole, the architect of the Royal Albert Hall, and was visited by a series of eminent guests, including the novelist Henry James. Today, the building has been converted into a nursing home and is known as Roslyn Court.

A large proportion of the common to the north of Thursley is a designated nature reserve, popular for its unusually large and varied population of dragonflies. The **Witley Common Information Centre** lies a few minutes' drive from Thursley Common on the eastern side of the A3. This purpose-built nature centre is managed by the National Trust and is set in woodlands at the edge of a substantial area of Trust-owned heathland. Inside, there is an audio-visual display and an exhibition outlining the history, geology and natural history of the area. The common is a designated Site of Special Scientific Interest.

Tigburne Court, which is regarded by many as Lutyens's finest work, is just over a mile south of Witley, standing right on the main Milford to Petworth road. It was built between 1899 and 1901 for Sir Edgar Horne. Lutyens was 30 years old when he designed Tigburne Court, and the house shows him at the height of his powers, yet still full of youthful exuberance. He playfully mixed Tudor styles with 18th-century classicism and used horizontal bands of tiles with the Bargate stone to create a powerful geometric effect. The gardens, like those of so many of the best Lutyens houses, are by his collaborator, Gertrude Jekyll.

HAMBLEDON

5 miles S of Godalming on the A283

Hydon's Ball

This scattered settlement contains a number of interesting buildings, including the tile-hung Court Farm, which stands near the part 14th-century church, the Old Granary, School Cottage, and Malthouse Farm and Cottage. The National Trust owns a small timber-framed dwelling in Hambledon known as Oakhurst Cottage, which has been restored as an old artisan's home and is open in the summer by appointment only.

A memorial to one of the Trust's founders, the social reformer Octavia Hill, stands at the top of nearby **Hydon's Ball**, an unusual conical hill, which at 593 feet above sea level, offers some fine views over the surrounding landscape.

HASLEMERE

9 miles S of Godalming on the A286

Educational Museum

The genteel town of Haslemere lies in the southwestern corner of the county. Now a quiet and comfortable home for well-to-do commuters, it has central streets filled with handsome Georgian and Victorian buildings, most of which were constructed following the arrival of the railway in 1859. The building styles, including stucco, redbrick and tile-hung, combine to form an attractive and harmonious architectural mix. Some of Haslemere's finest pre-Victorian structures include the Town Hall, rebuilt in 1814, the Tolle House Almshouses in Petworth Road, Church Hill House, the Town House, and two noteworthy hotels, the Georgian and the White Horse.

Towards the end of the last century, Haslemere became something of a centre for the arts. Alfred Lord Tennyson settled nearby, and a group known as the Haslemere Society of Artists was formed whose number included Birket Foster and the landscape painter Helen Allingham. At the end of World War I, the French-born musician and enthusiastic exponent of early music, Arnold Dolmetsch, founded what has become a world-famous musical instrument workshop.

OBJETS D'ART

2 High Street, Haslemere, Surrey GU27 2LY
Tel: 01428 643982 Fax: 01428 658438
e-mail: angela@objetsdart.biz
website: www.objetsdart.biz

Objets d'Art is one of the most interesting shops in Haslemere, occupying one of the oldest commercial premises in the town.

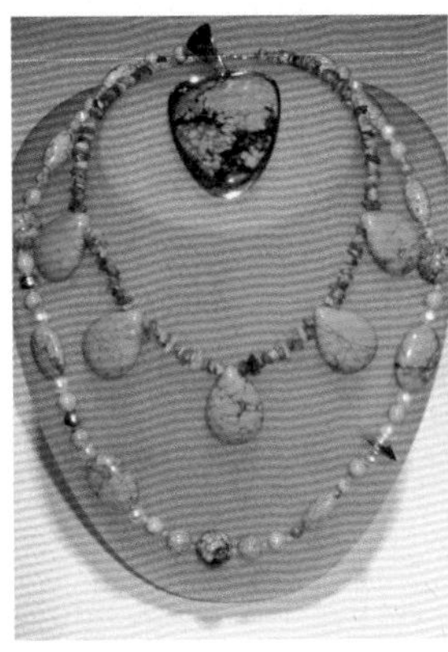

It has been owned by the French family for 32 years, founded by Helen and Bill French and joined by their daughter-in-law Angela in 1981who is a trained jeweller.

The aspect of the shop has changed over the years and although still stocking a large range of antiques including silver, glass, ceramics, bronzes and paintings the main focus is jewellery. This ranges from very modern silver and stone set items starting at very modest prices up to more valuable diamond and gem set jewellery.

There is also a full repair service including jewellery, watches, silversmithing, glass and china restoration.

Whether you are looking for a personal treat, something for the home or a very special gift, Objets d'Art is definitely a place to visit where there is undoubtedly something for everyone.

MEEKA

8-10 West Street, Haslemere,
Surrey GU27 2AB
Tel: 01428 644911
e-mail: enquiries@meeka.biz
website: www.meeka.biz

Meeka is a highly regarded ladies clothes shop in the centre of Haslemere which stocks a wide range of prestigious fashion clothing.

Brands stocked include Esprit, Fransa, Quba & Co, Joules, RM Williams, Aigle, Darling, Sea salt, In Town, Not The Same, The Barn, Nice Things, Calla Lily, Adini and Amari. New brands are added each season.

In addition to clothing, meeka also sells accessories including belts, boots, sandals, jewellery, hats & gloves together with other seasonal goods.

We look forward to welcoming you to our shop in the near future!

Dolmetsch's family went on to establish the Haslemere Festival of Early Music in 1925; it is still held each year in July.

Another of Haslemere's attractions is the **Educational Museum** in the High Street, an establishment that was founded in 1888 by local surgeon and Quaker, Sir James Hutchinson, and which now contains an imaginative series of displays on local birds, botany, zoology, geology, archaeology and history.

CHIDDINGFOLD

6 miles S of Godalming on the A283

St Mary's Church

With its three-sided green, waterlily-filled pond, part 13th-century church, medieval pub and handsome collection of Georgian cottages, this attractive settlement contains all the features of a quintessential English village. During the 13th and 14th centuries, it was an important centre of the glass-making industry, a once flourishing trade that used local sand as its main ingredient and employed skilled craftspeople from across northern Europe. Some fragments of medieval Chiddingfold glass can be seen in the small lancet window in **St Mary's Church**, below which a brass plaque is inscribed with the names of several early glass-makers. The church itself was much altered during the 1860s. However, its west tower is 17th century and contains a peal of eight bells, one of which is believed to be around 500 years old. The churchyard is entered through an exceptionally fine lych-gate, a covered gateway with a wide timber slab that was used to shelter coffins awaiting burial.

Of the many handsome buildings standing around Chiddingfold's village green, the Crown Inn is perhaps the most impressive. This is another hostelry that claims to be the oldest in England, its existence having first been recorded in 1383. The structure is half-timbered and incorporates a medieval great hall; Edward VI is reported to have stayed here in the 15th century. Other buildings in the village worthy of note are Chantry House, Manor House and Glebe House, the last two of which have elegant Georgian facades.

DUNSFOLD

6 miles S of Godalming on the B2130

Church of St Mary & All Saints

From Chiddingfold, a pleasant journey eastwards through country lanes leads to another settlement with fold (a Saxon term meaning 'forest clearing') in its name. Dunsfold is a narrow ribbon of a village, which lies on either side of a long unmanicured green. It contains a number of fine old brick and tile-hung cottages and houses, several of which date from the late 17th century, and an excellent pub, the Sun Inn, which stands beside a towering oak tree that is said to have a girth of over 20 feet.

Dunsfold's finest feature, however, is situated half a mile from the village on top of a raised mound, which may once have been the site of a pre-Christian place of worship. The **Church of St Mary and All Saints** dates from around 1280 and, apart from the addition of a 15th-century belfry, has remained virtually unchanged since. The structure was much admired by William Morris, the Victorian founder of the Arts and Crafts Movement, who particularly approved of the simple, rough-hewn pews, which were made around 1300 by the inhabitants of the surrounding farms. A leafy glade at the foot of the mound is the location of a holy well, whose water is reputed to be a cure for eye complaints and even blindness. The site of the holy well is marked by a timber shelter erected in the 1930s.

ALFOLD

9 miles S of Godalming on the B2133

Countryways Experience

A former clearing in the Wealden forest, Alfold is an exceptionally attractive village that was once an important glass-making centre. It reputedly supplied material for the windows of Westminster Abbey. Evidence of the medieval glassworks can still be made out in the woods on the edge of the village. The area around the church contains a number of interesting features, including an ancient yew tree in the churchyard, a charming Tudor cottage, and an old village whipping post and set of stocks. Just at the edge of the village is the **Countryways Experience**, a series of interactive exhibits that covers the history and natural history of this area, giving visitors some perspective on how living conditions adapted to new styles of farming over the centuries. Visitors can feed a range of animals, including lambs, goats, piglets, calves and chickens, with food from the farm shop.

ELLEN'S GREEN

9 miles SE of Godalming on the B2128

This tiny hamlet on the Sussex border is one of the best preserved Surrey villages. It is set in unspoilt Weald country, with thick woodlands giving way to small fields. Cottages line the green but in a way that has no suggestion of excessive self-consciousness. Although singularly lacking in dramatic sights, Ellen's Green offers the visitor the chance to see an example of the small villages that were once typical of the area, but are now much rarer.

CRANLEIGH

7 miles SE of Godalming on the B2128

The parish church, St Nicholas, in the quiet residential town of Cranleigh, contains a carving of a grinning feline that allegedly provided the inspiration for Lewis Carroll's Cheshire Cat. The town also contains the country's first cottage hospital, opened in the 1850s, and a public school founded by local

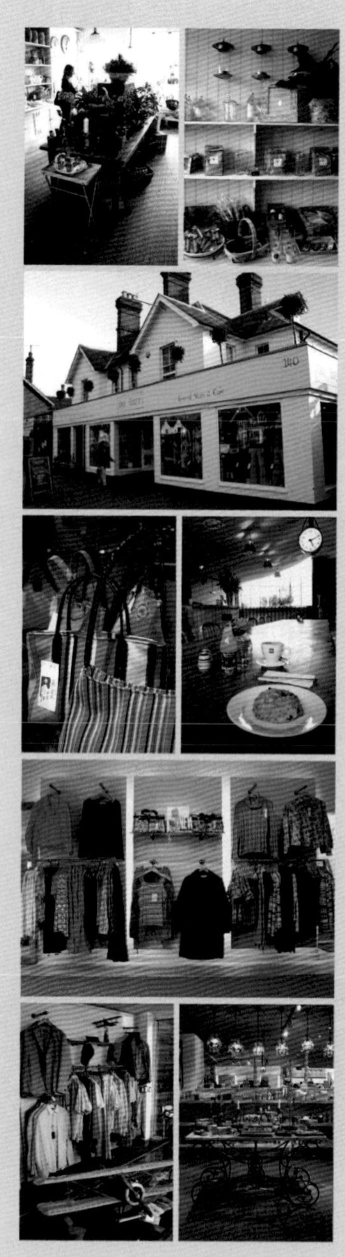

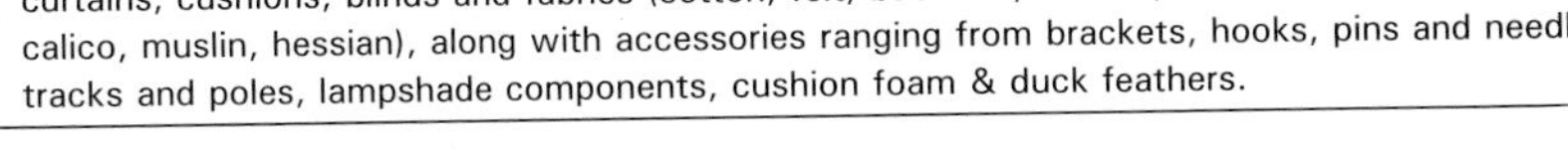

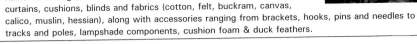

farmers in 1865, which still incorporates a working farm.

EWHURST

8 miles SE of Godalming on the B2127

Church of St Peter & St Paul

Ewhurst is a long village containing a sandstone church, **St Peter and St Paul**, whose nave and south door are considered to be among the finest examples of Norman church architecture in the county. The rest of the structure would have been of a similar age had it not been for an unfortunate attempt to underpin the tower in the 1830s, which resulted in the collapse not only of the tower, but of the chancel and north transept as well. The structure was eventually rebuilt in Norman style with an unusual shingled broach

DRAGONFLY

2 The Street (Unit 2), Ewhurst, nr Cranleigh,
Surrey GU6 7QD
Tel/Fax: 01483 278750

Ewhurst is an attractive village on the B2127 under the Surrey Hills. The sandstone Church of St Peter & St Paul brings many visitors to the village, which also boasts some fine 18th and 19th century buildings, but for anyone looking for a special gift or something to enhance the home the place to head for is **Dragonfly**, a wonderful boutique shop filled with an extensive selection of lifestyle ideas.

Jacqueline Miller and Derry O'Kelly, owners since 2007, source a range of goods from all over the country, some familiar, others you might not find in any other similar outlet. Dragonfly is a major stockist of Cath Kidson toiletries, and other items on display range from unusual pieces of jewellery to hand-made cushions, mirrors and furniture – in particular painted pieces.

With the stock changing constantly, every visit to Dragonfly will uncover new delights and surprises. Shop hours are 10 to 5 Tuesday to Saturday.

THE RUG CENTRE

68 South Street, Dorking, Surrey RH4 2HD
Tel: 01306 882202 Fax: 01306 882131
website: www.rugcentre.co.uk

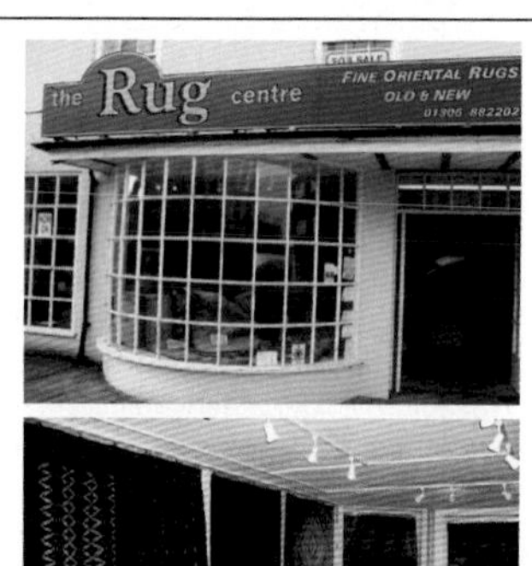

Fine hand-woven Oriental rugs are the speciality of **The Rug Centre**, located in handsome bow-fronted premises on South Street. The Centre has been in Dorking for only about 15 years, but owner Michael Woodman is an acknowledged expert, a 'rugman' with 40 years' experience. He finds rugs from all over the Middle East and Far East, from Turkey, India, Pakistan, Persia, Afghanistan, Tibet and Nepal. The sizes and styles vary enormously: exquisite silk or wool pieces from the famous towns of Isfahan and Qum; tribal-made rugs full of ethnic charm; chunky gabbehs in vibrant colours from Southwest Persia; rich-red Afghans from pillow-size pushtis to room size; round rugs; hearth rugs; kelims; tapestry-woven and needlepoint rugs; no-nonsense child-and pet-proof rugs; rugs for warmth, colour and sound insulation; rugs to cover worn patches; rugs for investment; heirloom rugs to be treasured down the generations. The rugs are beautifully displayed, with sizes and prices clearly marked. Michael has a fine eye for colour – customers can bring a fabric sample and ideal dimensions and he'll set off on a rug hunt, a hunt that usually ends in success! Customers can also try a chosen rug at home before making a purchase. Michael and manager Sheena Bamforth welcome one and all to come and see the wonderful range of rugs at the Centre, which also offers repair, cleaning, restoration and valuation services.

spire. Inside, there is a carved 14th-century font and a Jacobean pulpit, and outside, the churchyard contains a number of mature trees native to North America.

The remainder of the village, part of which is set around a small square, contains some fine 18th and 19th-century residential buildings, including the Woolpit, built for the Doulton family in the 1880s. The 843-foot Pitch Hill is situated a mile to the north and can be easily reached from the village along a pleasant footpath.

Dorking

North Downs Way · Holmwood Common

Dorking is a long-established settlement, which stands at the intersection of Stane Street, the Roman road that once connected London with Chichester, and the ancient Pilgrims' Way, the east-west ridgeway route, which is roughly followed by the course of the modern **North Downs Way**. Despite evidence of Saxon and Viking occupation, present-day Dorking is a congested commuter town that owes most of its character to the Victorians.

There are a small number of older buildings, most notably the part 15th-century former coaching inn, the White Horse, and the shops and houses in North Street, West Street, and at the western end of the High Street. One of the houses on West Street belonged to William Mullins (born 1572), one of the Pilgrim Fathers who, in 1620, sailed to America in the *Mayflower*. However, the town's two most distinctive architectural features are characteristically 19th century: the unexpectedly grand Church of St Martin with its soaring spire, and the Rose Hill housing development, an assortment of Victorian villas arranged around a green and entered from South Street through an unusual neo-Gothic arch. St Paul's Church in Dorking is a fine piece of architecture, designed by Benjamin Ferray and constructed in 1857.

Perhaps Dorking's most attractive feature is its close proximity to unspoilt countryside, a testimony to the success of the southeast's Green Belt policy. As well as the open spaces in the Downs to the north, **Holmwood Common**, two miles along the A24 to the south, is another tract of National Trust-owned land, which offers some pleasant way-marked walks through mature oak and birch woodlands, and disabled access to the pleasant picnic area around Fourwents Pond.

Around Dorking

BOX HILL

2 miles N of Dorking off the A25

Box Hill

The 563-foot **Box Hill** lies a couple of miles from Polesden Lacey on the eastern side of the River Mole. This popular local landmark, probably the best known part of the North Downs, rises sharply from the valley floor to an impressive tree-covered summit high above. The hill takes its name from the mature box trees that once grew here in profusion, but which were seriously depleted in the 18th century to supply the needs of London wood-engravers. By then, the site had already been known for over a century as a beauty spot and had been visited and recorded by, among others, the diarist John Evelyn.

Today, the National Trust owns over 800 acres of land around Box Hill, which has now been designated a country park. The area around the summit incorporates an exhibition centre, a late 19th-century fort and a café, and can be reached either by a footpath or by a narrow winding road leading up from Burford Bridge. The hillside is traversed by a series of nature walks, and there are several picnic sites, which enjoy breathtaking views across the Weald to the South Downs. Many species of orchids grow on the chalk grassland and butterflies abound, including the Adonis blue and the silver spotted skipper.

The Burford Bridge Hotel stands on the banks of the River Mole at the foot of Box Hill and is connected to it by stepping stones across the river. In the early 19th century, the establishment was known as the Hare and Hounds and it was here in 1805 that Admiral Nelson said his farewells to Lady Hamilton prior to the Battle of Trafalgar. Keats is also believed to have completed his second volume of poems, *Endymion*, here in 1818. Chapel

Box Hill from Ashcombe Wood

Farm at nearby West Humble is an open farm, where visitors can see at close quarters how a livestock farm works.

MICKLEHAM

3 miles N of Dorking on the A24

Church of St Michael

Mickleham is a highly picturesque village with a good pub, the Running Horses, and a restored Norman church, **St Michael's**, containing a rare Flemish stained-glass window. It is worth examining the churchyard because this is one of the few parish churches to preserve the Surrey tradition of grave-boards. These are wooden tombstone planks carried between two posts. Most of the grave-boards in St Michael's are 19th century and have been carefully preserved and renovated where necessary.

LEATHERHEAD

5 miles N of Dorking on the A24

Museum of Local History Fire and Iron Gallery

Leatherhead is a pretty Mole Valley town that manages to retain some measure of tranquillity despite being crossed by a number of major trunk routes.

Several buildings in the narrow streets of the old town are worthy of note, including the 16th-century Running Horse Inn and the attractive part 12th-century parish church of St Mary and St Nicholas. The grave of Anthony Hope (real name Sir Anthony Hawkins), the author of *The Prisoner Of Zenda*, can be found in the churchyard, and a short distance away in Church Street, the informative **Leatherhead Museum of Local History** is housed in a charming 17th-century timber-framed cottage with its own small garden.

On Oxshott Road stands the **Fire and Iron Gallery**, the world's leading metal art gallery, featuring spectacular work by top international blacksmiths and jewellers.

GREAT BOOKHAM

4 miles N of Dorking on the A246

Church of St Nicholas Polesden Lacey

Although heavily built up since World War II, the residential area to the west of Leatherhead manages to retain something of its historic past. The earliest mention of a settlement in the area dates back to the 7th century, when a manor at Bocheham is recorded as belonging to Chertsey Abbey.

Present day Great Bookham contains an exceptional parish church, the **Church of St Nicholas**, which has an unusual flint tower with a shingled spire dating back to the Norman era in the 12th century. A substantial part of the building, including the chancel, is known to have been rebuilt in the 1340s by the Abbot of Chertsey, and the church was again remodelled by the Victorians. Inside, there are some fine 15th-century stained glass windows and a number of noteworthy monumental brasses and memorials to the local lords of the manor. An early 18th-century owner of the Bookham estate, Dr Hugh Shortrudge, left an endowment in his will to four local churches on condition that an annual sermon be preached on the subject of the martyrdom of Charles I. St Nicholas continues to uphold the tradition of the 'Shortrudge Sermon', which is preached each year on the final Sunday in January.

Nearby Little Bookham has a small single-roomed church with a wooden belfry that is believed to date from the 12th century. The adjacent 18th-century manor house now operates as a school. Bookham Common and Banks Common to the northwest of Little

TASTE DELI & CAFÉ

27 High Street, Great Bookham, nr Leatherhead, Surrey KT23 4AA
Tel/Fax: 01372 457066
e-mail: deli@tastecontractcatering.co.uk
website: www.taste-deli.co.uk

Taste is a high-quality delicatessen, coffee shop and caterer in the heart of Great Bookham, owned and run by Alison Brown and Suzanne Ailes. The ladies and their staff serve an excellent selection of snacks and meals to eat in or take away, including soup, jacket potatoes, salads, sandwiches served in a variety of breads, pies and pasties. Cottage pies, fish pies and quiches from individual to family and party size are made in the kitchen on the premises. There's an enticing array of cakes and pastries, biscuits and chocolates, oils, vinegars, pickles and preserves, pasta, fruit juices and great coffee. From the deli section come cooked and cured meats, pâtés, 30+ cheeses, olives, marinated peppers, sun-dried tomatoes and anchovies. Taste will also make up individual hampers and caters for parties, celebrations, business lunches and other functions for up to 100. Among the specialities are lovely party canapés such as smoked salmon blinis or baby Yorkshire puddings filled with beef, crème fraîche, horseradish and chives.

Bookham provide some welcome relief from the commuter estates and offer some pleasant walking through relatively unspoilt open heathland. The commons are recorded in the Domesday Book as providing pannage, the right to graze pigs on acorns, for Chertsey Abbey. Now in the ownership of the National Trust, they are particularly known for their rich and varied birdlife.

Another National Trust-owned property, **Polesden Lacey** (see panel opposite), stands on high ground two miles to the south of Great Bookham. The estate was once owned by the writer R B Sheridan, who purchased it in 1797 with the intention of restoring its decaying 17th-century manor house. However, a lack of funds prevented him from realising his ambitions and, following his death in 1816, the building was demolished and the estate sold. During the 1820s, the architect Thomas Cubitt built a substantial Regency villa in its place, which was subsequently remodelled and enlarged by successive owners throughout the 19th century.

In 1906, the estate was acquired by Captain Ronald Greville and his wife Margaret, the daughter of a Scottish brewing magnate and a celebrated high society hostess. Over the following three decades, they invited a succession of rich and influential guests to Polesden Lacey whose number included Edward VII, and George VI and Queen Elizabeth (later the Queen Mother), who spent part of their honeymoon here in 1923. The Grevilles carried out a number of alterations of their own during this period and the extravagant 'Edwardian-Louis XVI' internal decoration remains as a testimony to Margaret Greville's taste - or lack of it.

Whatever the perspective, the house

contains an undeniably fine collection of furniture, paintings, tapestries, porcelain and silver, which the Grevilles accumulated over 40 years, and Margaret's personal collection of photographs provides a fascinating record of British high society at play during the early part of the century. The surrounding grounds amount to over 1,000 acres and incorporate a walled rose garden, open lawns, a youth hostel and a large area of natural woodland. An annual festival in late June and early July is held in the charming open-air theatre. This has expanded over the years and now presents a variety of theatre and entertainment, including Gilbert and Sullivan, light operetta, grand opera, ballet, classical concerts, jazz, big bands, music hall, folk dancing and spectacular fireworks. The programme always includes a Shakespeare production.

RANMORE COMMON

1 mile NW of Dorking off the A2003

Ranmore Common

Lying mainly to the south of Polesden Lacy, **Ranmore Common** enjoys excellent views from its location on top of the Downs. This unspoilt setting, which can feel remote in bad weather despite its proximity to Dorking, is a testament to enlightened Green Belt policy. The common is in reality a long green, with only a few houses dotted around it, thereby preserving its exposed nature. Owned in part by the Forestry Commission, it is a Site of Special Scientific Interest and provides an excellent habitat for wildlife. Butterflies, including purple hairstreak, white admiral and silver-washed fritillary, can be seen in the rides and clearings, as well as birds such as sparrow hawks and green, lesser and greater spotted woodpeckers.

EFFINGHAM

5 miles NW of Dorking on the A246

Effingham is an old village that was famous as the home of the Howards of Effingham, one of whom was the Commander-in-Chief of the English fleet that defeated the Spanish Armada in 1588. His home was Effingham Court Palace, which survives only as remnants at Lower Place Farm. There were two other

Polesden Lacey

Great Bookham, nr Leatherhead, Surrey RH5 6BD
Tel: 01372 452048
website: www.nationaltrust.org.uk

Polesden Lacey is an exceptional regency house remodelled by the Edwardian hostess The Hon. Mrs Greville DBE, with displays of her paintings, furniture, porcelain and silver. The Duke and Duchess of York (later to become King George VI and Queen Elizabeth The Queen Mother) spent part of their honeymoon here in 1923. In an exceptional setting on the North Downs, there are extensive grounds, lawns and a walled rose garden. A free easy-to-use map is available to guide you on country walks across woodland and farmland. There is also a free children's guide and activity sheets for the house and the garden, as well as seasonal trails and tracker packs. To complete your visit, refreshments are available at the tea room and there is an extensive National Trust gift shop and plant sales. A programme of family fun events runs throughout the year.

important manors in Effingham. One is the moated grange in Great Lee Wood, once the manor of Effingham la Leigh. The other was the medieval property of the Earls of Gloucester, East Court, which is now incorporated in a boarding school, St Theresa's Convent.

EAST HORSLEY

6 miles NW of Dorking on the A246

East Horsley Towers

Suburban building has caught up with East Horsley, leaving the town centre bereft of the sort of charm associated with Ranmore Common or some of the other villages that are nearer Dorking. It does, however, possess one of the more dramatic country houses in Surrey, at least as it is viewed from the road. **East Horsley Towers**, built in the 1820s, seems to capture the spirit of the 19th-century imagination as it moved from Romantic to the nostalgic re-creations so loved by the Victorians. A long entrance leads to the house, which presents itself with a huge round tower by the entrance. Another tower, to the west, is built in the Gothic style. The house itself displays Tudor influences, but has multi-coloured vaulting ribs throughout for support. Another tower, this time Germanic looking with a pointed roof, dominates the east wing of the house. It now operates as a luxurious management training centre.

OCKHAM

10 miles NW of Dorking on the B2039

All Saints Church

Ockham once possessed a fine Jacobean mansion, Ockham Park. A serious fire in 1948

F CONISBEE & SON

Park Corner, Ockham Road South, East Horsley, Surrey KT24 6RZ
Tel: 01483 282073 Fax: 01483 248859
website: www.fconisbee.co.uk

In a distinctive three-storey pebble-fronted building on a corner site in East Horsley, **F Conisbee & Son** are high-class butchers, poulterers, graziers and caterers who have been masters of their trade since 1760. The current head Conisbee is Neil, who runs the business with his sons Stephen and James.

They source the very best meat from local farms, from the Polesden Lacy Estate where they farm and from their own farms at Fetcham, Bookham and Shere, where they rear beef, cattle, sheep and prize-winning turkeys. All their meat is hung as carcasses or quarters, allowing the meat to mature naturally, ensuring tenderness and improved flavour without the tainting or discoloration often found in vacuum-packed meat. The business has a resident chef, Robert, who makes an excellent range of award-winning meat pies. He also produces meat platters, salads and specialities such as Beef Wellington – part of the full catering service offered by this outstanding firm. Another of the Conisbee specialities is a range of superb sausages in over 20 varieties (one is gluten-free) and they are widely known for their barbecues and spit roasts, providing whole or part pigs cooked on a spit over a bed of hot coals, with all the trimmings, all the equipment and all the staff to ensure a great occasion for up to 1,000 people. Shop hours: Monday 8am to 1pm; Tuesday 8am to 1pm & 2pm to 5pm; Wednesday 8am to 1pm; Thursday 8am to 1pm & 2pm to 5pm; Friday 7.30am to 1pm & 2pm to 5.30pm; Saturday 7.30am to 1pm & 2pm to 3.30pm.

destroyed everything except for the orangery, stables, kitchen wing, and a solitary Italianate tower. The **Church of All Saints** still stands within the grounds of the estate; this largely 13th-century building was constructed on the site of a pre-Norman structure and is known for its remarkable east window, a surprising combination of seven tall pointed lancets finished in marble with distinctive carved capitals. The window dates from around 1260 and is thought to have been brought here from nearby Newark Abbey following its dissolution in the 16th century. The church incorporates a brick chapel, which contains a robed marble effigy of the first Lord King, a former owner of Ockham Park who died in 1734. The name of Ockham is chiefly associated with the expression Ockham's Razor. William of Ockham was a 13th-century Franciscan intellectual whose maxim was that every hypothesis should be sliced to its essentials, and all unnecessary facts in the subject being analysed, should be eliminated. William is commemorated by a small stained-glass window in the church.

On Chatley Heath, a mile to the north of Ockham, there is a unique Semaphore Tower that was once part of the Royal Navy's signalling system for relaying messages between Portsmouth and the Admiralty in London. Although the semaphore mechanism soon fell into disuse, the structure has remained in good order and is open to the public at weekends. As well as offering outstanding views over the surrounding landscape, the Chatley Heath Semaphore Tower houses an interesting exhibition and model collection. It can be reached along a pleasant woodland pathway and is open throughout the summer at weekends and Bank Holidays.

EAST CLANDON

7 miles W of Dorking on the A246

Hatchlands Park

This attractive small village straddles the A246 Leatherhead to Guildford route. The road zig-zags between brick and half-timber cottages, several of which are clustered around the Norman church of St Thomas. This small church was extensively restored at the end of the 19th century, but the architects ensured that one of is most distinctive features - the bulky shingled bell tower - retained its original appearance.

The village also contains an interesting old forge and a lovely old manor farmhouse dating from the late 17th century. A striking National Trust property is located one mile to the northeast: **Hatchlands Park** is a distinctive brick-built house designed in the mid 18th century for Admiral Boscawen after his famous victory in the Battle of Louisburg. Inside, there are some splendid examples of the early work of Robert Adams, some fine period furniture and paintings, and a wonderful assortment of historic keyboard instruments, the Cobbe collection, which was moved here in 1988. Among the pianos are those owned or played by Beethoven, Mahler, Mozart, Chopin, Marie Antoinette and the Medici family. Elgar's piano is the very one on which he composed the *Enigma Variations*. The grounds, originally laid out by Humphry Repton, were remodelled by Gertrude Jekyll. In recent years, parts of the garden have been restored to the original designs and planting plans of Jekyll and Repton.

WESTCOTT

2 miles W of Dorking on the A25

Westcott is a tidy village that lies on the main road linking Dorking with Shere. Although

BURY HILL FISHERIES

The Boathouse, Old Bury Hill, Westcott, nr Dorking, Surrey RH4 3JU
Tel: 01306 883621
e-mail: info@buryhillfisheries.co.uk
website: www.buryhillfisheries.co.uk

Surrey's premier coarse fishery, **Bury Hill Fisheries** forms part of a beautiful 200-year-old estate, which lies in a secluded valley at the foot of the Surrey Hills. Although just 20 miles from Central London, Bury Hill is far removed from the stress of modern working life, a haven of peace and quiet amongst mature woodland and diverse wildlife.

Widely regarded as one of the finest day ticket coarse fisheries in the country, Bury Hill is an ideal venue for both beginners and experienced anglers of all ages boasting four lakes totalling 22 acres offering the finest sport for every discipline. If your aim is a genuine 40lb English carp, a bag of tench and bream, a big pike or double-figure zander, or simply a net of quality roach and perch, Bury Hill is a fishery where dreams are realised.

The Old Lake with its wooded island and prolific beds of lilies and irises is a traditional mixed fishery where carp top 35 lb with doubles and 20s commonplace, plus quality tench, bream, crucian, roach, rudd, perch, pike and zander. The two lakes in the lower valley are Milton and Bonds Lakes, bordered by irises with large lily beds, Milton has a huge head of crucian, tench, roach, golden rudd and perch whilst Bonds is home to hundreds of carp to 10 lb plus. The latest addition to the Bury Hill portfolio is Temple Lake, a purpose built specimen carp water, which is home to hefty English carp, which average close to 29lb and which top the magical 40 lb barrier.

And if you are new to fishing or a long time angler wanting to improve your skills, Bury Hill's Pro-Fish Angling Courses run May to September. With tackle and bait provided there is no easier way to be introduced to the fun of fishing.

Facilities are also first class with ample car parking, lakeside café with fantastic views over the Old Lake, a well stocked tackle and bait shop providing everything for an action packed day from floats, hooks and shot to boilies, groundbait, pellet and maggots and clean heated toilets which are also disabled friendly. Flat banks and gravelled paths also allow disabled access to large comfortable, purpose built swims. Add friendly, helpful staff and it's easy to see why Bury Hill attracts visitors from far and wide time and time again.

most of the houses are from the same Victorian period, they display a variety of building styles. This diversity stems from the fact that Westcott lies almost exactly at the junction of the chalk North Downs and the sandstone Surrey Hills. Both of these stone types figure in the design of the cottages, and sometimes both are used in the same house. Churtgate House, built in the 16th century, pre-dates nearly all the other buildings in Westcott; it is located on the main road at the corner of Balchin's Lane.

ABINGER

4 miles SW of Dorking off the A25

Church of St James

The parish of Abinger contains two villages, Abinger itself (or Abinger Common), which lies one mile west of Friday Street at the southern end of the parish, and Abinger Hammer, which lies on the A25 Dorking to Guildford road to the north. Abinger claims to be one of the oldest settlements in the country, having been settled by Middle Stone Age people around 5000BC. The remains of a Mesolithic pit-dwelling were discovered in a field near Abinger's old Manor House, which, when excavated in 1950, revealed over 1,000 tools and artefacts that are now on display in an interesting little museum.

Abinger's parish **Church of St James** is an unlucky building. This part 12th-century structure was largely destroyed by an enemy flying bomb during World War II. It was rebuilt, with great sensitivity, but was severely damaged in 1964 after being struck by lightning. In the churchyard is a war memorial designed by Lutyens, and in the corner of the three-sided village green, a set of old wooden stocks and a whipping post.

KINGFISHER FARM SHOP

Abinger Hammer, nr Dorking, Surrey RH5 6QX
Tel: 01306 730703 Fax: 01306 731654
e-mail: kfwatercress@btconnect.com

Kingfisher Farm Shop is famous for its home grown watercress. This family business has been growing this uniquely English product at Abinger Hammer since 1854. It is grown in natural spring water, which provides all the necessary nutrients without the aid of fertilisers or insecticides.

The Farm Shop has become an increasingly important part of the business since the family started selling fruit and vegetables in 1971 and the watercress shed at Abinger Hammer became the present shop in 1999. The shop provides high quality food for the discerning customer, sourcing as much regional and local food available.

An abundance of fresh vegetables and fruit greets the visitor and nearby shelves groan with locally produced breads, cakes and pies alongside jams and chutneys. Fresh meat from a local butcher is delivered six days a week. A selection of English wines, beers from Surrey and Sussex and cider from Herefordshire are stocked. Whether it's for breakfast, lunch or dinner, it is possible to gather all the ingredients in your basket from fresh produce to a ready made pud!

Outside are seasonal displays of herbaceous, perennial and bedding plants, herbs, pumpkins and squashes, and Christmas trees.

The latest addition to the offerings of this outstanding farm shop is the adjacent Flower Shop, which opened in October 2003. Fresh- cut British-grown seasonal flowers are sold as well as exotic stems, hand tied bouquets and spray arrangements (to order), growing mediums, terracotta pots and garden accessories. The experienced team of florists offer flowers for weddings, events, private parties and funerals.

The Farm Shop is open every day, the Flower Shop every day except Sunday and Monday. The small community of Abinger Hammer lies on the A25 Dorking-Guildford road in the Tillingbourne Valley.

'Jack the Smith' Clock, Abinger Hammer

Abinger Common is a delightful hamlet that lies one and a half miles north of Leith Hill, the birthplace of the first Archbishop of Canterbury whose name lives on in the title of a delightful pub, The Stephen Langton Inn.

Abinger Hammer, just over a mile to the northwest, lies in the valley of the River Tillingbourne, a fast-flowing stream, which, in the 15th and 16th centuries, was used to power the mechanical metal-working hammers from which the settlement takes its name. At one time, the village was known for the manufacture of cannon balls and a busy blacksmith's workshop can still be found here. Abinger Hammer's industrial past is reflected in the famous 'Jack the Smith' hammer clock, which was erected in 1909. This unique clock overhangs the road on the site of an old iron forge and is characterised by the figure of a blacksmith who strikes a bell with his hammer every half hour.

HOLMBURY ST MARY

6 miles SW of Dorking on the B2126

Until 1879 the village was called Felday and was a hideaway for smugglers, and many of the oldest stone cottages have unusually large cellars dug into the hillside - perfect for hiding goods in transit! Holmbury St Mary was the invention of well-to-do Victorians, one of whom, the eminent George Edmund Street, designed and paid for the church in 1879, giving it to the parish in memory of his second wife. The village is ideally situated for access to the 857-foot Holmbury Hill, an upland with an altogether wilder feel than Leith Hill, its taller neighbour across the valley. A pleasant walk leads to the remains of an eight-acre Iron Age hill fort whose fading earthwork fortifications lie hidden amidst the undergrowth on the hillside

COLDHARBOUR

5 miles SW of Dorking off the A29

Anstiebury Camp

A remote hamlet set 700 feet up in the Surrey Hills, Coldharbour has an atmosphere that is light years away from most people's preconception of Surrey as a county of cosy suburbs and fertile farmland. Sturdy, stone-built houses cling to the hilltop, from which there are magnificent views sweeping south over the Weald.

Just to the north of Coldharbour is **Anstiebury Camp**, an Iron Age fort probably dating from the 1st or 2nd century BC. The fort is oval in plan, covering more than 11 acres, and is defended by triple banks with double ditches to the north and northeast.

LEITH HILL

5 miles SW of Dorking on the B2126

Leith Hill Place · Leith Hill

The 965-foot National Trust-owned **Leith Hill** is the highest point in the southeast of England. In 1766, a 64-foot tower was built on the tree-covered summit by Richard Hull, a local squire who lived at nearby Leith Hill Place. He now lies buried beneath his splendid creation. Present-day visitors climbing to the top on a clear day are rewarded with a panorama that takes in several counties and stretches as far as the English Channel.

The part 17th, part 18th-century **Leith Hill Place** stands within beautiful rhododendron-filled grounds that are open to the public throughout the year. In its time, the house has been owned by the Wedgwood and Vaughan Williams families, and contains a fine collection of Wedgwood pottery and paintings by such eminent artists as Reynolds and Stubbs. An Edwardian country house designed by Sir Edwin Lutyens can be found on the northern slopes of Leith Hill. Goddards on Abinger Common, now the centre of activities of the Lutyens Trust, stands within attractive grounds laid out by Gertrude Jekyll.

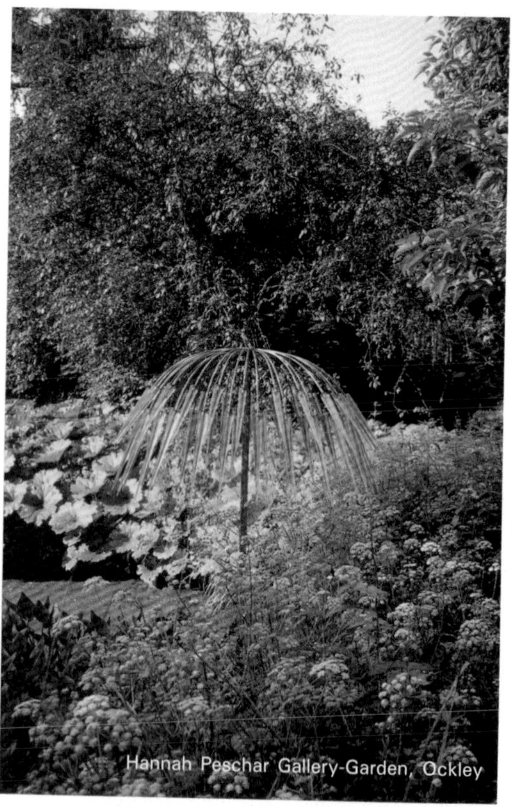

Hannah Peschar Gallery-Garden, Ockley

OCKLEY

8 miles S of Dorking on the A29

Hannah Peschar Gallery-Garden

At Ockley there is a village green, which, at over 500 feet in diameter, is one of the largest in Surrey. In summer, village cricket is played in this classic English setting, which is enhanced by a number of handsome period houses and cottages. Ockley has had a long and eventful history: the village once stood on Stane Street, the old Roman road between Chichester and London, now partially followed by the route of the A29, and in the mid 9th century, a momentous battle between the forces of King Ethelwulf of the West Saxons and the marauding Vikings reputedly took place near here. Following the Norman invasion, the surrounding woodlands were designated a royal hunting forest, and in the 12th century, the Normans built a fortification half a mile to the north of the present village green thatr has long since disappeared.

However, the nearby part 14th-century Church of St Margaret remains, although this was extensively remodelled by the Victorians during the 1870s.

Among the many other noteworthy buildings in Ockley are the 18th-century Ockley Court, which stands opposite the church, and the groups of cottages surrounding the green, built in a variety of styles and materials, including brick, tiling and weather-boarding. An interesting private sculpture and ceramics gallery, the **Hannah Peschar Gallery-Garden**, which incorporates a delightful water garden, can be found in Standon Lane.

A short distance to the southwest of Ockley, a chapel was built in the 13th century to serve the population of this once-isolated part of the Weald. Known as the Okewood Chapel, it was later endowed by a local nobleman after his son narrowly avoided being savaged by a wild boar when a mystery arrow struck and killed the charging animal.

NEWDIGATE

5 miles S of Dorking off the A24

A turning east off the A24 at Beare Green leads to the village of Newdigate. This historic settlement contains an interesting parish church, St Peter's, which is believed to have been founded in the 12th century by the Earl de Warenne as a 'hunters' chapel', a place of worship built to be used by Norman hunting parties during their expeditions in the Wealden forest. The tower, with its shingled spire, was constructed around a massive cross-braced timber frame in the 15th century, a time when Newdigate was relatively prosperous thanks to its flourishing iron-founding industry. The oak shingles on the spire had to be replaced in the

THE SIX BELLS

Village Street, Newdigate, nr Dorking, Surrey RH5 5DH
Tel: 01306 631276

The **Six Bells** is a splendid traditional inn dating back as far as the 17th century, built round a vast central chimney that is now an imposing inglenook fireplace. Smuggling tales abound here – traces remain of a tunnel that led from the cellar to the church – and, though much altered, the inn retains a great deal of its old-world character and atmosphere, with pictures of bygone village life to assist the period appeal. Landlord Martin Earp is the most welcoming of hosts, regaling his patrons with genuine warm hospitality, well-kept ales and good honest traditional pub food. Families with children are always made welcome, and when the sun shines the tables set out in the garden overlooking the Church of St Peter is very popular – a play area is guaranteed to keep the little ones busy and happy. (The church is well worth taking time to visit; it is believed to have been founded in the 12th century as a hunters' chapel, a place of worship for Norman hunting parties in the Wealden Forest.)

Also worth looking at are some splendid old timber-framed buildings in Newdigate, which is located not far from J9 of the M25 – take the A24 and turn off at Beare Green on the road signposted to Newdigate.

TANHOUSE FARM SHOP

Rusper Road, Newdigate, Surrey RH5 5BX
Tel:01306 631043 Fax: 01306 631891
email: tanhousefarmshop@btconnect.com
website: www.tanhousefarmshop.co.uk

Tanhouse Farm Shop, located on the road between Rusper and Newdigate, offers a warm welcome and a range of delicious, freshly produced, seasonal foods available seven days a week, throughout the year.

Julie Day, who founded the shop five years ago, has a strong commitment to offering her customers homemade meals and snacks, using only the best available ingredients, without the additives and preservatives so often found in other foodstuffs.

This commitment to wholesome fine food is reflected throughout the Tanhouse offering, from the scrumptious bread and cakes baked daily on the premises, to pickles, preserves and local honey, and to Gloucester Old Spot pork, premium lamb and Aberdeen Angus beef, which are raised on the farm with exceptional attention to animal welfare.

The farm shop boasts a delightful garden, with a heated, marquee dining room, which allows al fresco meals even in less than clement weather. The dining room and garden can also be reserved for private events, such as children's parties, birthdays, christenings or other family get togethers.

Anyone visiting with children will welcome the outdoor play equipment and toys provided to keep younger customers happy whilst Mum and Dad relax with a fair trade cappuccino, organic tea, or locally produced fruit juice. The lunchtime menu is also perfect for families, featuring flavoursome soups, Mediterranean-style treats and deli salad platters just perfect for sharing.

Alongside the food produced to eat on the premises or take home and enjoy, Tanhouse also offers local produce from growers in Surrey and Sussex and a range of cards and gifts, many of which are made by local artisans.

Tanhouse Farm has also built up an enviable reputation for its outside catering service, which again offers only fresh food with everything produced to order in the Farm Shop's own extensive kitchens. Chris Moon, who heads up the catering service, will be happy to discuss your event and work with you to develop the perfect menu.

Julie and the rest of her friendly team look forward to seeing you at Tanhouse Farm Shop, where you are guaranteed a warm welcome and the freshest, most delicious food for miles around.

late 1970s after their Victorian predecessors had warped in the hot summer of 1976.

Present-day Newdigate contains a number of exceptional old timber-framed buildings, several of which date back to the 16th century and earlier.

CHARLWOOD

8 miles SE of Dorking off the A24

A charming period village on the Sussex border, Charlwood is all the more admirable in that it is so near Crawley and Gatwick Airport and yet preserves so much of its own rural identity. Although it lacks the sense of remoteness that it must once have possessed, Charlwood still has many 18th-century cottages and a sprinkling of earlier, slightly larger yeomen's houses, such as the 15th-century Charlwood House to the southeast of the village centre.

The parish Church of St Nicholas was built in the 11th century and underwent a series of alterations, extensions and renovations beginning in the 13th century. The impression, surprisingly, is one of an organic building that has evolved with the centuries. One of its prized possessions is the late medieval screen, one of the most intricately carved pieces of ecclesiastical woodwork in Surrey.

BROCKHAM

1 mile E of Dorking on the A25

Brockham is a picture-postcard village set around a quintessential three-sided village green on which cricket is played in summer, a Guy Fawkes bonfire is lit in November, and Christmas carols sung in winter. The legendary cricketer W G Grace is even said to have played here. This delightful tree-lined setting is enhanced by a splendid view of Box Hill, some fine old cottages, and an elegantly proportioned parish church with a tall spire, which was built in the 1840s in uncomplicated Early English style. Other noteworthy buildings in the village include the late 18th-century Brockham Court, which can be seen on the eastern edge of the green, and the part 17th-century Feltons Farm, which lies a short distance away to the southwest. The remains of some 19th-century industrial kilns can be seen on the Downs above the village in the disused Brockham Quarries.

Southeast Surrey

The southeast corner of Surrey abuts both Kent to the east and Sussex to the south. Not surprisingly, there are elements of both counties in some of the Surrey border villages, noticeable in particular in the way that Kent weather-boarding features in the villages and hamlets near Lingfield.

The M25 marks the northern extremity of the area covered in this section. As with so many other parts of the county, the towns and villages lying just south of the motorway have fought - and largely won - a battle to preserve their sense of identity. Perhaps it is simply because they have had many centuries to grow accustomed to east-west traffic. The valleys and ridges here comprised the route followed by religious devotees on their way from London to Canterbury. Indeed many stretches of the original Pilgrims' Way, which is now a well-marked trail along much of its route, look down on its modern, secular, counterpart, the M25.

The countryside in this southeastern corner is far less wooded than south-central or southwestern Surrey. Instead, it is a land of open fields and church spires spotted on the horizon. Only at the southern edge,

ALANS PLANTS

Clifton Nursery, Clifton Lane, Reigate,
Surrey RH2 9RA
Tel: 0777 865 9525 / 01293 402071
e-mail: alanplants@hotmail.co.uk

Alans Plants was founded and is run by Alan Horlock, who has built up a fine reputation in the area for quality, reliability and value for money. In his small nursery he grows almost 90% of the plants sold, meaning that they are acclimatised to the prevailing weather and soil conditions of the region. There's always something of interest for the gardener, and each season also has its specialities. In January, February and March the nursery sells about 20 varieties of seed potatoes, along with shallots, onion sets and fruit bushes. March, April and May bring basket plants (they'll make up a basket if there's time) and bedding plants, with many varieties of geraniums and fuchsias.

In June, July and August potted rose bushes and fruit trees, ornamental trees, perennials and alpines come to the fore, while from September to December spring bulbs for planting, early primroses, wallflowers and pansies are in demand. Alan's plans for 2009/10 include stocking more hedging plants, soft fruit plants, herbs and grasses.

GORGEOUS

19 Bell Street, Reigate, Surrey RH2 7AD
Tel: 01737 222846
e-mail: heather@gorgeouslife.co.uk
website: www.gorgeouslife.co.uk / www.gorgeouswear.co.uk

Gorgeous is a Surrey-based interior design and fashion business owned and run by Heather Kemeys. She puts her 20+ years of experience into helping clients create beautiful rooms and homes to suit their personalities and takes great pride in the excellent reputation she has earned for design and personal service. The design consultancy covers houses old and new, large and small, and Heather can visit and advise on all aspects of interior design, from colour schemes to carpets and flooring, curtains, wallpapers, upholstery and soft furnishings.

The shop is stocked with a vast array of fabrics, paints, papers, carpets and furnishings, and also offers a bespoke service for making, measuring and fitting curtains and blinds. The front of the shop is filled with beautiful things, from cashmere cardigans and wraps to suede and leather handbags, silk scarves, kimonos, jewellery, scented candles and gifts.

where it nears the Weald of Kent, does the landscape begin to become defined by its dense woodlands.

Reigate

Priory

Reigate is a prosperous residential town whose expansion at the hands of postwar developers has done much to conceal its long and distinguished history. The settlement was once an important outpost of the de Warenne family, the assertive Norman rulers whose sphere of influence stretched from the Channel coast to the North Downs. As at Lewes, they built a castle on a rise above the village streets of which nothing remains today except for an arch, which was reconstructed in the 1770s from material recovered from the original castle walls. Today, this striking neo-Gothic reproduction stands at the heart of a pleasant public park.

A steep path leads down from the castle mound to the attractive mixture of Victorian, Georgian and older buildings, which line Reigate's High Street. The Old Town Hall, a handsome redbrick building constructed in 1729, stands at its eastern end, and a short distance away to the north, the entrance to a disused road tunnel can be seen. This was built beneath the castle mound in 1824 to ease the through-flow of traffic on the busy London to Brighton coaching route.

Other noteworthy buildings in this part of town include the timber-framed and tile-fronted La Trobes in the High Street, and the 400-year-old Old Sweep's House in the charmingly named Slipshoe Street.

As well as being effective administrators, the de Warennes were known for their devout

CAMEL & YAK

47a Bell Street, Reigate,
Surrey RH12 7AQ
Tel: 01737 222441
e-mail: claire@camelandyak.com
website: www.camelandyak.com

Owner Claire Dukes has established **Camel & Yak** as a haven of beautiful things, precious pieces that will enhance any home and delight children and adults alike. The shop, easily recognised by its red-painted frontage, stands opposite Priory Park, one of Reigate's main visitor attractions. The Park and the shop provide fun and interest for all the family – Dad and the kids enjoying the varied amenities of the Park, Mum having a great time among the lovely things in the shop. Camel & Yak is filled with elegant homeware, lifestyle items and gift ideas, most of them of French or Scandinavian origin. The ever-changing stock runs from glassware and stoneware to photo frames, candles, cushions and furniture ranging from individual pieces to complete dining sets. Among the best sellers are the pretty love hearts, which ladies love to collect. They come in all styles and sizes, including zinc hearts produced by the Danish firm of Walther. The same firm also produces lovely little zinc tea light houses and tiny zinc ballet dancers on a chain. Other suppliers include Greengate, another Danish firm, noted for its elegant, exclusive homeware, and the French company Jardin d'Ulysse, whose products include photo frames, beautiful glassware and carved wooden angel wings. Customers return time and again to seek out unusual, tasteful treats or gifts at Camel & Yak.

religious beliefs, and, as at Lewes, they founded a priory in the town some distance from the centre. After the Dissolution of the Monasteries, this became the home of Lord Howard of Effingham, the commander-in-chief of the English navy at the time of the Spanish Armada. **Reigate Priory**, now a Grade I listed building set in 65 acres of parkland, has been remodelled on a number of occasions, in particular during the Georgian era. It now operates as a school and museum. The interior contains some fine period features, including a Holbein fireplace and a fine 17th-century oak staircase. Also set away from the town centre, and probably standing on the site of pre-Norman Reigate, is the pale stone-built church of St Mary Magdalene. This contains a number of striking memorials, including one carved by Joseph Rose the Elder.

Around Reigate

BETCHWORTH

3 miles W of Reigate off the A25

Church of St Michael

Betchworth was once a much more important settlement than it is today. In the 14th century, it had its own fortress, Betchworth Castle, which stood beside the River Mole on a site now occupied by the local golf course. This has now virtually disappeared and the only reminder of Betchworth's past glory is the parish **Church of St Michael**, a surprisingly imposing structure that incorporates some ancient Saxon masonry, a Norman arch and a succession of more recent architectural modifications. Inside, there is a fascinating map of the local manor dated 1634, showing the vestiges of the feudal field system and a wooden chest that is reputed to have been made before the Norman invasion from a single piece of timber taken from a 1,000-year-old oak tree. There is also an unusual font dating from the 1950s. The church is situated at the end of a wide cul-de-sac, which also contains an early 18th-century vicarage, an old long barn, and a collection of attractive 17th and 18th-century cottages.

A number of interesting buildings can be seen in other parts of Betchworth, including the 16th-century Old Mill Cottage, the slender Queen Anne Old House, and Betchworth House, an impressive part-Georgian manor house that is surrounded by pretty parkland.

BUCKLAND

3 miles W of Reigate on the A25

Windmill Church

Buckland is a pretty settlement, which suffers from being sited on the busy main road. The road divides Buckland's tidy rectangular green from the parish church of St Mary, a part 13th-century structure whose interior is worth a look for its 15th-century stained-glass east window and 17th-century pews and oak panelling. The A25 to the east of Buckland passes along the northern edge of Reigate Heath. This narrow area of open heathland is the home of the unique **Windmill Church**, surely the only church in the world to be situated in a windmill.

Windmill Church, Buckland

LEIGH

4 miles SW of Reigate of the A217

Leigh (pronounced Lye) is a well-kept village, which, like at least a dozen others in Britain, takes its name from the Saxon term for forest clearing. Like Newdigate and Charlwood to the south, Leigh was an important centre of the Wealden iron-founding industry, which prospered from the 14th century until it was superseded by northern-based coal-fired smelting in the 18th century. Indeed, this now-tranquil area was once known as Thunderfield-in-the-Forest because of the number of iron furnaces it contained.

HORLEY

5 miles S of Reigate on the A23

The pleasant town of Horley lies on the Sussex border and not far from Gatwick Airport to the south. The proximity to the airport, surprisingly, has done little to alter the character of Horley, although the town did undergo a transformation in the Victorian era after the arrival of the main railway line. The present arrangement of streets, set mostly in a gridiron pattern, branched out from the railway line to provide housing for railway workers and shops to cater to their needs. This neighbourhood, which constitutes most of the core of Horley, is trim and neat, and the overall effect is pleasant. Dotted among the 19th-century buildings are a few survivors of earlier eras, including a lovely tile-hung cottage by the church.

OUTWOOD

5 miles SE of Reigate off the M23

Post Mill

Although Outwood is accessible from the M23, a more pleasant approach leads southwards from Bletchingley along a country road across the Weald. Outwood Common, the area of high ground to the east of the village, is best known for being the location of one of the most interesting windmills in the country.

The **Post Mill** is acknowledged as the oldest working windmill in England. It was built in 1665 and it is said that from the top of the mill, some 39 feet up, the Great Fire of London was visible 27 miles away. Unlike other ancient buildings in England, the Post Mill's early history is not shrouded in mystery and conjecture. It was built by Thomas Budgen, a miller of Nutfield, and the original deeds are still in existence.

The term 'post mill' describes the structure and mechanism of this remarkable building. The whole body of the mill, including its sails and machinery, balances on a huge central post. This post is made from oak, which, it is said, was carried seven miles by oxcart from Crabbet Park, near Crawley, where it was felled. It is supported by four diagonal quarter bars and two crosstrees. These in turn rest on four brick piers. The purpose of this post system is to allow the mill to be turned to face the breeze, and it is so finely balanced that a single person can turn the sails into the wind. Another special design feature, incorporated around 100 years later, allows the angle of the sails to be adjusted to suit different wind conditions using a system of elliptical springs.

For over a century, a second smock windmill stood nearby, and the pair were known locally as the Cat and Fiddle; sadly, the Fiddle blew down in a storm in the early 1960s.

BURSTOW

8 miles SE of Reigate off the B2037

Church of St Bartholomew Smallfield Place

The lanes to the south of Outwood lead through Smallfield to Burstow, a well-kept village whose **Church of St Bartholomew** has a surprisingly well preserved late medieval timber-framed tower. This hefty 15th-century structure supports a peal of six bells, the largest of which weighs over half a ton. The church itself is an attractive mixture of Norman, Perpendicular and Victorian influences; the chancel contains the remains of John Flamsteed, a former rector and the first Astronomer Royal, who is best remembered for his maps of the night skies, compiled in the late 17th century as an aid to marine navigation. Flamsteed was presented with the living of Burstow by Lord North in 1684.

About one mile north of Burstow is **Smallfield Place**, regarded by many as the best example of a stone-built country home in Surrey. Its almost forbidding appearance is at odds with the mellow brick or aged timber exteriors of so many Surrey manor houses. The house was built at the beginning of the 17th century and presents a long, largely unadorned two-storey Wealden stone face to the curious public.

LINGFIELD

12 miles SE of Reigate off the A22

Church of St Peter & St Paul · Racecourse

Lingfield is a large village, set within delightful wooded countryside in the southeastern corner of the county. Almost large enough to be called a town, 'leafy Lingfield' is perhaps best known to the world at large for its **Racecourse**, which stages racing throughout the year. However, the settlement has long been an important agricultural centre, whose largely Perpendicular **Church of St Peter and St Paul** has been enlarged over the centuries to create what has become known as the Westminster Abbey of Surrey. As well as having a rare double nave and an exceptional collection of monumental brasses, the church also contains a number of memorials to members of the Cobham family, the medieval lords of the manor who lived at the now demolished Starborough Castle, a mile and a half to the east. Each of the first four barons has a sizeable tomb showing an effigy of its occupant. These date from between 1361 and 1471 and are particularly fascinating to those with an interest in the development of late-medieval armour.

Lingfield Church

The broad thoroughfare leading down from the church is lined with characteristic weatherboarded and tile-fronted buildings, including Pollard Cottage, with its unusual 15th-century shop front, the 16th-century Old Town Stores, and the Star Inn Cottages, built around 1700. The county library on the opposite side of the church is a former farmhouse built in the 17th century on the site of a Carthusian college founded in the 1400s by Sir Reginald Cobham. Elsewhere in Lingfield, a couple of interesting features can be found near the pond in Plaistow Street: the 15th-century village cross, and the old lock-up, a small local jail built in 1772 and in use until 1882.

Greathed Manor, to the southeast of Lingfield, is a substantial Victorian manor house built in 1868 for the Spender Clay family.

CROWHURST

11 miles SE of Reigate off the A22

Crowhurst contains a yew tree estimated to be around 4,000 years old, thought to be one of the oldest in the country. Its branches are said to enclose an area over 30 feet in diameter. During the 1820s, a covered café was formed by removing some of the central branches and installing tables and chairs.

Crowhurst Place, to the southwest, was rebuilt after World War I on the site of a 15th-century moated manor house.

Bletchingley

Distance: *5.5 miles (8.8 kilometres)*
Typical time: *180 mins*
Height gain: *90 metres*
Map: *Explorer 146*
Walk: *www.walkingworld.com ID:537*
Contributor: *Nina Thornhill*

ACCESS INFORMATION:

Buses run to Bletchingley from Redhill and Oxted. Cars can be parked in the High Street on the A25. The walk starts from Castle Square opposite St Lychens Lane at the Red Lion pub end of the High Street, reached by heading uphill from the High Street.

ADDITIONAL INFORMATION:

Some of the walk is on bridleways, which are likely to be muddy after heavy rain, so boots are advisable. Bird lovers may find it useful to bring their binoculars, as Bay Pond Nature Reserve provides plenty of opportunities to see a wide variety of birds all year round. Just to the west of waymark one at the start of the walk, the remains of Bletchingley castle can be seen. Nothing of the castlle itself remains, just a series of mounds and ditches. Refreshments and supplies are available at Bletchingley, which has four pubs, and Godstone, which has two pubs and a sandwich bar. These are the only places where you are likely to find toilets.

DESCRIPTION:

This walk shows that there is more to the Surrey Hills than just the more widely-known North Downs. The Greensand Hills lie to the south of the North Downs, forming a ridge from Haslemere in Surrey to Hamstreet in Kent. This walk follows the Greensand Way for approximately 2½ miles from Castle Hill, Bletchingley, along Tilbustow Hill to Brakey Hill. Here we depart from the Greensand Way and head north to Godstone. En route a series of ponds are passed before entering Church Town, the older part of Godstone. It has quite a selection of period cottages and houses, some dating from the 16th century, as well as the church of St Nicholas. Right on Godstones' doorstep sits Bay Pond, a nature reserve managed by the Surrey Wildlife Trust. Godstone Green is an ideal place to stop and have lunch. There are two pubs here, one on either side of the green, both serve meals. On summer Sundays the green makes a good picnic spot where you can enjoy your lunch and watch a game of cricket! After Godstone, we head westwards over open farmland. It is here that we travel between the North Downs and the Greensand Hills. At Brewer Street, a half timbered farmhouse can be seen, dating from the 15th century. The walk ends at the village of Bletchingley, formed by the streams which gather into the Coombe Haven, that has several buildings of historic interest. The latter part of the walk takes you through the quiet residential streets of Bexhill. It ends at a car park beside a park in which are a museum and the ruins of a manor.

FEATURES:

Hills or fells, lake/loch, pub, church, wildlife, birds, great views.

WALK DIRECTIONS:

1 | From Bletchingley High Street, turn left into Castle Square. Keep ahead until a two-way fingerpost is reached. You are not going to take either of these paths, instead, turn around and face the way you came. You should see a single fingerpost on your right marked Greensand Way, this is the path to take. When you reach a road, turn right and walk along the road until you come to a fork.

2 | Turn left at this fork onto a bridleway. Keep to the path, ignoring a stile on the left (after a pond) and also ignore a path further on, to the right, until you arrive at a junction, by a tree stump.

3 | Bear right here, ignoring the path on the left. Keep ahead on the main path, ignoring any going off to the left until another fork is reached. Turn right here. When you reach a junction, turn left. After approx 50 yards, look out for a downhill path on your right. Go down this right-hand path and at the junction turn left. When you get to the road, turn left. Look out for a bridleway on the right after passing the white house.

4 | Follow the bridleway here. Be careful to keep to bridleway when you are going around the fields.

5 | Keep to the bridleway as it bears left and goes slightly uphill around the field. Do not take any paths that go through gaps in the hedgerow. When the road is reached, turn left. Look out for the bridleway on your right in approx 250 yards. Follow the GSW arrows (Greensand Way) on the bridleway, keeping straight ahead. When you come to Tilburstow Hill Road go over to the bridleway (marked GSW). Keep ahead on this bridleway, ignoring a path that comes up on the right, until you arrive at a junction.

6 | Bear right at this junction. After a few yards look out for a stile and path on the right. Turn right onto this path, which goes through a field heading towards the B2236. When the road is reached, turn left and walk along it until you get to a fork opposite a building suppliers.

7 | You need to turn right at the fork signposted Tandridge. At the millrace, look out for a stile on the left. Leave the Greensand Way and turn left onto this path by the millrace. Passing between two ponds at Leigh Place, ignore the path going off to the right. When a three-way fingerpost is reached, turn left to join the bridleway. Look out for another three-way fingerpost.

8 | Come off the bridleway and turn right onto the footpath here. Keep to the path until you reach a post. Once in the field, turn left to see a marked post. At this post, turn left into the wood and follow the path downhill and on past Glebe Water. Continue ahead through the graveyard, to pass through the lych gate. The path continues almost ahead on the other side of the road. This path passes Bay Pond Nature Reserve, then passes some buildings before coming out by the road at Godstone Green. Cross the green, making for the A25 on the other side. Cross over and turn left along this road until you come to a garden centre.

9 | Look out for the footpath on the right opposite the garden centre. This passes some sandworkings. When the road is reached turn left. In a few paces you should see 1 North Park Cottage on the right.

10 | Turn right onto this track by North Park Cottage. In a few yards turn left through a metal gate and keep to the sandy path until you reach the road. Do not turn right onto a cycle route track, instead, turn right and walk along Place Farm Road. You need to stay on this road, ignoring any paths going off. At the road junction turn left into Brewer Street. Keep ahead until the road forks off to the right.

11 | At this fork you leave the road and continue ahead on the track. Keep ahead on the path ignoring other paths going off. The path comes out by a road next to Dormers Farm.

12 | When this road is reached, be sure to take the path on the left that follows the road. In approx 200 yards a small workshop unit is reached on the left.

13 | You need to turn left onto this path by the workshop unit. When you reach a church, bear right around the front of the church. This path comes out behind Bletchingley High Street.

DORMANSLAND

12 miles SE of Reigate off the B2029

Old Surrey Hall

Dormansland presents itself as evidence for a bit of social history detective work. The cottages in this hamlet near the Sussex and Kent borders date from the Victorian era, with some 17th and 18th-century examples mixed in. However, they share a common limitation - their size. Other Surrey hamlets have workmen's cottages, but there is usually much more diversity in scale. Several social historians have proposed that these tiny cottages were built by people who were squatting in common land.

Just outside the village is an altogether grander structure, **Old Surrey Hall**, built in 1450 on the remote border with Sussex. Much of the 15th century section, with its close timbering exterior, survives, but the overall moated quadrangle of today's house dates from 1922 and represents a renovation work of near genius by the architect George Crawley.

REDHILL

2 miles E of Reigate on the A23

Redhill developed around the railway station after the London to Brighton line opened in the 1840s. The new rail line ran parallel to the corresponding road (now the A23) and cut through previously open landscape. Most of Redhill's buildings consequently date from that period or the decades shortly afterwards. The parish church of St John has an exceptionally tall and elegant spire, and the Harlequin Theatre in the Warwick Quadrant shopping precinct offers a full programme of drama, film and musical entertainment, in addition to having a pleasant bar, restaurant and coffee shop.

BLETCHINGLEY

4 miles E of Reigate on the A25

Bletchingley is a highly picturesque village and former 'rotten borough' which once had its own castle and street market. Traces of the Norman fortification thought to have been built by Richard de Tonbridge in the 12th century can be seen in the grounds of Castle Hill, a private house lying to the south of the A25. Closer to the centre, the old market in Middle Row is an exceptionally handsome thoroughfare, which, like the nearby High Street, contains some wonderful old timber-framed and tile-hung houses and cottages.

Some fine early buildings can also be found in Church Walk, the lane leading to Bletchingley's Perpendicular Church of St Mary. The oldest part of this sizeable sandstone structure, the Norman west tower, dates from the end of the 11th century; it had a spire until a bolt of lightning destroyed it in 1606. Inside are a 13th-century hermit's cell, a wonderful assortment of medieval gargoyles, a 16th-century monumental brass of a local tanner and his wife, and an extravagant sculpted monument to Sir Robert Clayton, a City money lender and former Lord Mayor of London who died in 1707. The church also contains the sizeable tomb of Sir Thomas Cawarden, the former owner of Bletchingley Place, who acquired the manor house from Anne of Cleves after she had been given it by Henry VIII as part of her divorce settlement.

A couple of interesting settlements lie within easy reach of Bletchingley. Pendell, a two-minute drive to the northwest, contains the striking Jacobean-style Pendell Court, which was built in 1624, and the neo-classical Pendell House, which was built 12 years later on an adjacent site. Brewer Street, one mile to the north, contains the remains of Anne of

Cleves's manor house, remodelled in the 18th century and known as Place Farm.

GODSTONE

6 miles E of Reigate off the A22

Bay Pond

Although Godstone is now thankfully bypassed by the A22, the A25 east-west route still passes through its heart, making a sharp change in direction as it does so. Fortunately, the village's Tudor and Elizabethan character has survived relatively intact. Godstone's most distinguished building, the White Hart Inn in the High Street, claims to have been visited by Richard II, Elizabeth I, Queen Victoria, and even the Tsar of Russia, who broke his journey here in 1815. A series of attractive lanes and alleyways connects the High Street to the village green, a broad open space with a cricket pitch, which is surrounded by a wonderful collection of 16th and 17th-century buildings, including the Tudor-built Hare and Hounds Inn.

Godstone's parish church of St Nicholas is situated half a mile east of the centre and can be reached from the White Hart along an old thoroughfare known as Bay Path. Although Norman in origin, the building was virtually rebuilt in the 1870s by Sir George Gilbert Scott, a local resident at the time. Inside, there is a marble memorial to a cousin of John Evelyn, the 17th-century diarist. The area around the church contains some fine old buildings, including a row of 19th century almshouses and the 16th-century timber-framed Old Pack House, which lies a short distance away to the south. Bay Path also leads to a former hammer pond, **Bay Pond**, which is now a designated nature reserve. At one time, its water would have been used to power the mechanical hammers in a nearby iron foundry, an indication of Godstone's lost industrial past, which also included the manufacture of gunpowder and leatherware. Godstone Farm, in Tilburstow Hill Road to the south of the village, is an open farm, where children can have a hands-on experience of life on a farm.

OXTED

8 miles E of Reigate off the A25

Titsey Place

Oxted is an old town that prospered because of its position just below the Downs and consequently a good trading link with the rest of Surrey. Today, however, Oxted constitutes two distinct parts. New Oxted lies between the original town and Limpsfield. It grew up around the railway station, which was built in the 19th century. Old Oxted is also largely Victorian to the eye, but occasionally the visitor notices some survivors of earlier centuries, such as the Forge House and Beam Cottages, with their medieval core and 17th-century exteriors. Streeters Cottage, built in the 17th century, presents a large timber-framed gable to the road.

At Titsey, north of Oxted on the other side of the M25, stands **Titsey Place**. Treasures at this fine Regency house nestling under the North Downs include four superb Canalettos of Venice, beautiful porcelain, portraits and objets d'art. In the 12-acre gardens are a rose garden, re-planted to commemorate Queen Elizabeth's Golden Jubilee, and a walled kitchen garden with three greenhouses.

LIMPSFIELD

9 miles E of Reigate on the B269

Detillens Limpsfield Chart

The churchyard at Limpsfield contains the grave of the composer, Frederick Delius, who died in France in 1934, but had expressed a wish to be buried in an English country graveyard. Sir Thomas Beecham, a great admirer of Delius, read the funeral oration and conducted an orchestra playing works by the composer. Sir Thomas died in 1961 and was originally buried at Brookwood cemetery near Woking. In 1991, his body was transferred to Limpsfield, where he was buried close to Delius. Also lying here are the conductor Norman del Mar and the pianist Eileen Joyce.

Detillens, a rare 15th-century 'hall' house, is also located in Limpsfield. This striking building has an unusual 'king-post' roof, and despite having been given a new façade in the 18th century, is a good example of a house belonging to a Surrey yeoman, a member of the class of small freeholders who cultivated their own land. Inside, there is an interesting collection of period furniture, china and militaria.

Limpsfield Chart, or simply The Chart, constitutes a hilltop common with some lovely views eastwards across Kent. Next to the common is a 17th-century Mill House. The windmill itself was removed in 1925. Elsewhere in The Chart there are handsome groupings of stone-built houses, cottages and farm buildings, best exemplified by the ensemble at Moorhouse Farm.

East Sussex

BATTLE
*Battle Abbey, High Street, Battle,
East Sussex TN33 0AD
e-mail: battletic@rother.gov.uk
Tel: 01424 773721*

BRIGHTON
*Royal Pavilion Shop, Pavilion Buildings, Brighton,
East Sussex BN1 1EE
e-mail: brighton-tourism@brighton-hove.gov.uk
Tel: 0906 711 2255*

EASTBOURNE
*Cornfield Road, Eastbourne, East Sussex BN21 4QA
e-mail: tic@eastbourne.gov.uk
Tel: 0871 663 0031*

HASTINGS
*Queens Square, Priory Meadow, Hastings,
East Sussex TN34 1TL
e-mail: hic@hastings.gov.uk
Tel: 01424 781111*

HASTINGS (OLD TOWN)
*The Stade, Old Town, Hastings, East Sussex TN34 1EZ
e-mail: hic@hastings.gov.uk
Tel: 01424 781111*

LEWES
*187 High Street, Lewes, East Sussex BN7 2DE
e-mail: lewes.tic@lewes.gov.uk
Tel: 01273 483448*

RYE
*The Heritage Centre, Strand Quay, Rye,
East Sussex TN31 7AY
e-mail: ryetic@rother.gov.uk
Tel: 01797 226696*

SEAFORD
*37 Church Street, Seaford, East Sussex BN25 1HG
e-mail: seaford.tic@lewes.gov.uk
Tel: 01323 897426*

Kent

ASHFORD
*18 The Churchyard, Ashford, Kent TN23 1QG
e-mail: tourism@ashford.gov.uk
Tel: 01233 629165*

BEXLEY
*Hall Place, Bourne Road, Bexley, Kent DA5 1PQ
e-mail: touristinfo@bexleyheritagetrust.org.uk
Tel: 01322 558676*

BROADSTAIRS
*Dickens House Museum, 2 Victoria Parade, Broadstairs,
Kent CT10 1QS
e-mail: visitorinformation@thanet.gov.uk
Tel: 0870 2646111*

CANTERBURY
*12/13 Sun Street, The Buttermarket, Canterbury,
Kent CT1 2HX
e-mail: canterburyinformation@canterbury.gov.uk
Tel: 01227 378100*

DEAL
*The Landmark Centre, 129 High Street, Deal,
Kent CT14 6BB
e-mail: info@deal.gov.uk
Tel: 01304 369576*

DOVER
*The Old Town Gaol, Biggin, Dover, Kent CT16 1DL
e-mail: tic@doveruk.com
Tel: 01304 205108*

FAVERSHAM
*Fleur de Lis Heritage Centre, 13 Preston Street, Faversham,
Kent ME13 8NS
e-mail: fata@visitfaversham.com
Tel: 01795 534542*

FOLKSTONE
*Harbour Street, Folkestone, Kent CT20 1QN
Tel: 01303 258594*

TOURIST INFORMATION CENTRES

GRAVESEND
Towncentric, 18a St George's Square, Gravesend, Kent DA11 OTB
e-mail: info@towncentric.co.uk
Tel: 01474 337600

HYTHE
Visitor Centre, Hythe Railway Station, Scanlons Bridge Road, Hythe, Kent CT21 6LD
Tel: 01303 266421

MAIDSTONE
Town Hall, Middle Row, High Street, Maidstone, Kent ME14 1TF
e-mail: tourism@maidstone.gov.uk
Tel: 01622 602169

MARGATE
12-13 The Parade, Margate, Kent CT9 1EY
e-mail: visitorinformation@thanet.gov.uk
website: www.visitthanet.co.uk
Tel: 0870 2646111

NEW ROMNEY
Visitor Centre, Romney, Hythe & Dymchurch Light Railway, New Romney Station, New Romney, Kent TN28 8PL
Tel: 01797 362353

ROCHESTER
95 High Street, Rochester, Kent ME1 1LX
e-mail: visitor.centre@medway.gov.uk
Tel: 01634 843666

ROYAL TUNBRIDGE WELLS
The Old Fish Market, The Pantiles, Tunbridge Wells, Kent TN2 5TN
e-mail: touristinformationcentre@tunbridgewells.gov.uk
Tel: 01892 515675

RAMSGATE
17 Albert Court, York Street, Ramsgate, Kent CT11 9DN
e-mail: visitorinformation@thanet.gov.uk
website: www.visitthanet.co.uk
Tel: 0870 2646111

SANDWICH
Guildhall, Cattle Market, Sandwich, Kent CT13 9AH
e-mail: info@ticsandwich.wanadoo.co.uk
Tel: 01304 613565

SEVENOAKS
Bus Station, Buckhurst Lane, Sevenoaks, Kent TN13 1LX
e-mail: tic@sevenoakstown.gov.uk
Tel: 01732 450305

SWANLEY
Swanley Library & , London Road, Swanley, Kent BR8 7AE
e-mail: touristinfo@swanley.org.uk
Tel: 01322 614660

TENTERDEN
Town Hall, High Street, Tenterden, Kent TN30 6AN
e-mail: tentic@ashford.gov.uk
Tel: 01580 763572

TONBRIDGE
Tonbridge Castle, Castle Street, Tonbridge, Kent TN9 1BG
e-mail: tonbridge.castle@tmbc.gov.uk
Tel: 01732 770929

Surrey

GUILDFORD
14 Tunsgate, Guildford, Surrey GU1 3QT
e-mail: tic@guildford.gov.uk
Tel: 01483 444333

RICHMOND
Old Town Hall, Whittaker Avenue, Richmond, Surrey TW9 1TP
e-mail: info@visitrichmond.co.uk
website: www.visitrichmond.com
Tel: 020 8940 9125

KINGSTON
Market House, Market Place, Kingston upon Thames, Surrey KT1 1JS
e-mail: tourist.information@rbk.kingston.gov.uk
Tel: 020 8547 5592

TWICKENHAM
The Atrium, Civic Centre, 44 York Street, Twickenham, Middlesex TW1 3BZ
e-mail: info@visitrichmond.co.uk
Tel: 020 8891 7272

West Sussex

ARUNDEL
1-3 Crown Yeard Mews, River Road, Arundel, West Sussex BN18 9JW
e-mail: arundel.vic@arun.gov.uk
Tel: 01903 882268

BOGNOR REGIS
Belmont Street, Bognor Regis, West Sussex PO21 1BJ
e-mail: bognorregis.vic@arun.gov.uk
Tel: 01243 823140

BURGESS HILL
Burgess Hill Town Council, 96 Church Walk, Burgess Hill, West Sussex RH15 9AS
e-mail: touristinformation@burgesshill.gov.uk
Tel: 01444 238202

CHICHESTER
29a South Street, Chichester, West Sussex PO19 1AH
e-mail: chitic@chichester.gov.uk
Tel: 01243 775888

CRAWLEY
County Mall, Crawley, West Sussex RH10 1FP
e-mail: vip@countymall.co.uk
Tel: 01293 846968

HORSHAM
9 The Causeway, Horsham, West Sussex RH12 1HE
e-mail: tourist.information@horsham.gov.uk
Tel:01403 211661

LITTLEHAMPTON
The Look & Sea Centre, 63 - 65 Surrey Street, Littlehampton, West Sussex BN17 5AW
e-mail: littlehampton.vic@arun.gov.uk
Tel: 01903 721866

MIDHURST
North Street, Midhurst, West Sussex GU29 9DW
e-mail: midtic@chichester.gov.uk
Tel: 01730 817322

PETWORTH
Petworth Area Office - CDC, The Old Bakery, Petworth, West Sussex GU28 0AP
Tel: 01798 343523

WORTHING CHAPEL ROAD
Chapel Road, Worthing, West Sussex BN11 1HL
e-mail: tic@worthing.gov.uk
website: www.visitworthing.co.uk
Tel: 01903 221066

WORTHING MARINE PARADE
Marine Parade, Worthing, West Sussex BN11 3PX
e-mail: tic@worthing.gov.uk
website: www.visitworthing.co.uk
Tel: 01903 221066

INDEX OF ADVERTISERS

ACCOMMODATION, FOOD AND DRINK

Arden House, Bexhill-on-Sea pg 173
B & B At Hartlip Place, Hartlip, nr Sittingbourne pg 42
The Barn at Penfolds Bed and Breakfast, Bury, nr Arundel pg 274
Bay View Guest House, Herne Bay pg 51
The Blue Bell Inn, Dockenfield, nr Farnham pg 354
The Bohemian, Deal pg 88
The Brewers Arms, Vines Cross, nr Heathfield pg 160
Burdfield's Country Market & Tea Room, Billingshurst pg 287
Cabbages & Kings, Halstead pg 20
Camelia Botnar Homes & Gardens, Cowfold pg 282
Castle Cottage Chilham B & B, Chilham, nr Canterbury pg 74
Castle House Hotel, Canterbury pg 58
The Cherry Tree Guest House, Eastbourne pg 211
Clayton Wickham Farmhouse, Hurstpierpoint pg 298
Coco Café & Sugar Lounge, Petworth pg 276
The Compasses Inn, Gomshall, nr Guildford pg 361
Country House Accommodation, Withy, nr Graffham pg 263
Cromwell Coffee House, Cranleigh pg 373
Cromwell House, Eastbourne pg 212
The Dining Room, Hersham pg 327
The Duke William, Ickham, nr Canterbury pg 68
The Evening Tide, Herne Bay pg 52
Eve's B & B, Bexhill-on-Sea pg 174
Field Place Country House Bed & Breakfast, Climping, nr Arundel pg 247
Fieldswood Bed & Breakfast, Hadlow, nr Tonbridge pg 135
The Five Bells, Eastry, nr Sandwick pg 94
Frogholt Bed & Breakfast, Frogholt, nr Folkestone pg 117
The Gables Bed & Breakfast, Eastbourne pg 210
The Garden of Eden, Newhaven pg 208
The George & Dragon, Sandwich pg 85
The Griffins Head, Chillenden, nr Canterbury pg 70
Haguelands Farm Village, Burmarsh, nr Romney Marsh pg 120
Hayden's, Rye pg 182
Henny's, Farnham pg 346
Hikers Rest Coffee & Gift Shop, East Dean pg 218
Holly Grove Bed & Breakfast, Little Landon, nr Heathfield pg 160
Holly House Bed & Breakfast, Borden, nr Sittingbourne pg 43
The Hop Pocket, Bossingham, nr Canterbury pg 73
The Horse Guards Inn, Petworth pg 278
igigi Café, Hove pg 194
Jeake's House Hotel, Rye pg 180
The Kings Arms, Fernhurst pg 260
Littlefield Manor, Littlefield Common, nr Guildford pg 359
The Lodge At Winchelsea, Winchelsea pg 187
Magnolia House, Canterbury pg 64
Merriland, Broadstairs pg 77
Michael's Country Kitchen, Steyning pg 286
Millstream Hotel and Restaurant, Bosham, nr Chichester pg 240
Minstrel's Rest, Hastings pg 164
Miss Molletts High Class Tea Room, Appledore pg 112
No 1 The Laurels Bed and Breakfast, Henfield pg 300
Nobles Restaurant, Battle pg 175
Number 7 Longport, Canterbury pg 63
The Old Manse Bed & Breakfast, Bexhill-on-Sea pg 171
One Forty, Cranleigh pg 374
The Pearsons Arms, Whitstable pg 47
Pekes Manor House, Golden Cross pg 224
The Queens Head Hotel, Rye pg 182
The Rose & Crown, Selling, nr Faversham pg 55
Rose Garden Tea Rooms, Westmarsh, nr Canterbury pg 66
The Royal Oak, Stonebridge, nr Dorking pg 377
Samphire, Whitstable pg 48
Savoy Court Hotel, Eastbourne pg 210
Sherwood Guest House, St Leonards-on-Sea pg 170
The Six Bells, Newdigate, nr Dorking pg 389
Solley Farm House, Worth, nr Deal pg 94
The Stephan Langton, Abinger Common pg 385
The Swingate Inn, Swingate, nr Dover pg 106
Sylvan Cottage, Canterbury pg 62
Taste Deli & Café, Great Bookham, nr Leatherhead pg 380
Terraces Bar & Grill, Brighton pg 189
Trading Boundaries, Sheffield Green, nr Fletching pg 152
Uppingham Bed and Breakfast, Steyning pg 285
West Faldie Bed and Breakfast, Lavant, nr Chichester pg 233
West Grange House B & B, Herne Common, nr Herne Bay pg 53
The White Hart Restaurant & Bar, West Hoathly pg 296
White Horses Bed & Breakfast, Felpham, nr Bognor Regis pg 251
White Rose Lodge, Sandwich pg 84

INDEX OF ADVERTISERS

The Whole World Café, Folkestone pg 115
Woodmansgreen Farm, Linch, nr Liphook pg 260
Woodstock House Hotel, Charlton, nr Chichester pg 262
Yew House Bed & Breakfast, Crowborough pg 148
Yew Tree, Barfreston, nr Canterbury pg 71
Yorke Lodge, Canterbury pg 61

ACTIVITIES

Broadstairs Art Courses, Broadstairs pg 78
Bury Hill Fisheries, Westcott, nr Dorking pg 384
Charlotte Rose, East Grinstead pg 291
Chichester Canal Trading Ltd, Chidham, nr Chichester pg 241
Chobham Rider & The Saddle Room, Chobham pg 343
Haguelands Farm Village, Burmarsh, nr Romney Marsh pg 120
Hempstead Equestrian Centre, Benenden pg 143
J.E.M'S Sewing Machine and Needlecraft Centre, Canterbury pg 59
Jo Letchford Mosaics, Folkestone pg 115
Uplands Riding School, Charing, nr Ashford pg 98
Wood Design Workshops & Mettle Studios, Angmering, nr Arundel pg 248

ANTIQUES AND RESTORATION

Antique Chandeliers, Copthorne pg 295
The Antiques Barn, Bethersden, nr Ashford pg 110
Artisan, Birchington pg 80
Fieldstaff Antiques, Rochester pg 31
Memories Antiques, Bramley, nr Guildford pg 364

ARTS AND CRAFTS

Adora Cards & More, Rainham, nr Gillingham pg 40
Amanda's, Selsey pg 237
Art & Sold, Miscellanea, The Sculpture Park, Brokenbog and Art & Investment, Churt, nr Farnham pg 355
Arts Hut, Herstmonceux pg 214
Battle Wool & Needlecraft Shop, Battle pg 178
Broadstairs Art Courses, Broadstairs pg 78
Carrera & Bronte, Ramsgate pg 86
Caxton Contemporary, Whitstable pg 47
Eternal Maker, Chichester pg 228
Francis Iles, Rochester pg 32
Francis Iles, Rochester pg 32
Frank, Whitstable pg 48
I Dig Dinos, Rochester pg 30
J.E.M'S Sewing Machine and Needlecraft Centre, Canterbury pg 59
Jo Letchford Mosaics, Folkestone pg 115
Just Paintings, Meopham pg 13
Kings Framers, Lewes pg 202
Lovelys, Cliftonville, nr Margate pg 79
The Pumpkin Patch, Hailsham pg 213
Rose Green Centre of Art & Craft, Aldwick, nr Bognor Regis pg 250
Stringers Gallery, Petworth pg 276
Swanstitch, Deal pg 89
Verité Gallery, Goring-by-Sea pg 257
Wa Waa's Wool 'n' Bits, Bexhill-on-Sea pg 173
Wood Design Workshops & Mettle Studios, Angmering, nr Arundel pg 248

FASHIONS

Ashford Guns & Tackle, Ashford pg 96
Baby Bea, Swan Street, nr West Malling pg 128
Chobham Rider & The Saddle Room, Chobham pg 343
The Dress Boutique, Guildford pg 358
Emmie Boutique, Hurstpierpoint pg 297
The Golden Fleece, Rye pg 183
Gorgeous, Reigate pg 392
igigi Menswear, Hove pg 195
igigi Womens Boutique, Hove pg 195
The Mad Hatter, Guildford pg 358
Meeka, Haslemere pg 371
Noa Noa, Reigate pg 393
One Forty, Cranleigh pg 374
Pardon my French!, Brighton pg 192
Ritzy Retro, Broadstairs pg 76
Trading Boundaries, Sheffield Green, nr Fletching pg 152
Vintage Styling by Lily Rose, Bexhill-on-Sea pg 172

GIFTWARE

Artful Teasing, Petworth pg 277
Baby Bea, Swan Street, nr West Malling pg 128
Bumbles, Ashtead pg 315
Camel & Yak, Reigate pg 394
Camelia Botnar Homes & Gardens, Cowfold pg 282
Charlotte Rose, East Grinstead pg 291
Dragonfly, Ewhurst, nr Cranleigh pg 376

INDEX OF ADVERTISERS

Gorgeous, Reigate pg 392
Graham Greener, Canterbury pg 62
I Dig Dinos, Rochester pg 30
Jane at Graham Greener, Whitstable pg 50
Jeni Wren Cookware & Kitchen Gifts, Shamley Green pg 363
Mad Hatters Emporium, Otford, nr Sevenoaks pg 19
One Forty, Cranleigh pg 374
Pardon my French!, Brighton pg 192
The Pavilion, Forest Row pg 155
Rose Green Centre of Art & Craft, Aldwick, nr Bognor Regis pg 250
Second Seed Bespoke Furniture, Unique Interiors and Gifts, Hove pg 196
sixtyseven, Brighton pg 190
Taking The Plunge, Whitstable pg 50
Trading Boundaries, Sheffield Green, nr Fletching pg 152
Villandry Home, Sheffield Green, nr Fletching pg 153
Vintage Styling by Lily Rose, Bexhill-on-Sea pg 172

HOME AND GARDEN

Alans Plants, Reigate pg 392
Antique Chandeliers, Copthorne pg 295
Aramas Interiors, Brighton pg 190
Artisan, Birchington pg 80
Bexhill Linens, Bexhill-on-Sea pg 172
Brass Monkeys, Hove pg 197
Camel & Yak, Reigate pg 394
Camelia Botnar Homes & Gardens, Cowfold pg 282
Carrera & Bronte, Ramsgate pg 86
Dragonfly, Ewhurst, nr Cranleigh pg 376
Fenestra Interiors, Cranleigh pg 375
The Forge & General Blacksmith, Ashurst Wood, nr East Grinstead pg 294
Forget-Me-Not, Rye pg 184
Giganteum, Ringmer pg 199
Gorgeous, Reigate pg 392
Graham Greener, Canterbury pg 62
Greatstone Secret Nursery, Greatstone, nr New Romney pg 121
The Greenhouse, Godalming pg 367
Horti. Halcyon, Fox Corner, nr Worplesdon pg 339
Hurstpierpoint Cookshop, Hurstpierpoint pg 297
igigi Homewear, Hove pg 194
Jane at Graham Greener, Whitstable pg 50
Jeni Wren Cookware & Kitchen Gifts, Shamley Green pg 363
Katherine Letts Interiors, Godalming pg 364
The Lighting Agency, Farnham pg 347
Mad Hatters Emporium, Otford, nr Sevenoaks pg 19
Memories Antiques, Bramley, nr Guildford pg 364
Objets d'Art, Haslemere pg 371
Old English Pine, Folkestone pg 116
Pardon my French!, Brighton pg 192
The Pavilion, Forest Row pg 155
Petals For Plants, Broad Oak, nr Heathfield pg 159
Pinecove Nursery, Leigh Green, nr Tenterden pg 111
Polka Dot Interiors, Hurstpierpoint pg 298
The Rug Centre, Dorking pg 376
Second Seed Bespoke Furniture, Unique Interiors and Gifts, Hove pg 196
sixtyseven, Brighton pg 190
Tower Forge Fires, Rye pg 181
Trading Boundaries, Sheffield Green, nr Fletching pg 152
Villandry Home, Sheffield Green, nr Fletching pg 153
Vintage Styling by Lily Rose, Bexhill-on-Sea pg 172
Walnut Hill Nurseries, Longfield Hill, nr Gravesend pg 12
Wing & a Prayer, Tenterden pg 109
Youngs of Cranleigh, Cranleigh pg 375

JEWELLERY

Artisan, Birchington pg 80
Brass Monkeys, Hove pg 197
Bumbles, Ashtead pg 315
Charlotte Rose, East Grinstead pg 291
Emmie Boutique, Hurstpierpoint pg 297
Gorgeous, Reigate pg 392
Jewelled Ltd, Godalming pg 365
The Jewellery Workshop Sussex Ltd, East Grinstead pg 290
Meeka, Haslemere pg 371
Noa Noa, Reigate pg 393
Objets d'Art, Haslemere pg 371
Punzi, Lewes pg 200
Ritzy Retro, Broadstairs pg 76
Wood Design Workshops & Mettle Studios, Angmering, nr Arundel pg 248
The Workshop, Lewes pg 200

INDEX OF ADVERTISERS

PLACES OF INTEREST

Amberley Museum and Heritage Centre, Amberley, nr Arundel pg 271
Anne of Cleves House Museum, Lewes pg 203
Art & Sold, Miscellanea, The Sculpture Park, Brokenbog and Art & Investment, Churt, nr Farnham pg 355
Arundel Wildfowl and Wetlands Centre, Offham, nr Arundel pg 246
Bateman's, Burwash, nr Etchingham pg 157
The Battle of Britain Memorial, Capel-le-Ferne, nr Folkestone pg 103
The Belmont Estate and Harris Belmont Charity, Throwley, nr Faversham pg 56
Bury Hill Fisheries, Westcott, nr Dorking pg 384
C.M. Booth Collection of Historic Vehicles, Rolvenden, nr Cranbrook pg 144
Chichester Canal Trading Ltd, Chidham, nr Chichester pg 241
Chichester Cathedral, Chichester pg 229
Chislehurst Caves, Chislehurst pg 10
Danson House, Bexleyheath pg 8
Doddington Place Gardens, Doddington, nr Sittingbourne pg 44
East Surrey Museum, Caterham pg 319
Farnham Maltings, Farnham pg 348
Firle Place, Firle, nr Lewes pg 206
Garden Organic Yalding, Yalding, nr Maidstone pg 134
Godinton House and Gardens, Ashford pg 97
Great Dixter House and Gardens, Northiam, nr Rye pg 167
Historic Days Out in East Sussex, Lewes pg 201
Historic Days Out in West Sussex, Chichester pg 228
The Historic Dockyard, Chatham pg 39
Ightham Mote, Ivy Hatch, nr Sevenoaks pg 23
Kent and East Sussex Railway, Tenterden pg 108
Knole House, Knole, nr Sevenoaks pg 15
Leonardslee Gardens, Lower Beeding, nr Horsham pg 281
The Museum of Rugby, Twickenham pg 307
Nymans House and Gardens, Handcross, nr Haywards Heath pg 301
Painshill Park, Cobham pg 330
Parham House and Gardens, Parham, nr Pulborough pg 269
Polesden Lacey, Great Bookham, nr Leatherhead pg 381
RHS Garden Wisley, Wisley, nr Woking pg 337
Royal Pavilion, Brighton pg 191
Rural Life Centre, Tilford, nr Farnham pg 350
Sarre Mill, Sarre, nr Birchington pg 82
Scotney Castle Garden and Estate, Lamberhurst, nr Tunbridge Wells pg 140
Shipwreck Heriatge Centre, Hastings pg 165
Tangmere Military Aviation Museum, Tangmere, nr Chichester pg 235
Titsey Place, Titsey, nr Oxted pg 401
Weald and Downland Open Air Museum, Singleton, nr Chichester pg 262

SPECIALIST FOOD AND DRINK SHOPS

Allotment, Deal pg 87
Burdfield's Country Market & Tea Room, Billingshurst pg 287
The Cheese Box, Whitstable pg 49
Coco Café & Sugar Lounge, Petworth pg 276
Crockford Bridge Farm Shop, Addlestone, nr Weybridge pg 321
F Conisbee & Son, East Horsley pg 382
Farm Fresh Express, Selham pg 259
Haguelands Farm Village, Burmarsh, nr Romney Marsh pg 120
J Wickens Family Butcher, Winchelsea pg 186
Janson's Deli & Greengrocers, Lenham, nr Maidstone pg 131
Kingfisher Farm Shop, Abinger Hammer, nr Dorking pg 386
The Little Stour Farm Shop, Wingham pg 67
Lower Hardres Farm Shop, Lower Hardres, nr Canterbury pg 73
Perry Court Farm Shop, Billing, nr Ashford pg 99
Sugar Boy, Whitstable pg 46
Sugar Boy, Canterbury pg 60
Sugar Boy, Deal pg 90
Sutton's Fish Shop, Winchelsea pg 186
Tanhouse Farm Shop, Newdigate, nr Dorking pg 390
Taste Deli & Café, Great Bookham, nr Leatherhead pg 380
Taywell Farm Shop, Goudhurst, nr Cranbrook pg 138

Looking for more walks?

The walks in this book have been gleaned from Britain's largest online walking guide, to be found at *www.walkingworld.com*.

The site contains over 2000 walks from all over England, Scotland and Wales so there are plenty more to choose from in this book's region as well as further afield - ideal if you are taking a short break as you can plan your walks in advance. There are walks of every length and type to suit all tastes.

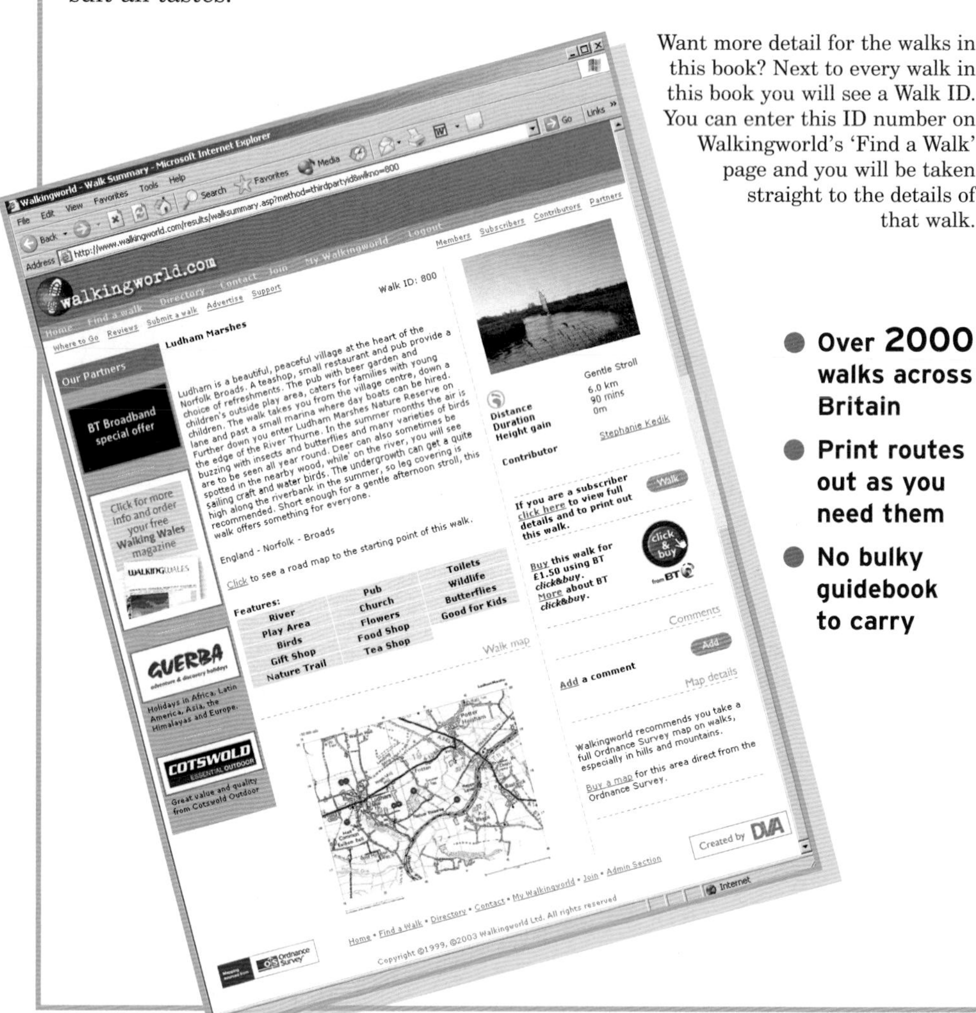

Want more detail for the walks in this book? Next to every walk in this book you will see a Walk ID. You can enter this ID number on Walkingworld's 'Find a Walk' page and you will be taken straight to the details of that walk.

- **Over 2000 walks across Britain**
- **Print routes out as you need them**
- **No bulky guidebook to carry**

INDEX OF WALKS

	Start	Distance	Time	Page
1	HOSEY COMMON *Hosey Common Car Park*	*5.7 miles (9.1km)*	*3½ hrs*	*16*
2	LOWER UPNOR *Upnor Road Car Park, Lower Upnor*	*3.5 miles (5.6km)*	*1½ hrs*	*36*
3	SOUTH FORELAND *St Margaret's Bay*	*5.6 miles (9.0km)*	*3 hrs*	*92*
4	BATTLE TO BEXHILL *Battle Abbey*	*5.3 miles (8.5km)*	*2½ hrs*	*176*
5	EAST DEAN *Off the A259 Eastbourne to Brighton Road*	*6.0 miles (9.6km)*	*3 hrs*	*216*
6	STOUGHTON *Village Green in Stoughton*	*4.3 miles (6.9km)*	*1¾ hrs*	*242*
7	HOUGHTON *North Stoke Village*	*4.3 miles (6.9km)*	*2½ hrs*	*272*
8	HORSTED KEYNES *Horsted Keynes Railway Station*	*5.9 miles (9.4km)*	*3¾ hrs*	*292*
9	FRENSHAM COMMON *Frensham Great Pond Car Park*	*5.8 miles (9.3km)*	*3 hrs*	*352*
10	GUILDFORD TO GODALMING *Guildford Railway Station*	*5.0 miles (8.0km)*	*3 hrs*	*366*
11	BLETCHINGLEY *Bletchingley High Street*	*5.5 miles (8.8km)*	*3 hrs*	*398*

ORDER FORM

To order any of our publications just fill in the payment details below and complete the order form. For orders of less than 4 copies please add £1 per book for postage and packing. Orders over 4 copies are P & P free.

Please Complete Either:

I enclose a cheque for £ ______ *made payable to Travel Publishing Ltd*

Or:

CARD NO: ______ EXPIRY DATE: ______

SIGNATURE: ______

NAME: ______

ADDRESS: ______

TEL NO: ______

Please either send, telephone, fax or e-mail your order to:

Travel Publishing Ltd, Airport Business Centre, 10 Thornbury Road, Estover, Plymouth PL6 7PP
Tel: 01752 697280   Fax: 01752 697299   e-mail: info@travelpublishing.co.uk

	Price	Quantity
Hidden Places Regional Titles		
Cornwall	£8.99	....
Devon	£8.99	....
Dorset, Hants & Isle of Wight	£8.99	....
East Anglia	£8.99	....
Lake District & Cumbria	£8.99	....
Lancashire & Cheshire	£8.99	....
Northumberland & Durham	£8.99	....
Peak District and Derbyshire	£8.99	....
Yorkshire	£8.99	....
Hidden Places National Titles		
England	£11.99	....
Ireland	£11.99	....
Scotland	£11.99	....
Wales	£11.99	....
Other Titles		
Off The Motorway	£11.99	....
Garden Centres and Nurseries of Britain	£11.99	....

	Price	Quantity
Country Living Rural Guides		
East Anglia	£10.99	....
Heart of England	£10.99	....
Ireland	£11.99	....
North East of England	£10.99	....
North West of England	£10.99	....
Scotland	£11.99	....
South of England	£10.99	....
South East of England	£10.99	....
Wales	£11.99	....
West Country	£10.99	....

TOTAL QUANTITY ______

TOTAL VALUE ______

READER REACTION FORM

The **Travel Publishing** *research team would like to receive readers' comments on any visitor attractions or places reviewed in the book and also recommendations for suitable entries to be included in the next edition. This will help ensure that the* **Country Living series of Rural Guides** *continues to provide its readers with useful information on the more interesting, unusual or unique features of each attraction or place ensuring that their visit to the local area is an enjoyable and stimulating experience. To provide your comments or recommendations would you please complete the forms below and overleaf as indicated and send to:*

The Research Department, Travel Publishing Ltd, Airport Business Centre, 10 Thornbury Road, Estover, Plymouth PL6 7PP

YOUR NAME:

YOUR ADDRESS:

YOUR TEL NO:

Please tick as appropriate: COMMENTS ☐ RECOMMENDATION ☐

ESTABLISHMENT:

ADDRESS:

TEL NO:

CONTACT NAME:

PLEASE COMPLETE FORM OVERLEAF

READER REACTION FORM

COMMENT OR REASON FOR RECOMMENDATION:

....

....

....

....

....

....

....

....

....

....

....

....

READER REACTION FORM

The **Travel Publishing** *research team would like to receive readers' comments on any visitor attractions or places reviewed in the book and also recommendations for suitable entries to be included in the next edition. This will help ensure that the* **Country Living series of Rural Guides** *continues to provide its readers with useful information on the more interesting, unusual or unique features of each attraction or place ensuring that their visit to the local area is an enjoyable and stimulating experience. To provide your comments or recommendations would you please complete the forms below and overleaf as indicated and send to:*

The Research Department, Travel Publishing Ltd, Airport Business Centre, 10 Thornbury Road, Estover, Plymouth PL6 7PP

YOUR NAME:

YOUR ADDRESS:

YOUR TEL NO:

Please tick as appropriate: COMMENTS ☐ RECOMMENDATION ☐

ESTABLISHMENT:

ADDRESS:

TEL NO:

CONTACT NAME:

PLEASE COMPLETE FORM OVERLEAF

READER REACTION FORM

COMMENT OR REASON FOR RECOMMENDATION:

....

....

....

....

....

....

....

....

....

....

....

....

TOWNS, VILLAGES AND PLACES OF INTEREST

A

Abinger 385
Church of St James 385
Abinger Hammer 387
Albury 361
Albury Park 361
Alciston 221
Medieval Dovecote 221
Alfold 373
Countryways Experience 373
Alfriston 220
Cathedral of the Downs 220
Clergy House 220
Market Cross 220
Star Inn 220
Alkham 104
Allhallows 37
Iron Beacon 37
Amberley 270
Amberley Castle 273
Amberley Wild Brooks 273
Amberley Working Museum 273
Appledore 113
Ardingly 289
Ardingly Reservoir 289
Wakehurst Place 289
Arundel 244
Arundel Castle 244
Arundel Museum and Heritage Centre 245
Cathedral of Our Lady and St Philip Howard 245
Wildlife and Wetland Centre 245
Ashdown Forest 154
Ashdown Forest 154
Ashford 96
Ashford Borough Museum 96
Godinton Park 97
Aylesford 129
Aylesford Priory 129
Kit's Coty House 129
Aylesham 69

B

Bagshot 342
Banstead 317
All Saints Church 317
Barcombe 198
Barfreston 72
Barham 107
Battle 175
Battle Abbey 178
Battle Museum of Local History 179
Battle of Hastings Site 175
Prelude to Battle Exhibition 178
Yesterday's World 179
Beachy Head 212
Beckley 188
Beddington 314
Carew Chapel 314
Bekesbourne 68
Howletts Wild Animal Park 68
Beltring 134
Hop Farm Country Park 134
Benenden 143
Betchworth 394
Church of St Michael 394
Bethersden 111
Bexhill-on-Sea 170
Bexhill Museum 174
De La Warr Pavilion 171
Bexleyheath 7
Danson Park 7
Hall Place 7
Lesness Abbey 8
The Red House 8
Biddenden 113
All Saints' Church 113
Biddenden Maids 113
Biggin Hill 24
Biggin Hill RAF Station 24
Bignor 273
Roman Villa 274
Billingshurst 287
Birchington 79
All Saints' Church 80
Quex House 80
Birdham 238
Sussex Falconry Centre 238
Bisley 341
Blackheath 362
Blean 75
Bletchingley 400
Bodiam 168
Bodiam Castle 168
Bognor Regis 249
Birdman Rally 250
Bognor Regis Museum 250
Borstal 34
Bosham 239
Bosham Walk Craft Centre 241
Bough Beech 27
Bough Beech Reservoir 27
Boughton 55
Farming World 55
Boughton Lees 99
North Downs Way 99
Boughton Monchelsea 132
Boughton Monchelsea Place 133
Box Hill 378
Box Hill 378
Boxgrove 234
Boxgrove Priory 234
Boxley 130
Bramber 284
Bramber Castle 284
St Mary's House 284
Bramley 363
Millmead 363
Brede 166
Brenzett 125
Brenzett Aeronautical Museum 125
Bridge 68
Brightling 158
Mausoleum 159
Sugar Loaf 159
Brighton 188
Booth Museum of Natural History 193
Brighton Museum and Art Gallery 191
Brighton Pier 193
Brighton Toy and Model Museum 193
Church of St John 191
Metropole Hotel 193
Preston Manor 192
Royal Pavilion 189
Stanmer Park and Rural Museum 192
The Dome 191
Theatre Royal 193
Broadstairs 75
Crampton Tower Museum 77
Dickens House Museum 77

TOWNS, VILLAGES AND PLACES OF INTEREST

Brockham 391
Brook 100
Agricultural Museum 100
Brookland 124
Church of St Thomas à Becket 125
Broomfield 132
Buckland 395
Windmill Church 395
Bulverhythe 170
Burgess Hill 296
Burmarsh 122
Burpham 246
Burstow 396
Church of St Bartholomew 396
Smallfield Place 396
Burwash 156
Bateman's 157
Buxted 150
Buxted Park 150
Hogge House 150

C

Cade Street 159
Camber 185
Camberley 341
Sandhurst Academy 341
Surrey Heath Museum 341
Canterbury 59
Canterbury Cathedral 59
Canterbury Festival 65
Canterbury Tales Visitor Attraction 63
Museum of Canterbury 65
Roman Museum 64
St Augustine's Abbey 59
St Martin's Church 63
The Kent Masonic Library and Museum 64
Capel le Ferne 104
Battle of Britain Memorial 104
Carshalton 313
Honeywood Heritage Centre 313
Caterham 318
East Surrey Museum 319
Tupwood Viewpoint 318
Chailey 153
Chailey Common 153
Chaldon 318
Challock 99
Beech Court Gardens 99
Eastwell Park 100
Charing 97
Charlwood 391
Chatham 38
Almshouses 39
Fort Amherst 38
Museum of the Royal Dockyard 38
The Historic Dockyard 38
Cheam 313
Lumley Chapel 313
Chertsey 332
Chertsey Museum 332
Chichester 229
Chichester Canal 232
Chichester Cathedral 229
Chichester District Museum 232
Chichester Festival Theatre 232
Guildhall 231
Pallant House 231
Pallant House Gallery 232
Royal Military Police Museum 232
St Mary's Hospital 231
Chiddingfold 372
St Mary's Church 372
Chiddingly 224
Chiddingstone 27
Chiddingstone Castle 27
Chilgrove 265
Chilham 74
North Downs Way 74
Chillenden 70
Chilworth 362
Chilworth Manor 362
Chipstead 317
Chislehurst 9
Chislehurst Caves 9
Chislehurst Common 9
Petts Wood 9
Chobham 342
Clandon Park 360
Clandon Park 360
Claygate 327
Clayton 299
Cobham 11, 329
Almshouses 11
Church of St Mary Magdalene 11
Cobham Bus Museum 329
Cobham Hall 11
Leather Bottle Inn 11
Owletts 13
Painshill Park 329
Coldharbour 387
Anstiebury Camp 387
Coldred 72
Compton 368, 265
Cooling 35
Coombes 254
Cootham 269
Parham 269
Coulsdon 317
Downlands Circular Walk 318
Farthing Down 318
St John the Evangelist Church 318
Court-at-Street 119
Cowfold 283
Church of St Peter 283
St Hugh's Charterhouse 283
Cranbrook 141
Cranbrook Museum 142
St Dunstan's 142
Cranleigh 373
Crawley 281
Crayford 7
World of Silk 7
Cross In Hand 159
Crowborough 148
Crowhurst 397
Croydon 314
Fairfield Halls 314
St John the Baptist Church 314
The Palace 314
Waddon Caves 314
Cuckfield 302
Borde Hill Gardens 302

D

Dartford 6
Deal 89
Deal Castle 90
Maritime and Local History Museum 90
Timeball Tower 90

TOWNS, VILLAGES AND PLACES OF INTEREST

Denton 105
Broome Park 105
Denton Court 105
Tappington Hall 107

Detling 129
Pilgrims Way 129

Ditchling 197
Anne of Cleves' House 197
Ditchling Beacon 197
Ditchling Common Country Park 197
Ditchling Museum 198

Doddington 43
Doddington Place 43

Dorking 377
Holmwood Common 378
North Downs Way 377

Dormansland 400
Old Surrey Hall 400

Dover 101
Dover Castle 101
Dover Museum 102
Maison Dieu 102
Princess of Wales' Royal Regiment Museum 102
Roman Painted House 102
Secret Wartime Tunnels 102
Women's Land Army Museum 104

Downe 24
Down House 24

Duncton 263

Dungeness 123
Dungeness Nature Reserve 123
Dungeness Power Station 123

Dunsfold 372
Church of St Mary and All Saints 372

Dymchurch 122
Lords of the Level 122
Martello Tower 122

E

Earnley 237
Earnley Gardens 237
Rejectamenta 237

Eartham 252

Easebourne 261

Eashing 369
The Meads 369

East Ashling 244
Kingley Vale National Nature Reserve 244

East Clandon 383
Hatchlands Park 383

East Dean 217
Seven Sisters 218
South Downs Area of Outstanding Natural Beauty 218

East Farleigh 133

East Grinstead 290
Church of St Swithin 291
Saint Hill Manor 294
Standen 294
Town Museum 294

East Hoathly 224

East Horsley 382
East Horsley Towers 382

East Molesey 323

Eastbourne 209
Beachy Head 212
Beachy Head Countryside Centre 213
Eastbourne Heritage Centre 211
Martello Tower No 73 212
Military Museum of Sussex 212
Museum of Shops 211
RNLI Lifeboat Museum 212

Eastchurch 44

Eastry 95

Edburton 301
Church of St Andrew 302

Edenbridge 28

Effingham 381

Egham 344
Royal Holloway College 344

Elham 105

Ellen's Green 373

Elmley Island 45
Elmley Marshes Nature Reserve 45

Elstead 351

Englefield Green 344

Epsom 314
Epsom Downs 315

Esher 328
Claremont House 329
Claremont Landscape Garden 328
Sandown Park 328

Etchingham 158

Ewell 316
Bourne Hall Museum 316

Ewhurst 375
St Peter and St Paul 375

Eynsford 21
Eagle Heights 21
Lullingstone Castle 21
Lullingstone Park and Visitor Centre 22
Lullingstone Roman Villa 21

F

Fairlight 169

Farnborough 18, 340
Farnborough Air Science Museum 340

Farnham 346
Farnham Castle 346
Farnham Maltings 348
Farnham Museum 348

Farningham 22
Darent Valley Path 22
Farningham Woods Nature Reserve 22

Faversham 53
Chart Gunpowder Mills 54
Fleur de Lis Heritage Centre 54
Guildhall 54
South Swale Nature Reserve 54

Felpham 250

Fernhurst 261
Black Down 261

Findon 254
Cissbury Ring 254

Fishbourne 239
Fishbourne Roman Palace 239

Fittleworth 274
Brinkwells 275

Folkestone 114
Church of St Mary and St Eanswythe 114
Folkestone Museum 116
Martello Tower No 3 116
The Folkestone Warren 116

Fontwell 252
Denman's Garden 252
Fontwell Park National Hunt Racecourse 252

Ford 249

Fordwich 65

Forest Row 155

French Street 18
Chartwell 18

Frensham 353

TOWNS, VILLAGES AND PLACES OF INTEREST

Frimley 340
Basingstoke Canal Visitors Centre 340
Friston 218

G

Gatwick Airport 280
Gillingham 40
The Royal Engineers Museum 40
Glynde 204
Glynde Place 204
Mount Caburn 204
Glyndebourne 204
Glyndebourne Opera House 205
Godalming 365
Charterhouse 367
Munstead Wood 367
Museum 365
Winkworth Arboretum 368
Godstone 401
Bay Pond 401
Gomshall 360
Goodnestone 69
Goodnestone Park Gardens 69
Goodwood 233
Goodwood House 233
Goodwood Racecourse 234
Goring-By-Sea 256
Highdown Gardens 257
Goudhurst 137
Bedgebury National Pinetum 139
Finchcocks 139
Gravesend 10
Church of St George 11
Milton Chantry 11
Great Bookham 379
Church of St Nicholas 379
Polesden Lacey 380
Great Mongeham 93
Great Tangley 362
Groombridge 149, 140
Groombridge Place 149, 140
Guestling Thorn 169
Guildford 357
Guildford Cathedral 357
Guildford Museum 359
River Wey Navigations 360

H

Hadlow 135
Broadview Gardens 135
Hadlow Down 149
Wilderness Wood 149
Hailsham 213
Halland 223
Bentley House and Motor Museum 223
Halnaker 234
Halnaker House 234
Hambledon 370
Hydon's Ball 370
Hammerwood 155
Hammerwood Park 155
Hampton Court 323
Hampton Court Palace 323
Hamsey 198
Handcross 302
High Beeches Gardens 302
Nymans 302
Harbledown 74
Bigbury Hill Fort 75
Hardham 273
Church of St Botolph 273
Hartfield 156
Pooh Corner 156
Haslemere 370
Educational Museum 372
Hastings 162
1066 Story 163
Fishermen's Museum 163
Hastings Embroidery 165
Hastings Museum and Art Gallery 165
Museum of Local History 165
Shipwreck Heritage Centre 164
Smugglers Adventure 163
The Stade 163
Underwater World 164
Hawkinge 104
Kent Battle of Britain Museum 104
Haywards Heath 288
Headcorn 114
Headcorn Manor 114
Lashenden Air Warfare Museum 114
Heathfield 159
Herne Bay 51
Herne Bay Museum Centre 51
Herne Common 52
Regia Anglorum 52
Wildwood Wealden Forest Park 52
Hernhill 53
Mount Ephraim Gardens 53
Hersham 326
Herstmonceux 214
Herstmonceux Castle 214
Herstmonceux Castle Gardens 215
Herstmonceux Science Centre 215
Hever 27
Hever Castle 27
Hextable 9
Hextable Gardens 9
Hextable Park 9
High Salvington 254
Higham 35
Gad's Hill Place 35
Hindhead 356
Hindhead Common 357
Hindhead Common 357
Hog's Back 350
Hollingbourne 130
Holmbury St Mary 387
Horley 395
Horsham 279
Christ's Hospital School 280
Horsham Museum 280
Horsmonden 137
Hove 193
13 Brunswick Place 193
British Engineerium 196
Foredown Tower 196
Hove Museum and Art Gallery 196
Hurst Green 179
Merriments Gardens 180
Hurstpierpoint 297
Hurstpierpoint College 297
Hythe 117
Hythe Local History Room 118
St Leonard's Church 118

I

Ide Hill 28
Emmetts Garden 28
Ightham 22
Ightham Church 22

TOWNS, VILLAGES AND PLACES OF INTEREST

Isle of Sheppey 43
Itchenor 238
Itchingfield 288
Ivy Hatch 23
Ightham Mote 23

J

Jevington 220

K

Kew 310
National Archives 310
Royal Botanic Gardens 310
Kew Gardens 310
Keymer 296
Kingston-upon-Thames 306
Chapel of St Mary Magdalene 307
Kingston Museum 307
Kirdford 268
Knowlton 72
Knowlton Court 72

L

Laleham 334
Laleham Riverside Park 334
Lamberhurst 139
Owl House Gardens 139
Scotney Castle 140
Laughton 223
Leatherhead 379
Fire and Iron Gallery 379
Leatherhead Museum of Local History 379
Leeds 130
Leeds Castle 131
Leigh 395
Leith Hill 388
Leith Hill 388
Leith Hill Place 388
Lewes 201
Anne of Cleves House 204
Barbican House Museum 202
Lewes Castle 202
Martyrs' Memorial 204
Leysdown 45
The Swale National Nature Reserve 45
Lightwater 341
Lightwater Country Park 342
Limpsfield 402
Detillens 402
Limpsfield Chart 402
Lindfield 289
Old Place 289
Lingfield 397
Church of St Peter and St Paul 397
Racecourse 397
Littlehampton 247
Littlehampton Museum 249
Littleton 334
Lodsworth 261
Long Ditton 326
Loose 132
Loseley Park 368
Loseley House 368
Lower Beeding 283
Leonardslee Gardens 283
Loxwood 268
Wey and Arun Junction Canal 268
Lurgashall 261
Lydd 123
All Saints' Church 123
Lydd Town Museum 123
Romney Marsh Craft Gallery 123
Lyminster 247
Knuckler Hole 247
Lympne 118
Lympne Castle 118
Port Lympne Wild Animal Park 118

M

Maidstone 126
Allington Castle 127
Maidstone Carriage Museum 127
Maidstone Museum and Bentlif Art Gallery 126
Museum of Kent Life 127
Mannings Heath 283
Manston 83
Spitfire and Hurricane Memorial Building 83
Marden 133
Maresfield 150
Margate 78
Margate Museum 79
Salmestone Grange 79
Shell Grotto 79
Matfield 137
Mayfield 161
Mayfield Palace 161
Meopham 13
Meopham Windmill 13
Mereworth 24
Mersham 119
Mickleham 379
St Michael's 379
Mid Lavant 232
Midhurst 258
Cowdray 258
Cowdray Park 258
Midhurst Grammar School 258
Milton Regis 41
Court Hall Museum 41
Dolphin Yard Sailing Barge Museum 41
Minster 43, 82
Agricultural and Rural Life Museum 83
Gatehouse Museum 43
Minster Abbey 43, 83
Mortlake 311

N

Nettlestead 134
New Malden 312
New Romney 119
Romney Hythe and Dymchurch Railway 121
Romney Toy and Model Museum 121
St Nicholas' Church 121
Newdigate 389
Newhaven 207
Newhaven Fort 208
Newhaven Local and Maritime Museum 208
Planet Earth Exhibition 208
Newick 154
Ninfield 174
Ashburnham Park 174
Nonington 69
North Lancing 256
Northbourne 95

TOWNS, VILLAGES AND PLACES OF INTEREST

Northiam 166
Brickwall House 167
Great Dixter House and Gardens 167
Kent & East Sussex Railway 168
Norton 236
Nutley 154
Nutley Windmill 154

O

Oatlands 326
Ockham 383
Church of All Saints 383
Ockley 388
Hannah Peschar Gallery-Garden 389
Old Romney 124
Derek Jarman 124
Romney Marsh 124
Orpington 9
Bromley Museum 10
Crofton Roman Villa 10
Ospringe 56
Maison Dieu 56
Otford 19
Becket's Well 20
Heritage Centre 20
Otham 130
Outwood 396
Post Mill 396
Oxshott 331
Oxshott Woods 331
Oxted 401
Titsey Place 402

P

Patrixbourne 69
Peacehaven 208
Penshurst 26
Penshurst Place 26
Peper Harow 351
Church of St Nicholas 351
Peper Harow Farm 351
Peper Harow House 353
Pett 169
Pett Level 169
Petworth 275
Petworth Cottage Museum 277
Petworth House 277
Pevensey 215
1066 Country Walk 217
Mint House 215
Pevensey Castle 215
Piddinghoe 207
Piltdown 150
Pirbright 340
Platt 22
Great Comp Garden 22
Plaxtol 23
Mereworth Woods 24
Old Soar Manor 23
Playden 185
Royal Military Canal 185
Pluckley 98
Plumpton 198
National Hunt Racecourse 198
Plumpton Place 198
Polegate 213
Windmill and Museum 213
Poynings 300
Devil's Dyke 300
Preston 66
Pulborough 267
RSPB Pulborough Brooks Nature Reserve 267
Puttenham 351
Pyecombe 299
Pyrford 336
Church of St Nicholas 336
Newark Priory 336

Q

Queenborough 45
The Guildhall Museum 45

R

Ramsgate 87
The Grange 89
Ranmore Common 381
Ranmore Common 381
Reculver 81
Reculver Country Park 81
Reculver Towers and Roman Fort 81
Redhill 400
Reigate 393
Reigate Priory 394
Richmond 309
Museum of Richmond 309
Richmond Hill 310
Ringmer 199
Ringwould 91
Ripley 338
River 105
Robertsbridge 179
Rochester 29
Guildhall Museum 33
Rochester Castle 31
Rochester Cathedral 33
Royal Victoria and Bull Hotel 33
Rodmell 205
Monk's House 206
Rolvenden 143
CM Booth Collection of Historic Vehicles 144
Rottingdean 209
North End House 209
The Elms 209
The Grange 209
Royal Tunbridge Wells 136
Church of King Charles the Martyr 136
Tunbridge Wells Museum and Art Gallery 136
Rudgwick 288
Runfold 349
Runnymede 344
Air Forces Memorial 345
Magna Carta 344
Rusper 280
Rusthall 141
Rye 180
Lamb House 183
Landgate 181
Mermaid Inn 183
Rye Castle Museum 185
Rye Harbour Nature Reserve 180

S

Sandgate 117
Sandhurst 144
Sandwich 83
Guildhall Museum 85
Richborough Roman Fort 86

TOWNS, VILLAGES AND PLACES OF INTEREST

Sarre 81
Sarre Mill 81
Seaford 219
Seaford Head 220
Seaford Museum of Local History 219
Sedlescombe 179
Selmeston 221
Charleston 222
Selsey 236
Lifeboat Museum 237
Selsey Bill 237
Selsey Windmill 236
Sevenoaks 14
Knole House 14
One Tree Hill 15
Sevenoaks Library Gallery 14
Shalford 362
Great Tangley 362
Water Mill 362
Wey and Arun Junction Canal 362
Sheerness 45
Sheerness Heritage Centre 46
Sheffield Green 151
Bluebell Railway 153
Sheffield Park 151
Sheldwich 55
National Fruit Collection 56
Shepherdswell 72
East Kent Railway 72
Shepperton 333
Shere 361
Church of St James 361
Shere Museum 361
Shipley 286
King's Land 286
Shoreham 20
Aircraft Museum 21
Shoreham-By-Sea 255
Marlipins Museum 255
Shoreham Fort 255
Sidlesham 236
Pagham Harbour Nature Reserve 236
Singleton 263
Weald and Downland Open Air Museum 263
Sissinghurst 142
Gardens 143
Sissinghurst Castle 142
Sittingbourne 41
Slindon 252
Slindon Estate 252
Small Dole 301
Woods Mill 301
Small Hythe 112
Smallhythe Place 112
Smarden 109
Smeeth 101
Snargate 125
Church of St Dunstan 125
Sompting 256
South Harting 265
Durford Abbey 267
Harting Down 266
Uppark 266
Southease 206
Speldhurst 141
St Leonards 169
St Leonards Gardens 170
St Margaret's at Cliffe 91
Church of St Margaret of Antioch 93
South Foreland Lighthouse 93
St Margaret's Museum 93
The Pines 93
St Mary in the Marsh 122
Staines 333
Great Thorpe Park 334
Spelthorne Museum 333
Staplehurst 133
Iden Croft Herbs 133
Stelling Minnis 100
Steyning 285
Steyning Museum 286
Stoke d'Abernon 331
Slyfield Manor 331
St Mary's Church 331
Stone-in-Oxney 125
Stopham 275
Stopham Bridge 275
Stopham House 275
Storrington 270
Church of St Mary 270
South Downs Way 270
Stourmouth 66
Strood 34
Temple Manor 34
Sullington 270
Long Barn 270
Sullington Warren 270
Sunbury-on-Thames 334
Surbiton 312
Sussex Weald 148
Sutton Place 338
Sutton Place 338
Swanscombe 13
Swingfield 104
MacFarlanes Butterfly and Garden Centre 104

T

Tangmere 235
Tangmere Military Aviation Museum 235
Tatsfield 319
Telscombe 207
Temple Ewell 105
Tenterden 108
Church of St Mildred 108
Colonel Stephens' Railway Museum 109
Kent and East Sussex Railway 109
Tenterden and District Museum 109
Teynham 57
Thames Ditton 326
St Nicholas' Church 326
The Devil's Punchbowl 356
Thorpe 332
Three Leg Cross 157
Bewl Bridge Reservoir 157
Throwley 56
Belmont 56
Thursley 353
St Michael's Church 356
Ticehurst 158
Pashley Manor Gardens 158
Tilford 349
Rural Life Centre 349
Tillington 278
Tonbridge 25
Tonbridge School 25
Tongham 350
Trottiscliffe 22
Coldrum Long Barrow 22
Trotton 267

TOWNS, VILLAGES AND PLACES OF INTEREST

Tudeley 25

Twickenham 307

Ham House 308

Marble Hill House 308

Museum of Rugby 308

Orleans House and Gallery 308

The Twickenham Museum 308

U

Uckfield 151

Upnor 35

Upnor Castle 35

Upper Beeding 284

Upper Dicker 222

Michelham Priory 222

Michelham Priory Gardens 223

V

Virginia Water 343

Savill Garden 343

Valley Gardens 343

Windsor Great Park 343

W

Wadhurst 161

Church of St Peter and St Paul 161

Walberton 252

Walderton 243

Stansted House 243

Stansted Park Garden Centre 243

Waldron 150

Walmer 91

Walmer Castle 91

Walton on the Hill 320

Walton-on-Thames 322

Church of St Mary 323

Warlingham 319

Warnham 288

Field Place 288

Washington 287

Chanctonbury Ring 287

Waverley Abbey 349

Waverley Abbey 349

West Chiltington 269

Church of St Mary 269

West Dean 219, 264

Charleston Manor 219

The Trundle 264

West Dean Gardens 264

West Firle 205

Firle Beacon 205

Firle Place 205

West Hoathly 295

Priest House 295

West Langdon 95

Langdon Abbey 95

West Marden 265

West Molesey 323

Molesey Hurst 323

West Sussex Weald 279

West Wittering 238

Cakeham Manor House 238

East Head 238

Westcott 383

Westerham 18

Quebec House 18

Squerryes Court 19

Westfield 166

Westham 217

Weybridge 321

Brooklands Museum 322

Elmbridge Museum 321

Whiteley Village 331

Whitfield 107

Dover Transport Museum 107

Whitstable 46

Whitstable Museum and Gallery 49

Willesborough 100

Wilmington 221

Long Man 221

Wilmington Priory 221

Wimbledon 311

All England Lawn Tennis and Croquet Club 311

Wimbledon Common 312

Wimbledon Lawn Tennis Museum 311

Winchelsea 185

Camber Castle 188

Winchelsea Court Hall Museum 187

Windlesham 342

Wingham 67

Norman Parish Church 67

Wingham Wildlife Park 67

Wisborough Green 268

Church of St Peter ad Vincula 268

Fishers Farm Park 269

Wisley 337

Wisley Garden 337

Withyham 156

Witley 369

Old Manor 369

Tigburne Court 370

Witley Common Information Centre 370

Wittersham 113

Woking 335

Wonersh 363

Chinthurst Hill 363

Woodchurch 111

South of England Rare Breeds Centre 111

Woodnesborough 83

Wootton 105

Worplesdon 338

Worth 83, 290

Church of St Nicholas 290

Worth Abbey 290

Worthing 253

Worthing Museum and Art Gallery 253

Wrotham 22

Wych Cross 155

Ashdown Forest Llama Park 155

Wye 100

Wye College 100

Y

Yalding 134

Yalding Organic Gardens 134

Yapton 249